# Dictionary of Afro-Latin American Civilization

—————— BENJAMIN NUÑEZ

With the assistance of the African Bibliographic Center

# Dictionary of Afro-Latin American Civilization

 Greenwood Press

WESTPORT, CONNECTICUT • LONDON, ENGLAND

**Library of Congress Cataloging in Publication Data**

Nuñez, Benjamín, 1912-
    Dictionary of Afro-Latin American civilization.

    Bibliography: p.
    Includes index.
·    1.   Latin American—Civilization—African
influences—Dictionaries.   2.   Caribbean area
—Civilization—African influences—Dictionaries.
I.   African Bibliographic Center.   II.   Title.
    f1408.N86      980'.003          79-7731
ISBN 0-313-21138-8

Library of Congress Catalog Card Number: 79-7731
ISBN: 0-313-21138-8

First published in 1980

Greenwood Press
A division of Congressional Information Service, Inc.
88 Post Road West, Westport, Connecticut 06881

Printed in the United States of America

10  9  8  7  6  5  4  3  2  1

To my wife, Marianne Watson Nuñez,
without whose devoted assistance
this book could not have been . . .

# Contents

# Illustrations ————————————————

# Foreword

It has been a long established aim of the African Bibliographic Center to attempt to publish works of particular use and value in continuing pertinent research at all levels of scholarly knowledge. Dr. Nuñez's book *Dictionary of Afro-Latin American Civilization* is clearly consonant with that aim. This book, one of the first of its kind, stands as a landmark, both in importance and value, in the fields of current and historic Afro-American, Latin, and African studies. It provides a unique documentation and illustration of the impact of African civilization and peoples upon—and contributions to—the New World. We are particularly proud to present this achievement in conjunction with Greenwood Press.

Perhaps Dr. Rafael L. Cortada's illuminating introduction best sums up the importance of this work in a historical perspective. Dr. Cortada provides additional insights into the perceptions of race and culture that have played a more predominant role in the development of both the Caribbean and Latin America than hitherto presented.

Dr. Nuñez's work is intended to spur further research and publishing along these lines. It is hoped that future scholars will refine and expand on this seminal effort, specifically with regard to the presence of blacks in the New World prior to the arrival of the Europeans, and also in the twentieth century, periods of time which require much study. The African Bibliographic Center's journal, *A Current Bibliography on African Affairs*, has published a number of articles relating to the former, specifically a series of articles by Legrand Clegg entitled "The Beginning of the African Diaspora: Black Men in Ancient and Medieval America?" (1969); "Ancient America: A Missing Link in Black History" (1972); and "The Black Origin of 'American' Civilization: A Bicentennial Revelation" (1976). Both Clegg and Nuñez have pointed the way into a much neglected, willfully forgotten cornerstone of world civilization, some "roots" of which have only recently recaptured the public imagination.

One last comment. Because of its sources, the *Dictionary* contains more words, phrases, and biographies from the Caribbean Islands than from continental Latin America. This reflects the importance of the Caribbean as the focal point in the African Diaspora, both as the staging point for European conquests of and trading routes to the American continents, and as the central repository and neo-acculturation "camps" of the slave trade. At one point or another, a majority of the African ancestors of American families, excepting those shipped directly to Brazil, passed through the Islands (see the illustrations "Destinations of the Atlantic Slave Trade, 1601-1700" and "Destinations of the Atlantic Slave Trade, 1701-1810" for a representation of the ship routes). Thus, the researcher looking into African origins *must* sift through the myriad cultures of the Islands to find the links of the Old World with the New.

Our thanks to our valiant staff for the many hours spent editing this manuscript. The ongoing fluidity of changes in terms of transliteration and flux from one language into another and from one idiom into another dialect through the years created a miasma of problems in terms of spelling, capitalization and accentuation. These discrepancies have been resolved to the best of our abilities without eliminating the interesting and important variations on words and themes which have naturally occurred over the centuries.

*Daniel Matthews*
March 1979

# Author's Note

The *Dictionary of Afro-Latin American Civilization* is a historical and descriptive dictionary of terms and phrases, with selected biographies of Afro-Latin political leaders, writers, and other important personalities caught in the complex neo-African sociocultural evolution in the New World. The *Dictionary* comprises a systematic and documented survey of Afro-Latin American civilization, and to the best of my knowledge it is the first of its kind in English. For the general reader, it will facilitate an understanding of the multicultured, multilingual African traditions in the New World.

The entries, taken from English, French, Portuguese, and Spanish sources, are listed in alphabetical order, and include generic terms (nouns, phrases, and idioms), selected biographies, and important historical events. Each term is defined in its geographical and historical context. The over 4,500 entries (totaling about 60,000 words) were selected on the basis of their intrinsic importance, as well as the frequency with which they appear in the sources cited in the bibliography. They have been collected from well-documented primary sources, such as reference books, encyclopedias, current historical literature, and scholarly journals.

In the research phase of this project, I encountered many problems in locating, studying, and selecting the most suitable material for the entries. While many people and institutions aided me, either directly or indirectly, it is with great appreciation that I mention the following: the Fulbright Commission; Georgetown University and West Chester State College, for the two leaves of absence (1965, 1977); Dr. William P. Houpt and the staff of the Francis Harvey Green Library, West Chester State College, West Chester, Pennsylvania; Dr. Harold E. Davis, American University; and Georgette E. Dorn and Everette E. Larson, Latin American-Portuguese and Spanish Division, Library of Congress.

Benjamin Nuñez
Member of the Scholars Committee
Library of Congress

# Introduction

The African cultural influence in Latin America is so pervasive but subtle that it is often overlooked. For example, Spain and Portugal dominated the colonization of Latin America, but Africans participated in every phase of the European invasion. Pedro Alonso Niño, a black man, piloted one of Columbus' ships. Núflo de Olaño, a free African, stood with Balboa as he viewed the Pacific Ocean for the first time. Africans fought on both sides when Hernán Cortés defeated Narváez for the right to plunder Mexico. It was a free black man whom Francisco Pizarro left as his representative to the Incas when he left Tumbés to explore the northern reaches of Peru. Blacks accompanied Ponce de León as servants and soldiers when he founded Saint Augustine, Florida. As the *conquistadores* extended their penetration and control, the numbers of Africans also grew. In 1820, Alexander von Humboldt estimated that 200,000 Africans populated Mexico's east coast, and about one million Africans lived on the Caribbean coasts of Colombia and Venezuela. The magnitude of the African migrations into Brazil and the Caribbean has remained evident. However, even such ostensibly white nations as Chile and Argentina accommodated huge black populations that predated the heavy migrations from Europe.

The distribution of the slave trade tends to support von Humboldt's unscientific census estimates. As many as sixty-five million souls may have been taken from Africa to the New World. About fifteen million survived the Middle Passage to set foot in the Americas. Only 5 percent of the Africans enslaved came to North America, and only half of the remainder were imported into Brazil. Thus, even with the numbers brought to the Caribbean Islands, simple arithmetic and reason tell us that African labor had to help build and populate every other colony started by the British, Dutch, French, and Spaniards.

Frank Tannenbaum's landmark 1947 work *Slave and Citizen: The Negro in the Americas* provides valuable insights into the conceptualization of race, blackness, and slavery in the Hispanic psyche. He clarifies valuable nuances on the interrelationships that may exist among perceptions of culture, economic status, and color in Latin America. Magnus Morner's valuable *Race Mixture in the History of Latin America* (1967) updates Tannenbaum's work. Together, these two works provide a useful context for Dr. Benjamin Nuñez's ambitious undertaking. Africans were a vital element in the evolution of Latin America. Although their impact has varied in each of the developing nations, the sum total of that impact is massive and pervasive. Africans have helped to mold the language, diet, music, literature, and psyche of every Latin nation, from Cuba and Mexico to Tierra del Fuego. That contribution has never been studied, dissected, and documented fully. Dr. Benjamin Nuñez's *Dictionary of Afro-Latin American Civilization*, then, is a first effort in that direction; it provides a resource that will give better balance to Latin American research in the years to come.

*Rafael L. Cortada*
December 1978

# Format of Dictionary ——————

Each entry is followed by an abbreviation such as (Afr.) indicating its presumed linguistic association. The abbreviations used are as follows:

| | | | |
|---|---|---|---|
| (Afr.) | African | (Fr. Cr.) | French Creole |
| (Ar.) | Arabic | (Pap.) | Papiamento |
| (Bant.) | Bantu | (Pg.) | Portuguese |
| (D.) | Dutch | (Sp.) | Spanish |
| (Eng. Cr.) | English Creole | (Yor.) | Yoruba |
| (Fr.) | French | | |

Dictionary and historical sources are cited as appropriate at the end of entries in shortened form. For the full citations, see the Bibliography at the end of this work.

Cross-references are indicated by (q.v.) and see or see also.

Some glossary entries have more than one meaning. In such cases, definitions are given in their presumed historical order of development.

When there are variant names for the same entry, the most common name is listed first, followed by all other names.

# Maps

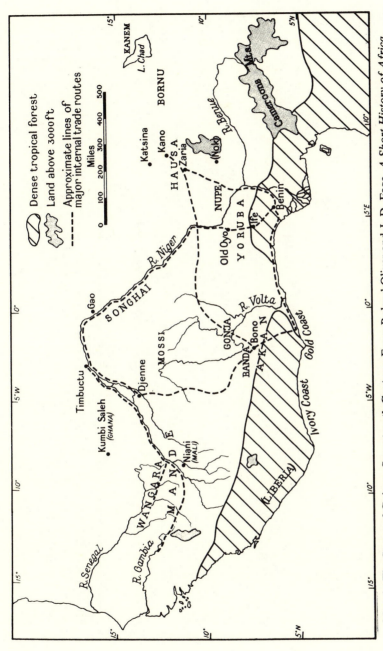

**Map 1. The States of Guinea, Seventeenth Century.** From Roland Oliver and J. D. Fage. *A Short History of Africa*. Penguin African Library, 1975, p. 103, Plate B. © Roland Oliver and J. D. Fage, 1962, 1966, 1970, 1972, 1975. Reprinted by permission of Penguin Books Ltd.

Dense tropical forest

Land above 3000ft

Approximate lines of major internal trade routes

Miles
0  100  200  300  400  500

KANEM

L. Chad

BORNU

R. Benue

Cameroons Mt.

Katsina

Kano

Zaria

(Nok)

HAUSA

NUPE

Benin

Ife

YORUBA

Old Oyo

R. Niger

Gao

SONGHAI

R. Volta

GONJA

Bono

BANDA

AKAN

MOSSI

Gold Coast

Ivory Coast

(LIBERIA)

Djenne

Timbuctu

Kumbi Saleh
(GHANA)

Niani
(MALI)

MANDE

WANGARA

R. Senegal

R. Gambia

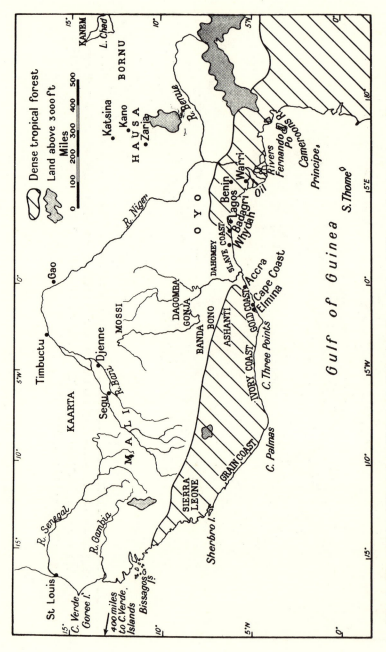

**Map 2. West Africa, Fifteenth to Eighteenth Centuries.** From Roland Oliver and J. D. Fage. *A Short History of Africa.* Penguin African Library, 1975, p. 119, Plate 9. © Roland Oliver and J. D. Fage, 1962, 1966, 1970, 1972, 1975. Reprinted by permission of Penguin Books Ltd.

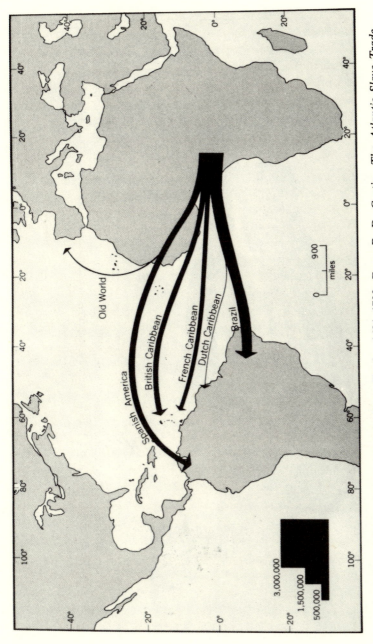

**Map 3. Destinations of the Atlantic Slave Trade, 1601–1700.** From P. D. Curtin. *The Atlantic Slave Trade*. University of Wisconsin Press, 1969, p. 120, Figure 9. Reprinted by permission of the University of Wisconsin Press.

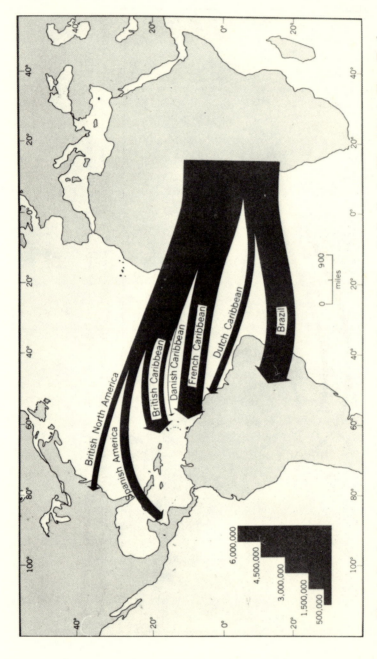

**Map 4. Destinations of the Atlantic Slave Trade, 1701-1810.** From P. D. Curtin. *The Atlantic Slave Trade.* University of Wisconsin Press, 1969, p. 215, Figure 14. Reprinted by permission of the University of Wisconsin Press.

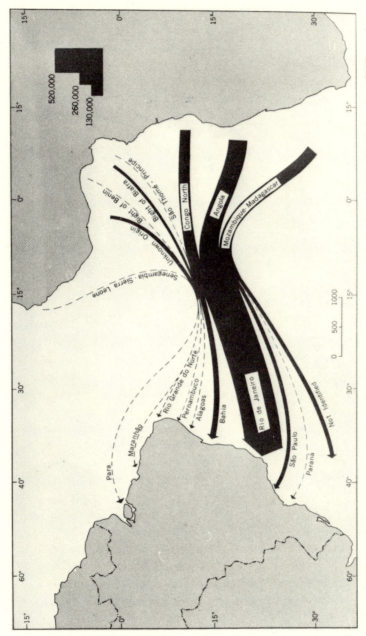

**Map 5. The Brazilian Slave Trade, 1817-1843.** From P. D. Curtin. *The Atlantic Slave Trade.* University of Wisconsin Press, 1969, p. 239, Figure 18. Reprinted by permission of the University of Wisconsin Press.

# Figures

**Figure 1. A Spanish Master Punishing His Slaves.** From F. P. Bowser. *The African Slave Trade*. Stanford University Press, 1974, p. 102, Figure 3.

**Figure 2. A Black Slave Approaching an Indian Prostitute with Silver Stolen from His Master.** From F. P. Bowser. *The African Slave Trade*. Stanford University Press, 1974, p. 152, Figure 4.

**Figure 3. A Spanish Slaveowner and His Wife Abusing Their Slaves.** From F. P. Bowser. *The African Slave Trade*. Stanford University Press, 1974, p. 194, Figure 5.

**Figure 4. Two Afro-Peruvians at Their Devotions.** From F. P. Bowser. *The African Slave Trade*. Stanford University Press, 1974, p. 244, Figure 6.

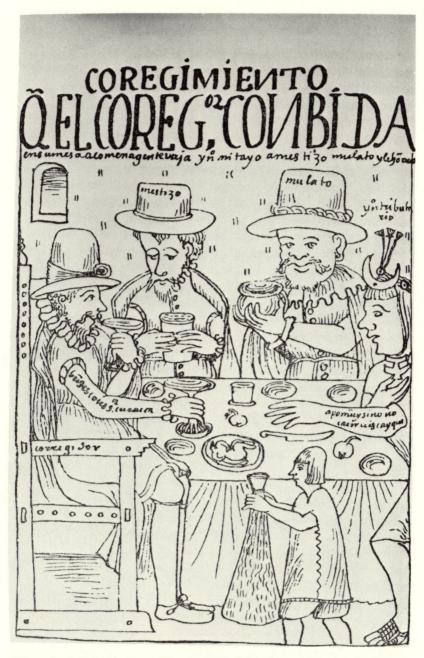

**Figure 5. A Spanish Corregidor and His Mulatto and Mestizo Underlings Being Served by Indians.** From F. P. Bowser. *The African Slave Trade.* Stanford University Press, 1974, p. 284, Figure 7.

**Figure 6. Slave Brands Recorded in Lima.** Notarial Documents. A sequence of brands (as in the top row) indicates the black changed hands one or more times. From F. P. Bowser. *The African Slave Trade.* Stanford University Press, 1974, p. 82, Figure 2.

**Figure 7. A Black Slave of a Spanish Corregidor de Indios Flogging an Indian.**
From F. P. Bowser. *The African Slave Trade.* Stanford University Press, 1974,
p. 6, Figure 1.

# Dictionary of
# Afro-Latin American
# Civilization

# a

**AAN, AANT** (Eng. Cr.), among Afro-Jamaicans, stepmother, also aunt.

**AAPETEBI USAKA** (Afr.) ("The crows will eat you [when you are dead]"), an African aphorism preserved in Jamaica. (Cassidy, *Dictionary*, p. 1.)

**ABADA** (Ar.), in Brazil, a burial garment used by Moslem blacks.

**ABA KOSO** (Afr.), in Trinidad, a male god of African origin worshippéd among the black population. His favorite foods are sheep, cock, honey, and milk, and his colors are red and white. He is usually identified with Saint Anthony. (Herskovits, *Trinidad Village*, pp. 331-33.)

**ABAKWÁ** (Afr.), an Afro-Cuban cult, usually, though not always, restricted to blacks, which blends African religions and Catholicism. It has a very sophisticated ritual that accommodates and integrates various beliefs, philosophies, social conditions, and cultural and artistic elements. Neo-African music is one of its main features. (Roberts, *Black Music*, pp. 32, 36.)

**ABARÁ** (Afr.), an Afro-Brazilian food consisting of bean paste seasoned with pepper and *dendé* palm oil (q.v.).

**ABASÍ** (Afr.), the Christian crucifix that occupies a place of honor in the rituals of the Afro-Cuban folk religion; it usually appears with a candle on either side. In an initiation ceremony, Abasí is carried by a priest flanked by two assistants. One of them sprinkles holy water with a feather cluster made of basil leaves, and the other swings a basin of sacred smoke and sings songs of praise. The initiates carry large altar candles, although, in the past, they are said to have carried torches.

**ABASONGO** (Afr.), a chief priest in the Afro-Cuban folk religion.

**ABBA, ABBAH** (Afr.). 1. African day-name (q.v.) for a female born on Thursday. 2. A flat African hand basket used by blacks in the fields.

**ABBAY, ABBEY, ABI** (Afr.), in the West Indies, the African oil-palm *(Elaeis guineensis)*, which grows to a height of 20 to 30 feet; also, the fruit of this tree, about 2 inches in diameter, resembling very small coconuts. Apparently brought from Africa in slavery times.

**ABÉ** (Afr.), an Afro-Brazilian goddess of thunder who lives in the sea.

**ABEDÊ** (Afr.), ocean shell used by priests in Afro-Brazilian cults, mainly in the *gêgé-nagó* (q.v.) fetish cult. (Mendonça, *A Influencia*, p. 108.)

**ABENG** (Afr.), a cow's horn used as a musical instrument and for signalling, especially among the Maroons (q.v.). 1. It is blown, not from the end, but from a mouth hole on the concave side. The hole at the small end is stopped with the thumb, which gives a variation of about one tone. 2. By extension, a conch shell or any other form of Maroon bugle. (Cassidy, *Dictionary*, p. 2.)

**ABENITA** (Afr.), African day-name (q.v.) for a girl born on Sunday, used in slavery times throughout the Caribbean region. (Bastide, *African Civilizations*, p. 56.)

**ABENITANTA,** a black character in modern Guianan theater; his usual role is as a commentator criticizing persons and events. (Voorhoeve, *Creole Drum*, p. 17.)

**ABERDEEN BILL,** a bill sponsored by Lord Aberdeen, introduced into the House of Lords on July 7, 1845, authorizing the seizure of any slave cargo going to Brazil. Both Houses of Parliament passed this law ordering that any condemned slave ship be destroyed. Passage of the Aberdeen Bill aroused great indignation in Brazil.

**ABERÉM** (Afr.), an Afro-Brazilian variety of corn or rice cake which is baked or fried and then wrapped with banana leaves.

**ABERISUN** (Afr.), in the Afro-Cuban folk religion, the priest in charge of killing a he-goat as sacrifice to the gods.

**ABI** (Afr.). See **ABBAY.**

**ABINA** (Afr.), an important female ancestor among Surinam Bush Negroes (q.v.).

**ABOBO** (Afr.). 1. ("May it do you good.") A sacred exclamation said in several Afro-Haitian cults before every libation or pouring of ritual water. (Jahn, *Muntu*, p. 35.) 2. In Afro-Haitian rituals, a phrase meaning "the end." Also *ai abobobi*. (Courlander, *The Drum*, p. 356.)

**ABOLICIONISMO** (Sp.). See **ABOLITION MOVEMENT.**

**ABOLICIONISTA ESPAÑOL, EL** (Sp.), a short-lived antislavery newspaper founded in Madrid in 1864 by a Puerto Rican, Julio L. de Vizcarrondo y Coronado (q.v.) As the organ of the Sociedad Abolicionista Española (q.v.), it unified and encouraged the abolition movement (q.v.) in Spain and in the colonies. (Corwin, *Spain and the Abolition*, p. 158.)

**ABOLITION BILL**, a law passed by the British Parliament on March 25, 1807, declaring the slave trade illegal on British ships. Engaging in the trade was subsequently made a felony and, later, was considered an act of piracy.

**ABOLITION MOVEMENT** (1753-1888), a generally enlightened movement inspired by rational humanitarianism and the evangelical religious conscience of Protestantism. It sought the end of the immensely lucrative slave trade to overseas plantations and, ultimately, the overthrow of the entire slave system. By the beginning of the nineteenth century, the slave trade and African bondage were considered an anachronism in a world animated by the new spirit of egalitarianism and brotherhood. In England, one of the first champions of the abolition movement was George Fox (q.v.), the founder of Quakerism. The movement in Britain ended with the suppression of slavery in the West Indies and all the overseas colonies by the British Act of Emancipation (q.v.) on August 1, 1834. In France, the abolition movement inspired the National Convention's decree on February 4, 1794, to suppress the system of slavery "in all the territory of the Republic, including Saint Domingue." (Ott, *The Haitian Revolution*, p. 82.)

**ABOLITION OF SLAVERY**, accomplished in every Latin American country and island between 1794 and 1888—in France and Saint Domingue in 1794; in Martinique and Guadeloupe in 1848; in Argentina in 1813; in Gran Colombia, 1821; in Mexico, 1829; in the British colonies, 1834; in Puerto Rico, 1873; in Cuba, 1880; and in Brazil, 1888.

**ABORTION**, in plantation America, in order to save their offspring from undergoing the cruel life they themselves were leading, often practiced by women by drinking a brew concocted from wild herbs.

**ABOUKANI** (Afr.), in the language of the Accompong Maroons (q.v.) of Jamaica, a bull.

**ABOUKRESS** (Afr.), in the language of the Accompong Maroons (q.v.) of Jamaica, a cow.

**ABOURISHA** (Afr.), a bride of the god Eshu (Exu) (q.v.), who acquired her status after fourteen years of service in an Afro-Brazilian *candomblé* (q.v.).

**ABRIDGEMENT OF THE MINUTES OF EVIDENCE,** a shortened account of the Minutes of Evidence (q.v.) regarding the slave trade, prepared by Thomas Clarkson (q.v.) with the help of other abolitionists for public convenience. It appeared in London in 1791. (Mannix, *Black Cargoes*, p. 291.)

**ABU** (Afr.), clayish earth of a dark reddish-black or dun color, occurring in shale-like formation in damp places. It has a sweetish taste and was once eaten by slaves in the Caribbean. See DIRT-EATING.

**ABUJA** (Afr.), an African term for a glow worm or firefly *(Photorus* and *Pyrophorus)* found in the Caribbean region.

**ABUNÂ** (Pg.), an Afro-Brazilian delicacy, made of turtle or *tracajá* eggs which are "smoked" before gestation has been completed. Thus, the small turtle or tortoise still has a portion of the yolk attached to its breast. *Abunâ* is eaten with salt and flour.

**ABURU** (Afr.), an Afro-Jamaican cornmeal mush highly seasoned with country pepper; usually eaten by blacks.

**ABUXÓ** (Afr.), a kind of edible vegetable cultivated mainly in Bahía, Brazil, apparently imported from West Africa, where it is still very popular. (Mendonça, *A Influencia*, p. 111.) See also AGUX.

**ACAÇA, ACASSA** (Pg.), an Afro-Brazilian gelatin made of a corn and water mixture. After the mixture has been brought to a boil, and while it is still on the fire, it is stirred with a wooden spoon; with the same spoon, it is dipped out in small portions and laid in rolls upon banana leaves. It is also a drink, made by fermenting a mass of cracked corn (or rice), sugar, and water.

**ACAJOU DE SÉNÉGAL** (Fr.), an African tropical tree with a dark brown trunk and mixed dark and light grain, brought to the Caribbean in colonial times. Since the seventeenth century, its hard wood has replaced ebony in cabinet-making.

**ACANISTA** (Pg.), a black chief and merchant who, in colonial times, conducted the trade of slaves, elephant tusks, and sometimes gold between African chiefs and the Portuguese and other Europeans. He was paid in articles equal to the value of his merchandise. The *acanistas* were independent traders and shrewd merchants. (Goslinga, *The Dutch*, p. 348.)

**ACANSAN** (Afr.), an Afro-Haitian dish of Nigerian-Dahomean origin made of cooked balls of cornmeal. Sometimes, as a sacred dish, it is offered to *loas* (q.v.) (Mendonça, *A Influencia*, p. 109.)

**ACARÁ** (Yor.), an Afro-Brazilian pastry made from boiled rice which is fried in *dendé* palm oil (q.v.) and seasoned with *malagüeta* (q.v.) pepper. See also ACAÇA.

**ACARAJÉ** (Yor.), a Brazilian food of African origin, consisting of small croquettes of bean paste and shrimp, seasoned with onion and pepper and fried in *dendé* palm oil (q.v.). It is heated in a clay frying-pan. This is one of the finest offerings of the Bahian kitchen. (Freyre, *The Masters*, p. 464.)

**ACASSA.** See ACAÇA.

**ACCOMPONG** (Afr.). 1. The Supreme Being of the heavens who, according to the Jamaican Maroons (q.v.), is the creator of all things. 2. A black of Maroon origin. (Cassidy, *Dictionary*, p. 3.)

**ACCOMPONG, CAPTAIN,** a famous Maroon (q.v.) slave chief of Jamaica who, as second in command to his brother, Captain Cudjoe (q.v.), played an important role in the Maroon War (q.v.) of 1725 to 1739. He was one of the signers of the Articles of Pacification on March 1, 1738, on behalf of the Maroons of Trelawny town. (Price, *Maroon Societies*, p. 237 ff.)

**ACCOMPONG TOWN,** a Jamaican Maroon (q.v.) village which was part of the Leeward slave settlement located in Saint Elizabeth parish. It was named after the chief of that name. (See ACCOMPONG, CAPTAIN.)

**ACEA, ISIDRO** (d. 1912), a Cuban mulatto liberal leader, assassinated in Güira de Melena, Cuba, on November 10, 1912. He was a hero of the War of Independence and an assistant to the black General Máximo Gómez y Maceo.

**ACHÊCHÊ** (Afr.), Yoruba (q.v.) funeral rites among Afro-Brazilians.

**ACHŌGUN** (Afr.), an assistant priest who performs animal sacrifices in certain Afro-Brazilian cults; possibly of *gêgé-nagó* (q.v.) origin.

**ACKEY** (Afr.), a unit of currency used in the slave trade in Dahomey (q.v.) around 1793; 1 ackey was worth 2s. 6d. or 1 galinha (q.v.). (Davidson, *Black Mother*, p. 91.)

**ACKRA** (Afr.). See ACRA.

**ACON** (Afr.), an Afro-Haitian calabash rattle used in sacred dances.

**ACOSTA, JOSÉ J.**, a Puerto Rican leader, one of the founders of the Sociedad Abolicionista Española (q.v.), organized in Madrid on December 7, 1864. (Corwin, *Spain and the Abolition*, p. 154.) See also VIZCARRONDO Y CORONADO, JULIO L. DE.

**ACOUBA** (Afr.), African day-name (q.v.) for a girl born on Thursday; used among slaves in the Caribbean.

**ACRA, ACKRA** (Afr.), in Trinidad and elsewhere, an African dish made from boiled salt-fish (q.v.) fried in fat and coconut oil. It is a favorite black delicacy.

**ACT FOR SETTLING THE MILITIA,** a statute passed by the Assembly of Jamaica in 1681 setting up a militia to defend the island and secure internal peace from slave rebellion. It consisted of local freemen, including whites, mulattoes, blacks, and Jews, between the ages of sixteen and sixty. Militiamen were responsible for supplying their own uniforms and small arms and were mustered once a month for drill. Military duty was compulsory. The average militia had about 8,000 men. (Brathwaite, *The Development*, p. 26.)

**ACT FOR THE ABOLITION OF SLAVERY,** an act of the British Parliament passed in 1830 abolishing slavery in the West Indies. This bill, forced on the Jamaican Assembly, inspired a slave rebellion there in December 1831. Once the short-lived uprising was crushed, Jamaican authorities established a state of half-slavery in which slaves served their masters as "apprentices" for seven years, earning wages for one-fourth of the work week. See also APPRENTICESHIP.

**ACTION DE GRÂCE** (Fr. Cr.), in the Afro-Haitian folk religion, a ritual composed of Roman Catholic prayers and hymns. It precedes any service for the African gods and *loas* (q.v.).

**ACT OF EMANCIPATION,** an act of the British Parliament passed on August 28, 1833 abolishing slavery in the West Indies and in the other overseas colonies. The law became effective on August 1, 1834.

**ACTOR-BOY,** in Afro-Jamaican folklore, a kind of John Canoe dancer (q.v.).

**AÇUBA** (Afr.), in Brazil, a Moslem religious service performed on the first day of the week.

**ACUTIERRE,** a black *quilombo* (q.v.) organized in northeast Brazil around 1670.

**ADAMISIL WEDO** (Afr.), an Afro-Haitian water-goddess, identified with Saint Anne.

**ADARRUM** (Afr.), in Afro-Brazilian fetish cults, a special beat on a sacred drum. The faithful believe that its repeated rhythm induces the phenomenon of possession.

**ADARUNZA DIPLOMATIC MISSION,** an official delegation sent by the petty king Adarunza of the Gold Coast (q.v.) to Portugal, by way of Bahia, Brazil, on May 26, 1795. The king demanded that the port of Ajudá (q.v.) become his exclusive market on the coast of Mina (the Gold Coast) (q.v.) for the supply of slaves for the plantations. He further demanded that the gold mines of his territory be commercially exploited by a combined labor force, under Portuguese supervision, and that the forces stationed at the trading post be increased to protect it from the dominant power of his rival, the king of Dahomey, (q.v.). Apparently the mission was not successful because Adarunza dispatched another mission in 1804. (Rodriques, *Brazil and Africa*, p. 31.) See also DAHOMEY EMBASSY; DAHOMEY EMISSARY.

**ADIOULA** (Afr.), in French Guiana, an African day-name (q.v.) for a girl born on Tuesday. Its origin seems to be Fanti-Ashanti (q.v.).

**ADIXÁ** (Afr.), in Brazil, the fifth and last daily service performed by black Moslems; it is always an evening prayer meeting. Also called *vitri* (q.v.) and *lixari* (q.v.). (Ramos, *As Culturas Negras*, p. 145.)

**ADJA** (Afr.). 1. In the Afro-Haitian pantheon, a female *loa* (q.v.) associated with the art of pharmacy. The Yoruba (q.v.) of Nigeria had a similar spirit, also called Adja, who took men and women off into the forest to teach them the medicinal properties of roots and herbs. Adja's favorite foods are cookies and chicken. Persons possessed by her sometimes eat broken glass. 2. An African tribe in the Bight of Benin (q.v.) from which many slaves were shipped to Saint Domingue between 1781 and 1790. Also called Adia. (Curtin, *The Atlantic Slave*, p. 194.) 3. A musical instrument consisting of a small metal bell with a long handle, shaken at the height of the heads of ceremonial dancers by the leader in an Afro-Brazilian cult. The sound of the bell is supposed to speed the arrival of a deity during the ceremonial dancing. The *adja* is also used to invite cult members to the ritual known as "the feeding of the saint."

**ADJANIKON** (Afr.), in the Afro-Haitian religion, a black initiated into the cult who acts as an assistant priest. He waves the banners used to salute the gods, sings the songs for the *loa* (q.v.), aids in bringing the possessed dancers out of their trance, and performs other ritual tasks.

**ADJASOU** (Afr.), in northern Haiti, a powerful *loa* (q.v.) with protruding eyes who is always in a bad humor. He lives under the mombin tree near a spring and makes the water rise. His servitor runs around in an excited manner. Adjasou's favorite foods are duck, turkey, pigeon, and goat meat; he drinks vermouth, rum, and cognac.

**ADJI-BOTO** (Afr.), a game of counters among Afro-Surinamese blacks. This game is also played in the Caribbean and West Africa. Its Ashanti name is *wari* (q.v.). (Herskovits, *Rebel Destiny*, p. 346.) See also A-I-U-.

**ADO** (Afr.), a black Yoruba (q.v.) tribe of southwestern Nigeria. Many of its members were brought to the West Indies as slaves in the eighteenth century. (Curtin, *The Atlantic Slave*, p. 187.)

**ADOC** (Afr.), a black slave who, in 1749, launched a ten-year war against the colonists in Dutch Guiana. He ultimately obtained independence for all the slaves under his command. (Bastide, *African Civilizations*, p. 52.)

**ADRUE, ADRUI ADRUU** (Afr.). 1. A Jamaican medicinal plant *(Cyperus articulatus)* consisting of a reed with a chive-like blossom, used by blacks as a dressing for fresh cuts and wounds; usually it is crushed and mixed with rum. 2. A preparation made from this plant used as an ingredient in recipes to drive away ghosts.

**ADÚM** (Afr.), a traditional Afro-Brazilian dish consisting of a cake made from corn flour. It is seasoned with fragrant and savory spices, mixed with onions and shrimp, rolled in leaves and cooked in a large pan. Made by black mothers or grandmothers for their children, this food could last two or three months without spoiling. It symbolized deeply felt maternal affection. In Brazil, it was called "blacks' tasty morsel" (*Negro bom bocado*). (Pierson, *Negroes*, p. 242.)

**AFANA** (Afr.), in Jamaica, a bush knife or cutlass, probably imported from West Africa during slavery times.

**AFASIA, AFASYAH** (Afr.), in the Caribbean, a wild yam (q.v.) *(Christaller)* of poor quality; formerly a staple food for slaves.

**AFFONSO I OF CONGO,** an African ruler, son of João I (see NZINGA A \KUWU), the first African king of the Congo (q.v.). Affonso was converted to Christianity and baptized by the Portuguese in 1491. His reign lasted almost forty years, from 1506 to 1545. Allied with the Portuguese invaders, he tried to attract missionaries and teachers and made efforts to organize the kingdom's trade. It was during his reign that the massive exportation of slaves to Brazilian plantations took place. His African name was Nzinga Mvemba. (Birmingham, *Trade and Conflict*, pp. 23-25.)

**AFFRANCHI** (Afr.), in Saint Dominigue, a small, special social class, consisting primarily of mulattoes who, in prerevolutionary times, had gained their liberty and developed large economic interests. Under the Code Noir (q.v.) of 1685, they were considered French citizens with corresponding rights, including the right to own slaves. Many of the *affranchis* regarded themselves as Frenchmen. (Leyburn, *The Haitian People*, pp. 37-38.)

**AFI** (Afr.), an Afro-Surinamese day-name (q.v.) for a girl born on Friday; this term is found in Jamaica as Kofi and Kwaku. It is also known in the United States. In the Gold Coast (q.v.), as in Surinam, the name is associated with the soul. (Herskovits, *Rebel Destiny*, p. 346.)

**AFIBA** (Afr.), an African day-name (q.v.) for a girl born on Saturday; used by French Guiana blacks. (Bastide, *African Civilizations*, p. 56.)

**AFOCHE** (Afr.), in Brazil, a black carnival, apparently of Congo (q.v.) origin.

**AFOFIÉ** (Yor.), an Afro-Brazilian flute made of tacuara with a wooden mouthpiece.

**AFOO.** See AFU.

**AFRANKERI** (D.), in certain black Surinamese comedies, a black character who was the defender of high morals.

**AFRICA FOR THE AFRICANS,** a slogan of the black nationalist movement led by Marcus Garvey (q.v.). It was a fundamental tenet of the Universal Negro Improvement Association (q.v.).

**AFRICAN.** 1. In the West Indies, synonymous for black; often a derogatory term. 2. In Saint Thomas parish, Jamaica, a black group living in the lowlands around Morant Bay; its members and their religious practices.

**AFRICAN DAY-NAME.** See DAY-NAME.

**AFRICAN INSTITUTION SOCIETY,** an English society based on abolitionist philosophy and practice sponsored by the government at the end of the eighteenth century to advance the cause of enslaved people. After the abolition of the English slave trade by the Parliament in 1807, the African Institution set out to block the African slave trade in the West Indies and elsewhere.

**AFRICANIZACIÓN DE CUBA** (Sp.) (''Cuba's Africanization''), a slogan that inspired a political movement, organized mainly by Cuban slaveholders in 1853, to oppose the Spanish policy of suppressing the slave trade. This policy had been adopted under pressure from British Prime Minister Lord Palmerston (q.v.). The planters claimed that Spain would send blacks to the island and free them after a short period of enforced contract labor and that slaves would then take over the island, thus destroying morality and Christianity. All this they saw as part of the diabolical plot of Africanization. (Foner, *The Spanish-Cuban-American War*, V. II, p. 79.)

**AFRICAN MALLOW.** See FRENCH SORREL.

**AFRICAN MIDDLEMAN,** AFRICAN SUPPLIER, a West African chief engaged in providing slaves for the New World market.

**AFRICANO** (Pg.). In Brazil: 1. An African-born slave. 2. A *candomblé* (q.v.).

**AFRICANOS** (Pg.), a generic term applied in Bahia, Brazil, to a small group of Brazilian-born blacks who, after being more or less completely incorporated into the European world, still hold onto certain of their own ideas, attitudes, customs, and practices. They represent another world tolerated by the upper class of modern Brazil. Despite social disapproval, the *africanos* have retained their ancestral beliefs.

**AFRICANOS LIVRES** (Pg.), in Brazil, a group of unskilled free blacks imported from Africa around 1840-1860 to work on public projects, including the most onerous and unpleasant jobs in the cities.

**AFRICAN ROSE,** in the West Indies, an unidentified plant in the rose family.

**AFRICAN SLAVE,** in the Caribbean and elsewhere, an African-born slave brought to the New World against his will; he was thought to be proud and recalcitrant, with a propensity to run away as soon as the opportunity presented itself. Unlike the Creole slave (q.v.), who temporarily fled to another plantation or town and continued, if illegally, as a functioning member of the society, the Africans tended to take to the wilderness, forming gangs of aggressive marauders or organizing self-contained, Maroon-like communities. (Brathwaite, *The Development*, p. 164.)

**AFRICAN SLAVE WOMAN,** the slave woman, either African-born or Creole, generally enjoyed more opportunities and fewer restrictions than her male counterpart, especially in the nineteenth century. In Brazil, a female slave, either black or mulatto, easily formed a permanent liaison with her master on the plantation or with whites in the cities. In order to earn money for her manumission (q.v.), she was often allowed to work outside the household as a street seller, in the market, or even as a prostitute.

**AFRICAN SUPPLIER.** See AFRICAN MIDDLEMAN.

**AFRICAN TALK,** a Jamaican dialect thought to be of African origin.

**AFRICAN TRADITION,** in Latin America, a way of life reminiscent of West African societies and cultures from which most of the New World's slaves originally came. This way of life was variously perpetuated in plantation America.

**AFRIKETE,** among Guianan Bush Negroes (q.v.), an African god of the crossroads.

**AFRO-AMERICAN CULTURE,** a term used in ordinary discourse to denote a cultural and/or ancestral legacy from Africa. Scholars in the United States recently developed this concept in recognition of the distinct cultural heritage of black Americans as evolved from African origins and the black experience in America.

**AFRO-ARAB LITERATURE,** oral or written literature which originated in the Islamic-African world.

**AFROCUBANISMO** ("Afro-Cubanism"), an artistic and literary movement that developed in Cuba between 1928 and 1940. In *afrocubanismo,* poetry, dance, and music seek to imitate African rhythms and verbal repetitions, following the pattern of traditional African folk ceremonies in which sound reiteration is used to induce a trance-like state in the initiates. Through this movement, the poetry of a brilliant generation of writers gave powerful expression to Africa as a living entity flourishing in the islands of America. It blends both an African vocabulary and African onomatopoeic phrases with guttural slang or Creolized Spanish, and sonorous Yoruba (q.v.) drum rhythms with voluptuous melodies that originated among the Afro-American cultures. The movement has its roots in the Cuban black's art, mode of life, and sensitivity. *Afrocubanismo* is not an anti-European or anti-Christian movement; rather, it aims to stress the magical and telluric values of an urbanized black folklore.

**AFROCUBANO** (Sp.), a second-generation black slave, called *criollo* (q.v.) in late colonial Cuba. Well-acculturated and fluent in Spanish, *afrocubanos* were often employed as domestics in the cities.

**AFRO-JAMAICAN CULTURE,** the product of a fairly well-developed acculturation process involving West African slaves who lived and worked in a white European socioeconomic system, the tropical plantation. It incorporated diverse African elements as well as some European traditions, always tending to emphasize the elements common to all groups. The process of cumulative adaptation and amalgamation of neo-black cultures continued in this fashion for a century and a half. By 1830, the time of the abolition of slavery in Jamaica, the Afro-Jamaican culture was solidly established and was passed on to each new generation, as it had already been passed on, by a process of acculturation and assimilation, to new arrivals from Africa and Europe. (Curtin, *Two Jamaicas*, p. 25.)

**AFRO-LATIN AMERICANA,** a field of study dealing with the socially learned behavior of Afro-Latin American peoples as expressed in artifacts, ideas, social facts, languages, tradition, values, and the like. This socially acquired behavior and its consequences are principally, though by no means exclusively, perpetuated by the descendants of African slaves whose histories involved forced transatlantic migration, protracted servitude, and persistent social isolation, exclusion, and discrimination. (Hymes, *Pidginization*, p. 6.)

**AFROMESTIZO** (Sp.), in modern Latin America, a person of mixed blood with at least some black element. Both ethnically and culturally, this individual is predominantly European.

**AFU, AFOO** (Afr.), a common variety of hard yellow yam (q.v.) *(Dioscorea aculeata)*. It is grown and eaten mainly by blacks in Jamaica.

**AFUGURU** (Afr.), among Black Caribs (q.v.), one of the three spirits present in an individual. It is the person's double, which reproduces his physical form on the spiritual plane and remains on this earth until the time is ripe for it to become a *gubida* (q.v.). The *afuguru* of evildoers, together with those of murdered persons, Protestants and Freemasons, are doomed to wander near the earth forever, assuming the form of ghosts who persecute the living. (Bastide, *African Civilizations*, pp. 79-80.)

**AFURÁ** (Afr.), in Bahia, Brazil, a ball or cake made of fermented rice.

**AGALLÚ** (Afr.), a female *orisha* (q.v.), promoter of evil in the Afro-Cuban folk religion.

**AGANMAN** (Afr.), in the Afro-Haitian voodoo (q.v.) pantheon, a male deity characterized as a zondolite, a small lizard capable of changing colors. A person ''mounted'' or possessed by Aganman sometimes climbs trees or posts. Some believers claim that such a person will change color, from dark to light. (Courlander, *The Drum*, p. 325.)

**AGAYÚ** (Afr.), in the Afro-Cuban religion, the *orisha* (q.v.) or spirit of those who carry burdens. He dances with large strides, lifting up his legs as if he were getting over obstacles, and picking up children and carrying them away. Agayú is identified with Saint Christopher.

**AGÊ** (Afr.), PIANO DE CUIA (Pg.), an Afro-Brazilian musical instrument consisting of a large gourd filled with pebbles and covered with a small cotton net to which cowries (q.v.) have been fastened; it is shaken by hand.

**AGIDA** (Afr.), in Afro-Surinamese folklore, a spirit; also a sacred drum.

**AGIDAVI** (Afr.), an Afro-Brazilian drumstick. (Slonimzki, *Music*, p. 257.)

**AGIDI** (Afr.), an Afro-Jamaican pudding made from the fine sediment of grated corn meal, seasoned and boiled in a banana leaf.

**AGISYMBA,** a term used by Ptolomy, the Egyptian astronomer and geographer (210 A.D.), to refer to the land mass extending in ancient times south of Libya into "the unknown."

**AGO** (Afr.). 1. An African ethnic group of Dahomean culture, located in the Gulf of Guinea (q.v.), from which many slaves were brought to the New World. 2. An African plant which blacks in Brazil used in folk medicine; brought from Saō Tomé (q.v.) in slavery times.

**AGOARDENTE DA TERRA** (Pg.), in colonial Brazil, a name applied to rum and sugar cane (q.v.) brandy, important byproducts of the sugar industry. These fiery distilled spirits found a large export market in the slave trade with the West Indies, for they were in great demand by the blacks of Angola (q.v.) and Guinea (q.v.). The excessive consumption of *agoardentes da terra* by soldiers, slaves, and sailors in the coastal towns of Brazil and Portuguese Africa led to drunken fighting and alcoholism, and ultimately increased mortality. (Boxer, *The Golden Age*, p. 151, 258ff.)

**AGÔGÔ** (Afr.), an Afro-Brazilian bitonal instrument consisting of two hollow iron cones joined together and struck with an iron pin; it is part of black orchestras. In some Afro-Brazilian cults, the *agôgô* sounds the first note of each invocation of a deity and then accompanies the drums during the rest of the invocation. (Pierson, *Negroes*, p. 369.)

**AGOSU** (Afr.), in Afro-Surinam, a name applied to a child born feet first. (Herskovits, *Rebel Destiny*, p. 346.)

**AGOUÉ** (Afr.), an Afro-Haitian god of the sea, patron of navigators and fishermen; a member of a large family of deities.

**AGRICOLE, EUGÈNE** (1834-1901), a political leader born in Basse-Terre, Guadeloupe. Agricole settled in Fort-de-France, Martinique, where he played an important role in establishing the secular education system in the French Antilles. He also encouraged the development of small rural property in Martinique with the idea of promoting mass education and social freedom for the black descendents of former slaves. As a poet, he began the tradition of black militant literature and rejected the emphasis on classics in the religious schools. His poems appeared in magazines and newspapers. After his death, his friends and disciples published *Les Soupées et les rêves* (1936). (Corzani, *Littérature antillaise, poésie*, pp. 84-86.)

**AGUA DE MENINOS** (Pg.), in colonial Brazil, a famous slave market in Bahia noted for its cruel spectacles, details of which have been well documented by foreign writers of the period. Here, slaves were landed almost naked, or at best scantily clad in a coarse cotton sarong. Their sale took place in the open, with the price varying according to racial type and physical appearance. (Ramos, *The Negro*, p. 30.)

**AGUIDA** (Fr. Cr.), a special drumstick played in Afro-Haitian cults.

**AGUILERA, FRANCISCO V.** (1821-1877), a wealthy Cuban planter, son of a Spanish general and daughter of General Kindelan, governor of Santiago, Cuba. He traveled extensively throughout Europe and America. At the outbreak of the island revolution in 1868, he was an ardent patriot; Aguilera freed all his slaves. Later, he became minister of war and eventually vice president under C. M. de Céspedes. He died in New York. (Calcagno, *Diccionario*, p. 24.)

**AGUXÓ** (Afr.). See ABUXÓ.

**AGWÉ** (Afr.), an Afro-Haitian god of the sea; thunder and lightning over the ocean are thought to be Agwé shooting his cannon. He is usually symbolized in pictures by a sailing or steam vessel. His colors are blue and white, and his primary sacrificial animal is a male goat. High rituals for Agwé are begun in a chapel and consummated in a sailing boat on the open sea, from which a highly decorated and stylized miniature ship is launched containing food for the deity. This tiny craft is known as the *barque d'Agwé*. Shrines honoring him often have a small boat hanging from the rafters. His wife, La Sirène (q.v.), is a mermaid. (Jahn, *Muntu*, p. 43.)

**AGWETTA WOYO** (Afr.), in the Afro-Haitian religion, one of the wives of Agwé (q.v.). In Dahomey (q.v.), she was considered to be his daughter.

**AHPETTI** (Afr.), an amulet worn by Jamaican blacks as protection against harmful duppies (q.v.). (Cassidy, *Jamaica Talk*, p. 249.)

**AI ABOBO.** See ABOBO.

**AIÉ** (Afr.), a New Year festivity celebrated by the Nagó (q.v.) slaves in Brazil; it originated in slavery times.

**AI-LÁ, OI-LÁ** (Ar.), the second daily prayer said at noon by Afro-Brazilian Moslems; it was introduced by slaves converted to Islam.

**AINHUM** (Afr.), in Brazil, a disease that attacks blacks and mestizos, characterized by a progressive thickening of the skin and the consequent formation of a fibrous ring at the base of one or more of the toes that eventually mutilates them. (Freyre, *The Masters*, p. 475-77.)

**AINSI PARLE L'ONCLE** ("So the Uncle Speaks"), a series of essays by Haitian writer Jean Price-Mars (q.v.), published in Port-au-Prince in 1928. In the essays, Price-Mars repudiates French and Anglo-American traditions and values, and calls for a return to the stories, legends, proverbs, rituals, music, and dancing of peasant folklore. He also stresses the need to study African civilization and African elements in Haitian life, and he exalts the mystique of Africa, still very much alive in Haitian folklore. Price-Mars bitterly denounces the racial prejudices of the Haitian elite and its snobbish worship of French or foreign literature and ideas.

**A-I-U-, AIÚ** (Afr.), in colonial Brazil, a game which black slaves played during their leisure hours. It consisted of a small wooden board made up of a dozen or more hollow segments into which small, hard, lead-colored seeds were bounced in and out. The process of working each seed from compartment to compartment constituted a rich source of amusement and diversion. This simple game was originally introduced from Africa. (Ramos, *The Negro*, p. 33.) See also ADJI-BOTO; WARI.

**AJAJA** (Afr.), a male god of African origin worshipped among the black population of Trinidad. His favorite colors are red and white, and his favorite foods are red cock, land turtle, guinea bird, and rum. Ajaja lives in the sea and is characterized as "a big man" or as a king. He is identified with Jonah.

**AJAOUNTO** (Fr. Cr.), a small, sacred drum played as an accompaniment to dancing and singing in Afro-Haitian rituals. See also BOULA.

**AJUDÁ FORT, WHYDAH,** a fortified trade post on the Guinea Coast (q.v.), built by the Portuguese under the name of São João de Ajudá in 1698 for the purpose of exporting slaves to Brazil. It was part of the territory of the black kingdom of Ardra (q.v.). Between 1728 and 1748, 90,800 black slaves were exported to Bahía, Brazil. Around 1750, when the slave trade declined, the port of Luanda (q.v.) became more important than Ajudá. In 1849, the British Foreign Office sent a consul to Ajudá to keep an eye on the slaving activities. Today Ajudá is called Ouidah. (Boxer, *The Golden Age*, pp. 154-55.)

**AJUDÁ SLAVES,** primarily Sudanese slaves of the Dahomey (q.v.) culture who were exported through the Ajudá (q.v.) trade fort. Around 1728, Ajudá slaves became irreplaceable in the mining of gold and diamonds in Minas Girais, for they were believed to have a peculiar gift for discovering new gold-bearing deposits. By 1731, the Portuguese crown levied duties on slaves passing through the fort; the profits from this branch of the slave trade paid for the upkeep of churches and military fortifications and for the establishment of the island of São Tomé (q.v.). At that time, it was estimated that between 10,000 and 12,000 Ajudá slaves were imported yearly into Bahía, Brazil. (Boxer, *The Golden Age*, pp. 46, 175-77, 400.) See also AJUDÁ FORT.

**AKAM** (Afr.), an African wild yam (q.v.) *(Discorea alata)* imported into Jamaica and the West Indies during the slavery period. The part that is eaten is not the tuber-like cultivated yam but rather the large seeds that grow on the vine; they are the size of a fist and are shaped like an Irish potato. In Africa, *akam* is eaten in times of famine. (Cassidy, *Dictionary*, pp. 340-94.)

**AKAN KINGDOM,** a short-lived empire in West Africa which, between 1680 and about 1730, expanded, like the eastern Gold Coast (q.v.) and the western Slave Coast (q.v.) in an attempt to control all the trade between the hinterland and the south. A few years later, the Ashanti (q.v.) took over its place as a major Gold Coast power. (Oliver, *A Short History*, pp. 104-105, 122, 244.)

**AKAN SLAVES,** in Jamaica and elsewhere, Coromantee (q.v.) black slaves of original Akan-speaking stock from southern Dahomey (q.v.). Several of the Maroon (q.v.) black leaders were Akan-speaking slaves. (Curtin, *The Atlantic Slave*, p. 155.)

**AKANTAMASU** (Afr.), among the Surinamese blacks, the god of the ant hill; the name comes from the Gold Coast (q.v.).

**AKEE** (Afr.), the fruit of a shrubby tree *(Blighia sapida)* from tropical West Africa, known widely as the *akee* (or *akee akee*). This tree was introduced to Jamaica in 1778, along with breadfruit (q.v.), to provide inexpensive food for black slaves. African explorers had already found the *akee* to be a favorite with black peoples in the area from which the slaves came. (Beckwith, *Black Roadways*, p. 44; Cassidy, *Dictionary*, p. 7.)

**AKETTA** (Afr.), an Afro-Jamaican bugle probably connected with *kête*, an African flute or pipe. (Cassidy, *Jamaica Talk*, p. 263.)

**AKPALÔ** (Afr.) ("raconteur"), a professional Afro-Brazilian storyteller; part of an African institution that flourished in Brazil in the person of the old black woman who went from plantation to plantation telling stories to other black women, especially to the nurses of white children. (Freyre, *The Masters*, p. 342.)

**AKRA** (Afr.), in the Afro-Surinamese religion, one of the two souls of an individual. Akra is born and dies with a man. It defends him against the forces of evil. (Bastide, *African Civilizations*, pp. 60, 100.)

**ALABÉ** (Pg.), the head drummer of an Afro-Brazilian cult.

**ALAFIA** (Ar.) ("all goes well"), an expression used particularly in the system of divination with sacred coconuts, a prevalent practice among black slaves in colonial Cuba. (Montejo, *The Autobiography*, p. 35.)

**ALAKU** (Afr.), another name for the Bush Negro Creole (q.v.) language.

**ALASARI.** See AY-A-SARI.

**ALBARRAZADO** (Sp.), an archaic term used to designate the offspring of a mulatto man and an Indian woman.

**ALBIZU CAMPOS, PEDRO** (1891-1965), a mulatto political leader of the independence movement in Puerto Rico. As head of the Nationalist party in the 1930s, he fought for the separation of the island from the United States. (Farr, *Historical Dictionary*, p. 5.)

**ALCABALA** (Sp.), in colonial Spanish America, a general sales tax of 6 percent imposed by the Crown on the sale of each slave. This duty was reduced during 1780-1783, but to the great discontent of planters in Cuba and elsewhere, it was restored a few years later. (Aimes, *A History of Slavery*, p. 38.)

**ALEIJADINHO** (1730-1812), born Antonio Francisco Lisbôa, the mulatto son of a Portuguese man and a black slave woman; the most brilliant artist of his time in Brazil. He was given the nickname Aleijadinho ("the maimed") because of an illness he developed after the age of forty. Leprosy gradually deformed his appendages, incapacitating him for all work with his hands; his masterpieces were done with a chisel held tightly in the crook of his elbow. He painted churches, especially in Ouro Preto, and was also a great architect and sculptor. He usually worked in absolute solitude, accompanied and aided by a single black slave. An artistic genius, Aleijadinho represents the culminating expression of centuries of colonial development. He was the first visual artist to create a strictly Brazilian school of art. (Ramos, *The Negro*, p. 133.)

**ALENCAR, JOSÉ DE** (1829-1877), a Brazilian poet, playwright, and statesman. Although Alencar was not an active abolitionist, he wrote two social dramas, *O Demonio Familiar* and *Mãe*, in which he expressed his opposition to slavery. (Sayers, *The Negro*, p. 130.)

**ALEXIS, JACQUES STEPHEN** (1922-1962), a black Haitian novelist and theorist of négritude (q.v.) who strove for a clearer definition of the négritude movement. Along with other Afro-Haitian intellectuals, he proposed négritude as an antidote to the traditional view of Haiti as a cultural province of France. Alexis thought of the movement as a dynamic one which would unite all Africans throughout the world. For him, Afro-Haitian art, based on a racial and ethnic mystique, was powerful, primitive, non-logical, and deeply emotional. As part of a national revival, according to Alexis, négritude was to be considered the common denominator of all black intellectuals. Among his works are *Le négre masqué* (1933); *Compère Général Soleil* (Paris, 1955); and *Les Arbres musiciens* (Paris, 1957). (Coulthard, *Race and Colour*, pp. 64, 68-70.)

**ALFÂNDEGA** (Pg.), in colonial Brazil, a customs house which collected royal revenues. One of its special tasks was to prevent the loss of duties from smuggling.

**ALFANDOQUE** (Sp.), a kind of *maracas* played by blacks in Colombia.

**ALFONSO, JUAN DE DIOS** (d. 1877), a Cuban mulatto clarinet player and orchestra conductor. As a composer of dances and waltzes, he enjoyed great popularity. He died in Guanabacoa. (Calcagno, *Diccionario*, p. 30.)

**ALFOR, ALFOR COUSIN** (Fr.), in rural Haiti, a peasant's straw knapsack without which no mountain man makes a journey; it has a charm and grace that is not diminished by its humble and inexpensive construction. Decorated with sisal braid and tassels, and colored with green and magenta dyes, each *alfor*, upon close inspection, is seen to be unique. These geometric patterns and figures of flowers and animals are apparently of Dahomean origin.

**ALFORRIAS NA PIA** (Pg.), in colonial Brazil, a traditional practice consisting of the manumission (q.v.) of an infant on the occasion of his baptism by the acceptance by his master of a small amount of money (5 to 50 milreis). This custom became very common, especially when the child was light-skinned. (Pierson, *Negroes*, p. 87.)

**ALGEMA, ANJINHO** (Pg.), in Brazil, an instrument of torture made from iron. It held the slaves' hands tightly, crushing the thumbs, and was used for serious offenses such as escape.

**ALÍ-BABÁ** (Ar.), a child-god worshipped by Moslem blacks in Brazil.

**ALIBAMBO** (Pg.), in colonial Brazil, an instrument of torture used to punish rebellious slaves. It gripped the unfortunate victim at the neck and also served to chain two slaves together to a tree.

**ALIGENUM** (Pg.), among Afro-Brazilians, a magical talisman invoked by Moslem blacks in their ritual.

**ALI-LÁ** (Ar.), the third daily prayer recited by Moslem blacks in Brazil.

**ALI-MANGARIBA** (Ar.), the fourth daily prayer, recited by Afro-Brazilian Moslems at sunset. (Ramos, *As Culturas Negras*, p. 145.)

**ALIMBAMBAS** (Pg.), in colonial West Africa, gangs of slaves consisting of eight to twelve persons bought by an agent, usually in central Angola (q.v.) and brought in chains to the port of Luanda (q.v.) to be shipped to Brazil. Since they usually had to travel hundreds of miles and consequently reached the port in very poor condition, they were placed in *barracoons* (q.v.) by the seashore. During this time, they were baptized in groups. (Boxer, *The Golden Age*, p. 5.)

**ALLADA KINGDOM.** See ARDRA KINGDOM.

**ALLIGATOR APPLE,** in the West Indies, a tropical shrub *(Annona palustris)* the fruit of which has a fine sweet-scented smell; supposedly a strong narcotic formerly used by slaves.

**ALLÍ TE ESTÁS** (Sp.) ("There you are!"), in early colonial Spanish America, a humorous expression referring to the offspring of Creole parenthood with a mixture of Indian, Negro, and Spanish blood. It expresses one of the most important facts of Latin America, the common mixing of races.

**ALMAS PENADAS** (Pg.), in Afro-Brazilian folklore, wandering souls in torment who, having left this world without atoning for their sins, are condemned to come back to expiate them. When they come back, they smear children's faces with "ghost broth"; for this reason, it is said that no child should neglect to wash his or her face or to take a bath first thing in the morning.

**ALMEIDA, MANUEL ANTONIO DE** (1831-1861), a Brazilian novelist who wrote about slavery at the beginning of the nineteenth century. The slaves are shown as they go about their household tasks and take part in the life of Rio de Janeiro. Some of his historical characters, such as Leonardo, Vidinha, and Chico-Juca, are supposedly popular blacks of the days of D.

João VI who lived in that city as regent and king from 1807 to 1821. The author stressed how the mulattoes were completely integrated into society. (Sayers, *The Negro*, pp. 169-70, 171-73.)

**ALÓ** (Afr.), in Brazil, usually an African story narrated by an *akpalô* (q.v.). These stories of animals fraternizing with human beings, talking like them, marrying, feasting, and so on, came to be combined in colonial times with Portuguese tales. The language of the *aló* has an almost African flavor.

**ALÓA, ALÚA** (Afr.), in Brazil, a refreshing drink made of boiled rice and flour, or toasted corn, which is mixed with sugar and water and allowed to ferment in clay jars. In Minas Gerais, it is made with pineapple rind. It is very popular among Afro-Brazilians.

**ALOVI** (Fr. Cr.), a Haitian marauding *loa* (q.v.), or dwarf-like spirit, who likes to disarrange things and play practical jokes. Persons possessed by *alovi* may break up gatherings, scare spectators and dancers, and generally make a nuisance of themselves. Some believers regard this *loa* as belonging to the Pétro (q.v.) group rather than to the Dahomean one.

**ALUÁ.** See ALOÁ.

**ALUFÁ** (Afr.), an Afro-Brazilian cult organized by descendants of Moslem blacks. The faithful worship Allah, also known as Olorum-ulua, and practice circumcision and observe Ramadan (q.v.) which ends in a great feast that includes the sacrifice of a lamb and the exchange of gifts.

**ALUGADA** (Pg.), in colonial Brazil, a domestic female slave; today, a black prostitute.

**ALUJÁ** (Afr.), a sacred dance in Afro-Brazilian *candomblés* (q.v.).

**ALVARES, AFONSO** (d. 1650)), a mulatto bastard whose father was black and who was born and raised in the palace of Don Afonso of Portugal, bishop of Evora. Alvares married the daughter of a saddler, had children, and acted as occasional secretary of a Franciscan convent. Apparently, he was the first author of African descent to write in a European language. He wrote dramatic works and satires and seems to have earned a respectable place in the society of his day. His published works are *Auto de Santo Antonio* (Lisboa, 1613); *Auto de Santa Barbara, virgem e martyr* (Lisboa, 1613); *Auto de S. Thiago Apostolo* (Lisboa, 1639); and *Auto de San Vincente* (Lisboa, 1658). (Jahn, *Neo-African Literature*, pp. 15, 24.)

**ALVARO I OF CONGO** (d. 1587), a Christian king of the Congo (q.v.) who attempted to reorganize the kingdom. Around 1571, he reached an agreement with the Portuguese to expand trade in goods and slaves. As a result, the slave traffic developed rapidly, and, in a few years, 14,000 slaves were exported to work on Brazilian plantations. (Birmingham, *Trade and Conflict*, pp. 42-43.)

**AMA DE CRIAR** (Pg.), in colonial Brazil, a colored nursemaid slave, or sometimes a former slave, who was considered a member of the family. She always lived under the same roof with her masters and enjoyed various privileges.

**AMA DE LEITE** (Pg.), in colonial Brazil, a slave woman who served as wet nurse for her master's child. She was generally chosen from among female slaves who gave birth at the same time.

**AMALA** (Afr.), an Afro-Cuban dish made of cornmeal and water which is wrapped in banana leaves and shaped into balls. It is eaten with or without sugar.

**AMA SECA** (Pg.), an old black woman who takes care of the white master's children; a nanny.

**AMARELO** (Pg.), a Brazilian term for a mulatto.

**AMARIZIADO** (Pg.), a type of Afro-Brazilian family organization that has no legal or religious sanction but is nonetheless very stable and socially accepted among black people (in contrast to European concubinage which is not socially acceptable). It is thought to be a revival of an African social relationship common among urban free blacks. Often in modern Brazil, a man of European descent lives with a black woman who cares for their offspring and with whom the man has sexual relations; thus they are considered *amariziados* or lovers.

**AMARO** (Pg.), the name of a Negro *quilombo* (q.v.) organized in the wilderness of northeast Brazil around 1660. (Ramos, *The Negro*, p. 58.)

**AMBA** (Afr.), African day-name (q.v.) for a female child born on Wednesday; used by Guianan Bush Negroes (q.v.).

**AMBER,** in the West Indies, a piece of amber which blacks use for divination purposes in the practice of obeahism (q.v.) and myalism (q.v.).

**AMBER-HEAD,** in Jamaican folklore, a talisman which a black sorcerer receives from the spirits during the course of a religious dance. It is used to cure sickness.

**AMBRIZ,** an Angolan port located north of Luanda (q.v.) which, between 1836 and 1840, was one of the most important outlets for the export of black slaves to Brazil. It was at the end of the main route from the interior of the colony to the coast. (Curtin, *The Atlantic Slave*, pp. 26-62.)

**AMBROZÓ** (Afr.), an Afro-Brazilian dish made of corn flour and spices.

**AMBUJO** (Sp.), in Spanish America, the offspring of a mulatto and a black woman.

**AMBUNDU** (Afr.), an African ethnic group located in the Congo-Angola (q.v.) region from which slaves were taken to the New World.

**AMELIORATION ACT OF 1788,** a bill approved by the General Assembly of the Leeward Islands to provide more protection for the slaves, to encourage their increase, and in general to improve their health and working conditions. (Goveia, *Slave Society*, p. 57.)

**AMERICAN SLAVING SQUADRON,** an American naval force established in 1843 to patrol the West African coast with the aim of ending the slave trade. It was part of a coordinated effort involving British warships as well. The American squadron was based on Cape Verde (q.v.), a thousand miles from the slave-trading area.

**AMÉRICO, PEDRO** (1845-1905), a Brazilian mulatto painter who began his formal study of art in Rio de Janeiro. In 1859, Américo traveled to Europe, visiting several capitals, and studied with Ingres and Hyppolyte Flaudrin in Paris. On his return to Rio, he set out to paint a veritable gallery of national heroes and historical scenes. His most highly regarded works are "The Battle of Avalu," "Battle of Campo Grande," and "The Proclamation of Independence."

**AMERIND NEGROES,** descendants of escaped colonial slaves who settled along the Atlantic coast of Central America. This group can be further divided according to the degree of adaptation to different local traditions.

**AMINE** (Fr. Cr.), an Afro-Haitian goddess who is fond of perfumes.

**AM I NOT A MAN AND A BROTHER?,** a famous sentence engraved on a 1787 medallion sculpture by the English potter Josiah Wedgewood (q.v.). It represents a slave in chains, with one knee on the ground and both hands lifted up to heaven. In 1795, the abolitionists adopted it as their official seal.

**AMOMBO** (Afr.), a leader, male or female, of the Shangó (q.v.) cult in Haiti.

**AMURÉ** (Ar.), a Moslem marriage between Afro-Brazilian slaves, performed by an *imam* (q.v.).

**ANAGÓ** (Afr.), an Afro-Cuban dialect spoken by Lucumí blacks.

**ANAMABÚ** (Afr.), in colonial Mexico, black slaves introduced from Anamabou, in the Gold Coast (q.v.), where the British built a trading post around 1673.

**ANAMANGUÍ** (Afr.), the god of the dead in the Afro-Cuban folk religion.

**ANAMBUCURU** (Pg.), an Afro-Brazilian female deity who is thought to live in the sea, lakes, rivers, and streams. She is also known as the goddess of the waters. She is dressed in white and dark blue, and her favorite foods are goat and hen.

**ANAMÚ** (Afr.), a wild plant *(Petivera alliacea)* which, when eaten by cattle, gives a garlic taste to the animal's milk and meat. The plant was probably brought from Africa in slavery times. Today it is found in Puerto Rico and the Caribbean region.

**ANANCY, ANANSI** (Afr.), a central dramatic character of African origin, extremely popular in Jamaica and in other parts of the Caribbean. In Jamaica, Anancy is a little bald-headed man with a falsetto voice and cringing manner. He lives by his wits and treats outrageously anyone on whom he can impose his superior cunning. He is a famous fiddler and something of a magician as well. In some stories, he has the form of a man; and in others, that of a spider. He has a wife and a set of children who share in his expoits, including a quick-witted son who eventually outdoes his father. In Haitian folklore, Anancy is the spider trickster-hero and buffoon, although his name occurs rarely. (Beckwith, *Black Roadways*, p. 219.)

**ANANCY ROPE,** in the Afro-West Indies, a spider web.

**ANANCY STORY, NANCY STORY** , a widely used Afro-Caribbean term for certain highly eclectic tales favored by the peasantry and Jamaican children in general. An Anancy story is either a beast fable (in which case it is usually of African origin, and specifically Ashanti [q.v.], with Anancy [q.v.], the spider, as its prominent figure), or a fairy tale (in which case it is usually of European origin). Sometimes features of both types are combined. Anancy, originally the Ghanaian word for spider, is given numerous cosmopolitan traits. The Anancy stories often preserve the old device, almost universal in Africa, of interjecting a short song at crucial moments. (Cassidy, *Dictionary*, p. 10.)

**ANANSI.** See ANANCY.

**ANDALAQUITUCHE** (Pg.), a Brazilian *quilombo* (q.v.) located 25 leagues northwest of Lagoas. Ruled by a brother of Zambi (q.v.), it was one of the largest fortified *quilombos* which flourished between 1672 and 1694. In 1694, it was destroyed by the Afro-Portuguese army. (Pescatello, *The African*, p. 201.)

**ANDREONI, JOÃO ANTÔNIO.** See ANTONIL, ANDRÉ JOÃO.

**ANDRESOTE,** a runaway black slave who was one of the leaders of a settlement organized in 1732 in the Coro region of Venezuela. (Bastide, *African Civilizations*, p. 66.)

**ANGANA** (Afr.), an Afro-Brazilian term of address for mistress; used by black slaves. (Mendonça, *A Influencia*, p. 112.)

**ANGEL,** a currency used by African chiefs and Europeans in exchange for slaves and goods. The rate of exchange in Dahomey (q.v.) (circa 1555) was a measure of two ells of cloth for a weight of 2 angels. (Polanyi, *Dahomey*, p. 146.)

**ANGEL-MAN,** a practitioner of *myalism* (q.v.) in the Afro-West Indies.

**ANGLO-AMERICAN NEGRO,** a descendant of African slaves brought to the English Antilles and Guiana during the colonial period to work as a laborer on the sugar plantations. Whether of pure blood or mixed, such descendants exhibit a strong continuity with the colonial period, and in many instances, they have adopted the language, values, and manners of their masters. The degree of their Anglo-Saxon assimilation varies considerably throughout the Caribbean Islands. (Olien, *Latin Americans*, p. 123.)

**ANGLO-SPANISH TREATY** (1836), in this treaty, England and Spain agreed to the mutual search of ships suspected of being slavers (q.v.). Spain also adopted stringent measures to end the Cuban slave trade and to give liberty to all Africans found on captured Spanish slave ships.

**ANGOLA.** See ANGOLA AFRICAN STATE; ANGOLA COLONY.

**ANGOLA AFRICAN STATE,** a Negro kingdom founded on the west coast of central Africa just before the first Europeans arrived in the region. Its growth was closely associated with the beginning of Portuguese activities and the opening of the Atlantic slave trade (q.v.) (1483-1565). Its ruler, called Ngola, was the dominant power in sixteenth-century Africa. Around 1626 it became a puppet state controlled by the Portuguese, and in 1671 it disappeared as an independent kingdom. Its African name was Ndongo (q.v.). (Birmingham, *Trade and Conflict*, pp. 20, 26.)

**ANGOLA CLOTH,** a clothing fabric made of palm or twill weave, with cotton warp and wood weft. It was used as currency in the slave trade.

**ANGOLA COLONY,** a land made up of desert and savanna, except for a narrow coastal strip. It extended about 1,000 miles along the Atlantic coast of Africa, between the Congo River in the north and the Kunene (Cunene) River in the south. The Portuguese first settled here around 1575, when São Paulo de Loandas was founded. The colony was populated by Bantu (q.v.) peoples and supplied most of the slaves sent to Brazil.

**ANGOLA, FRANCISCO,** a black slave, possibly a native African, who as the second in command with Yanga (q.v.) helped the latter to establish in 1608 a runaway slave settlement in the modern state of Veracruz. He was a courageous leader who insisted that their rebellion was justified, for blacks had every right "to liberate themselves from the cruelty of the Spanish, who without any right pretend to be determiners of our liberty." Angola together with Yanga and his followers were defeated but were given their freedom in 1611 by the Viceroy of Mexico Don Luis de Velasco. (Rout, L.B., *The African Experience in Spanish America*, p. 106.)

**ANGOLA GRASS, PARÁ GRASS,** in Brazil, a perennial pasture and green forage grass *(Panicum purpurascens)* grown in tropical areas. It probably was imported from Angola (q.v.) in slavery times.

**ANGOLA PEA.** See PIGEON PEA.

**ANGOLAR.** 1. The basic monetary unit of the Angola Colony (q.v.), established in 1928 and equal to the Portuguese escudo. 2. A currency note representing an angolar.

**ANGOLARES,** in Brazil, native slaves of the island of São Tomé (q.v.) off the West African coast.

**ANGOLA SLAVES,** a broad term applied to black slaves, usually of Bantu (q.v.) culture, who were exported to the New World, especially to Brazil. The Angolas were thought to be physically weak, talkative, quarrelsome, and much given to merrymaking and dancing. They knew how to work metal, weave, and make pottery; they were also familiar with cattle raising. In Brazil, they were preferred for domestic work.

**ANGOLA TRADE,** in the early seventeenth century, a type of trade that was conducted with sea shells, European trinkets, and beads in exchange for palm-cloth. Later, this cloth was the most widely accepted currency in Angola for buying slaves.

**ANGOLENSE.** See ANGOLO.

**ANGOLINHA** (Pg.), in Brazil, guinea-fowl (q.v.) *(Numida melearis)* brought from Angola (q.v.) in the colonial period.

**ANGOLO, ANGOLENSE** (Pg.), in Brazil, an Angolan-born slave brought to work on the sugar plantations.

**ANGOMBE** (Afr.), an African bird brought to Brazil by slaves.

**ANGÚ** (Afr.), an Afro-Brazilian dish made of corn, manioc, or rice, with water, salt, and spices; apparently, a Yoruba (q.v.) meal.

**ANGÚA** (Afr.), a current Afro-Cuban dialect, spoken by former slaves.

**ANGUITE** (Afr.), in Brazil, an edible herb imported from Africa.

**ANGUZADA** (Afr.), in Brazil, a mixture of herbs and ingredients used in African dishes.

**ANGUZO** (Afr.), an Afro-Brazilian dish prepared with herbs mixed with corn meal or manioc and water. (Mendoça, *A Influencia*, p. 112.)

**ANIGI** (Afr.), a human life-force residing in the head and blood of a person, which, according to the Black Carib (q.v.) belief, disappears after death. (Bastide, *African Civilizations*, p. 79.)

**ANIMALIZAÇÃO DO NEGRO,** the process of animalization or debasement of the freed Brazilian black. The process persists to this day as an almost indelible stigma, making it impossible for him to stand on equal footing with descendants of the slave-holding generation. Only those branded with such a stigma know what it means in terms of the imbalance in the blacks' competition with whites. In making the tremendous effort to overcome this stigma, the black became "animalized." (Fernandes, *The Negro*, pp. 49-50.)

**ANISOW** (Eng. Cr.), an Afro-Jamaican cough medicine made from anise seed and rum; also good for fever.

**ANJINHO** (Pg.). See ALGEMA.

**ANJOS FERREIRA, MANOEL FRANCISCO DOS,** a black general who, in 1839, organized a *balaiada* (q.v.) in northeast Brazil. He was the chieftain of 300 peasants and runaway slaves, who fought effectively for three years until regular government troops suppressed them. At one time, he controlled the entire provice of Maranhão. He died heroically, from his wounds, in Caxias. (Ramos, *The Negro*, p. 53.)

**ANNALS OF JAMAICA, THE,** a book about the history of Jamaica, constituting a full-scale defense of slaving, written by the Reverend George Wilson Bridges (q.v.) in 1828. Although the author detested the institution of slavery, considering it barbarous and a curse, he nevertheless justified it for Jamaica and thought the emancipation of slaves would be impractical. (Curtin, *Two Jamaicas*, p. 62.)

**ANNE LICEAT INVITOS IN SERVITUTEM DARE?** (Lat.) ("Is it right to make slaves of others against their will?"), a question proposed in 1785 by Dr. Peckard, vice-chancellor of Cambridge University, as the dissertation subject for a Latin prize. Dr. Peckard himself opposed slavery. The winning essay was by Thomas Clarkson (q.v.), a young student who had been awarded two earlier prizes. In preparation for his essay, Clarkson read A. Benezet's *Historical Account of Guinea*. (Ragatz, *The Fall*, p. 249.)

**ANO BOM, ANNABON** (Pg.), an island off the Guinea coast (q.v.). It was used as a slave-trading post by Brazilian-Dutch forces (1625-1683) until Pernambuco acquired exclusive rights to export black slaves.

**ANTANA** (Afr.), a large string bag for carrying burdens on one's back; used mostly by blacks in Jamaica.

**ANTILLANITÉ** (Fr.), a deep feeling for the regional culture developed by Afro-French intellectuals in the modern Antilles. The regional culture is seen as rooted in French values and traditions. This sentiment has survived négritude (q.v.) and simultaneously stresses both African and French values. Rather than disclaiming any European heritage, it rejects isolation and claims that the only difference between a Frenchman and an Afro-Antillean is the geographical distance between them. (Corzani, *Littérature antillaise, poésie*, p. 30.)

**ANTI-SLAVERY MONTHLY REPORT,** a militant London periodical founded in 1825 as the chief organ of the African Institution Society (q.v.). The editor was Zachary Macaulay (q.v.). Its low price of a half penny per copy helped secure a wide readership.

**ANTI-SLAVERY SOCIETY,** an abolitionist society organized in London in January 1823 and similar to the African Institution Society (q.v.). It declared slavery to be "opposed to the spirit and precepts of Christianity as well as repugnant to every dictate of natural humanity and justice." It further stated that its intention was to secure the immediate amelioration of the condition of black slaves and, ultimately, their freedom. The members of the society included a duke as president and five peers and fourteen members of Parliament as vice-presidents. Many of the members were persons of high social standing, including prominent British Quakers. This society was originally organized under the name of Society for the Mitigation and Gradual Abolition of Slavery Throughout the British Dominions (q.v.). (Jakobsson, *Am I not*, p. 234.)

**ANTI-SLAVERY-TRADE SOCIETY,** a militant group formed in London in 1787 to promote the abolition of the slave trade. It began with twelve members, nine of whom were Quakers, and included no noblemen among its members. (Jakobsson, *Am I not*, pp. 234, 446.)

**ANTONIL, ANDRÉ JOÃO** (1649-1716), an Italian Jesuit born João Antônio Andreoni who came to Bahía in 1681. Apart from brief visits to Pernambuco and Rio de Janeiro, he remained in Bahia for more than forty years. In addition to his accomplished scholarly works in Latin, he published *Cultura e Opulencia do Brasil por sus Drogas e Minas* (Lisbon, 1711), considered to be the best book on the economic and social conditions of Brazil during the first half of the eighteenth century. In his examination of the agricultural society, Antonil shows a much more complete understanding of the importance of the black than previous Brazilian writers had. Antonil does not dismiss the slave or the mulatto freedman; rather, he shows the slave to be the basic element of his owner's capital, the "hands and feet of his master." (Sayers, *The Negro*, pp. 45-47.)

**ANYÉ-EWO** (Afr.), an Afro-Haitian deity, protector of the family; a member of a large group of deities of Dahomean origin.

**APADRINHAMIENTO** (Pg.), in colonial Brazil, personal protection given by a master or a private individual to a fugitive slave who implored his mercy. It saved the unfortunate slave from punishment or even death. (Ramos, *The Negro*, p. 67.)

**APANHA-O-BAGO** (Afr.), an Afro-Brazilian dance.

**APARTHEID,** the legal and social separation of blacks and the white minority. In Afro-Jamaican society during colonial times, the plantation blacks lived apart from white quarters in their own "villages" and could not move beyond certain statutory limits without a ticket. In the towns, there were black ghettos. All nonwhites, both slave and free, were legally discouraged from drinking in town shops, riding along the streets, and coming into intimate contact with whites. Some whites allowed themselves certain sexual exceptions from the system. (Brathwaite, *The Development*, pp. 176, 178, 183.)

**APETEBI** (Afr.), in Afro-Brazilian cults, a female assistant of a *babalâo* (q.v.).

**APINTI** (Afr.), in the Afro-Surinamese culture, a tenor drum. The same name is found in western Nigeria and Dahomey (q.v.).

**APONTE, ANTONIO** (d. 1812), a free black born in Havana, who organized a slave rebellion in Cuba in 1812 in emulation of Toussaint L'Ouverture (q.v.). His headquarters were in Jaruco, a few miles from Havana. This large-scale uprising involved sugar estates in the provinces of Puerto Principe, Holguin, Bayamo, Trinidad, and Havana. Many overseers and other white dependents on these estates were killed, and factories were burned. Slaves in many estates were implicated. Eventually, the rebellion was crushed. Aponte and eight of his accomplices were caught on March 15, 1812 and conducted to Havana, where they were tried and executed; their corpses were exposed publicly to terrorize the slaves. (Calcagno, *Diccionario*, p. 55.)

**APÓSTOL DE LOS NEGROS, EL** (Sp.) ("The Apostle of the Blacks"), a Spanish Jesuit, Pedro Claver (1585-1654), who labored among slaves who had just arrived at Cartagena, Colombia. Father Claver devoted forty years of his life to improving the conditions of the slaves. He boarded the ships on their arrival and assisted the sick in finding places in the hospital. To those who needed no physical ministration, he administered baptism and the consolation of the church.

**APPRENTICE,** in colonial Jamaica and elsewhere, a former slave who, under the Emanicipation Bill (q.v.) of 1833, was allowed to become a free laborer for one quarter of the work week. During this time, he could earn wages by selling his labor, or he could work for himself on a plot provided by his owner. After a seven-year period, he could buy his freedom by using the proceeds of the wages or profits from his own small holding. Fearing that the local judiciary would be less than fair in dealing with former slaves, the British government sent several judges out from England specifically for the purpose of adjudicating disputes over work, wages, and manumission (q.v.). (Hurwitz, *Jamaica*, p. 153.)

**APPRENTICESHIP SYSTEM,** in Jamaica and the West Indies, a system of training slaves to do plantation work as freemen after their emancipation on August 1, 1834. The apprenticeship system lasted four years. On August 1, 1838, the Jamaican Assembly abolished the system altogether and freed praedial slaves (q.v.) as well as nonpraedial slaves . (Curtin, *Two Jamaicas*, p. 95.)

**APRÈ BÔ-DIÉ, SE HÉTA** (Fr. Cr.) ("After God Is the State"), a popular saying among the impoverished Haitian masses, especially the peasants. Since the majority of them live divorced from the urban society that taxes and rules them, the only world meaningful to them, after God and a few spirits, is the state, distant and indifferent. The saying seems to echo Louis XIV's "L'état c'est moi."

**APRIGIO,** a black slave leader, who organized an unsuccessful revolt of Hausa Moslem slaves (q.v.) in Bahia, Brazil, in 1835. (Ramos, *The Negro*, p. 50.)

**APUKU** (Afr.), among Surinamese blacks, gods of the bush (q.v.). Whenever natural clearings appear in the forest, they are said to have been made by the Apuku gods. (Herskovits, *Rebel Destiny*, p. 347.)

**AQUIA** (Afr.), an ethnic group located on the windward coast of Africa from which slaves were brought to Saint Domingue between 1771 and 1780.

**ARABI,** a black slave, probably a Moslem, who in 1757 and 1761 led several insurrections against colonists in Dutch Guiana. By the Treaty of Auca, he was granted the right to found a republic on the condition that he give no further asylum to black fugitives. (Bastide, *African Civilizations*, p. 52.)

**ARABÚ** (Afr.), an Afro-Brazilian gourmet dish made solely with flour and the yolk of turtle eggs.

**ARADA, RADA** (Afr.), an Afro-Haitian sacred dance; Dahomean in origin.

**ARADA DRUMS,** in Haiti, drums similar in shape but with stylistic variations, used primarily with the dances and rituals of black cults. They usually come in sets of three. The largest, the *mamman* (also called *hountor* [q.v.] or *hountogri* [q.v.]), may be three or four feet high. The middle-sized drum, or *second* (also called *grande* or *moyen*), is about two feet high. The smaller, the *bula* or *bete* (sometimes called *dundun*), is about eighteen or twenty inches high. They are sometimes called by the Yoruba (q.v.) name *bana*, which was originally applied to a two-headed instrument. Arada drumheads are made of cowhide, held in place by hardwood pegs set into the bodies of the drums at an angle. The drums are tuned by driving in or loosening the pegs. In Cuba, the drums of the Arada (they are called Arara) cult are made in precisely the same way. (Courlander, *The Drum*, pp. 190-193.)

**ARADA KINGDOM.** See ARDRA KINGDOM.

**ARANGO, SECUNDINO** (b.1850), a mulatto composer and musician born in Havana, Cuba. For many years Arango was an organist in the Church of La Merced. He played violin and cello, taught piano, and wrote many dances and *guarachas* (q.v.). Among his popular compositions is "La viuda de Placido." (Calcagno, *Diccionario*, p. 58.)

**ARARIPE JUNIOR, TRISTÃO DE ALLENCAR** (1848-1911), a Brazilian writer best known for his romantic novel *O reino encantado* (1878). The work is about a fortified *quilombo* (q.v.) located at the site of a magical rock and ruled by Frei Simao, a black *feiticeiro* (q.v.). Although the author pays lip service to the ideal of slave emancipation, the tone of the book is antiblack. The main black characters are villains, and the slaves are portrayed as almost animal-like in every instance in which they appear in a group. (Sayers, *The Negro*, pp. 96, 198-200.)

**ARBRES MUSICIENS, LES** (1957), an Afro-Caribbean novel by Haitian writer Jacques Alexis (q.v.). The work describes the earthly spirituality of voodoo (q.v.) mysticism as a kind of nature philosophy set against the backdrop of a romanticized, happy Africa, which it contrasts with the sufferings and struggles of slaves under colonialism and the white man's cruelty. Africa, a vague geographical region, is depicted as the imaginary and emotional fatherland of all the blacks of the world.

**ARCAS DE NOÉ** (Sp.), in early Mexican history, public registries of slaves.

**ARDOUIN, COROLIAN** (1812-1835), an Afro-Haitian poet who, inspired by the romantic movement, sought solace from his anguish and sadness in the bosom of nature. His works, all published posthumously, include *Poésies: reliques d'un poète haïtien* (Port-au-Prince, 1837); *Poésies de Coriolan Ardouin.* Intr: B. Ardouin (Port-au-Prince, 1881); and *Poésies complètes* (Port-au-Prince, 1916).

**ARDRA,** a trading port on the African Slave Coast (q.v.) controlled by the Dutch West Indies Company where, around 1838, slaves were bartered nearly exclusively for sugar. A company director-general was in charge of all transactions, especially those involving licensed slave-trade ships. In colonial times, the port was in direct contact with Bahía, and there were heads of commercial business in both cities. At the end of the nineteenth century, a bank called Porto Seguro was founded in Ardra to repatriate freedmen. In the mid-1600s, the triangular round trip from Ardra to Curaçao to Amsterdam lasted about 15 months. (Goslinga, *The Dutch*, p. 349.)

**ARDRA KINGDOM,** an old African kingdom located in the coastal Dahomey (q.v.) -Togo region; between 1790 and 1800, its rulers sold slaves mainly to Saint Domingue and the West Indies. The kingdom is also known as Allada and Arada. (Curtin, *The Atlantic Slave*, p. 186.)

**ARDRA SLAVES,** a broad term used to refer to black slaves imported into Brazil through the trading port of the ancient kingdom of Ardra (q.v.) on the Slave Coast (q.v.). These slaves were Gêgê (q.v.) and Dahomean blacks and were considered to be thick-headed, slow, and hard to accustom to the routine of plantation life. They were supposedly so fiery that they would slash everything with a single stroke. They frequently rose up against their overseers and showered them with blows. (Freyre, *The Masters*, pp. 301, 302, 376.)

**ARGUIM,** a trading fort on the Guinea Coast (q.v.), south of Cabo Blanco, built by the Portuguese between 1448 and 1452 to facilitate commercial relations between Portugal and the West African coast. It was one of the first fortified outposts ever established on the black continent.

**ARINGA** (Afr.), an Afro-Brazilian fortified camp in the colonial period. See also ROCHELA.

**ARISTOCRATA CLUBE,** an association of lower class Brazilian blacks who, at the turn of the twentieth century, were preoccupied with imitating the life-style of the white propertied elite. They strongly aspired to higher social status. These impulses, reflected in a desire for lavish foods and immaculate, showy clothes and shoes, were apparently the result of long deprivation and an almost uncontrollable urge to display the new status they were acquiring. (Fernandes, *The Negro*, p. 280.)

**ARMAS Y CÉSPEDES, FRANCISCO DE,** a Cuban abolitionist author best known for *De la Esclavitud en Cuba* (1886). In a chapter entitled "Brief Reflection on Legislation," he declares: "The supporters of the status quo [regarding slavery] greatly eulogize our legislation in this matter; limiting themselves to citing only the most favorable prescriptions in favor of slaves." After a summary of the legislation in favor of the slaves, however, Armas concludes that "the greater part of the Spanish laws are not in use." (Corwin, *Spain and the Abolition*, p. 165.)

**ARMAZOENEN** (D.), in colonial times, the slave cargoes which were carried across the Atlantic by Dutch slave traders and sold or bartered in Brazil or the Caribbean for such local products as tobacco, hides, coffee, cacao, and wood. (Goslinga, *The Dutch*, p. 437.)

**ARO** (Afr.), a famous and influential oracle, residing in the territory of an Ibo (q.v.) clan in the Bight of Biafra (q.v.). In colonial times, it was known by various names such as Arochuku, Chukwa, and Umu-chukwu, the "children of God." The oracle had great authority, and the Ibo clans, called Aroas, organized Aro colonies along the trade routes of the interior of West Africa. The Aro priests became the sole operators of the slave trade between much of Iboland and the busy ports of the eastern delta through which thousands of slaves were sent to the New World, especially in the seventeenth and eighteenth centuries. (Davidson, *Black Mother*, p. 211.)

**AROKIN** (Afr.), in colonial Brazil, a black narrator of chronicles.

**AROTIRENE** (Afr.), a Brazilian *quilombo* (q.v.) located 5 leagues from Porto Clavo in the northeast. It was one of the largest and least fortified slave camps. It flourished between 1672 and 1694 when it was captured and destroyed by the colonial government. (Pescatello, *The African*, p. 21.)

**AROZARENA, MARCELINO** (b. 1912), a black Cuban poet who has helped Afro-Cuban folklore gain world-wide recognition. He is the master of a fascinating lyric poetry inspired by the emotional and romantic theme of the "rebirth of Africa out of the soul." At the same time, he depicts the earthly eroticism of black girl dancers possessed by voodoo (q.v.) music. His *Canción negra sin color* (1939) contains a vivid description of the Cuban *santería* (q.v.) and includes one of his greatest poems, "Cubandalucia." (Jahn, *Neo-African Literature*, pp. 225-28.)

**ARRÊTÉ** (Fr.), in Haitian folklore, protective magic in a broad sense. The *arrêté* is used to protect not merely an individual but an entire household or even a group of households. In addition to warding off supernatural creatures and shielding people from assassins, it is a neutralizing agent against various forms of black magic. The *arrêté* is usually in the form of a package hung in the house or in a nearby tree or buried somewhere in the ground. (Courlander, *The Drum*, p. 98.)

**ARRONDISSEMENT** (Fr.), in Haiti, a group of communes forming a district. It is presided over by an army officer of high rank, appointed by the president of the country to exercise civil and military authority.

**ARROZ DE HUAÇA** (Pg.), an Afro-Brazilian delicacy made of rice, dried fish, and pepper. Boiled rice is placed in water without salt, and it is mixed with sauce containing malagüeta (q.v.) pepper, onions, and shrimp. All are grated on a stone with *dendé* palm oil (q.v.).

**ARRUMÁ** (Afr.), a black Brazilian leader in the revolts of Moslem Hausa slaves (q.v.) from 1807 to 1816. The revolts were centered in Bahía. (Ramos, *The Negro*, p. 44.)

**ARTISAN SLAVES,** in the colonial West Indies, skilled and highly priced slaves who worked on the plantations as carpenters, millwrights, coppersmiths, wheelwrights, coopers, sawyers, distillers, boilers, blacksmiths, and bricklayers, as well as other specialists like head drivers (q.v.), mule men, cattlemen, and midwives. Towards the end of the eighteenth century, the most valuable slaves in this category were the carpenters, millwrights, and coppersmiths. They enjoyed perhaps the greatest amount of freedom on sugar plantations; they were encouraged to "job" outside the estate and pay the planter a weekly sum. Black slaves in some trades, such as tailoring, were permitted to work for themselves, paying the master a fixed rate, such as a dollar a week, for the privilege. (Brathwaite, *The Development*, p. 154.) See also DOMESTIC SLAVE.

**ARYANIZAÇÃO PROGRESSIVA** (Pg.) ("progressive Aryanization"), a theory held by some Brazilian intellectuals that the population is constantly becoming less Negroid and more and more European in appearance. There is a general tendency for the predominantly white population to absorb the lighter mixed-bloods, while the mulattoes in turn absorb the blacks. (Pierson, *Negroes*, p. 123.) See also BRANCARÃO.

**ASAGWE** (Fr. Cr.), a salute to the gods in some Afro-Haitian cults.

**ASAMBIA** (Afr.), the supreme deity of a major Afro-Cuban cult.

**ASASI** (Afr.), among Surinamese Bush Negroes (q.v.), an African goddess worshipped as the mother of the earth.

**ASENTADO** (Sp.), in colonial Spanish America, a black slave who, with his master's permission, offered his services for wages or training. In this manner, an *asentado* often obtained his freedom. See also ESCLAVO COARTADO.

**ASENTISTA** (Sp.), in colonial Spanish America, a merchant who had bought the right from the Spanish Crown to import slaves into the colonies. The *asentista* was given the opportunity to buy numerous licenses, and he was obliged to pay the Crown an annual lump sum for the licenses that was slightly less than their total value. He derived his profit from the difference between the two figures, plus whatever he could make on the few licenses he was allowed to use himself. Thus, the *asentista* was essentially a middleman between the government and the slave merchant, an agent responsible for finding buyers for the licenses, smoothing out any differences between slave merchants and government officials, collecting (with the aid of factors) the contract's revenues, and helping enforce the regulations that governed the trade.

**ASHAM** (Afr.), in the Afro-Jamaican dialect, guinea corn (q.v.) which has been parched, finely ground, and mixed with sugar. Also called Black George, Brown George, Coction, Kak Sham, and Sham-Sham.

**ASHANTI KINGDOM,** a small West African kingdom situated inland from the Gold Coast (q.v.). Early in the seventeenth century, it began expanding and forming tributary states like Bono, Banda, Gonja, and Dagomba. It vigorously resisted British and European intrusions into its territory. When it reached the Guinea Coast (q.v.), however, where the Europeans had already become firmly entrenched, it had to associate with the British and was unable to set up its own slave exportation system, as Dahomey (q.v.) had done early in the sixteenth century. In 1874, the British made it a colony and, in 1895, conquered all its territory. The British sacked its capital, Kumasi, in 1900. (Oliver, *A Short History*, p. 122-123.)

**ASHANTI SLAVES**, African slaves imported into the New World, most of whom were subjects or captives sold by the rulers of the Ashanti Kingdom (q.v.). These slaves were considered the proudest and most warlike in all the lands bordering on the Gulf of Guinea (q.v.). Their culture was Sudanese, and, among other things, they brought with them the art of weaving and other crafts; they were among the most advanced and progressive blacks of their day. Their number is undetermined, but the rise in the number of slaves exported through the 1740s correlates well enough with the rise and consolidation of the Ashanti Kingdom. (Ramos, *The Negro*, p. 30.)

**ASHANTI OATH**, in Mexico, (circa 1660), an oath taken by an African-born slave to prevent another from doing him bodily harm. (Engerman and Genovese, *Race and Slavery*, p. 318.)

**ASHAROKO** (Afr.), in Trinidad, a male god of African origin worshipped by the black population. His favorite foods are land turtle and guinea-bird (q.v.) and his drink, rum; his sacred day is Wednesday and his colors are brown and white. Characterized as a very big man, he is identified with the Sacred Heart.

**ASHOGUN** (Afr.), in some Afro-Brazilian cults, the priest in charge of sacrificing animals.

**ASHOLA AGUENGUE** (Afr.), in the Afro-Cuban folk religion, a goddess worshipped as the mother of the waters; she is identified with Our Lady of Charity.

**ASIENTO DE NEGROS** (Sp.) ("slave trade permit"), a trade contract granted by the Spanish Crown to foreign ship owners and merchants, allowing them the exclusive right to import African slaves into the colonies. The first *asiento* was given by Charles V in 1518 to his "favorite," Laurent de Gouvernat, a Dutch merchant; this license was for ten years. When the license expired in 1528, it was transferred for four years to Henrich Ehinger and Hieronymus Seiber, employees of the Welseers, the German bankers. Between 1534 and 1580, the *asiento* was handled as a state monopoly by the government; later, it passed from the Dutch to the French and finally to the English. (Goslinga, *The Dutch*, p. 339.)

**ASIENTO DE TRABAJO** (Sp.) ("labor contract"), in colonial Spanish America, an agreement whereby a worker, often a black slave, agreed to work for a certain period of time in return for which the employer was to provide either money, clothing, room and board, or training in a skilled profession. In Santiago, Chile, between 1565 and 1585, *asientos de trabajo* were entered into by colored saddlers, sailors, and tailors. (Mellafe, *La esclavitud*, p. 41.)

**ASOCIACIÓN CONTRA LA TRATA** (Sp.) (Association Against the Slave Trade), a Cuban group organized by leading reformers in Havana in 1845 to carry out the plan for the gradual abolition of slavery. Among the organizers were Cuban slaveowners and intellectuals, backed by some Spaniards who, among other things, pledged not to buy slaves smuggled onto the island from the United States after 1865. (Foner, *The Spanish-Cuban-American War*, V. II, p. 134.)

**ASSIQUI** (Afr.), an Afro-Brazilian talisman or charm worn by blacks in fetish cults.

**ASSOCIAÇÃO ACADEMICA PROMOTORA DA REMISSÃO DOS CAPTIVOS** (Pg.) (Academic Association for the Promotion and Emancipation of Slaves), an abolitionist association organized in 1860 by a group of students in Recife. (Eisenberg, *The Sugar Industry*, p. 162.)

**ASSOCIAÇÃO CENTRAL EMANCIPADORA** (Pg.) (Central Association for Emancipation), an antislavery group founded in Rio de Janeiro in 1880. Like similar societies of that period, it sponsored lectures and encouraged meetings to which intellectuals, writers, artists, and others were invited. (Ramos, *The Negro*, p. 72.)

**ASSOCIAÇAO DE SOCORROS MUTUOUS E LENTA EMANCIPAO DOS CATIVOS** (Pg.) (Association for the Mutual Aid and Slow Emancipation of Slaves), a private abolitionist group founded in 1859 by Bishop João da Purificação Masques Perdigão in Recife. It did not survive very long. (Eisenberg, *The Sugar Industry*, p. 162.)

**ASSOCIAÇÃO DOS BRASILEIROS DE CÔR** (Pg.) (Association of Colored Brazilians), a group organized in São Paulo (circa 1889) by a black named Marcos Rodrigues for the purpose of promoting black education and political awareness. (Ramos, *The Negro*, pp. 178-179.)

**ASSOCIAÇÃO LIBERTADORA** (Pg.) (Liberator Association), an active abolitionist group organized in December 1877 whose aim was the abolition of slavery in São Paulo. It was established by planters when they began to experience mass waves of slave escapes. These planters emphasized a delayed rather than an immediate abolition because they wanted time to prepare for the free-labor system without disruption of work. (Toplin, *The Abolition*, p. 226.)

**ASSON** (Fr. Cr.), *tiatia*, an Afro-Haitian gourd rattle webbed with beads and snake vertebrae to which a small bell is attached. It is used as a symbol of authority by the *houngan* (q.v.) or priest.

**ASSOT** (Fr. Cr.), in Afro-Haitian folklore, a board for striking; used as a percussion instrument.

**ASSOTOR** (Fr. Cr.), in Haiti, a very sensitive drum which is said to vibrate like the Aeolian harp in the breeze. It is the greatest of all things in the voodoo (q.v.) temple. In making an *assotor*, first a religious service is held, and then the priest goes into the woods to find a suitable large tree. The trunk must be big enough so that the drum is at least as tall as a man. Most *assotors* are six feet high or more.

**ASSOUBA** (Afr.), the first daily prayer, recited at dawn, by black slaves in Brazil who were followers of Mohammed. (Ramos, *As culturas negras*, p. 144.)

**ASSUMY** (Afr.), in colonial Brazil, the annual fast observed by Moslem black slaves from Dahomey (q.v.), Mali, Bornu (q.v.), and elsewhere in Africa.

**ASUNU** (Afr.), in Jamaica, an elephant who appears as a character in Anancy stories (q.v.); his identity is now obscure. (Cassidy, *Dictionary*, p. 14.)

**ATABAQUE, TAMBAQUE** (Pg.), in Afro-Brazilian fetish cults, a sacred wooden drum used in sets of three of varying sizes; apparently of Yoruba (q.v.) origin.

**ATALAIA** (Pg.), on the West African coast, a big house composed of many dwellings placed side by side and having a common roof. It is a standard traditional residence for polygamous African families.

**ATARÉ** (Yor.), an African pepper brought by Yoruba (q.v.) slaves to Brazil; also known as "pepper of the Coast" *(pimenta da Costa)*. (Ramos, *As culturas negras*, p. 78.)

**ATELIER** (Fr. Cr.), in the colonial French Antilles, a slave gang (q.v.) working under an overseer.

**ATLANTIC PASSAGE.** See MIDDLE PASSAGE.

**ATLANTIC SLAVE TRADE,** a commercial and legal system of bringing black slaves from the west coast of Africa to tropical America. Almost 90 percent of the slaves went to Atlantic coastal areas, from Brazil through the Guianas to the Caribbean Coast and the islands. These blacks were transported against their will from about 1510 to 1807, when the British Parliament officially abolished the trade. Africans and Europeans alike participated in this commercially profitable activity, and both societies were deeply influenced by it. (Pescatello, *The African*, p. 35.)

**ATRAPALHADO** (Pg.), in colonial Brazil, a slave who spoke his own African tongue to other Africans and a "mixed up" Portuguese to his master and overseers.

**ATTIBON LEGBA** (Afr.). See LEGBA SE.

**ATTOO** (Afr.), a plant *(Cassia viminea)* whose roots were once used by black slaves in Jamaica to clean their teeth.

**ATTORNEY**, in the West Indies, a term for one who manages a plantation or property for an absentee owner. During the colonial period, many attorneys mismanaged or destroyed the estates. Their aim was to upset the affairs of the plantations to such an extent that their services would seem to be required for a longer period of time until, finally, the property under their charge would be turned over to them completely. An attorney, even though absent, might undertake the general management of several plantations. In 1770, a single Jamaican attorney frequently superintended the affairs of many properties, and in 1823, in Tobago, an attorney once had charge of thirty-six estates at one time. (Cassidy, *Dictionary*, p. 14.) See also ATTORNEYSHIP.

**ATTORNEYSHIP**, a system of plantation management of nonresident estates in the West Indies during the colonial period. The negative consequences of this system were numerous—even under the best conditions—but as actually operated in the sugar colonies, they beggar description. A nonagriculturist usually held the attorneyship; thus, physicians, lawyers, and even clergymen were sometimes given charge of estates. (Ragatz, *The Fall*, p. 54-55.) See also ATTORNEY.

**AUGUST MORNING**, in Jamaica, the celebration of the end of slavery on the eve of Emancipation Day (q.v.) (August 1, 1834). Blacks refer to this event as bringing in the August Morning.

**AUTOBIOGRAPHY OF A RUNAWAY SLAVE, THE,** an autobiographical narrative by a black Cuban Maroon (q.v.), Esteban Montejo, edited by M. Barnett (London, 1968).

**AVALOU.** See YANVALOU.

**AVENÇAS** (Pg.), **AVENECIAS** (Sp.) ("agreements"), contracts for slave exportation concluded between Portuguese revenue collectors for West Africa and slave traders. These agreements were required for all merchants wishing to export Africans from these regions. They necessitated the payment of duties, whether the slaves were destined for Lisbon, Brazil, or Spanish America.

**AVERÍA** (Sp.), in colonial Spanish America, a tax paid by slave traders based on the estimated value of the cargo.

**AVERÍA DE LOS NEGROS BOZALES** (Sp.) ("head tax on black slaves"), the head tax collected on slaves imported into the Spanish colonies. In 1622, the Spanish Crown collected 20 reales per head. (Diaz Soler, *Historia*, p. 80.)

**AVIRONS,** magic oars, symbols of the great Agwé (q.v.), the ruler of the seas in Afro-Haitian folk cults.

**AWASA** (Afr.), an Afro-Surinamese dance.

**AWKA** (Afr.), the name of an Afro-Surinamese tribe. In southern Nigeria, there is a group of Ibo-speaking people known as the Awka people.

**AXEM.** See AXIM.

**AXÊXÊ** (Yr.), an Afro-Brazilian term for a ritual preceding the service celebrated on the seventh day after death. It is used only by blacks in Bahia, Brazil.

**AXIM, AXEM** (Afr.), a fort built by the Dutch in the Gold Coast (q.v.) around 1645 as a slave-trading post.

**AXÔGUN** (Afr.), in Afro-Brazilian fetish cults, players of musical instruments, particularly, those who perform on the sacred drums.

**AY-A-SARI, ALASARI** (Ar.), the third daily prayer recited in the afternoon by Afro-Brazilian Moslems. (Ramos, *As culturas negras*, p. 148.)

**AYIDA WEDO** (Afr.), in Afro-Haitian folk cults, the wife of Damballa (q.v.). Her symbols are the snake and the rainbow, and her color is white. In Dahomey (q.v.) and Nigeria, Ayida Wedo is known as a male rather than female spirit and is regarded as the same divinity as Damballa, or Dji. When a rainbow appeared after a rain, it was said that Ayida Wedo had come out from under the earth to drink the fresh water.

**AYIZAN** (Afr.), the goddess of the markets and the highest goddess of the Arada Olympus. She is the wife of the powerful Dahomean god, Legba Se (q.v.).

**AYLELOLÉ!, AYLOLOLÉ, LOLOLÁ!** (Yor.), an Afro-Spanish exclamation used in rhythms. (Alvarez Nazario, *El elemento negroide*, p. 291.)

**AZA** (Afr.), an Afro-Haitian god, symbol of happiness, who, according to the faithful, dances at religious meetings.

**AZAKA MÉDÉ** (Afr.), in Afro-Haitian cults, the name of a stream which Dahomeans believe all the dead must cross. (Courlander, *The Drum*, p. 324.)

**AZANQ** (Afr.), in the Dutch West Indies, a magical spirit-barrier made of palm fronds. It is placed before the entrance of every black village to brush away the evil spirits from visitors entering the town. It is also put in place wherever there is an epidemic. The word is of Dahomean origin.

**AZEITE DE DENDÉ** (Pg.), an oil made from the *dendé* (q.v.) palm fruit, called *cocos*. There are several kinds; the oil made at home by Afro-Brazilians is generally richer and tastier than the one made in factories. During slavery times, merchants from Bahía used to buy *azeite de dendé* and slaves in the Costa da Mina (q.v.). In 1798, 1,000 drums of oil from the Costa da Mina and 500 drums from São Tomé (q.v.) were imported into Bahía. The best *azeite de dendé* was bought in the port of Lagos, Nigeria. In Africa, this oil has many names, such as *ade-quoi, adesran, abe Pa*, and *abobobe* in the Gold Coast (q.v.); and *de-yara, de-kla, de-gbakum, vot-chi, fade*, and *kinede* in Dahomey (q.v.). (Carneiro, *Ladinos e Crioulous*, pp. 72-76.)

**AZENHA** (Pr.), in colonial Brazil, a primitive water mill for grinding cane which relied on the power of water falling over a large wooden wheel. It employed few slaves, and its output was very limited. See also ENGENHO.

**AZETO** (Afr.), a witch or a werewolf in Afro-Haitian folklore.

**AZEVEDO, ALUIZIO** (1857-1913), a Brazilian writer, author of several successful antislavery novels such as *O mulatto* (q.v.) (1881), *O Cortiço, A Casa de Pensão*, and *Homem*. He made good use of the methods of the naturalist writers to expose the sordid misery and abuses in Brazilian society.

His descriptions of a cruel and unjust world are brilliant and incisive. (Sayers, *The Negro*, pp. 145, 199, 204.)

**AZEVEDO, ARTHUR** (1855-1908), a Brazilian playwright and poet, author of many comedies and short stories in some of which he attacks slavery. In his plays *O Escravocrata* and *O Liberato*, Azevedo exposes the inhumanity and exploitation of the slave system.

**AZIRI** (Afr.), a spirit, apparently of Dahomean origin, belonging to a large family of gods worshipped in Afro-Haitian cults.

**AZIZAN** (Afr.), among Trinidadian blacks, supernatural beings or "little folk" living in the forests; they are feared by hunters.

**AZOTES DE CUJES O LÁTIGO** (Sp.) ("flogging with a fiber or leather whip"), flogging (q.v.), the most convenient form of slave punishment in plantation America. In 1789, a Spanish law limited the number of lashes to twenty-five and stipulated that only masters could impose them. (Hall, *Social Control*, p. 104.)

**AZUZI** (Afr.), in the Afro-Haitian folk religion, a snake diety.

# b

**BA, BAA,** in the Afro-Jamaican dialect, an abbreviation of *baada*, used for: 1. Brother. 2. A term of intimate address for a man of one's own age. 3. A reciter of folk tales at Accompong (q.v.). (Cassidy, *Dictionary*, p. 15.)

**BAABA** (Yor.), in the West Indies, a Yoruba (q.v.) term for father, grandfather, or senior member of a household.

**BAADA** (Afr.). See BA.

**BAAKINI** (Bant.). In Jamaica, 1. a black ring game or play constituting part of a nine-night (q.v.) ritual or other funeral observance. 2. A funeral meeting, usually the one held on the second night; characterized by ring play.

**BAAMI** (Eng. Cr.). See BAMMY.

**BAANDI** (Afr.), in the West Indies, a type of yam (q.v.) *(Dioscorea)* eaten by blacks.

**BABA**, an ethnic group of the Bight of Biafra (q.v.) from which slaves were taken to the West Indies.

**BABÁ** (Afr.), a priest or priestess of an Afro-Brazilian cult who acts as a powerful intermediary between man and the gods. Babá is known by a variety of names, including *babá* or *baboloxi* in Rio de Janeiro, *babalâo* (q.v.) in Bahia, and *babalorixá* in Recife. When officiating at the altar in the ceremonial house, he is called *pai de santo* (q.v.) or, if female, *mãe de santo* (q.v.). In Africa, women, being of inferior social status, may not be received into the priesthood, but in Brazil many of the *babás* are female. The *babá is* usually the repository for the secrets of the cult and the director of the rituals. (T. L. Smith, *Brazil*, pp. 534, 732.)

**BABAÇA** (Afr.), an Afro-Brazilian word meaning twin brothers.

**BABACUARA** (Afr.), an Afro-Brazilian term for a lower-class laborer on a sugar plantation, usually a black.

**BABACUÉ** (Afr.), an Afro-Brazilian fetish song.

**BABALÁ, BATALÁ** (Afr.), in the Afro-Cuban folk religion, a term for witchcraft.

**BABA-LAD** (Afr.), in Jamaica, a term of intimacy and friendship.

**BABALÂO** (Afr.), in certain Afro-Brazilian cults, a priest whose primary function is to foretell the future. As such, he has considerable prestige among the faithful. At first, his essential mission was, as in Africa, purely religious and magical, but in the New World it changed greatly, losing many of its original qualities. *Babalâos* are found elsewhere in Latin America, especially in Cuba. In 1952, in Havana, the number of these leaders acting in the Cuban *santería* (q.v.) was calculated to be between 200 and 300. (Ramos, *The Negro*, p. 95.)

**BABALÚ-AYE, BABAYÚ-AYÉ,** an African male god who causes leprosy and also cures it. He is thought to be a sickly man afraid of flies and insects. Whenever anyone comes near him, he warns the person by shaking a little placard that hangs around his neck as a sign of infection. An *orisha* (q.v.) in the Afro-Cuban *santería* cult (q.v.), he was a god of infectious diseases in Yorubaland. (Jahn, *Muntu*, p. 68.)

**BABASSÚ,** in Brazil, a species of palm *(Orbignya Sp.)* found in the tropical forest. Slaves and poor people have used its leaves to make baskets and as thatching; its nuts were an important source of oil and, in the past, a staple food for slaves.

**BABAYÚ-AYÉ.** See BABALÚ-AYE.

**BABOULE** (Afr.), an Afro-Haitian dance performed on the occasion of building a new house in the countryside.

**BABWA!** (Afr.), in the Afro-Jamaican dialect, an expression of wonder formerly used by slaves. On sugar estates (q.v.), planters considered it disgraceful. (Cassidy, *Jamaica Talk*, p. 19.)

**BABY-PUZZLE,** an Afro-Jamaican phrase for the tea fed newborn children. (Beckwith, *Black Roadways*, p. 198.)

**BACALHAU** (Pg.), a twisted raw leather hide used as an instrument of torture to punish slaves in Brazil. It was the customary punishment for small faults, such as the theft of a chunk of meat or of cane. The person was tied face down on the ground and then beaten with the *bacalhau* from nine to thirteen consecutive nights. Some were incapable of withstanding the punishment and expired before the end of the ninth night. (Ramos, *The Negro*, pp. 34-35.)

**BACHATA** (Sp.), an Afro-Spanish word for a noisy and joyful celebration, a merrymaking.

**BACKRA, BUCKRA** (Afr.). In the West Indies: 1. A white man or woman (the latter, also *backra* lady, *backra* mistress, and so forth); also, collectively, white people. 2. A term of polite address, equivalent to sir, master, boss; also master or boss. 3. A term used to refer to people of light enough color to be associated with whites rather than blacks. 4. One who, though not white, lives like a white man or moves in white society. See also BLACK BACKRA; SAMBO BACKRA. 5. As an adjective: fit for the white man or master, hence good (or the best), quality, excellent. See also BACKRA CALALOU; BACKRA PINE. 6. As an adjective: introduced to the black by the white man, hence considered by the black as characterizing or pertaining to whites. See also BACKRA BOOK; BACKRA SWEAR. 7. Used in the possessive as an equivalent to "my." (The speaker's sense of possession evidently made him feel like a master.) 8. A species of the genus *Phytolacca*, a type of *calalou* (q.v.). 9. Probably the tree water mahoe *(Hernandia catalpifolia).* (Cassidy, *Dictionary*, p. 18.)

**BACKRA BOOK** (Afr.), in Jamaica, the Bible. See also BACKRA.

**BACKRA CALALOU** (Afr.), an Afro-Jamaican term for a fine variety of *calalou* (q.v.). See also BACKRA.

**BACKRA COUNTRY** (Afr.), Jamaica, to which slaves were brought against their will by the white man. See also BACKRA.

**BACKRA HALL** (Afr.), in Jamaica, the parlor of an overseer's house on an estate. (Cassidy, *Dictionary*, p. 19.) See also BACKRA.

**BACKRA HOUSE** (Afr.), in Jamaica, the overseer's house on an estate. See also BACKRA.

**BACKRA PINE** (Afr.), in Jamaica, a fine variety of pineapple. See also BACKRA.

**BACKRA SWEAR** (Afr.), in Jamaica, an oath taken on the Bible. See also BACKRA.

**BACKRA YAM** (Afr.), in the West Indies, a delicate variety of yam (q.v.) *(Dioscorea)* universally cultivated by blacks. See also BACKRA.

**BACK-TIE,** a Jamaican term for a piece of cloth tied on a black mother's back to carry her baby.

**BA-CONGOS,** in colonial Brazil, black slaves, most of them Bantu (q.v.) brought from the Congo (q.v.) Kingdom.

**BACOUA, BAKOUA** (Afr.), a big, colorful straw hat, conical on top, with the brim turned up; worn especially by peasant black women in the French Antilles. (Corzani, *Littérature antillaise, poésie*, p. 305.)

**BACOULOU-BAKA**, an Afro-Haitian god, master of black magic.

**BAD CANDLE, BAD LAMP,** an Afro-Jamaican term for a candle or lamp used in sympathetic magic practices. As it is burned, the life, breath, luck, etc., of the person against whom it is directed is supposed to dwindle away. (Cassidy, *Dictionary*, p. 19.)

**BADJICAN** (Afr.), the keeper of the altar in the Afro-Haitian cult. As an assistant to the priest, he is highly respected by the faithful. (Courlander, *The Drum*, p. 10.)

**BADOO** (Afr.), an African name for a plant *(Nimphaee lotus)*. In Jamaica, it is applied to a variety of *coco* (q.v.) with a large, light-red rhizome or "head" which is eaten. Blacks considered it less desirable than the regular *coco*. (Cassidy, *Dictionary*, p. 20.)

**BADOO-BILL,** an Afro-Jamaican term for a short blade or hoe, both edges of which are sharpened. It is often attached to a handle and used as a tool by blacks for digging cocos (q.v.), yams (q.v.), and other roots.

**BADYAT KON** (Afr.), a special bobbin-like stick used by blacks to play sacred drums in the Afro-Haitian cult.

**BAFAN** (Afr.). 1. In Africa, a child who did not learn to walk the first two to seven years. 2. In Jamaica, a useless clumsy person; applied as an epithet —for example, a clumsy maidservant. (Cassidy, *Jamaica Talk*, p. 135.)

**BAFINI** (Afr.), in the Afro-Jamaican dialect, a disfigured or crippled child; one who does not learn to walk properly.

**BAGI** (Fr. Cr.), in the Afro-Haitian folk religion, a sacred place in a shrine dedicated to a particular god.

**BAGI** (Eng. Cr.). In Jamaica: 1. A side-bag used by blacks in the field. 2. A baby's knicker. (Cassidy, *Dictionary*, p. 20.)

**BAGUETTE** (Fr. Cr.), in Afro-Haitian folk music, a single crooked stick held in the right hand by the drummer, while the left hand strikes the drumhead with the fingers. The drumstick itself is struck either against the drumhead or against its wooden side, thus permitting a further variation in tone.

**BAGUETTES GUINÉES** (Fr. Cr.), in Afro-Haitian rituals, crude wood carvings of popular deities, iron carved *marassa* (q.v.) bowls, and grotesquely shaped drumsticks covering the inner wall of many chapels.

**BAHIANO** (Pg.), an Afro-Brazilian dance and its music, apparently originating in Bahia. The participants freely improvise rhythm and movements while the players keep time and harmony by varying the tempo and tones. After several movements, the pair of dancers exchanges places with another couple by going over to them and striking them with their bellies; this new couple then takes up the dance. The rhythm becomes progressively livelier, and after a while, the group breaks into popular songs and poetical improvisations. (Ramos, *The Negro*, p. 121.)

**BAIGNE DE MAMBU** (Fr. Cr.), in Afro-Haitian voodoo (q.v.), a bottle filled with a foul, evil-smelling lotion used in incantations.

**BAIGNEUR DES MORTS** (Fr. Cr.), in Afro-Haitian funerals, the person or functionary who bathes the corpse and watches over it.

**BAILE DE BOMBA** (Sp.), an Afro-Spanish drum used to accompany black dances.

**BAILE DEL SANTO** (Sp.), in colonial Buenos Aires, Sunday feast day at noon, celebrated by African "nations" (q.v.) such as the Congos, the Mozambiquans, Mandingos and the Benguelas. Included in the festivities were prayers, dances, songs, and a colorful procession to the Plaza de la Victoria where banners and African instruments were paraded around the square. Each group was led by a king and a queen and sang and invoked its deities in its own native tongue. It is said that at the end, the crowd passed into a trance.

**BAILELE** (Sp.), in Afro-Cuban folklore, an individual with both male and female reproductive organs.

**BAILING** (Eng. Cr.), in Jamaica, a container for produce used by blacks.

**BAIN** (Eng. Cr.), in Jamaica, a word for buttocks; used mainly by blacks.

**BAIN DE NOEL** (Fr. Cr.), an Afro-Haitian ritual whose main feature is the pulverizing of leaves in a mortar. This is done by males, to the accompaniment of drumming and singing by the *hounsi* (q.v.). Later, a sacred "lotion" is made from the powdered leaves and is shared by all.

**BAIYERI YAM,** in the West Indies, a yellow yam (q.v.) *(Dioscorea)* eaten mainly by blacks.

**BAKA** (Afr.), in Afro-Haitian folklore, an evil spirit akin to former Christian representations of evil. The *bakas* are described as small, mischievous creatures, human in appearance with red eyes and legs or arms covered with skin but not flesh. They change into animals at will and may roam the countryside in the form of cats, dogs, or cattle. They are notorious sorcerers, known for performing malevolent acts.

**BAKA LOAS** (Afr.), in Afro-Haitian folklore, a group of small, malevolent creatures with beards and flaming eyes, thought to be "doubles" of sorcerers.

**BAKA SANI** (Afr.) ("a white man's thing"), a phrase used idiomatically by Bush Negroes (q.v.) in Surinam for everything outside their own culture. In this sense, "a white man's thing" is a car, a flashlight, a phonograph, a book, a pill, and the like. (Herskovits, *Rebel Destiny*, p. 347.)

**BAKER, MOSES,** a North American former slave who, at the close of the American Revolution, settled in Jamaica. A loyalist and former member of the George Liele (q.v.) black church in Georgia, he began converting black slaves on the island in 1784, enjoying a remarkable degree of success. (Ragatz, *The Fall*, p. 29.)

**BAKOUA.** See BACOUA.

**BAKULU BAKA** (Afr.), in Afro-Haitian folklore, a malevolent *loa* (q.v.)· who eats and destroys people. Sometimes, when thought of as separate spirits, both Bakulu and Baka are akin to demons.

**BAL** (Fr. Cr.), in Haiti, a black country social dance held on Saturday or Sunday afternoons.

**BALAFON** (Afr.), in the French Antilles, an African musical instrument consisting of a calabash, which serves as a resonance box, and a thin wooden plate that the player hits with a small hammer.

**BALAFOU** (Afr.) 1. In Africa, a xylophone. 2. In Jamaica, an old African wind instrument akin to a harmonica. (Cassidy, *Dictionary*, p. 21.) See also BALAFON.

**BALAIADA, BALAIÃOS** (Pg.), in northeast Brazil, a rebellion of peasants and runaway slaves against the landowners, planters, and government that broke out in Maranhão in 1839. One of its leaders, Manoel Francisco dos Anjos Ferreira (q.v.), gathered around him a force of some 300 men. In 1842, after several skirmishes and after being hounded relentlessly by the government troops, the *balaiada* was suppressed and its forces fled to the forests. (Ramos, *The Negro*, p. 53.)

**BALAIÃO**, nickname of Manoel Francisco dos Anjos Ferreira (q.v.).

**BALAIO** (Pg.), in Brazil 1. A large basket made of palm leaves. 2. A black dance. 3. Nickname of Raymundo Gomes (q.v.) chief of the *balaiada* (q.v.). 4. A follower of the *balaiada* (q.v.).

**BALDEMOA, TRINIDAD,** a free mulatto promoter and leader of the slave insurrection called the Conspiracy of the Ladder (q.v.), an unsuccessful plot crushed by the Cuban government in 1844. Under the advice of British consul David Turnbull (q.v.), Baldemoa, together with mulattoes Félix Rodríguez, José del Carmen Beitia, and José de C. Zamorano, toured the country and later went to Demerara (Jamaica) to promote the slave rebellion. Apparently, Turnbull financed Baldemoa's activities. After Baldemoa's return to Havana, he and Zamorano were jailed, put on trial before a military tribunal, and accused of abolitionist activities. (Calcagno, *Diccionario*, p. 96.)

**BALDORIOTY DE CASTRO, ROMÁN** (1822-1889), a leading political and literary figure in Puerto Rico during the nineteenth century. As a deputy to the Spanish Cortes in 1870, he worked tirelessly for the abolition of slavery.

**BALÉ** (Sp.), an Afro-Cuban word meaning a plantation overseer.

**BALELE** (Sp.), an old black dance in Puerto Rico.

**BALJAAREN** (D.), in Surinam, a boisterous African dance, popular since slavery times. It provides the occasion for social gatherings at which there is great consumption of wine, beer, gin, and brandy, as well as expensive pastries and other foods. Undoubtedly, *baljaaren* has been one of the most popular Afro-dances because, from 1698 until the present day, there has been a large body of edicts regulating it. Around 1728, plantation owners were prohibited from allowing slaves to have *baljaaren*; in 1828, black slaves were at liberty to have these dances in Paramaribo during the month of January. (Lier, *Frontier Society*, pp. 144-45, 150.)

**BALLAGAS, EMILIO** (1908-1954), a white Cuban poet who identified himself with *afrocubanismo* (q.v.). Ballagas did much to make black art and poetry respected in Latin America. His poems exploit the exoticism of Afro-Cuban dancing and singing. His verbal repetitions depend entirely on the effects of sounds, and the words have little, if any, connotative, expressive value. Ballagas's essential poetic rhythm is not an idiomatic one, but rather that of a percussion instrument accompanying the human voice. It operates as a polyrhythm, a sort of rhythmic counterpoint. His works are *Júbilo y fuga* (1931); *Cuaderno de poesía negra* (1934); *Sabor eterno* (1939); *Mapa de la poesía negra* (1946); and *Cielo en rehenes* (1951).

**BALLAHOO** (Afr.), in Afro-Brazilian folklore, a spectral dog of popular tales. It is imagined to be the size of a calf, and its appearance is accompanied by the clanking of charms.

**BALLANO, KING,** a black slave who organized a *cimarron* (q.v.) settlement in the mountains of San Blas in the isthmus of Panama in 1552. For six years he led attacks against the mule trains carrying commodities, silver, and other goods eastward to Porto Bello, or slaves and imported wares westward to Panama City. King Ballano was caught, castrated, and released in 1553. His eventual fate is still disputed. (Rout, L.B., *The African Experience in Spanish America*, p. 118.)

**BALM,** an Afro-Jamaican term for the healing influence experienced at a balm-yard (q.v.). (Cassidy, *Dictionary*, p. 22.)

**BALM-MAN,** an Afro-Jamaican term for a black man who keeps a balm-yard (q.v.). See also BALM.

**BALM-OIL,** an Afro-Jamaican term for any of the supposedly curative oils or other ingredients in the medicines prescribed at a balm-yard (q.v.).

**BALM-YARD,** in Jamaica, the headquarters and ritual site of a black balm-man (q.v.), or shepherd, who administers herbs and other remedies such as balm-oils (q.v.). At his yard, he leads a form of worship featuring revivalist preaching and the singing of Sankey and Moody hymns, accompanied by drumming and dancing which induce a trance-like state in the dancers. At the end of this ritual, healing may take place, followed by a feast.

**BAMBAI** See BAMBY.

**BAMBARA TAIBA** (Afr.), one of the numerous Afro-Haitian *loas* (q.v.) symbolized as a sea crab who moves and dances like a crab. (Courlander, *The Drum*, p. 329.)

**BAMBELÔ** (Afr.), an Afro-Brazilian dance of Bantu (q.v.) origin performed in two rows, men opposite women, or else in a circle with a couple dancing in the middle, miming the choice of sexual partners. (Bastide, *African Civilizations*, p. 176.)

**BAMBOUCHE** (Fr. Cr.), name for an Afro-Haitian recreational dance; often applied to a serious voodoo (q.v.) dance. Also a party.

**BAMBOULA, BAMBULÉ** (Bant.), drum dances of the West Indies blacks; common until 1865 in Saint Thomas when street masquerading began to replace it. African in origin, the name is related to bamboo, of which the drum is made. (Farr, *Historical Dictionary*, p. 90.)

**BAMBUCO** (Afr.), one of the most characteristic Afro-Colombian airs and dances. Its name comes from Bambara, a West African ethno-linguistic group; apparently, it was imported into Colombia by slaves. It is called a pursuit dance, in that the male partner pursues the female until they unite and continue the dance together. Usually sung to the accompaniment of a guitar, it combines African, Andalusian, and Indian strains and ardor.

**BAMBULÉ** (Bant.). See BAMBOULA.

**BAMBY, BAMBAI** (Afr.), an Afro-Jamaican term for a portion of food put aside to be eaten later. Also called *iit-an-left*.

**BAMMY, BAAMI** (Eng. Cr.) (Afr.), an Afro-Jamaican dish consisting of a flat, round cake (about one inch thick) formed from cassava flour and baked in a heavy iron mold, pot, or pan. Afro-Jamaicans are extremely fond of this delicacy; no choicer offering can be made to a resident of the northwest side of the island, where cassava is not grown, than a package of homemade *bammy* from the drier south. (Beckwith, *Black Roadways*, p. 22.)

**BAMMY CHIPS,** an Afro-Jamaican term for thin cassava cakes made by a quashee (q.v.).

**BAMMY PRESSER,** an Afro-Jamaican bag in which grated cassava is pressed to squeeze out the juice; used in making *bammy* (q.v.).

**BANANA CUDJOE,** an Afro-Jamaican word for a kind of dark banana *(Bodianus rufus)*, eaten mainly by blacks.

**BANANA ENGLISH,** an English Creole (q.v.) spoken in Trinidad.

**BAÑANI** (Afr.), in the Afro-Cuban folk religion, a deity, brother of Changó (q.v.).

**BANCRA** (Afr.). See BANKRA.

**BANDA** (Eng. Cr.), in Jamaica, a large African drum.

**BANDE** (Fr. Cr.), an Afro-Antilles word for a group of black children working for wages under an overseer on a plantation.

**BANDO DE BUEN GOBIERNO** (Sp.) ("Act of Good Government"), in colonial Cuba, a law promulgated in Havana in 1792 forbidding the blacks of Guinea (q.v.) from erecting altars in honor of Catholic saints when they held their great dances on grounds belonging to the *cabildos de negros* (q.v.). It also barred them from carrying the bodies of deceased members on the association's premises and from mourning them according to their native customs. (Bastide, *African Civilizations*, p. 94.)

**BANDO DE BUEN GOBIERNO Y POLICIA DE LA ISLA DE CUBA** (Sp.) ("Act of Good Government and Order on the Island of Cuba"), a decree issued by Captain-General Geronimo Valdez in 1842 ordering that any free colored person (q.v.) had to obtain a license from his or her local town council before seeking employment. It also forbade free blacks from carrying arms, although whites were permitted to do so.

**BANDO NEGRO** (Sp.), a "Black Decree" proclaimed by Marshal Juan Prim, Spanish governor of Puerto Rico in 1830; its purpose was to discourage slave rebellions.

**BANGA** (Afr.), in the West Indies, a word for dancing and singing.

**BANG-BANG** (Eng. Cr.), in Jamaica, a paddle-shaped stick used by black women to beat clothes against a stone when washing them.

**BANG-BELLY,** an Afro-Jamaican term for the protruding stomach of an ill-nourished child. (Cassidy, *Jamaica Talk*, p. 138.)

**BANGGARANG, BANGGERANG** (Afr.), an Afro-Jamaican term for a great noise or disturbance among people; quarreling.

**BANGUÊ** (Pg.), in colonial Brazil, a litter used to carry dead slaves for burial.

**BANGUELA, BENGUELA** (Afr.), an Afro-Brazilian word for fight, confusion.

**BANGUINHA** (Pg.), in Brazil, a small bench where young girls sit down to sew.

**BANGULA** (Afr.), an Afro-Brazilian term for a small fishing boat.

**BANGULÊ** (Afr.), an Afro-Brazilian dance in which blacks hold their palms in their hands and stamp their feet while dancing.

**BAHIAN DAY.** See BANYAN DAY.

**BANI.** See BANNIE.

**BANIKLEVA.** See BANNIE.

**BANJO: A STORY WITHOUT A PLOT,** a novel published in 1929 by Jamaican Creole author Claude McKay (q.v.), a leading writer of the Negro Renaissance (q.v.). It describes the adventures of black workers from the

West Indies and from Africa on the waterfront of Marseilles. McKay, who feels a fascination for Africa, states that the African working-class blacks are far superior spiritually and morally to those of the Caribbean and the United States. According to him, they are more "primitive" and less "savage." (Jahn, *Neo-African Literature*, pp. 182-83.)

**BANJU SALE** (Afr.), in the Afro-Jamaican dialect, a public sale of used articles.

**BANK,** in Jamaica, a game played mainly by blacks consisting of throwing cashew nuts into a hole in a bank of earth.

**BANKRA,  BANCRA** (Afr.), in the West Indies, a square-cornered basket used by black country people. It consists of a group provision hamper, about eight to ten inches high, which is fitted with a close cover and a double handle. The handle is made from two strips of withe, which have been wrapped together with palm thatch (q.v.) and sewn to the bottom of the basket, about four inches apart. It may be carried by hand or on the head.

**BANNER BEANS, BONNABEES,** in the West Indies, edible beans *(Leguminosae)*, apparently imported in slavery times from the Cape Verde (q.v.) island of Bona Vista.

**BANNIE, BANI, BANIKLEVA, BOMI.** An Afro-Jamaican word for: 1. Sour, curdled milk. 2. The creamy froth on top of boiled corn meal.

**BANSÁ** (Pg.), an Afro-Brazilian musical instrument, consisting of an arched bow with a cord that is rubbed by a piece of wood or a bone.

**BANTA, BANTAM** (Eng. Cr.), in the West Indies, a form of rivalry which consists of trying to imitate somebody in dress and fashion; common among blacks.

**BANTÉ** (Afr.), in the Afro-Cuban folk religion, a sacred garment or apron worn by the god Shangó (q.v.).

**BANTER-SING** (Eng. Cr.), in the West Indies, a black group song sung while digging yam-hills (q.v.), building huts, and the like.

**BANTU,** a member of one of the great family of Negroid tribes occupying equatorial and southern Africa. The Bantu languages constitute the most important linguistic family in Africa south of the Sahara.

**BANWALÁ** (Afr.), in the Afro-Cuban religion, a god, son of Obatalá (q.v.).

**BANYA** (Afr.), a song dance among Surinam Bush Negroes (q.v.).

**BANYAN DAY, BAHIAN DAY,** among Jamaican blacks, a day on which (as on shipboard) no meat is served; hence a day of fasting or austerity. This is one of the many nautical terms that was adopted into Jamaican use. Its present folk form appears to be Ben Jonson Day (q.v.). (Cassidy, *Dictionary*, p. 27.)

**BANZ** (Eng. Cr.), an Afro-Jamaican word for a great crowd or mass.

**BANZA** (Afr.), an Afro-Brazilian string instrument.

**BANZÉ** (Afr.), an Afro-Brazilian term for disorder, riot, disturbance.

**BANZEIRO** (Afr.), an Afro-Brazilian term for a very sad and depressed individual.

**BANZO** (Afr.), in Brazil, a deep sadness and depression that affected many slaves brought to the colony against their will. Many died along the way; many of those who survived and lived to endure their torment were driven to drinking, the use of narcotics, and dirt-eating (q.v.). Those slaves unable to bear their situation committed suicide by hanging themselves or by consuming the poisonous herbs and brews provided by sorcerers. (Freyre, *The Masters*, pp. 18, 476.)

**BAPTISMAL TAX,** in the kingdom of Angola (q.v.) at the end of the seventeenth century, a tax of 300 reis paid by slave traders for every captive slave they embarked for Brazil. (Davidson, *Black Mother*, p. 158.)

**BAPTISTA, PEDRO JOÃO,** a Portuguese slave trader who in 1806, together with Amaro José (q.v.), made the first attempted crossing of central Africa. The two traveled from inland Angola (q.v.) to the Portuguese settlement of Tete on the Lower Zambezi River, thus anticipating David Livingston by half a century. Baptista left a journal which shows (as Livingston would later confirm) that the trails were relatively safe and easy once the goodwill of two or three African chiefs was obtained. (Davidson, *Black Mother*, p. 155.)

**BAPTISTE, JOHN,** a black slave who led a rebellion in Saint Domingue on August 22, 1791. He was killed in the early phase of the fighting. (Ott, *The Haitian Revolution*, p. 47.)

**BAPTIST MISSIONARY SOCIETY** (BMS), a Baptist society that, after 1807, when the campaign against the slave trade was raging, became interested in sending missionaries to the West Indies. One of its leaders, John Ryland, wanted to work among the slaves in Jamaica. In 1813, the first missionary, John Rowe, was sent to Jamaica at the request of an aged black Baptist preacher. This group was a leading force in the abolitionist movement (q.v.), and William Knibb (q.v.) was one of its great missionaries. (McCloy, *The Negro*, p. 288.)

**BAPTIST MOVEMENT.** See NATIVE BAPTIST MOVEMENT.

**BAPTIST TICKET,** around 1761, a printed card given once a month to every Jamaican black attached to a congregation. Every Sunday, members were obliged to present these tickets to the Baptist minister, who, upon receipt of a macaroni (a coin worth 1 shilling and 8 pence), filled in one of the blank spaces, thus certifying that the slave had attended chapel and presented the offering. If two or three Sundays passed without a ticket being marked, the ticket holder was expelled from the congregation. Hundreds of Baptist tickets were found on many estates during the Baptist War (q.v.). (Cassidy, *Jamaica Talk*, p. 233.)

**BAPTIST WAR,** the name given to the slave rebellion in Jamaica in 1831. The Baptists were blamed for it because they had encouraged the slaves in their demands for emancipation. The uprising, led by Samuel Sharp (q.v.), a slave and a Baptist minister, was strongly under the influence of the black Baptist church. During the insurrection, several estates were burned, and many whites and slaves were killed.

**BAQUAQUA, MAHOMMAH G.,** a black slave from Zoogas, in the interior of West Africa, who was brought to Brazil in the 1830s. After his Brazilian experience, Baquaqua traveled to New York as a slave sailor on a merchant vessel. There he was freed. Later, he went to Haiti, where he was converted to Christianity; from there he went to Canada. His autobiography was published in 1854 in Detroit by Samuel Moore.

**BAQUINÉ** (Afr.), an Afro-Caribbean term for a wake held for an infant. As befits the passing of an innocent, it is a joyful and happy gathering, with prayers, songs, and dances. (Alvarez Nazario, *El elemento negroide*, p. 276.)

**BARA** (Afr.), a god in some of the Afro-Brazilian cults who acts as the obligatory intermediary between mortals and spirits. As a result, he is always the first deity to be worshipped in any service. His origin is Yorubaland. (Bastide, *African Civilizations*, p. 117.)

**BARÂO DO CHOCOLATE** (Pg.) ("Chocolate Baron"), in Brazil, prominent mixed-blood citizens with Negroid features who were elevated to the nobility by Emperor Dom Pedro II in the 1840s. In the European community, these individuals were characterized as brilliantine parvenus, sporting scandalous waistcoats and wearing too much jewelry.

**BARBA, DOROTEO,** a black Cuban teacher who, around 1795, opened the first school for black pupils. Previously, the only educational facility for blacks was the Belén school of Havana which selected black students could attend. (Calcagno, *Diccionario*, p. 99.)

**BARBACOA** (Afr.), in colonial Antilles, a big room or a section of the slaves' quarters used for storing grains and nonperishable products. It was usually situated across from the main gate of the compound.

**BARBADOS ACT FOR THE BETTER ORDERING AND GOVERNING OF NEGROES,** a comprehensive code approved by the Barbados Assembly on September 2, 1661, stating the rights and obligations of masters, slaves, and servants. The master always had almost total authority over his slaves, but markedly less power over his servants. He was obliged to give his blacks new clothing once a year (a pair of drawers and cap for every male, a petticoat and cap for every female), but no rules were laid down about slave food or slave working conditions. The master could correct his slaves in any way he liked, but if, while beating a black for a misdemeanor, he happened to maim or kill him, he was liable to a penalty. (Dunn, *Sugar and Slaves*, p. 239.)

**BARBALHO, LUIZ,** a black hero of the war against the Dutch invaders from 1626 to 1630. He was the leader of the defeated Brazilian army which fled to the Sertão. (Senna, *Africanos no Brasil*, p. 42.)

**BARBOSA, JOSÉ CELSO,** a Puerto Rican mulatto politician who, in 1880, graduated from the University of Michigan Medical School in Ann Arbor, Michigan. Immediately afterwards, he returned to practice on the island. In 1882, Barbosa began his political career by organizing the Partido Liberal Reformista (Liberal Reform party). Later, in 1889, he founded the Partido Republicano (Republican party). In 1900, U.S. President William McKinley appointed him a member of the executive council of the island.

**BARCALA, LORENZO** (1775-1835), an Argentine, born in Mendoza as a legal slave. He was freed by the National Assembly legislation of 1813. He fought in the independence war; with unusual gifts of leadership and ability to organize, he rose to the rank of colonel. He was known as the "Black

Caballero." He fought in provincial wars in Brazil and civil wars until his capture, court martial and execution in Mendoza, his native city, in 1835.

**BARICA-SUBÁ** (Ar.) ("May God give you a good day!"), a friendly greeting which Moslem slaves used in colonial Brazil. (Ramos, *O Negro*, p. 77.)

**BARK BATH,** in the West Indies, a medicinal bath which blacks commonly used to cure fevers. Its essential ingredient is quinquina bark.

**BARK JACKET** (Eng. Cr.), in the Caribbean region, powdered quinquina bark which is sprinkled upon a patient until it covers him like a jacket; common among blacks.

**BARK-TREE,** the mahoe tree whose bark is stripped and used in making rope. In the West Indies, blacks and country people make all their ropes from it.

**BAROKO** (Afr.), a he-goat offered as a sacrifice by a black priest in the Afro-Cuban religion.

**BARON CHITA** (Fr. Cr.), in the Afro-Haitian pantheon, a god who sits on graves.

**BARON CIMITIÈRE,** an African male god of death, worshipped by blacks in Haiti. The faithful make him offerings of food and drink and sacrifice clean live animals to him.

**BARON LACROIX,** in the Afro-Haitian religion, a male god of death.

**BARON PIQUANT,** a god in charge of grave-digging, worshipped by Haitian blacks.

**BARON SAMEDI,** the god of black magic in the Afro-Haitian pantheon.

**BARRACÃO** (Pg.), in Afro-Brazilian cults, the pavilion where ritual dances are performed.

**BARRACÓN** (Sp.), in colonial Spanish America, a public building rented by slave traders as a temporary quarters for blacks until they were sold. In these compounds, often away from the center of the city, buyers examined the slaves, paid taxes to government officials, and formalized their sales. In colonial Cuba, some *barracones* grew into huge compounds that could house as many as 200 slaves with their families.

**BARRACOON,** in West Africa, a huge coastal warehouse where slaves were kept until ships came for them. Originally, *barracoons* were collection centers set up by the most powerful black chieftains; later, the Europeans themselves established floating *barracoons*, hulks permanently anchored in a creek or estuary for the storage of slaves. The coast of the Bonny River, with its miles of rotting mud water, was one of the most popular areas for bulding these floating compounds. The *barracoon* was a stockade within a stockade and resembled a corral for cattle. A long shed ran down the center to protect the slaves from the sun and rain. Down the middle of the shed was stretched a long chain fastened to a stake at either end. The male slaves were secured at intervals along the chain; the women and children were allowed to run loose. At one corner of the *barracoon*, there was usually a tower where an armed guard kept watch over the captives. (Davidson, *Black Mother*, p. 214; Mannix, *Black Cargoes*, p. 76.)

**BARRETO, TOBIAS.** See MENEZES, TOBIAS BARRETO DE.

**BARRIÈRE** (Fr. Cr.), in Afro-Haitian cults, the entrance of a chapel.

**BARROWBY BEANS** (Eng. Cr.), in the West Indies, a species of edible beans *(Leguminosae)*, formerly a standard slave food.

**BARROW-CROOK** (Eng. Cr.), on Caribbean plantations, a machete with a hooked end used by black laborers in the fields.

**BARUBA** (Afr.), in colonial Cuba, an African ethnic group represented by many of the slaves who worked on the plantation.

**BASILIQUE** (Fr. Cr.), in Afro-Haitian folklore, a magic tree whose leaves are used by black sorcerers to prepare different kinds of infusions.

**BASKET HOOK** (Eng. Cr.), in the West Indies, a round basket made of withe; used by blacks to carry produce.

**BASKET WITHE,** on Caribbean plantations, a coarse basket made of any of several plants *(Tournefortia, Chamissoa)*; formerly used by slaves to carry dung.

**BASSE** (Fr. Cr.), in Haiti, a finger drum resembling a tambourine. Constructed in the pattern of an African prototype, its head is made of goatskin and is usually fifteen to eighteen inches in diameter. Small metal disks are sometimes inserted in the frame to act as rattles. The head, kept well coated with resin or beeswax, is tapped and rubbed with the fingers. The *basse* is used only for secular music, except in rare instances when it is played in the Congo (q.v.) service. (Courlander, *The Drum*, p. 196.)

**BASSETERRE, PETER,** a black slave leader of Saint Kitts who, in 1778, organized a slave uprising against the white planters. The plot was discovered, and Basseterre was tried, convicted, and sentenced to a public whipping and a month's imprisonment. (Goveia, *Slave Society*, p. 96.)

**BASSIN** (Fr. Cr.), in Afro-Haitian folklore, a deep pool in a stream, the favorite residence of water spirits.

**BASTÃO** (Pg.), in Brazil, a sacred stick or cane used by black sorcerers to drive out spirits.

**BASTARD OKRO (OKRA),** a wild plant that grows chiefly in rich, low-lying areas. Slaves in the Caribbean widely used its tender buds, full of mucilage, for food.

**BATA** (Pg.), a long, white, loose-flowing blouse worn by Afro-Brazilian black women. It is usually made of cotton, though sometimes of silk, and is ordinarily trimmed with wide lace.

**BATÁ-COTÔ,** an Afro-Brazilian drum which played a prominent role in many slave insurrections. It has long since disappeared.

**BATALÁ.** See BABALÁ.

**BATÉ-BAÚ** (Pg.), an Afro-Brazilian dance popular in Bahia, Brazil, similar to the *samba* (q.v.).

**BATONNI** (Fr. Cr.), in Haiti, a wild dance performed by men dressed in female clothing. They crouch in circles and do baton-tapping dances to the accompaniment of drumming and singing. *Batonni* usually occur at Mardi Gras. (Courlander, *The Drum*, p. 106.)

**BATUCADA** (Pg.), in Bahia, Brazil, an Afro-Brazilian carnival parade composed of twenty young men, invariably blacks or dark mulattoes, who carry small drums and march in single file. The music is monotonal. (Pierson, *Negroes*, p. 201.)

**BATUCAGÉ** (Pg.), a wild, noisy Afro-Brazilian dance accompanied by shouts and stamping.

**BATUQUES** (Pg.), in colonial Brazil, black dances which were usually performed on Sundays when slaves came together to enjoy and renew their common traditions and beliefs. This recreation was one of the official activities of the different ethnic groups, called "nations" (q.v.), through which blacks automatically and unconsciously renewed their ancestral feelings, which otherwise tended to vanish in the general atmosphere of degradation and exploitation. In modern Brazil, *batuque* is a noisy dance accompanied by drums. (Bastide, *African Civilizations*, p. 91.)

**BATUQUEIRO** (Pg.), a player or dancer of Afro-Brazilian songs.

**BAVAROISE** (Fr. Cr.), in the Antilles, an Afro-French beverage prepared with milk, ice, and rum or sometimes gin.

**BAXTER, JOHN,** a shipwright by profession and an ardent follower of John Wesley (q.v.) who, in 1783, arrived from England in Antigua, West Indies, to promote the expansion of the Wesleyan church among the slaves. He built a chapel and within three years, the local black membership approached the 2,000 mark. (Ragatz, *The Fall*, p. 29.)

**BAYERE YAM** (Afr.), in Jamaica, a yellow cultivated yam (q.v.) eaten by blacks; originally imported from Africa.

**BAY ISLAND FARM, THE,** a New World *barracoon* (q.v.) established in 1840 on one of the Bay Islands off the coast of Honduras. There slaves fresh from Africa were fattened and taught a few words of English before being marketed in small consignments to the Cotton States of the southern United States. (Mannix, *Black Cargoes*, p. 235.)

**BEARD-MAN,** in Jamaica, an adherent of the Afro-Creole cult of Rastafarians (q.v.). He often wears a beard and has plentiful hair, although he occasionally trims both.

**BEAU MARIAGE** (Fr.), in Martinique and elsewhere in the French Antilles, a legal union between two wealthy people, both belonging to esteemed, usually white, families. It assumes a formal church ceremony and a reception. (Comitas and Lowenthal, *Slaves, Free Men*, p. 261.)

**BEAUVOIS, LOUIS,** a Haitian mulatto leader of the slave rebellion that began on September 3, 1791. A member of a mulatto family which had been rich and free, he was educated in France and later served in Savannah, Georgia, during the American War of Independence. After his service, he returned to Saint Domingue and taught until the outbreak of the Haitian revolution. (Ott, *The Haitian Revolution*, pp. 51, 61.)

**BEDWARD, ALEXANDER** (b. 1859), a black preacher, born a laborer on the Mona Estates in Kingston, Jamaica. In 1892, Bedward proclaimed himself a reincarnation, first of Jonah, then of Moses, later of Saint John the Baptist, and finally of Christ. He promised salvation and the violent destruction of the white race. In 1894, he founded the Jamaican Baptist Free church, an Afro-Creole sect very similar to the Father Divine congregation. (Bastide, *African Civilizations*, p. 166.)

**BEDWARDISM,** a Jamaican religious movement inspired by Alexander Bedward (q.v.). Organized in 1876 in the August Town area, it was essentially a black proletarian sect centered around two doctrinal elements: the vow ceremony and the strick observance of fasting. In 1894, its leader founded the Jamaican Baptist Free church in August Town to promote his revivalistic ideas. This anachronistic Afro-Creole movement was dramatized by Bedward's final bizarre attempt at celestial ascent. (Lewis, *The Growth*, p. 175.)

**BEGUINE** (Fr. Cr.), in the Antilles, an Afro-French dance once considered to be the most popular dance in the Caribbean region. It was made famous by Cole Porter's tune, "Begin the Beguine." (Slonimzki, *Music*, p. 297.)

**BEHANZIN,** a Dahomean king exiled by the French to Fort-de-France, Martinique, around the turn of the nineteenth century. There he kept his colorful African court, his concubines, his royal umbrella, and his kingly attire, all according to his ancestral traditions. In contrast, his son Danilo accepted European values and customs. Danilo studied and practiced law in Bordeaux, enlisted in the French army, and was killed in battle in 1914. (Corzani, *Littérature antillaise, poésie*, pp. 34-35.)

**BEHN, APHRA** (1640-1689), an Englishwoman, author of the novel *Oroonoko, or The History of the Royal Slave*, c. 1678 (q.v.) in which the literary figure of the Noble Negro (q.v.) appeared for the first time in Europe. (Sayers, *The Negro*, p. 38.)

**BEJI** (Afr.), an Afro-Brazilian *orisha* (q.v.) of twin birth. See also MARASSA.

**BE JUCO DE ANGOLA** (Sp.), a medicinal plant used to cure broken bones and bone ache; imported from Africa into the New World during the slavery period.

**BÉKÉ** (Fr. Cr.), in Martinique, a white Creole descendent of the French colonists who were born on the island. The identification criteria are: race, wealth, education, and generations of ancestors settled in Martinique. Con-

fined for generations to a tiny island, isolated from France, fighting the economic demands of the metropolis, and observing suspiciously the rise of the
colored bourgeoisie, the *békés* have found it easy to develop an independent
way of life as well as a strong feeling of identification with their own group.
These white Creoles view themselves, with some ethnocentricity, as the descendants of slave-holding planters and rank themselves above others on the
grounds that their ancestors were masters and soldiers of fortune. The
majority belong to the wealthy landlord class on the island. The term *béké* is
not used in Guadeloupe. (Comitas and Lowenthal, *Slaves, Free Men*, p.
243.)

**BÉKÉ GOYAVE, BITAKO** (Fr. Cr.), in Martinique, a poor rural white distinguished by his rustic manners and lack of style and education. He speaks
Creole rather than French. Some *békés goyaves* own a few hectares of land
and manage to increase their means of subsistence by growing vegetables
and raising a few animals for domestic consumption. Most are employed by
other white Creoles, sometimes as managers but more often as foremen,
mechanics, cashiers, and the like. Without the means to become independent or, in most cases, to gain education, they are soon immersed in the task
of earning a living. Lacking the power to assert their rights, they are often
exploited. They participate in no trade union activities for if they try to do
so they are rejected by the white community. (Comitas and Lowenthal,
*Slaves, Free Men*, p. 255.) See also BÉKÉ.

**BÉKÉ MOYEN** (Fr. Cr.), in Martinique, one of the many members of the
white middle-class subgroup of natives. He is usually a civil servant or an
employee in an enterprise owned by a *grand béké*. In the country, he
generally owns small farms, cultivates cane or bananas, practices stock
farming, or operates small distilleries. He recognizes the existence of a
ruling white minority and is conscious that only wealth separates him from
it. He is unhappy about the exclusivity of high society and about the meager
extent of his contact with it. The *béké moyen* group, like all middle classes,
is the most difficult to delineate, for its members are the most apt to change
levels in the hierarchy, given an opportunity for social mobility. As a rule,
*békés moyens* never mix with the black population. (Comitas and
Lowenthal, *Slaves, Free Men*, pp. 250-51.) See also BÉKÉ.

**BEL-AIR, BELÉ** (Fr. Cr.), in the French Antilles, a song and dance
accompanied by an Afro-Caribbean drum that the player keeps between his
legs.

**BELCHOIR,** a Brazilian black Moslem slave who was a leader in the ill-
fated revolt of Hausa slaves (q.v.) in Bahia, Brazil, in 1835. (Ramos, *The
Negro*, p. 50.)

**BELÉ.** See BEL-AIR.

**BELEMBE** (Afr.), a kind of wild fig tree *(Xanthosoma brasiliense Desf.)* introduced into Brazil by Angolan slaves during colonial times.

**BELL-A-RING,** a black shanty-song in the West Indies.

**BEM AREIADO** (Pg.), in Bahía, Brazil, a light, mixed-blood individual categorized as belonging to the white class.

**BEMBA, BEMBO** (Afr.), an Afro-Cuban individual with Negroid features.

**BEMBE** (Afr.). In the Afro-Spanish dialect: 1. Thick lips, mainly those of a black. 2. A black dance brought to Cuba by slaves. 3. A small orchard or vegetable garden of slavery tradition. (Ortiz Fernández, *Glosario*, p. 48.)

**BEMBO.** See BEMBA.

**BEMBÓN** (Afr.), in the Antilles, an Afro-Spanish derogatory name for the fully everted lips commonly associated with the Negroid racial phenotype. (Ortiz Fernández, *Glosario*, p. 49.)

**BENCH DRUM,** a small, square wooden frame over which a goat's skin is stretched tightly. When struck briskly several times in quick succession with one hand, and once only with the other, it produces a monotonous sound with only a slight vibration. (Cassidy, *Dictionary*, p. 38.)

**BENDENGUÉ** (Afr.), an Afro-Brazilian dance.

**BENDER** (Afr.), an Afro-Jamaican string instrument consisting of a bow with two or three wires which the player struck with a stick. It was brought by Whydah (see AJUDÁ FORT) slaves from Africa, among whom it was very popular. (Beckwith, *Black Roadways*, p. 211.)

**BENEBA** (Afr.), in Jamaica, an African day-name (q.v.) given to a female child born on Tuesday. In colonial times, it was common among black slaves; now it is rarely used. See also CUBBENA. (Cassidy, *Dictionary*, p. 38.)

**BENGALA** (Afr.), an Afro-Brazilian term for a cane or walking stick.

**BENGO** (Bant.). 1. An Afro-Brazilian word for a cow path, a country road. 2. In Angola (q.v.), a village. (Mendoça, *A Influencia*, p. 118.)

**BENGUELA.** See BANGUELA.

**BENGUELA KINGDOM,** in colonial times, a small chiefdom centered in the Atlantic seaport of Benguela in the Angola (q.v.) territory. In the seventeenth century, the Portuguese converted it into an important slave-trading post; after 1575, it was part of the Angola Colony. In 1705, the French sacked the port. Later, around 1800, the Portuguese established a penal settlement at Benguela. (Woodson, *The African Background*, p. 131.)

**BENGUELA SLAVES,** in colonial Brazil and elsewhere in the New World, this term was applied broadly to Bantu (q.v.) slaves imported from the Atlantic seaport of the same name. These blacks were gathered together in the Angolan hinterland, brought to Benguela (q.v.), and from there embarked for the New World, especially for Brazil. In the sixteenth century, they were employed in the sugar cane (q.v.) fields of the northeast. Later, during the gold rush (1714-1770), these slaves were very much in demand in Minas Gerais. (Boxer, *The Golden Age*, p. 175.)

**BENIN KINGDOM,** an ancient African kingdom located in the south-central Nigerian forest, not far from the Guinea Coast (q.v.). It was founded at the beginning of the thirteenth century. Before the coming of the Europeans, it was the center of a network of trade routes linking towns and villages throughout almost the entire western Sudan. Around 1482, when the Portuguese reached the Guinea Coast, Benin was already a powerful state where the industrial arts and the art of working gold, ivory, bronze, and iron were well developed. Hence, the Portuguese found considerable opportunities for trade expansion there. Benin flourished during the sixteenth and seventeenth centuries when it achieved extraordinary artistic development, which in many respects equaled that of Europe. Between 1680 and 1730, the devastation of the slave-raiding wars began to destroy its trade and its political structure. Even so, it remained a powerful kingdom until the end of the nineteenth century. (Woodson, *The African Background*, p. 117.)

**BENIN SLAVES,** in colonial Brazil, Moslem slaves imported from the Benin Kingdom (q.v.). These blacks were skilled in iron, gold, and bronze work, and introduced into the northeast a highly advanced metallurgic art. The vast majority of the so-called Benin slaves brought to the New World during the nineteenth century came from a narrow coastal region—from the present state of Togo in the west to the Cameroons in the east. (Ramos, *The Negro*, pp. 130-31.)

**BEN JONSON,** in Jamaica, a legendary figure whose story was often related in slaving annals. He was a black slave merchant on the west coast of Africa in the eighteenth century. He kidnapped and sold a young girl into slavery, then was himself kidnapped by her brother who took him to the slave ship and exchanged him for his sister. (Cassidy, *Dictionary*, p. 39.)

**BEN JONSON DAY,** in the West Indies, the day before pay day, a day of short provision and austerity, a day when the prospect of life is unpleasant, a day of reckoning. The term probably originated in slavery times. See also BEN JONSON.

**BENKO, KING,** a black slave known as Dionisio (or Domingo) Bioho, who in 1732 declared himself king of the *palenque* (q.v.) San Basilio in Colombia, in the highlands near Cartagena. He assumed the name of King Benko. (Rout, L.B., *The African Experience in Spanish America*, p. 110.)

**BENTA** (Afr.), a crude wind instrument used by Whydah (see AJUDÁ) slaves in Jamaica, producing a trembling, querulous, yet delightful harmony. It was made out of a bent stick, the ends of which were kept bent by a slip of dried grass. The upper part of the grass was gently compressed between the lips and blown gently, producing a soft and pleasing vibration. The other end was played by tapping it with a slender stick that controlled the natural acuteness of the sound. The instrument was very popular among slaves in Jamaica. (Cassidy, *Jamaica Talk*, p. 264.)

**BENTO, ANTONIO** (b. 1843), an ardent Brazilian abolitionist who, around 1880, organized an underground movement to help black slaves escape from *fazendas* (q.v.) and farms. Called Brazil's John Brown, he systematized the operations in São Paulo by organizing a kind of religious brotherhood whose members were called *caifazes* (q.v.). Under Bento's inspiration, farmers and black freemen appealed to slaves on the *fazendas*, railroad coachmen guided the fugitives on trains and lawyers and businessmen sheltered them in their houses. After abolition in 1888, groups of former slaves gathered in front of Bento's home each year on the anniversary of emancipation to celebrate and dance the *samba* (q.v.). (Toplin, *The Abolition*, pp. 204-205.)

**BENZEDOR** (Pg.), in colonial Brazil, a black healer who cured physical diseases. For tuberculosis, he prescribed *herva de Santa Maria* (Saint Mary's herb), pounded with a mortar and pestle and drunk in the morning on an empty stomach. For dysentery, he prescribed a tea made of *sete-sangria* poured into a bath of tepid water in which the patient remained until the water cooled. There were similar prescriptions for several other diseases. (Stein, *Vassouras*, p. 189.)

**BERBESI,** an African ethnic group situated in the Guinea-Bissau coastal region from which many slaves were taken to Peru between 1548 and 1560.

**BERE BERE** (Afr.), an Afro-Cuban word for slowly.

**BEREKÉ** (Afr.), an Afro-Cuban deity, keeper of the crossroads and of the house doors, a messenger of the god Olofi (q.v.); also called Elegua. (Cabrera, L., *Anagó*, p. 81.)

**BEREN, BERIN** (Eng. Cr.), an Afro-Jamaican word for funeral; also burying.

**BERGEAUD, EMERIC** (1818-1858), a black Haitian writer inspired by the romantic movement. He wrote what appears to have been the first Haitian novel, *Stella*, published posthumously in Paris in 1859.

**BERI KULA** (Afr.), in the Afro-Cuban religion, a faithful still waiting to be initiated into the cult.

**BERIMBAU** (Pg.), an Afro-Brazilian musical instrument consisting of a wire strung upon a stick to form a bow, with a dried gourd, open at the top, attached to the lower end. The instrument is beaten to produce numerous complex rhythms by using a wooden-reed bow in the right hand, while a copper coin in the left hand is alternately pressed against the wire and released.

**BERI MENEYE** (Afr.), an Afro-Cuban word for quarrel or fight.

**BERIN.** See BEREN.

**BERKSHIRE, BOKSHA,** in Jamaica, an inoffensive nickname for a very black man; derived from the color of Berkshire hogs.

**BESSE, BISSY,** in the Caribbean, the kola nut (q.v.) tree *(Cola acuminata)* and its fruit; used by blacks in folk medicine.

**BESSY,** in Jamaica, a busybody black who always puts in an appearance at public functions.

**BETANCES, RAMÓN EMETERIO** (1827-1898), a Puerto Rican mulatto poet, essayist, and ardent abolitionist. Together with other political leaders, he took part in the National Assembly of the first Spanish Republic on March 22, 1873, which promulgated the Law of Abolition of Slavery in Puerto Rico and thereby emancipated some 30,000 black slaves. In 1853, Betances received a medical degree in Toulouse, France. During the cholera epidemic of 1855, he ordered the burning down of the filthy slave cabins and issued hygienic regulations governing the treatment of slaves. As an opponent of slavery, he was forced to leave the island and settle in other Caribbean countries. Later, he traveled to Europe. He died in Paris.

**BETANCOURT, JOSÉ MERCEDES** (b. 1836), a Cuban mulatto composer and teacher of music born in Puerto Príncipe. For years Betancourt conducted the local orchestra in his native city. A prolific composer, he wrote many pieces of popular music and, in Havana in 1861, he published a musical collection called *Ecos de Tinima*, dedicated to the countess of San Antonio, wife of General Francisco Serrano, governor of the island. He toured the country giving concerts with his orchestra. After a short sojourn in Havana, he returned to Puerto Príncipe where he died a young man. (Calcagno, *Diccionario*, p. 108.)

**BETHUNE, LEBER** (b. 1937), a black poet born in Kingston, Jamaica. After finishing his secondary studies in his native city, Bethune joined his parents in New York where he graduated from New York University. He has traveled extensively in Africa and, for a time, lived in Tanzania. His first book, *A Juju of My Own* (Paris, 1965), is a collection of twenty poems, some of which originally appeared in *Présence Africaine*. (Hughes, *The Best Short Stories*, p. 497.)

**BÉVILLE, PAULO.** See NIGER, PAUL.

**BEVERAGE**, among Jamaican blacks, lemonade.

**BEX** (Eng. Cr.), in the West Indies, a word for anger used mainly by blacks.

**BEYI** (Afr.), in the Afro-Cuban dialect, twins.

**BEYI-AYAI** (Afr.), an Afro-Cuban word for a child born after twins.

**BIAFADA.** See BIGHT OF BIAFRA.

**BIAFARA,** an ethnic group located in Biafra (Guinea-Bissau), many of whose members were brought to the New World as slaves early in the sixteenth century.

**BIAFRA.** See BIGHT OF BIAFRA.

**BIAFRA SLAVES,** a term broadly applied in the eighteenth century to a great number of slaves exported from a few city-states in the area of the Oil

Rivers and the estuary of the Cross River in the Bight of Biafra (q.v.). The rise in exports from this region after 1700 was associated with political and economic reorganization. Between 1711 and 1810, the export of Biafra slaves reached its highest point.

**BIAH, BYA** (Afr.), among Afro-Jamaicans, to lull a child to sleep as "biah baby to bed."

**BIAH-BABY,** in Jamaica, a nanny's lullaby sung by blacks.

**BIAN** (Afr.), an Afro-Cuban folklore, a black devil, spreader of smallpox.

**BIASSOU,** a black slave owned by the Fathers of Charity, a Catholic congregation established in Le Cap, Haiti. He ran away and became one of the earliest leaders of the great slave rebellion of 1791. Later, he quit the fight, and, in 1796, he left for France. Upon his return to the island, he joined the white colonists against the slave forces. He was eventually murdered. Toussaint L'Ouverture (q.v.) gave a pension to his widow. (Ott, *The Haitian Revolution*, p. 56.)

**BIATATA** (Pg.), an Afro-Brazilian mythical female, inhabitant of the sea. She appears above the waters at night, gradually increasing in size until she assumes a monstrous shape. Soon after, Biatata suddenly disappears into the darkness.

**BIBAYE** (Afr.), an Afro-Cuban word for corpse.

**BIBI** (Eng. Cr.). In Jamaica: 1. a black mistress, a sweetheart. 2. An affectionate term of address to a friend or a child; darling.

**BIBILÁ** (Afr.), an Afro-Cuban term for an oil lamp.

**BIBLE,** the Scriptures, used by blacks in Trinidad to protect a growing child. Usually, an open Bible, preferably open to the Twenty-third Psalm—"The Lord is My Shepherd"—is laid on his or her bed near or under the pillow. On the open pages is placed a pair of scissors with "points sharp, sharp." If anyone comes for the baby's shadow, "scissors jukes [stabs] him." (Herskovitz, *Trinidad Village*, p. 241.)

**BIBLE POINTER,** in Jamaica, a black female assistant at revivalist and similar meetings who reads out the Scriptures upon which the black preacher expounds.

**BICHE** (Eng. Cr.), in the West Indies, the kola nut (q.v.) tree *(Cola acuminata)* and its fruits; greatly valued by blacks in folk medicine.

**BICHO** (Pg.), in Afro-Brazilian folklore, a vague term for a "fear-inspiring creature"; usually applied to any animal, insect, or human being endowed with mythical characteristics. It represents a horrible, undeniable being, only vaguely known. The Brazilian child of today has a quasi-instinctive fear of the *bicho*. (Freyre, *The Masters*, pp. 139-40.)

**BICHO DA COSTA** (Pg.), in colonial Brazil, a parasite brought by black slaves from West Africa.

**BICHO DE PÉ** (Pg.), a type of flea that burrows beneath the skin of the foot and lays eggs in a neat little sack. It especially attacked barefoot slaves. A female slave was usually in charge of removing the *bichos de pé* from the great-house (q.v.) children.

**BICHY, BISSY** (Afr.), in Jamaica, a bush imported from Guinea, West Africa, whose seeds are eaten mainly by black peasants. Today the seed is used to cure malaria and high blood pressure, and as an antidote for poison. (Cassidy, *Jamaica Talk*, pp. 355-56.)

**BIDONVILLE** (Fr. Cr.), an Afro-Caribbean shanty-town (q.v.) on the fringes of a large city. This new, densely populated community is inhabited by an impoverished rural black peasantry, partially attracted by the allure of industrialized urban life. The hovels, sometimes built on the ruins of abandoned residential areas, are important centers of syncretistic cults and surviving African cultural elements. A bidonville is usually surrounded and governed by a white or Creole administration, and its inhabitants remain culturally, economically, and politically a minority group. (Bastide, *African Civilizations*, pp. 199, 213.)

**BIG HOUSE.** See CASA GRANDE.

**BIGHT OF BENIN,** the coastal zone between the Volta and the Benin rivers in West Africa. In the eighteenth century, the core of this region was vaguely known as the Slave Coast (q.v.). Today it includes Togo and Dahomey (q.v.). From this general area, many slaves came to the New World. (Curtin, *The Atlantic Slave*, p. 128.)

**BIGHT OF BIAFRA,** a coastal zone in West Africa, west of the Cameroons. Its bounds were the Benin River on the west and Cape Lopez to the south in present-day Gabon. From this region, the majority of black slaves were brought to the New World during the nineteenth century.

**BILAD-ES-SUDAN** ("Land of the Blacks"), an Arabic name used since the sixteenth century for the region south of the Sahara.

**BILALU** (Afr.), songs sung in the Afro-Jamaican *cumina* (q.v.) cult. These country religious songs are in a language which blacks refer to as African.

**BILL TO PREVENT PREACHING BY PERSONS NOT DULY QUALI-FIED BY LAW,** a law passed by the Jamaican Assembly in 1802 forbidding the preaching by ill-disposed, illiterate, or ignorant enthusiasts to meetings of black slaves and freemen who were unlawfully assembled. Although this bill was rejected in Britain on the grounds that it unduly limited religious freedom, Jamaican authorities eventually got around this setback by requiring the would-be preachers to have a license by a magistrate and by limiting the preaching to specified hours and places. (Brathwaite, *The Development*, pp. 10, 260.) See also SLAVE PREACHER.

**BILONGO** (Afr.), an Afro-Cuban mythical creature that can be used by a sorcerer to cause physical or mental evil. It is believed that his master can transfer the *bilongo* from one person to another for wicked purposes.

**BILTONG** (Afr.), in the Afro-Antilles region, jerked meat prepared by smoking over a slow fire on a wooden grill called a *boucan*.

**BIM,** a native of Barbados, often of mixed blood.

**BIMA** (Afr.), an Afro-Jamaican term for an old sore or ulcer on the foot or leg which does not heal easily.

**BIMBICHA** (Pg.), an Afro-Brazilian word for a child's penis; used as a term of endearment by black wet nurses.

**BIMBO** (Afr.), in the Caribbean, a fermented palm wine once highly valued by slaves.

**BINGA** (Afr.), in the Afro-Brazilian dialect, a horn or an antler.

**BIOGRAPHY OF MAHOMMAH G. BAQUAQUA,** an autobiographical narrative published in 1854 by S. Moore. This document is particularly valuable for its comparison of the living conditions among slaves in northern and southern Brazil between 1830 and 1840. See also BAQUAQUA, MAHOMMAH G.

**BIOHO,** an African ethnic group, the modern-day Bisago, located in the Guinea-Bissau region from which many slaves were taken to the New World.

**BIOHO, DOMINGO,** a black slave chieftain who, in 1732, founded the *palenque* (q.v.) San Basilio in Colombia. (Bastide, *African Civilizations*, p. 66.)

**BIRD PEPPER** (Eng. Cr.), in the West Indies, a variety of capsicum peppers, small and conical, which grow wild but are also easily cultivated. Blacks often use them in cooking, and they are much favored by birds.

**BIRIMBAU** (Pg.), an Afro-Brazilian musical instrument.

**BIRTH BELIEFS,** the belief that a child born with a caul will be strong in combating evil spirits. If a child is born with his navel cord wrapped about his throat, he is thought to be destined for leadership.

**BIRTH NAME,** an Afro-Jamaican custom reflecting a West African custom according to which each child at birth receives a name based on the day of the week on which he or she is born. (Cassidy, *Dictionary*, p. 44.) See also DAY-NAME.

**BISSIMILAI** (Afr.) ("In the Name of God"), a doxology used by Moslem blacks in Brazil in their religious meetings. Once the congregation is ready, the *imam* (q.v.) begins the service with this invocation. (Ramos, *As culturas negras*, p. 145.)

**BISSAGO** (Afr.), an Afro-Haitian mystical secret society whose members appear at night wearing horns and holding candles. They are believed to be able to change into animals when they do their evil works. The Bissago meets at night in the open country.

**BISSY (BUSH).** See BICHY.

**BISSY (NUT TREE).** See BESSE.

**BITAKO.** See BÉKÉ GOYAVE.

**BIZANGO, KIMBUNGO,** (Afr.), an Afro-Haitian creature, a kind of African werewolf, which devours children and swallows them through a hole in its back. Some rural Haitians imagine it to be a kind of enormous dog that runs in parks at night seeking people to eat.

**BIZOTON AFFAIR,** an incident which began on December 27, 1863, in Bizoton, Haiti, when a little black girl named Claireine disappeared from her home while her mother was absent. After a search of several days, it was discovered that she had been killed and used as part of a sinister sacrifice by religious fanatics. An inquest resulted in the arrest and conviction of eight men and four women who were executed in Port-au-Prince on February 13, 1864. (Leyburn, *The Haitian People*, p. 131.)

**BLACK ANANCY** (Afr.), in Afro-Jamaican folklore, a usually harmless spider.

**BLACK-AND-WHITE DANCE,** an Afro-Jamaican memorial dance sponsored by a family for one or more of its deceased members, so-called because black and white insignia are worn on the occasion. The term is used in black revivalist cults.

**BLACK-ART MAN,** in Jamaica, an *obeah* man (q.v.).

**BLACK BACKRA** (Afr.), in Jamaica, a term of respect for a black.

**BLACK BETTY** (Eng. Cr.), in the Caribbean, a kind of red pea *(Vigna unguiculata)*, formerly a staple food among slaves.

**BLACK BLAST,** in colonial Jamaica, a disease that attacked black slaves working in sugar cane (q.v.) fields. Its carriers were insects attached to the stems and leaves of the cane.

**BLACK CARIB,** a variant of West Indian black culture. The Black Carib population, reflecting a mixture of Amerindian and African features, is settled in the rural area along the coast of Belize and Central America. Most of these blacks are descendants of slaves deported from Saint Vincent and of others who escaped to the Atlantic Coast from neighboring islands at the end of the eighteenth century. (Olien, *Latin Americans*, p. 120.)

**BLACK CARIB CREOLE,** a fairly conservative English-based dialect spoken in British Honduras and along the Atlantic Coast from Belize to Costa Rica and Panama. It contains many words of African origin, together with many features in common with Jamaican English Creole (q.v.). (Hymes, *Pidginization*, p. 512.)

**BLACK DOG,** a coin, probably of silver, current in the West Indies during slavery times. It was of the lowest value. (Cassidy, *Dictionary*, p. 48.)

**BLACK ISRAELITE,** a member of one of the Pocomania (q.v.) cults in Jamaica.

**BLACK IVORY,** a name given to slaves brought to the New World in the sixteenth century. As early as 1502, they were considered a precious commodity in the Caribbean region. (Hurwitz, *Jamaica*, p. 32.)

**BLACKMAN, THE,** a daily newspaper founded in Kingston, Jamaica, by black leader Marcus Garvey (q.v.) which lasted only two years, from 1929 to 1931. It campaigned for self-government and for the political and civil rights of the black population.

**BLACK NAYGA** (Eng. Cr.), in Jamaica, a black with more purely African features.

**BLACK-NAYGA HAM** (Eng. Cr.), in Jamaica, codfish; a very common food among blacks since slavery times.

**BLACK POWER,** the capacity for action displayed by the black preachers and white missionaries in Jamaica around the middle of the eighteenth century. It was the most dramatic manifestation of Christian brotherhood in the Jamaican white and black society. (Brathwaite, *The Development*, p. 252.)

**BLACK PREACHERS,** in colonial Jamaica, Christian slave preachers (q.v.), often itinerant and entirely independent of white control, who used to speak to unlawfully assembled slaves under the pretense of being ministers of religion. Many of them were not recognized as acceptable Christian ministers by the white missionaries because they were generally illiterate and were considered morally unfit. In 1802, the Jamaican Assembly passed a law restricting their activities. (Brathwaite, *The Development*, pp. 260-61.) See also BILL TO PREVENT PREACHING BY PERSONS NOT DULY QUALIFIED BY LAW.

**BLACK PROVINCE (PROVINCIA NEGRA),** a name given to Panama by Colombia in 1821, at the time of the emancipation of slaves. The black population was so numerous then that many white families left the Isthmus.

**BLACK SHOT.** In the colonial British West Indies: 1. A trusted and well-trained black or mulatto soldier. 2. A trusted slave permitted to bear firearms. (Cassidy, *Dictionary*, p. 50.)

**BLACK SLAVE TRADERS,** in West Africa, black chieftains engaged in selling slaves to foreign merchants. They usually bought their slaves at well-organized fairs in the coastal region within 200 miles of the Atlantic. They also used to buy blacks in groups of five to ten which were frequently brought to their houses by those who made a practice of kidnapping and procuring slaves. The purchased blacks were cleaned and oiled with palm oil and then offered for sale to ship captains. (Dow, *Slave Ships*, p. 140.)

**BLACK TROY,** a name given by some Brazilian historians to Palmares (q.v.), the largest slave hideaway in northeast Brazil.

**BLACK WASH,** a dark-colored drink made of sugar and water; a favorite beverage of West Indies blacks.

**BLANCO, DON PEDRO** (d. 1854 or 1856), a native of Málaga, Spain, originally a mate on a sailing vessel, who, in 1821, settled along the unclaimed Grain Coast (q.v.) now Liberia. From 1822 to 1839, he built up a large slave-trading business, contriving to ship to Cuba, Puerto Rico, Brazil, South Carolina, Georgia, and the Bahamas an average of 5,000 slaves annually. Blanco employed Spanish, Portuguese, American, and Russian ships for his slave transports. He and his agents obtained their slaves chiefly from the Gallinas lagoon, Mende, Gora, Busi, Vai, and Kpwesi tribes and from other peoples behind the Bassa and Kru coasts. In 1839, Blanco retired; he lived in Cuba for a while, and then moved to Genoa. (Johnston, *The Negro*, p. 41.)

**BLEIAL, DANIEL.** See BOUKMAN, DANIEL.

**BLOODY FLUX,** an African disease caused by various forms of bacillary dysentery that affected and decimated the black slave population during their Atlantic crossing to the New World. See MIDDLE PASSAGE.

**BLUES AND REDS,** in Jamaica in the late eighteenth and early nineteenth centuries, troupes of young black girls who vied with each other in fancy dress parades at Christmas time and at New Year's. (Cassidy, *Dictionary*, p. 55.)

**BLYDEN, EDWARD WILMOT** (1832-1912), the first black from the Virgin Islands to achieve wide recognition as a linguist, scholar, and educator. He translated both Christian and Islamic literature. Since his color prevented his acceptance at U.S. schools, he taught in Liberia and eventually became Liberian secretary of state. He was hailed as a "Champion of the Negro Race" for his extensive efforts throughout Africa on behalf of the blacks. (Farr, *Historical Dictionary*, p. 92.)

**BOATING,** a West African slave trade term for the practice of sailing out for days or weeks at a time, along the coast and up the rivers, to buy small groups of slaves from local black traders. (Mannix, *Black Cargoes*, p. 89.)

**BOATSWAIN,** in colonial Jamaica, an "officer" on a sugar estate (q.v.) who was formally in charge of a slave gang (q.v.).

**BOBBIN,** an Afro-Jamaican term for the refrain or burden of a song, rhythmically sung by blacks working in the fields in slavery times. (Cassidy, *Jamaica Talk*, p. 274.)

**BOBÓ** (Afr.), an Afro-Brazilian dish made of yam (q.v.) mixed with *azeite de dendé* (q.v.), *camarão*, and pepper.

**BOCOR** (Afr.), in Haiti, a black magician or medicine man who has acquired power by the purchase of spirits; he does not officiate in religious ceremonies. Sometimes, a *bocor* is a diviner who, through contact with the spirits, can answer questions about the future, the whereabouts of lost objects, or the supernatural causes of certain events.

**BODOO** (Afr.), an African drum played in the Caribbean region.

**BOF** (Eng. Cr.), food pounded soft in a mortar, a traditional black method of preparing food.

**BOGLE, PAUL** (d. 1865), an uneducated former black slave who worked tirelessly for the rights of the black population in Jamaica. An able and energetic person, he was one of the leaders of the Morant Bay rebellion (q.v.) on October 11, 1865, who ordered the burning of houses in the town and several plantations. Twelve days after the rioting, Bogle was captured and hanged. In 1969, he was awarded the rank of national hero.

**BOGOBI** (Afr.), an African word for a small river fish in the Caribbean.

**BOGRO-SALT** (Afr.), an Afro-Jamaican word for coarse salt.

**BOG WALK,** in Caribbean black revivalist meetings, a call to end the singing.

**BOHÍO** (Sp.), in colonial Cuba, the Antilles, and along the Caribbean coasts of South America, living quarters for slaves working on sugar estates (q.v.). They consisted of a one-room hut with a thatched roof and a dirt floor.

**BOILING HOUSE,** on West Indian plantations, a building in which cane juice is evaporated in manufacturing sugar, formerly operated by specially trained slaves.

**BOIS BOURIGUE.** See VACCINE.

**BOIS D'ÉBÈNE** (Fr.), in the colonial French Antilles, a slave. See also EBONY; MADERA DE ÉBANO.

**BOJA** (Eng. Cr.), an Afro-Jamaican word meaning a sneak thief.

**BOJO** (Eng. Cr.), in the West Indies, a cloth or straw bag with a loop by which it can by slung over the shoulder; used by blacks since slavery times for carrying food to the fields.

**BOKRA** (Afr.). See BACKRA.

**BOKSHA** (D.) See BERKSHIRE.

**BOKSN, BUXEN** (Eng. Cr.), in Jamaica, a small edible wild yam (q.v.) *(Dioscorea)*, formerly a staple food for slaves.

**BOLÃO DE ANGU** (Pg.), an Afro-Brazilian dough made of rice, okra (q.v.), and pork, and seasoned with *dendé* palm oil (q.v.) and spices. See also CARURU.

**BOLERO** (Sp.), *bolero-son*, a Cuban song-dance, apparently introduced into the island in the second half of the nineteenth century by Spanish colonists from the Canary Islands. Its rhythms are in 2/4 time in contrast with the Spanish bolero in 3/4 time. Later, it spread beyond the island and was further influenced by African and Mexican elements. Its present ultra-sentimental quality seems to have come from an urban middle-class, emotional music which was popular in the nineteenth century.

**BOLLO** (Eng. Cr.). In Jamaica: 1. A black fellow-worker. 2. A system of relief work in hard times.

**BOLOW** (Eng. Cr.). Among Afro-Jamaicans: 1. A fellow comrade, friend. 2. A black female, sweetheart.

**BOLUNGUEIRO** (Pg.), an Afro-Brazilian sorcerer; formerly, in Angola (q.v.), a tribal magician.

**BOMBA** (Afr.) In the Antilles: 1. An African drum which is given sexual attributes, as in Ghana, being called in slavery times by female names; a carryover of African personalization of instruments. 2. A black dance held on Sundays at which the spectators formed the chorus for response singing. The music was supplied by two drums, maracas, and two sticks tapped on a bench. The rhythm was set, not by the drummers, but by the lead dancer. The form of the *bomba* was like many African dances in which the voices start out unaccompanied and then are joined by drums, which come in with dramatic effect. 3. Today, a song-dance.

**BOMBA DE LOS NEGROS** (Sp.), an Afro-Antilles dance popular in Puerto Rico, formerly danced by slaves. The accompanying instrument was a drum, a kind of African kettledrum or tom-tom. Today, it is danced by mixed couples, separate or in groups, with the two sexes facing one another, but not touching. The rhythm, monotonal and enervating, is very sensual and suggestive.

**BOMBÉ SERRÉ** (Fr. Cr.), a highly suggestive black dance popular in Martinique. See also BOMBA.

**BOMBO** (Bant.), in the Antilles in slavery times, a Bantu (q.v.) word meaning the pudendum. Today, buttocks.

**BOMBÓ** (Bant.), an Afro-Cuban word for a tropical plant and its fruits *(Abelmoschus esculentus* or *Hibiscu esc. L.)*; a staple food for slaves brought from Africa in the colonial period.

**BOM BOCADO.** (Pg.). See ADÚM.

**BOMBOLA,** an Afro-Spanish word for amusement, recreation.

**BOMBOTÓ** (Bant.), a hard, round, Afro-Caribbean cake prepared with wheat flour and brown sugar.

**BOMI** (Eng. Cr.). See BANNIE.

**BOM JESUS NA CRUZ** (Pg.) ("Jesus on the Cross"), the name of a runaway slave settlement in the interior of northeast Brazil. In 1676, it was taken and destroyed by the colonial militia.

**BOMMA** (Eng. Cr.), in the West Indies, a black leader of a group singing work songs.

**BOMP-A-CHUAT** (Eng. Cr.), an Afro-Jamaican word for Adam's apple.

**BONAPARTE, JOSEPHINE** (1743-1814), wife of Napoleon I and empress of France, born in Trois Islets, Martinique. In 1797, she warned her husband against restoring slavery in Saint Domingue and removing Toussaint L'Ouverture (q.v.) from his position of power. In Paris, the empress befriended the two young sons of the Liberator, Isaac (q.v.) and Placide (q.v.), who were attending school there. Earlier, in 1793, Josephine wrote to L'Ouverture regarding her mother's plantation, which was then in ruins. L'Ouverture repaired and restored the estate at the expense of the colony and ordered all the revenues from its operations to be sent to the empress in Paris. Apparently, Josephine kept the estate until 1806, because until then her mother was still living on the family plantation. (James, *The Black Jacobins*, p. 262.)

**BON DIEU BON** (Fr. Cr.). 1. A common expression used by black peasants in Haiti to express a deep feeling of acceptance of life and of things as they are. The basic concern is to keep oneself out of harm's way, if possible, but if it comes to bear it stoically. 2. The supreme god of all Afro-Haitian deities; the creator of the world. He is so high above man that he is not concerned with man's existence. The peasants believe that Bon Dieu Bon just laughs at the sufferings of mankind. (Leyburn, *The Haitian People*, p. 9.)

**BON DIÉ MANIÉ MOIN** (Fr. Cr.) ("The good God has touched me!"), a thankful exclamation used by Martinique fishermen on their safe return with a bountiful catch.

**BONFIM, MARTINIANO ELISEAU DO** (1860-1943), a black Brazilian religious leader and scholar. In about 1930, Bonfim traveled to Nigeria for initiation into an African cult. On his return, he introduced into the priestly hierarchy of the Brazilian fetish cult of Opó Afonga Candomblé (q.v.) the twelve ministers of Xangó (a.v.)—a direct borrowing from the royal court of Oyo (q.v.) in West Africa. In 1937, he founded and presided over the Union of Afro-Brazilian sects of Bahia, Brazil. In 1941, together with other distinguished blacks, he signed a petition to the governor of Bahia asking for official recognition of the Afro-Brazilian sects. (Bastide, *African Civilizations*, p. 130.)

**BONG** (Afr.), in Jamaica, a dirty, untidy house.

**BONGO** (Afr.). 1. Name of a tribe of the Chari-Wadai area of Africa. 2. An Afro-Jamaican sect that still flourishes today under its African name *bongo*, or in English as the "Convince Cult." Its black followers seek to establish real contact with the spirits of the dead rather than with God and Christ whom they consider too closely connected with whites. It establishes a hierarchy according to the power of the spirits, dividing them into the spirits of (a) Africans, (b) former slaves or Maroons (q.v.), and (c) blacks more recently deceased. The object is to obtain immediate material benefits, such as the healing of illnesses, the securing of good fortune, or the ability to manufacture magical objects. At one time, this movement was a focal point for black protest against white domination. Today, it is chiefly a fraternal organization. (Bastide, *African Civilizations*, p. 167.)

**BONGÓ BONGÓO** (Afr.), a small Afro-Antilles drum about six inches in diameter, held between the knees and played with bare hands. The Cuban twin bongos have gained great popularity.

**BONI** (Afr.), another name for a Bush Negro Creole (q.v.) dialect in Guiana.

**BONNABEES.** See BANNER BEANS.

**BONNEVILE, RENÉ** (1870-1902), a mulatto journalist born in Saint Pierre, Martinique. As a political activist, he was often accused of being a traitor to his black brothers. His romantic poetry is less noteworthy than his prose, especially his narratives of the historical past of Saint Pierre and Martinique. The themes of his short stories are contemporary events. According to Bonneville, the deeply rooted Afro-French tradition is an essential part of Martinique. Among his works are *Le Triomphe d'Englantine*, (1899); *Fleurs des Antilles* (1900); *Les Soeurs ennemies* (1901); *Les Voluptueuses* (1902); and *Mal d'amour* (1902). He died a victim of the Mont Pelée eruption in 1902. (*Corzani, Littérature antillaise, poésie*, p. 99.)

**BORN-DAY,** an Afro-Jamaican expression for the day of the week on which one is born, as reflected in one's day-name (q.v.).

**BORNÉ** (Fr. Cr.), in the Afro-Haitian folk religion, action taken by the leader of the cult to prevent a malign spirit from inflicting harm on the person or family to whom it has come.

**BORN NEAR THE PLANTATION ROOT** (Eng. Cr.), in the West Indies, a phrase applied to a black peasant who is totally uneducated.

**BORNU,** an old black kingdom centered west of Lake Chad in the central Sudan. After it converted to Islam, it became a powerful state, monopolizing the trade routes across central Sahara to Tunis and Tripoli. In 1430, it was an ally of the Kano Kingdom of northern Nigeria. It flourished during the sixteenth century; then, in 1603, it was conquered by the Moors of North Africa.

**BORNU SLAVES,** Moslem blacks of the western Sudan imported into Brazil. Physically, these slaves were a mixed-blood type of Negro with Hamitic and possibly Berber strains. They generally had a broad-faced, heavy-boned physiognomy, which, especially in their women, was considered to be far from pleasing. (Freyre, *The Masters*, p. 313.)

**BOSSA NOVA,** a modern Afro-Brazilian jazz form related to the *samba* (q.v.), generally quiet and smooth with poetic lyrics. It has brought Brazil considerable publicity all over the world. Sprung from an ultra-cool attitude to the *samba* and rather tenuous connections with modern jazz, it has developed the "whitest" of styles, such that it can fairly easily be played by non-Brazilian musicians. (Wagley, *An Introduction*, p. 283.)

**BOUBA** (Pg.), a tumor produced by a bacterium very similar to that which causes syphilis. Among Afro-Brazilians, *bouba* is considered an illness common to all males. "It began with the world," it is said, "and everyone has it, even horses, although it may never show up."

**BOUC, BOURG** (Fr. Cr.), in Haiti, an isolated hamlet, often deep in the country, which serves as a marketplace for black women traders. The size of the *bouc* appears to be proportional to the size of the market.

**BOUKMAN,** a black slave who became a religious and political leader in the great slave rebellion of Haiti that began on the night of August 14, 1791. A fugitive from Jamaica and a voodoo (q.v.) priest, he used the deep roots of this African cult among the slaves as a communication system to organize the uprising. He was killed early in the fighting.

**BOUKMAN, DANIEL** (b. 1936), pseudonym of the poet Daniel Bleial, born in Martinique and educated in Paris. Drafted during the Algerian War, Boukman, together with a group of other young Antillean intellectuals, deserted in 1961 to join the liberation movement. He settled in Algeria, where he took an active part in the war against French colonial power. His pseudonym is taken from the leader in the Haitian uprising of 1791 (see Boukman). His aggressive political views are clearly expressed in his poetry. For Boukman, "négritude" (q.v.) is a banner in the fight for the liberation of Martinique, the federation of the Antillean islands, and the destruction of French colonialism. Among his books of poetry are *Chants pour hâter la mort du temps des Orphées* (1967); and *Le Meutre ritual d'Orphée*. (Corzani, *Littérature Antillaise, poésie*, pp. 220-25.).

**BOULA** (Afr.), a small, sacred drum played to the accompaniment of dancing and singing in Afro-Haitian folk religion. Also called *ajaounto* (q.v.).

**BOULAILLER** (Fr. Cr.), in Haiti, the player of a sacred drum. See also BOULA.

**BOURG.** See BOUC.

**BOURIKI,** a black English-derived dialect spoken in Trinidad.

**BOYER, JEAN-PIERRE** (1776-1850), a Haitian-born free mulatto who received his education in Paris. He served under Toussaint L'Ouverture (q.v.) in Haiti's struggle for independence from France in the 1790s. Following the division of the country into a black kingdom in the north and a mulatto republic in the south, Boyer became president after Petión's (q.v.) death. He conquered Santo Domingo in 1822 and negotiated French recognition of Haitian independence in 1825. After consolidating the entire island of Hispaniola under his rule, he was forced into exile in 1843—first to Jamaica, and later to Paris where he died. His dictatorial regime (1818-1843), the longest in Haitian history, was characterized by economic stagnation, little social progress, and an unpopular compulsory labor law.

**BOZAL** (Sp.), a slave born in Africa who was bought there and then sold in the Spanish-American colonies. In the first years after the granting of the *asiento* (q.v.), blacks were heavily imported from West Africa. These slaves, like all other slaves, by law were supposed to have been baptized at the port of entry. Like the Indians, they fell into the same legal, tutorial status regarding the church. The *bozales* could not be married by a priest until both parties were instructed and baptized.

**BOZÓ** (Pg.). 1. An Afro-Brazilian magical technique for causing harm to a person or thing. Evil forces may be invoked through the mysterious influence of *bozó* and bring illness, blindness, insanity, and even death. Rituals vary. 2. An Afro-Brazilian form of dice game. (Freyre, *The Masters*, p. 346.)

**BOZU-A,** in Trinidad, a male god of African origin, a messenger of Ogun (q.v.), worshipped by the black population; he is honored on Wednesdays. He likes to eat goat, pigeon, and land turtle, and his colors are red and white.

**BRAI** (Afr.), in Brazil, a small tropical shrub brought from Guinea (q.v.) in slavery times.

**BRAM** (Afr.), an Afro-Jamaican outdoor dance, thought to be of higher class than the *bruckins* (q.v.).

**BRAMANTE** (Sp.), in the Spanish Caribbean, a coarse cotton fabric used to manufacture slaves' clothing. Also called *rollo* and *listado*.

**BRAMBRA** (Afr.), an Afro-Jamaican word for breadfruit (q.v.), formerly a standard food for slaves.

**BRAM-BRAM, BRANG-BRANG** (Afr.), in the West Indies, an African term for small bits of stick or wood for burning, kindling wood. In Twi (q.v.), *fram-fram*.

**BRAN** (Afr.). 1. in the Caribbean, an African word for a boar, especially a castrated one. 2. An ethnic group located in the Guinea-Bissau region of Africa from which slaves were brought to Peru and elsewhere early in the sixteenth century.

**BRANCAL** (Pg.), in Brazil, a term applied to a whitish or pale person, often associated with Negroid features.

**BRANCÃO** (Pg.), in Brazil, a wicked white man; used as a derogatory term.

**BRANCARANA** (Pg.), in Brazil, a light-colored mulatto girl or woman.

**BRANCARÃO** (Pg.), in Brazil, a very light-skinned mulatto—so light as to appear almost white. A transitional physical-cultural type, he represents the product of a general and consistent whitening process which, according to some Brazilian intellectuals, will eventually end in a totally white, Caucasian population. (Freyre, *The Masters*, p. 484.) See also ARYANIZAÇÃO PROGRESSIVA.

**BRANCO** (Pg.) ("white"), in Brazil, any person of exclusively or predominantly Caucasian features. This concept includes physical appearance and social rank, not race or color as such. A mixed-blood, such as a light mulatto, is a *branco* if his occupation, education, or accumulation of wealth are those of the upper class. *Branco* is thus an ethnic classification made on the basis of social position.

**BRANCO DA BAHIA** (Pg.) ("a Bahian white"), in Brazil, a mixed-blood person belonging to the middle, and occasionally to the upper social class in Bahia. A lighter mulatto has a tendency to climb the occupational ladder. A well-educated *branco da Bahia* enjoys full acceptance in white social circles, and his participation in any endeavor has no limitations. This Brazilian concept tends to emphasize the individual as a person and as a member of the community, regardless of color and race. (Pierson, *Negroes*, p. 139.)

**BRANCO DA TERRA** (Pg.) ("white of the land"), in Brazil, a person of Negro blood ancestry with Caucasian fair skin, fine features, and straight hair; phenotypically, a white. Sometimes, the *branco da terra* shows traces of *caboclo* (q.v.), as well as Negro and white characteristics. He is always called white and both whites and nonwhites treat him as they would any white person. (Hutchinson, *Village and Plantation*, p. 118.)

**BRANCO POR PROCURAÇÃO** (Pg.) ("white by law"), in Bahia, a light mixed-blood individual in the white category.

**BRANCO(S) RICO(S)** (Pg.) ("rich whites"), in rural Brazil, the group of rich and well-to-do townsfolk, predominantly whites and wealthy mulattoes and blacks. Although the descendants of African slaves are considered inferior to the whites, nevertheless high rank can be achieved in spite of, though never because of, the fact that one is black.

**BRANDENBURG AFRICAN COMPANY,** a trading company established in the late seventeenth century by Frederick Wilhelm, elector of Brandenburg, and the Danish king. Its base was a plantation and factory in the Virgin Islands. Besides exporting sugar and tobacco, the company was interested in importing slaves from West Africa for sale in the Spanish colonies. The king of Spain refused direct importation of slaves and insisted on indirect dealing instead. In 1685, the company negotiated a treaty with Denmark, and Saint Thomas became a slave port and distribution point. (Farr, *Historical Dictionary*, p. 92.)

**BRANDING,** performed on African slaves, men and women alike, on the African coast before their embarkation. If the ship's surgeon found them sound, the slaves were set aside for branding with a hot iron on the breast (later on the shoulder) with the mark of the company or the individual trader. They were branded so as to prevent the natives from substituting slaves in poor condition. Care was usually taken that the women not be burned as deeply as the men. Before 1680, slaves sold in New Spain always bore the brand of the captains who introduced them on their own account. On March 12, 1685, Baltazar Caymans (q.v.) obtained legal authority from the king of Spain to brand slaves with a sign or mark of the *asentista* (q.v.). The mark under consideration was composed of a *B* and an *a* interwined. In 1676, the Royal African Company (q.v.) branded slaves with the letters *D Y* (q.v.), the initials of the duke of York, a shareholder of the corporation. (Dow, *Slave Ships*, p. 10.)

**BRANQUEADO** (Pg.) ("whitened"), in Brazil, a nearly white person, a transitional condition in the process of blacks becoming white. See also ARYANIZAÇÃO PROGRESSIVA; BRANCARÃO.

**BRANQUEAMENTO** (Pg.) ("whitening"), a supposedly Brazilian racial ideal that stresses unrestricted miscegenation with the aim of ultimately obliterating the characteristic physical traits of the three main component races—Portuguese, Negro, and mulatto—in the move towards progressive whitening. This "mystique of whiteness," present in modern Brazil, expresses the common tendency of the European portion of the population to absorb the higher mestizos, while the mulattoes absorb the Negroes. *Branqueamento* means that the Brazilian population is constantly acquiring a more European and less Negroid appearance. (Rodrigues, *Brazil and Africa*, pp. 83-85.) See Also ARYANIZAÇÃO PROGRESSIVA; BRANCARÃO; BRANQUEADO.

**BRANQUIDADE** (Pg.), in Brazil, a deep desire to have pure white ancestry.

**BRAVI** (Pg.), in colonial Brazil, a term applied to black slaves whose task was to defend the big house on the plantation against attacks by Indians, to fight in the wars against the Dutch, to attack settlements of runaway slaves, and to protect the estate's autonomy from city and central government intrusion. (Freyre, *The Masters*, pp. 358, 480.)

**BRAWTA** (Afr.), an Afro-Jamaican practice among black people of giving a little extra in a market transaction; thus, a seller always adds one or two onions, a carrot, or an orange for a regular client. *Brawta* "sweetens" the load, as in a "baker's dozen."

**BRAZILIAN-AFRO-ASIAN TRIANGLE,** a three-way trade system, established in the eighteenth century, with Brazil as center; it was dissolved following Brazilian independence from Portugal. Imports into Brazil, in addition to carpets, pepper, and Oriental textiles of cotton, silk, and damask, included slaves from Angola (q.v.) Mina, and Bissau, and wax from Luanda (q.v.). Exports were brandy, tobacco, flour, manioc, sugar, and dried meat. (Rodrigues, *Brazil and Africa*, p. 28.)

**BREADFRUIT TREE,** a member of the mulberry family *(Artocarpus altilis),* brought from Tahiti to the West Indies and introduced as a staple food for black slaves. In 1792, Captain William Blight introduced it to Jamaica.

**BREAD KIND,** in rural Jamaica, all vegetables normally cultivated by blacks and used as staples, like yam (q.v.) *coco* (q.v.), sweet potato, and plantain (q.v.).

**BREDA,** a famous Haitian plantation located in the mountainous region of Cap François. It was owned in the eighteenth century by the family of the Comte de Noé and managed around 1780 by Bayon de Libertad. Here, Toussaint L'Ouverture (q.v.), the Liberator, was born a slave in 1746. (Ott, *The Haitian Revolution*, pp. 57-58.)

**BREDDA MONKEY,** a character of African origin, found in Jamaican versions of the Anancy story (q.v.).

**BREDDA RABBIT,** an Anancy story (q.v.) character representing the hare; its origin is African.

**BREDDA TIGA,** a character representing the leopard in Jamaican Anancy stories (q.v.); it originated in Africa.

**BRETHREN OF THE COAST,** a group of pirates, godly Puritan capitalists, and irreligious "desperados," effectively united by their greed and common hatred of Spain. At the beginning of the seventeenth century, they engaged in piratical activities against Spanish shipping and coastal towns of the Antilles. By 1630, these buccaneers (q.v.) were well organized as slave traders on the island of Tortuga.

**BRICHY, BRUCHY,** in colonial Jamaica, a tattooed black; the tattoo showed the tribe or caste to which the individual belonged. (Cassidy, *Jamaica Talk*, p. 134.)

**BRIDGES, GEORGE WILSON,** an English churchman who came to Jamaica in 1816. By 1820, he was rector of several churches as well as a magistrate and an assistant judge of the Court of Common Pleas. In 1837, he returned to England. He published several proslavery works, including *A Voice from Jamaica* (1823); *Dreams of Dulocracy* (1824); *Emancipation Unmask'd* (1835); *The Annals of Jamaica* (1828); and *A Statistical History of the Parish of Manchester* (1924). (Ragatz, *The Fall*, pp. 430-36.)

**BRIÈRRE, JEAN FERNAND** (b. 1902), a black Haitian poet, very much influenced by Oswald Spengler's ideas regarding the decadence of white civilization. Committed to the destruction of the white world, he violently attacked bourgeois culture for the crime of slavery and humiliation of the blacks. Among his works are *Le Drame de Marcheterre* (1930); *L'Adieu à la Marseillaise* (1930); *Le Drapeau de demain* (1931); *Le Petit Soldat* (1932);

*Chansons secrètes* (1933); *Nous garderons le Dieu* (1945); and *Poèmes* (1945). (Coulthard, *Race and Colour*, pp. 53-54.)

**BRISÉ GÉNÉRAL,** in the Haitian pantheon, an enormously large and ferocious spirit who is worshipped by the country people. Although stern, he is fond of children. His symbol is the owl, and his home is the Chardette tree. (Courlander, *The Drum*, p. 329.)

**BRITISH AND FOREIGN ANTI-SLAVERY SOCIETY,** An abolitionist group formed in England in 1829 under the leadership of Joseph Sturge. While this society kept up public agitation, the British government sought to obtain international agreements to stop the slave trade by means of an effective naval patrol.

**BRITISH SOUTH SEA COMPANY,** a chartered company founded in 1711 for the purpose of general trading with the overseas territories of Spain, including the Pacific Islands. By the Asiento Treaty with Spain in 1713, a monopoly was granted to transport a total of almost 5,000 slaves to the Spanish colonies for a period of thirty years.

**BRITO, FRANCISCO DE PAULA** (1809-1861), a Brazilian mulatto and self-educated journalist. Brito was the publisher of *O Homem de Cor* ("The Coloured Man") (q.v.), a periodical that appeared in Rio de Janeiro on September 14, 1833; with the appearance of its fourth issue, its name was changed to *O Mulatto*. It was the first periodical devoted to the interests of the Brazilian colored population.

**BROAS DA CASTANHA DOS NEGROS** (Pg.) ("Negroes' cashew nut cakes"), a delectable Afro-Brazilian cornbread made and sold by black women in the street.

**BROCA** (Afr.), an Afro-Caribbean drum played in popular dances.

**BROTHER DUPPY,** in Jamaica, a personified character in Anancy stories (q.v.).

**BROUARD, CARL** (b. 1902), a black Haitian poet. Together with several distinguished young intellectuals, Brouard returned from Paris to Port-au-Prince in 1927. Inspired by the new African renaissance, he became a close collaborator on *La Revue indigène* (1927-1928) and *Les Griots* (1938-1939), in whose pages he set forth the principles and philosophy of the black movement. He enthusiastically set out to describe, defend, and glorify the native Afro-Haitian folk culture which, until then, had been neglected. He learned French Creole (q.v.) and peasant customs, especially the old and very much alive black religious beliefs. In a collection of poetry entitled *Le Tam-Tam angoisse* (1927), he wrote on the title page what became a motto for Haitian nationalism: "It is absurd to play the flute in a country where the national instrument is the mighty assotor" (q.v.). That same year, he published *Nostalgie*, a touching evocation of Mother Africa. In *La Doctrine de l'ecole nouvelle* (1927), he discusses black aesthetics.

**BROWN GEORGE,** an Afro-Jamaican dish made of parched dry corn, beaten fine in a mortar and served with sugar and salt; eaten mostly by blacks.

**BROWN GIRL,** a Jamaican mulatto or colored girl. In the plural, the term was formerly used in Jamaica to suggest the beauty of these girls and their supposed amorous accessibility.

**BROWN MAN,** in Jamaica, a colored man, between black and white. Among blacks, the term often implies resentment and scorn.

**BROWN-SKIN,** in Jamaica, someone whose skin is light brown; a mulatto.

**BRU-BRU** (Afr.), in Jamaica, disorderly, untidy; applied by Afro-Jamaicans to lower class people of no account.

**BRUCHY.** See BRICHY.

**BRUCKINS** (Eng. Cr.), in Jamaica, a noisy, rollicking black dance of rustic origin dating back to the slavery period.

**BRUCK-ROCK-STONE** (Eng. Cr.). See ROLL ROCK-STONE.

**BRULÉ ZIN** (Fr. Cr.) ("the boiling pot"), in the Afro-Haitian religion, a ceremony performed in various ways according to the tradition of the particular priest. Common to all is the dipping of hands into boiling oil.

**BRULIS** (Fr. Cr.), in the Afro-French Anilles, soil fertilized by the ashes of burnt trees and vegetation, an old agricultural technique very prevalent in Africa.

**BRUSHA** (Afr.), in Jamaica and elsewhere in the West Indies, a white overseer on a plantation.

**BRUXARIA** (Afr.), among Afro-Brazilians, any object or instrument used in black magic. The *bruxaria* is sometimes put in a doorway in the form of a doll stuck through with pins.

**BUCCANEER** (Fr. Cr.), originally, a shipwrecked sailor or deserter who preyed upon early Spanish vessels around Tortuga Island, off Hispaniola. Later, in the seventeenth and eighteenth centuries, the buccaneers became organized, with strong leaders, and were notorious slave traders. See also BRETHREN OF THE COAST.

**BUCKRA.** See BACKRA.

**BUCKRA PANYARING** (Afr.), the kidnapping of blacks by white men, around 1771, along the west coast of Africa. Always a fairly common practice, it seems to have been especially prevalent after the dissolution of the Royal African Company (q.v.) in 1750. (Mannix, *Black Cargoes*, p. 92.)

**BUCKY MASSA** (Afr.), an Afro-Jamaican term of address, respectfully affectionate or pleading.

**BUDDOE.** See GOTTLIEB, MOSES.

**BUDUM** (Afr.), in Brazil, the body odor reputedly characteristic of blacks or mulattoes; their extravagant use of perfumes seems to have been an over-compensation. (Freyre, *The Masters*, p. 279.) See also CATINGA.

**BUELTA Y FLORES, TOMÁS,** a free Cuban black, born in Havana, who became a popular orchestra leader. Between 1830 and 1843, he composed many *guarachas* (q.v.), contradanzas, and other melodies. In 1843, he was accused by the government of being a member of the Conspiracy of the Ladder (q.v.). He was jailed, tortured, and finally expelled from the island. (Calcagno, *Diccionario*, p. 131.)

**BUFFRO-BUFFRO** (Afr.), an Afro-Jamaican term for a clumsy, stout person.

**BUFF-TEETH** (Eng. Cr.), an Afro-Jamaican phrase meaning protruding teeth, common among blacks.

**BUFU-BUFU** (Eng. Cr.), in the West Indies, a term used mainly by blacks for a very big, clumsy, worthless person.

**BUGABOO,** an Afro-Jamaican word for a hobgoblin or ghost.

**BUGABOO'S MAN,** an Afro-Jamaican term for a ghost or supernatural being; used to threaten or frighten small children.

**BUGIA** (Afr.), in Brazil, a kerosene lamp; possibly related to Bugia, a town in North Africa (Algeria) known for its wax candle factories.

**BUGIO** (Pg.), an Afro-Brazilian term for monkey.

**BUG-JARGAL,** a legendary African prince who was enslaved for the murder of his father, the king of Kakongo. He was brought to Haiti as a slave and became a national hero. Bug-Jargal is described in one of Victor Hugo's poems.

**BUGUYAGA** (Afr.), an Afro-Jamaican word for a worthless, slovenly, clumsy person; an unkempt person.

**BUIAI, BUYÉ** (Fr. Cr.), the priest of the Black Carib (q.v.) cult. He often succeeds his father in office, although this kinship is regarded more as an inspiration than an inheritance. The *buiai* must not be confused with a witch doctor or seer. (Bastide, *African Civilizations*, p. 81.)

**BULL-BUCKER,** in Jamaica, a man who thinks he is strong enough to buck a bull; a belligerent person. The term is used mainly by blacks in connection with *duppy conqueror* (q.v.). (Cassidy, *Dictionary*, p. 77.)

**BULLDOG, DON'T BITE ME,** a black shanty-song in the West Indies.

**BULULÚ** (Afr.). 1. An Afro-Spanish word for turmoil. 2. In early sixteenth-century Spain, an itinerant comedian, performing alone in towns and villages. (Alvarez Nazario, *El elemento negroide*, p. 202.)

**BUMBA MEU BOI** (Pg.), in Brazil, a traditional pantomime festival in which one dancer wears a bull's head mask and is tormented by other dancers, while a chorus sings appropriate folk songs. The bull costume is made by hanging a cloth over a frame of wooden slats; the head is made from a decorated skull of a cow. The pantomime consists mainly of "sacrificing" the ox, then "resurrecting" it, and finally "eating" it. The "meat" of the animal is distributed among the participants in the festival. It is a favorite play among blacks. (Pierson, *Negroes*, p. 103.)

**BUMBO** (Afr.), an Afro-Jamaican word for buttocks, rump.

**BUNDA** (Afr.), an Afro-Brazilian word for buttocks, rump.

**BUNDO** (Afr.), in colonial Brazil, a black slave born in Angola (q.v.).

**BUNGA** (Afr.), in the Afro-Cuban dialect, a small band.

**BUNGAY.** See BUNGY.

**BUNGGUZU, BUNGUZUNG** (Afr.), an Afro-Jamaican word for sorcerer, wizard, *obeah* (q.v.).

**BUNGO** (Afr.), in Jamaica, an insulting term meaning very black, ugly, stupid; "African," with an offensive connotation. (Cassidy, *Dictionary*, p. 80.)

**BUNGO BEE,** (Afr.), an Afro-Jamaican name for the carpenter bee *(Xylophaga mordax)*, a large, black bumblebee.

**BUNGO BESSY** (Afr.), an Afro-Jamaican word for a Creole woman whose bushy hair is considered regressive, lower class, or highly undesirable.

**BUNGO CREOLE,** another name for Jamaican English Creole (q.v.).

**BUNGO MAN** (Afr.), in Jamaica, a black who, while dancing and singing, utters words which are said to be in African *bungo* (q.v.) language.

**BUNGO OKRO** (Afr.), an Afro-Jamaican term for a short, thick, coarse type of okra (q.v.).

**BUNGO STORY** (Afr.), in Jamaica, a type of black story formerly popular among slaves, which showed the stupidity of the Bungo (sometimes Congo [q.v.] and other) peoples. (Cassidy, *Dictionary*, p. 80.)

**BUNGO TALK** (Afr.), in Jamaica, a term for the language used in African *bungo* stories (q.v.) dealing with ignorant, stupid bush people.

**BUNGUZUNG** (Afr.). See BUNGGUZU.

**BUNGY, BUNGAY** (Afr.), an Afro-Jamaican word for a large, clumsy dugout canoe used by blacks for carrying freight; later, applied to various modern-day boats.

**BURAÇO DE TATÚ** (Pg.), in colonial Brazil, the name of a black *quilombo* (q.v.) organized outside Bahía, northeast of the city. It was a well-established village laid out in a rectilinear pattern of six rows of mud huts, divided by a large central street. At the time of its destruction by a Portuguese-led military expedition on September 2, 1763, there were thirty-two rectangular dwellings with approximately sixty-five adults. Upon capture, its inhabitants were incarcerated; thirty-one, whose only crime was to have escaped slavery, were branded with the letter *F* for *fugido* ("fugitive") by royal order; the leaders were sentenced to public flogging, several years as galley slaves, and then exile. (Price, *Maroon Societies*, pp. 211-22.)

**BURN WANGLA** (Afr.), in Jamaica, the ritual burning of seeds of the *wangla* (q.v.) to secure, by its magic smoke, the catching of a thief. Blacks procure the seeds of this wild tree and, with pepper and salt, burn them on the road where the thief is known to travel during the night. (Cassidy, *Dictionary*, p. 82.)

**BURU** (Afr.). In Jamaica: 1. A wild, sometimes indecent, Afro-Jamaican dance, or an occasion when such a dance takes place, especially funeral celebration dancing. 2. A place where lascivious or indecent dancing is done. 3. A type of music, especially, such as is used for *buru* dancing; also a drum and a group of musicians who play *buru* dance music. 4. A black cult similar to *cumina* (q.v.) in which wild dancing to drums is a prominent feature. (Cassidy, *Dictionary*, p. 83.)

**BURU-MAN** (Afr.), in the West Indies, a black man who does *buru* (q.v.) dancing.

**BURUNDANGA** (Afr.), an Afro-Spanish term for a mess, turmoil, confusion.

**BUSH.** 1. Wild or uncleared woodland and thickets, a place of refuge for runaway slaves in the colonial West Indies. 2. Any plant used by blacks in folk remedies, in teas, and in other domestic ways; also, in Jamaica, the tea itself. 3. Specifically, the concoction of an *obeah* man (q.v.) in which medicinal or poisonous herbs are an important ingredient. (Cassidy, *Dictionary*, p. 83.)

**BUSHA, OBISHA** (Eng. Cr.). In Jamaica: 1. A term of respect applied by slaves to a white overseer on a sugar estate (q.v.). 2. Today, a term expressing respect to any man of some local standing.

**BUSHA HOUSE** (Eng. Cr.), the overseer's dwelling on a sugar estate (q.v.) during slavery times in Jamaica.

**BUSH-BAG** (Eng. Cr.), an Afro-Caribbean word for a temporary bag made of grass or other material available in the fields; formerly used by slaves.

**BUSH-BATH** (Eng. Cr.), in the West Indies, a bath with hot water in which local herbs have been steeped. Among blacks, the water is commonly applied to the body with a cloth and is followed by a rubdown with rum. Some of the wild plants used are leaf-of-life, horse-bath, fiddle-wood, and black-giant. A bush-bath is supposedly good for aches and pains.

**BUSH-CLOTHES,** on Caribbean plantations, old sturdy clothes; formerly worn by slaves.

**BUSH-DOCTOR** (Eng. Cr.), in the West Indies, a black, especially a practitioner of magic, who practices herb remedies under the guise of medicine.

**BUSH-FIGHT** (Eng. Cr.), on Caribbean sugar estates (q.v.) in slavery times, a fight by stealth, not by the rules of organized warfare. Generally used to refer to the Maroons' (q.v.) way of fighting.

**BUSH-MAN** in the West Indies, a black sorcerer or *obeah* man (q.v.).

**BUSH NEGRO,** in Dutch Guiana, a descendant of former slaves of English colonists left behind when the English withdrew or were expelled from the region. These English-speaking slaves fled to the trackless forests of the interior where they organized themselves into several tribes. Until the last century, they lived in isolation and carried on continuous warfare with the colonial government. Their language is English-based, with elements drawn from Portuguese and other languages. See also BUSH NEGRO CREOLE.

**BUSH NEGRO CREOLE,** an English-based Creole dialect spoken by descendants of former slaves in Dutch Guiana. It has retained many Portuguese elements and a far higher proportion of words of African (especially Kikongo) origin than any other Surinam Creole.

**BUSH-TEA,** in the West Indies, a medicinal beverage prepared by blacks from the leaves, seeds, and roots of an enormous variety of plants, over 200 of which have been listed.

**BUSU** (Afr.), in Jamaica, a wicked, mischievous black.

**BUTA** (Afr.), in the West Indies, a black member of an African cult.

**BUTLERESS,** in the Afro-Jamaican dialect, a black woman servant who, among other things, waits at table.

**BUXEN** (Eng. Cr.). See BOKSN.

**BUXTON, THOMAS FOWELL** (1786-1845), a British philanthropist and abolitionist. In 1818, Buxton was elected member of Parliament, and, in 1824, he replaced William Wilberforce (q.v.) as head of the abolitionist movement (q.v.) in England. He actively participated in the organization of the Society for the Extinction of the Slave Trade and the African Civilization Society.

**BUYÉ.** See BUIAÍ.

**BUZIO** (Pg.), a cowry, or small, ivory-colored, glossy shell of a mollusk found on the shores of the Indian Ocean. During slavery times, it was used for money in parts of Africa and Brazil. In the Costa da Mina (q.v.) in 1759, a pound of *buzios* was worth $320. In Brazil today, they are worn by some women in Afro-Brazilian cults and by black women fortune-tellers. (Carneiro, *Ladinos e Crioulous*, p. 196.)

**BUZO,** in colonial Brazil, a game popular among new slaves from Africa.

**BWANGA** (Afr.), an Afro-Haitian term for a magical faith in the transcendental value of one's own being. It suggests a magical power that reinforces an individual's personality, a kind of stoic force, ever present and indispensable in facing the miseries of a hostile social environment.

**BYA.** See BIAH.

**BYE-CHILD,** an Afro-Jamaican term for the offspring of a concubinage, often a mixed-blood child who generally stays with the mother. (Cassidy, *Dictionary*, p. 84.)

**"BY INCH OF CANDLE,"** a public auction of black slaves held by slave traders in the West Indies. The ship captain went over the cargo and picked out the slaves who were maimed or diseased. These were carried to a nearby tavern and auctioned off with a lighted candle beside the auctioneer; bids were received until an inch of candle had burned. The price of these "refused" slaves sold at auction was usually less than half that paid for healthy blacks. (Mannix, *Black Cargoes*, p. 128.)

# C

**CABAÇA** (Afr.), an Afro-Brazilian word for the first-born of twins.

**CABAÇO** (Afr.), an Afro-Brazilian term for: 1. The second-born of twins. 2. Hymen, virginity. (Mendonça, *A Influencia*, p. 120.)

**CABANADA** (Pg.), in Brazil, a peasant and slave revolt that first occurred in Pernambuco and Alagoas in 1832 when 6,000 men gathered in an uprising against landowners and the government. The struggle was violent and bloody. There were several other *cabanadas* until 1839, when the government finally established an agreement with the rebels. (Ramos, *The Negro*, p. 52.)

**CABANO** (Pg.), in colonial Brazil, a member of an armed peasant-slave rebellion. See also CABANADA.

**CABELEIRA** (Pg.), in Afro-Brazilian folklore, a ghostly and terrifying creature used to frighten children. According to tradition, the old black nanny had but to shout at the weeping youngster: "Cabeleira's coming," and the child at once stopped crying. Originally, Cabeleira was a bandit of the sugar cane (q.v.) fields of Pernambuco who was finally hanged in early colonial times. (Freyre, *The Masters*, p. 340.)

**CABESS** (Pg.), a unit of currency used in slave trading in Dahomey (q.v.) around 1793. One cabess was worth 10s. 0d., or 4 ackeys (q.v.). (Davidson, *Black Mother*, p. 91.)

**CABILDO AFROCUBANO.** See CABILDO DE NEGROS.

**CABILDO DE NEGROS** (Sp.), in Cuba and elsewhere in Spanish America, an association of black slaves of both sexes, established for mutual aid and recreation. In some cases, *cabildos* were organized societies with houses and halls outside town where the members met periodically to celebrate their festivals under the presidency of a "king" or "queen." Throughout the year, the society acted as a communal aid association, the chief aiding his members if they were sick. Their general funds were also used to pay burial expenses and sometimes to free old, invalid slaves. The chief presided at the celebration of their patron saints, held annually by the members of the *cofradía de negros* (q.v.). The *cabildos de negros* were eventually recognized as legitimate political agents for the slaves and freedmen in dealing with local authorities, thus providing outlets for political organization and leadership. As early as 1573, *cabildos* were active in the municipal government in Havana. (L. Foner, *Slavery*, pp. 148-49.)

**CABINDA, KABINDA** (Afr.), an Atlantic sea-trading post located a short distance north of the mouth of the Congo River which, in the sixteenth century, was part of the Congo (q.v.) Kingdom. Around 1575, the Portuguese slave traders began exporting black slaves through this post to northeast Brazil to work on the sugar plantations. They also started training and arming bands of native "allies" to make war on the tribes around Cabinda in order to get slaves. (Woodson, *The African Background*, p. 131.)

**CABINDA CULT**, an Afro-Brazilian urban cult centered around the worship of Christian saints and the spirits of the family ancestors. This congregation, of Bantu (q.v.) origin, uses a syncretic liturgical service based on African and European traditions. (Ramos, *The Negro*, p. 101.)

**CABINDA SLAVES**, a broad term applied to Bantu (q.v.) black slaves imported through the port of Cabinda in the Angola (q.v.) territory. These slaves, thought to be physically weak, talkative, quarrelsome, and given to excessive merrymaking, were preferred in Brazil for domestic service early in the colonial period. Later, they were employed mainly in the mines in Minas Gerais. Their color was a dark brown or chocolate that differed from the yellow or light-brown, reddish skin of the Sudanic blacks. (Freyre, *The Masters*, pp. 300, 303-304.)

**CABOCEER, CABOCEIRO** (Pg.), an important slave trader, operating mainly along the Slave Coast (q.v.) in West Africa. Since he was usually under the supervision of coastal African kings, his activities acquired an air of legality. Some *caboceers* were Portuguese half-castes, professing to be Christian but maintaining several wives; some were honest native merchants; and others were gangsters leading bands of professional kidnappers. (Davidson, *Black Mother*, p. 95.)

**CABOCLINHO** (Pg.), an Afro-Brazilian song-dance.

**CABOCLO** (Pg.). In Brazil: 1. An acculturated pure-blood Brazilian Indian. 2. A Brazilian of mixed Indian and white blood. 3. A South American rural half-breed with a reddish or bronze tinge to his skin color, more prominent cheekbones than the Africans or whites, and a tendency toward almond-shaped eyes.

**CABOOSE** (Eng. Cr.), in Jamaica, a black's small house, a hut.

**CABORÉ.** See CABURÉ.

**CABORGE** (Pg.), an Afro-Brazilian term for witchcraft.

**CABOVERDE,** in Brazil, a very dark person with Caucasian features and black, glossy "straight" hair, thin lips, and a straight narrow nose; he is almost a "black white man."

**CABRA** (Pg.). In Brazil: 1. A brave young mèstizo, an offspring of African-white-Indian ancestry. 2. A hired black gunman on a plantation.

**CABRA-CABRIOLA** (Pg.) ("capering nanny goat"), in Afro-Brazilian folklore, an imaginary goat-like creature or goblin character who comes at night to suck the wet nurse and eat the child.

**CABRAL, MANUEL DEL** (b. 1907), a white Dominican poet who violently and abusively rejects négritude (q.v.) and denounces it as arrogant nothingness. His works include *Doce poemas negros* (1935) and *De este lado del mar* (1949).

**CABRERA, LYDIA** (b. 1900), a Cuban scholar and writer who has investigated in depth black historical and oral traditions. Her widely published works include *Cuentos negros de Cuba* (1940); *Refranes de negros viejos* (1955); and *Anago, Vocabulario lucumi* (1970).

**CABROCHA** (Pg.), in Brazil, a dark-skinned female mestizo who, during colonial times, served variously as domestic, concubine, and even lawful wife of her white master. This black woman exerted a powerful influence on Brazilian society. Her mixed-blood children, whether fathered by the planters legitimately or illegitimately, tended to break up the feudal allotments and the landed estate system.

**CABULA,** a nearly extinct Bantu (q.v.) cult that held three annual festivities devoted mainly to honoring Saints Barbara, Mary Magdalen, Cosmos, and Damian. Their meetings were held in secret, usually in the forest. The present-day *macumba* (q.v.) is apparently a direct outgrowth of this cult.

**CABUNGO** (Pg.), an Afro-Brazilian term for chamber pot.

**CABURÉ, CABORÉ.** (Pg.). 1. In colonial Brazil, the offspring of black and Indian parents. 2. Today, a poor rural laborer.

**CAÇAMBA** (Afr.), an Afro-Brazilian word for a bucket used to carry water from a well.

**CAÇANJE** (Afr.), in colonial Brazil, a Creole Portuguese dialect spoken by black slaves imported from Angola (q.v.).

**CACHEU** (Pg.), a river on the Guinea Coast (q.v.) where the Portuguese established a post in 1680 to export black slaves to Brazil. Six years later, the post at Cacheu became a village, with a governor, a garrison of about thirty soldiers to man the camp, and a convent of Capuchins. (Alvarez Nazario, *El elemento Negroide*, p. 49.) See also COMPANHIA DE CACHEU.

**CACHIMBO** (Bant.), an Afro-Brazilian word for a smoking pipe.

**CACHOT EFFROYANT** (Fr. Cr.), in late colonial Haiti, tiny maximum-security cells, probably without lights, where slaves accused of crimes such as armed rebellion and poisoning were jailed. After 1760, *cachots effroyants* were constructed on practically every plantation with more than 150 slaves. (Price, *Maroon Societies*, p. 119.)

**CACIMBA** (Afr.), an Afro-Brazilian word for an artificial water well.

**CACOON** (Afr.), a well-known Jamaican vine with a bean pod often three or more feet long and beans large enough to serve as money purses. It was used by the Maroons (q.v.) to disguise themselves when in ambush. With its beans, the blacks prepare an antidote for bites from spiders, wasps, centipedes, and other insects. It is probably of African origin.

**CACOS** (Fr. Cr.), Afro-Haitian highlanders, half peasants and half bandits, traditionally used as political armies by presidents and men of power. In 1918, during the period of intervention by the United States, the *cacos* resisted an order for compulsory labor on the roads; they fought for two years, and almost 2,000 people lost their lives. These professional warriors were finally suppressed by the U.S. Marines.

**CAÇULA** (Afr.), an Afro-Brazilian word for the last daughter of a family.

**CAÇULO** (Afr.), an Afro-Brazilian term for the last son of a family.

**CAÇUMBU** (Afr.), an Afro-Brazilian word for a worn-out hoe.

**CADGER,** in Kingston, Jamaica, a street vendor who cries his wares with a peculiar musical inflection. See also HIGGLER.

**CAESAR BOY, CAESAR,** a black shanty-song in the West Indies.

**CAFAJESTE** (Afr.), an Afro-Brazilian word meaning a person of low social condition or bad manners.

**CAFANGA** (Afr.). An Afro-Brazilian word for: 1. Squeamishness; touchiness. 2. Simulated or false apology. 3. Pretended refusal.

**CAFÉ MANDINGUEIRO** (Pg.) ("witch's coffee"), in Brazil, a love potion made by a black female sorcerer. It consists of strong coffee mixed with much sugar and a few clots of the menstrual fluid of the sorcerer herself. See also MACUMBEIRO.

**CAFIOTO** (Afr.), in Afro-Brazilian cults, a male novice initiated as an assistant to the priest.

**CAFRE** (Afr.), a black slave, often a Moslem, brought to Brazil from Africa.

**CAFÚ** (Afr.), an Afro-Cuban word for a fellow black slave; now a popular character in folklore.

**CAFÚA** (Afr.), an Afro-Brazilian term for a schoolroom where delinquent students were kept for punishment.

**CAFUNDÓ** (Afr.), an Afro-Brazilian word for a gulch or gorge; often used as a mountain refuge.

**CAFUNÉ** (Afr.), an Afro-Brazilian term for stroking or gently scratching the head. In colonial times, black women slaves used to give *cafunés* with their hands when looking for lice or caressing children.

**CAFUNGE** (Afr.), in Brazil, a rascal child.

**CAFUSO** (Afr.), in Brazil, a back country offspring of black and Indian parentage.

**CAHIER DES DOLÉANCES** (Fr.) ("Book of Complaints"), a list drawn up by a group of French planters in Saint Domingue in 1789 requesting the National Assembly in Paris to grant permission to the whites to govern the colony without any interference from France.

**CAHIER D'UN RETOUR AU PAYS NATAL** (Fr.) ("Notebook of a Return to the Fatherland"), a long poem published by Aimé Césaire (q.v.) in 1938 in which the author violently and aggressively rejects Europe and its Christian tradition, and stresses the loyal and fraternal courage of the black man, symbol of an eternal and inexhaustible strength. It is in this poem, published in Paris 1938, that the term négritude (q.v.), now in common use, appeared for the first time. The poem begins with a bitter evocation of the poverty and deprivation of colonial Martinique and then passes into an expression of deep hatred for the white world. In his revolt against the French Enlightenment, Césaire turned to African primitivism.

**CAIFAZES** (Pg.), underground Brazilian abolitionists, organized in a kind of religious brotherhood, who, around 1880, systematically helped black slaves escape from *fazendas* (q.v.) and farms in São Paulo and elsewhere. With evangelical zeal, they made extensive arrangements to coordinate escape plots, assisted by people from many different social classes. If a *caifaz* had relatives who were slaveowners, he was expected to cooperate in the escape of at least one slave from his kinsfolk. (Toplin, *The Abolition*, pp. 204-205.)

**CAILCEDRAT** (Fr.), a hardwood tree apparently brought to the New World from tropical Africa. In Senegal (q.v.), it is known as *acajou* (q.v.).

**CAILLE** (Fr. Cr.), in Haiti, a native one-room hut, usually with a hand-hewn wooden frame. The poorest is walled with mud-daubed wattles and thatched with palm branches or guinea-grass (q.v.). The plaster of the best *cailles* is sometimes painted over with a color design superimposed on top. In addition, the better *cailles* have ceilings and wooden floors and often a tin roof and porch. There are also two- and three-room *cailles*.

**CAILLE MYSTER** (Fr. Cr.), in Haiti, a voodoo (q.v.) temple. See also HOUNFORT.

**CAILLE-PAILLE** (Fr. Cr.) ("palm hut"), in rural Haiti, a peasant hut. In general, it is a one- or two-room thatched cottage whose walls are loosely made of twilled bamboo or other flexible creepers coated with mud and lime. The shelter tends to be small, averaging ten to twelve feet, with a beaten-earth floor but no ceiling. Its roof thatching is of straw, palm leaves, or similar material. Cooking is done outside. Despite general uniformity, some variations exist in the *caille-paille*, reflecting both the owner's economic status and the region in which he lives. See also CAILLE.

**CAIPIRANHO** (Pg.), a Brazilian Creole Portuguese spoken in rural areas by some Brazilians of African ancestry.

**CAJÚ** (Pg.), the cashew tree *(Anacardium occidentale)* from which cashew nuts are obtained. Its astringent fruit also makes an excellent drink. In slavery times, cashew nuts were a source of cheap food for plantation slaves all over tropical America.

**CALABAN, CALAMBAM** (Afr.), a pyramidal wicker trap made of reeds; used widely to catch birds in the West Indies. The word appears to have been spread very early in the Caribbean, probably by blacks.

**CALABAR,** a West African slave port located at the tip of the Niger River Delta, sometimes known as the Bight of Biafra (q.v.). Slaves from this port were usually from the Ibo (q.v.) ethnic group.

**CALABAR, DOMINGOS,** a Brazilian mulatto who fought in Pernambuco (circa 1692) under Mathis d'Albuquerque. He later passed over to the side of the Dutch invaders and was responsible for several Portuguese defeats. He was finally captured and hanged. (Freyre, *The Masters*, p. 269.)

**CALAFATE, MANOEL,** a Brazilian Moslem slave who played a leading role in the unsuccessful Hausa uprising of 1835 in Bahía, Brazil. (Ramos, *The Negro*, p. 50.)

**CALALOU, CALALU** (Afr.), a generic name given to several tropical plants with edible leaves; eaten as greens in soups or used as medicine. These plants were introduced from the Guinea Coast (q.v.) in colonial times.

**CALALOU-GOMBO** (Afr.), in Haiti and the French West Indies, a soup made of *calalou* (q.v.) and other ingredients; eaten as part of a ritual in a wake. Also known as *calalou des morts*.

**CALALU.** See CALALOU.

**CALAMBAM.** See CALABAN.

**CALAMBUCO** (Afr.), a black sorcerer in the Afro-Cuban *santería* (q.v.) cult.

**CALCAGNO, FRANCISCO** (1827-1903), a Cuban educator and writer born in Güines, Havana province. Son of an Italian physician, Calcagno attended schools in Güines as well as the University of Havana, and traveled widely in Europe and the United States. In his native town, he founded the first periodical and the Academy of Languages. Among his works are *Diccionario biográfico cubano* (1886) and *Poetas de color—Placido,*

*Manzano, Rodriguez, Echeverría, Silveira, Medina* (q.v.) (1878); some of the poets in the latter book were former slaves.

**CALDAS BARBOSA, DOMINGOS** (1738 or 1740-1800), a Brazilian mulatto musician and writer.Caldas Barbosa was the son of a Portuguese man and a black woman from Angola (q.v.). His inspired songs, often sung to the accompaniment of the viola, were very popular in both Brazil and Portugal. He was sent for military service to the province of Sacramento (Uruguay); soon after he left for Lisbon where, in 1755, his first poems were published. He was also a secular priest. In Lisbon, he helped found the Academy of Fine Arts, becoming its first president. Caldas Barbosa was extremely talented and attained considerable fame in the salons of Rio de Janeiro and later in Lisbon. He was a prolific writer and composer. Among his works are *Epithalamio* (Lisboa, 1777); *A Doença* (Lisboa, 1777); *Os Viajantes Ditosos* (Lisboa, 1790); *A Saloia Namorada, ou O Remédio é Casar* (Lisboa, 1793); *A Vingança da Cigana* (Lisboa, 1794); *A Escola dos Ciosos* (Lisboa, 1795); and *Viola de Lereno* (Lisboa, 1796-1826). (Ramos, *The Negro*, p. 127.)

**CALDERÓN, LOUISA,** a fifteen-year-old mulatto mistress of a Spanish resident in Trinidad whom she and her paramour were accused of robbing. She denied her guilt in the face of clear evidence. Consequently, with the consent of Sir Thomas Picton, former governor of Trinidad, she was treated in accordance with Spanish law covering such a situation. This episode, widely exaggerated, was used by the abolitionists as an argument against slavery. Louisa's subsequent arrival in London with Colonel and Mrs. William Fullerton created a furor. The whole matter was thoroughly aired in a series of pamphlets from 1804 to 1806. In 1806, Picton was brought to trial on the specific charge of having ordered Louisa tortured and was found guilty. In 1808, the case was retried. When Picton proved that his action had been taken in accordance with the law of Castile, he was released from bail without judgment being given. (Ragatz, *The Fall*, p. 274.)

**CALEMBE, CALIMBE** (Afr.), in the West Indies, a black song-dance of African origin. Often performed at wakes, it consists of two men holding a pair of sticks parallel, while a third dances upon them to the strains of the song. (Cassidy, *Dictionary*, p. 89.)

**CALENDA, CALINDA** (Afr.), a lascivious, sexual dance popular throughout the Caribbean region in colonial times. It was brought to the area by Guinea slaves. Blacks reputedly used to dance the *calenda* for days at a time.

**CALENDRÉE** (Afr.), in the French Antilles, a black woman wearing a stiffly starched head scarf of colorful madras (q.v.) fabric, a fashion of African origin.

**CALHAMBOLA** (Pg.), in colonial Brazil, a runaway slave who often killed cattle and domestic animals in order to keep alive. Classified as bandits and robbers, such slaves indulged in illicit diamond and gold mining, finding refuge in the *quilombos* (q.v.).

**CALIBASH ESTATE,** an Afro-Jamaican phrase referring to the practice among black slaves of stealing sugar from the curing house in calabashes. When caught, they pleaded that they were "carrying sugar to Calibash estate!" (Cassidy, *Jamaica Talk*, p. 94.)

**CALICO NEGRO.** See NEGRO CALICO.

**CALIMBE.** See CALEMBE.

**CALINDA.** See CALENDA.

**CALINGA.** See CARINGA.

**CALIPSO, CALYPSO,** in the West Indies, a song consisting of a spoken or intoned story or comment on the news, or on a celebrity in the news, accompanied by drumming and guitar strumming. It contains rhymes of a sort, usually in couplets, but no regular meter. Its fascination lies in the singer's ability to fit in any number of words in each line. The words are in English.

**CALOMBO** (Afr.), an Afro-Brazilian word for a swelling in the body.

**CALUGE** (Afr.), an Afro-Brazilian word for a straw hut.

**CALUNDU** (Afr.), in Brazil, a black dance; also weariness, boredom.

**CALUNGA** (Afr.). 1. An Afro-Brazilian word for a doll made out of wax or cloth by a black sorcerer which is used in black magic rituals. 2. In Brazil, a Bantu (q.v.) divinity worshipped by Angolan slaves.

**CALYPSO.** See CALIPSO.

**CALZA Y RAMAL** (Sp.), an instrument of slave torture consisting of a twelve-pound piece of iron fastened around the foot. The unfortunate victim carried it for a stipulated period of time.

**CAMARINHA** (Pg.) ("the little room"), the sacred room of a *candomblé* (q.v.) center in Brazil where the cult's followers undergo several initiation rituals. They sleep there with their heads together; while they are in the *camarinha*, they do not attend any ceremonies.

**CAMBÔNE, CAMBÔNDE** (Pg.), in the Afro-Brazilian cult of the *macumbas* (q.v.), the assistant of the high priest during the rituals of evocation of the spirits.

**CAMILLE, ROUSSAN** (b. 1915), a Haitian writer who began his education at Jacmel, his native town. He continued his schooling at the Tippenhauer Institute and at the Lycée National Alexandre Pétion in Port-au-Prince. In 1935, he joined the staff of the *Haiti Journal*. Two years later, he was appointed first secretary of the Haitian legation in Paris. In 1940, he returned to Port-au-Prince and was given an important position in the Department of National Education. Later, he became editor-in-chief of the *Haiti Journal*. After a while, he was sent to New York as vice-consul. He has traveled to many countries and has frequently represented his country as a cultural envoy. His works are *Assaut à la nuit* (1940) and, in collaboration with J. F. Brièrre (q.v.) and F. Morisseau-Leroy (q.v.), *Gerbe pour deux amis* (1945). (Hughes, *The Poetry*, p. 391.)

**CAMONDONGO, CAMUNDONGO** (Pg.), an Afro-Brazilian word for mouse.

**CAMPBELL, GEORGE** (b. 1917), a black writer born in Kingston, Jamaica, where he attended school. He later attended Saint George College. In Jamaica, he worked as a newspaper reporter on the *Kingston Daily Gleaner*. Soon after he emigrated to New York. Among his works are *First Poems* (1945) and *A Play without Scenery* (1947).

**CAMPO, DIEGO DE**, a runaway black slave who between 1545 and 1548 led with his band bloody attacks against Spanish settlements throughout the island of Santo Domingo. Captured in 1546, he was pardoned and joined the Spaniards in the fight against his former followers. (Rout, L.B., *The African Experience in Spanish America*, p. 118.)

**CAMUNDONGO.** See CAMONDONGO.

**CANBOULAY** (Fr. Cr.), in colonial Trinidad and elsewhere in the Caribbean, a torchlight procession to commemorate one of the few excitements of the plantation, a fire in the cane fields. *Canboulay* eventually became a symbol of emancipation. It was celebrated yearly by black laborers on August 1 as a counterpart to the more decorous annual public dinners in

Port-of-Spain. Probably during the 1840s, *canboulay*, with its torches and stick fights, merged into the carnival, perhaps adding a sense of racial solidarity and past suffering to the mood of the participants. It certainly brought fire and torches to the processions; these were held to be a main cause of the troubles that often marred later carnivals.

**CANDOMBE** (Afr.), an old Afro-Argentine dance in mildly syncopated rhythm. Apparently, it has now been combined with the *tango*, (q.v.). Its origin is African. (Slonimzki, *Music*, p. 299.)

**CANDOMBLÉ** (Afr.), in Brazil, a fetish cult of African origin. It is still a vigorous institution and numbers among its adherents some of the most widely known members of the urban lower classes. The language, ceremonial dress, dance, song, and pantheon of the *candomblés* vary a great deal. In the so-called *candomblé* of Bahia, there are three principal divisions: the *gêgé nagó* (q.v.), the Angola, and the *candomblé-caboclo* (q.v.). The Afro-Brazilian Congress, which met at Bahia in January 1937, addressed a petition to the governor of the state asking for official recognition of the *candomblé* as a religious sect with rights and privileges equal, under the Brazilian Constitution, to those of all other forms of religious expression. (Pierson, *Negroes*, pp. 275-77.)

**CANDOMBLÉ ANNUAL** (Afr.) ("annual *candomblé*"), an Afro-Brazilian week of festivities in honor of the saints and *orishas* (q.v.) of the *candomblé* (q.v.) cult. It follows a prescribed schedule: Monday—Exú (q.v.) and Osmolu; Tuesday—Namamburucu and Oxumaré; Wednesday—Xangó (q.v.) and Yansan (q.v.); Thursday—Oxossi (q.v.) and Ogun (q.v.); Friday —Oxalá (Obatalá) (q.v.); Saturday—Yemanjá (q.v.) and Oxúm (q.v.); and Sunday—all the *orixas*. (Ramos, *As Culturas Negras*, p. 89.)

**CANDOMBLÉ-CABOCLO** (Afr.), in Brazil, an Amerindian folk cult which mixes, in varying degrees, African and Indian rituals, dances, and deities. It is carried on in Portuguese, with the addition of certain phrases of African origin and a few words of Tupi derivation. Feathers, the bow and arrow, and other Indian cultural elements enter into the liturgy. Apparently, it has only recently been organized. (Pierson, *Negroes*, p. 276.) See also CABOCLO; CANDOMBLÉ.

**CANDOMBLÉ FUNERÁRIO** (Afr.), an elaborate Afro-Brazilian ritual that takes place some time after death. It includes the celebration of a mass in a Catholic church attended by the relatives, friends, and members of the *candomblé* (q.v.) brotherhood. It lasts one or two days, during which there are dances, songs, prayers, and animal sacrifices to the soul of the dead person and to the spirits. The clothing of the departed is often given to the attendants. (Ramos, *As Culturas Negras*, p. 91.)

**CANDUNGO, CANDONGO** (Bant.), in the Afro-Antilles, a bucket made from a tropical tree *(Cucurbita legendaria L.)* known variously as *marimba, carracho, güidaro,* or *güiro.*

**CANDUNGUÉ** (Bant.), a vivid, indecent dance popular among Neo-Africans in Puerto Rico.

**CANGIRISTA** (Pg.), in Brazil, a black healer who employs a variety of remedies (including herbs and other substances), prescribed in accordance with set magic rituals.

**CANGUÉ, CANGUÁ** (Afr.), in Brazil, a nocturnal meeting of plantation slaves to perform mysterious ceremonies which they believed could cure certain diseases, prevent corporal punishment, and help them earn money. (Stein, *Vassouras*, p. 200.)

**CANJICA** (Pg.), an Afro-Brazilian delicacy made from green-corn paste seasoned with sugar, butter, coconut milk, and cinnamon. This dish is usually prepared at Christmas and for Saint João's Day.

**CANNING'S RESOLUTION,** a crucial act passed by the House of Commons and signed in 1823 by the foreign minister, George Canning (1770-1827), stating the intention of the British government to abolish slavery in the West Indies and other colonies. In Jamaica, it touched off a violent wave of opposition organized by the white planters.

**CANOA RANCHERA** (Sp.), in the Pacific Colombian lowlands, a special canoe built by blacks to explore the sea coast, rivers, and swamps. A sleeping structure is attached to the stern and indicates the canoe's use for long trips or a change of residence.

**CANTO** (Pg.), in Brazil, a group of black slaves who used to meet periodically in suitable places in a town to engage in traditional crafts such as pottery, leather work, and wood carving, and to share their African religious customs. A *canto* was a kind of informal, institutionalized social activity under the supervision of an elected chief *(capitão).* (Nina Rodrigues, *Os Africanos*, p. 156.)

**CANYANGUE** (Bant.), an Afro-Spanish dance popular among black slaves in the Plata River region in colonial times.

**CANZO** (Afr.), in the Haitian voodoo (q.v.) cult, a series of ritual ceremonies that all novices must pass through before becoming full-fledged
participants in the cult. The ritual includes the covering of the initiate with a
sheet while he handles hot stones or walks over live coals.

**CANZUÁ, GANZUÁ** (Afr.), an Afro-Brazilian cult center; the word is
derived from "Gantoiz," the name of a fetish temple in Bahia, Brazil.

**CAOBA, JOSÉ EMERSON** (d. 1877), a black Cuban slave, born in Sagua,
who was owned by a German planter. He was a leader of a slave revolt in
the Cinco-Villas district and died fighting in 1877. (Calcagno, *Diccionario*,
p. 154.)

**CAPATAZ DE CABILDO** (Sp.), in Cuba and elsewhere the black chairman of an African slave mutual aid society who was in charge of maintaining the good behavior of its members during the festivals held on Sundays
and on days of important fiestas. These gatherings took place along the city
walls. If there were any violations of the city ordinances, the chairman had
to pay a fine to the authorities.

**CAPE VERDE ISLANDS,** Archipelago and Portuguese colony in the
Atlantic, about 375 miles west of Dakar. The area came under Portuguese
rule in the late fifteenth century and became a busy slave-trading post
between Africa and Brazil.

**CAPIM DE ANGOLA** (Afr.), a type of weed brought to Brazil by African
slaves.

**CAPIM GORDURA** (Afr.), an African weed brought to Brazil during the
slave trade.

**CAPIM MEMBECA** (Afr.), an African weed brought to Brazil by African
slaves.

**CAPITÁNA DE NEGRAS ESCLAVAS** (Sp.), in colonial Spanish America,
a female black chief in charge of a gang of women slaves working in the
mines or on the farms. (Pescatello, *The African*, p. 102.)

**CAPITÁN DE BANDERA** (Sp.) ("captain of the flag"), an American citizen whose only function was to take temporary command of a slaver (q.v.)
illegally carrying black slaves to the Spanish colonies and Brazil when it was
boarded by an English cruiser. This practice was introduced after 1807
when slavery was outlawed. Then a flag, especially if it were American,
could provide legal protection. In the event of British navy intervention, the

captain simply sold the vessel to any American sailor on board for 1 dollar and thus avoided condemnation of the cargo. (Mannix, *Black Cargoes*, pp. 201-202.)

**CAPITÁN DE CUADRILLA** (Sp.), in Colombia and elsewhere a black slave in charge of a slave gang (q.v.) working in the mines. His duties included the disciplining of his men, the distribution of food supplies, and the collection of the week's take of gold. A man respected by his master, he was often given special treatment and rations. (Pescatello, *The African*, p. 101.)

**CAPITÃO DO CAMPO** (Pg.), in colonial Brazil, a police officer appointed by the governor or police chief to be in charge of apprehending runaway black slaves. Almost without exception, the men chosen were Creole blacks of unquestionable courage. They were authorized to arrest and return to their owners any slaves who were absent from their plantations without their master's consent. They operated in the countryside.

**CAPITÃO DO MATTO** (Pg.) ("bush captain"), in Brazil, a black or mulatto chief of an army unit in charge of apprehending runaway slaves in towns and cities. At ports of entry, he also sought to prevent any large gatherings of African slaves from the same ship or ethnic group. He was usually a Brazilian-born black or mulatto, with trained dogs, which helped net him a steady income. Selected by the landowners and planters, the *capitão do matto* became a symbol of despotism and oppression.

**CAPITATION** (Fr.), a poll tax. In the French Antilles, a tax paid by slave-owners and by free blacks and mulattoes for each slave. There were many exemptions, either because of job classifications or because of the identity of the owners. Officials in the colonial government, military officers, religious orders, and hospitals were granted exemptions for a certain number of slaves. In Guadeloupe, free blacks and mulattoes aged fourteen to sixty and not serving in the militia were taxed at 25 livres each. Slaves working in the cultivation and manufacture of sugar or as domestics were also taxed at 25 livres. Those occupied in the raising of livestock were taxed at 10 livres. (McCloy, *The Negro*, pp. 26-28.)

**CAPLATA** (Fr. Cr.), in the Afro-Haitian folk religion, a sort of jack-of-all-trades who professes to be able to achieve whatever is demanded of him in magic, whether beneficial or harmful.

**CAPOEIRA** (Pg.), in Brazil, a black or mulatto dancer who accompanied religious processions. He wore light sandals on his feet, carried a razor or a sharp, pointed knife, and wore his hair combed in the shape of a turban. He performed a variety of difficult steps and movements of incredible agility. Later, the *capoeira* became an "idler" who practiced feats of bodily skill and dexterity in the lowest quarters and taverns of the cities to the delight of sailors, seamen, and laborers. On the plantations, *capoeiras* were under strict supervision and sometimes their masters, fearful for their slaves' safety, outlawed them. Today, they have survived as sophisticated black ballet dancers. *Capoeiras* probably originated in Africa. (Freyre, *The Masters*, pp. 41-42.)

**CAPOEIRA DE ANGOLA** (Pg.), in urban Brazil, a black wrestler.

**CAPOEIRAGEM** (Pg.), in Brazil, the art and skill of a black dancer.

**CAPRESSE** (Fr. Cr.), in the French Antilles, the offspring of mulatto man and a black woman.

**CARABELAS** (Sp.), in colonial Cuba, Peru, and elsewhere in Spanish America, African slaves who traveled on the same ship across the Atlantic. The horrors of the voyage resulted in the formation of strong and lasting bonds of friendship, as with brothers and sisters in disgrace. In order to survive in the hostile plantation society, some *carabelas* organized fraternities and clubs for mutual aid and recreation. (Comitas and Lowenthal, *Slaves, Free Men*, p. 28.)

**CARABELÍ** (Afr.), in Cuba, black slaves, presumably from the Ibo (q.v.) ethnic group, brought to the island in the nineteenth century.

**CARACUMBÉ** (Afr.), an Afro-Spanish dance still popular in Colombia.

**CARBERRY, H. D.** (b. 1922), a Jamaican poet educated in Spanish Town and Mandeville. He later entered Saint Andrew College in Kingston and received a law degree at Saint Catherine's College, Oxford, England. His poems "Nature," "I Shall Remember," and "Return" originally appeared in the Jamaican weekly *Public Opinion*.

**CARGAZOENEN** (D.), a slaver (q.v.) cargo consisting of gum, cloth, brandy, and other European goods. Dutch merchants carried the goods to the west coast of Africa where they were traded for slaves destined for the Caribbean region. (Goslinga, *The Dutch*, p. 347.)

**CARIAPEMBA, CARIPEMBA** (Pg.), an Afro-Brazilian word for a demon who in slavery times was said to pursue the slaves and take possession of their bodies. This spirit is still mentioned in the *macumba* (q.v.).

**CARIJÓ** (Afr.), in colonial Brazil, the offspring of a black father and an Indian mother.

**CARIM.** See CAURIS.

**CARIMBO** (Afr.), an iron mark, or official stamp, branded on each African slave legally entering the New World colonies. This kind of marking was introduced around 1525 by the Spanish Crown as part of the *asiento* (q.v.) system. The practice of branding (q.v.) slaves was abolished by a royal order of the king of Spain on November 4, 1784.

**CARINGA, CALINGA** (Afr.), an Afro-Cuban dance popular in the nineteenth century, especially among white country peasants. Supposedly of African origin, the *caringa* took the form of a scurrilous song accompanied by drums. It was performed during fiestas by couples and groups in the parks and the streets.

**CARIPEMBA.** See CARIAPEMBA.

**CARLOTA,** in Brazil, the name of a black *quilombo* (q.v.) located in Mato Grosso. In 1795, after twenty-five years of resistance, it was destroyed. (Price, *Maroon Societies*, p. 172.)

**CARMO, ETESBÃO DO** a black slave leader of the black community in Bahia, Brazil, who, around 1835, led an uprising of Moslem Hausa blacks in that city. He was an *Alufá* (q.v.) and attained great influence among his own people. (Ramos, *The Negro*, p. 51.)

**CARPENTIER, ALEJO** (b. 1904), an outstanding Cuban intellectual and one of the leaders of the *afrocubanismo* (q.v.) movement. He welcomes the primitivism of the black as a positive quality and pronounces himself in favor of "Negrism" as a corrective to the overcivilization of the white world with its frustrations and failures. Carpentier seeks to recreate the enchanted magic of the Afro-Cuban religion and to give slaves' descendants a sense of self-confidence and pride. The main struggle, he feels, is not between Europe and Africa, but between oppressors and oppressed. The African theme is a substantial element in most of Carpentier's writings. Some of his best works are *Ecué-Yamba-O* (1933); *El reino de este mundo* (1949); and *El siglo de las luces* (1963).

**CARR, ERNEST A.** (1902-1975), a short-story writer born in Trinidad who ridicules the racial snobbery of many mulattoes whom he describes as "time-serving, boot-licking agents to the whites." In *Gan-Gan*, a short story published in 1953, he criticizes the middle-class mulatto group which tries to pass as white. In an earlier story, *Civil Strife* (1950), Carr writes about a mulatto woman who married an Englishman and developed a pathological repugnance for people of her own color. The irony of the tale is that her husband is greatly attracted to mulattoes, and what most attracts him to her physically is her Negroid appearance. (Coulthard, *Race and Colour*, pp. 101-102.)

**CARRAPATÚ** (Pg.), an Afro-Brazilian mythical creature used to frighten children.

**CARREFOUR** (Fr. Cr.), in Afro-Haitian folklore, a crossroad thought to be guarded by a powerful spirit named Maît' Carrefour (q.v.), the protector of the highways.

**CARTA DE LIBERTAD, CARTA DE HORRO, CARTA DE MANU- MISION,** (Sp.), in Cuba, starting in 1844, an official letter of emancipation given to an *emancipado* (q.v.) slave stating he was a freedman.

**CARURU** (Pg.), a Brazilian food of African origin prepared with okra (q.v.), fish, shrimp, and other ingredients seasoned with oil of dendé palm (q.v.) and pepper. It is considered a delicacy of fetish deities.

**CARURU DE COSME-DAMIÃO** (Pg.), a religious ceremony held by Brazilian-Yorubas in honor of twins whose patrons are Saints Cosmas and Damian. It is celebrated on Thursday and includes a sacred supper.

**CASA DE CANDOMBLÉ** (Pg.), an Afro-Brazilian cult center that has been maintained for generations. It comprises a sacred dancing place, the fetish sanctuary, the holy room in which initiates are interned during the period of their preparation, and the living quarters for the priest and his retinue. (Pierson, *Negroes*, p. 279.) See also TERREIRO.

**CASA DE GUINÉ** (Pg.), a Portuguese trading company which, in 1444, established a warehouse in Lagos, Nigeria, with the primary purpose of exploiting African commerce and fishing. Later, this concern was instrumental in bringing to Portugal trade in slaves, gold, ivory, oils, crafts, and other products. (Diffie, *Latin American*, p. 31.) See also CASA DE GUINÉ E MINA.

**CASA DE GUINÉ E MINA** (Pg.), a warehouse transferred from Lagos, Nigeria, to Lisbon in 1481-1482. Its original name was Casa de Guiné (q.v.). All goods from overseas territories, including slaves, had to be brought here for registration, payment of taxes, and sale.

**CASA DE LA MARIMBA** (Sp.), a house where black women usually dance to the tune of the *marimba* (q.v.). Almost all the black settlements in the Pacific lowlands of Colombia have one such house. In rural, scattered areas, a *casa de la marimba* is available within four to six hours' canoe travel. (Whitten, *Black Frontiersmen*, p. 108.)

**CASA DOS ESCRAVOS** (Pg.) ("the slave market"), in Lisbon, a public market where all slaves from Africa and elsewhere had to be brought by law for recording their age, race, and sex, and for the payment of sales taxes. It became an important trade center around 1481-1482, when the Casa de Guiné e Mina (q.v.) was transferred from West Africa to that city.

**CASA GRANDE** (Pg.) ("the big house"), in Brazil, a manor house where the plantation owner lives; a symbol of the power of the landed aristocracy. It is considered as part, though not the center, of the Portuguese system of colonization and the patriarchal society which still survives in the country. In colonial times, it embraced several generations (children, parents, grandparents, great-grandparents, and often great-great-grandparents) whose lives where inextricably intertwined. In addition, there were hosts of collateral kinsmen (cousins, aunts, uncles, nephews, and nieces) of many and varied degrees of consanguinity. This huge patriarchal kinship group—the major economic unit and the seat of political and judicial power—also involved large numbers of servants and other retainers with no blood relationship to the head of the clan. The exceptions were the illegitimate offspring of the patriarch or those of his children and grandchildren. The patriarchal domestic unit itself was eventually interwoven through an elaborate system of tracing descent to notable ancestors and maintaining a feeling of kinship solidarity. (T.L. Smith, *Brazil*, p. 204.)

**CASA GRANDE E SENZALA** (Pg.), the title of a well-known historical essay by Gilberto Freyre (1933) which caused a sensation in its interpretation of the Brazilian ethos to the world and to the Brazilians themselves. Its thesis has been challenged, but it continues to defy scholars' efforts to refute it. It was published in English in 1933 with the title *The Masters and the Slaves.*

**CASANGA** (Afr.), an African ethnic group located in the Guinea-Bissau region from which slaves were taken, mainly to Peru, between 1524 and 1560.

**CASINO ESPAÑOL** (Sp.), a powerful Cuban association founded in Havana in 1869, supposedly for social purposes but actually to provide a center where wealthy members of the landed oligarchy, the slaveowners, and the rich commercial families could unify their efforts to maintain Spanish domination on the island. The Casino Español corporation had headquarters in Santiago and other important cities. (Foner, *The Spanish-Cuban American War*, V. II, p. 181.)

**CASSÉUS, MAURICE** (b. 1909), a black Haitian poet who, like many of his generation, looks to Africa as a lost paradise. He was very active in the négritude (q.v.) movement. One of his major poems, ''Tambour racial,'' appeared in *Les Griots* (1939).

**CASSUIS DE LINVAL, CLEMENCE** (b. ca. 1900), a Creole writer born to an old traditional family in Saint-Pierre, Guadeloupe. She writes under the pen-name of Jean Max. In her work *Réminiscences* (1921) she evokes the primitive landscape of her native town. Her book *Coeur martiniquai* is a nostalgic description of the Pelée volcano eruption in 1902 and the loss of some of her relatives.

**CASTAS** (Sp.), in colonial Spanish America, a class of persons of mixed-blood ancestry; sometimes employed as a derogatory term referring to persons of mixed black background.

**CASTEE** (Eng. Cr.), in colonial Jamaica, the third-generation offspring of a white man and a black woman. See also MUSTEE.

**CASTILOA** (Pg.), in Brazil, a gum tree *(Castilla ulei)* probably imported from Africa in slavery times.

**CASTLES,** in colonial West Africa, forts built like castles, with thick brick walls and protected on the landward side by two moats cut into solid rock. Some had over 400 cannons mounted to repulse land or sea attacks. In the dungeons, there was room for approximately 1,000 slaves. The first Portuguese castle was at Elmina (q.v.) on the Gold Coast (q.v.) and was constructed in 1481. (Mannix, *Black Cargoes*, p. 74.)

**CASTRO, A. URBANO PEREIRA DE,** a Brazilian writer. In 1853, two years after the appearance of Harriet Beecher Stowe's *Uncle Tom's Cabin*, Castro translated it into Portuguese under the title *Cabana do Pai Thomas, ou a Vida dos Negros na America*. It was advertised on book jackets for years after its publication in Portuguese. (Sayers, *The Negro*, p. 116.)

**CASTRO ALVES, ANTONIO DE** (1847-1871), a Brazilian poet and playwright and chief Brazilian representative of the romantic movement. An ardent abolitionist, Castro Alves wrote a great deal of poetry in which the emancipation of slaves was one of his major themes. He has had a deep and lasting appeal in Brazilian letters. Among his numerous poems are "Vozes d'Africa" and "Navio Negreiro"; his main works include *Espumas Volantes* (1870); *Os Escravos* (1883); and a play, *Gonzaga, ou A Revolução de Minas* (1875).

**CAT (SHACKLE)**, a device used by slave ship captains in the Guinea trade as the principal means of enforcing discipline among black slaves and often among merchantmen and sailors as well. The cat consisted of a handle or stem, made of a rope about three and one-half inches in circumference and eighteen inches in length. At one end were fastened nine branches, or tails, composed of long lines with three or more knots in each. These knots would cut the flesh from the back of the slave or sailor. (Mannix, *Black Cargoes*, pp. 143-44.)

**CATANGA** (Afr.), among Afro-Hispanics of the Pacific lowlands of Gran Colombia, a pot used for boiling shrimp and crayfish.

**CATÃO, OLIMPO** (1850-1908), a Brazilian writer. His melodrama *O Negro* (1879) illustrates the point that an educated black differs only in color from a white of the same intellectual level. His hero moves in society as a sort of "Angel of Justice." The author declares that he cannot expect his play to be well received because he is black and a member of the lower class.

**CATERETÊ** (Pg.), a Brazilian dance of African origin. Its vivid and irregular rhythm includes a high degree of syncopation.

**CATÊTÊ** (Pg.), the last thick lumps of *dendé* oil (q.v.) at the bottom of the pot. The Afro-Bahianos in Brazil believe they have a special flavor.

**CATIMBÓ** (Pg.), in Brazil, the practice of sorcery among blacks, seemingly derived from an African fetish cult. It is officially banned throughout the country.

**CATIMBOZEIRO** (Pg.), in Brazil, a sorcerer or priest in charge of the *catimbó* (q.v.) cult. He alone receives the spirits on behalf of the faithful. There is a well-defined hierarchy of prestige, based on the number of spirits which the *catimbozeiro* deals with. In cult ceremonies, the gods are invoked to come down and take physical possession only of the priest. (Bastide, *African Civilizations*, pp. 83, 85.)

**CATINGA** (Pg.), in Brazil, a bed smell or stench; sometimes applied to the reputed body odor of blacks.

**CAURIS, CARIM, COWRIE** (Afr.), the shell of a marine gastropod *(Cypraea)* used as money on the African coast and imported into colonial Brazil by black slaves. Threaded into a collar, the shells were easy to carry. Each was worth one-130th of a penny sterling.

**CAVALO DE SANTO** (Pg.), in Bahia, Brazil, a black priestess of the Xangó (q.v.) cult used by the god to manifest himself.

**CAXAMBÚ** (Afr.), in colonial Brazil, a slave festival based upon drumming, versifying, and dancing. It occupied an intermediate position between religious ceremony and secular diversion. Saturday nights and saints' days were the occasions for requesting the planter's consent for *caxambú*. After the chores were completed, wood piled on the drying terrace located near the slaves' huts was lit. On one side of the fire were drums, and on the other side sat the crowd surrounding the old black slaves. The drummer tapped out rhythms, and wild, noisy dancing began. Supervising the whole meeting was the king of caxambú, sometimes joined by his queen. Participants walked first to greet the king and kiss his hand. Then the king entered the circle and sang a riddle, while assembled slaves repeated the refrain, clapped hands, and joined the dancing group. Dancers moved in a counterclockwise circle. Even children entered the circle. The feast lasted the whole night. As late as 1890, *caxambú* was prohibited in town streets and in any house within town limits. (Stein, *Vassouras*, p. 297.)

**CAXIXI** (Afr.), an Afro-Brazilian musical folk instrument made of a tiny reed or straw basket containing small pebbles.

**CAYAMBOUGUE** (Fr. Cr.), in Haiti, a decorated container made by blacks from a divided calabash, with the top ingeniously cut to fit into the lower part. It was often carved with geometric designs, usually crude and haphazard, but on occasion meticulously executed.

**CAYAN BUTTER, CAYENNE BUTTER,** salt ground with hot pepper *(Capsicum)*, a favorite sauce among blacks in the Caribbean.

**CAYAN PEPPER,** a very hot pepper *(Capsicum)* formerly eaten mainly by plantation slaves in the West Indies.

**CAYENNE BUTTER.** See CAYAN BUTTER.

**CAYMANS, BALTAZAR,** a Spanish slave trader who, on March 12, 1685, obtained royal authorization to brand slaves with a sign or mark of the *asentista* (q.v.). The mark was composed of a *B* and an *a* intertwined. See also BRANDING.

**CECILIA VALDEZ,** an antislavery novel written by Cirilo Villaverde (q.v.) of Cuba. The first part appeared in Havana in 1839, and the second part in New York in 1879. The heroine, a free mulatto girl, is the illegitimate daughter of a Spaniard and a black woman. Beyond the suffering of the slaves on the plantations, the cruelty and abuses of the masters and their moral corruption, the author deals with the ambivalent social position of half-castes. This glimpse at mulatto psychology constitutes one of the most original features of the novel.

**CEDAR** (Fr. Cr.), a black albino in the West Indies.

**CÉDULA DE GRACIAS AL SACAR** (Sp.), a legal decree declaring a mulatto person white. In colonial Spanish America, this decree was obtained by paying a fee. The policy aimed at improving the status of mixed-blood persons in the Caribbean at the end of the eighteenth century, and was dictated both by fiscal interest and by the desire for political counterbalance. (Liss and Liss, *Man, State and Society*, p. 112.)

**CÉDULA DE LIMPIEZA DE SANGRE** (Sp.) ("document of purity of blood"), in colonial Spanish America, an official church document certifying that a person did not have any black or Indian blood.

**CENTRAL** (Sp.), in Cuba, a sugar mill (q.v.).

**CENTRO CIVICO DE PALMARES** (Pg.) ("Civic Center of Palmares"), a Brazilian association founded in São Paulo in 1927 for educational purposes. It soon became a nucleus for the organization of blacks and an active center in the struggles against color prejudice.

**CENTRO DA LAVOURA** (Pg.) ("Laborers' Center"), a pro-slavery planters' club organized in 1880 in Rio de Janeiro and in other cities to oppose the immediate abolition of slavery.

**CENTRO DE CULTURA AFRO-BRASILEIRA** (Pg.) ("Afro-Brazilian Cultural Center"), an idealistic cultural institution founded in 1937 in Recife, Brazil, by a group of distinguished blacks. Its aims have been racial unity and the promotion of civic and educational awareness. The association has undertaken several research projects designed to better the conditions of those descended from slavery. It has also sponsored research on black folklore.

**CEPO** (Sp.), in colonial Cuba and elsewhere, stocks for punishment of slaves. The most common *cepo* consisted of an enormous fixed board with holes for the head, hands, and feet of the victims, either separately or in combination. Left in the open and unable to protect themselves, the slaves suffered from the weather as well as from the many varieties of insects found in the tropics. (Knight, *Slave Society*, p. 77.)

**CERASEE** (Afr.), in the West Indies, a plant *(Momordica charantia* and *M. balsamina)* valued by blacks in Jamaica as bush tea (q.v.) to clear the blood. In use since slavery times, it is noted for its bitterness. Also called *ganah*.

**CERCA REAL DO MACACO** (Pg.) ("the Royal Camp of Macaco"), name of one of the most famous runaway slave camps established in the interior of northeast Brazil between 1660 and 1695. It was ruled by the black King Ganga Zumbá (q.v.). See also QUILOMBO.

**CÉSAIRE, AIMÉ** (b. 1913), black poet and politician born in Martinique. Césaire attended local schools after which he went to Paris. At the Sorbonne, he became one of the leaders of the négritude (q.v.) movement and an outspoken champion of the black mystique. His chief concerns include the return to one's African roots, the rehabilitation of the ordinary and exploited black peasant and his culture, and the violent rejection of bourgeois capitalism and the Christian religion which he considers responsible for the spiritual and economic subjection of the black race. Everything white is rejected, while négritude is exalted. Césaire believes that the black world will eventually emerge and triumph over the inhumanity and exploitation of its past. Among his works are *Cahier d'un retour au pays natal* (Paris, 1938); *Soleil cou-coupé* (Paris, 1938); *Les armes miraculeuses* (Paris, 1950); *Corps perdu* (Paris, 1950); *Discours sur le colonialisme* (Paris, 1950); *Et les chiens se taisaient* (Paris, 1956); and *Toussaint L'Ouverture: La révolution française et le problème colonial* (Paris, 1960).

**CHA, CHO** (Afr.), an Afro-Caribbean exclamation expressing scorn or annoyance.

**CHAAW** (Eng. Cr.), an Afro-Jamaican word for a between-meal snack.

**CHABIN** (Fr. Cr.), in the French Antilles, a person of racially mixed ancestry showing contrasting racial features, such as a black with blue eyes and tightly curled hair or a near-white individual with black facial features.

**CHACHÁ.** 1. An Afro-Cuban song-dance. 2. An Afro-Caribbean rattle.

**CHACÓN, PETRONA,** a female black slave who, in 1840, in the Conspiracy of the Ladder (q.v.) in Cuba, was elected ''queen'' by the black conspirators. (Hall, *Social Control*, p. 59.)

**CHACONA MULATA** (Sp.), a wild dance of African origin popular in the American colonies and in Spain during the sixteenth century.

**CHAGAS, FRANCISCO,** an outstanding Brazilian mulatto sculptor. He was one of the most perfect creators of religious images, some of which can still be seen in churches in Bahia, Brazil. Little is known of his life, not even the exact dates of his birth or death.

**CHAKA, CHAKA-CHAKA** (Afr.), an Afro-Caribbean term for a disorderly manner; sloppy, untidy, muddy.

**CHALONEC, FRANTZ** (1929-1967), a mulatto poet born in Lorrain, north of Martinique. Chalonec attended the Lycée Schoelcher in Fort-de-France, but unable to pay for his education, he left school to work in commerce. A self-made man and gentle young poet, he published his poems in magazines and periodicals on the island.

**CHALUSKA** (Fr. Cr.), an Afro-Haitian Mardi Gras dance characterized by comic mimicry in which the participants are dressed as nineteenth century generals. Also referred to as Charles Oscar.

**CHAMBA** (Afr.), in the West Indies, a tattooed black slave brought from northeast Nigeria or Cameroon; he had deep, curved incisions on each cheek, from the ear to the mouth. (Cassidy, *Jamaica Talk*, p. 134.)

**CHAMPONG-NANNY,** an Afro-Caribbean term for a semilegendary female black bully and fighter.

**CHANGÓ** (Bant.). 1. A black living on the Ecuadorian Pacific Coast. 2. An Afro-Haitian deity usually known as Ogoun Changó (q.v.).

**CHANGO PRIETO** (Sp.), an Afro-Spanish term for a black in Puerto Rico.

**CHANGÜÍ** (Bant.), an Afro-Spanish dance popular among black slaves in Puerto Rico and elsewhere in the New World.

**CHANLATTE, JUSTE.** See ROSIERS, COMTE DE.

**CHANTERELLE, CHANTRELLE** (Fr. Cr.), a sacred song sung by a special soloist in the Afro-Haitian folk religion.

**CHANTYING.** See SHANTYING.

**CHAPELLE** (Fr. Cr.), in Trinidad, a small room of a house used by the family group to worship a single god; sometimes other gods come, but only to visit. Blacks and friends meet in the *chapelle* to celebrate the sacred days of Afro-Christian deities.

**CHAS-CHAS** (Fr. Cr.), in the Virgin Islands, a near-white person descended from French colonists who lives in very poor, closed communities.

**CHATENAY, LIBERT** (b. 1905), a black poet born in French Cayenne. He began his studies at the Cayenne schools and then went to the University of Toulouse (France) where he obtained his medical degree. He collaborated on *L' Express du Midi, Mercure de France*, and other periodicals, and also wrote poems, novels, and political essays. In 1935, he published *Décret d' insurrection*, a social and political pamphlet. He was taken prisoner in 1940 and later wrote for *Chantelier*, a prison camp journal. (Damas, *Poètes d'expression*, p. 172.)

**CHAUVET, HENRI** (1863-1928), a Haitian poet. Chauvet was born in Port-au-Prince and was educated both in his native city and in Paris. His themes are Haitian traditions and customs. He often wrote in French Creole (q.v.) as in *Macaque au chien*. His works include *La Fleur d'or: Poème patriotique haïtien* (1892); *Toréador par amour, comédie bouffe en un acte* (1892); *Les Quisqueyennes, la fille du kacik, drame en 5 actes, en vers* (1894); and *Fleurs et fleurs* (s.d.).

**CHAUVET, MARIE** (b. 1918), a Haitian poetess. Chauvet was inspired by black themes and describes the psychology of peasants. Her novel *Fond des Nègres* was awarded the Grand-Prix France-Antilles. Among her works are *Fille d'Haïti* (Paris, 1954); *La Danse sur le volcan* (Paris, 1967); and *Amour, colère et folie* (Paris, 1968).

**CHAVANNES, MARC,** (d. 1791), a mulatto born in Saint Domingue who was educated on the island. Chavannes was one of the many free mulattoes who fought in the American War of Independence. Later, back in Saint Domingue, he became closely associated with Vincent Ogé (q.v.), chief of the mulatto party, an antislavery group. Chavannes, in alliance with other black leaders, organized the slave uprising on October 30, 1790, in which a massacre of whites took place. The rebels were defeated; Chavannes fled to Spanish Santo Domingo and was hanged on March 9, 1791.

**CHECHE, CHENCHE** (Afr.), in colonial Cuba, a black slave.

**CHEF D'ESQUADE** (Fr. Cr.), in Haiti, a black farmer at whose behest others come to do cooperative agricultural labor.

**CHEGA AFRICANA** (Pg.) (The Arrival of the Africans), in Bahia, Brazil, the name of a carnival club formed mainly of mulattoes and blacks. In the annual, noisy carnival parade, members portray themes related to African traditions, while an enormous crowd of blacks and mulattoes sings African songs and dances in the streets.

**CHEIO DE MANHA** (Pg.) ("full of little tricks"), in modern Brazil, a black who uses ingenious feats designed to puzzle or amuse in order to appear white.

**CHEMIN DE L'EAU** (Fr. Cr.), in the Afro-Haitian religion, a ritual in which a spirit arrives and departs from the service by way of water—a river, a waterfall, or a spring. The spring being the primary source of fresh water, it is the most direct means for contact between the land and spirit. The spirits are said to be accustomed to traveling by the "water road."

**CHENCHE.** See CHECHE.

**CHEVAUCHÉ** (Fr. Cr.), in Haitian voodoo (q.v.) cults, the possession of the faithful by a spirit or a *loa* (q.v.).

**CHÉVERE** (Afr.), an Afro-Cuban term meaning something well done.

**CHEVRY, ARSENE** (1867-1915), a Haitian poet. Inspired by the romantic movement, Chevry tried to evoke the "happy and enchanted life of the Indians." In classical verses, he praised the nobility of the exploited natives. His works include *Les Areytos: Poésies indiennes* (Port-au-Prince, 1892); *Voix perdues: Poésies, première série* (Port-au-Prince, 1896); *Les Voix du* *centenaire: Poèmes héroïques* (Port-au-Prince); and *Voix de l'exile, fatal expiation* (Saint Thomas, Virgin Islands, 1908).

**CHEWAL** (Fr. Cr.), in Haitian voodoo (q.v.), the devotee while possessed or mounted by a spirit.

**CHIBA** (Pg.). 1. A Brazilian of African origin. 2. A Brazilian dance very popular among blacks.

**CHICO-REI** (b. 1790), in Brazil, a legendary character, supposedly a petty chief in West Africa, who was taken prisoner with his ethnic group and sold into slavery. His name was Francisco, and it is said that with the capture of his entire people, his wife and children accompanied him to the New World. He and his people were sent to Ouro Preto, Minas Gerais, where he was allowed to keep his royal rights and later amassed a small fortune. Little by little, he bought his freedom and that of his children and all his people. He built a palace and a church and organized a black fraternity to free slaves. (Ramos, *The Negro*, pp. 79-83.)

**CHIGUALO** (Sp.), among blacks of the Pacific Colombian lowlands, a wake for a still born child, with dancing, singing, and praying. After the tiny corpse is baptized by a midwife, the mother's ritual co-parents hold the child wrapped in white, and other women form a circle around them. This one-hour ritual is also held for a child who dies shortly after birth. (Whitten, *Black Frontiersmen*, p. 132.)

**CHINEY-RIAL,** in the Caribbean, the offspring of a Chinese man and a black woman.

**CHIRINOS, JOSÉ LEONARDO,** a black slave who led a bloody rebellion to free the slaves in 1795 near Coro, Venezuela. Based on the principle of the Codigo Negro (1792) promulgated by King Charles IV of Spain and the doctrine of human equality established by the French Revolution (1789-1793), Chirinos declared a "French Republic." In May 1795, a dozen whites were killed and several *haciendas* (q.v.) burned to the ground. These events caused a large number of free blacks, mulattoes, zambos (q.v.), and Indians to join the movement. But Chirinos and his followers were defeated. Many were condemned to death and others were incarcerated for indefinite periods at Puerto Cabello. Chirinos was captured, tried, and executed on December 10, 1796. (Rout, L. B. *The African Experience of Spanish America*, pp. 115-116.)

**CHO.** See CHA.

**CHOCALHO** (Pg.), an Afro-Brazilian word for a hollow metal instrument like a dumbbell, with one enlarged extremity containing small pebbles. See also XAQUE-XAQUE.

**CHOMBO** (Afr.), in Panama, a black laborer descended primarily from Jamaican blacks. He has a hispanicized name, has joined the church, and takes advantage of the Constitution, which makes it easy for those born on Panamanian soil to become citizens. As a group, *chombos* have no political voice and remain the target of discrimination by Panamanians.

**CHRÉTIENS VIVANTS** (Fr. Cr.) ("living Christians"), voodoo (q.v.) priests in charge of caring for the faithful while they are possessed or mounted by the spirits. See also HOUNSI.

**CHRISTOPHE, HENRI** (1767-1820), a former Haitian slave who was a leader in the struggle for independence. In 1791, Christophe joined the anti-slavery rebellion and became a great fighter for freedom. He aided Toussaint L'Ouverture (q.v.) in the liberation of Haiti and, in 1802, was appointed army chief. Elected president of Haiti in 1806, he disputed control of the island with Pétion (q.v.) until 1811 when he proclaimed himself Henry I, king of Haiti. He restored the sugar and coffee economy. A strict disciplinarian and ardent admirer of France, especially of Louis XIV, Christophe set up elaborate protocol and noble titles. Although uneducated himself, he surrounded himself with scholars from abroad, built schools, established newspapers, and proclaimed the Code Henri. He recruited 4,000 blacks from Dahomey (q.v.) to form his National Guard and keep order in the countryside. He governed until October 8, 1820, when beset by dissidents and suffering partial paralysis, he committed suicide.

**CHUMBA** (Afr.), a sacred container used to receive the blood of slaughtered animals in rituals of the Afro-Cuban folk religion.

**CHUMBO** (Sp.), an insulting name given to a West Indian born or English-speaking black who has settled in the Republic of Panama.

**CHURCH OF THE UNITED BRETHREN.** See MORAVIAN CHURCH.

**CHURUSCO** (Sp.), in Panama, a person with woolly hair, a thick nose, and dark skin, indicating various degrees of Negroid blood.

**CHUZO** (Sp.), a hard, wooden weapon carried by black slaves in *palenques* (q.v.). It consisted of a long stick of hard wood, sharpened and scorched at the end to render it still harder.

**CIMARRON** (Sp.), in the Caribbean islands and elsewhere, runaway slave settlements in the innermost mountain areas. By the mid-sixteenth century, *cimarrones* were identified exclusively with blacks. The inhabitants eventually became sedentary farmers with fields in the outlying regions and stockaded villages. See also CUMBES; PALENQUE; QUILOMBO.

**CIMARRONISMO** (Sp.), in colonial Afro-Hispanic territories, the persistent and violent rebellion of runaway slaves in search of freedom. This social phenomenon began early in the sixteenth century and continued into the nineteenth century, at which time it was stimulated and aided by the rising wars of independence. By the second half of the eighteenth century, it had become a threat to the new Afro-Hispanic society. *Cimarronismo* exerted great pressure on the Spanish authorities who were often forced to recognize the freedom of those who lived in the runaway slave communities. See also MARRONAGE.

**CINÉAS, JEAN-BAPTISTE** (1895-1958), a black Haitian writer who was part of a nationalistic literary revival. Cinéas, like others of his generation, was attracted to the Haitian peasants' simple life. His chief concern was to explain and interpret the peasants' religion, ideals, and values. His works include *Le Drame de la terre* (Port-au-Prince, 1933); *La Vengeance de la terre: Roman paysan* (Port-au-Prince, 1933); *L'Heritage sacré: Roman paysan* (Port-au-Prince, 1945); and *Le Choc en retour* (Port-au-Prince, 1948).

**CINQUE, JOSEPH** (1814-1876), a black slave, also known as Joseph Singbe, born in Mani, a farming village in the Dzhopoa district of the Mende tribe in West Africa. In the spring of 1839, he was kidnapped, brought to Havana, sold as a slave, baptized, and given a Christian name. On June 27 of that same year, while sailing from Havana to a port near Puerto Príncipe, Cinque led a mutiny of about fifty slaves. After killing the captain and sending the sailors ashore, Cinque took command of the schooner and ordered the two remaining white officers to steer it to Africa. After seven weeks of sailing, the vessel reached Montauk, Long Island, where it was seized. The Spanish government demanded the return of the slaves to Cuba for speedy trial as murderers. Abolitionists entered the case, and John Quincy Adams, the former president, spoke for Cinque and his comrades before the Supreme Court in 1841. The Court ruled that all the Guinea (q.v.) slaves on board the ship *Amistad* had been introduced into Cuba illegally and therefore ordered them back to Africa. On November 25, 1841, all the slaves, including Cinque, returned to their homeland, accompanied by some white missionaries. After reaching Freetown, Liberia,

Cinque went to Mendeland (Sierra Leone—q.v.) to become a slave trader, but he did not prosper. He soon went back to the mission, remaining there as an interpreter until his death. (Mannix, *Black Cargoes*, pp. 217-18.)

**CLAIRIN** (Fr. Cr.), in Haiti, a rum or sugar cane (q.v.) brandy spiced with pepper; used in folk religion rituals.

**CLAPHAM SECT,** a dissenting movement within the Church of England dedicated, among other things, to working for the betterment of the slaves in the West Indies. In 1788, it sought practical ways to serve God by improving the conditions of black slaves; it opposed slave revolts and violence.

**CLAPPS, JOÃO,** a white Brazilian businessman who, in 1883, served as president of the Abolitionist Confederation *(Confederação Abolicionista)* in Rio de Janeiro. The owner of a china shop and other commercial enterprises, he centered his antislavery operations in the cities of Rio de Janeiro and Niteroi. While working to impress political leaders through organizational activities and the dissemination of propaganda, he opened night schools for slaves and freedmen. Clapps also secretly arranged to have fugitive slaves spirited out of Rio.

**CLARK, DUGALD** (d. 1798), a Jamaican mulatto who, as a self-made man, became thoroughly acquainted with mathematics and the principals of mechanics in general. In 1771, he applied the power of a steam engine to the working of his newly constructed sugar mills (q.v.). In 1787, he invented various methods for applying the power and motion of waves to freeing vessels at sea. Clark obtained 100 pounds from the Assembly as full compensation for the models of various discoveries and inventions which he exhibited at different times to the House. Like Prince de Bundo (q.v.), he was an extraordinary person. In 1798, Clark died in a debtor's prison in Kingston, appointing in his will the Honorable Charles James Fox and William Wilberforce (q.v.), among others, as his executors. (Brathwaite, *The Development*, pp. 172-73.)

**CLARKSON, THOMAS** (1760-1846), a leader of the English antislavery movement. Clarkson wrote a history of the abolition of the slave trade as well as numerous other pamphlets, books, and articles on the subject. Besides being an ideologist and a propagandist, he was the organizer for antislavery forces in England, riding on horseback to the various towns, cities, and counties to recruit members for the committees being formed throughout England and Scotland.

**CLASH THE CYMBALS,** a religious hymn sung by Afro-Jamaicans at wakes and other rituals.

**CLASS LEGISLATION,** in Jamaica, legislation designed by planters to oppress small settlers (usually free blacks) and force them to work on estates for wages. Examples of such legislation are the Policy Acts of 1835 and 1838 and the Vagrancy Acts of 1834 and 1839. (Cassidy, *Jamaica Talk*, p. 108.)

**CLAVER, PEDRO.** See EL APÓSTOL DE LOS NEGROS.

**CLAVES** (Sp.), in Cuba, a musical instrument consisting of cylindrical blocks of hard wood. When held in each hand and tapped together, the cupped palm of the hand provides resonance. The *claves*, a West African instrument, has played an important role in the development of the *rumba* (q.v.) and other Afro-Cuban dances.

**CLEAN-FACED MAN,** in Jamaica, an adherent of the Rastafarian (q.v.) cult who does not wear the beard and long hair characteristic of regular members.

**CLÉRIGO DE BANGUÉ** (Pg.), in colonial Brazil, a Catholic chaplain in charge of conducting burial services for black slaves. Such services were introduced circa 1651.

**CLERY, PIERRE** (b. 1930), a black poet born in Rivière-Pilate, Martinique. Clery, the son of a justice of the peace, attended schools in Fort-de-France but left law school to pursue a career in writing. Also an accomplished musician and painter, he published his first verses in 1951. Most of his poems are scattered in magazines and anthologies.

**CLOCHETTE** (Fr. Cr.), the tiny hand bell of priests in Afro-Haitian cults; used along with a gourd rattle webbed with beads as a symbol of authority.

**CLUB DE LA HABANA** (Sp.) (The Havana Club), an association organized in 1837 by wealthy Cuban planters, prominent merchants, professionals, and intellectuals to promote the annexation of the island to the United States. The organization was dominated by slaveholders and had agents in New York, Miami, and other American cities.

**CLUBE CUPIM** (Pg.), an antislavery association organized in Pernambuco, Brazil, in 1884, dedicated to the freeing of slaves by any means. Its members arranged emancipation with the slaveowners' consent, but they also held secret meetings, infiltrated slave quarters to incite escapes, and kept their identities hidden behind *noms de guerre*.

**CLUBE DA LAVOURA** (Pg.) (Labor Club), an antislavery group formed in Ceara, Brazil, in 1883, to champion the gradual abolition of slavery and to oppose intransigent abolitionism. The club's program urged guarantees of private property, faithful execution of the Free Womb Law (see LEI DO VENTRE LIBRE), public workhouses for free slaves, and education of slaves' children under twenty-one years of age. The club membership included eighty-eight landowners, thirteen tenants, a lawyer, and a doctor. (Eisenberg, *The Sugar Industry*, p. 168.)

**CLUBE DOS LIBERTOS DE NITEROY** (Freedmen's Club of Niteroy), an antislavery association formed in 1883 by prominent citizens of Niteroy, Brazil, to promote the end of slavery.

**COAL BOY,** in the West Indies, a black man employed to carry coal, often known for his chanting and walking with a characteristic swing up the gangway onto the steamships.

**COAL GIRL,** in the West Indies, a black woman employed to carry coal into steamships. These hard-working women often sang as they trouped up the gangway to empty their baskets into the hold.

**COARTACIÓN** (Sp.), a legal practice that developed in Cuba and elsewhere in Spanish America whereby a slave could purchase his freedom on an installment plan. It consisted of definitively fixing the value of a slave by agreement between master and slave, so that at no time thereafter could a larger sum be exacted for his or her liberty. It was well recognized by customary law in a royal decree issued in 1766. The laws governing *coartaciòn* were placed in the official slave code in 1843. A well-behaved slave could attain freedom through this process in seven years.

**COARTADO** (Sp.), in colonial Cuba, a freedman who had legally purchased his freedom through the practice of *coartaciòn* (q.v.).

**COCHON ROUGE** (Fr. Cr.), an Afro-Haitian legendary being, half-demon and cannibal, who lives in the forests.

**COCHONS GRIS** (Fr. Cr.). 1. Afro-Haitian mythical creatures, half-demon cannibals, who meet in secret in the hollow heart of the *mapou* (q.v.), a legendary tree. They are dressed in comic ancient military attire, complete with swords, epaulets, medals, and outlandish beards. 2. A well-organized Afro-Haitian secret society of sorcerers; its hierarchy includes an emperor, queen, president, ministers, and minor officials. It is believed to be of African origin. (Bastide, *African Civilizations*, p. 145.)

**COCHONS SANS POILS** (Fr. Cr.) ("hairless pigs"), an Afro-Haitian secret society of sorcerers who meet in the open country at night and are very much feared by the peasants because of their reputation for working all kinds of evil. The society is supposedly of African origin. See also COCHONS GRIS.

**COCKATY** (Afr.), an Afro-Jamaican term for a boastful, selfish person.

**COCO,** a fruit produced by the coconut palm (q.v.) *(Cocos nucifera* and *Colocasia esculenta)*, the most important product of the tropics. Its dried meat yields coconut oil. A staple food for plantation slaves, it was probably domesticated in the New World and eaten by Indians.

**COCOA,** in West Indies, an early spelling of *coco* (q.v.).

**COCOA-WALK,** on West Indian plantations, coconut palms (q.v.), usually placed in rows with other trees between to shade them.

**COCOBAY,** in Jamaica, a kind of leprosy or elephantiasis once prevalent among blacks. The name was later transferred to yaws (q.v.) and similar diseases.

**COCOFIO** (Sp.), in Venezuela, a black leader and fetish priest who, around 1740, led a runaway slave settlement in the region of Coro, on the north coast of Venezuela.

**COCOLO** (Sp.), in Puerto Rico, black slaves brought to the island from the Minor Antilles.

**COCOMACAGUE,** a kind of dwarf palm. Sticks made from this tree are used in Afro-Haitian religious dancing.

**COCO-MACCA, COCO MACO,** a heavy bludgeon used by blacks in Jamaica; originally made from the cocomacague tree (q.v.).

**COCO-NEGUE** (Fr. Cr.), in the Afro-French Antilles, an earthen vessel made and used by blacks.

**COCONUT.** See COCO.

**COCONUT PALM,** in the West Indies, a new variety of coconut tree, especially *Colocasia esculenta*, apparently developed by blacks around 1740. This Afro-Jamaican rootstock with edible tuber was later introduced from the Caribbean region into Africa. In Jamaica, it is also known as *negro coco* (q.v.).

**COCORICO** (Sp.), an Afro-Spanish term for an extremely ugly or extravagantly dressed person.

**COCOTTE** (Fr. Cr.), in Haitian Creole, a loose woman, a tart.

**CODE NOIR** (Fr.) ("Negro Code"), a general slave law promulgated by Louis XIV in 1685 for Saint Domingue and the French colonies. It clarified the legal status of slaves, whose ownership and sale were to be regulated by royal ordinances and customs. It limited the planters' punishment of blacks and also prescribed minimum conditions for feeding and housing them. It affirmed the slaves' rights to formal trial, promulgated important civil rights regarding marriage, and prohibited the separation of families. It stated that a slave acquiring freedom, either by gift or purchase, was to become a full French citizen, with all rights, including the right to own slaves of his own.

**CODE RURAL** (Fr.) ("Rural Code"), a civil code proclaimed by President Jean-Pierre Boyer (q.v.) of Haiti in 1826 for the purpose of attaching peasants to their land and requiring a certain fixed rate of production. This code failed because its provisions were not enforced; the peasants, who had had a taste of liberty after their emancipation, simply ignored it.

**CÓDIGO NEGRO CAROLINO** (Sp.) ("Caroline Negro Code"), a special code promulgated by the Spanish Crown in 1785 in an attempt to ameliorate the conditions of black slaves and to promote plantation agriculture in Cuba and elsewhere in the colonies. Written in the style of the Code Noir (q.v.), it delineated slaves' rights, called for a large number of slaves to be imported from Africa, and decreed the compulsory enlisting of slaves and free blacks into agricultural labor. It severely restricted emancipation. (Hall, *Social Control*, p. 102.)

**CÓDIGO NEGRO ESPAÑOL** (Sp.) ("Spanish Negro Code"), a code proclaimed by the Spanish government in 1789 for the purpose of clarifying the Còdigo negro carolino (q.v.) and improving the living and working conditions of the slave population in the colonies. Apart from the usual religious requirements of baptism, daily prayers, Christian instruction, and Mass, the code freed the slaves from working on holidays, except during the harvest when it was customary to grant permission for them to do so. The masters had to feed their slaves and dress them in a way which conformed to that of free workers. This code was implemented in 1842 under pressure from the British.

**CODRINGTON, CHRISTOPHER** (1668-1710), a soldier, planter, and scholar born in Barbados and educated at Oxford. In 1699, King William appointed him captain-general of the Leeward Islands. His two Barbados estates, now known as the "Society" and the "College," together with part of the island of Barbuda, were left to the Society for the Propagation of the Gospel in Foreign Parts (q.v.) for the foundation of a college. At his death, Codrington was a rich planter serving as governor of the Leeward Islands.

**CODRINGTON COLLEGE,** a college established in Barbados with funds left by Christopher Codrington (q.v.). It was built between 1714 and 1742 for the purpose, according to its founder, of bringing together a convenient number of professors and scholars, all under vows of poverty, chastity, and obedience, to study and practice physics, surgery, and divinity, and to educate the youngsters of the colony. The college was to be maintained with the income from several plantations and at least 300 black slaves. (Ragatz, *The Fall*, p. 12.)

**CODRINGTON ESTATES,** two Barbados estates with over 300 slaves left to the Society for the Propagation of the Gospel (q.v.) by Christopher Codrington (q.v.) in 1710 for the establishment of an educational institution. This was the origin of Codrington College (q.v.). When the question of the slave trade was before Parliament in 1789, slavery at Codrington Estates became a problem for the society. In 1820, substantial reforms for the welfare of the slaves were introduced. Finally, in 1831, the society pledged itself to employ every means for the accomplishment of emancipation. (McCloy, *The Negro*, p. 258.)

**COFFLE, COFILA** (Pg.), in West Africa, a common name for a caravan of bound slaves driven for weeks, or even months, to the rivers or seashore where they were sold to Europeans. In making up the *coffle* for the long trip, the slave traders discarded the sick, maimed, and feeble blacks. A *coffle* consisted of hundreds of slaves.

**COFI, KOFI** (Afr.), in Guiana, an African day-name (q.v.) for a boy born on Saturday; still used in Ghana today. (Bastide, *African Civilizations*, p. 56.)

**COFRADÍA DE NEGROS** (Sp.) ("Negro Brotherhood"), in colonial Spanish America, a religious brotherhood of free blacks in the church in areas of great concentration of slaves. Around 1540, there were several *cofradías* in Lima and other cities. By 1750, Negro *cofradías* played a vital role in the social life of both slaves and freedmen, having their own festivities with parades and carnivals. Usually organized by regional African origin, its members coming from the same "nation" (q.v.) or geographical locality, these associations were of both a religious and strongly benevolent nature. (Mellafe, *La esclavitud*, p. 84.)

**COICOU, MASSILLON** (1867-1908), a black Haitian writer and poet. He was an early nationalist, who tried to justify the excesses of rebellious slaves as punishment for the cruelty and abuses of the French colonists. Long after the abolition of slavery, planter exploitation still remained a poetic theme that fit very well with the denunciation of colonialism and European imperialism. Among his works are *Poésie nationale* (Paris, 1892); *Liberté*, a play produced in 1894 at Port-au-Prince; *Les Fils de Toussaint* (Port-au-Prince, 1906); *Fefé Candidat* (Port-au-Prince, 1906); *Fefé Ministre* (Port-au-Prince, 1906); and *L'Empereur Dessalines* (Port-au-Prince, 1906).

**COKE, THOMAS** (1747-1814), an English Methodist bishop called the Father of Wesleyan missions among slaves in the West Indies. On September 2, 1784, John Wesley (q.v.) ordained him and sent him to preach the faith to African slaves in the Caribbean. He always took a firm stand against slaveholding and consequently met with little opposition in his mission. Coke was also a scholar and writer. Among his numerous books is *A History of the West Indies* (Liverpool, 1808).

**COLA NUT.** See KOLA NUT.

**COLETA** (Sp.), a cheap cotton fabric, the most common material used in the Spanish Antilles to clothe black slaves.

**COLLAR DE HIERRO** (Sp.) ("iron necklace"), an instrument of slave torture consisting of a heavy iron chain placed around the victim's neck.

**COLLIER-CHOU** (Fr.), a necklace or string of gold beads, part of a traditional Afro-Antilles costume. In colonial times, *collier-chou* was a child's birthday gift. The wearing of several collars of different sizes, each with two or three beads, was a status symbol among blacks. The nannies used to receive two or three *collier-chou* on occasions of family celebrations, especially on the birthdays of the infants under their care.

**COLLYMORE, FRANK** (b. 1893), a black poet born and educated in Barbados. After graduation in 1910, Collymore became a school teacher on the island. Later, a scholarship allowed him to study in England. His works include *Thirty Poems* (Bridgetown, Barbados, 1944); *Beneath the Casuarinas* (Bridgetown, Barbados, 1945); *Flotsam* (Bridgetown, Barbados, 1948); *A Dozen Short Poems* (Georgetown, Guiana, 1952); and *Collected Poems* (Bridgetown, Barbados, 1959).

**COLONIAL CHURCH UNION**, a Jamaican religious extremist group organized by white planters in 1832. Its main purpose was to persecute Protestant missionaries active in the abolition movement (q.v.) whom the planters considered responsible for the slave insurrection of 1831-1832. The group was suppressed by April 1833.

**COLONO-EMPREITEIRO** (Pg.), in Brazil in the post-abolition period, a resident laborer, hired to replace a black slave working in a specific job. See also EMPREITEIRO.

**COLONOS AFRICANOS** (Sp.) ("African colonists"), another name for African slaves illegally brought from West Africa to Peru between 1841 and 1850 when their direct importation was outlawed.

**COLONS AMÉRICAINS** (Fr.), in Saint Domingue, a political pressure group made up of mulatto planters, led by Julien Raimond (q.v.) and Vincent Ogé (q.v.), who fought in the Paris National Assembly for the rights of French colonists. As a result of their efforts, in 1791 the Assembly granted full citizenship to all mulattoes, including the American colonists who had settled on the island. (Ott, *The Haitian Revolution*, pp. 29, 30.)

**COLORED PERSON,** in Jamaica and the West Indies, one who is of mixed African and European descent. He represents a unique phenomenon in the mixed-race world. Such individuals are generally almost entirely ignorant of African culture and despise what little they know as being primitive and undesirable. According to their color, they are prey to much anxiety as to whether they will be able to achieve acceptance by the white minority. Even if this ideal is unattainable, there is still the conscious drive to appear white in their ways and ideas. The intensity of this anxiety varies from individual to individual, but is apparent in all. (Henriques, *Family and Colour*, pp. 51-53.) See also QUASHEE.

**COLOR ES ACCIDENTE PERO EL PELO NO MIENTE** (Sp.) ("Color is an accident, but the hair tells no lies"), a Panamanian expression used by persons of a mixed-blood family to defend the ones who happen to be darker. Many prominent Panamanians keep their hair trimmed very short to disguise its woolliness.

**COLOR LE OFENDE, EL** (Sp.) ("His color holds him back"), an expression used in Panama to refer to a person whose black ancestry may be a stumbling block to higher status.

**COLOROCRACIA** (Pg.) ("colorocracy"), in Brazil, a social-political movement which began around 1835, characterized by the rising of the black elite to high government positions. Throughout the country, Brazilians carried forward the work of interracial harmony, of adjustment without regard to color, and of always valuing moral and intellectual achievements above variants of race and color. (Rodrigues, *Brazil and Africa*, pp. 70-71.)

**COMANDEUR** (Fr. Cr.) ("commandant"), in the colonial French Antilles, an overseer, usually a black or mulatto slave, in charge of a plantation slave gang (q.v.). He often was more cruel and demanding than his master.

**COMBOLO, COMBOLOW, CUMBOHLOH, CUMBOLO** (Afr.). 1. A traditional African song-dance performed at wakes; widely spread throughout the Caribbean region. 2. Among blacks, a sexual partner.

**COME-BETWEEN** (Eng. Cr.), in Jamaica, a derogatory term for a black albino.

**COMPAGNIE DE GUINÉ** (Fr.), a slave-trading company organized in France around 1685 to promote commerce between France and West Africa and to transport slaves to the Antilles.

**COMPAGNIE DES CHASSEURS DE GENS DE COULEUR** (Fr.), a regiment consisting of volunteer free blacks and mulattoes organized by the government in Saint Domingue on April 29, 1762, to be in charge of the defense of the colony. In 1768, it was employed in the systematic pursuit of fugitive slaves and deserters and in the policing of neighborhoods on the island. (Hall, *Social Control*, p. 116.)

**COMPAGNIE DES CHASSEURS ROYAUX** (Fr.), a corps of free black citizens organized by the central French government in 1779 to protect Saint Domingue on the eve of the great slave rebellion. All blacks, mulattoes, and free colored men between fifteen and sixty years of age were ordered to serve one year in the company.

**COMPAGNIE DE SÉNÉGAL** (Fr.), a commercial trading company organized in France in 1674 to trade between French and West African ports. It played an important role in the slave traffic between African and the Caribbean plantations. It was discontinued, in 1685.

**COMPAGNIE DES INDES** (Fr.), a trading corporation established in France in 1720 to promote commerce between the metropolis and the African coasts and to supply slaves to the French colonies. It operated until 1769.

**COMPAGNIE DES INDES OCCIDENTALES** (Fr.), a slave-trading company organized in France in 1664 by Jean Baptiste Colbert to supply black slaves for the plantations in the French Antilles. It collapsed in 1645.

**COMPAGNIE DES ISLES D'AMERIQUE** (Fr.), the first French slave-trading company, organized in 1631 to supply black slaves for the French Caribbean plantations. One of its promoters was Cardinal Richelieu.

**COMPAGNIE ROYALE D'AFRIQUE** (Fr.), a slave-trading company established in France in 1720 to transport black slaves to the French islands in the Caribbean.

**COMPANHÍA DA COSTA DE AFRICA** (Pg.), a slave-trading company established by Brazilian colonists in 1723 to export black slaves from the Guinea Coast (q.v.) to Brazil. The same year the viceroy of the colony was authorized to rebuild the fortress of Ajudá (q.v.). The company enjoyed a trade monopoly for fifteen years. (Mendonça, *A Influencia*, p. 23.)

**COMPANHÍA DE CABO VERDE E CACHEU DE NEGOCIOS DOS PRETOS** (Pg.), a Brazilian trading company established in 1690 to transport black slaves from Cacheu (q.v.) and the Cape Verde Islands (q.v.) to the plantations of northeast Brazil.

**COMPANHÍA DE CACHEU** (Pg.), a Portuguese slave-trading company engaged in trade between West Africa and the New World. In 1693, this company provided an annual delivery of 4,000 slaves to the Spanish colonies, distributed by sex, age, and physical condition in such a way as to make up 2,000 *piezas de Indias* (q.v.). (Pescatello, *The African*, p. 37.)

**COMPANHÍA DE LAGOS** (Pg.), a slave-trading company organized in 1442 at Lagos, southern Portugal, to introduce African slaves. Three years later, in 1445, it brought 927 slaves to Lisbon, the main slave market in Europe at that time. (Alvarez Nazario, *El elemento negroide*, p. 23.)

**COMPANHÍA DO ESTANCO DO MARANHÃO** (Pg.), a Brazilian slave-trading company founded in 1679 to transport and sell black slaves to the plantations of northeast Brazil.

**COMPANHÍA DO GRÃO PARÁ** (Pg.), a Brazilian trading company chartered in 1678 by Portuguese merchants who were backed with privileges, subsidies, and loans from the government to exploit the Amazon Valley and to import and sell black slaves to the plantations of the northeast.

**COMPANHÍA DO GRÃO PARÁ E MARANHÃO** (Pg.), a Brazilian commercial concern established by the marquis de Pombal in 1755 in order to supply slaves needed in the extensive gold mines, on the tobacco and sugar plantations, and in the sugar mills (q.v.) of the colony. It traded chiefly with the Costa da Mina (q.v.).

**COMPANHÍA REAL DE GUINÉ** (Pg.), a Portuguese slave-trading company organized in 1693 to export slaves, mainly to the Spanish colonies. It disappeared in 1706.

**COMPAÑÍA DE NEGROS ESCLAVOS** (Sp.), a military unit of 100 black slaves established by the Spanish government in Havana, Cuba, in 1765. These men were used for multiple purposes within the artillery corps, chiefly in the ammunition and storage sections.

**COMPAÑÍA DE NEGROS Y MULATOS LIBRES** (Sp.), a military unit organized for defense purposes by the Spanish Crown at the beginning of the seventeenth century throughout the New World colonies. It gave free blacks and free mulattoes a decent status in order to promote loyalty to the king and thus secure the empire against European piracy. The corps was dissolved in 1844.

**COMPAÑÍA DE PARDOS LIBRES** (Sp.), a military company of 100 free mulattoes, founded in Havana in 1600. Years later (circa 1717), this force was extended into four full companies with a total of 400 men. By this time *pardo* (q.v.) companies were established in Santiago, Cuba, and in other provincial centers. With bright uniforms, these units performed at parades and other social functions. (Klein, *Slavery*, p. 214.)

**COMPANIONATE FAMILY,** in modern rural Jamaica, a black "family" in which members live together for pleasure and convenience, usually for less than three years. (Simey, *Welfare and Planning*, p. 43.)

**COMPANY OF ROYAL ADVENTURERS OF ENGLAND TRADING TO AFRICA,** an English company chartered in 1663 under the duke of York, brother of Charles II, to supply a minimum of 3,000 slaves yearly to the West Indies. As a tribute to the duke, its slaves were branded with the letters *D Y* (see also BRANDING). It started by establishing a chain of new forts and camps along the Guinea Coast (q.v.), but, in 1667, the Dutch captured all these trading forts, and the company lost nearly all its investments. (Davidson, *Black Mother*, pp. 28-29.)

**COMPÉ ANANCY,** a spider-trickster character in black Anancy stories (q.v.)

**COMPELLING POWDER,** among Jamaican blacks, a magic powder supposed to be able to compel someone to love another.

**CONDOREISMO** (Pg.), a Brazilian poetic form created by the black poet Antonio de Castro Alves (q.v.). Its name was inspired by the flight of the majestic condor *(Vultur gryphus)* found in the highest Andes.

**CONFRÈRE** (Fr. Cr.), a term of polite greeting used by black Haitian peasants.

**CONGA** (Afr.), a modern Afro-Hispanic dance that probably originated in slavery times. See also CONGADA.

**CONGADA** (Afr.), an Afro-Hispanic dance that originated with the election of "Congo kings" on the plantations. These dignitaries, like the governors of Protestant America, were elected with a view to disciplining the behavior of slaves and to acting as intermediaries between masters and slaves. In some *congadas*, there were processions with a king, queen, standard-bearer, and ladies-in-waiting as in an African court; in others, ambassadors and officials paraded before the Congo king, who sat in state on the public square to receive the delegations. The *congada*, with some variation, was popular throughout Catholic Afro-Latin America in the colonial period.

**CONGO.** 1. In plantation America, a general term for the African country of origin of many slaves. 2. A Congo-born slave. 3. Among blacks today, used to suggest blackness, stupidity, backwardness, and other mostly unfavorable qualities.

**CONGO-ANGOLA** (Afr.), an Afro-Brazilian cult in which a Bantu (q.v.) dialect is spoken. The sect is well organized, performing its services according to dignified, fixed, traditional rites.

**CONGO-BREADFRUIT,** in the Caribbean, a term applied to a variety of breadfruit (q.v.) with rough skin and considered not as delectable as others.

**CONGO-GUINÉE CULT,** in Haiti, a black cult made up of Congo (q.v.), Bambana, Guinea (q.v.), and other African pagan elements. Its deities and rites are often regarded as heathen.

**CONGO JACK,** a runaway slave who, after capture, was flogged until dead on a Saint Kitt sugar estate (q.v.) in 1807. His master, William Rawlins, an Anglican clergyman, was charged and convicted of murder. He was sentenced to three months in jail plus 200 pounds fine. (Ragatz, *The Fall*, p. 402.)

**CONGO JÉRUOUGE,** a malevolent Afro-Haitian spirit.

**CONGO-JOE.** 1. In Jamaica, a basket made of woven palm thatch (q.v.) (sometimes of canvas, hemp, and the like), usually with a cover. It hung at one's side from a strap over the shoulders and was used by blacks to carry market produce. It was often associated with magic. 2. A field-bag used by black peasants to transport grated cassava and provisions while working in the fields.

**CONGO LOA.** 1. An Afro-Haitian god who acts like an idiot. As a subordinate *loa*, he has no powers, and is usually quiet and shy during rituals. 2. A family of independent *loas* whose number and characteristics are ill defined. 3. A black social dance.

**CONGO MAHOE,** in Jamaica, a tropical plant, originally grown on the coast of the island. Its name was probably given by slaves because of its resemblance to a plant named mahoe in Africa.

**CONGO MANZONE** (Fr. Cr.), an Afro-Haitian dance in which men and women pair off and dance face to face, making contact occasionally but only briefly. Their arms are stretched forward as though to embrace each other around the waist; loin movement is free, and there is restrained sexual intensity, although explicit lewdness is not necessarily present.

**CONGO MAPIONGLE, CONGO MAPIONNE** (Fr. Cr.), a malevolent Afro-Haitian spirit.

**CONGO MARDI GRAS.** See CONGO PAILLETTE.

**CONGO "NATION",** in colonial Montevideo, Uruguay, a well-organized black brotherhood with elected officials, patron saints, and a meeting place where its members met regularly to celebrate festivals, enjoy social gatherings and collect funds to purchase members' freedom. Around 1780, the

Congo nation was divided into six provinces: Gunga, Guanda, Angola, Munjolo, Basundi, and Boma. On Saint Balthazar's Day, in addition to the usual Catholic processions, funeral wakes were organized in honor of the deceased, presided over by a "permanent judge of the dead." (Bastide, *African Civilizations*, p. 97.)

**CONGONHA-DA-AFRICA** (Pg.), in Brazil, a kind of shrub *(Psoralea pisinata L.).*

**CONGO PAILLETTE,** an Afro-Haitian carnival parade and dance.

**CONGO PEA.** See PIGEON PEA.

**CONGO PEGGY** (Eng. Cr.), in the Caribbean, a kind of large ant *(Formicidae).*

**CONGO PLAIT** (Eng. Cr.), an Afro-Jamaican style of hair-plaiting using only two portions of hair rather than the usual three. One plait is rolled over the other continuing around the head and gradually bringing in fresh tufts.

**CONGO PLAYS,** popular Brazilian comedies or "autos" dating from the seventeenth century. They consisted of dramatizations of the coronation of black kings in Africa, in which slaves crowned a king and queen as heads of their brotherhoods. They were a pretext for banquets, parades, singing, and dancing on the plantations. (Ramos, *The Negro*, p. 100.)

**CONGO SAVANE** (Fr. Cr.), a fierce Afro-Haitian deity; represented as a monster who grinds people in a wooden mortar, as a similar Dahomean god did in Africa. Also called Congo Zandor.

**CONGO TOMBE,** an African dance performed by slaves in colonial Surinam.

**CONGO TONY,** in the Caribbean, a word applied by black fishermen to various fish, alluding to their blackness. Also KANGGATUONI.

**CONGO-WORM** (Eng. Cr.), an Afro-Jamaican term for a kind of worm *(Lytta)* that supposedly eats the body after burial.

**CONGO YAMINGAN,** a benevolent Afro-Haitian god usually associated with curing and protecting the sick.

**CONGO ZANDOR.** See CONGO SAVANE.

**CONHECENÇAS** (Pg.), nature's signs—including the color and run of the sea, the type of fish and sea birds, and the varieties of seaweed; encountered and registered by Portuguese pilots in their early deep-sea expeditions around the coast of Africa and elsewhere. (Boxer, *Four Centuries*, p. 11.)

**CONNAISSANCE** (Fr. Cr.), an Afro-Haitian term for the knowledge and power of folk cult priests in curing and in controlling the deities.

**CONNU FESTIVAL,** in colonial Jamaica, a black Christmas parade in masquerade through the streets, led by tall, robust blacks dressed in grotesque costumes with a pair of oxhorns on their heads. It was a kind of slave Mardi Gras. This celebration was later called John Canoe (q.v.).

**CONSOLIDATED SLAVE ACT,** a provision laid down by the Jamaican Assembly in 1781 giving norms to ensure the humane treatment of slaves and to soften their economic exploitation. This code set an eleven-hour day as the maximum working day for the slave and further stipulated that every other week the slave should be given a free day to work on his provision ground. This was the first slave code ever provided in the colony. It was revised in 1787 and 1788, and reenacted in 1792.

**CONSORCIO** (Pg.) ("arrangement"), in Brazil, a conjugal union either legal or outside marriage; common among blacks. A white-black *consorcio* involving a member of the upper class is ordinarily extralegal.

**CONSPIRACY OF THE LADDER (CONSPIRACIÓN DE LA ESCALERA"),** a Cuban slave rebellion scheduled to start in March 1844 and to take power immediately. It was well organized and spread through the plantations and towns all over the island. In the Yumuri district, nineteen estates and over 6,000 black slaves were involved in the uprising. The repression of the plot was extremely cruel. Of the 4,000 blacks and mulattoes tried by military courts, 98 were executed, about 600 imprisoned, and over 400 deported. Many slaves committed suicide. (Hall, *Social Control*, pp. 57-58.)

**CONSTITUCIÓN SINODAL** (Sp.), a church Synodical Constitution promulgated in June 1680 by the Havana diocese in Cuba. It repeated the proviso of the Imperial Spanish Code ordering that all slaves be instructed in the Roman Catholic faith and be baptized within a year of admittance to the New World. It provided that slaves born in Africa and remaining pagan could not be married by a priest until both parties were baptized; if they were married outside the church and the parties wanted to live together in that bishopric, after being baptized their marriage would have to be ratified *in facie ecclesiae* (in the sight of the church). (Klein, *Slavery*, p. 94.)

**CONTOON** (Afr.), a kind of heavy work cloth worn by slaves. Today, it refers to a woolen cloak worn by black laborers in the Antilles.

**CONUCO** (Sp.), in colonial Cuba, the small slave-worked plot of land on a plantation which provided a source of food and private gain for the slave and his family. In the nineteenth century, the planter took over the *conuco* to grow more sugar cane (q.v.); he then relied on imported flour, salt pork, and codfish to feed his slaves.

**CONUGUERO** (Sp.), in colonial Cuba, a slave who, for his own benefit, cultivated tiny patches of land provided by the owner of a sugar estate (q.v.). See also CONUCO.

**COOBA** (Afr.), in Jamaica in slavery times, a casual black maid. Today, a *cooba* is a homosexual man whom women often address as Miss Cooba.

**COOBLA** (Afr.), among Jamaican blacks, a small or young calabash (usually with a handle) or a portion of shell used as a drinking vessel.

**COOK-UP**, in Jamaica, a black dish made of meat, rice, and vegetables cooked together.

**COPPER-COLOUR**, in Jamaica, a mulatto or a black albino.

**CORDÃO** (Pg.), a carnival masquerade of blacks and mulattoes who, during Mardi Gras, march through Brazilian cities and towns gaily dancing, singing songs of African derivation, and beating their palms.

**CORDE COUPE CORDE** (Fr. Cr.) (''cord cuts cord''), an Afro-Haitian saying.

**CORDERO, RAFAEL** (b. 1790), a Puerto Rican son of free blacks who was a self-made man. An indefatigable reader, he taught himself and acquired sufficient knowledge to teach children. In 1810, he opened a school in San German to instruct black and mulatto children. He was acclaimed as Maestro Rafael (Raphael, the Teacher).

**COROMANTEE** (Afr.). 1. The first fort and trading post built by the English (circa 1631) on the Gold Coast (q.v.). It was an important center from which many slaves were exported to the New World. In 1665, it was captured and held by the Dutch. 2. A generic term applied in the West

Indies to black slaves brought over from this post; they belonged to the Ashanti-Fanti (q.v.) culture and were considered strong, good workers but prone to rebellion and therefore dangerous. Their dreaded reputation, originating in Africa, spread across the Atlantic so that French and Spanish colonists refused to take them as slaves.

**COROMANTEE FLUTE,** a musical instrument of African origin in use among blacks in Jamaica. It is made from the porous branches of the trumpet tree and is about a yard in length and nearly as thick as the upper part of a bassoon. It usually has three holes at the bottom.

**COROMANTEE TALK,** in Jamaica, the "secret language" of the Maroons (q.v.).

**CORONILLA** (Sp.), "R" shaped brand used to mark slaves arriving at ports of entry.

**COROSSOL,** in the Caribbean region, a small bush resembling the European pear whose fruit, trimmed with soft thorns, has juicy, fragrant, and refreshing pulp. The blacks assign magic powers to it and use it as a medicinal plant.

**CORPS DE CHASSEURS VOLONTAIRES DE GENS DE COULEUR DE SAINT DOMINQUE** (Fr.), a military police organized by the French government in 1779 in each district of the colony. All blacks, mulattoes, and free colored men fifteen and sixteen years of age were ordered to serve one year in this regiment.

**CORTÉS, JUAN,** a black slave, perhaps an African native, who as a servant of Hernán Cortés came with the expedition that conquered Mexico in 1519.

**CORUMÍN** (Afr.), in Brazil, a young black slave boy acting as servant and companion of a white youngster and usually a victim of his caprices.

**CORVÉE** (Fr.). 1. In rural Haiti, cooperative day-work done by a group of blacks; sometimes organized in a society whose members hire themselves out to any landlord in need of a large force in exchange for a good meal. 2. In colonial Africa, a forced labor gang organized by the government for public works.

**CORVÉE ACHETÉE** (Fr.), cooperative day-work done by black peasants in rural Haiti for money payments.

**COSTA** (Pg.). 1. In colonial Brazil, a generic term applied loosely to the west coast of Africa and to Africa in general. 2. The name of a black slave religious association in northeast Brazil; it had a patron saint and elected officers responsible for the celebration of special festivities. (Ramos, *The Negro*, p. 101.)

**COSTA, CEZARIO ALVES DA,** a black Brazilian hero of the Tri-Alliance War (1865-1870) against Paraguay. As a corporal, he fought so valiantly that he was promoted to the rank of sergeant and was later awarded the Cruzeiro decoration by the count d'Eu, chief of the army.

**COSTA, CLAUDIO MANÔEL** (1729-1789), a Brazilian poet. Costa's long narrative poem, *Vila Rica* (1773), praises the black slaves working in the mines and on the plantations.

**COSTA, JOÃO SEVERIANO MACIEL DA** (1769-1832), a Brazilian historian and politican who took an early antislavery position at the time of independence from Portugal. He was president of the Constituent Assembly (1825) and was rewarded with the title of marquis de Queluz. In 1821, he published a book, *Memoria sobre a Necessidade de Abolir a Introdução dos Escravos Africanos no Brazil.* He was not opposed to slavery on humanitarian grounds. In fact, he agreed with those who believed it was beneficial to Africans to be taken away from their native continent. He further contended that blacks were as talented as Europeans and were not inferior as workers. His rejection of slavery was based on economic grounds because he felt slave labor was inferior to that of freedmen. (Sayers, *The Negro*, pp. 67, 69.)

**COSTA DA MINA** (Pg.) ("Mina Coast"), a vague geographical term whose use began around 1700. For the Portuguese, it included what the English termed the Ivory, Gold, and Slave Coasts (q.v.), extending roughly from Cape Palmas to the Cameroons. Around 1740, Costa da Mina exports included the greater part of Pernambuco tobacco, sugar, sugar cane brandy, gold, jaguar's skin, hammocks, and European goods. Twenty years later in 1760, traders from Bahia, Brazil, carried on a considerable slave trade with this region. At that time, twelve to fifteen ships sailed annually with 60,000 bundles of tobacco, returning with 6,000 to 7,000 slaves, including boys and girls. (Rodrigues, *Brazil and Africa*, pp. 25, 26.)

**COSTA DA MALAGUETA** (Pg.) ("the Malagueta Coast"), in colonial times, the West African coast between the Senegal River in the north and Sierra Leone (q.v.) in the south. Also known as Guinea Portuguesa.

**COTTA,** in Jamaica, a carrying pad for the head usually worn by black women to transport produce to the market. It was originally made of dried plantain (q.v.) leaf; now it is often made of cloth. Among blacks, on the voluntary separation of a man and woman, it is cut in two and each party takes half.

**COTTON TREE,** in the West Indies, a large tree *(Ceiba pentandra)* used mainly for dugout canoe. It is revered by blacks as a favorite hiding place for ghosts and duppies (q.v.). This parasitic tree is characterized by curious branch-like roots above the ground. Lurking in the great chambers formed by these tree roots, it is said, are spirits and phantoms; they come out from seven in the evening to five in the morning. It has been related to the sacred Akata tree of the Ashanti religion.

**COTTON-TREE WORM** (Eng. Cr.), in the colonial West Indies, the macaca worm, formerly eaten by slaves as a delicacy.

**COTTONWOOD TREE.** See COTTON TREE.

**COUAMI** (Afr,), among Guiana blacks, an African day-name (q.v.) for a boy born on Sunday; still used in Ghana today.

**COUIS** (Fr. Cr.), in the Afro-Haitian folk religion, a colorful ritual calabash bowl, decorated with abstract designs, magic symbols, and sometimes human and animal figures which are carefully painted on the inner or concave surface of the bowl.

**COUMBITÉ** (Fr. Cr.), among Haitian blacks, a cooperative work group organized for mutual self-help. Besides strenuous physical labor, it involves the stimulus of working with one's fellows, the pleasure of gossiping with friends, and the partaking of the feast which marks the climax of the day. *Coumbité*, held in the fields, a formalized institution for the exchange of labor, originated in slavery times. The work is done to the accompaniment of music played on drums, bamboo trumpets, or conch horns.

**COUNDJAILLE** (Fr. Cr.), a noisy Afro-Haitian religious dance.

**COUNTRY HIGGLER,** in Jamaica, a black woman trader who buys produce from growers near her rural home and sells it in the town market. She specializes in trading root vegetables and other available items. She is careful in establishing and maintaining commercial relations, both with farmers and buyers in town. If she is unable to do her daily run for any reason, such as illness, she will send someone to buy her load and take it to her regular customers. (Horowitz, *People and Cultures*, pp. 341, 356.)

**COUNTRY SCARS, COUNTRY MARKS,** in the West Indies, scars caused by tattooing before the slaves left Africa. These ritualistic marks were usually tribal in origin. Later, they served to identify runaway slaves.

**COUP DE MAIN** (Fr. Cr.), in rural Haiti, a small black cooperative work group.

**COUPÉES, COLAS JAMBES** (d. 1743), a black slave of Saint Domingue who was officially accused of being a sorcerer. He was charged with escaping several times from irons and prisons and of poisoning several blacks. He ran away to the Spanish part of the island, seduced and carried away other blacks, and led an armed band which robbed passersby in broad daylight and even attacked whites. He was arrested, tortured, and executed on June 4, 1723. (Hall, *Social Control*, p. 38.)

**COURTIER** (Eng. Cr.), in the Caribbean, a black lover (either male or female); he or she usually appears in African tales such as Anancy stories (q.v.).

**COURTINGSHIP** (Eng. Cr.), an Afro-Jamaican word for courtship.

**COUSCOUS** (Afr.), in the West Indies, a gruel made of boiled parched corn or grated banana cooked in oil. Originally an African dish, couscous was a standard food for slaves in the colonial period. Today, a wheat grain (semolina) steamed like rice and similar in taste and texture; eaten throughout the Middle East, North and West Africa.

**COUSIN ZAKA,** an Afro-Haitian deity, patron of the country farmer and the people of the mountains. He is always portrayed wearing the blue denim costume of the peasant, carrying a woven rustic knapsack with a stick and smoking a clay pipe. Persons possessed by this spirit are dressed in the same way and speak in the manner of the mountain people.

**COUTO, DOMINGOS DO LORETO,** a Brazilian Benedictine monk born in Pernambuco, about whom little is known. He is the author of *Desagravos do Brazil e glorias de Pernambuco* (1757), a long, intimate, and liberal account of Brazilian history which includes anecdotes and biographies of black heroes, warriors, and slaves. Couto especially admired Henriques (q.v.) and Domingos Calabar (q.v.) whom he considered proud, ambitious, and valiant blacks. (Sayers, *The Negro*, pp. 55, 58.)

**COUVERT SEC** (Fr. Cr.), in the Afro-Haitian folk religion, minor offerings to the deities which do not include any animal sacrifice or blood.

**COWRIE, COWRY.** See CAURIS.

**COWSKIN HERO,** in Jamaica, a nickname for a sugar estate (q.v.) manager alluding to his power over slaves by means of the cowskin whip.

**COYMANS, BALTAZAR,** a Dutch slave trader to whom the Spanish Crown granted an *asiento de Negros* (q.v.) on February 23, 1685, to import 3,000 African slaves every year. Coymans, like previous *asentistas* (q.v.), did not carry on the trade directly from Africa; rather, he obtained his slaves in the nearby island of Jamaica and Curaçao, principally the latter.

**COZ, (COUSIN),** in Jamaica, a term of address apparently used for any relative of any generation, regardless of age, with or without blood connection. It is common among Afro-Jamaicans.

**CRABIENNE, CARABIENNE,** in the West Indies, a black ritual dance.

**CRAB-YAWS,** in Jamaica, a form of frambesia that often afflicted black slaves. Today, there are two distinct diseases included under this name: one is a painful infection of the palms of the hands and the soles of the feet; the other is a disease of the outer layer of the skin.

**CRAW-CRAW** (Afr.), an Afro-Jamaican term for a malignant species of postulous itch prevalent among black women. In colonial times, it was common on the African coast up to about Sierra Leone (q.v.).

**CRAWL** (Eng. Cr.), in the West Indies, a pen where slaves fed and bred hogs.

**CREOLE CULTURE,** in the West Indies, a generic term applied to a cultural complex based on slavery, the plantation system, and colonialism. Its cultural content mirrors a racial mixture in which European and African elements predominate in a fairly standard combination and relationship. The ideal forms of institutional life, such as government, religious formality, kinship, law, property, education, economy, and language, are of European derivation, affected in different degrees by colonial African traditions. Metropolitan and local influences produce various types of mostly undefined Creole cultures because, despite their shared traditions, the cultures differ in orientation, values, habits, and modes of life. (M. G. Smith, *The Plural Society*, p. 5, 6.)

**CREOLE MAMA,** in colonial Dutch Surinam, an old black slave woman whose special task was to look after the children of field slaves.

**CREOLESE,** an English-based dialect spoken by blacks in Guiana.

**CREOLE SLAVE,** in the colonial West Indies, a black slave born on the islands who was considered more attractive and valuable in shape, features, and complexion than one born in Africa. The white planters preferred Creole slaves for a variety of reasons and appraised them at three times the price of an African. On the whole, they were regarded as having accepted their condition. In many instances, they were indeed faithful and acquiescent because of their contact with European civilization and had a good command of Pidgin English, Spanish, or Creole. These slaves were regarded with suspicion by African-born blacks who systematically excluded them from rebellions plotted against whites. (Brathwaite, *The Development*, p. 164.)

**CREOLISED ENGLISH.** See ENGLISH CREOLE.

**CREOLISED FRENCH.** See FRENCH CREOLE.

**CREOLISED PORTUGUESE.** See PORTUGUESE CREOLE.

**CREOLIZATION,** in Afro-Latin America, a complex process of sociocultural change, in which African, European, and Indian elements combine with the New World geographic and economic environment. It is usually associated with social and linguistic components, and is interdependent with various colonial slavery factors.

**CRESPO, ANTONIO CANDIDO GONÇALVES** (1846-1883), a black Brazilian poet who, at the age of fourteen, was sent to Portugal where he lived and died. After graduating from Coimbra University, he began writing romantic poetry. His influence in Brazil between 1860 and 1870 was extraordinary. He was indeed the only specifically Afro-American poet fully recognized in Central Europe prior to 1900. His poem "A Escrava" (1876) vividly describes a slave girl's sufferings. His feelings for Africa, the land of his ancestors, are deep and touching. Crespo married a white woman, the daughter of a general, herself a famous writer in the second half of the nineteenth century. Among his works are *Miniaturas* (Lisboa, 187?) and *Nocturnos* (Lisboa, 1888).

**CRESPO Y BORBÓN, BARTOLOMÉ JOSÉ** (1811-1871), a poet born in Galicia, Spain, who later settled in Havana, Cuba. Under the pen-name of Creto Gangá, he wrote Afro-Cuban rhymes, farces, plays, and satirical articles, using the so-called *bozal* dialect spoken by black slaves brought from Africa. Even the titles of his satires show Afro-Spanish influence. Among his numerous works are *Un Ahijado, o la Boda de Pancha Jutia y Cañuto Raspadura* (Havana, 1847); *El Chasco* (Havana, 1838); *Laborintos y trifulcas de carnavá* (Havana, 1864); *Debajo del tamarindo* (Havana, 1864); *Los pelones* (Havana, s.d.); and *Los Habaneros pintados por si mismos en miniatura* (Havana, 1847).

**CRETO GANGÁ.** See CRESPO Y BORBÓN, BARTOLOMÉ JOSÉ.

**CRIA** (Pg.), in colonial Brazil, a mulatto child born and reared within the planter's house. The *cria* usually acquired a social status similar to that of a member of the family.

**CRIAÇÃO, SISTEMA DE** (Pg.), a system of rearing black children who were born within the master's home as persons of the house; somewhat comparable to poor relations in the households of medieval Europe.

**CRIB** (Eng. Cr.), in the West Indies, a slatted box used by blacks as a hamper, often in pairs slung over the back of a donkey or mule.

**CRIC CRAC!** (Fr. Cr.). 1. In Haiti, a phrase introducing a tale: once the listeners are gathered and ready, the storyteller says "Cric?" as if to say "Shall I tell you a story?" To this, the listeners reply "Crac!"—"We are listening!" The two words together establish rapport between raconteur and audience. 2. An Afro-Haitian short story.

**CRICHE** (Fr. Cr.), in Afro-Haitian cults, an earthen jar or bottle used to contain the *loa* (q.v.) removed by a sorcerer from the head of people who have died.

**CRIER** (Eng. Cr.), in Jamaica, a piece of leather placed by request into a locally made boot or shoe to make it squeak; it is a source of pride among uneducated blacks.

**CRIOLLERA** (Sp.), in colonial Cuba, an old black woman who looked after infant slaves and supervised the nursery.

**CRIOLLO** (Sp.) ("Creole"), an American born person of Spanish blood, or of Spanish-Indian ancestry.

**CRIOLLO DE CURAZAO** (Sp.), in the Caribbean region (circa 1815), a free mulatto born in Curazao who settled in the Spanish islands. He was characterized by his speech, costumes, songs, and dances.

**CRIOLLO MORENO** (Sp.). 1. A "black creole" born in the New World. In some instances these slaves were tradesmen such as brick masons, carpenters, blacksmiths and for this reason very valuable. In 1805 in the Cartagena slave-market, the price of a *criollo moreno* was between 500 and 600 pesos compared with half of this amount for a prime bozal (q.v.). (Rout, L. B. *The African Experience in Spanish America*, p. XV, 74.)

**CRIOULO** (Pg.), a Brazilian-born black. In 1703, the fair market price in Bahia for a good *crioulo* craftsman was 500 drams. (Boxer, *The Golden Age*, p. 331.)

**CROCUS** (Eng. Cr.), in the West Indies, a coarse material, formerly of linen, widely used like osnaburgh (q.v.) for the clothing of slaves.

**CROCUS BAG** (Eng. Cr.), a crude field-bag made of crocus (q.v.), widely used by black laborers for agricultural products. In slavery times it was called Osnaburgh bag.

**CRODUCK** (Eng. Cr.), an Afro-Jamaican term for a smart black.

**CROMANTY** (Afr.), name of a town and settlement area of the Gold Coast (q.v.), variously spelled Calamente, Cormanti, Coromantee (q.v.), Coromantine, Kormanty, and Koromantyn.

**CRONGOE, CRUNJO** (Afr.), in Jamaica, a yam (q.v.) which grows wild in the fields; a favorite food of blacks. When roasted it compares favorably with the best Irish potato.

**CROOKIE,** in Jamaican folklore, the wife of Anancy in the Anancy story (q.v.).

**CROPOVER,** in the West Indies, a black funeral rite held on the ninth night after burial. This mourning ritual is only for men.

**CRUNJO.** See CRONGOE.

**CRUZ, SOR JUANA INÉS DE LA** (1651-1695), a Mexican poet who raised her voice against slavery in the seventeenth century. In one of her poems, she tells of a poor slave who has been taken to Mexico from Puerto Rico, and de la Cruz wonders whether there is redemption and grace for the blacks since they are people just as the whites.

**CRUZ JUNIOR,** a Brazilian poet, author of "A Escrava," a romantic poem published in 1852. The central character is a melancholy female slave who sings songs of her fatherland and longs to return to Africa so that she may enjoy her liberty and embrace her parents. The poem contains vivid descriptions of the tortures and abuses of slaves by white planters.

**CU-, COO-,** in the West Indies, a prefix added to the day-name (q.v.) root of a black male, reflecting an old African custom.

**CUA** (Bant.), in the Afro-Antilles, a small drum played by blacks.

**CUADRILLA DE NEGROS** (Sp.) (''Negro gang''), a gang of black slaves employed in mining in Spanish America. The size of the gang ranged from five or six to more than one hundred, depending upon the extent of the workings. It was composed of men and women and was led by a trusted black slave captain.

**CUADRILLERO** (Sp.), in colonial Spanish America, a freed mulatto or black slave employed by a town as a police officer to apprehend runaway slaves.

**CUARTELES DE ESCLAVOS** (Sp.), in the Spanish Antilles, slave quarters built on a plantation near the master's big house.

**CUARTERÓN** (Sp.), in Spanish America, the offspring of a white man and a mulatto woman.

**CUARTERÓN Y GRIFO** (Sp.), in the Spanish Antilles, any offspring with black blood.

**CUBBA** (Afr.), in the West Indies, an African day-name (q.v.) for a black female born on Wednesday.

**CUBBENA** (Afr.), in the West Indies, an African name for a black male born on Tuesday; often confused with Cubba (q.v.).

**CUCALAMBÉ** (Afr.), a popular Afro-Spanish dance in Venezuela.

**CUCKOO** (Eng.), an Afro-Jamaican word for corn dumpling.

**CUCUMBY** (Afr.), an Afro-Brazilian folk play or farce from the seventeenth century, dramatizing the crowning of black kings in Africa. The play follows a fairly general pattern, with variations in details rather than in the basic plot or argument.

**CUDJOE** (Afr.). 1. In the West Indies, a day-name (q.v.) for a black male born on Monday. 2. A slave trader in colonial times. See also JUBA.

**CUDJOE, CAPTAIN,** a black slave leader in the Maroon War (q.v.) (1734-1738) in Jamaica. At the end of the fighting, Cudjoe signed a treaty with the Jamaican government which set the Maroons (q.v.) apart from the rest of the black population on their own reservation.

**CUDJO-RUBBA, CUFFY-ROUTEN,** (Afr.), in the West Indies, a skin disease peculiar to blacks, resembling a finer form of eczema. The term seems to be connected with African day-names (q.v.).

**CUEMBÉ** (Afr.), an Afro-Spanish dance, apparently already known in Africa during the sixteenth century.

**CUFFEE** (Afr.). 1. In the West Indies, an African day-name (q.v.) for a black male born on Friday. 2. A derogatory term for a backward or stupid black. 3. A Jamaican black slave taken in 1754 to the Bay of Honduras. There he was sold to Don Emanuel, a Cuban planter. In 1762, Cuffee was given his freedom for having fought valiantly with British forces in the capture of Havana. (Black, *History of Jamaica*, p. 95.)

**CUFFEE, CAPTAIN** (d. 1686), a black slave leader of a Maroon settlements (q.v.) in the Windward region of Jamaica who fought against the white colonists between 1673 and 1686. A skillful and shrewd chief, he was killed in battle in April 1686.

**CUFFEE WOOD** (Afr.), an African plant name applied in Jamaica to a timber *(Zuelania quidonia)* used for building. There are several species.

**CUFFY-ROUTEN.** See CUDJO-RUBBA.

**CUGOANO, OTTOBAH** (b. 1745), a black writer born in Ajumaco, Ghana, who was kidnapped at the age of twelve and taken to the West Indies where he was sold into slavery. He eventually obtained his freedom, after which he traveled to London, where he became a barber and an occasional domestic servant. He married an Englishwoman, and, in 1787, he published his two-volume autobiography, *Thoughts and Sentiments on the Evil and Wicked Traffic of Slavery, and Commerce of Human Species*, in which he covers the period from his childhood near the Niger River to slavery in the New World. (Curtin, *Africa Remembered*, p. 14.)

**CUIA** (Pg.), a small gourd used by black plantation slaves in Brazil to store beans, rice, or pork fat.

**CUICA** (Pg.), an Afro-Brazilian musical instrument composed of a hollow wooden cylinder which is closed at one end and a stick covered with resin which hangs from the center of the drum head. It produces a muffled, pulsating sound.

**CUMAMA** (Afr.), in Jamaica, an African word for the calling of a dead mother in black cults. See also CUMINA.

**CUMBA** (Bant.), an Afro-Cuban drum brought from Africa in slavery times.

**CUMBANCHA** (Afr.), an Afro-Cuban word for a wild, noisy celebration; an orgy.

**CUMBÉ** (Afr.), a well-organized black settlement in Parahyba in northeast Brazil. It was destroyed by royal order in 1731.

**CUMBES** (Afr.), in Venezuela, black slave settlements established in the Coro region in 1795. These isolated runaway slave communities, unable to guarantee the survival of African customs, were eventually destroyed by the colonial authorities. See also PALENQUE; QUILOMBO.

**CUMBIA** (Afr.), in rural Colombia and Panama, an Afro-Spanish dance, notably African in rhythm and in its erotic movements.

**CUMBOHLOH, CUMBOLO.** See COMBOLO.

**CUM-CUM-TEK.** See KONGKONTE.

**CUMINA, KUMINA** (Afr.), a memorial ceremony for calling down ancestral spirits and African deities; still practiced by blacks in Jamaica and elsewhere in the West Indies. It is similar to some Haitian and Afro-Brazilian mourning rituals.

**CUMUNO** (Afr.), a drum made from hollowed logs in the form of a conga drum with one head; very popular among blacks of the Colombian Pacific lowland.

**CUNHA** (1737-1809), a black slave artist. Around 1760, Cunha painted ceilings and walls in several churches in Rio de Janeiro. Owned by Canon Januario de Cunha Barbosa, he began his formal training in Brazil. After he obtained his freedom, Cunha traveled to Lisbon to continue his studies in painting. His master portrait is that of the "Count of Bobdelle" which, according to critics, possesses artistic qualities of the highest order.

**CUNHA AZEVEDO DE COUTINHO, JOSÉ JOAQUIN,** a Brazilian bishop of Pernambuco. In his book *A Analyse sobre a Justiciado Commercio do Resgate dos Escravos da Costa d'Africa* (Lisbon, 1791), he upheld slavery as having existed since the beginning of the world.

**CUNNIE-MON'N-FATHER,** a son trickier than his father, a character in Anancy stories (q.v.).

**CURAÇALEÑO.** See PAPIAMENTO.

**CURASSESSE.** See PAPIAMENTO.

**CURIBOCA** (Pg.), in northern Brazil, the offspring of a black man and an Indian woman, especially if they are illiterate and live in the backlands.

**CURRO** (Sp.), in early colonial Cuba, a black slave brought from Spain, who considered himself an aristocrat among local slaves.

**CURRULAO** (Sp.), an Afro-Hispanic *marimba* (q.v.) dance with the xylophone as its central instrument; popular among blacks in the Colombian Pacific lowland.

**CURUMIN** (Afr.), in colonial Brazil, a young black slave companion and victim of young white masters. Each big house had one or more *curumin* boys who served a variety of purposes. Even today, in rural Brazil small white boys may be seen playing horse-and-buggy with black boys, and even with black girls, the daughters of their nurses. (Freyre, *The Masters*, p. 350.)

**CUSCUTA,** in Jamaica, a parasitic yellow weed that grows upon a bush or hedge. Blacks considered it a "love weed."

**CUSTOS,** in Jamaica, an elected mayor of a parish (county), the equivalent of an American state governor or of an English lord lieutenant. This office has never been held by a black in Jamaica.

**CUSTOS ROTULORUM,** in colonial Jamaica and elsewhere, the chief magistrate of each parish (county) who, together with the justices, the rector of the Church of England, and the vestrymen, were elected annually by the freeholders of the parish and formed the organ of representative local government. Blacks were excluded from this office by customary law.

**CUTACOO** (Afr.), in Jamaica, a long, flat field-bag made of canvas, hemp, or woven palm thatch (q.v.) used by blacks to grate cassava. It has a cover and is usually slung by a strap over the shoulder so that it hangs at one side. Some associate it with the *obeah* man (q.v.) as the container for his "things."

**CUTTING,** in the *obeah* (q.v.) cult, the black practitioner's talking of an unknown language when possessed by the spirits; while he babbles, he is said to be cutting an obscure tongue.

**CUZCUZ** (Pg.), an Afro-Brazilian dish made of steamed rice, manioc, or cornmeal; probably of African origin.

# d

**DA** (Fr. Cr.), in Martinique and the French Antilles, the black nanny of Creole children, often considered to be a member of the family. Her loyalty and affection are legendary.

**DA ALUWA** (Afr.), among Trinidadian blacks, a male god of African origin considered to be a king living in the sea. His colors are white and red, and his favorite foods are goat, pigeon, and land turtle. Usually identified with Saint John, he is worshipped on Wednesdays.

**DA COSTA** (Pg.), in Brazil, an expression referring vaguely to the west coast of Africa from which slaves and goods were imported in colonial times. At that time, traders and even slaves maintained direct contact with this part of Africa. Trade gradually decreased until by 1905 it had almost entirely disappeared.

**DADÁ** (Afr.), in the Afro-Cuban *santería* (q.v.) cult, a Yoruba (q.v.) god, protector of the newly born.

**DAGAN** (Afr.), in some Afro-Brazilian fetish cults, a group of black minor priestesses of the god Exu (q.v.) who have more than seven years of service in the cult.

**DAGOWE** (Afr.), among Bush Negroes (q.v.) of Guiana, a male god who lives on the banks of the rivers where fishermen throw him offerings. He is a Dahomean deity.

**DAHOMEY,** a powerful West African kingdom off the Bight of Benin (q.v.) that flourished in the early eighteenth century and soon became a main source of slaves for tropical America. From its capital in Abomey, the king established contact with the Portuguese trading post of Ajudá (q.v.). The kingdom was frequented by European traders as well as Luso-Brazilians. At one point, relations between Dahomey and Bahía were so intimate that heads of commercial houses in San Salvador received honorary distinctions from the government of the West African kingdom. The French conquered it in 1823. In 1960, Dahomey became an independent state and, in 1975, changed its name to the People's Republic of Benin. Beginning about 1710, with the rise of their power, the Dahomean kings exported many slaves to the New World. Planters, considering these slaves to be docile and given to merrymaking, employed them generally in domestic service. There were many Dahomeans among leaders of the 1835 slave uprising in Brazil, however.

**DAHOMEY EMBASSY,** an official mission sent by the king of Dahomey (q.v.) in 1750 to Portugal by way of Bahia, Brazil. His purpose was to dis-Ajudá (q.v.) be declared the central slave-trading port and be given a monopoly in the trade. (Carneiro, *Ladinos e Crioulous*, p. 66.)

**DAHOMEY EMISSARY,** an ambassador sent by the king of Dahomey (q.v.) in 1750 to Portugal by way of Bahía, Brazil. His purpose was to discuss the control of the port of Ajudá (q.v.), then one of the most important sources of slave labor in Brazil. The ambassador was received with honors in Bahia but, for unknown reasons, did not continue to Lisbon.

**DAMAS, LÉON GONTRAN** (1912-1977), a black French Guiana poet and writer who, together with Aimé Césaire (q.v.) and Léopold S. Senghor, was considered a leader of the négritude (q.v.) movement. Greatly influenced by Oswald Spengler, he stressed the decline of the white race and the superiority of blacks. His violent racial hatred was based partially on the cruel degeneration brought by slavery upon millions of blacks in the Caribbean region and elsewhere in the New World. As a stylist, Damas emphasized the phonic value of words, the sequence of vowels and consonants, repetitions, alliterations, and the so-called Caribbean dance rhythms. His volumes of poetry include *Pigments* (Paris, 1937); *Graffiti* (Paris, 1952); *Black-Label* (Paris, 1956); and *Névralgies* (Paris, 1966). He is also the author of an important anthology, *Poètes d'expression française* (Paris, 1947).

**DAMBALLA** (Afr.), an Afro-Haitian deity believed to bring rain and good crops whose symbol is the serpent; his devotees dress in white. He is identified with Saint Patrick.

**DAMBALLA WEDO,** (Afr.), one of the most venerable deities in the Afro-Haitian pantheon and the husband of Ayida Wedo (q.v.) He is associated with rainfall, springs, and fertility.

**DAMBRUGANA** (Afr.), a black *quilombo* (q.v.) settled in the interior of northeast Brazil around 1670.

**DANDAH** (Afr.), in Jamaica, an old black woman.

**DAN-DAN** (Afr.). In the Afro-Antilles: 1. Baby-dress. 2. A black man excessively concerned about clothes and appearance.

**DANDY-FEVER.** See DENGUÉ FEVER.

**DANISH WEST INDIES COMPANY,** a commercial corporation organized in 1671 for the purpose of developing a profitable trade between Denmark and the Virgin Islands. In 1674, the company entered the black slave trade and set up operations in Africa for procuring slaves. That year its name became the Danish West Indies and Guinea Company. It lasted eighty-four years. (Farr, *Historical Dictionary*, p. 99.)

**DANSE CHICA,** a lascivious Afro-Haitian dance popular around 1809.

**DANSE CONGO,** an Afro-French black dance in Guiana.

**DANTAS, MANOEL PINTO DE SOUZA** (1831-1894), a liberal Brazilian politician and senator from Bahia. He held many high government posts and traveled widely throughout Europe. In 1886, he proposed a plan for the total abolition of slavery in the county.

**DANZÓN** (Sp.), a lively Afro-Cuban dance played on pianolas with accordions and gourds. It is said that it was introduced to the island in 1879 by a black composer, Miguel Failde. Soon after it became a popular folk dance.

**DAN WEDO** (Afr.). See DAMBALLA WEDO.

**DAR COMIDA A LA CABEZA** (Sp.) ("to feed the head"), a ritual of initiation on an Afro-Brazilian *candomblé* (q.v.); it must be performed on the first visit of a spirit.

**DASH,** a gift or a bribe paid to African chiefs by slave traders and captains of slaving vessels. *Dash* was an essential part of the long-drawn-out process of purchasing slaves in West Africa. Today it is commonly employed in social and business transactions. (Davidson, *Black Mother*, p. 27.)

**DASHEEN,** in Jamaica, an edible root crop, a staple food among blacks. It is sold by black women in the town markets.

**DAY CLEAR,** an Afro-Jamaican idiom for daybreak.

**DAY-DAY.** In Jamaica: 1. An expression blacks use to show courtesy to a superior. 2. Among blacks, an expression meaning good-bye.

**DAY FOR DAY,** in Jamaica, the practice common to small black land-holders of getting together to cut down bush (q.v.), to help with harvest, and to move or build houses in the countryside.

**DAY-NAME,** among West Indian black slaves, the name given to a child according to the day of the week of his or her birth. This custom, with local variations, was common among Ashanti (q.v.) and other African ethnic groups. Today it survives in Jamaica as born-day (q.v.) name and birth name (q.v.). See also CUDJOE; JUBA; QUASHEBA; QUASHEE.

**DEAD LETTER,** in the colonial West Indies, laws enacted by local legislatures regarding community affairs, including the relationships between masters and slaves, the construction and repair of chapels, and the duty of clergymen to instruct slaves in religion.

**DEALING STICK,** in Afro-Jamaican cults, a sacred stick or staff with magical powers to drive out unfriendly spirits.

**DÉBOIS** (Fr. Cr.), in Haiti, a carved wooden puppet with a short handle below. It is usually painted and sometimes dressed. During the Mardi Gras, it is an object of endless fun among blacks.

**DÉCLASSÉ** (Fr. Cr.), in the French Antilles, a poor, white, illiterate who lives like a black.

**DÉDÉ** (Fr. Cr.), in the French Antilles, a word for good-bye.

**DÉDÉ-MOTHER,** an Afro-Jamaican phrase for a mother whose child dies on the ninth day after birth.

**DEEBU** (Afr.), an Afro-Jamaican kinship term for maternal-blood relations, i.e., my mother's sisters and brothers, her mother and all her children.

**DE ESTE LADO DEL MAR** (Sp.) *(On This Side of the Sea)*, a book of poetry written in 1949 by Manuel del Cabral (q.v.) in which the author bitterly denounces black poetry as barbarous and backward.

**DEFICIENCY LAWS,** in the colonial West Indies, a number of decrees adopted during the early eighteenth century in an attempt to increase the number of whites on the islands. They required the maintenance of a certain proportion of blacks and whites working on each estate. Both racial ratio and the amount of fines for violations varied from time to time. Thus, in Antigua, before 1750, all slaveowners were obliged to employ one white man for every thirty blacks, with a fine of 20 pounds per deficiency. (Ragatz, *The Fall*, p. 8.)

**DE L'AIR** (Fr. Cr.), an Afro-Haitian deity identified with the sky; good protector of the family.

**DELORMÉ, DEMESVAR** (1831-1901), a black Haitian poet who was an ardent romantic and an imitator of Goethe, Hugo, and Alexandre Dumas. His works include *Les théoriciens au pouvoir: Causeries historiques* (Paris, 1870); *Francesca: Les jeux du sort* (Paris, 1873); and *Le Damné* (Paris, 1877.)

**DÉ MORNE PAS CAPAB' RENCONTRE, DÉ MOUNE CAPAB'** (Fr. Cr.), (''Two mountains cannot meet, two men can''), an Afro-Haitian saying. (Courlander, *The Drum*, p. 336.)

**DENDÉ PALM** (Pg.), a tropical palm *(Eloesis quineensis)* native to West Africa; introduced into Brazil in slavery times. A tall columnar trunk, 120 meters high and more, bears a crown of gigantic leaves. Its fruit, the *coco* (q.v.), has a pulp which is eaten raw, boiled, or roasted mainly by blacks. In Bahia, blacks make *dendé* wine (q.v.).

**DENDÉ PALM OIL,** a product of the *dendé* palm (q.v.) used in Brazil since slavery times for cooking and in folk medicine.

**DENDÉ WINE,** in Brazil, a fermented beverage made mainly by blacks from the *dendé* palm (q.v.); introduced from Africa in slavery times.

**DENGO** (Afr.), an Afro-Brazilian word for child.

**DENGOSO** (Afr.), an Afro-Brazilian term meaning fastidious, overnice.

**DENGUÉ** (Afr.). 1. An Afro-Spanish work for infant, child. 2. An Afro-Brazilian term for darling, minion, affectation, showiness. 3. Grippe, influenza. (Alvarez Nazario, *El elemento negroide*, p. 250.)

**DENGUÉ FEVER, DANDY-FEVER.** (Afr.). In the West Indies: 1. A sudden cramp-like seizure. 2. Evil spirit, plague.

**DE NIMRODBEWEGING** (D.) ("The Nimrod Movement"), a weekly periodical published in Paramaribo and devoted to the spiritual and material well-being of blacks in the colony of Surinam. This paper appeared from December 1, 1918, to October 4, 1919, and contributed to the awakening of black consciousness.

**DENTLÉ, DENTLI** (Afr.), an Afro-Haitian musical instrument consisting of a notched stick played with a bamboo scraping blade.

**DEPA** (Afr.), in the West Indies, a yam (q.v.) *(Dioscorea)* eaten mainly by blacks.

**DEPESTRE, RENÉ** (b. 1926), a black Haitian poet. Depestre was born in Jacmel and educated at the Lycée Pétion, Port-au-Prince. Partly because of his Marxist ideas and radical activities, he was forced to leave Haiti in 1946 and settled in Paris. In 1958, he returned briefly to his country, but had to leave once again. Since then, Depestre has lived in Communist nations, notably Cuba. He is a prolific writer. Among his works are *Etincelles* (Port-au-Prince, 1945); *Gerbes de sang* (Port-au-Prince, 1946); *Végétations de clarté* (Paris, 1951); *Traduit de grand large* (Paris, 1952); *Minérai noir* (Paris, 1956); *Journal d'un animal marin* (Paris, 1964); and *Un Arc en ciel pour l'Occident chrétien* (Paris, 1967).

**DEPORTES, GEORGES** (b. 1921), a mulatto poet born in Balata, Martinique. Deportes was educated in Fort-de-France and is a member of an aristocratic black family. He is a champion of blacks whom he depicts as victims of white racism and colonialism. As an intellectual, he claims to be a progressive humanist fighting against racial and social prejudices. He is dedicated to the principles of négritude (q.v.). His published works are *Les Marches souveraines* (Paris, 1956); *Soliloques pour mauvais rêves* (Fort-de-France, 1958); and *Sous l'oeil fixe du soleil; poèmes masqués* (Paris, 1961).

**DERECHO DE COARTACIÓN** (Sp.) See COARTACIÓN.

**DERMIÈRE PRIÈRE** (Fr. Cr.) ("the last prayer"), in the Afro-Haitian culture, the final burial service which takes place nine days after death.

**DESPACHO** (Pg.), in Afro-Brazilian cults, a sacrificial offering made to a deity, especially Exu (q.v.), at the opening of each service. It ordinarily consists of food, a dead chicken, coins, a piece of red cloth, or a candle. The *despacho* is frequently left at a crossroads or at the foot of trees.

**DESSALINES, JEAN-JACQUES** (1758-1806), the great black liberator of Haiti. Born a plantation slave, he joined the slave rebellion of 1791. As a lieutenant of Toussaint L'Ouverture (q.v.), he distinguished himself as a fighter. In 1804, Dessalines proclaimed the independence of Haiti and became president. He used forced labor on plantations to increase production, confiscated white lands, and launched a campaign to exterminate the French colonists. He was killed by A. S. Pétion (q.v.)

**DÉSSOUNIN, DÉSSOUNÉ** (Fr. Cr.), in the Afro-Haitian folk religion, the ritual of dispossessing a spirit from the head of a deceased person.

**DE SURINAAMSCHE LETTERVRIEDEN** (D.) (The Surinam Literary Society), a literary society founded in 1786 by residents of Paramaribo, Surinam, then a Dutch colony. Although a short-lived group, it promoted intellectual interests at a time when a large number of books published in various modern languages were imported from Europe. (Lier, *Frontier Society*, p. 82.)

**DEVIL-MAN,** the blackest person in the Afro-Caribbean. John Canoe dance (q.v.).

**DÉVINEUR** (Fr. Cr.), in Haiti, a black professional fortune-teller.

**DEYE-DOS** (Fr. Cr.), in Haiti, a beverage made with native leaves by black peasants.

**DEYE MORNE GAINYAIN MOURNE** (Fr. Cr.) ("Behind the mountains are mountains"), an Afro-Haitian proverb that stresses the limitlessness of power. (Courlander, *The Drum*, p. 37.)

**DIABLESSE** (Fr. Cr.), in the French Antilles, an evil female spirit. In Haiti, she is thought to be a spinster who must live in the woods for several years before being admitted to heaven as punishment for having died a virgin.

**DIA DE DAR O NOME** (Pg.), in Afro-Brazilian cults, the day when a female novice is given her sacred name by the priest. This ritual, which comes after months' or even a year's probation, includes prayers, songs, and the pouring of animal blood on the head of the initiate.

**DIA DE PAGODÉ** (Pg.) ("play day"), in colonial Brazil, Saturday nights and invariably Saints' days on which the slaves, with the permission of their masters, sang, danced, and greatly enjoyed the rhythm of the drums, flutes, and other African instruments.

**DIALOGOS DAS GRANDEZAS DO BRASIL** (Pg.), an anonymous, historical account of the early geography, economics, and social development of Brazil published in 1618. In it the author gives the black slaves due credit for being the developers of the country and for having created a "new Guinea."

**DIAMBA** (Afr.), a variety of European hemp *(Cannabis sativa,* var. *indica L.)* whose leaves and flowers are impregnated with a narcotic, the effects of which are similar to those of opium. This tropical plant was widely used by black slaves in colonial Brazil. In 1830, its users were fined and condemned to three days' imprisonment. (Freyer, *The Masters*, p. 317.)

**DIARIO DE VIAGEM** (Pg.) ("Travel Diary"), a well-informed report about Palmares (q.v.) by a Dutch Captain, João Blaer, who visited the black republic in 1645. He found the old settlement abandoned as unhealthy and a new one in the process of formation.

**DIAS, ANTONIO GONÇALVES** (1823-1864), a brilliant mulatto poet, playwright, and scholar, the son of a Portuguese merchant and a mulatto maid. Dias went to Coimbra where he received a law degree with the highest academic honors. As a romantic poet, Dias is the voice of tropical Brazil and of a poet living in perpetual communion with nature. Among his works are *Primeiros Cantos* (Rio de Janeiro, 1846); *Leonor de Mendonça* (Rio de Janeiro, 1847); *Os Tymbiras, Poema Americano* (Rio de Janeiro, 1848); *Sequndos Cantos e Sextilhas de Frei Antão* (Rio de Janeiro, 1848); and *Ultimos Cantos* (Rio de Janeiro, 1851).

**DIAS, HENRIQUE** (d. 1645), a black Brazilian who was a hero in the war against the Dutch (1624-1654). With other black slaves, he led a rebellion against the invaders of Pernambuco in 1645. He fought with courage and died in battle. As an author of letters describing his fighting, Días is probably the first black writer in Brazilian history. (Sayers, *The Negro*, p. 38.)

**DIAS, MARCILIO** (1838-1865), a black Brazilian sailor who fought in the Paraguayan War in 1864 and died of his wounds. To honor his heroism, the Brazilian navy established the Casa Marcilio Dias for the education of the children of men in the ranks of the navy.

**DIAS JUNIOR,** a black painter honored by the Brazilian National Academy with the prize of a visit to Europe in 1914. Caught by the outbreak of the war, he took refuge in Corsica where he died. His masterpiece is the canvas "Abel e Cain."

**DÍAZ, JOSÉ DEL CARMEN,** a Cuban slave poet born in Guinea (q.v.). Díaz began writing in 1867 and soon became very popular among intellectuals in Havana. It is reported that the authorities jailed him because slaves were forbidden to read and write. In 1879, Díaz was able to purchase his freedom with the profits from the book *Los poetas de color* which included some of his poems; the book had been published by Francisco Calcagno (q.v.) in 1868.

**DIEGO, ELISEO** (b. 1920), a Cuban poet and ardent follower of the afrocubanismo (q.v.) movement. The black is one of his main sources of inspiration. Among his work are *En las Oscuras Manos del Olvido* (Havana, 1942) and *El la Calzada de Jesus del Monte* (Havana, 1946).

**DIGGING MATCH,** among Jamaican blacks, a communal planting whereby a number of peasants agree to work together to clear and plant each other's ground. Drink and food are provided by the owner of the land being cleared. See also CORVEÉ; COUMBITÉ.

**DIGGING SONG,** in the colonial West Indies, a slave song chanted with great spontaneity by a soloist and chorus during digging work. In tone and spirit, these songs were laments about the slaves' cruel and oppressive life or direct complaints about harsh treatment by an overseer. This collective chanting is of African origin.

**DIMAJAI** (Afr.), in West Africa, a native-born slave who could not be alienated or mutilated by his master at will, but only by permission of a court which took responsibility for such penalties. (M. G. Smith, *The Plural Society*, p. 127.)

**DIMMO** (Afr.), in Jamaica, a lame black.

**DINDINHO** (Pg.), in Brazil, grandfather or godfather; a term of endearment used by the black wet nurse.

**DINÉ MACHETE** (Fr. Cr.), among black Haitians, afternoon communal work during harvest time. It ends with a dinner served by the owner of the land being worked. It is comparable to an American threshing party.

**DINKIES, DINKY MINNY, JUMP DINKY** (Eng. Cr.), in Jamaica, the ninth-night celebration held by blacks after a funeral; it usually ends with a festive party.

**DIREITO DE NÃO TRABALHAR** (Pg.) ("the right not to work), a Brazilian expression referring to the privilege claimed by any white citizen or planter as a free man. The expression dates from slavery times when work was considered the black burden.

**DIRI** (Afr.), in the Afro-French Antilles, a word for rice.

**DIRT-EATING,** in the West Indies, the habit of eating clay earth to which many black slaves were addicted. It was a form of geophagy. See also MAL D'ESTOMAC.

**DIRTY MOTHER** (Eng. Cr.), in Jamaica, a children's game in which a big girl, chosen as a *muma*, has a set dialogue with the others at the end of which they insult her and run away. Apparently, the game originated in slavery times. Also called *dog muma* and *dutty muma*.

**DJAB** (Fr. Cr.), in Afro-Haitian folklore, a kind of demon.

**DJÉVO** (Fr. Cr.), an Afro-Haitian term for the inner room of a fetish temple.

**DJODJO** (Afr.), among the Bush Negroes (q.v.) of Guiana, one of the two souls which serves as a life protector of a person and wanders on the earth after death.

**DJUBA-BELÉ** (Afr.), in the French Antilles, a type of African dance.

**DJUKA CREOLE** (Afr.), a Bush Negro (q.v.) dialect spoken in Surinam. It is unique among Creole languages in that it has developed a syllabic writing system which has remarkable similarities with various indigenous scripts of West Africa.

**DOCA** (Afr.), among Haitian blacks, the first female child born after twins; she is thought to be specially qualified to be a priestess. Her patron is the goddess Marassa Doça (q.v.).

**DOCKER** (Eng. Cr.), in the colonial West Indies, a skirt, petticoat, or similar garment worn by female slaves. Also known as *dacas*.

**DOCTEUR FÉ** (Fr. Cr.), in Haiti, a black medicine man, expert in dispensing herbs.

**DOCTOR-MAN,** in colonial Jamaica, a slave attendant in a slave hospital.

**DOCTRESS, DOCTORESS** (Eng. Cr.), in colonial Jamaica, a slave nurse working in a slave hospital.

**DOÇU, DOSU** (Afr.), among Afro-Haitians, the first male child born after twins; he is believed to be even more powerful than twins themselves. He plays an important role in some black cults.

**DODINE** (Fr. Cr.), in Haiti, a rocking chair of the tropics very much used by blacks.

**DOES** (D.) in colonial Surinam, folk plays staged annually by black slaves. The government prohibited them in 1794 in order to prevent blacks from congregating in public places. (Lier, *Frontier Society*, p. 140.)

**DOG-DRIVER,** in the colonial West Indies, a black or mulatto slave on a sugar estate (q.v.) who was in charge of slaves working in the plantation sugar fields and in the sugar mills (q.v.). He is said to have treated the slaves under his command like dogs. See also DRIVER.

**DOG MUMA.** See DIRTY MOTHER.

**DO-GOOD** (man), in some Afro-Jamaican cults, an *obeah* man (q.v.) thought to have healing powers.

**DOIS-DOIS** (Pg.), twin deities worshipped in several Afro-Brazilian cults of *gêgé-nagó* (q.v.) origin. They are frequently identified with Saints Cosmas and Damian.

**DOKPWÉ** (Afr.), in the Afro-West Indies, a cooperative work group of Dahomean origin. This black self-help system, organized in Africa along a lineal descent line, is widely spread throughout the New World. It has survived today under different names. See COUMBITÉ; CORVÉE; DIGGING MATCH; TROCA DIA.

**DOKUNU** (Afr.), in Jamaica, a kind of pudding made from starchy food which is sweetened, spiced, and traditionally wrapped in plantain (q.v.) or banana leaf. A favorite black dish, it can be boiled, baked, or roasted.

**DOKUNU TREE** (Afr.), an Afro-Jamaican term for an imaginary tree that bears *dokunus* (q.v.). It figures in some Anancy stories (q.v.).

**DOMESTIC SLAVE,** in the colonial West Indies, a specialized slave working in or about his owner's house. His master and fellow slaves considered him to be in a more "honorable" position than the field slaves (q.v.). He belonged to a privileged group of slaves, being selected for his good disposition, loyalty, and truthfulness. His standard of living and his earning power were much higher than those of unskilled slaves. In general, a domestic slave had the most promising opportunity for purchasing his freedom and was better clothed, better fed, and had easier work than the agricultural slaves.

**DOMICI WEDO** (Afr.), an Afro-Haitian deity, the wife of Damballa Wedo (q.v.).

**DON PÉTRO** (Fr. Cr.), a legendary black slave of Spanish origin born in Hispaniola who, at some time in prerevolutionary Haiti, settled in the mountains in the commune of Petit-Goâve. There he organized a folk cult with deities and rituals of local origin. Upon his death, Don Pétro came to occupy an honorable place in the Afro-Haitian pantheon, leaving in his name a whole progeny of gods.

**DOSU** (Afr.). See DOÇU.

**DOUDOUS** (Fr. Cr.), in the French Antilles, a black native beauty. As a term of endearment, it is also applied by a woman to a male friend.

**DOUVANT JOU** (Fr. Cr.), among black Haitian peasants, early morning communal work done during the harvest.

**DRAM** (D.), in Surinam, an alcoholic beverage distilled from sugar; greatly enjoyed by urban and rural blacks. It differs from rum in the way it is made and in its alcoholic content.

**DRAPEAU DE DEMAIN** (Fr.) ("Tomorrow's Flag"), a famous poem by black writer Jean F. Brièrre (q.v.) in which he voices a violent reaction against the American occupation of Haiti (1915-1934). He considered the occupation an unjust and cruel invasion similar to the French slave planta-tion system. Published in 1931, it reflects the nationalistic feelings of the négritude (q.v.) movement.

**DRES-MAMA** (D.), in colonial Surinam, a female black.

**DRES-NEGER** (D.), in colonial Surinam, a black male nurse.

**DRIETTE** (Fr. Cr.), in the French Antilles, a long dress worn by black women with a wide skirt of ankle length or longer and a tight bodice; worn with a matching kerchief at religious cult services.

**DRIVER,** in the colonial West Indies, a black or mulatto slave in charge of slaves or slave gangs (q.v.) on plantations and in sugar mills (q.v.). He kept a constant and strict surveillance over the labor force. Commonly called dog-driver (q.v.), he carried a whip as a symbol of his position.

**DRIVERESS,** in the colonial West Indies, a black slave woman in charge of a gang of black children over five or six years old who did the weeding.

**DROGUE** (Fr. Cr.), in Haitian folklore, a powerful magic charm which protects its owner against all inimical forces. It consists of a beverage especially prepared by a sorcerer. Once a man drinks *drogue*, he is regarded as immune to poison, sorcery, illness, and all kinds of enemies.

**DUCKANOO, DUCKUNU** (Afr.), an Afro-Jamaican dumpling made of corn meal, sweet potatoes, or yellow yam, (q.v.), and baked or boiled in a plantain (q.v.) or banana leaf.

**DUGGY-MAN,** in Jamaica, a black with short legs.

**DUNDEE** (Afr.). 1. In the West Indies, an African tribal name. 2. In Jamaica, a black albino.

**DUNDO** (Afr.), in colonial Jamaica, a small drum played by slaves.

**DUNDOOZE, DUNDOZE** (Afr.), in Jamaica, a black folk term for a darling, a much-loved person; used as a term of endearment by an older person to a young boy or girl.

**DUNDUN** (Fr. Cr.), in Haiti, the smallest drum of the *arada* (q.v.) group.

**DUNGA** (Afr.), an Afro-Brazilian term for mister.

**DUNGA TARÁ** (Afr.) ("How are you, master"), an African greeting used by slaves to hail an overseer or a planter on Brazilian plantations. (Mendonça, *A Influencia*, p. 135.)

**DUNG BASKET,** in Jamaica, a basket formerly used by slaves to carry manure to the cane fields.

**DUNJU** (Eng. Cr.), in the West Indies, a black albino.

**DUPPY** (Afr.), in the West Indies, a ghost or spirit attached to every person, child or adult, throughout his life. Even after death, a duppy is capable of returning to aid or to harm living beings, directly or indirectly. Among black slaves, and even today among blacks, the duppies are feared but not worshipped. At some black wakes, there is a ceremony designed to catch duppies and lay them to rest.

**DUPPY BIRD,** in Afro-Jamaican tradition, any bird associated with duppies (q.v.) or ghosts, such as doves, owls, and wild pine sergeants. Blacks believe that if a duppy bird flies into a church, someone will die.

**DUPPY CATCHER,** in some Afro-Jamaican cults, an *obeah* man (q.v.) skilled in catching duppies (q.v.) or ghosts.

**DUPPY CONQUEROR,** in Jamaica, a belligerent or bullying black; a derisive epithet.

**DUPPY PEA,** in the West Indies, a species of wild pea *(Crotolaria verrucosa* or *C. retusa)* which looks like an edible pea but is not. The dry pods rattle loudly when the bush is moved or shaken. Blacks use it in magic.

**DUPREY, PIERRE** (b. 1911), a mulatto journalist and historian born in Fort-de-France, Martinique. He studied on the island and in Paris. His chief interests are the Islamic culture of North Africa and the history of the Gold Coast (q.v.), where he settled in 1935. His main works are *Le coupeur de bois* (1945); *Bli, homme pensant* (1948); *Histoire des Ivoriens* (1962); and *La Côte d'Ivoire de A à Z* (1970).

**DURAND, LOUIS HENRY** (b. 1897), a black poet born in Cap-Haitien, Haiti. After attending local schools, Durand was sent to the Lycée Janson de Sally in France. His poetry is exquisite and delicate. His works include *Poésies* (Port-au-Prince, 1916); *Cléopâtre*; *pièce en quatre tableaux et en vers* (Port-au-Prince, 1919); *Roses rouges* (Paris, 1930); and *Trois poèmes* (Port-au-Prince, 1930).

**DURAND, OSWALD** (1840-1906), a black Haitian poet. Durand is considered the first to show the realities of his country in simple and tender images and to write in French Creole (q.v.), thus making it acceptable in written literature. His writing captures black Haitian women, and half-caste girls whose beauty, sensuality, and charm he continually celebrates. Among his works are *Choucoune* (an anthology, 1884); *Rires et pleurs*, (poems, 2 v., 1896); *Quatre nouveaux poèmes* (Cap-Haitien, 1900); and *Fefé Candidat and Fefé Ministre* (a play, 1906).

**DURÃO, FREI JOSÉ DE SANTA RITA** (1722-1784), the oldest Brazilian poet of the Escola mineira, author of "Caramuru," a poem inspired by Camões. In his patriotic rendering of early history, Durão writes about the greatest heroes, including the black Henrique Días (q.v.). He was the first to incorporate the figure of the Noble Negro (q.v.) into Brazilian poetry.

**DURRA** (Afr.). See GUINEA CORN.

**DUTCH-AMERICAN NEGRO,** a descendant of African slaves brought to the Dutch Antilles during the colonial period to work on sugar plantations. As a result of a high degree of miscegenation over the years, the Dutch-American Negro is the product of many different cultural elements, including Spanish, Portuguese, English, and French. He speaks papiamento (q.v.).

**DUTTY MUMA.** See DIRTY MOTHER.

**D Y,** a slave trade mark, standing for the duke of York, one of the shareholders of the Company of Royal Adventurers of England Trading to Africa (q.v.) and a brother of Charles II. In 1676, in the port of New Calabar, on the Niger River, the representative of the company branded exactly 100 slaves, including men women and children. This cargo was taken aboard the *Sarah Bonaventura*, a company vessel, to Barbados. (Davidson, *Black Mother*, p. 90.) See also BRANDING.

**DYALI** (Afr.), in the French Antilles, a black troubadour who recites an ode or an epic poem accompanied by the African harp *(kora)*.

# e

**É A MULATA QUE É MULHER** (Pg.) ("The female mulatto is the real girl"), a Brazilian proverb meaning that a mixed-blood woman is the ideal sexual partner. (Boxer, *Four Centuries*, p. 78.)

**EARTH-BOUND GODS,** in the Afro-Jamaican *cumina* (q.v.) cult, a number of African deities such as Macoo, Appei, and Beeco. They are supposedly very much concerned with man's problems and sufferings. (Cassidy, *Dictionary*, p. 167.)

**EARTH-EATER,** on Caribbean plantations, a slave addicted to dirt-eating (q.v.).

**EATING-MATCHING** (Eng. Cr.), in Jamaica, a religious feast celebrated by blacks at wakes.

**EATING-THE-PARROT,** in colonial Brazil, a children's game in which a white boy flew a kite having a bit of glass hidden in the folds of the tail, supposedly to play a trick on his slave playmates. (Freyre, *The Master*, p. 391.)

**EBELAIT, EBOE-LIGHT** (Eng. Cr.), in the West Indies, a tropical palm *(Erthroxylon areolatum)* once used by slaves for torches and walking sticks.

**EBERY DAAG T'INK HIMSELF LION IN A HIM MASSA YARD**(Eng. Cr.) ("Every dog thinks himself a lion in his master's yard"), an Afro-Jamaican saying. (Beckwith, *Jamaica Proverbs*, p. 44.)

**EBIFÁ, EFIFÁ** (Yor.), an Afro-Brazilian term for a kind of witchcraft.

**EBÓ** (Afr.), an Afro-Brazilian rice-cake prepared with *dendé* palm oil (q.v.) or honey; often eaten by Moslem blacks in Bahia at religious ceremonies. (Freyre, *The Masters*, p. 465.)

**EBOE, IBO** (Afr.). 1. An ethnic group living near the Bight of Biafra (q.v.) from which many slaves were brought to the New World during the colonial period. Some planters considered these slaves a poor investment since they were alleged to be chronically despondent and required gentle treatment. Moreover, while the women were sufficiently industrious, the men were reputed to have an inborn aversion to any form of exertion. Their reputation for suicide extended throughout the hemisphere, including the English colonies. 2. A sacred sacrificial offering in various Afro-Brazilian cults; also known as *despacho* (q.v.). It consists of a dead chicken, popcorn, pigeon, a piece of cloth, a silver or copper coin, candles, and African dishes which are left at a crossroad. (Mendonça, *A Influencia*, p. 135.)

**EBOE-DRUM** (Afr.), in Jamaica and the West Indies, a large drum, yellow in color, with out-thrust lower jaw. It was a favorite Ibo (q.v.) instrument connected with sorcery.

**EBOE-LIGHT.** See EBELAIT.

**EBONIM** (Afr.), in some Afro-Brazilian cults, the rank reached by a god's bride after seven continuous years of service in the sect.

**EBONY,** in the West Indies, a slave trade term meaning African blacks regarded as articles of commerce to be sold. (Alvarez Nazario, *El elemento negroide*, p. 338.)

**EBO-TAYA** (Afr.), in Jamaica, a kind of *coco* (q.v.) associated with Eboe (q.v.) slaves.

**É CHEIO DE ARTE** (Pg.), in modern Brazil, a black who tries to appear white.

**ECHEMENDÍA, AMBROSIO** (b. 1839), a black Cuban poet born a slave on a plantation in Trinidad. As a child Echemendía was brought to Cienfuegos where his master sent him to a school that placed white and black children on an equal footing. He became a very popular poet, giving readings and circulating handwritten poems. In 1865, he was publicly acclaimed an outstanding bard by the city of Cienfuegos. That year a group of intellectuals collected 500 pesos; another 500 pesos were collected at a banquet honoring D. Eduardo Asquerino, an abolitionist visitor from Madrid. Thus, the sponsors of the slave poet obtained the 1,000 pesos necessary to buy his freedom. Echemendía's poetry appeared only in periodicals. In 1869, he married a mulatto woman, Dolores Susanne. (Calcagno, *Los poetas de color*, pp. 49-50.)

**ÉCOLE INDIGÉNISTE** (Fr.), a Haitian literary movement deeply rooted in the native soil and in Afro-peasant traditions. It was a nationalist awakening whose followers tried to study and investigate black folklore and find the African cultures that had previously been ignored. The movement began in 1927 with *La Revue Indigène*, published by Emile Roumer (q.v.) and Normail Sylvain (q.v.). The following year Jean Price-Mars (q.v.) published his famous essay *Ainsi parle l'Oncle*, an interpretation of Haitian culture. L'École Indigéniste, whose strong influence continues to the present, was neither anti-European nor anti-white. (Pompilus, *Manuel illustré*, p. 326.) See also ÉCOLE PRIMITIVE DU NORD.

**ÉCOLE PRIMITIVE DU NORD** (Fr.), an artistic movement organized in Cap-Haitien, Haiti, in the 1940s by Philomé Obin (b. 1892), his brother Sénèque, and his son Antoine. This school of painting was profoundly realistic, with careful attention to detail and a vivid, attractive naïveté. Though there was an emphasis on composition and detail, the paintings were never cluttered, retaining a great deal of open space.

**ECUÉ, EKUÉ** (Afr.), in colonial Cuba, an African god worshipped by Calabar black slaves who were organized into a secret society. Its members met periodically in a temple to pray, to sacrifice goats, and to celebrate holy communal feasts. There were also special offerings to the ancestors. During the service, it was said that at appropriate moments Ecué's groans were heard.

**ECUÉ-YAMBA-O** (Afr.) ("Jesus Christ Be Blessed"), The title of an Afro-Cuban novel by Alejo Carpentier (q.v.) published in 1933. Carpentier depicts the life of a humble mulatto boy, Hermenegildo, who lives in the enchanted world of the *santería* (q.v.) Far from feeling inferior to whites, he derives a deep sense of superiority from his primitive life, free from complications and full of magical emotions. This novel both exposes the conditions of blacks on Cuban plantations and documents their customs and their inner feelings. See also BWANGA.

**É DE RAÇA** (Pg.) ("He is a black"), in Brazil, a black who tries to appear white.

**EDOUARD, EMMANUEL** (1860-1895), a black Haitian poet born in l'Ansé-à Veau in 1860. After studying in Port-au-Prince, Edouard was sent to France to further his education and received a law degree from the Sorbonne in Paris. His works include *Rimes haïtiennes, poésies* (Paris, 1847-1881); and *Le Panthéon haïtien: Précédé d' une lettre à LL. MM. l'Empereur du Brésil, et le roi d' Espagne* (Paris, 1885).

**EFAN** (Afr.), in Brazil, a black slave with tattooed face, an ethnic distinction.

**EFIFÁ.** See EBIFÁ.

**EFIK** (Afr.), an ethnic group living off the Bight of Biafra (q.v.) from which many slaves were brought to the West Indies beginning in the 1730s.

**EFÓ** (Afr.), an Afro-Brazilian delicacy; a kind of ragout made of shrimp and herbs, seasoned with *dendé* palm oil (q.v.) and pepper.

**EFUM** (Yor.), an Afro-Brazilian fetish cult which includes a sacred dance performed by the initiates with their heads painted white, blue, and red.

**EGBÁ** (Afr.). See EUBÁ. An Afro-Brazilian ritual, part of the *candomblé* (q.v.).

**EGUSSI** (Afr.), in Brazil, melon pips or seeds; a condiment of African origin much favored by blacks.

**EIDON** (Afr.), in Afro-Jamaican folklore, the ghost of a baby who dies before christening. He is considered dangerous because he has no human knowledge. See also DUPPY.

**EKEDI** (Afr.), in various Afro-Brazilian cults, a girl dedicated to a god who acts as a maid-in-waiting, helping the dancers during their performances and trances.

**EKOBIO** (Afr.), a brother or member of the Afro-Cuban *santería* (q.v.) who undergoes an elaborate initiation process.

**EKÓN** (Afr.), in the Afro-Cuban folk religion, the sacred bell that calls the faithful to the service. See also SANTERÍA.

**EKUÉ.** See ECUÉ.

**EKUENON** (Afr.), in the Afro-Cuban religion, a master of ceremony.

**ELE É UM POUCO OSCURO, MAS O CABELO É BOM** (Pg.) ("He is a bit black, but his hair is good"), a Brazilian maxim expressing the popular belief that in a mixed-blood individual, hair texture is much more important than the color of the skin. (Pierson, *Negroes*, p. 1441.)

**ELEGBARÁ** (Afr.), in the Afro-Cuban *santería* (q.v.), a fetish god who personifies the devil; his cult is secret.

**ELEGUÁ** (Afr.), an Afro-Cuban god, guardian of the house doors, the roads and the highway; a messenger of Olofi (q.v.) who has about 21 different representations. An important god identified with the souls of Purgatory, the Niño de Atocha in the Catholic Church.

**ELEGUÁ ODÉ MATA** (Afr.), an Afro-Cuban god who lives in the countryside and is a protector of the peasants.

**ÉLÉQUELÉ** (Bant.), an Afro-Cuban word for calabash.

**ELE TEM DEDO NA COZINHA** (Pg.) ("He has a finger in the kitchen"), a Brazilian saying applied to an individual with black blood.

**ELE TEM GENIPAPO** (Pg.), an Afro-Brazilian idiom referring to the possession of a Mongolian blue spot, considered to be an index of black ancestry. See also GENIPAPO.

**ELIE, ABEL** (1841-1876), a black Haitian poet born in Port-au-Prince. After finishing his studies in his native city, Elie was sent to France (in 1858) to continue his education. After three years, he returned to Haiti and began writing poetry in the periodical *Le Bien Public,* published in Port-au-Prince. He left an unpublished book, *Premiers accords.*

**ÉLITE** (Fr.), in modern Haitian society, the mulatto class, as opposed to blacks who are considered inferior, utterly ignorant, and incapable of progress. The elite or aristocracy comprises only 3 percent of the total population; to this mixed-blood minority belong all the professions, most government and military offices, and the large business enterprises. A cardinal rule in Haiti is that mulattoes do not work with their hands; such work is done exclusively by the blacks or the lower classes.

**ELMINA, EL MINA** (Pg.), a trading post and fortress located at the mouth of the Mina River on the Gold Coast (q.v.) (Ghana). This famous slave trade port, built by the Portuguese in 1481, was called the Key to the Gold Coast and was one of the main sources of black labor for the New World. The Dutch conquered it in 1637 after invading Pernambuco, Brazil; it remained under their control until 1872.

**EMANCIPADO** (Sp.), in colonial Spanish America, a black slave freed by purchase or manumission (q.v.).

**EMANCIPATED BLACK CHILDREN,** in the West Indies, the offspring of a master and his slave concubine, free by customary law. The father was in charge of the child's care until he or she came of age. These mixed-blood children formed a special class of freedmen, always distinguished from the other classes of free blacks. (Hall, *Social Control*, p. 140.)

**EMANCIPATION BILL,** a law passed on August 28, 1833 by the British Parliament, giving restricted freedom to all black slaves; it became effective on August 1, 1834. It stipulated that all slave children under six years of age should be freed immediately; adults spent a six-year period as apprentices (q.v.). The planters were compensated by cash payment.

**EMANCIPATION DAY,** August 1, 1834, the day set by the British Parliament in the Emancipation Bill (q.v.) for freeing all black slaves in the West Indies and in the British Empire. It was viewed with intense anxiety in both Great Britain and the Caribbean. The situation was tense, though restrained, on the part of the government, the planters, and the exultant Africans. The long-awaited day finally came and passed, without any incident to mar the inauguration of a new epoch in British imperial history.

**EMANCIPATORY MOVEMENT,** a modern black struggle for their civil rights. The goals are to end discrimination in political and social life, to improve their standard of living, and to obtain better education for the descendants of slaves in the French Antilles and elsewhere in the Caribbean. The literary expression of this racial awakening is négritude (q.v.).

**EMBAIXADA AFRICANA** (Pg.) (The African Embassy), name of a black carnival club in Bahia, Brazil, which organizes festivities and parades portraying African characters and black themes. Only blacks and mulattoes take part in its activities, which are usually noisy and tumultuous.

**EMBÁKARA** (Afr.), in the Afro-Cuban *santería* (q.v.), an assistant priest in the cult. One of his duties is to untie the sacrificial he-goat and turn it over to the main priest.

**EMBANDA** (Pg.), a high priest of the Afro-Brazilian *macumba* cult (q.v.). See also QUIMBANDA.

**EMBIGADA, UMBIGADA** (Pg.), an Afro-Brazilian belly dance.

**EMBÓ** (Afr.), in the Afro-Cuban folk religion, an elaborate magic ritual centered around a witchcraft bundle; considered by blacks to be a powerful charm that can help or hurt a person.

**EMBRÍKAMO** (Afr.), in Afro-Cuban cults, the black drummer who introduces the solemn procession led by the priests and their attendants that precedes the sacrifice of an animal. The drummer plays continuously, with a commanding sound that reaches a climax when the executioner kills the he-goat on the altar.

**EMPACASSEIRO** (Pg.), in Angola (q.v.), a black aid who helped the Portuguese and Brazilians conquer and dominate indigenous ethnic groups. He facilitated slave-kidnapping and slave trading for over two centuries. (Boxer, *Four Centuries*, p. 31.)

**EMPEGÓ** (Afr.), an assistant priest in the Afro-Cuban *santería* (q.v.) who is in charge of drawing complicated signs and patterns representing magic figures and scenes on the floor of the altar or on the walls of the chapel where the rituals are held. When the purpose of the sacrifice is to increase the stock of fish in the river, the *empegó* draws his magic signs on the bank of an actual stream or even along the Bay of Havana. This ceremonial designer is of African origin. See also VÈVÉ.

**EMPÊTRE,** in colonial Haiti, a shackle used to punish delinquent slaves. It confined the legs in two rings which were closed by either a padlock or hinges. The lower part of the legs was put in these rings, protected by a piece of cloth to prevent abrasions. The chain was light enough to allow the victim to walk very slowly. If the slave was so strong that the rings failed to impede his movement, a weight was added to the chain.

**EMPREITADA** (Pg.), in Brazil, a system of employing former slaves as free agricultural laborers for specific tasks; a wage-labor practice introduced immediately after the abolition of slavery in 1888.

**EMPREITEIRO** (Pg.), in Brazil, a labor contractor who, after the abolition of slavery, made deals with planters whose slaves had deserted them to furnish the necessary gang labor at a flat rate. He picked up workers from the pool of unemployed freedmen wandering in towns and organized itinerant work gangs of about fifty blacks. The *empreiteiro* provided the men with food and lodged them in huts located in the sugar fields. Once a job was done, the contractor and his gang moved on to another plantation.

**ENCOMENDERO DE NEGROS** (Sp.), in early colonial Spanish America, an agent, or factor, employed by slave traders in the ports to handle the sale of black slaves.

**ENDOGUE** (Pg.), an Afro-Brazilian term for sorcerer.

**EN ESTOS TIEMPOS EL NEGRO QUIERE SER BLANCO Y EL MULATO CABALLERO** (Sp.) ("Today the black wants to be white and the mulatto a knight"), an Afro-Spanish aphorism reflecting negative feelings about the social advances of blacks and mulattoes.

**ENGAGÉ** (Fr.), a bondsman, usually a white Frenchman, who, in pre-revolutionary times, repaid his passage to Haiti by working on a plantation for a number of years. During this time, the *engagé* was treated like the black slaves, and at the expiration of the term, usually three years, he was as destitute as when he arrived from his native France.

**ENGAGEMENT** (Fr. Cr.), in the Afro-Haitian religion, a pact between a black man and a spiritual power which binds him to fulfill exacting obligations in return for a fixed reward; always a matter of evil magic. The pledge sometimes includes giving a member of the family to the evil spirit in return for important gains.

**ENGAGEMENT À TEMPS** (Fr.), in the French Antilles, a system of slave indenture for a period of fourteen years. Between 1817 and 1848, the French allowed the government of Senegal to buy slaves for its own use and then "liberated" these blacks by sending them to work as indentured slaves in Guiana and the neighboring islands. (Curtin, *The Atlantic Slave*, p. 250.)

**ENGENHO** (Pg.), in colonial Brazil, a rural settlement which was totally autonomous. It included the sugar factory, the owner's house (with a few rooms for his extended family and servants), a chapel, and rows of huts for the slaves. It also included a warehouse in which the sugar underwent the process of claying, pens for the cattle, carts, heaps of timber, and a small pond through which water ran to the mill.

**ENGENHO D'AGUA** (Pg.) ("a water-wheel"), a primitive sugar mill (q.v.) powered by water, introduced by the Dutch (circa 1630) in Pernambuco, Brazil.

**ENGENHO DE BANGUÉ** (Pg.), in Brazil, a regional term for a sugar cane (q.v.) plantation and for a smaller, older, and more primitive mill than the *engenho d'agua* (q.v.).

**ENGLISH CREOLE,** a descriptive term for an English-based dialect used in the West Indies, West Africa, and Asia. It has long coexisted with standard English, apparently with surprisingly little interlingual influence. It represents English learned incompletely since slavery times, with a strong infusion of various African languages; it has continued traditionally in much the same fashion to the present. As in the past, it is spoken by Afro-Caribbean peasants and laborers who remain unaffected by English education and educational standards. (Cassidy, *Jamaica Talk*, p. 3.)

**ENKANDEMO** (Afr.), in Afro-Cuban cults, the priest in charge of preparing sacred meals served to the gods and the faithful. He offers the flesh of animals sacrificed in rituals to Ecué (q.v.) and other supernatural powers, just as his ancestors in Africa once did.

**ENKOBORÓ** (Afr.), in Afro-Cuban cults, the head-ghost who precedes the priest in the processions, dancing and leaping to frighten off evil spirits.

**ENKOMO** (Afr.), in Afro-Cuban folklore, a small drum of African origin. It is made from a tree trunk which is burned out inside and covered with a parchment. It was one of several drums used as a means of communication in the African forests. In late colonial times, the Spanish authorities felt obliged to forbid the manufacture of *enkomos* and similar drums to forestall outbreaks of black unrest. (Slonimzki, *Music*, p. 304.)

**ENTERO** (Sp.). See ESCLAVO ENTERO.

**ENVOI-MORTS** (Fr. Cr.), an Afro-Haitian magic curse uttered by a black sorcerer in a cemetery with the object of afflicting the consultant's enemies with sickness or death.

**EQUIANO, OLAUDAH** (1746-1801), a black born at Essaku near Benin, Nigeria. At twelve, he was kidnapped and sold to British slavers. Brought to Barbados in 1756, he was taken to Virginia and sold to a British naval officer who gave him the name of Gustavus Vassa and took him to England as a servant. Equiano served with his master in the British navy during the Seven Years' War. At the end of the war, his owner returned him to the West Indies and sold him to a Quaker merchant of Philadelphia who was trading in the Leeward Islands. He soon became assistant to the captain of one of his schooners. Through this captain's support, he was able to earn enough money to buy his freedom in 1766. The following year, he returned to London where he qualified as a barber and worked ashore as a personal servant with service afloat. He traveled widely to the Levant, New England, Nicaragua, and Greenland, and, in 1786, he was appointed commissary of provisions of a Sierra Leone expedition. He became associated with the British antislavery movement and petitioned the queen to support the abolition of the slave trade. He married an Englishwoman. His memoirs, *Interesting Narrative of the Life of Olaudah Equiano, or Gustavus Vassa, the African, Written by Himself* (London, 1789, 2 v.), represent a uniquely detailed account of an African's movement out of slavery. (Curtin, *Africa Remembered*, pp. 60-61.)

**EQUIPACIÓN** (Sp.). See ESQUIFACIÓN.

**ERAM-PATETE** (Afr.), an Afro-Brazilian dish made of rice and *dendé* palm oil (q.v.) with *iere* and *ataré* condiments, eaten at religious ceremonies by Muslim blacks in Bahía.

**ÉRÉ** (Afr.), in Afro-Brazilian cults, the spirit's initial possession of a novice. It precedes the formal and total possession which comes when the initiate becomes a full member of the sect.

**ERIBANGANDO** (Afr.), in Afro-Cuban cults, the purifier of the chapel who dances around the cauldron containing the sacred meal and throws bits of meats in all directions to appease the spirits. Once this is done, the service begins.

**ERIBÓ** (Afr.), a sacred drum decorated with skins, shells, and feathers, a dominant instrument in the Afro-Cuban folk religion. At one point it is carried by the high priest, with the cock that has been sacrificed lying on top. See also SANTERÍA.

**ERVILHA DE ANGOLA** (Pg.), a variety of pea introduced into Brazil during slavery times. See also CONGO PEA.

**ERZILIE.** See EZILIE.

**ESCLAVISTA** (Sp.), a defender of slavery.

**ESCLAVO COARTADO** (Sp.), in Cuba and elsewhere in Spanish America, a black slave who had the right by customary law to purchase his freedom under specific and clearly stated conditions. By accepted practice, a slave was allowed to accumulate funds through his own labor and to pay for his freedom in installments. The price was set in advance.

**ESCLAVO DE GANHO** (Sp.). See NEGRO DE GANHO.

**ESCLAVO DE TALA** (Sp.). See FIELD SLAVE.

**ESCLAVO DOMÉSTICO** (Sp.). See DOMESTIC SLAVE.

**ESCLAVO ENTERO** (Sp.), in colonial Spanish America, a black slave who could not change masters without his master's consent except in certain cases established by law. His status was much lower than that of the *esclavo coartado* (q.v.).

**ESCLAVO JORNALERO** (Sp.), in colonial Spanish America, a black slave who, under orders from his master or with his master's permission, worked for wages on plantations and in towns. After 1849, the owners of these slaves had to report to the government their names, numbers, sex, and earned wages. See also ESCLAVO DE GANHO.

**ESCORTE** (Fr. Cr.), in Afro-Haitian cults, the mutual assistance that the gods give to each other in their efforts to assist human needs.

**ESCURO** (Pg.), in Brazil, a person with light skin and thin facial features, but tight, kinky hair. Also called *moreno* (q.v.).

**ESHU** (Afr.). See EXU.

**ESPINOSA, MANUEL,** a black slave, who on June 24, 1750, led a slave rebellion against the Spaniards in the city of Caracas. The plan was to rise, murder all the whites, and take over control of the town. The rebellion was crushed; Espinosa and all of his followers were executed. (Rout, L.B., *The African Experience of Spanish America*, p. 119.)

**ESQUIFACIÓN,** in colonial Spanish America, the slave's issue of work clothes. According to government regulations, the master had to provide *esquifación* three times a year. The men were given a pair of trousers with large pockets, a shirt, and a wool cap for the cold; the women received blouses, skirts, and petticoats. (Alvarez Nazario, *El elemento negroide*, p. 342.)

**ESQUIFE** (Pg.), a simple litter used for the burial of slaves in colonial Brazil. It was later replaced by the *tumba de arco* (q.v.).

**ESTADO DE SANTO** (Pg.), in Afro-Brazilian cults, the holy condition of an initiate after receiving the gods; a blessing. It is ordinarily induced by fasting, prayer, the pungent odors of certain sacred herbs, and the continued beating of drums.

**ESTATE ATTORNEY.** See ATTORNEY.

**ESTATE SLAVE-COMMUNITY,** in the West Indies and elsewhere, a hierarchical organization based on occupational divisions. The offices of superior rank involved rights of ownership and management, while a large number of subordinate black slaves remained without rights and were socially and morally debased. It included illegal slave courts within the plantation where the highest ranking slave adjudicated and had final authority. On some estates the owner also presided, as sole judge, in a court of his own. Parties dissatisfied with the verdicts of either tribunal had little redress except to run away or take revenge with magic and poison. (M. G. Smith, *The Plural Society*, p. 103.)

**ESTEBAN.** See ESTEBANICO.

**ESTEBANICO,** a black slave, a Moslem African native, a servant of Pánfilo de Narvaez's ill-fated Florida expedition in 1528. He later accompanied A. Nuñez·Cabeza de Vaca in a transcontinental trip from the Texas coast, near Galveston and the mouth of the San Antonio River, to northeastern Sonora, an eight-year expedition which ended in 1536 in Mexico City. Estebanico did not obtain his freedom because when acting as a guide for Friar Marcos de Niza in 1538, he was killed by Zuni Indians in a small village on the upper Rio Grande. (Rout, L.B., *The African Experience in Spanish America*, p. 76.)

**ESTERADO** (Sp.), a fishing screen used across estuaries or within small bay zones on a beach by black residents in the Pacific lowland of Colombia.

**ESUSU, SUSU** (Afr.), a Yoruba (q.v.) system for saving money which is still practiced by blacks in Barbados and Guiana. It consists of a cooperative pooling of earnings by members of a group of laborers so that each member may benefit by obtaining, in turn, and at one time, all the money paid in by the entire group on a given date. Each member contributes the same amount. Both men and women may belong to one or several *esusus*. (Herskovits, *Trinidad Village*, pp. 76-77.)

**ETÉ** (Afr.), an Afro-Brazilian word for pest or plague.

**ETHIOPE RESGATADO, EMPENHADO, SUSTENTADO, CORREGIDO, INSTRUIDO E LIBERADO,** the title of a book published in Lisbon in 1758 by Manoel Ribeiro da Rocha (q.v.), a graduate of Coimbra University. The author advocated the abolition of the slave trade, apparently for the first time in Portugal.

**ETHIOPIAN,** in colonial Afro-Latin America, an African slave.

**ETHIOPIAN BREAKDOWN,** an Afro-Jamaican rollicking, noisy dance or entertainment.

**ETÍOPE CRIOLLO** (Sp.), epithet given to the black Cuban poet Ambrosio Echemendía (q.v.).

**ETUDIANT NOIRE, L'** (Fr.), the name of a famous journal founded in Paris in 1934 by Léopold Senghor, Aimé Césaire (q.v.), and Léon Gontran Damas (q.v.). This periodical became the leading mouthpiece of négritude (q.v.), one of the most innovative literary movements in contemporary literature.

**EUBÁ, EGBÁ** (Afr.), a black dialect spoken in Rio de Janeiro, Brazil.

**É UMA AFRICA!** (Pg.) ("It's an Africa!"), a traditional Luso-Brazilian saying signifying something heroic, a feat, a difficulty hard to overcome. It conveys the image of a land harsh because of its natural conditions, the barbarity of its people, and the number and ferocity of its wild animals. (Rodrigues, *Brazil and Africa*, p. 10.)

**EVERY DAY YOU GOAD DONKEY, ONE DAY HIM WI' KICK YOU** (Eng. Cr.) ("Every day you beat donkey, some day he will kick you"), an Afro-Jamaican saying. (Beckwith, *Jamaica Proverbs*, p. 45.)

**EVERY JOHN-CROW T'INK HIM PICKNEY WHITE** (Eng. Cr.) ("Every John-crow—i.e., carrion crow—thinks his own child is white"), an Afro-Jamaican saying. (Beckwith, *Jamaica Proverbs*, p. 46.)

**EWE.** 1. A black people of Ghana, Togo, and the border regions of Dahomey (q.v.). 2. A Kwa language of the Ewe people.

**EXASPERATION ZONE.** See ZONE OF EXASPERATION.

**EXPEDITION** (Fr. Cr.), in Afro-Haitian sorcery, black magic.

**EXU, ESHU** (Afr.), in Afro-Brazilian cults, a mischievous spirit dressed in red and black who is the incarnation of evil. His day of worship is Monday.

**EYE-WATER,** an Afro-Jamaican word for tears.

**EZILIE** (Afr.), in the Afro-Haitian religion, a female spirit envisaged as a pale, trembling woman, sometimes living in the water. A fabulously wealthy lady, she wears silk clothes of brilliant colors and golden necklaces and rings. Her favorite foods are white chicken, fine cakes, and desserts, and she drinks fine, nonalcoholic liqueurs. She is identified with Mater Dolorosa. (Herskovits, *Life in a Haitian*, p. 316.)

**EZILIE DOBA, EZILIE DAROMAIN,** (Afr.), in the Afro-Haitian religion, a goddess of Dahomean origin who symbolizes purity. She is sometimes identified with the Virgin Mary. Her favorite color is white, and services to her include a ritual of sweeping and sprinking the floor of the temple and perfuming the air. Food offerings to her include corn meal and eggs. Mystic marriages are performed with her, and her "horses" or servants are obligated to refrain from sexual intercourse on certain days which belong to her. There are a number of Ezilies, all of whom are regarded as members of the same family or, in certain cult centers, as different manifestations of the same deity. (Courlander, *The Drum*, p. 319.)

**EZILIE FRÉDA** (Afr.), in the Afro-Haitian religion, a goddess who is a member of the Ezilie (q.v.) family. She is the giver of wealth.

**EZILIE JEROUDE** (Afr.), an Afro-Haitian goddess, erratic and unpredictable; a member of the Ezilie (q.v.) family.

**EZILIE WÉDO** (Afr.), an Afro-Haitian deity, a sister or daughter of Ezilie Doba (q.v.).

# f

F (Pg. *fugão*), the letter *F*, standing for fugitive; a mark branded on a captured runaway slave during slavery times in Brazil. This punishment, first ordered by the Portuguese Crown in March 1741, was part of a campaign to stop the increasing desertion of slaves. Each town council kept a branding iron for this purpose. It was alleged that many slaves were proud of their branded *F*, regarding it as a badge of honor rather than of infamy. (Boxer, *The Golden Age*, p. 172.)

FABULÉ, FRANCISQUE, a black slave brought by the Dutch and sold in Guadeloupe before 1656. Later he became a leader of Maroon (q.v.) gangs who fought for several years against the white planters. Eventually, he commanded 300 or 400 runaway slaves, organizing a successful guerrilla war. On March 2, 1665. French authorities signed a peace agreement with Fabulé, giving him land, freedom, and general amnesty. (Hall, *Social Control*, p. 64.)

FAIR MAID, in Afro-Jamaican folklore, a supernatural being who lives in deep holes in the rivers and combs her black hair at midday on the river banks. A goddess of the waters, she disappears the moment she is espied.

FAITHFUL CONCUBINAGE, in rural Jamaica, a stable and lasting union of a man and a woman without any formal or legal sanction. The woman usually has a greater share in the economic activity of the couple. This kind of patriarchal family organization is very common among Jamaican blacks, especially in the countryside.

FALA BONITO (Pg.) ("He talks pretty"), in modern Brazil, a black who beguiles people with his elegant speech with the aim of appearing white.

FALCONBRIDGE, ALEXANDER (d. 1792), an English surgeon forced by poverty to practice his profession on board slave ships. He made several voyages to Bonny, Old and New Calabar, and Angola (q.v.) on the coast of Africa from which he traveled with slave cargoes to the West Indies. He forcefully depicted the horrors he was compelled to witness in a book entitled *An Account of the Slave Trade on the Coast of Africa* (London, 1788). It soon became a classic narrative, widely used by abolitionists in antislavery campaigns.

**FALUCHO,** a nickname for a black soldier of the Regiment of the Rio de la Plata, a native of Buenos Aires, stationed in the port of Callao, near Lima. On February 7, 1824, after a mutiny, Royalist troops took the rebel barracks and raised the Spanish flag. The Argentine regiment was ordered to mount guard and salute the flag against which it had so often fought. The black freedman broke his musket against the flag-staff and was shot, shouting "Viva Buenos Aires!" (Pilling, W., *The Emancipation of South America*, pp. 447-448.)

**FAMBÁ** (Afr.), in the Afro-Cuban dialect, a chapel; also a brothel.

**FANG** (Afr.). See PAHOUIN.

**FANDANGO,** an Afro-Spanish dance popular to all Latin Americans, which originated in colonial times. It is a dance with much shaking of the hips to a sensual rhythm. It was rejected as immoral by a bishop in Puerto Rico as early as 1691. In Chile it was popular in the 18th century and there also it was condemned by the ecclesiastical authorities as "an infamous dance cultivated in the low class, which leads to excesses of bestiality." (Roberts, *Black Music of Two Worlds*, pp. 38, 44, 78.)

**FANGA** (Afr.), in Jamaica, a magic powder used by a black *obeah* man (q.v.) as a charm to do either good or evil, according to circumstances.

**FA NODOE** (Eng. Cr.) ("Do what is necessary"), a black Surinamese expression denoting the moral obligation to participate in ethnic religious and recreational meetings.

**FANON, FRANTZ** (1925-1961), a political theorist, anti-racist, revolutionary, physician and writer born in Martinique, French West Indies. He volunteered for the French army during W.W. II and then after his service went to France to study medicine and psychiatry from 1945 to 1950. In 1953 he was appointed Head of the Psychiatry Department of a government hospital in Algeria. As a Marxist, he deeply identified with Algeria's revolutionary struggle for independence. Fanon stressed the need to reject

Europe's culture and to accomplish the revolution alone. In 1960 he served as Ambassador to Ghana for the Algerian Provisional Government. After treatment in the Soviet Union for leukemia, he went to the United States to seek further treatment but died there in 1961. His works include *Black Skin, White Masks* (1952) and *The Wretched of the Earth* (1961).

**FANTA** (Afr.), in colonial Brazil, the supper served to slaves at 4:00 P.M. in the fields while working during the *zafra* (q.v.).

**FANTI-ASHANTI** (Afr.), a term applied by scholars to a West African culture surviving in varying degrees among Bush Negroes (q.v.) of Guiana and black communities of the Caribbean region. Especially on the religious level, it has been found that myalism (q.v.), an old Fanti-Ashanti tradition, has remained alive, although it has been reinterpreted in Christian terms.

**FANTÔME** (Fr. Cr.), in the Afro-Haitian folk religion, a ghost.

**FARINE GUINÉE** (Fr. Cr.), in Afro-Haitian folk religion, a magic powder used by black sorcerers to paint mysterious figures and designs on the floor or walls of chapels. See also VÈVÉ.

**FAROFA, FAROFIA** (Pg.), an Afro-Brazilian dish made of manioc cooked to form a mush, with butter or other fat added.

**FATHER,** a rank and title among black revivalist sects in the Caribbean.

**FATTEN-BARROW** (Eng. Cr.), in the West Indies, certain wild plants which blacks use to fatten pigs, rabbits, and cattle. Also called Jack o' woods.

**FAUBERT, PIERRE** (1806-1868), a black Haitian poet born in Cayes. Faubert, the son of a general of the Independence, was educated in Port-au-Prince and later in Paris. From 1837 to 1842, he was director of the Lycée Nationale; he then entered the diplomatic service. He died in Vances near Paris. His works include *Ogé ou le préjugé de couleur*, (a drama, 1842) and *Les poèmes fugitives* (Paris, 1856).

**FAVELA** (Pg.), in Brazil, an urban shanty town without public services, often insecure from violence. The poverty of many of the squatters is extreme. There is a high incidence of unemployment or low pay, lack of medical facilities, and lack of education for the children, especially in Rio de Janeiro.

**FAZENDA** (Pg.), in Brazil, any large estate. It was a self-sufficient sugar estate (q.v.) community, owned and managed by a recognized lord and his patriarchal family; the labor force consisted mainly of a vast black slave population. The *fazenda* provided the major sociocultural pattern for colonial Brazil.

**FAZENDEIRO** (Pg.), in colonial Brazil, the owner of a *fazenda* (q.v.) and the acknowledged master of his extended family, the freedmen, and the black slaves working on his land. He was a powerful local chief and holder of public office, very often spending much time in neighboring towns and cities. After the abolition of slavery in 1888, the *fazendeiro* lost power, prestige, and social influence.

**FAZENDEIRO CREOLE,** a rudimentary Afro-Brazilian dialect spoken in São Paulo by Brazilians of mixed Italian and black ancestry.

**FAZER SALA** (Pg.), the morning and evening prayer, recited daily by Afro-Brazilian Moslems.

**FAZER SANTO** (Pg.), in the Afro-Brazilian *candomblé* (q.v.), the complete rite of initiation into the service of the gods. It comprises an initial offering to Exu (q.v.), total immersion in *azeite de dendé* (q.v.) or honey, and special invocations by the priest of the sect.

**FÉ DE ENTRADA** (Sp.), in colonial Spanish America, the official certification that a slave was legally imported and the proper duties paid.

**FEIJÃO DE CÔCO** (Pg.), an Afro-Brazilian dish made of beans, coconut, spices, and various fats.

**FEIJÃO FRADINHO** (Pg.), an Afro-Brazilian delicacy made of beans, spices, and fat, and placed on a stone with a dressing of onion and salt.

**FEIJOADA** (Pg.), a popular Afro-Brazilian stew made of beans and rice plus some meat, preferably fatty meats such as sausage or pork, and liberally sprinkled with manioc flour. It is considered the Brazilian national dish.

**FEITA** (Pg.) ("made"), the female initiate of one of the Afro-Brazilian fetish cults after she has undergone all the ceremonial preparation and is ready to become a medium through which the gods express themselves. The ritual includes the receiving of a sacred name, the immersion of her head in the blood of sacrificed animals, and a solemn feast of consecration. The blacks consider her the "horse of the saint."

**FEITICEIRO** (Pg.), in Brazil, a black medicine man who works black magic for a price. The *feiticeiro* has great prestige and influence among the masses, and is always consulted in afflictions and troubles. Some *feiticeiros* are professionals who act as advisers, consultants, and priests of Afro-Brazilian fetish cults. See also BABÁ, HOUNGAN.

**FEITIÇO** (Pg.), in Brazil, any object of devotion which through proper ritual procedure supposedly has been endowed with mysterious wonder-working or spiritual powers. Fetishes are represented by statues of saints, symbolizing a polytheistic system of belief and a magic of African influence. *Feitiços*, especially African *feitiços*, penetrate the full fabric of the Brazilian masses.

**FEITOR** (Pg.). 1. In Portuguese Africa, a royal manager of the exchequer in charge of collecting tributes from the black chiefs, of purchasing goods for the Crown, and, in general, of attending any commercial transaction; also responsible for exacting the sales tax on slaves. 2. Later, in colonial Brazil, an intermediary between the planters and the exporters and also between planters and bankers. The planter-*feitor*-banker relationship was based on a triangle of debts in which slavery played an important role. 3. A foreman who supervised slave laborers on a plantation; he moved around, whip in hand, checking the work of the gang members. The *feitor* was in charge of discipline and had to impose respect and authority.

**FEITORIA** (Pg.), in colonial West Africa, a trading post used by the Portuguese and Brazilians to buy slaves and raw materials in exchange for sugar, rum, and European goods.

**FELONY ACT,** an act of the British Parliament passed in 1811 declaring that any subject of His Majesty who participated in the slave trade was guilty of a felony. (Ragatz, *The Fall*, p. 386.)

**FELUPO** (Afr.), in Brazil, a black slave who was a member of the Felupo ethnic group in West Africa.

**FENNAY** (Afr.), in the Afro-Jamaican dialect, a word for suffering, swoon.

**FER COUPE FER** (Fr. Cr.) ("Iron cuts iron"), an Afro-French aphorism meaning that even the strongest person is not invincible.

**FERMAGE** (Fr. Cr.), in colonial Saint Domingue (Haiti), a system of seizing abandoned plantations and renting them. Half of the profits from such a property went to the state, while the remainder was equally divided between workers and proprietors. Other features of the system included regulation of working hours, permission for a worker to quit a plantation, and advice to the planter that he should labor with his slaves. Its origin is controversial, but its practice started early, around 1795. (James, *The Black Jacobins*, p. 130.)

**FERMIER** (Fr. Cr.) ("tenant"), in rural Haiti, a black sharecropper who holds a written legal contract as a tenant and pays a fee to the landlord. The contract must be signed before a civil official and must extend through the harvesting of one crop. Even then, tenants could not abandon their contracts except after a three-month notice, with a formal declaration to the local official. (Leyburn, *The Haitian People*, p. 51.)

**FERNANDES VIEIRA, JOÃO,** a Brazilian mulatto hero, the son of a white man and a mulatto woman. In colonial history, he is considered the most outstanding leader in the war against the Dutch in 1645. His forces, consisting of black slaves, mulattoes, and Amerindians, helped to defeat the invaders.

**FERREIRA, JOÃO,** a Brazilian prophet of Sebastianismo (q.v.) who, around 1870, led a group of fanatic black slaves from several *fazendas* (q.v.) to the interior of the country where an enchanted kingdom was supposed to appear. Encouraged by their leader, the black masses attacked towns and plantations and often practiced orgiastic, bloody rites in the wilderness.

**FERREIRA DE MENEZES, JOSÉ** (b. 1845), a black abolitionist in Brazil. Ferreira de Menezes studied law and the social sciences. His legal practice gave him an opportunity to be active in speaking, writing, journalism, and politics. He was also an outstanding poet, novelist, and essayist.

**FERY, ALIBÉE** (1818-1896), a black Haitian writer and army general. He was apparently the first short-story writer to be inspired by peasant black folklore. He followed the classic tradition, and his tales are full of ghosts, legends and African customs. His main work is *Essais littéraires* (4 v.; Port-au-Prince, 1876).

**FEVER BUSH,** among Jamaican blacks, a generic term for several weeds and seeds used to treat fevers.

**FIELD SLAVE, FIELD NEGRO, PRAEDIAL SLAVE** in the colonial West Indies, an unskilled black slave working on a sugar plantation, usually in gangs under the discipline of the whip. As a beast of burden, he worked long hours on all the heavy, exhausting tasks of the estate community. It was universally agreed that of all the slaves he had the most laborious work. Compared to most of the other slaves, he also lived on more meager allowances and had fewer opportunities to earn a cash income. The field slave suffered from all the diseases that afflicted the slave population, including scurvy, dysentery, leprosy, yaws (q.v.), smallpox, tetanus, worms, dropsy, venereal diseases, a variety of fevers, and dirt-eating (q.v.). (The last-named appears to have been a result of malnutrition.) As a group, they were more unhealthy than domestic slaves (q.v.). At the end of the eighteenth century, field slaves made up the great majority of the slave population in the West Indies and elsewhere in Afro-Latin America. (Brathwaite, *The Development*, pp. 152-153.)

**FIGA** (Pg.), an Afro-Brazilian charm made from wood, ebony, coral, gold, silver, or jade in the form of a closed fist with the thumb inserted between the index and the middle finger. Blacks wear this amulet to protect themselves from the "evil eye."

**FILÃO** (Pg.), a tree whose foliage resembles a willow, native to Madagascar, and brought to the Antilles during slavery times. Today, as a decoration it lends grace to Afro-Antilles cemeteries.

**FILARIA** (Pg.), nematode worms *(Nematoda)*, including pinworms, trichina, and Guinea worms (q.v.) brought by slaves into Brazil from West Africa.

**FILHA DE CRIAÇÃO** (Pg.) ("a foster daughter"), in Brazil, an adopted daughter, usually of African descent, who is raised to be a servant to the white family. She is loved, rewarded, and treated as an "equal" by relatives and friends as long as she is submissive, respectful, conscious of her place, hard working, and servile.

**FILHA DE SANTO** (Pg.), in Afro-Brazilian cults, a young black priestess who after long preparation has been consecrated a servant of the gods and an intermediary of the deity to whom she has been dedicated. Throughout her life, the *filha de santo* rigorously observes fasts, as well as drink and sex taboos; on days of obligation (Fridays especially) she must wear a ceremonial costume. Among some West African tribes, the *filhas de santo*, called *kosi*, were destined to sacred prostitution. See also FILHO DE SANTO.

**FILHO DE CRIAÇÃO** (Pg.), in Brazil, a foster black or mulatto child adopted by a white family; usually an illegitimate offspring of a kinsman. This child is raised partly as a servant and partly as a member of the family.

**FILHO DE SANTO** (Pg.), in Afro-Brazilian cults, a black servant of the gods. Before consecration he must go through a rigorous initiation ritual. He is assigned to a temple where he conducts services and acts as spiritual and social adviser to members of the sect. He enjoys great prestige among his followers. See also FILHA DE SANTO.

**FILHOS DE AFRICA** (Pg.) ("The sons of Africa"), name of a black club in Bahia, Brazil. In the carnival parade, its members portray colorful African rituals, followed by a large crowd of blacks and mulattoes singing, dancing, and mimicking.

**FILLE DE COULEUR** (Fr. Cr.), in colonial Saint Domingue (Haiti), a black or mulatto female, often the preferred sexual partner of a white colonist. She was thought to be more amorous and fertile than white women. A *fille de couleur* frequently married newly arrived white settlers. In 1865, the Code Noir (q.v.) legalized the marriage of a *fille de couleur* and a Frenchman. Also called *mulâtresse libre*.

**FIMBO** (Afr.), an Afro-Brazilian word for a light javelin, a slender hardwood spear usually tipped with iron and imported from West Africa by black slaves.

**FINE-PLAY NIGHT,** among Afro-Jamaicans, any of the nights, from the second to the eighth, of a funeral wake observance; in contrast to the first night (burial) and the ninth night (games and dancing).

**FIOFÍO** (Afr.), among Haitian blacks, a magic insect which is thought to enter the body when a quarrel between intimates has not been followed by sincere reconciliation.

**FIRE DOWN BELOW,** a black shanty-song in the West Indies.

**FIRST GANG,** in the West Indies, the first of three gangs of slaves working on a plantation, consisting of the most healthy and able-bodied men and women. At crop time, they cut ground and carried the cane to the mill. At other seasons, they cleared, weeded, and hoed the fields and planted the cane. This crew performed the most exhausting tasks on the estate. See also SECOND GANG; THIRD GANG.

**FIRST NIGHT,** in the West Indies, the night after death when the wake takes place. This black ritual is of African origin.

**FIXED MELANCHOLY,** in the West Indies, a state of deep depression experienced by many African slaves which usually ended in suicide. The newly arrived blacks lost their desire to live, stopped eating and drinking, and died. Mass and individual drownings were also common. Some slaves killed themselves by suffocation with their own tongues or by hanging. This mental disease produced a high suicide rate among certain ethnic groups which was attributed to their belief in the transmigration of souls. They were convinced that when they died, they would return to Africa and to their family and friends.

**FLENKEE,** an Afro-Jamaican revivalist cult.

**FLEURY BATTIER, ALCIBIADE** (1841-1883), a prolific black Haitian poet. Fleury Battier wrote patriotic poetry glorifying Haiti's national heroes, including the founders of the Haitian republic such as Dessalines (q.v.), Pétion (q.v.), and Toussaint L'Ouverture (q.v.). Among his works are *La Journée d'adieux* (Port-au-Prince, 1869); *Lumena ou le Génie de la liberté* (Port-au-Prince, 1869); *Le Génie de la patrie* (Port-au-Prince, 1877); *Sous les bambous* (Paris, 1881); and *Par mornes et par savanes; rimes glanées* (Port-au-Prince, s.d.). (Jahn, *Neo-African Literature*, p. 144.)

**FLIBUSTIER** (Fr. Cr.), in the colonial French Antilles, a white or mixed-blood freebooter (q.v.) who plundered coastal towns and plantations on the islands.

**FLIIK** (Eng. Cr.), in the West Indies, a black albino.

**FLOGGING,** in colonial Afro-Latin America, the most common form of slave punishment. In some regions, as in Cuba, it was legally limited to twenty-five lashes, but it was often given on a brutal installment of nine consecutive nights. Some estates had a special flogging place. (Knight, *Slave Society*, p. 76.) See also NOVENARIO; TUMBADERO.

**FLORES, ANTONIO,** a Cuban mulatto hero whose service was typical of the life of a black militiaman. Volunteering as a private in 1708, he served in the ranks for nine years before being promoted to sergeant. After three decades, he finally reached the senior grade of company captain. During this time, he served on guard duty at outlying forts of the island, fought against British and French pirates, and finally went on an expedition to east Florida where he was taken prisoner and sent to France, not returning to Cuba for eighteen months. He then fought in an expedition against the British colonies in which he served with distinction. (Klein, *Slavery*, p. 215.)

**FOE MEMRE WIE AFO** (D.) ("In Memory of the Fathers"), a booklet published in Paramaribo, Surinam, in 1940 by a black school teacher,

J.A.C. Koenders, for the purpose of regulating the spelling of black English, which he called Surinaamsch. The author's aim was to provide a standard spelling of names for the descendants of black slaves imported into Surinam. (Lier, *Frontier Society*, p. 282.)

**FOETE** (Sp.) a whip used to flog slaves on Spanish American sugar estates (q.v.).

**FOLLOW FASHION JUBA NEBER BWOIL GOOD SOUP** (Eng. Cr.) ("Follow the fashion of Juba, never boil good soup"), an Afro-Jamaican aphorism. (Beckwith, *Jamaica Proverbs*, p. 49.) See also JUBA.

**FON** (Afr.). 1. An old and well-established black ethnic group of lower Dahomey (q.v.), West Africa, distinguished by its intellectual, artistic, and political achievements. 2. A black slave culture that has survived in varying degrees throughout Afro-Latin America. Two mythological features are regarded as fundamental elements of Fon colonial culture: first, a dual system of dividing the gods according to age, whereby the role of the elder ones, who are regarded as mischievous spirits, is to prepare the way for the descent of the younger gods; and second, a category of young female goddesses or "little girls," over and above the first group, who descend only on special occasions when they induce trances of a childlike character. (Bastide, *African Civilizations*, pp. 135-36.)

**FONSECA DA SILVA, VALENTIM** (1750-1813), a brilliant Brazilian mulatto artist, popularly known as Maestro Valentim. Fonseca da Silva was born in Minas Gerais and was educated in Rio de Janeiro where he developed his artistic talents. He was a master craftsman, specializing in gold and silver work. He devoted special attention to the making of sacred vessels, candlesticks, tabernacles, cruets, and other religious articles. He also enriched the churches and parks of Rio with statues, carved benches, and fountains. Maestro Valentim inspired a whole school of sculptors and woodworkers. (Ramos, *The Negro*, p. 134.)

**FONTES, HERMES** (1890-1930), a Brazilian mulatto poet who was a leader of the modernist movement in poetry in Brazil. His verses are characterized by nostalgic feelings and the quiet evocation of a world of silence, purity and mystery. Among his numerous works are *A Fonte de matta . . . 1830-1930* (Rio de Janeiro, 1930); *Poesias Escolhidas* (Rio de Janeiro, 1944); *Apoteosis*; *Ciclo de Perfeição*; *Desperatar*; *Epopéia da Vida*; *A Lâmpara Veluda*; and *Microcosmo, Elogio dos Insectos e das flores*. (Jahn, *Bibliography*, p. 201.)

**FORCED CROP,** in colonial Jamaica, a sugar cane (q.v.) crop for which land and slave laborers were used to maximum capacity. The blacks were driven by force, from morning until night, to produce the largest possible yield.

**FORCE VITALE** (Fr.) ("vital force"), a philosophical concept, supposedly Afro-Haitian, that stresses a deep faith in the transcendental values of a person, especially a person of African descent. It proclaims the indomitable spirit of the Negroid race and suggests that, despite the chains in which the blacks must live, their true self belongs to a superior being and will someday be recognized by the society at large. *Force vitale* is seen as a universal and supreme value.

**FORMATURA** (Pg.), in Brazil, a slave roll call on a plantation at dawn and at nightfall.

**FORMIGUEIRO** (Pg.), on a Brazilian plantation, a trained black slave whose job was to seek out spots where red earth had been laid bare by ants in order to eradicate the ants' nests. He did this by building smouldering fires at the mouths of the tunnels and blowing smoke through them.

**FORMULIEREN VAN CARGAZOENEN** (D.), a list of the cargo brought from Africa to Brazil by Dutch merchants early in the seventeenth century. The law required a detailed statement of the freight. Slaves' listings included name, sex, age, and price. (Goslinga, *The Dutch*, p. 348.)

**FORT.** See CASTLES.

**FORTUNA,** a black slave who, in June 1675, dutifully warned her master, Captain Giles Hall, a planter of Bridgetown, Barbados, of a slave uprising organized by Coromantee (q.v.) blacks from the Gold Coast (q.v.). All the leaders of the plot were captured and executed.

**FOUCHÉ, FRANK** (b. 1915), a black poet born in Saint Marc, Haiti. Fouché was educated in his native town and in Port-au-Prince where he received a law degree. His main work is *Message* (Port-au-Prince, 1946).

**FOULA** (Fr. Cr.), in Afro-Haitian cults, the sacred spraying of brandy spiced with pepper; done by a priest.

**FOUR-EYED,** in Jamaica, a black member of myal (q.v.) cults, supposedly able to see spirits and to communicate with them. See also MYAL MAN.

**FOURMI PAS JAM' MOURI EN BAS BARRIQUE SUC'** (Fr. Cr.) ("The ant never dies under a barrel of sugar"), an Afro-Haitian aphorism. (Courlander, *The Drum*, p. 337.)

**FOWL NYAM DONE, WINE HIM MOUT' A GRUND** (Eng. Cr.) ("When a fowl is through eating, it wipes its mouth on the ground"), an Afro-Jamaican aphorism implying ingratitude for hospitality. (Beckwith, *Jamaica Proverbs*, p. 50.)

**FOX, GEORGE** (1624-1691), the English founder of the Society of Friends. Fox turned from organized religion to a direct, personal relationship with God through the "inward light" of Christ. He traveled to North America and the West Indies in 1671-1672. In Barbados, he exhorted converts to treat their slaves well, to give them religious instruction, and to grant them freedom after some years of service. His writings include his noted *Journal* (London, 1694).

**FRANCISCO, EL INGENIO O LAS DELICIAS DEL CAMPO** (Sp.) ("Francisco: The Plantation or the Delights of Country Life"), an anti-slavery novel by the Cuban writer Anselmo Suárez y Romero (q.v.), written in 1838 and published in New York in 1880. It depicts the horrible plight of black slaves on the island's plantations. Suárez considers slavery an evil and tries to show the repugnant aspects of the institution and to arouse indignation in the reader.

**FRANÇOIS, JEAN,** a black slave who was one of the leaders of the rebellion of Haitian slaves in 1791.

**FRAQUIA** (Pg.), a sacred grove highly revered by the faithful in some Afro-Brazilian cults; it is a place of worship.

**FRECKLE-NATURE** (Eng. Cr.), a Jamaican English term for a black albino.

**FREEBOOTER,** in colonial Jamaica, a runaway black slave who was a member of a predatory gang which plundered plantations and towns.

**FREEBORN,** in the colonial West Indies, a black or mulatto who was born free.

**FREE COLORED,** in colonial Jamaica, a freeborn mulatto. He usually could not vote in either local or Assembly elections, and he was excluded from holding public office. He had to bear arms in the militia, but he could not serve in the cavalry and could not rise above the rank of sergeant.

**FREE COLORED BALL,** in Jamaica, an elaborate, formal dance to which only blacks are admitted.

**FREE COLORED MAN,** a legal term used in Jamaica (circa 1820) to refer to a large number of mixed-blood individuals who enjoyed basic civil rights, including the right to own slaves and land, although mainly by inheritance from their white progenitors. A free mulatto man who had been educated and trained at his father's expense was allowed to act as a lawyer, account-ant, and even medical doctor. The harsh attitude of free mulatto men toward their black slaves is noted by all available sources. (M. G. Smith, *The Plural Society*, p. 131.)

**FREE COLORED WOMAN,** in Jamaica (circa 1820), a black or mulatto female born free from slavery. Though her racial and social status was inferior, she enjoyed greater opportunities, preferences and even "privi-leges" than most white women. Her behavior, goals, and attitudes were similar to those of the white population, but her social mobility was often restricted by traditional limitations on occupation. A free black or mulatto woman's aspiration was often to form a concubinage relationship with a white man, hence avoiding marriage to a free black or mulatto man.

**FREED BLACK,** in the colonial British West Indies, a black slave freed through purchase or by manumission (q.v.). In both cases, the former slave surrendered all his customary rights to allowances of food, clothing, housing, medical attention, and other benefits from his master. He ceased to be a member of the estate community, becoming an isolated individual with no rights to land. He then faced the grim task of earning his livelihood in a closed society which had little place for free labor.

**FREEDMAN,** in the British West Indies, a black or mulatto slave set free from slavery through purchase or manumission (q.v.).

**FREEHOLDER,** in the colonial West Indies, a white property holder with ten or more acres who was not a servant. He could vote and be elected as-semblyman, vestryman, and juror. (Dunn, *Sugar and Slaves*, p. 92.)

**FREEMAN,** in Barbados and elsewhere in the West Indies (circa 1690), a white landowner with less than ten acres who was not a servant. He could neither vote nor be elected to any public office.

**FREE-PAPER.** 1. In colonial Jamaica, a personal document of manumis-sion (q.v.) or emancipation from slavery. 2. A slave's pass or ticket allowing him to be away from his plantation for a limited time. See also BAPTIST TICKET.

**FREE-PAPER BURN,** in colonial Jamaica, an overdue slave's pass or ticket; once the holiday or leave was over, the holder had to be back on the estate.

**FREE-SOIL,** in the British West Indies, an area in which slavery was prohibited, usually during the period immediately after abolition (1833).

**FREE VILLAGE SYSTEM,** in Jamaica and Trinidad, a post-emancipation practice of establishing small independent settlements of former slaves under the leadership of a Baptist or other missionary. The idea, originating with William Knibb (q.v.), was to people large areas of underdeveloped lands in the mountains, away from the plantation estates, where the freed slaves could grow their own food. The acquisition of a small plot of land on which to live in independence became the chief desire of the West Indian black and has remained so ever since. (Simey, *Welfare and Planning*, p. 56.)

**FREE WARD,** in Jamaica (circa 1820), a junior kinsman of a black slave, loosely protected and cared for by his master until maturity. A free ward could marry in church and inherit property from his guardian, and was not subject to conveyancing.

**FREI SIMÃO,** a legendary character in Brazilian literature sometimes represented as an old African sorcerer, who might at first glance seem to be an Abyssinian priest. He is shrewd and intelligent. Frei Simão does not hesitate to shed blood or to permit the sacrifices required by his cult. Because of his greed for power, he hates all whites.

**FREKE** (Eng. Cr.), an Afro-Jamaican dish made of coconut milk mixed with oil and spices.

**FRENCH-AMERICAN NEGRO,** a descendant of African slaves brought to the French Antilles plantations as a laborer. His degree of physical and cultural blackness, as well as his political influence, varies a great deal from country to country. In Haiti, 90 percent of the total population is full-blooded black, and the remaining 10 percent, classified as mulattoes, is made up of people of mixed black and European, especially French, descent. The black practice subsistence agriculture, speak French Creole (q.v.), and are illiterate; the mulattoes, well educated and deeply identified with French language, tradition, and values, constitute the aristocracy and the dominant power. In Guadeloupe and Martinique, this extreme racial and cultural gap is less pronounced. (Olien, *Latin Americans*, p. 121.)

**FRENCH CREOLE,** a French-based dialect spoken in Haiti and elsewhere, informally by everyone and exclusively by black peasants. It was already well developed when the mass of African slaves arrived in the colony. As with any dialect, French Creole has its own patterns of sounds, grammatical conventions, and a vocabulary adequate for the cultural demands of its native users, although there is not yet a standard orthography. It has helped keep the peasant masses isolated since slavery times. It has long coexisted with standard French, apparently with little interlingual influence. Today there are about four French Creole dialects in the Caribbean (all mutually intelligible): Haiti, French Guiana, Louisiana, and Lesser Antilles. (Hymes, *Pidginization*, p. 17.)

**FRENCH SET-GIRLS,** in colonial Jamaica, troupes of young black women who celebrated Christmas in the French Creole (q.v.) fashion. There were three groups, the "Royalists," "Mabiales," and "Americans." See also SET GIRLS.

**FRENCH SORREL,** in Jamaica, an early and once common name for a small ericaceous tree *(Hibiscus sabdariffa)* with white flowers and sour, evergreen leaves; used by black slaves to make "sorrel" (q.v.), a popular Christmas drink. Also called African mallow.

**FRENCH WOMAN.** See OBEAH WOMAN.

**FRENTE NEGRA BRASILEIRA** (Pg.) ("Brazilian Negro Front"), a national movement founded in São Paulo in September 1931 in order to unify all blacks throughout Brazil. The first board of directors included leading mulattoes and blacks from all walks of life. Among other goals, it envisaged a social movement promoting the moral, intellectual, physical, and professional elevation of the Negroid race.

**FRESH-CUT,** in the West Indies, a generic term for herbs used by blacks in folk medicine.

**FRÊTE CACHE** (Fr. Cr.), in Afro-Haitian cults, the cracking of the whip by the priest to wake up the sleeping spirits.

**FRÊVO** (Pg.), an Afro-Brazilian march-polka characterized by insistent, unsyncopated rhythms and strident, noisy instruments. Originally soft, Christmas music, once it was assimilated by black slaves it acquired African characteristics. (Slonimzki, *Music*, p. 116.)

**FREYRE, GILBERTO DE MELLO** (b. 1900), a Brazilian anthropologist, sociologist, historian and journalist, born in Recife, Pernambuco, Freyre was educated in Recife and the United States at Baylor and Columbia Universities. As a scholar he emphasizes the African influence in Brazilian ideas and in the making of the country. He has studied the structure and development of the traditional plantation family, rural slavery, and the status of women. One of his more recent and most controversial theories is that of *lusotropicalismo* (q.v.). Among his most important works are: *Casa grande e senzala* (1933), translated into English as *The Masters and the Slaves* (1946); *Sobrados e mocambos* (1936), translated into English as *The Mansions and the Shanties* (1963); *The Portuguese and the Tropics*, Lisbon (1961); *Vida social no Brasil nos meados do seculo XIX* (1964) in translation *Social Life in Brazil in the Middle of the Nineteenth Century* (1922) originally written in English.

**FRIEN' KILL FRIEN', DRITTY WATER OUT FIRE** (Eng. Cr.) ("Friend kills friend, dirty water puts out fire"), an Afro-Jamaican aphorism implying that a man has been betrayed by his friend. (Beckwith, *Jamaica Proverbs*, p. 51.)

**FRIJOL, EL,** a Cuban settlement organized by runaway slaves, situated in the Sierra del Cristal in the mountains of Oriente.

**FROMAGER** (Fr. Cr.), in the French Antilles, a tall, majestic tropical tree brought from Africa during slavery times. Under its sacred shade, the black sorcerers perform witchcraft rituals.

**FRUTA-PÃO** (Pg.), in Brazil, the breadfruit tree (q.v.) *(Artocarpus incisa)* of the Malvacea family, a standard food for slaves in colonial times.

**FUA** (Bant.), in the Afro-Antilles, a small drum very popular among blacks.

**FUBÁ** (Afr.), an Afro-Brazilian term for corn or rice flour.

**FUFU** (Twi), an Afro-Jamaican dish made of eddoes, okra (q.v.), mashed plantain (q.v.) with crabs, and pungent cayenne pepper; its ingredients vary greatly. It is well known along the West African coast from Senegambia (q.v.) to the Congo (q.v.) region.

**FUGU** (Afr.), an Afro-Jamaican starch food eaten boiled and pounded or further prepared and cooked. Today it is less popular than previously, but the food is still known throughout the island. (Cassidy, *Dictionary*, p. 191.)

**FULAH, FULANI** (Afr.), originally a non-Negroid ethnic group, exclusively pastoral, which settled in West Africa. In the fourteenth century, these pagan herders were associated with the native people of the lower Senegal River; they later established themselves upstream along the Niger

River. They converted to Islam. Many Fulani were brought to northeast Brazil during the colonial period. These Sudanese slaves had straight hair, light-skinned faces, prominent noses, and physical traits nearer to those of the Europeans. They were well educated, versed in cattle raising and pasturing of herds, and were skillful iron workers. Some were school teachers, priests, and political leaders. At the beginning of the nineteenth century, these slaves led various revolts against the planters and the government.

**FULBE,** an ethnic group and a kingdom of West Africa from which many slaves were brought to the New World.

**FUM-FUM,** in the West Indies, the flogging (q.v.) of slaves.

**FUMO** (Pg.), a Bantu (q.v.) chief in southeast Africa. (Boxer, *The Portuguese Seaborne*, p. 388.)

**FUNCHE** (Afr.), an Afro-Caribbean dish prepared with manioc flour boiled in hot water and served with fish or meat soup.

**FUN-FUN,** in Jamaica, repetition done in fun or in play for amusement or as a game; chiefly a game for black children.

**FUNGEE, FUNGA** (Bant.). In the Afro-West Indies: 1. Corn or cassava meal boiled down until it is hard; now more often called cornmeal *pane* or *musa*. Other ingredients may also be added. 2. Coconut milk boiled with cassava flour.

**FUNK-BUSH,** in the West Indies, an unidentified wild plant used by blacks in bush medicine.

**FUTA** (Afr.), in West Africa, Fulbe (q.v.) kingdoms from which many slaves were brought to the New World. These states were often prefaced by Futa, e.g., Futa Toro, Futa Jallon (q.v.), and sometimes Futa Bondu.

**FUTA JALLON** (Afr.), a Fulbe (q.v.) kingdom located near Timbuktu, West Africa, whose chief called for a religious war or *jihad* in 1804. This uprising apparently had some influence on the slave rebellion of January 1832 in Jamaica. (Curtin, *Africa Remembered*, pp. 27, 163-64).

# g

GA (Afr.), an ethnic group of West Africa from which many black slaves were brought to the West Indies.

GAGE (Fr. Cr.), in Haiti, a game played by black children, usually with the objective of making someone "it." It is sometimes played at funeral services.

GALINHA, GALLINHA, GALINHA DE BUZIO (Pg.), a Portuguese unit of currency used in slave trading (circa 1793) in Dahomey (q.v.). One galinha was worth 6d. or 5 tockys (q.v.).

GALLINA DE GUINEA (Sp.). See GUINEA-FOWL.

GALLINAS, GALINHAS (Sp., Pg.), a generic term applied to black slaves exported through the Gallinas River trading post northwest of Monrovia, Liberia. Between 1822 and 1839, many Gallinas slaves were imported to Cuba and Brazil.

GALLINHA. See GALINGA.

GAMA, JOSÉ BASILIO DA (1741-1795), a Brazilian mulatto poet and soldier. Gama studied in Rio de Janeiro and Lisbon, and upon his return to Brazil, he became a member of the Escola Mineira, a nativist movement in literature and art. His works incorporated the new qualities of individualism and feeling for nature which were characteristic of the Arcadian lyricism. His poem "Uruguay," in which he censured the Jesuit method of colonization, signaled the birth of Brazilian literature. In this poem appeared the figure of the Noble Negro (q.v.) Quitubia (q.v.). (Sayers, *The Negro*, pp. 39, 60.)

GAMA, LUIS GONZAGA PINTO DA (1830-1882), pseudonym Getulino, a Brazilian mulatto poet, journalist, and abolitionist leader. Gama was the son of a dissolute Portuguese planter and a free black woman, Luiza Nahin (q.v.). In 1840, his father sold him into slavery and took him first to Rio de Janeiro and from there to São Paulo. As a servant in São Paulo, he managed to learn to read and write. In 1848, he fled from his master's home after learning the illegality of his enslavement. Later, he served six years in the militia, and, in 1854, he reappeared in São Paulo as a clerk. He soon became recognized as a man of letters. A self-educated lawyer, Gama was the co-editor of an antislavery journal, *O Radical Paulistano*. By 1880, he had become a prominent and unchallenged leader of the national abolition movement (q.v.). His main works are *Primeiras Trovas Burlescas de Getulino* (Rio de Janeiro, 1861) and *Trovas Burlescas e Escritos em Prosa*. (Ramos, *The Negro*, p. 145.)

**GAMBIA ADVENTURERS,** a British company which had a legal monopoly on the Senegambia slave trade until the end of 1677 when the Royal African Company (q.v.) took over the trade.

**GAMELEIRA, GAMELLEIRA** (Pg.), a wild fig tree (*Moraceae* family) considered by some Afro-Brazilians to be a religious fetish. In Bahia, it is called tree of Loko *(a arvore do Lôko)*, an African god.

**GAMELLE, GAMMELLE** (Fr. Cr.), among Afro-Haitians, both a wooden washing bowl and a wooden mortar for grinding grain.

**GANG.** See SLAVE GANG.

**GANGÁ** (Afr.). 1. A black slave brought to the Spanish colonies from the coast and interior of Sierra Leone, north of Liberia. 2. In Cuba, a black sect whose main function is to arrange funeral rites for its members. 3. A sorcerer in the Afro-Cuban religion.

**GANGÁ-ARRIERO** (Sp.), in colonial Cuba, a mutual aid association; sometimes a religious brotherhood of black slaves.

**GANGAN** (Afr.), in Haiti, an important voodoo (q.v.) priest and practitioner of black magic; also pronounced *n'gan*.

**GANGA ZUMBÁ** (Afr.) (d. 1685), a powerful black king of Palmares (q.v.) who was at the peak of his power around 1672. He and his family resided in a palace, and he was attended by guards and officials who had their own quarters. All the residents were runaway slaves and treated him with the consideration due a monarch. Leading a force of 6,000 blacks, he successfully resisted several government expeditions. He was assassinated by his nephew Zambi (q.v.) in 1685. (Ramos, *The Negro*, p. 61.) See also ZAMBI.

**GANG-GANG** (Afr.), among Afro-Jamaicans, an affectionate term of address for a grandmother or other older woman.

**GANHADOR NO CANTO** (Pg.), in colonial Brazil, a free black who worked in the cities as a day laborer. He was a beast of burden, street cleaner, wagon driver, and the like, performing all the menial work shunned by the whites. The *ganhadores no canto* normally gathered on special corners or street crossings, and squatted on little stools in lively conversation until called upon to do the various jobs. Many were diligent craftsmen. (Ramos, *The Negro*, p. 32.)

**GANZÁ** (Afr.), in Brazil, a musical instrument, probably of African origin, consisting of a hollow cylindrical gourd with a notched surface which is rubbed with a stick to make a rasping noise. It is sometimes also called *chocalho*.

**GANZUÁ.** See CANZUÁ.

**GARCÍA, ANTONIO,** a Spaniard who, together with Sebastián de Siliceo (q.v.), obtained an official grant on December 15, 1674, to introduce 4,000 slaves a year into the Spanish colonies for a five-year period. The total annual payment to the Crown was 450,000 pesos. This liquidation was to be made at the ports of entry, mainly Cartagena de Indias.

**GARDE, GARDE CORPS** (Fr. Cr.), in the Afro-Haitian religion, a protective charm against evil. The making of a magic *garde* is an elaborate ritual, performed in a house with all shutter doors closed.

**GARDE D'HAITI, LA,** an elite army, divorced from politics, created in 1915 by the U.S. Marines. It recruited men from the rural areas, educated them, and raised many of these former peasants to command the Garde by the time the Americans withdrew in 1934.

**GARDE D'HABITATION** (Fr. Cr.), an Afro-Haitian magic amulet devised to protect a household and its surroundings.

**GARDE MAÎT CARREFOUR** (Fr. Cr.), an Afro-Haitian magic charm that enabled its owner to go out at night unharmed.

**GARI** (Fr. Cr.), in the French Antilles, an African dish prepared with manioc and various other ingredients.

**GARIMPEIRO** (Pg.), in colonial Brazil, a freedman, white or black, who engaged in illicit diamond mining.

**GARIMPO** (Pg.), in colonial Brazil, illegal diamond mining.

**GAROTO** (Pg.), in Brazil, a word for blackguard or wag.

**GARRIDO, JUAN,** a black slave, possibly an African native who as a servant accompanied Hernán Cortés in the Conquest of Mexico in 1519.

**GARVEY, MARCUS** (1887-1940), a Jamaican-born black who unsuccessfully tried to organize a great community of American and African blacks. This community was to become economically self-sufficient by the creation of a black merchant marine, the Black Star Line. Garvey founded the African Orthodox church, a black religion with a black God, and preached against miscegenation and for racial purity. In conjunction with the "Back to Africa" movement, he evolved a scheme for running the African black continent with a top-level cadre of U.S. blacks. American imperialists supported Garvey, for in this prospect they saw an instrument whereby Africa might be deflected from the European to the American colonial orbit. In 1923, Garvey was convicted of mail fraud and sent to jail. After President Coolidge commuted his sentence in 1927, he was deported to Jamaica where he sought to keep his movement alive. He later moved his headquarters to London where he died on June 10, 1940.

**GAYAP** (Afr.), in Trinidad, a black system of cooperative harvesting in which the owner of the field provides meals and entertainment at the end of the day's work. The helpers are invited by the beat of a drum. The practice is considered a survival from slavery times.

**GAYAP SONG** (Afr.), black songs sung by peasants in the fields while helping each other at harvest time. These songs of praise and derision comment obliquely on the foibles of workers and villagers who have been the objects of gossip. *Gayap* songs are common in rural Trinidad and elsewhere in the West Indies where they serve to lighten the task at the end of the day.

**GAYUMBA** (Afr.), in the Dominican Republic, a musical bow made of a flexible piece of wood with a cord attached to a plank covering a hole in the ground; formerly played by slaves.

**GBAN** (Afr.), in the French Antilles, an African musical instrument played by blacks. It was apparently introduced by slaves.

**GÈDÉ** (Afr.), a large family of Afro-Haitian deities with different names and manifestations.

**GÈDÉ L'ORAILE** (Fr. Cr.), an Afro-Haitian god of thunder closely associated with death. He is repulsive in appearance, with a dwarf-like stature, and is considered a malevolent force.

**GÈDÉ NANSOU** (Fr. Cr.), an Afro-Haitian deity, a member of the Gèdé (q.v.) family.

**GÈDÉ NIMBO** (Fr. Cr.), an Afro-Haitian god who is a spirit of the grave-yard, a sexual rascal, and a violator of property. He is usually dressed in a black frock coat, black top hat, and black trousers. He is often represented as carrying a cane and smoking a pipe.

**GEDEONSU** (Fr. Cr.), an Afro-Haitian deity, a member of the Gèdé (q.v.) family.

**GÈDÉ TIWAWÉ PANCHÉ** (Fr. Cr.), an Afro-Haitian god who makes mischief as he enters religious services.

**GÈDÉ VI** (Fr. Cr.), an Afro-Haitian female deity, the wife of Gèdé Nimbo (q.v.).

**GÈDÉ ZECLAI** (Fr. Cr.), an Afro-Haitian deity thought to be responsible for death by lightning.

**GÊGÉ** (Afr.). 1. In colonial Brazil, a West African language spoken by some black slaves throughout the eighteenth century and until at least the middle of the nineteenth century. 2. A "nation" (q.v.) of black slaves concentrated in Bahia, Brazil.

**GÊGÉ CANDOMBLÉ** (Afr.), an Afro-Brazilian cult of Yoruba (q.v.) origin.

**GÊGÉ NAGÓ** (Afr.), an Afro-Brazilian fetish cult of Sudanese origin, the most widespread black sect in Brazil. It has a pantheon of deities, an organized priesthood, large congregations, temples, fetishes, and highly emotional rituals with music, dances, and songs. The highest level of excitement is reached in the so-called phenomenon of possession by the gods.

**GELDING,** in the West Indies, slave punishment consisting of chopping off half the foot with an ax. This cruel torment was common for minor crimes.

**GELOFE, GALOFO,** (Afr.), an African ethnic group, today known as Wolof, located in Senegal, many of whose members were shipped as slaves to Peru and the Caribbean. Because of their insubordination and tendency to run away, the planters considered these Moslem slaves to be a very dangerous influence.

**GEMBO** (Afr.), an Afro-Haitian divining device made of a small shell, about the size of a lemon, through which a long cord is passed. When there is no tension on the cord, the shell can easily be slid back and forth. When the cord is taut, the shell will not slide. The typical *gembo* is decorated with beads, old coins, religous medals, snake bones, and fragments of mirror. It is used by black sorcerers.

**GENEALOGICAL COLOR,** in West Indian society, the biological status of a mixed-blood individual as defined in terms of purity of racial descent and physical appearance.

**GÉNÉRAL CLERMEIL,** an Afro-Haitian god thought to be the father and patron of all light-skinned children born to dark parents. Men who wrongly accuse their wives of infidelity because of the lightness of their children are sometimes punished by this god. Also known as President Clermeil.

**GENIPAPO** (Pg.), in Brazil, a bluish spot near the base of the spine which is thought to be a strong indication of the nearness of black ancestry. This birthmark, which the mother will take care not to let visitors see, disappears after the child is seven or eight months old. The *genipapo* is known as the Mongolian blue spot.

**GENS CASÉS,** in Martinique and elsewhere in the French Antilles, a gang of black laborers housed rent free on a sugar plantation under the control of the landlord.

**GENS DE COULEUR** (Fr. Cr.). 1. In colonial Haiti, all free persons who had African blood. These former slaves, having secured their liberty either by cash purchase or by manumission (q.v.) of their white masters (or white fathers), were regarded as full French citizens. The *gens de couleur* could own land and slaves, dispose of their wealth, bear testimony in legal cases (even against whites), marry as they pleased, vote, bear arms, travel freely, embrace any career, and free their own slaves. 2. In modern Haiti, a mulatto or Afro-European who is a descendant of the French colonists and, by tradition, a member of the aristocracy or elite. These individuals are highly educated, speak standard French, and control the economic, political, and social life of the country. The mulattoes constitute about 2 percent of the population.

**GENTE DE CASTA LIMPIA** (Sp.), a term used in the Spanish colonies in the early sixteenth century to refer to a class of persons free from the "taint" of black blood; a white or a Spaniard.

**GENTE DE COLOR** (Sp.), a group of free blacks organized in Cuba in 1860. They established a powerful political minority that apparently aided slaves in their revolts against the white planters.

**GENTE LLEVADA** (Sp.), among blacks of the Pacific Colombian lowlands, condemned persons who die sinners without repentance and wander in terribly disfigured form in the other world. Such people, controlled by the devil, may seek reburial. They come and go from hell, entering and leaving by the cemetery. (Whitten, *Black Frontiersmen*, p. 101.)

**GENTE PEQUENA** (Pg.), in colonial Brazil, a free mulatto child who was the illegitimate son of a Portuguese man and a black slave woman. If his Negroid features were too pronounced, he was left in bondage with his mother, although his father would partially recognize and help him. He occupied a low social status.

**GEREUR** (Fr. Cr.), in the French Antilles, a Creole of Afro-French overseer in charge of a plantation owned by an absentee proprietor.

**GETULINO.** See GAMA, LUIS GONZAGA PINTO DA.

**GEZO,** a black king of Dahomey (q.v.) and a powerful slave trader with agents in the British West Indies. In 1850, Queen Victoria sent a diplomatic mission to him, asking him to stop the slave trade. Gezo refused to abandon his profitable activities, saying that his people could not live without them. (Mannix, *Black Cargoes*, p. 222.)

**GHOST BROTH.** See ALMAS PENADAS.

**GIBB, GEORGE,** an African-born black who was taken to Virginia as a planter's slave and was later brought to Jamaica (ca. 1780). He settled on a plantation in the northern part of the island, around Saint Mary's parish, where he helped found the Baptist Movement (q.v.). He departed from orthodoxy by emphasizing the spirit of the Gospel rather than the Bible (q.v.) or the written word. He gathered large crowds of slaves, and, eventually, the white planters became quite alarmed by his activities as an *obeah* man (q.v.). A runaway slave, he was twice married, his first wife being a black woman. (Curtin, *Two Jamaicas*, p. 32.)

**GIGIRI** (Afr.), in the French Antilles, a method blacks employ to preserve fruits by using sorghum and sugar cane (q.v.) syrup.

**GILAFO, PEDRO,** a runaway black slave leader of a slave uprising in Costa Rica in 1540. After twenty days of skirmishes against the Spanish settlers, he was caught near the town of Orisco. Accused of being in company of "warlike Indians," he was tried and condemned to death and boiled alive. (Rout, L. B., *The African Experience in Spanish America*, p. 99.)

**GILBERT, NATHANIEL,** a planter and speaker of the Assembly in Antigua, West Indies. While in England he, together with ten of his slaves, was baptized by John Wesley (q.v.), the founder of Methodism. Upon his return to Antigua in 1760, he established a congregation in his own house. The organization languished after his death, but in 1778 on the arrival of John Baxter (q.v.), a new start was made.

**GIRAUD, OCTAVE,** a white Creole poet and abolitionist born in Guadeloupe. As an infant Giraud was taken to France where he was educated and spent most of his life. In poetry, he was a follower of Victor Hugo, and, in politics, he was a declared enemy of racial discrimination on the island. In his writings, Giraud was concerned with the miseries and poverty of the former slaves. From February to November 1860, he lived on the island and wrote *Fleurs des Antilles* (1862), a book of poems describing the beauty of the tropics. Other books include *Les Devoirs du poète* (1857); *Rêves d'avenir* (1859); and *L'Abolition de l'esclavage* (1861).

**GLIMPSE** (Eng. Cr.), in Jamaica, a black albino.

**GLISSANT, EDOUARD** (b. 1928), a mulatto writer born in Sainte-Marie, Martinique. Glissant was educated in the Lycée Schoelcher in Fort-de-France. He later went to Paris where he studied philosophy at the Sorbonne and ethnology at the Musée de l'Homme. His first novel, *Le Lézarde* (1958), evokes the revolutionary ideals of a young Martiniquan. He has been very active in political movements, advocating the independence of the French Antilles in order to organize a federation without racial barriers. Recently, he served as principal of a private school in Fort-de-France. His writing style is brilliant and his language is poetic and enchanting. His works are *Soleil de la conscience* (1956); *Le Lézarde* (1958); *Le Sel noir*

(1960); *Le Sang rivé* (1961); *Monsieur Toussaint* (1961); *Poèmes* (1961); and *L'Intention poétique* (1969). (Corzani, *Littérature antillaise, poésie,* p. 206.)

**GOAT-MOUTH,** in Jamaica, a mouth like a goat's which, according to blacks, indicates the possession of prophetic powers and the power to inflict bad luck, disease, or evils.

**GOD-BROTHER,** in Jamaica, a term of intimate address for a man of one's own age. It is very common expression among black Maroons (q.v.) in the Accompong region.

**GOD-BUSH,** in Jamaica, a parasitic bush (*Loranthaceae* family) also known as West Indian mistletoe. Blacks believe it has magical power because it grows by spreading over every branch and eventually kills its host. It thrives without ever touching the ground.

**GODDIE,** among Jamaican blacks, godmother; an intimate term of address.

**GOD-HORSE,** an Afro-Jamaican term for the stick insect; also, the praying mantis. Among Hausa slaves (q.v.), it originally meant Allah's horse.

**GOD-OKRO,** in Jamaica, a parasitic tree *(Cereus triangularis)* which, according to black belief, grows without its roots touching the ground because of its supernatural or magical powers. Its crimson fruit, known as strawberry pear, contains a pleasant, sweet bulb enclosing numerous black seeds.

**GODO WOSO** (Afr.), in Surinam, a treasure hut where a black man with more than one wife keeps his personal belongings, free from the prying eyes of his spouses.

**GOLA,** an ethnic group located in modern Liberia from which slaves were brought to Mexico and Peru early in the sixteenth century.

**GOLD AND SILVER ROLL,** in the Panama Canal Zone, an official sign in front of the U.S. Disbursing Office indicating the two divisions of the entire labor force working under the American government; it meant "gold" for American workers and "silver" for blacks, Panamanians, Europeans, and other non-Americans. The Administration seized upon this division as a convenient way of segregating the white and black races, and extended the terms *gold* and *silver* to all aspects of life. It established gold and silver towns, gold and silver commissaries, gold and silver windows at the post office, and even gold and silver lavatories and drinking fountains. The euphemisms were used until 1947. (Biesanz and Biesanz, *The People of Panama*, p. 56.)

**GOLD COAST,** the land bordering the Gulf of Guinea (q.v.), coinciding roughly with modern Ghana. The first slave trade fort, Elmina (q.v.), was built here by the Portuguese in 1481; in 1637 it was taken by the Dutch. At the height of the slave trade, this region was one of the chief centers for collecting and exporting black slaves to the New World.

**GOLDEN CIRCLE,** a circle of new slave states to be formed under the leadership of southern U.S. cotton-growing states around the Caribbean and the Gulf of Mexico. The dream of a Golden Circle, a minor cause of secession and war, was promoted in the United States throughout the 1850s. (Mannix, *Black Cargoes*, p. 271.)

**GOMBAY.** See GOOMBAY.

**GÓMES, RAYMUNDO,** a black Brazilian herdsman, who, in 1839 was the principal leader of the *balaiada* (q.v.), a peasant and slave rebellion in the province of Maranhão. He is also known by the nickname Balaio.

**GÓMEZ, JUAN GUALBERTO,** a Cuban mulatto, a son of slaves, born in Sabanilla del Encomendador and educated in a local religious school. In 1869, his parents sent him to France to learn the art of cabinetmaking; instead, he studied the humanities and political science in Paris. Upon his return to the island, he became active in politics. Gómez was a leader in the War of Independence and was later elected senator.

**GÓMEZ, KEMP, VICENTE** (b. 1914), a white Cuban poet attracted and inspired by Afro-Cuban themes and music. His poetic style is characterized by a verbal repetition of sounds, a rhythmic imitation of dancing, and mystical exaltation of the African colonial tradition on the island. His major work is *Acento negro* (1934).

**GÓMEZ REYNAL, PEDRO,** a Spanish slave trader who, on January 30, 1595, was granted an *asiento* (q.v.) contract to transport 38,250 black slaves to the Spanish colonies over a period of nine years. For this privilege, Gómez Reynal had to pay the Royal Treasury 900,000 ducats in annual installments of 100,000. The city of Cartagena, Colombia, then Nueva Granada, was established in the *asiento* as port of primary entry.

**GOMMIER** (Fr. Cr.), in Martinique, a slender, heavy, keelless boat with a small motor or two crude spars and a rough sail. It is used by blacks along the coast of the island and does not sail beyond 20 miles of the shore. These boats often have colorful names.

**GONGÁ** (Afr.). 1. An Afro-Spanish word for a very popular dance. 2. An Afro-Brazilian term for a basket with lid used mainly by blacks.

**GONG-GONG** (Afr.), in the Afro-Cuban religion, African evil spirits Christianized under the name of *diablitos* (little devils). They play an important role in the *santería* (q.v.) Christmas celebration and carnival parades. (Klein, *Slavery*, p. 102.)

**GONGOLÍ** (Bant.), an Afro-Spanish generic term for a worm *(Spirolus grandis Julus)* introduced into the New World from the west coast of Africa in colonial times.

**GONZAGA, TOMÁS ANTONIO** (1744-1807), a Brazilian lyric poet. In his works, Gonzaga describes the strength and skill of black laborers. In his book *Cartas chilenas*, he shows great sympathy for the humble elements of society—the black slaves and mulattoes working in the mines in Minas Gerais. At times he strikes a humanitarian note, new in the Brazilian poetry of his day. He depicts how the slaves are forced to build the handsome buildings that grace Ouro Preto, and he boldly defends the runaway blacks.

**GONZÁLEZ DE MENDOZA, ANTONIO,** a wealthy Cuban lawyer who in 1865 founded an antislavery trade association in Havana. Its members were Creoles and Spaniards, and they were concerned not only with the trade itself but also with the eventual demise of the entire system of slavery.

**GOOD AFRICAN,** an antislavery phrase coined and used during the second half of the eighteenth century in England.

**GOOD WIFE BETTER DAN ESTATE WAGON** (Eng. Cr.) ("A good wife is better than a sugar plantation wagon"), an Afro-Jamaican aphorism from slavery times. (Beckwith, *Jamaica Proverbs*, p. 55.)

**GOOMBAY, GOOMBAH, GOMBAY, RULÚ-KULU,** (Afr.), in Jamaica, a large drum fashioned from a hollow log covered with sheepskins. It was beaten by one man with a stick about six inches in length, while another man rolled a stick over a notched piece of wood fixed across one end of the instrument. At one time the *goombay* was forbidden on the plantations because it was used for war and by sorcerers. It was brought from Africa by black slaves.

**GOOMBAYER** (Afr.), in Jamaica, a black who plays a *goombay* (q.v.).

**GORDON, GEORGE WILLIAM** (1820-1865), a Jamaican mulatto, the illegitimate son of a black woman and her white master. His father, Joseph Gordon, had come to the island from England as an attorney for a number of absentee-owned sugar estates (q.v.) and later bought several properties himself. With little help from his father, young Gordon taught himself to read, write, and keep accounts. In 1836, he set himself up as a produce dealer in Kingston. In 1842, he was able to send his twin sisters to England and France to be educated at his expense and, later on, an older sister as well. Three years later, he married Lucy Shannon, the white daughter of an Irish editor. When his father, after taking a white woman as wife, lost his wealth, Gordon, as a loving son, paid his debts and helped support his family—although the children never received their brown half-brother in the house and did not recognize his relationship to them in any way. He also never forgot his slave mother. He was a deacon in the Baptist church, a journalist and a member of the Assembly. Accused of being a supporter of the black rebellion at Morant Bay (q.v.) in 1865, Gordon was arrested, tried, and hanged on October 7, 1865, less than two weeks after the uprising. In 1969, he was posthumously awarded the rank of national hero by the government in Jamaica. (Black, *History of Jamaica*, pp. 188-89.)

**GOTTLIEB, MOSES,** a young black slave from the British islands known as Buddoe, who was a secret organizer and avowed leader of the slave revolt on Saint Croix in 1848. On July 4 of that same year, Gottlieb led a band of blacks and threatened Frederiksted, the capital of the Danish West Indies. The government abolished slavery at once. Buddoe was later deported to Trinidad and never returned to the colony. (Farr, *Historical Dictionary*, p. 103.)

**GOURD COUVRI GOURD, OR COUIS COUVRI COUIS** (Eng. Cr.) ("Gourd covers gourd, or bowl covers bowl"), an Afro-Jamaican aphorism meaning that for every force, there is an equal or superior power. (Courlander, *The Drum*, p. 337.)

**GOUTÉ DÜ** (Fr. Cr.), an Afro-Haitian sacred dish made of rice freshly taken from the field and cooked with Congo beans; it is eaten as part of black rituals.

**GOUVERNEUR LA-PLACE** (Fr. Cr.), in rural Haiti, a black leader in charge of political and social activities in a small rural village; usually centered around a large extended family.

**GOVIS** (Fr. Cr.), an Afro-Haitian sacred vessel or glass bottle in which gods and spirits are kept in the temple. See also criche.

**GRACIAS AL SACAR** (Sp.). See CÉDULA DE GRACIAS AL SACAR.

**GRAGE** (Fr. Cr.), sheet metal used by Afro-Haitians as a scraping device in secular music.

**GRAIN COAST,** the shoreline of upper Guinea (q.v.), in the region of Liberia. European traders of the eighteenth century gave it this name because it was the region where *malagüeta* (q.v.) pepper was obtained.

**GRAINS OF PARADISE,** aromatic seeds *(Aframomum melegueta)* of tropical West Africa used to give pungency to cattle powders and some liquor. Taken to the New World in colonial times, the plants were widely cultivated by black slaves.

**GRANBO** (Fr. Cr.), in Haiti, an African instrument consisting of a stamping tube made of bamboo reed which is beaten rhythmically against a hole in the ground covered with wooden planks.

**GRAND ALOUMANDIA** (Afr.), in Afro-Haitian folk religion, a demon.

**GRAND BLANC** (Fr. Cr.), in colonial Saint Domingue, the owner of large plantations, a wealthy merchant, and often a high official of the state. As an aristocrat he lived in stately mansions surrounded by domestic slaves. Many *grands blancs* spent their time in Paris, ostentatiously squandering their riches. Most of these aristocrats died violent deaths or were exiled during the Humanitarian Revolt (q.v.) of 1791.

**GRAND DON** (Fr. Cr.), in modern Haiti, a wealthy black peasant; a rural leader who controls the economic and political power in the countryside. As a rule, he controls the selection and appointment of local officials such as justices of the peace, sheriffs, teachers, and tax collectors.

**GRANDE CULTURE** (Fr. Cr.), in Haiti, the modern sugar and sisal plantation which to a great extent has replaced the colonial slave community plantation.

**GRANDEE** (Eng. Cr.), in colonial Jamaica, a black midwife. On every sugar estate (q.v.), a house was built for the grandee; pregnant slave women were brought there and placed under her sole care. See also DOCTRESS.

**GRANDE FAMILLE** (Fr. Cr.), among Haitian blacks, the eldest person in the family.

**GRANDE LAVOURA** (Pg.), in colonial Brazil, a large-scale plantation owned by white masters and exploited through the use of slaves. See also PEQUENA LAVOURA.

**GRANDE MULÂTRE** (Fr. Cr.), in Martinique, a light-skinned mulatto, usually a planter or a professional linked by life-style with the white elite; a mulatto aristocrat.

**GRAND GOUT** (Fr. Cr.), in French Creole (q.v.), hunger. See also MOIN GRAND GOÛT.

**GRAND LESSAIGNE**, in Afro-Haitian folklore, an aged, dwarf-like deity, who is the guardian and protector of children.

**GRANDMA-HAIR** (Eng. Cr.), in the West Indies, a type of machete with a broad flaring, turned-back end; used by black laborers in the fields.

**GRANDMAISON, DANIEL** (b. 1901), a Creole poet born in Saint Pierre, Martinique. Educated in local schools, Grandmaison began writing at an early age. In 1925, he was secretary of *Lucioles*, a literary magazine founded by local intellectuals. His poetry, inspired by the tropical landscape of the Antilles, is simple and romantic. In his works of fiction Grandmaison describes the customs and intrigues of Creole society which still holds values and ideas rooted in the slavery tradition. His major works are *Amour et coxalgie* (poems, 1930), and *Rendez-vous au Macouba* (a novel, 1948).

**GRANDMARKET** (Eng. Cr.), in the West Indies, a large market held by blacks at stated times or on special occasions.

**GRAND MARRONAGE** (Fr. Cr.), in the French Antilles, the permanent flight of a slave who, after escaping from a plantation, never returned.

**GRANDMOTHER FAMILY** (Eng. Cr.), in the West Indies, a black family in which the grandmother or some other old relative performs the functions of the natural parents.

**GRAND SIMBA** (Afr.), in the Afro-Haitian folk religion, a female deity.

**GRANDY** (Eng. Cr.). In the West Indies: 1. A black grandmother; also a title and a term of address. 2. A term of address for a black woman older than oneself; a mother. 3. A midwife, whose duties on estates in slavery times included the rearing of infants.

**GRAND-ZOMBI** (Afr.), in Jamaica, an African god worshipped by blacks; the power which guards and overshadows the voodoo (q.v.) worship of the serpent. He protects his devotees against evil and sickness.

**GRANG-GRANG** (Afr.), an Afro-Jamaican term for bits of sticks used as kindling.

**GRAN KAPITIN** (Eng. Cr.), among Surinamese Bush Negroes (q.v.), the headman of the main village serving as center of a neighborhood.

**GRAN'-LICKNY,** in black Jamaican folklore, a grandchild.

**GRANMAN** (Eng. Cr.), among Surinamese blacks, a head of an ethnic group. Formerly appointed by the Dutch governor to control various villages, he was assisted by local chiefs.

**GRAN NÈGRE** (Fr. Cr.), in Haiti, a successful and prestigious black sorcerer.

**GRANNY** (Eng. Cr.), in the West Indies, a pet name used by blacks for a grandfather or a grandmother.

**GRASIMÁ** (Sp.), a black dance in the Spanish Antilles.

**GRASS-GANG,** in Jamaica, one of the gangs of slaves on sugar estates (q.v.), usually made up of the younger or weaker slaves. It was employed to gather grass and fodder for cattle and to perform light jobs in the fields.

**GRATIANT, GILBERT** (b. 1895), a Creole poet born in Saint-Pierre, Martinique. Gratiant studied at Montpellier and Paris. From 1923 to 1925, he taught in Martinique and, at the same time, was engaged in revolutionary activities. He is an ardent militant in the négritude (q.v.) movement, but does not reject European values and ideals. He believes that biological hybridization between blacks and whites produces a new racial and cultural type, the *sang-mêlé* (q.v.), a moral, intellectual and artistically enriched man. Gratiant wrote in Freench Creole *Fab' compé Zicague*, a book in which he praises a living Afro-Christian syncretism. His chief works are *Cris d'un jeune; poèmes en vers faux* (1931); *Une fille majeuce, credo des sang-mêlés*; *Martinique conditionel Eden*; *Fab' compé Zicaque* (1958); *Martinique à vol d'abeille* (1961); and *Sel et Sargasses* (s.d.). (Corzani, *Littérature Antillaise, poésie*, p. 234.)

**GRAVE-DIRT,** in Trinidad, cemetery dust used in magic by black sorcerers who sprinkle it in the yard of an enemy to hurt him. Blacks consider it a favorite food of the gods.

**GREAT ATTORNEY,** in the West Indies, a white administrator who, in slavery times, used to be in charge of twenty or more sugar estates (q.v.) simultaneously. See also ATTORNEYSHIP.

**GREAT-GANG,** in the West Indies, the crew composed of the strongest slaves, in charge of the heaviest tasks on a sugar estate. See also FIRST GANG.

**GREAT-HOUSE,** in the colonial West Indies, the residence of the planter or, in his absence, that of the overseer. The first such residences were crudely constructed dwellings, but after 1750 the masters' houses became imposing structures. They usually stood in a commanding position, frequently facing the sea. They were almost invariably set some distance back from the main road and the slave quarters, being approached by an avenue of cedars, palmettos, or coconut trees. They were built of wood, stood clear of the ground on stone supports, and were one story in height. (Ragatz, *The Fall*, pp. 7-8.)

**GREY-BO** (Eng. Cr.), in Jamaica, a black albino.

**GREY-BOZA** (Eng. Cr.), in colonial Jamaica, a black slave recently imported from Africa who spoke English badly. See also BOZAL.

**GREY HOG ARE DE HARDEST HOG FE DEAD** (Eng. Cr.) ("The grey hog is the hardest hog to kill"), an Afro-Jamaican maxim reflecting the belief that the hog possessed by spirits is the hardest to kill. (Beckwith, *Jamaica Proverbs*, p. 55.)

**GREY-JANE, GREY-JOE,** a derogatory Jamaican term for a female or male black.

**GREY PEOPLE,** a Jamaican folk word for a black albino.

**GREY PUSS** (Eng. Cr.), a Jamaican term for a black albino.

**GREY-WHITE NIGGER** (Eng. Cr.), in Jamaica, a mulatto; an insulting term.

**GRIFERÍA** (Sp.), a trait or peculiarity, usually negative, characteristic of a black or mulatto.

**GRIFFE** (Fr.), GRIFO (Sp.), the offspring of a mulatto and a black; a mulatto.

**GRIFFONNE** (Fr.), a Creole woman with a black features and hair, but light, yellowish skin.

**GRIFO** (Sp.). See GRIFFE.

**GRILLETE** (Sp.), a shackle used in Cuba and elsewhere to punish delinquent slaves. It varied from simple chains and padlocks to heavy logs tied to the ankles of the victims.

**GRILLO, DOMINGO,** a Genovese slave trader who, on July 5, 1662, obtained permission to introduce 24,500 slaves into the Spanish colonies. The term of the contract was nine years, and the total fee to be paid to the Spanish Crown was 2.1 million pesos.

**GRIMARD, LUC** (b. 1886), a black Haitian poet born in Cap-Haitien. Grimard was educated in his native town and in Port-au-Prince where he obtained a law degree. He was a distinguished educator and diplomat. In 1922, he was appointed consul general of Haiti in Le Havre, France. Upon his return in 1926, Grimard became curator of the National Museum. His main works are *Sur ma flute de bamboo* (Paris, 1927); *Ritornelles* (Paris, 1927); *Quelques poèmes* (Port-au-Prince, 1947); *La Corbeille* (Port-au-Prince, 1947); *Du Sable entre les doigts* (Port-au-Prince, 1941); and *L'Offrande du laurier* (Port-au-Prince, 1950).

**GRIS GRIS** (Afr.). 1. Among Haitian blacks, a bird used for the making of charms. 2. In Brazil, witchcraft.

**GROANING,** in Jamaican black cults, the heavy sucking in and expulsion of breath during dancing.

**GRONDÉ** (Fr. Cr.). Among Haitian blacks: 1. To grumble. 2. The middle-size *arada* drum (q.v.).

**GROS BON ANGE** (Fr. Cr.), the "big good angel" that, according to black Haitian belief, is linked to the body of a person and becomes a ghost after the person's death.

**GROS (GRAND) BÉKÉ** (Fr. Cr.), in Martinique, a member of one of the upper-class families and a descendant of French colonists. Both rich and powerful, each *gros béké* is part of a closed society, living on his own estate with his family and having many relatives bearing the same patronym. Today, the *gros békés* constitute a minority. See also BÉKÉ; BÉKÉ GOYAVE.

**GROS HABITANT, GROS NÈGRE** (Fr. Cr.), in Haiti, a rich black land-lord; a powerful town leader. His landholdings are above average, and he is active in politics and commerce. Below the *gros habitant* stand the largest percentage of black rural freeholders who work their own small plots.

**GROS-KA** (Fr. Cr.), in Guadeloupe, a black drum.

**GROS NÈGRE** (Fr. Cr.). See GROS HABITANT.

**GROOT** (D.), in colonial Brazil, a Dutch word for *quilombo* (q.v.).

**GROUND-ANANCY** (Eng. Cr.), among Jamaican blacks, a black spider with a red spot under its abdomen; it is not poisonous.

**GRUDE** (Pg.), an Afro-Brazilian delicacy made of dried tapioca and grated coconut, baked in an open oven and wrapped in banana leaves. This dish is cooked and sold on the streets by black women.

**GUANDÚ** (Afr.), a species of cultivated Angola pea (q.v.) *(Cajanus indicus; Cytisus cajanus)* introduced to the Caribbean region from West Africa during slavery times.

**GUARACHA** (Sp.), in Cuba, a lively song-dance often performed with *rumba* (q.v.) rhythms in double meter. It is of Spanish origin, but greatly influenced by African elements. It combines Spanish and African vocal traditions by using improvised solo quatrains answered by regular choral refrains. It began in the brothels in the nineteenth century and was taken over by the popular theater. It tends to have satirical lyrics, somewhat along the lines of the Trinidadian *calipso* (q.v.). Some *guarachas* printed in the 1880s both began and ended with a solo verse, which is normally a strong African element. (Slonimzki, *Music*, p. 306.)

**GUARAPO** (Bant.), an Afro-Antillean word for an alcoholic beverage made of sugar cane (q.v.). It was very popular among slaves.

**GUARD,** among Trinidadian blacks, a spirit that, through magic, can help an individual achieve personal happines and ward off evil.

**GUARD D'HAITI.** See GARDE D'HAITI.

**GUARDIAN.** See SLAVE WARDSHIP.

**GUATEGUE** (Bant.), in colonial Antilles, a noisy and lascivious black dance.

**GUBIDA,** among black Caribs (q.v.), the spirit of the ancestors which must be honored by their descendants. If the descendants are remiss in their duties, the *gubida* sends them a reminder in a dream. If they ignore this warning, sickness or misfortune will strike the members of their family.

**GUÉDE** (Afr.), in the Afro-Haitian pantheon, a spirit associated with cemeteries and death. He often appears as a scarecrow, with old frock coat and top hat, and sometimes as a corpse. His favorite foods are fish with much pepper, black chickens, and fried plantains (q.v.). *Guédes* are fond of uttering obscenities.

**GÜEMILERE** (Yor.), in the Afro-Cuban folk religion, a special service honoring the gods.

**GUERRA PRETA** (Pg.) ("Black War"), in Angola (q.v.), a slave-raiding expedition organized by Portuguese and later by Brazilian slave traders.

**GUIABLESSE** (Fr. Cr.), in Martinique, Afro-French makeup and fancy dress traditionally worn during carnival parades.

**GÜIJE, JIGÜE** (Sp.), in Cuba, a black dwarf.

**GUILBAUT, TERTULIAN MARCELIN** (1856-1899), a black Haitian poet born in Port-de-Paix. After finishing school in Haiti, Guilbaut attended the Sorbonne in Paris where he obtained a law degree. He was a school inspector in Cap-Haitien (1891-1894) and founded a free law school in that city. Later, he became secretary of education and ambassador to Paris. Among his works are *Higuenamota* (1876); *Moeurs électorales* (comedy, 1878); *Les Chants de soir* (1878); *Patrie* (1885); and *Feuilles au vent* (1888).

**GUINAIN** (Fr. Cr.). In the French-Antilles: 1. A Guinean black. 2. A derogatory term for a savage and primitive black inferior to any black Creole.

**GUINEA.** 1. In Old Portuguese, "Land of the Negroes"; in modern geographical usage, the forested southern half of West Africa, including part of Nigeria. The Portuguese reached the Guinea region in 1471 and the next year built Elmina (q.v.) to exploit gold and to engage in limited trade. Guinea later became one of the main sources of slaves exported to the New World. 2. An English gold coin issued from 1663 to 1813; first struck out of gold from Guinea. In 1717, its value was fixed at 21 shillings (at par, $5.11). Today it is still a prestige monetary unit. 3. Short for guinea-fowl (q.v.). 4. A slave brought from the Guinea region. 5. A word used mainly in compounds to denote real or supposed connections with Guinea. 6. A nation in West Africa, formerly a territory of French West Africa.

**GUINEA-BIRD** (Eng. Cr.), in Jamaica and the British West Indies, a derogatory name given to an African black slave brought directly from West Africa.

**GUINEA-CHICK** (Eng. Cr.), a guinea hen or fowl.

**GUINEA COAST,** the shoreline bordering the Gulf of Guinea (q.v.). The coast itself was considered to begin at the Senegal River (latitude 16° N) and curve down and away to South Angola (latitude 16° S).

**GUINEA CORN,** a variety of a grain-yielding sorghum *(Zorghum vulgate)* widely grown for food in West and North Africa. Also called *durra.*

**GUINEA-CORN GRUNT** (Eng. Cr.), an Afro-Jamaican term for a variety of grunt fish with a mottled color pattern resembling guinea corn (q.v.).

**GUINEA-CORN YAWS** (Eng. Cr.), in Jamaica, one of the types of yaws (q.v.) in which the skin becomes mottled, thereby resembling guinea corn (q.v.). It commonly affected black slaves.

**GUINEA-FOWL,** an African bird with a full body, a small, partially naked head, and a shorter, depressed tail; especially the common domesticated bird *(Numida melearis)* which is dark gray with small white spots. It was apparently introduced from the West African coast to the Caribbean area.

**GUINEA-GRAIN.** See GRAINS OF PARADISE.

**GUINEA-GRASS,** in the West Indies, a grass *(Panicum jumentarum)* imported from tropical Africa during slavery times. It is a very sweet grass with blades from three to four feet in length and a stem ten to twelve feet high. It is utilized as building material for huts. Today it is one of the most valuable grasses for stock on the islands.

**GUINEA-HEN.** See GUINEA-CHICK.

**GUINEA-HEN PARROT,** a Jamaican variety of the parrot fish, speckled like a guinea-hen (q.v.).

**GUINEA-HEN QUOK,** in Jamaica, the night heron with speckled plumage which, according to black belief, is supposed to indicate youth.

**GUINEA-HEN WEED,** in Jamaica, a strong-smelling wild plant *(Petiveria alliacea)* used in medicinal preparations although disliked for its taste. Brought from Guinea (q.v.) by slaves, it is widely distributed in tropical America.

**GUINEA-MAN.** 1. A ship engaged in the Guinea (q.v.) slave trade between England, West Africa, and the West Indies. 2. A sea captain who traded in goods and slaves between England, Guinea, and the Caribbean. Guineamen were known for their cruelty and abuses of seamen and slaves carried in their ships. 3. A black slave born in Guinea and brought to the West Indies.

**GUINEA MINT,** in Jamaica, a medicinal plant known to have been used in Africa. Its fresh leaves are commonly made into a tea for indigestion, flatulence, and other illnesses. It is a standard medicine among blacks.

**GUINEA PEPPER,** in the West Indies, another name for *malagüeta* (q.v.); in use since slavery times.

**GUINEA-PLUM,** in the West Indies, a plant-like fruit of a large African tree *(Parinarium excelsum)*, hardly edible on account of its scant, dry, farinaceous pulp and large stone. Brought from Africa in colonial times, it is distributed extensively in the tropical islands.

**GUINEA-SHIP,** formerly in the West Indies, a vessel bringing slaves from Guinea (q.v.).

**GUINEA-WOOD,** a kind of red wood (species of *Erythroxylon*) formerly exported from Jamaica as a dyewood.

**GUINEA WORM,** a very slender thread-like nematode worm *(Filaria medinensis)* common in tropical Africa and also found in tropical America where it was brought by slaves. The adult worm is sometimes six feet long. It enters the human stomach in drinking water, and from there it makes its way to the subcutaneous connective tissues, especially of the legs and feet, where it causes abscesses. Black slaves were commonly affected with Guinea worms.

**GUINEA YAM,** in the West Indies, a variety of yam like white yam (q.v.), but coarser grained. It is called Guinea yam because the plants were first brought from Africa during slavery times.

**GUINEA YARD,** in the West Indies, an open building or enclosure where new slaves were brought after disembarkation.

**GUINÉE** (Fr. Cr.). In Haiti: 1. A god worshipped by blacks. 2. Africa and African traditions among the black population.

**GUINÉE PANTHÉON** (Fr. Cr.), in Haiti, a very large family of gods of African origin.

**GUINEO** (Sp.), in Afro-Spanish America, a tropical fruit *(Musassapientum L.; Musa canvendishii)* commonly known as the banana. It was introduced early in the slavery period and became a standard slave food.

**GUIRAO, RAMÓN** (1908-1949), a Cuban poet and leader of *afrocubanismo* (q.v.). Guirao's first poem was "Bailadora de rumba." In his poetry, he depicts black types and customs by using a very colorful and striking Afro-Spanish slang. Guirao admits that the movement is undeniably influenced by European fashion and the traditional black folklore. Among his main works are *Bongó* (Havana, 1934); *Orbita de la poesía afrocubana* (Havana, 1936); and *Poemas* (San Radad, Mendoza, Argentina, 1947).

**GULF OF GUINEA.** 1. A gulf on the western coast of Africa between latitude 6° 30′ N. and 1 °S. 2. A large region of western Africa bordering on the Gulf of Guinea; it included the Bight of Benin (q.v.) and the Bight of Biafra (q.v.) from which many slaves were brought to the New World.

**GUNDA** (Afr.), in Afro-Spanish America, a plant *(Dioscorea aerea bulbifera, Tuberculifera Barret)* that produces a fruit similar to the potato; apparently brought from Africa by slaves. In Cuba it is known as *ñame cimarrón* (q.v.).

**GUNDA PEA** (Afr.), in the West Indies, a white yam (q.v.) that lasts from five to seven years in good soil whence it derives the name seven-year pea. It continues bearing for several months of the year until Christmas and, in Jamaica, therefore, it is also called the Christmas pea. It is widely cultivated and eated by blacks and was apparently brought from Africa during slavery times.

**GUNDÚ** (Afr.), in colonial Brazil, a sickness that affected blacks, characterized by bony excrescences on the nose and cheekbones.

**GUNOCÔ** (Afr.), in Brazil, an African forest god worshipped in several black cults.

**GURNEY BIRD,** in colonial Jamaica, a derogatory term for an imported black slave suggesting that this new African was prone to drunkenness and thievery. Such slaves were usually kept away from Creole blacks born in the New World.

**GUYANA CREOLE,** another name for Creolese (q.v.).

**GUYS' TOWN,** a large Maroon settlement (q.v.) in the windward region of Jamaica named after its leader. It was well planned and contained about 200 well-armed men, and even more women and children. It tended to play a passive role during the Maroon War (q.v.) of 1730-1739, fighting only to defend its passes and scattered fields of plantains (q.v.) and yams (q.v.). (Price, *Maroon Societies*, p. 262.)

**GUZO** (Afr.), an Afro-Brazilian word for strength, vigor, vitality.

**GUZU, GUZUM** (Afr.), in Jamaica, a deity or ancestral spirit worshipped in the Ashanti (q.v.) religion; also witchcraft.

**GUZU-MAN** (Afr.), in Jamaica, a sorcerer.

**GYAASHANI** (Afr.), a bull in Anancy stories (q.v.).

**GYOU** (Eng. Cr.), an Afro-Jamaican word for falsehood, pretentiousness. (Cassidy, *Dictionary*, p. 217.)

# h

**HABANERA,** an Afro-Cuban dance-song characterized by a swaying rhythm similar to the Argentine *tango* (q.v.). Its melodic-rhythmic components are of European and African origin. Some scholars have traced the *habanera* to an English country dance of the seventeenth century, imported into Cuba by Spaniards where it became *danza habanera*. (Slonimzki, *Music*, p. 307.)

**HABITANT** (Fr. Cr.). 1. In the Afro-French Antilles, a colonist who owned rural property. The origin of the term goes back to early settlers who formed bourgs or enclaves in the country. Later it meant a group of small landowners engaged in agriculture and sugar planting. 2. Today, in Haiti, a black peasant.

**HABITATION** (Fr. Cr.), in Haiti, a small rural property including land, the owner's house and the laborers' huts. It served as a center for black peasants who were often culturally and socially isolated.

**HA-BUO** (Afr.), in Jamaica, a black albino.

**HACENDADO** (Sp.), in colonial Cuba and the Spanish Antilles, the owner of a sugar mill (q.v.) or "central" (q.v.) and master of a large slave force. See also SENHOR DE ENGENHO.

**HACIENDA** (Sp.), in the colonial Antilles, a large sugar estate (q.v.) which was self-sufficient in its supply of slaves. It contained a sugar mill, (q.v.), the owner's great-house (q.v.), a boiling and curing house, slave quarters, extensive sugar cane (q.v.) fields, and pasture for cattle, domestic animals, and fowl. It emerged soon after the Spanish Conquest.

**HACIENDA COMUNERA** (Sp.), in colonial Cuba, a communal country estate operated by slaves and owned by members of the same family. Each heir or purchaser received an interest in the use of the land instead of a share.

In the eighteenth century, the crops and cattle ranching were replaced by sugar and tobacco, and the *hacienda comunera* became a slave estate held without subdivision by a number of claimants. In modern times, it was divided into many small pieces, giving rise to a large class of small landowners.

**HACIENDA DE CAÑA** (Sp.), in the Spanish Antilles, a landed estate where sugar cane (q.v.) has been cultivated to produce sugar, molasses, alcohol, and other commercial goods. In the colonial period, it was worked by slaves brought from Africa.

**HAIR STRAIGHTENING,** among Jamaican and other blacks or mulattoes, the practice of trying to make kinky hair appear straighter and more European.

**HAITIAN CREOLE,** the equivalent of French Creole (q.v.).

**HAITIAN RENAISSANCE,** a new birth or revival of the traditional black arts of Haiti. The movement began twenty-five years ago. Many Afro-Haitian painters, sculptors in wood and ceramics, and ironworkers draw heavily on national lore and legend for inspiration and subject matter. These artists, inspired by the "primitive" countryside, have been gaining increasing respect and praise in the world of arts. (Courlander, *The Drum*, p. 125.) See also NÉGRITUDE; NEGRO RENAISSANCE.

**HALF A FAM'BLY BETTER DAN NONE AT ALL** (Eng. Cr.) ("Half a family is better than none at all"), an Afro-Jamaican aphorism. (Beckwith, *Jamaica Proverbs*, p. 55.)

**HALL, PRINCE** (circa 1748-1807), a mulatto born in Bridgetown, Barbados, the son of an Englishman and a mulatto woman. In 1765, when he was seventeen years old, Hall arrived in Boston where he soon was struck by the indignities visited upon the blacks in Massachusetts. He entered the Methodist ministry and took a positive stand on all questions related to the freedom of slaves. In 1784, Hall and fourteen of his black brethren were initiated by the Grand Lodge of England into African Lodge, No. 459, with Prince Hall as master. This lodge spread the idea of Masonry among the blacks of America. His only published work is *A Charge Delivered to the African Lodge, June 24, 1797, at Menotomy, Mass. by the Right Worshipful Prince Hall.*

**HALOU,** an African-born slave who, in 1792, organized in Cul-de-Sac, Saint Domingue, a Maroon (q.v.) force of 12,000 slaves to attack the colonists. A self-proclaimed prophet, he carried a white rooster as his symbol and was often surrounded by a group of black sorcerers singing and playing drums. The white rooster was supposed to give him inspiration and the blessing of God. (Fouchard, *Les Marrons*, p. 538.)

**HANGKRA** (Twi), in Jamaica, a metal pack or basket which blacks use to cure and preserve meat or fish; it is often hung above the fireplace.

**HANGING JOHNNY,** in the West Indies, a black shanty-song.

**HANG-'PON-ME** (Eng. Cr.), in Jamaica, a basket made of thatch (q.v.) with a square pocket hung from the neck. It is used by blacks.

**HARD LIBIN' MEK MAN BWOIL CALLALU** (Eng. Cr.), ("Men boil greens when living is hard"), an Afro-Jamaican aphorism. (Beckwith, *Jamaica Proverbs*, p. 57.)

**HARD PUSH MULATTO WOMAN KEEP SADLER SHOP** (Eng. Cr.) ("The mulatto woman keeps a sadler's shop because she is hard pushed for support"), an Afro-Jamaican aphorism. (Beckwith, *Jamaica Proverbs*, p. 57.)

**HARLEM RENAISSANCE.** See NEGRO RENAISSANCE.

**HARRIS, RAYMOND,** a renegade Spanish-born Jesuit of English extraction who worked for a Liverpool trading house. In 1788, he wrote a book, *Scriptural Researches on the Licitness of the Slave Trade*, in which he undertook to prove that the trade was in conformity with the laws of nature, the laws of Moses, and Christian dispensation as set forth in the Bible.

**HARRIS, WILSON,** a prolific British Guianan novelist. For fifteen years, Harris traveled throughout British Guiana as a land surveyor. He sets the final seal on the West Indian sense of identity and proclaims that its heterogeneous, multiracial society must create and express a new and authentic personality rooted in an Afro-European tradition. Among his works are *Eternity to Season* (Georgetown, Guiana, 1954); *Palace of the Peacock* (London, 1960); *The Far Journal of Oudin* (London, 1961); *The Whole Amour* (London, 1962); and *The Secret Ladder* (London, 1963).

**HAUSA KINGDOM,** an ancient black kingdom in northern Nigeria which converted to Islam in the thirteenth century (circa 1203). It flourished throughout the Middle Ages and, in about 1500, emerged as a powerful military state in West Africa. It was conquered by the Fulah (q.v.) in 1870.

At one time, the Hausa language was spoken throughout the western Sudan.

**HAUSA SLAVES,** in Brazil and elsewhere in tropical America, a generic term applied to a large number of black slaves brought from northern Nigeria. They were a mixed-blood group with Hamitic and possible Berber strains, although negroid characteristics were predominant among them. They were distinguished by a stubby beard. They led rigorous and even austere lives, refusing to mix with the other slaves. These blacks, members of Islam, were largely responsible for the slave uprisings in the Brazilian province of Bahia in the first half of the nineteenth century. The Hausas had powerful secret societies such as the Obgoni (q.v.) which generally followed the same lines as those in West Africa. Their language was spoken in Bahia during the entire nineteenth century and perhaps even in the eighteenth century. Though relatively few in number, their influence was considerable. After abolition in 1888, many Hausas were repatriated to the city of Ardra (q.v.). (Freyre, *The Masters*, p. 305.)

**HAUT CHANT** (Fr. Cr.), in Afro-Haitian religious cults, songs saluting a deity, usually one of the warrior group.

**HAUTE QUADRILLE** (Fr. Cr.), a black dance performed only in Martinique. See also QUADRILLE.

**HEAD BOILER,** in Jamaica and the West Indies, a black or mulatto, perhaps the most skillful slave on a sugar estate (q.v.), who had to know how the cane had been raised and treated, its species, the kind of soil it had grown in, and whether it had been arrowed, bored, or rat-eaten. Such knowledge would determine the juice's tempering with lime, how long it would have to be boiled, and hence the quality of the sugar.

**HEAD CATTLE AND MULE,** on a West Indies sugar estate (q.v.), a reliable black slave who was responsible for the livestock, for transporting the cane from the fields to the mill, and for taking the crops to the warehouses and wharves. He kept the steers and mules in good order and selected the animals best fitted for field, treadmill, and road work. He regulated the system of relays and periods of rest, and was expected to understand all about animal foods, diseases, and cures.

**HEAD DRIVER,** on colonial West Indies sugar estates (q.v.), a black or mulatto slave who controlled all the other slaves, including each gang and every black working in the fields and in the manufacture of sugar. A Creole slave was thought to make the best head driver; this driver was often a middle-aged or elderly black who had long been employed on the estate. As the life and soul of the entire enterprise, he was expected to be sober, reliable, of good character, and respectful to white people.

**HEAD-FORM SHAPING,** among Haitian blacks, the molding of a child's head. This process begins right after birth and often lasts for two months.

**HEAD NEGRO,** in the West Indies, a polygamous black man possessing from two to four wives. Only one wife is the object of a particularly steady attachment; the rest, although called wives, are actually occasional concubines or drudges whose assistance the man claims in the cultivation of his land, the sale of his produce and so on. In return, he repays them with acts of friendship and support when they are in need. In Jamaica in 1920, there were 10,000 head Negroes. (Brathwaite, *The Development*, p. 215.)

**HEAD PEOPLE,** in colonial Jamaica and elsewhere, a small group of privileged slaves who held the key to the effective control and efficient management of the slaves on a sugar estate (q.v.). As incentives, this elite was given preferential treatment and the lion's share of material goods set aside for the slaves.

**HEALER,** in Jamaica, a medicine man in the black Shouters' (q.v.) cult who heals all kinds of diseases by magic. Blacks often consider healer and doctor to be synonymous.

**HELGAARD, ANNE** (1790-1859), a mulatto woman of wealth and experience who became the famed mistress of Peter von Scholten (q.v.), the Danish governor of the Virgin Islands. She probably asked her lover to free the slaves in the Virgin Island in 1848. After emancipation took place, she reportedly canceled a large debt owed to her by von Scholten. (Farr, *Historical Dictionary*).

**HENRIQUE,** a black Yoruba (q.v.) slave who, in 1835, led a great slave revolt in Pernambuco, Brazil. In the fight he was badly wounded; although almost speechless from agony, he refused to betray his brethren.

**HENRIQUE, PRINCIPE DOM** (1495-circa 1535), Prince Henry, the son of King Alfonso (q.v.) of the Congo (q.v.), born in 1495 and educated in a seminary in Portugal. In 1513 Prince Henry, then eighteen years of age, headed a mission to Rome, accompanied by gifts of ivory, rare skins, and fine-woven raffia textiles of the Congo. Five years later, on May 5, 1518, he was elevated to the rank of bishop by Pope Leo X, returning to his native land three years later. During this time, the slave traffic between the Congo

Kingdom and Brazil was on the increase, and Prince Henry was apparently unable to stop it. (Davidson, *Black Mother*, p. 126.)

**HENRIQUES,** in colonial Brazil, black militia units named after the famous black hero Henrique Días (q.v.), a leader in the war against the Dutch invaders (1624-1654).

**HERÉ CHÉCHÉRÉ,** in Brazil, a copper rattle that is shaken in ceremonies by the "holy daughters" of a cult.

**HERMOSO, ANDRÉS,** a runaway slave who, in October 1771, escaped with several other slaves from the Capaya estate in the vicinity of Cartagena de Indias, Colombia. He eventually joined the Ocoyta settlement, a well-organized black community. The colonial militia attacked and destroyed the village later that same year. Hermoso was taken prisoner and condemned to 200 lashes as provided by law for such offenders. (Price, *Maroon Societies*, pp. 68, 70.)

**HERNÁNDEZ CALVO, DIEGO,** a Spanish captain who was head of the colonial militia in Cartagena de Indias, Colombia. Around 1600 the raids and attacks led by fugitive slaves threatened the prosperous plantations established near the city which at that time was the most important slave trade center on the Colombian coast. By order of the provincial governor, Hernández Calvo organized several successful expeditions against the black settlements located in the forested and marshy areas of the Maturana River. (Price, *Maroon Societies*, p. 78.)

**HERNÁNDEZ FRANCO, TOMÁS RAFAEL** (1904-1952), a writer and poet born in Tamborli, Dominican Republic. Hernández Franco was one of the most inspired representatives of the Antillanité (q.v.) literary movement. He began as a modernist poet, but soon took up the African theme. Among his many poems is "Yelia," about a mulatto girl, the daughter of a Norwegian man and a black woman, Suquiette. His main work is *Canciones del litoral alegre* (Ciudad Trujillo, Dominican Republic, 1936).

**HERRAR LA MULA** (Sp.) ("shoeing the ninny"), an Afro-Cuban dance in which a female dancer, on all fours, represents the she-ass, while the male dancer portrays the smith who is shoeing her "hoofs." This is one of the many degenerations of the Afro-Cuban dance, created only for the entertainment and exploitation of foreign tourists.

**HERRERA, JOSÉ,** a Havana-born black who enlisted in the regiment of Loyal Blacks *(batallón de pardos honrados)* and was widely acclaimed for his loyalty and heroism in the fight against runaway slaves between 1868 and 1877. On August 1, 1877, he was assassinated by a fugitive slave. (Calcagno, *Diccionario*, p. 347.)

**HERRING ROLL,** on West Indian sugar estates (q.v.), a list of slaves indicating the number of herrings given out to each at stated times.

**HIGGLER,** in Jamaica, a market seller who is nearly always a black or mulatto woman. The higgler may keep a shop in town where she sells produce bought in the country, or she may sell door-to-door all over the district. Each higgler has her own musical cry which rises and falls with a peculiar inflection, generally with an upward turn at the end.

**HIGGLER BASKET,** in Jamaica, the kind of basket used by higglers (q.v.) for produce.

**HIGGLERING,** in Jamaica, a system of trading in agricultural produce by black or mulatto women. It is a true middle-woman transaction in that the higgler (q.v.) buys almost everything that she sells, and her trade purchases are made for resale. Higglering requires a minimum initial capital investment, usually obtained from relatives and kin group. The system performs an essential socioeconomic function by making available to consumers goods that are produced in small quantities on scattered, outlying farms. Higglering usually takes place on Fridays and Saturdays. (Horowitz, *People and Cultures*, p. 370.)

**HIMBA** (Afr.), in the Afro-Antilles, a kind of edible wild yam (q.v.) that grows in shady places in the high woods. It is a favorite black food.

**HIP-SAW** (Eng. Cr.), in colonial Jamaica, a hip-shaking dance common among blacks.

**HITTOE** (Afr.), the name of an African ethnic group from Calabar, West Africa; in Jamaica, a slave from the Hittoe people.

**HOHOVI** (Afr.), among Trinidadian blacks, twins; thought to bring good fortune, they are held in high esteem and are much honored.

**HOLE,** among Haitian blacks, a hole dug in the room where a birth occurs for the burial of the placenta. A preferred spot for the hole is beneath a bed or at the threshold.

**HOLING,** in the Caribbean Islands, the digging with hoes of parallel lines of holes about two feet wide and six inches deep. In colonial times, slaves worked in pairs, the weaker laborers doing the easier part of the task while the stronger ones did the more difficult. "Holing" was the hardest work in the cultivation of sugar cane (q.v.) and was performed by a large number of black slaves, some of whom were especially hired for the job.

**HOLLAR, CONSTANCE** (1880-1945), a black poetess born in Port Royal, Jamaica. Hollar was educated on the island and spent most of her life there. After completing her schooling, Hollar went to study in England. Upon her return to Kingston she opened a kindergarten. Her major work is *Flaming June* (Kingston, 1941).

**HOMEM DA FAZENDA** (Pg.), in colonial Brazil, an overseer on a sugar estate (q.v.) known for his mistreatment of slaves.

**HOMEM-MARINHO** (Pg.), in Afro-Brazilian folklore, a sailor and terrifying mythical creature who haunts beaches and devours people's fingers, noses and private organs.

**HOMENS BONS** (Pg.), in colonial Brazil, white members of the upper plantation class. They had the right to vote and to be elected members of municipal councils.

**HOMENS DO POVO** (Pg.), in colonial Brazil, ordinary Portuguese citizens who, especially at the beginning of the colonization period, were excluded from land grants. They were excluded primarily because of their humble origins and their lack of capital to buy the tools, slaves, and other requisites needed in the production of sugar and rum for the domestic market.

**HOMME MOYEN SENSUEL** (Fr. Cr.), in Trinidad and elsewhere in the Antilles, a social type, often a black or a mulatto playboy, whose ideal is to enjoy illicit sexual liaisons and to earn just enough money to satisfy his present needs.

**HONTO** (Afr.), among the Afro-Haitians, a small sacred drum.

**HORATIO, AUGUSTUS FREDERICK.** See PRINCE DE BUNDO.

**HORRO** (Sp.). In colonial Spanish America: 1. A legally free black slave who legally has the same social status as a Spaniard. 2. A domestic black slave.

**HORSE-HEAD,** in Jamaica, a traditional character in the black John Canoe (q.v.) masquerade; he wears either a horse-head mask or the actual skull of a horse. He may be historically related to the "hobby horse" figure of English mumming.

**HOSTOS, EUGENIO MARÍA DE** (1839-1903), a Puerto Rican politician, writer, reformer, and journalist. Hostos fought for the abolition of slavery on his native island and campaigned on behalf of emancipation all over the Antilles until slavery was finally outlawed in Puerto Rico in 1873 and in Cuba in 1880.

**HOT HOUSE PIECE,** in the West Indies, a slave hospital on a sugar estate (q.v.). It was usually located on a hill or elevation since this was regarded as the healthiest spot on the plantation. It was generally kept warm and was under the care of a black nurse.

**HOUNAI, HOUNAIÉ** (Fr. Cr.), among Haitian blacks, a spirit who enters the body of the faithful during religious rituals or dances. An individual possessed by Hounai often exhibits changes in personality, voice, manners, and attitudes.

**HOUNFORT, HUMFORT** (Fr. Cr.), in Afro-Haitian cults, the house where the gods are worshipped. It usually has two rectangular rooms, each with a separate entrance and a platform for offerings to the gods. Some are painted green "for hope," some red "for victory," while others have designs of flowers painted on the walls above the platform. There is a special chamber in which the secret part of the rituals takes place and an open peristyle or cloister for public ceremonies. The *hounfort* also serves as a clubhouse, dance hall, theater, music hall, court, and council chamber.

**HOUNGAN** (Fr. Cr.), in the Afro-Haitian religion, a black priest, healer, and diviner. Besides praying and offering sacrifices for the people, he determines by divination who is responsible for the misfortunes that plague the faithful. The *houngan* also provides security, wealth, and social advances, and acts as a leader and protector of the community against supernatural forces and human perils. As a medicine man, he is thought to have supernatural powers to cure illnesses caused by the adverse magic of one's enemies. Foretelling the future is one of his most important tasks, and no black family would make any important decision without first consulting the *houngan* to determine the propitiousness of the time.

**HOUNGÉNICON** (Fr. Cr.), in some Afro-Haitian cults, the top ranking priest among the servitors of the gods; he is also called emperor.

**HOUNSI** (Fr. Cr.), an initiate in one of the several Afro-Haitian cults; as a servitor of the gods, his main task is to dance and be possessed by a god.

**HOUNSI-BOSSALE** (Fr. Cr.), in Afro-Haitian cults, an initiate occupying the lowest order among the gods' servitors. He is still not sufficiently well trained to be able to control the spirit who enters his body. Accordingly, in the ritual, the *hounsi-bossale* screams, jerks, and acts hysterically because his god is wild and untamed.

**HOUNSI KANZO** (Fr. Cr.), in Haiti, an initiate or gods' servitor who, in some Haitian black cults, has passed through a fire ordeal demonstrating that he has the favor and protection of the spirit who is his master.

**HOUNTOGRI** (Fr. Cr.), in Haiti, the largest of the three *arada* (q.v.) drums played in black rituals.

**HOUNTOR** (Fr. Cr.), among Haitian blacks, the spirit of a drum.

**HOUSE JOHN CANOE,** in Afro-Jamaican folklore, one of the types of John Canoe (q.v.) masquerade, traditionally a part of the Christmas celebration among blacks.

**HOUSEMOVING SHANTY,** in the West Indies, a black work song.

**HOUSE SYSTEM,** in colonial West Africa, a cooperative trading corporation based in coastal river posts. It was organized around 1600 by black kings and by Portuguese and other European merchants engaged in trading guns, clothing, ivory, gold, rare skins, sugar, rum, and, most of all, slaves. Small houses were controlled by independent white merchants, and royal ones were owned by powerful local chiefs with thousands of officers and servants. The original center of these activities was the Congo River Delta and Angola (q.v.). Later, many houses spread to the Slave Coast (q.v.), the Gold Coast (q.v.), and the Niger River Delta. (Davidson, *Black Mother*, p. 208.)

**HOW SWEET THE NAME OF JESUS SOUNDS,** a famous religious hymn written by John Newton (q.v.), a slave captain, while waiting on the West Coast of Africa to transport slaves to the West Indies. (Mannix, *Black Cargoes*, p. 133.)

**HUIDOR** (Sp.), in colonial Spanish America, a runaway slave. In 1572, the City Council of Lima ordered that such slaves be branded with the letter *H* on the cheek. The Audiencia rejected the idea. (Bowser, *The African Slave*, p. 84.)

**HUMANITARIAN REVOLT,** a violent slave rebellion in Haiti that stemmed from the French Revolution's proposition of liberty, fraternity, and equality for all men. It began in 1791 and ended in 1798 when the blacks took control of the colony. The revolt soon spread to all the French Antilles islands.

**HUNGRY BELLY AND FULL BELLY NEBER WALK ONE PASS,** (Eng. Cr.) ("The hungry belly and the full belly do not walk the same road"), an Afro-Jamaican aphorism. (Beckwith, *Jamaica Proverbs*, p. 60.)

**HUNGRY FOWL WAKE SOON** (Eng. Cr.) ("The hungry fowl wakens early"), an Afro-Jamaican aphorism. (Beckwith, *Jamaica Proverbs*, p. 60.)

**HYACINTH** (b. 1770), a black slave leader in the Haitian uprising of 1791. At the age of twenty-one, he went from plantation to plantation claiming he was divinely inspired. With a bull's tail in his hand, Hyacinth assured the black fighters that his talisman would chase death away.

# i

**IAIÁ** (Pg.), in colonial Brazil, a term of address used by slaves in talking to the master's wife or daughter.

**IALÉ** (Yor.), in Brazil, a Yoruba (q.v.) term for the favorite wife in a polygamous slave household.

**IANMAN IBO** (Afr.), an Afro-Haitian god who protects his devotees against evil and sickness.

**IANSAM** (Afr.), an Afro-Brazilian term for Saint Barbara.

**IAO** (Afr.), in Afro-Brazilian *candomblés* (q.v.), the bride of a god.

**IBÁ** (Afr.), in Brazil, a term used by Yoruba (q.v.) slaves for payment made to a sorcerer.

**IBÁ-BALÓ** (Afr.), the patio or court of Afro-Cuban temples.

**IBEJI** (Yor.). In Brazil: 1. The spirit who protects twins. 2. A *candomblé* (q.v.) ritual that includes a sacred supper honoring the gods, usually held on Thursday.

**IBO** (Afr.). 1. An ethnic group in southeastern Nigeria. 2. A generic term applied to black slaves brought to the New World from the Niger Delta regions; they were supposedly prone to fixed melancholy and to suicide. 3. A secondary god in the Afro-Haitian pantheon.

**IBO FOULA** (Afr.), a friendly Afro-Haitian god, protector of the family.

**IBO HEQUOIKÉ**, an Afro-Haitian deity belonging to the Ibo (q.v.) family of gods, who looks after members of the family.

**IBO JEROUGÉ** (Afr.), in the Afro-Haitian religion, a malevolent female deity with red eyes. Her favorite foods are pigeons and cocks.

**IBO KAMA** (Afr.), an ambivalent Afro-Haitian deity, protector of the family group.

**IBO LAZILE** (Afr.), a god worshipped by blacks in Haiti, a protector of the family. His favorite food is goat, offered to him by the faithful.

**IBO LÉLÉ** (Afr.). See IANMAN IBO.

**IBOS PEND COR A YO** (Fr. Cr.) ("The Ibos hang themselves"), an expression still used in Haiti to refer to the Ibo (q.v.) slaves' traditional tendency to fits of despondency that often resulted in suicide. (Mannix, *Black Cargoes*, p. 19.)

**IBO WANÈME** (Afr.), a friendly Afro-Haitian deity who helps and protects members of the family; worshipped since slavery times.

**ICHE MOIN** (Fr. Cr.), a French Creole (q.v.) idiom meaning "my child"; used as a term of endearment by Haitian blacks.

**IDÉS** (Pg.), a tin bracelet or charm, symbol of Oxun (q.v.), worn by Afro-Brazilians.

**IEGYU, AGUE** (Eng. Cr.), an Afro-Jamaican word for an acute or violent fever.

**IERERÊ** (Afr.), in Brazil, seeds similar to those of the coriander *(Coriandrum sativum)* used extensively by blacks in seasoning.

**IFÁ** (Afr.), in Brazil, an African god worshipped in the *gêgé-nagó* (q.v.) cult who is closely associated with divination. The process of foretelling is called "to see Ifá." The diviner employs a chain into which he inserts halves of mango (q.v.) seeds or fruits from a palm tree.

**IFÁ GUENSI** (Afr.), an Afro-Cuban word for *babalâo* (q.v.).

**IFÁ NECKLACE,** a charm worn by a diviner of the *gêgé-nagó* (q.v.) cult in Brazil; it is made of mango (q.v.) seeds or of palm tree fruits.

**IFE** (Afr.), a Yoruba sacred town in West Africa, located on the Niger River Delta, from which many slaves were brought to the New World.

**IFEFE** (Afr.), an Afro-Cuban word for wind, hurricane.

**IFENIA** (Afr.), in West Africa, a cassava product often served at breakfast; it was a standard slave food in the New World.

**IFÉ RE RESI** (Afr.), in the Afro-Cuban religion, an Ifá's (q.v.) blessing.

**IFÓ** (Afr.), an Afro-Cuban term for pain.

**IF YOU CAN'T KECHT QUACO, YOU KETCH HIM SHIRT** (Eng. Cr.) ("If you can't catch Quaco, you catch his shirt," i.e., if the man himself escapes, vengeance may be taken upon his children), an Afro-Jamaican saying from slavery times. (Beckwith, *Jamaica Proverbs*, p. 65.) See also QUACO.

**IF YOU FOLLOW WHA' BLACK NEGER SAY, YOU LOSE YOU' WAY** (Eng. Cr.) ("If you follow a black's directions, you will lose your way"), a derogatory aphorism used in Jamaica and elsewhere in the Caribbean.

**IGALA** (Afr.), an ethnic group established in the Niger River Delta from which slaves were brought to the New World.

**IGBIRA** (Afr.), an ethnic group settled in the Niger River Delta from which many slaves were brought to the West Indies and elsewhere.

**IGBÓ** (Yor.), in the Afro-Cuban dialect, forest, jungle.

**IGBODU** (Yor.), the most holy place of a temple in the Afro-Cuban folk religion. The term is derived from the Yoruba (q.v.) idiom *igbo-odu*, meaning forest oracle.

**IGÉ** (Yor.), an Afro-Cuban word for twins.

**IGNAME.** See YAM.

**IGO** (Yor.), in the Afro-Cuban dialect, honeybee.

**IGÚ** (Yor.), an Afro-Cuban word for an evil spirit.

**IGUEDÉ** (Afr.), a sacred garment worn by a black sorcerer while performing rituals to honor the god Ogun (q.v.).

**IGÜÍ** (Yor.), in the Afro-Cuban folk religion, a ghost, the shadow of a dead person.

**IJIMERE** (Yor.), among Trinidadian blacks, supernatural beings or little people found by hunters and fishermen; their encounters and callings are dangerous.

**ILÉ AVON AFONJÁ** (Afr.) (''House of Xangó''), an inscription found on the wall of a Xangó (q.v.) temple in Bahia, Brazil (circa 1945). (Pierson, *Negroes*, p. 296.)

**ILEOCHO** (Yor.), in Afro-Cuban folk cults, the temple or house of images.

**ILÚ** (Afr.), the largest Afro-Brazilian drum, usually measuring between two-and-one-half and seven feet tall.

**IMAGUAS** (Afr.), in the Afro-Cuban religion, twins, a symbol of man's eternity.

**IMBABURA** (Sp.), a special canoe with higher sides than an ordinary one; used to travel along riverine forests by blacks in the Pacific lowlands of Colombia. It is also called *panga*. (Whitten, *Black Frontiersmen*, p. 69.)

**IMAM** (Afr.), in Brazil, a spiritual leader among Moslem blacks.

**IMBANGALA** (Bant.), an Angolan state which, during the 1780s and 1790s, played an important role in exporting slaves to northeast Brazil.

**IMMIGRANT PLANTER,** in Jamaica (circa 1820) and elsewhere in the West Indies, any whites who settled on the island. These immigrants fell into three groups: planters or owners of large sugar estates (q.v.); their employees (overseers, bookkeepers, and technicians); and those who, having settled in the colonies with small estates after long years of employment, relied on the hire of their slaves as jobbing gangs for part of their income. (M. G. Smith, *The Plural Society*, p. 93.)

**IMPHEE,** in Barbados, a species of wild sugar cane (q.v.) *(Holchus saccha-atus)*; also called African or Chinese sugar cane. Formerly used as fodder, now it is rarely cultivated. (Collymore, *Notes*, p. 48.)

**INDIGÉNISME** (Fr.). See ÉCOLE INDIGÉNISTE.

**INFERNO DOS NEGROES, PURGATORIO DOS BRANCOS, A PARAIZO DOS MULATOS E MULATAS** (Pg.) ("A hell for blacks, a purgatory for whites, and a paradise for mulattoes"), a saying used in characterizing Brazil (circa 1711). (Boxer, *Four Centuries*, p. 78.)

**INGENIO DE AZÚCAR** (Sp.), a large, well-equipped mill which characterized the nineteenth-century sugar plantation in Cuba and much of the Caribbean. It was first run by water power and later by steam. Most *ingenio* plantations were large, family-owned estates, although corporate ownership was not absent. Depending on the time and place, the labor force was either slave or free. In early colonial times, a Cuban sugar estate (q.v.) with mill produced 100 long tons of sugar each season with a labor force of 100 slaves. (Knight, *Slave Society*, p. 31.)

**INGENUO** (Pg.), in Brazil, an infant slave born after the passage of the Rio Branco Law (see LEI DO RIO BRAVES) in 1871. The planters were given the option of freeing *ingenuos* at the age of eight with indemnification or freeing them at twenty-one without compensation. After 1871, no child was born a slave, but all children of slave mothers continued to be raised as slaves as in the past.

**INGLESSOUS** (Fr. Cr.), in the Afro-Haitian folk religion, a fiery god who drinks the blood of his victims and whose worship is held at night by a fire in the jungle.

**INHAMBALANCE** (Afr.), an ethnic group settled in Mozambique from which many slaves were brought to Brazil.

**INHAME** (Pg.). See YAM.

**INHERITANCE OF THE SOUL**, in the West Indies, the slave belief that one's soul is inherited from an ancestor within the family; a traditional African belief.

**INLE** (Yor.), in the Afro-Cuban *santería* (q.v.), a male god who takes the form of a fisherman and gatherer. He dances zig-zag, searching everywhere, and pulls in nets and picks berries. Among the Yoruba (q.v.) in West Africa, he was a hunter known as Erinle.

**INNOCENT, ANTOINE** (1874-1960), a black Haitian novelist inspired by the naturalist movement. He depicts African and Haitian scenes and characters with photographic exactness. He presents facts and reactions without any moral or psychological commentary, except for the insertion of evolutionist and scientific arguments to explain the black peasant's backward behavior. Innocent was apparently the first writer to focus on the African tradition in Haitian folklore. Among his works is the novel *Mimola ou l'histoire d'une cassette; petit tableau des moeurs locales* (Port-au-Prince, 1906).

**INTERESTING NARRATIVE OF THE LIFE OF OLAUDAH EQUIANO OR GUSTAVUS VASSA, THE AFRICAN, WRITTEN BY HIMSELF,** the vivid and unique story of an Ibo (q.v.) slave published in London in 1789. Equiano describes how he was kidnapped when alone with his sister in his family compound, gagged, tied up, and carried to the woods. He was sold to some traders from the coast and was forced aboard ship together with the rest of the black cargo. The atmosphere became absolutely pestilential, and he was overcome with extreme depression. Then followed the indescribable horror of the Middle Passage (q.v.). Finally, he was sold in the West Indies to a white planter. See also EQUIANO, OLAUDAH.

**INTERLOPER,** an illegal, independent slave trader engaged in transporting black slaves between the African coast and the West Indies. Interlopers were very active in the seventeenth century. By government account, these traders, operating in the years 1679-1682, were credited with 29 percent of the English slave trade of that period. (Curtin, *The Atlantic Slave*, pp. 54, 125.)

**IN THE CASTLE OF MY SKIN,** an autobiographical novel by the Barbadian writer George Lamming (q.v.) in which he depicts the struggle and frustration of a black youth growing up in a society dominated by the myth of white supremacy. The book was published in London in 1953.

**IOIÓ.** See YOYO.

**IOIÓ, FAZÉ BUCHICHIM!** (Pg.) ("Master, puff out your cheeks!''), in colonial Brazil, a friendly expression used by a slave barber to get his master to fill his mouth with air to make his cheeks stand out for easier shaving.

**IRMANDADE** (Pg.), in colonial Brazil, a religious brotherhood made up exclusively of blacks. It is under the patronage of Saint Benedict and Our Lady of the Rosary. In Bahia, at least, these all black organizations persist to this day.

**IRMÃO** (Pg.) ("Brother"), an honorific title given by African chiefs to Portuguese and Brazilian slave traders. (Mendoça, *A Influencia*, p. 23.)

**IRÚ** (Afr.), in Brazil, a variety of small bean extensively used as seasoning by lower class blacks.

**ISAIAHS,** in Jamaica, members of a black revivalist sect founded in 1833 by Edward Alexander, a black converted to Christianity just after the emancipation. In the early days the members worshipped in the open, sacrificing goats and cows. Today the Isaiahs conduct meetings by day, dancing and singing as the revivalists do.

**ISANCIO** (Afr.), in the Afro-Cuban folk religion, a major female deity identified with Saint Barbara.

**ISAROKO** (Afr.), in the Afro-Cuban *santería* (q.v.), the place of sacrifice, usually under a cotton-silk tree.

**ISLES, SAMUEL** (d. 1764), an English Moravian missionary who arrived in Antigua in 1754 to work among the black slaves. He visited their huts and fraternized with them. In 1757 he baptized the first black slave after which his success grew rapidly. He died seven years later.

**ISUÉ** (Afr.), the highest priest or bishop who presides over the rituals in the Afro-Cuban *santería* (q.v.). At the end of the services, Isué carries the head of the cock that has been sacrificed, holding it between his teeth. In his hand he holds the sacred drum on which the body of the cock is lying. (Jahn, *Muntu*, p. 75.)

**ITÁS DA XANGÓ** (Pg.) ("Xango's rocks"), in Afro-Brazilian folklore, sacred stones thought to have fallen from heaven during thunderstorms. They are used in the preparation of medical prescriptions and are considered to possess miraculous healing power. Also known as *petras de Santa Bárbara*.

**ITEQUES** (Bat.), tiny wooden sculptures made for religious purposes by Brazilian blacks, descendants of slaves from Angola (q.v.) and Mozambique.

**ITÓN** (Afr.), the sacred staff used by an executioner to kill a he-goat in the Afro-Cuban *santería* (q.v.) cult.

**IUANI** (Afr.), among Black Caribs (q.v.), a spiritual entity which, together with the body and the soul, is part of a man's personality. (Bastide, *African Civilizations*, p. 79.)

**IVONET, PEDRO** (d. 1912), a black Cuban, born a slave on a coffee plantation in Caney, Oriente Province. He was a general and a hero in the War of Independence in 1898 and later became the leader of the Colored People's Independent party (see PARTIDO INDEPENDIENTE DE LA GENTE DE COLOR). He was assassinated by his political opponents on July 12, 1912.

**IVORY COAST,** the shoreline of the Gulf of Guinea (q.v.) between Cape Palmes and the Volta River which during the slave-trading period was an important center for collecting and exporting black slaves to the New World.

**IYA KÊKÊRE** (Afr.) ("Little Mother"), in Afro-Brazilian cults, a black priestess.

**IYALORISHA** (Afr.), in an Afro-Brazilian *candomblé* (q.v.), a priestess, the bride of the god Exu (q.v.). Before reaching this rank, she must serve the cult for fourteen years and be able to lead her own *candomblé*.

**IZEMODZÁ** (Afr.), a Yoruba (q.v.) goddess worshipped in the Afro-Cuban *santería* (q.v.).

# j

**JABADO, JABAO** (Sp.), in the Antilles, the offspring of a white man and mulatto woman with white skin and blond, kinky hair.

**JABOTÃO, ANTONIO DE SANTA MARIA** (1704-1768), a Brazilian friar who, in 1745, delivered a sermon in a Recife church, arguing that mulattoes were superior to black and whites. As evidence he read a long list of famous mulattoes and declared a holy mulatto, Gonçalo Garcia, to be the patron of all mixed-blood persons. This original thesis is exposed in his book *Novo Orbe Seraphico Brasilico ou Chronica da Frades Menores de Provincia do Brasil*, written in about 1761. (Sayers, *The Negro*, p. 52.)

**JACKASS ROPE** (Eng. Cr.), in Jamaica, a locally grown tobacco whose leaves are dried and twisted by blacks into a kind of rope.

**JACK MANDORA,** in Jamaica, a black character in the Anancy story (q.v.) of African origin.

**JAGAS,** an Angolan ethnic group, many of whose members were brought as slaves to northeast Brazil. A large number of Jagas reached Brazil after a military expedition organized in 1624. It is probable that these slaves were the founders of the Republic of Palmares (q.v.). (Price, *Maroon Societies*, p. 175.)

**JAGWA-TAAK,** another name for Jamaican English Creole (q.v.).

**JA JA** (b. 1821), an African king born into domestic slavery in Bonny, West Africa. After earning his freedom, he organized a prosperous palm oil exportation center in the Congo Delta. Because of internal wars, he moved from Bonny to Adoni country, a few miles to the east. There he founded a new state, Opebo, of which he became king. After a bitter struggle with British commercial competitors, Ja Ja was jailed, tried, and condemned to five years of exile in the West Indies where he died. (Davidson, *Black Mother*, pp. 261-64.)

**JALOFO.** See GELOFE.

**JAMAICA FISH,** fish caught off the New England coast and sold exclusively to West Indian planters to feed their slaves during the colonial period. Each black was given six or seven of these fish per week, almost his only source of protein. (Mannix, *Black Mother*, p. 159.)

**JAMAICAN ENGLISH CREOLE, QUASHEE CREOLE,** an English-based dialect which, syntactically, phonologically, and lexically is the farthest removed from standard Jamaican English. It is spoken in several closely related forms by most of the country's black people.

**JAMAICA NEGRO CODE,** an official slave code passed by the Jamaican General Assembly in 1831.

**JAMAICA PEAS,** in the West Indies, a variety of lima bean *(Phaseolus)*; a staple slave food in the colonial period.

**JAMAICA PEPPER,** in the West Indies, a tropical plant (genus *Piper*) whose dried leaves yield a pungent condiment greatly valued by blacks. Also called *pimento*.

**JAMAICA REBELLION.** See MORANT BAY REBELLION.

**JAMAICA RED MAN.** See JAMAICA WHITE.

**JAMAICA SORREL.** See RED SORREL.

**JAMAICA WHITE,** a dark-skinned man who looks like an Englishman might look after a sojourn in the tropics; a racial type difficult to distinguish except to the eyes of a "native" observer.

**JAMBES COUPÉES, COLAS,** a runaway slave residing in Saint Domingue who, in 1723, organized and armed bands of blacks to attack plantations and rob passersby in broad daylight. He was captured, tortured, and executed on June 4, 1723. (Hall, *Social Control*, p. 38.)

**JAMETTE CARNIVAL,** in Trinidad, a colorful black celebration popular around 1875. It was described as a festival organized by lower class mixed-bloods, including vagabonds and derelicts.

**JAMMA** (Afr.), an Afro-Jamaican folk song sung by slave gangs (q.v.) while working in the fields. Today it is performed at wakes.

**JANGKO FIES** (Afr.), in Jamaica, a mask worn by blacks in the John Canoe (q.v.) celebration.

**JANGKO RIID** (Eng. Cr.), in the West Indies, a wild tropical plant with a strong smell; used by blacks in folk medicine.

**JAN-JAN** (Eng. Cr.), in Jamaica, small bits of wood or rubbish; a term used mainly by blacks.

**JANKRA** (Afr.), in the Caribbean region, a word meaning untidy or careless-looking; probably of African origin.

**JANVIER, LOUIS JOSEPH** (1855-1911), a black Haitian novelist who was a disciple of Honoré de Balzac and a follower of the naturalist movement. Among his works is *Une chercheuse* (Paris, 1888).

**JARDIN LOIN GOMBO DUR** (Fr. Cr.) ("When the garden is far, the okra is hard"), an Afro-Haitian aphorism. (Courlander, *The Drum*, p. 336.)

**JAW-BONE,** in Jamaica, a black slave musical instrument of the rattling type.

**JAW-FALL,** in Jamaica, a black childhood disease, usually tetanus, characterized by convulsions. In colonial times, it was perhaps the most fatal malady among slave children. It was responsible for the deaths of nearly one-half of the infants of all blacks, free or slave.

**JEAN BATEAU,** an Afro-Haitian deity whose devotees, when possessed, can speak several tongues.

**JEAN CHACHÉ, JEAN TROUVÉ** (Fr. Cr.) ("Jack seeks, Jack finds"), an Afro-Haitian aphorism meaning that if you look for trouble, you will find it. (Courlander, *The Drum*, p. 335.)

**JEAN LE BLANC,** an Angolan-born slave brought from Africa and sold by the Dutch (circa 1650) to French colonists in Martinique. In 1656, while working on a plantation in Guadeloupe, Jean le Blanc planned to massacre the whites, keep their wives, and set up two Angolan kingdoms, one at Basse-Terre and the other at Capterre. For ten or twelve days the slaves pillaged the plantations and slaughtered the French settlers. When the colonists finally crushed the uprising, Jean le Blanc and several of his followers were executed. (Hall, *Social Control*, p. 62.)

**JEAN-LOUIS, VICTOR** (b. 1915), a mulatto Bohemian poet born in Sainte-Anne, Guadeloupe. Among his ancestors he included the sultan of Timbuktu. An ardent follower of négritude (q.v.), Jean-Louis visited Cameroon where he wrote poems inspired by Islam. His works are *Issandr le mulattre* (1949); *Les Jeux du soleil* (s.d.); and *Ouvrages techniques divers* (s.d.).

**JÊGUEDÊ** (Afr.), in Brazil, a black dance of African origin performed as part of ritualistic ceremonies.

**JELENGUE** (Afr.), an Afro-Spanish word for tumult, commotion, hurly-burly.

**JE N'AIME PAS L' AFRIQUE** (Fr.) ("I don't love Africa"), the title of a sarcastic, violent poem by Paul Niger (q.v.), published in Paris in 1945. Inspired by the négritude (q.v.) movement, it contains an insolent attack on established Christian values and traditions, using sarcasm and vulgar slang.

**JENIPAPO.** See GENIPAPO.

**JENKOVING** (Afr.), in Jamaica, an African instrument consisting of two jars with medium-sized openings tapped by the player's hands. It was very popular among slaves in colonial times.

**JENSIMAN BRITISSE** (Fr. Cr.), an Afro-Haitian deity depicted as having white skin.

**JERK.** See JORK.

**JESUS** (1790-1847), a Brazilian mulatto who was one of the most famous painters of his time. In his portraits and panels, which adorn several churches and monasteries in Bahia, critics point to his use of disconcerting forms, forceful tones, and original conceptions. Jesus, a profound individualist and unbridled artist, refused to address his Majesty, the Emperor Dom Pedro II, when the latter visited Bahia in 1840. (Ramos, *The Negro*, p. 136.)

**JEU DE MAYAMBA** (Afr.) ("Mayamba game"), in Haiti, a black game played with four chips made of shell, baked clay, or broken chinaware. One side of the chip is white, the other is usually blue; any number of players may participate, and, as in dice, all compete against the thrower.

**JE WÈ BOUCHE PÉ** (Fr. Cr.) ("The eyes see, the mouth shuts"), an Afro-Haitian aphorism meaning don't talk about everything you know. (Courlander, *The Drum*, p. 338.)

**JIBONAM** (Afr.), in Afro-Brazilian *condomblés* (q.v.), an assistant priestess in charge of the ceremonial dancers and of the offerings to Exú (q.v.); also called the little mother *(pequena mãe)*.

**JIGGA NANNY** (Eng. Cr.), in Jamaica, a black dancer who jiggles at the center of a singing ring-game.

**JIGGER,** in Jamaica, the choice *(Tunga penetrans)* or flea, common in the Caribbean; formerly the cause of deformity among black slaves.

**JIGGER-FOOT,** in Jamaica, a black slave whose foot was infected or deformed by jiggers (q.v.).

**JIGGER NO CARE FE BOCKRA FOOT** (Eng. Cr.) ("The jigger does not pay respect to the white man's foot"), an Afro-Jamaican aphorism meaning misfortune is no respecter of persons.

**JIGGEY** (Eng. Cr.), in Jamaica, a powerful charm consisting of a bunch of sacred herbs used by black sorcerers.

**JIGÜE.** See GÜIJE.

**JIHAD** (Ar.), a term commonly used to refer to the proselytizing wars of Moslem religious fanatics. In colonial Brazil, it was loosely applied to slave rebellions led by Hausas (q.v.).

**JIMAGUA** (Ar.), in the Afro-Cuban religion, a fetish of twins consisting of a wooden doll dressed in red and sometimes painted black. Some of these magic statues still bear a resemblance to African idols, their ancestors. Jimaguas are used in sorcery, and often inside their hollow bodies are found dust, bones, rocks, needles, as well as human hair and nails. (Ortiz Fernández, *Los negros brujos*, pp. 40-41.)

**JIMBO** (Afr.), in colonial Brazil, shellfish used as coins by Black slaves.

**JIMÉNEZ, JOSÉ JULIÁN** (b. 1823), a black Cuban born in Trinidad on January 9, 1823, the son of an orchestra conductor. Because of his great talent as a violinist, he was sent to Germany to further his studies. He acquired fame by giving concerts in Leipzig and in other European centers. In 1849, he returned to Trinidad, his native city, where he organized his own orchestra. He composed dances, *guarachas* (q.v.), and other popular melodies. In 1869, he again visited Leipzig. He was the father of two Cuban composers, José Manuel Jiménez (q.v.) and Nicasio Jiménez (q.v.). (Calcagno, *Diccionario*, p. 354.)

**JIMÉNEZ, JOSÉ MANUEL** (b. 1855), a black Cuban musician, son of José Julián Jiménez (q.v.), born in Trinidad on December 7, 1855. He studied piano in Leipzig, Germany, and then toured Europe. In 1876, as a student of Marmontel, he won first prize at the Paris conservatory. He gave concerts in Paris in the mansion of Felipe Herz. On his return to Havana he was acclaimed throughout the island. Among his well known compositions are *Eleguia* (1881) and *Rapsodias Cubanas*. He was the most famous musical performer and composer of the Jiménez family, exceeding his father José Julián, and brother Nicasio in both fame and popularity. (Calcagno, *Diccionario*, p. 354.)

**JIMÉNEZ, NICASIO** (b. 1847), a black Cuban musician, son of the maestro José Julián Jiménez (q.v.). He studied the violin with his father who then sent him to Leipzig, Germany, to pursue his musical studies. There he became an accomplished violinist and cellist. After graduation, he accompanied his father and brother on their European tours. He settled in Tours, France, around 1884 where he taught music.

**JING-BAND** (Eng. Cr.), among Afro-Jamaicans, a word for noisy, dirty, disreputable people.

**JOÃO I.** See NZINGA A NKUWU.

**JOBABO REBELLION,** a bloody slaves' uprising that took place in the Jobabo copper mines in Cuba in 1553. Four rebel leaders were hung, drawn, and quartered; their heads were put on stakes. In 1713, black slaves organized several uprisings against the Spanish authorities. Finally in 1798 they were ordered freed by the government. (Rout, L.B., *The African Experience in Spanish America*, p. 120.)

**JOBBER,** in colonial Jamaica, a white settler who supplied slave labor to sugar estates (q.v.) for holing, cutting, and transporting cane. At harvest time jobbers were in great demand. Rural townships and cities relied on these jobbers to supply slaves for work on roads and buildings.

**JOBBING GANG,** in the West Indies, a group of slaves hired out by their owners and managers to do temporary work on sugar estates (q.v.), repair roads, and build houses. A jobbing gang generally comprised twenty to forty stout male and female blacks.

**JOBBING SLAVE,** in the West Indies, a black slave whose owner hired him out for heavy tasks like digging cane holes, weeding, and transporting cane to the mills on sugar estates (q.v.), or for work on road construction and repair. He represented an important added source of income for his owner.

**JOHN CANOE (CONNU),** in colonial Jamaica and elsewhere, the name of the black men who led the Christmas parades. Each group of slaves had its own Canoe to lead dozens of dancers and singers on the streets. The original John Canoe was a Johnny Conny, revered by blacks along the Guinea Coast (q.v.). (Hurwitz, *Jamaica*, p. 81.)

**JOHN CANOE (CONNU) DANCE,** a Christmas festival dance held by black slaves in colonial Jamaica and the West Indies. Its chief performer wore a traditional headdress in the form of a model boat looking something like a stylized Noah's ark. With this on his head and a wooden sword in his hand, he performed a dance through the streets of the town, accompanied by a group of followers and musicians with drums, gourds filled with the seeds of the Indian shot plant, and other African rhythmic instruments. It was closely associated with the survival of African religion and magic. See JOHN CANOE (q.v.).

**JOHN-CROW.** 1. In Africa, a large kind of fowl with sparse plumage. 2. A bird that symbolizes the unfavorable traits attributed to blacks by other blacks; a favorite Afro-Jamaican figure in proverbs, tales, and myths. 3. A carrion crow or scavenger.

**JOHN-CROW BEADS** (Eng. Cr.), in the West Indies, seeds *(Abrus protorius)* or scarlet peas with a prominent black spot, frequently strung into necklaces and worn by blacks. Also called crab-eye and John-Crow eye.

**JOHN CROW EYE.** See JOHN-CROW BEADS.

**JOHN CROW ROASTING PLANTAIN,** an Afro-Jamaican phrase signifying the prediction of a person's imminent death or downfall. (Cassidy, *Dictionary*, p. 250.)

**JOHN-CROW SAY HIM A DANDY MAN, SAME TIME HIM HAB SO-SO FEDDER** (Eng. Cr.) ("John-Crow says he's a dandy man, but he has nothing but [only] feathers"), an Afro-Jamaican aphorism applied to a poor black man who puts on fine clothes and appears prosperous. (Beckwith, *Jamaica Proverbs*, p. 76.)

**JOHNNY JUMPER.** See JUMPER.

**JOLLIFICATION,** in Nevis, West Indies, cooperative work in which small black landholders get together to cut down bushes and trees, plant yams (q.v.), reap crops, and move or build a house.

**JONGLEUR** (Fr. Cr.) ("jester"), in Haiti, a strong black man who performs feats such as dancing while holding a fully set table off the ground with his teeth.

**JONGO** (Pg.), in colonial Brazil, a song sung by slaves. There were several forms of *jongos*. A very popular one was that of a riddle which could conceal bitterness with words, expressions, or situations subject to more than one interpretation. Words were often African, and persons were replaced by trees, birds, and animals of the forest. There was a premium on terseness; the fewer the words, the more obscure the meaning. The better *jongos* were those more difficult to decipher. Jongo was also a song-dance performed in religious services. Its origin is African. (Stein, *Vassouras*, pp. 207, 209.)

**JONG SANG DOO** (Afr.) ("the land where slaves are sold"), an expression supposedly popular among blacks along the African coast (circa 1600) expressing their readiness to starve and die at home rather than be carried across the ocean to the New World and sold to white cannibals. (Mannix, *Black Cargoes*, p. 49.)

**JONGUEIRO** (Pg.), in colonial Brazil, a black slave who sang *jongos* (q.v.).

**JORDON, EDWARD** (1800-1869), a light-colored freeman born in Kingston, Jamaica, on December 6, 1800; his father was from Barbados and his mother may have been from Jamaica. He was a tailor's apprentice in Kingston and later worked as a printer. At the age of twenty he became a fighting abolitionist. With his friend Robert Osborn, a mulatto printer, Jordon organized a planned resistance to the oppression of the black people in Jamaica and with him edited *The Watchman* (q.v.), a small weekly paper. In 1835, he was elected a member of the House of Assembly, and, in 1860, he was made a Companion of the Bath by Queen Victoria. Jordon has been acclaimed one of the great men of the island.

**JORK, JERK** (Eng. Cr.), in the colonial West Indies, cured meat from wild hogs, a staple slave food on the plantations. Also called jork hog.

**JORKING PUOK** (Eng. Cr.), in the West Indies, the cutting or scoring of the flesh of a wild hog which was then smoked; a task formerly performed by slaves on the plantations.

**JOSÉ, AMARO,** a Portuguese slave trader who, in 1806, accompanied by Pedro João Baptista (q.v.), opened the long trail across central Africa. They walked from inland Angola (q.v.) to the Tete settlement on the lower Zambezi River and thus anticipated David Livingston by half a century. (Davidson, *Black Mother*, p. 155.)

**JOSEPHINE.** See BONAPARTE, JOSEPHINE.

**JOUCOUJOU** (Fr. Cr.), in Haiti, a battery of gourd rattles carried on a pole.

**JOU' FÉ TOMBÉ DANS DLEAU C'EST PAS JOU LI COULÉ** (Fr. Cr.) ("The day a leaf falls into the water isn't the day it sinks"), an Afro-Haitian aphorism meaning the battle isn't over yet. (Courlander, *The Drum*, p. 336.)

**JOÚ MALHEUR LAIT CAILLÉ CASSÉ TETE OU** (Fr. Cr.) ("On a bad day clabbered milk breaks your head"), an Afro-Haitian proverb meaning that things are going badly; even clabbered milk can hurt you if it falls on you. (Courlander, *The Drum*, p. 334.)

**JUBA** (Afr.). 1. In colonial Jamaica, the day-name (q.v.) for a girl born on Monday. 2. In Haiti, a black social dance.

**JUBA ('S) BUSH** (Eng. Cr.), in Jamaica, a wild plant *(Iresine panicuta)* used by blacks in folk medicine.

**JUDGE,** in Trinidad, a black leader in the Shouter (q.v.) sect.

**JUGEMENT DE BAGUETTE** (Fr. Cr.), in Haiti, a folk ritual used by black sorcerers for identifying a thief or other guilty person. A long stick is pointed at one man, then at another, and when the tip vibrates in a circular manner the guilty party has been found.

**JUJU** (Afr.), a West African secret society very influential among blacks in Jamaica. Its members wear ritual dress and try to convince simple folk that they are dead men who have been revived by the power of magic medicine. (Beckwith, *Black Roadways*, p. 106.)

**JULIEN LUNG-FOU, MARIE-THÉRÈSE** (b. 1909), a mulatto poet born in Rivière-Salée, Martinique. Julien Lung-Fou was educated on the island and in Paris. In 1937, she was awarded first prize in sculpture by the French government. The next year she was honored with a bronze medal at the Paris International Exposition of the Grand Salon of French Artists. In 1938 she married Julien and took the name of Lung-Fou to honor her two grandfathers—one born in Dieppe, France, and the other in Canton, China —and her two mulatto grandmothers. Her main works include *Fables créoles transposées et illustrées* (1958); *Nouvelles fables créoles* (s.d.); *Trois bonnes fortunes* (s.d.); *Trois comédies* (s.d.); and *L'Amour universel* (s.d.). (Corzani, *Littérature antillaise, poésie*, p. 268.)

**JUMBY** (Afr.). 1. In colonial Jamaica, a magical place-spirit, feared and propitiated by black slaves; it was not worshipped. 2. In Trinidadian black folklore, the spirit of an evil person who, neither in life nor in death, can enjoy peace. 3. A generic term associated with magic and divination; used throughout the Afro-Caribbean region.

**JUMBY BEADS,** in Jamaica, a talisman worn by blacks to protect themselves against evil spirits. It consists of a string of red seeds with black spots.

**JUMBY MAN,** in Jamaica, a black sorcerer.

**JUMBY TOWN,** in Afro-Jamaican folklore, the place where jumbies live. See JUMBY.

**JUMINER, BESTÈNE** (b. 1927), a mulatto writer born in Cayenne, French Guiana, on August 6, 1927. His father was a Guianan, and his mother was from Pointe-à-Pitre, Guadeloupe. He studied at the Lycée Carnot in Pointe-à-Pitre and at the medical school at the University of Montpellier, France. As a medical doctor, he worked in Tunis, Iran, and other countries. In 1967, he was appointed professor of medicine at the University of Dakar, Senegal (q.v.). He has been very active in the political arena and, in 1958, he met with F. Fanon and joined forces to fight against French colonialism for the independence of Guiana. His works are *Les Batards* (1961); *Au Seuil d'un nouveau cri* (1963); and *Le revanche de Bozambo* (1968).

**JUMP DINKY.** See DINKIES.

**JUMPER,** in colonial Jamaica, a black slave in charge of whipping delinquent or recalcitrant blacks. Also called Johnny jumper.

**JUMPING-UP,** in Jamaica, a slave dance performed at wakes; today a black social dance.

**JU NETYE** (Fr. Cr.), among Haitian blacks, a word for daybreak.

**JUNGO** (Afr.), any kind of fungus or fungus-like plant, edible or inedible, growing on the ground or on wood. In the Caribbean, this word is always associated with blacks, implying African origin.

**JUNTA DE POBLACÍON BLANCA** (Sp.) (Committee for White Immigration), a Spanish government agency established in Havana, Cuba, in 1815 for the purpose of attracting white settlers. Among other privileges, it provided underdeveloped lands in the interior of the island. Few Spanish immigrants responded, but many refugee sugar planters from Saint Domingue, Louisiana, and Florida took advantage of the act. (Corwin, *Spain and the Abolition*, p. 33.)

**JUNTA PROTECTORA DE EMANCIPADOS** (Sp.) (Committee for the Protection of Freedmen), an agency established in Cuba by the Emancipation Law (1872) to protect former slaves. Among other regulations, it provided strict supervision of working conditions, salaries, clothing, and medicine. The liberated slaves were expected to obey and respect their former masters "as if the latter were their own father," and they could not change masters without the consent of their original owners. The freedmen were given the choice of remaining in Cuba or returning to Africa. See also LEY MORET.

**JUREMA** (Pg.), a toxic substance used by Afro-Brazilian sorcerers to induce a state of trance.

# k

**KÂ,** an Afro-Antillean wooden drum consisting of a small barrel with one end open and the other covered by a piece of sheepskin.

**KABINDA** (Afr.), in Trinidad, a black song-dance with percussion accompaniment. It is featured in carnival torchlight processions, along with stick men singing and performing stick fights.

**KAFFIR POX** (Ar.), in Jamaica, a mild form of smallpox that affected black slaves.

**KAFFRARIAN** (Afr.), in the West Indies, a black slave brought from the Mozambique coast to Brazilian plantations.

**KAGGA** (Afr.), in Jamaica, the ring around the smallest, hourglass-shaped drum played by blacks; of Yoruba (q.v.) origin.

**KAMISA** (Sp.), among the Bush Negroes (q.v.) of Guiana, a dhoti-like cotton shirt worn by a boy or girl at the age of fourteen as a symbol of their having became an adult in society.

**KANA** (Afr.), in Jamaica, a vessel or pot hung in a kitchen to keep meat.

**KANDA** (Afr.), an Afro-Jamaican word for a palm bough, especially the large lower sheath which holds it to the tree.

**KANGA** (Afr.), an ambivalent "stern" deity in the Afro-Haitian pantheon; protector of the family. A devotee "mounted" by him plays with fire and eats hot peppers.

**KANGA LANGA** (Afr.), an Afro-Haitian deity who takes care of members of the family.

**KANGA TROIS** (Fr. Cr.), a god in Afro-Haitian mythology, protector of the family.

**KANGKRA.** See KRENG-KRENG.

**KANUBA** (Afr.), a deity in Afro-Jamaican folk cults of unknown origin.

**KANURI** (Afr.). 1. In northeast Brazil, mixed-breed black slaves brought from central Sudan in West Africa. 2. An African language spoken in colonial Bahia, Brazil, by Bornu and Guinea black slaves.

**KANZO** (Afr.), in Afro-Haitian cults, a test of fire that an initiate must undergo to advance beyond the lowest status in the sect hierarchy. It is a formalized ritual, demonstrating that the power of the cult and the spirit of the individual are superior to the pain produced by the flames.

**KARITE,** in the French Antilles, a tropical fruit tree whose pale green, oiled berries are eaten by blacks. It was probably brought from Africa in slavery times.

**KEBIOSU** (Afr.), in the Afro-Haitian pantheon, a god of thunder who hurls stones to the earth when angered. He is also worshipped in Dahomey (q.v.). Persons killed by lightning are thought to be enemies of Kebiosu and are given special treatment at burial.

**KEEPER,** in the West Indies, a woman who lives with one or several men. This informal cohabitation can be short-lived or can endure for the better part of the participants' lifetime. It sometimes serves as a kind of trial marriage.

**KEEPER FAMILY,** an informal, often durable family association, very common among blacks in the West Indies, whereby the man and woman live together, with both working to support themselves and their children. The female partner must live with the insecurity of her position; if the union is broken up, either party may be held liable, and the other may resort to violence or magic against him or her.

**KEEP SENSA FOWL FE PICK OBEAH** (Eng. Cr.) ("One keeps a frizzled fowl to work sorcery"), an Afro-Jamaican aphorism. (Beckwith, *Jamaica Proverbs*, p. 78.)

**KEKE** (Afr.), an Afro-Jamaican term for the female sexual organs.

**KÉLÉ** (Afr.), in Afro-Brazilian *candomblés* (q.v.), a sacred necklace worn by a priestess of Exu (q.v.) symbolizing her subjugation to the god's service.

**KEMBE** (Afr.), in Afro-Haitian folk religion, magic power used by black sorcerers against their enemies.

**KEN CUFFEE** (Afr.), in colonial Jamaica, a band of Maroons (q.v.), possibly led by the famous black Captain Cuffee (q.v.).

**KENGE, KENGGE** (Afr.), an Afro-Jamaican term for a sore on the foot. See also YAWSY-KENGE.

**KETTLE HA' CUSS POT SAY HIM BOTTOM BLACK** (Eng. Cr.) ("The kettle curses the pot, says its bottom is black"), an Afro-Jamaican aphorism. (Beckwith, *Jamaica Proverbs*, p. 78.)

**KETU** (Afr.), the name of an Afro-Brazilian sect established in Bahia. Ketu is also the name of a town in Dahomey (q.v.) (Benin; q.v.).

**KEY,** in Jamaica, a black revivalist word for a stone, cloth, or piece of wood endowed with magic powers; a fetish.

**KIAKE** (Afr.), in Jamaica, a cow's horn used as a bugle by black Maroons (q.v.). See also ABENG.

**KIBUNGO** (Afr.), in Afro-Brazilian folklore, a mythical and terrifying ghost—half man, half animal—with an enormous hole in the middle of its back which opens when the creature bends its head. According to folklore, the *kibungo* was especially fond of visiting houses where naughty boys live. (Pierson, *Negroes*, p. 107.)

**KICKERABOO, KICKERABOO!** (Afr.) ("We are dying, we are dying!"), the cry of black slaves confined to overcrowded quarters under the deck of a slave ship during the Middle Passage (q.v.). After stowing the slaves below, the sailors closed and barred the hatchway gratings, and the slaves were not brought out on deck. The air became so thick and poisonous to breathe that sometimes at night the sailors heard from below "an howling melancholy noise and the anguishing cry 'Kickeraboo, kickeraboo!'" (Mannix, *Black Cargoes*, p. 117.)

**KILL-BUCKRA,** the Jamaica buttercup *(Tribulus cistoides).* It flourished at the season of fevers when many white men died and was therefore thought by the slaves to cause their death. See also BUCKRA.

**KILL-HOG,** among Jamaican Maroons (q.v.), a family celebration announcing that one's daughter has reached marriageable age.

**KILLING THE OBEAH,** an Afro-Jamaican phrase for the practice of putting the object causing an illness into a basin and throwing lime juice, and ashes over it. See also OBEAH.

**KIMBO** (Afr.), in the Afro-Jamaican dialect, the hip.

**KIMBUNGO** (Afr.). See BIZANGO.

**KINA** (Afr.), in Guiana, a charm that Bush Negroes (q.v.) believe protects the members of a matrilineal clan.

**KING CHRISTOPHE.** See CHRISTOPHE, HENRI.

**KING-FREE,** in the West Indies, a black child up to six years of age freed by the Emancipation Act in 1834; a slave child six years of age or older remained bound under the apprenticeship system.

**KINGO, JOHANNES CHRISTIAN,** an ordained missionary, pastor in Christiansted, Virgin Islands, whose ordination in 1771 was the first and only such ordination in the Danish West Indies. He was also the first minister to the slaves on Saint Thomas. In 1764, he translated Luther's *Small Catechism* into Dutch Creole; it was published in Copenhagen in 1770. (Farr, *Historical Dictionary*, p. 109.)

**KING RASTA,** a name for the Emperor Haile Selassie given by the Rastafarian (q.v.) black sect in Jamaica; who believe him to be the son of King Solomon and the Queen of Sheba.

**KING SUGAR,** a name given to the West Indies by English slave traders operating along the coast of Africa during colonial times.

**KIN-OUL** (Eng. Cr.), a Jamaican term for witch. Blacks believe she sheds her skin at night, takes the form of an owl, and flies out to suck people's blood.

**KISHEE, CAPTAIN,** a black commander in the Maroon War (q.v.) of 1730-1739 in Jamaica. He was eventually assassinated by a black traitor.

**KISIMBA** (Afr.), a major deity in the Afro-Cuban religion, identified with Saint Francis of Assisi.

**KITCHEN GARDEN,** in the West Indies, a small plot of land given by planters to black slaves to grow their own food. Each hut was surrounded by a separate garden filled with a profusion of oranges, shaddocks, coconuts, yams (q.v.), peppers, and okra (q.v.); there were also hogs and poultry.

**KITIBU** (Afr.), an African term applied in Jamaica to the dick-beetle or firefly *(Pyrophorus plagioph thalmus)* whose two luminous spots on its thorax are often mistaken for eyes.

**KITIBU AFU** (Afr.), an African word applied in Jamaica to a kind of yam (q.v.) *(Dioscorea alata)*, an edible starchy root plant with prominent eyes. See also KITIBU (q.v.).

**KITIBUM** (Afr.), a term, probably African in origin, applied in Jamaica to an entertainment at which there is dancing, singing, and other lively amusements.

**KITTY-KATTY,** a simple Afro-Jamaican percussion instrument made of wood and beaten with two sticks.

**KLEIN** (D.), a Dutch word used to describe a *quilombo* (q.v.) in colonial Brazil.

**KNIBB, WILLIAM,** one of the most famous British Baptist missionaries who, in 1830, successfully organized the antislavery forces in Jamaica. He was a member of the Baptist Missionary Society (q.v.). Accompanied by two Wesleyan agents, he went to England in 1831 to lay his case before the country and the Parliament. After the abolition of slavery in 1834, Knibb organized a system of free villages (q.v.) to settle former slaves as independent farmers. (Ragatz, *The Fall*, pp. 443, 448.)

**KNIFE-AND-SCISSORS MAN,** in Jamaica, a black sorcerer, so-called because of the symbolic use he makes of knives and scissors to indicate his supposed power to cast off evil.

**KNOCK,** among Afro-Jamaicans, spirits of the dead who are believed to be capable of returning for a relative or friend who has injured them. These persons, especially children, suddenly suffer convulsive fits and are knocked down by ghosts.

**KOBI** (Afr.), an Afro-Jamaican term for a variety of yam (q.v.) *(Dioscorea alata* or *Dioscorea sativa)* grown on the island.

**KOENDUS, J.A.G.,** a Surinamese black teacher who, in 1940, published a booklet aimed at regulating the spelling of black English spoken in the colony.

**KOFI.** See COFI.

**KOFI-ROUTN** (Afr.), an Afro-Jamaican term for a skin disease such as eczema.

**KOJO-RUBA** (Afr.), in the colonial West Indies, a generic term for a number of skin diseases such as eczema usually associated with African blacks as distinct from Creole blacks.

**KOKIO** (Afr.), in the Afro-Haitian folk religion, a chicken sacrificed by the priest to honor the gods.

**KOLA** (Ar.), in colonial Brazil, the circumcision of young children practiced by Islamic black slaves.

**KOLA NUT** (Afr.), the brown bitter nut of two trees *(Cola acuminata* and *C. vesa)* cultivated in tropical America and apparently brought from Africa in slavery times. The nuts contain much caffeine and are chewed by Caribbean blacks in great quantity.

**KONGK** (Afr.), an Afro-Jamaican term for a blow on the head.

**KONGKONGSA** (Afr.), an Afro-Jamaican word for falsehood, deceit; a deceitful person.

**KONGKONTE, CUM-CUM-TEK** (Afr.), in Jamaica, a black delicacy made of cassava flour, plantain (q.v.), or green banana; it is eaten as porridge in the form of dumplings.

**KONGORIOCO** (Afr.), a deity in Afro-Cuban *santería* (q.v.). He is said to have arrived too late at the distribution of divine powers by the great Jambampungo, so he only obtained the power of seeing and forewarning.

**KOOKOO** (Afr.), in Jamaica, a gang of blacks boys who performed for money at carnival time. Its name derives from the chorus they sang imitating the sound of an empty stomach.

**KORA** (Ar.), in the Afro-Antilles, an African harp with from sixteen to thirty-two chords played by blacks while reciting poems. *Kora* players are called black minstrels *(troubadours noirs)*.

**KOROMANTY.** See COROMANTEE.

**KOS KOS** (Afr.), an Afro-Jamaican word for quarrel, contention, trouble.

**KOSI OBA KAN AFI OLORUM** (Afr.) ("There is no god but Olorum"), an inscription in Nago, a Yoruba language, that occasionally was seen around 1895 on cult buildings and on small commercial establishments owned by blacks in Bahia, Brazil. (Pierson, *Negroes*, p. 72). See also OLORUM.

**KPOSDZIEM** (Afr.) ("going-out ceremony"), in Jamaica, a ritual held by blacks on the eighth day after birth. Two female relatives bring the infant to the outside yard where he is laid naked on the ground under the leaves. The godfather then proceeds to "baptize" him and to give him a name. (Brathwaite, *The Development*, p. 214.)

**KRA** (Afr.), among Surinamese blacks, a person's soul; someone's *kra* can be called up by a black sorcerer by means of spells and chants, sometimes to the accompaniment of drums. (Lier, *Frontier Society*, p. 289.)

**KRAAL** (Afr.), in Portuguese Angola (q.v.), a black settlement of thatched huts scattered in the eastern savanna. Thousands of *kraal* residents, most of them Bantu (q.v.), were brought as slaves to Brazil in the colonial period.

**KRACH-KRACH.** See SCRATCH-SCRATCH.

**KRENG-KRENG** (Afr.). 1. An Afro-Jamaican term for brambles, presumably fit for use as kindling-wood. 2. In Jamaica, a basket or container hung above the fire from the roof of a kitchen to receive the smoke; it is used to preserve and store meat or fish. Also called a *kangkra*. (Cassidy, *Dictionary*, p. 307.)

**KROMANTI FLUTE.** See COROMANTEE FLUTE.

**KUKU** (Afr.). In Jamaica: 1. Plentiful. 2. Pure rum.

**KULU-KULU** (Afr.). See GOOMBAY.

**KUMINA.** See CUMINA.

**KUMUNA DANCE** (Afr.), an Afro-Jamaican religious dance ceremony held on the occasion of a birth, betrothal, nine-night (q.v.), or memorial. During the ceremony, the dancers are believed to become possessed by ancestral spirits. (Cassidy, *Dictionary*, p. 267.)

**KUNU** (Afr.), an Afro-Jamaican term for fishing boat, a canoe. Sometimes quite large, they frequently ventured about twenty or thirty leagues from shore. (Cassidy, *Dictionary*, p. 267.)

**KWAAB** (Afr.), in Jamaica, a black albino.

**KWAAMIN** (Afr.). See QUAMIN.

**KWA-KWA** (Afr.), an Afro-Haitian name for the common gourd rattle.

**KWISEL** (Eng. Cr.), in Jamaica, a black albino.

**KYAMFYA** (Afr.), an Afro-Jamaican term for a type of yellow yam (q.v.) *(Dioscorea sativa, D. alata).*

**KYNANDO** (Yor.), an Afro-Jamaican word for the smallest hourglass-shaped drum.

**LABAT, JEAN BAPTISTE** (1663-1738), a Dominican priest born in Paris who arrived on the island of Guadeloupe in 1693. He was a missionary, a planter, and a builder of boats and roads. A great writer and prolific chronicler of his voyages, he traveled extensively around the island. For his interest in bettering the conditions of slaves working on the plantations, he was attacked by the whites and the mulatto settlers. He retired to France in 1705 and later visited Spain and Italy. In 1709, he went to Rome where he stayed until 1716. Père Labat became a legendary figure, and even today black peasants believe he became a *zombi* (q.v.). Among his works are *Voyage aux îles d'Amérique* (autobiography, 1722); *Relation sur l'Afrique occidentale d'après les ennemis d'André Brue* (1728); *Vogage du chevalier de Maesay en Guinée et à Cayenne* (1730); *Voyages en Espagne et en Italie* (autobiography, 1730); *Relation de l'Ethiopie occidentale* (1732); and *Mémoires du chevalier d'Arvieux . . . contenant ses voyages à Constantinople, dans l'Asie, la Syrie, la Palestine, l'Égypte, et la Barbarie . . .* (Paris, C.J.B. Delespine, 1735). (Corzani, *Littérature antillaise, prose,* p. 46.)

**LABORERS' RIOT OF 1878,** a violent riot of black laborers that erupted in Saint Croix in October 1878. After the 1848 emancipation, black laborers on plantations were still legally obligated to work under one-year contracts with strict provisions. Blacks complained that the Labor Act was merely a new kind of slavery, providing only a 10-cent per day wage. The rioters sacked the city of Christiansted and attacked several plantations. Once the rebellion was put down, the Labor Act was repealed. (Farr, *Historical Dictionary*, p. 109.)

**LABRA, RAFAEL MARÍA** (1840-1915), a Cuban-born mulatto, the son of a Spanish army officer and a mulatto woman. Soon after his birth, the family moved to Spain where young Labra was educated. Later he became a newspaperman and ardent abolitionist, and was a charter member of the Sociedad Abolicionista Española (q.v.). He believed that slaves should be free in a democratic society and that emancipation was in the best interest of both the colonies and Spain. A prolific and didactic writer, Labra would prove to be the Spanish Wilberforce (q.v.) of the abolition movement (q.v.). He was a man of exceptionally high moral stature. (Corwin, *Spain and the Abolition*, p. 160.)

**LACERDA, CARLOS DE,** a Brazilian journalist who was a leader of the antislavery movement (1884-1888). He was the editor of a radical abolitionist newspaper in Campos, his native city. He concealed fugitive slaves in his home at great risk to his own life and wrote editorials encouraging black slaves to burn the sugar cane (q.v.) fields and flee. At the time, his name elicited extreme emotions among planters and blacks in the Campos region.

**LACERDA, QUINTINO,** a black Brazilian leader who, in 1886, organized the Jabaquara shanty town (q.v.) for runaway slaves. This community, located outside the city of Santos, had more than 10,000 residents by the end of 1887.

**LACOUR, LAKU** (Fr. Cr.), in Haiti, a rural black hamlet inhabited by related families. A kind of rural community in which residents share a common social life and work together in the surrounding fields. The *lacour* is often made up of landless house renters who work whenever they can find odd jobs for wages.

**LACROSIL, MICHÈLE,** a prominent contemporary writer born on the island of Guadeloupe. Orphaned at an early age, she attended private schools on the island and then was sent to Paris to further her education. There she met and married Henri Galliar, a member of the French Academy of Medicine. Lacrosil is deeply concerned with African themes, racial prejudice, and the social tensions between whites, mulattoes, and blacks on her native island. Her works include *Sapotille et le serin d'argile* (Paris, 1960) and *Demain, Sab-Herma* (Paris, 1967). (Corzani, *Littérature antillaise, prose*, p. 261.)

**LADANE, LADANO** (Pg.), in Brazil, the assistant of the high master of worship in the Moslem religion; an acolyte of the *imam* (q.v.).

**LADEIRA** (Pg.), in colonial Brazil, a settlement of runaway slaves. See also QUILOMBO.

**LADINO** (Sp.). 1. As originally used, a Christianized African slave who spoke Spanish or had some knowledge of Spanish culture. Subsequently the term came to include any descendant of African slaves born in the New World and eventually any Hispanized black. 2. Today in Guatemala and elsewhere an urban Spanish person as opposed to an Indian one.

**LAFOREST, EDMOND** (1876-1915), a black poet born in Jérémie, Haiti. After receiving a degree in education, Laforest taught for many years in his native town and was also a school inspector and journalist. Among his works are *L'Evolution* (Port-au-Prince, 1901); *Poèmes mélancholiques* (Port-au-Prince, 1894-1900); *La Dernière fée, fantasie en vers* (Port-au-Prince, 1909); *Sonnets-médallions du dix-neuvième siècle: Ornés de quatre-vingt-six portraits authentiques et de douze fleurons originaux* (Paris, 1909); and *Cendres et flammes* (Paris, 1912).

**LAGUIDIBÁ** (Pg.), in Brazil, a chain of beads of different sizes made of horn. Blacks, especially children, wear them around their neck or waist as a magic charm.

**LAHIRA** (Ar.), in the belief of Moslem Hausa slaves (q.v.) in colonial Brazil, the abode of sanctified souls after death, paradise.

**LAILLÉ** (Fr. Cr.), an Afro-Haitian term for the swirling of skirts in a dance.

**LAKU** (Fr. Cr.). See LACOUR.

**LALEAU, LÉON,** a black Haitian poet inspired by African themes and an ardent follower of négritude (q.v.). Convinced of the greatness of black traditions, Laleau expressed despair at wearing European clothes, speaking the French language, and being constrained by the patterns of white thought. At one point, he declared that Senegal, not Haiti, was his real home. Among his numerous works are *Amitiés impossibles* (Port-au-Prince, 1901); *Jusq'au bord* (Port-au-Prince, 1916); *La danse des vagues* (Port-au-Prince, 1919); *A voix basse* (Port-au-Prince, 1919); *Abbréviations* (Paris, 1929); *Musique nègre* (Port-au-Prince, 1931); *Orchestre* (Paris, 1937); and *Apothéoses* (Port-au-Prince, 1952).

**LAMBI** (Fr. Cr.), in Haiti, a black's drum, made from a conch shell. In colonial times, it played a decisive role in calling the slaves to rise up against their masters. Today *lambis* often mark poor people's graves in cemeteries.

**LAMMING, GEORGE** (b. 1927), a Barbadian novelist. Lamming is deeply concerned with the plight of blacks as victims of white discrimination at home and abroad. He idealizes Africa and African values and looks to the African continent with nostalgia, sadness, and vague longing. He dislikes his own colonial society which he considers defiled by racial prejudice and discrimination. Lamming's fictional characters live in constant tension and painful insecurity, consumed by the problem of having to adapt to the world around them. His works include: *In the Castle of My Skin* (q.v.)

(New York, 1953); *The Emigrants* (London, 1954); *Of Age of Innocence* (London, 1958); and *The Pleasures of Exile* (London, 1960).

**LAMPION** (Fr. Cr.), in Haiti, metal candelabra or oil lamps carried by groups of marching blacks at carnival time.

**LANÇADO** (Pg.), in colonial Guinea (q.v.), West Africa, a Portuguese or black adventurer who controlled much of the bartering and procurement of slaves for plantations in Brazil. See also TANGAMÃO.

**LAND IN ANCESTRAL CULT,** among Haitian blacks, the practice of setting aside land for the worship of ancestors; an African custom brought to Haiti by slaves.

**LANDSKINDEREN** (D.), in Surinam, a Dutch word for a native-born mulatto.

**LANGAGE** (Fr.) ("language"), in Afro-Haitian cults, the tongue or tongues spoken by the priest or possessed persons during services.

**LANGGULALA** (Afr.), an Afro-Jamaican word for a tall, slim black.

**LAPLACE** (Fr. Cr.), in Haiti, the assistant priest in some black cults who assumes responsibility for running the temple in the absence of his chief. The *laplace* frequently inherits the cult temple and all that goes with it.

**LARA, ORUNO** (b. 1879) a mulatto poet and self-made man born on January 20, 1879, in Pointe-à-Pitre, Guadeloupe. Orphaned at an early age, Lara left school at eleven, unable to pay for his education. He was blessed with a brilliant mind, however, and went on to become a well-known newspaperman, a popular literary critic, and a leader in the regional renaissance of Afro-Antillean literature. Like other black intellectuals of his time, he became interested in Africa, but he did not reject his own black traditions. He tried to reconcile his black ancestry with the dominant French influence and heritage, and proclaimed his loyalty to Antillanité (q.v.) rather than to the radical négritude (q.v.) movement. His main works are *L'Année fleurie* (1901); *Guadeloupe et Martinique* (1903); *L'Idylle rose* (1907); *Fleurs tropicales* (1908); *Les Emblemès* (1909); *L'Art des vers* (1911); *Sous le ciel bleu de la Guadeloupe* (1912); *Essai sur la littérature antillaise* (1912); and *Histoire de Guadeloupe* (1923).

**LAS SIETE PARTIDAS** (Sp.) ("The Seven Laws"), a medieval Spanish legal system that provided a slave code applied in the New World. Influenced both by Latin Roman law and by Christian philosophy, it held as a fundamental principle that slavery was against natural reason because "slavery is the most evil and the most despicable thing that can be found among men." Although slavery was accepted as a historical institution, the law insured the slave his God-given humanity, and the slave was considered a human being, legally possessing a series of rights such as sanctity of marriage, parenthood, fraternization, and rights and obligations as a child of the Christian church. (Klein, *Slavery*, p. 59.)

**LA SIRÈNE**, an Afro-Haitian female deity of the sea who appears as a mermaid.

**LATINO, JUAN** (1516-1606?), a black poet and writer, born in Guinea (q.v.) and brought to Spain. He and his mother were slaves in the household of the daughter of Gonzalo Fernández de Córdoba, Doña Elvira. In 1530, his mistress sent him to school at Baena where he studied the humanities, learning Greek and Latin. He later continued his education at the University of Granada. Juan was so outstanding in Latin that he renounced his slave name, Juan de Sessa, and called himself Juan Latino. He was soon known for his scholarship; in addition, he played the organ, lute, and guitar. He was later mentioned by Lope de Vega in the play *La dama boba*. Around 1548, he married a white woman who bore him three daughters. In 1556, he graduated from the University of Granada, and, in 1557, he became a professor there. His main work is *Austrias*, a series of poems in Latin praising the great Spanish hero Don Juan de Austria, son of Charles V. In 1586, when he was seventy, he gave up his professorial chair for health reasons. (Jahn, *Neo-African Literature*, pp. 31-32.)

**LAVADO** (Sp.), in Puerto Rico, a mulatto with light skin and delicate features.

**LAVAGEM** (Pg.), in Bahia, the washing and garnishing of a chapel by black women, members of an African cult house, and their joyous dancing in the streets asking for alms. The entire procedure is called *lavagem*. It is said to be a Yoruba (q.v.) religious ceremony.

**LAVAGEM DAS CONTAS** (Pg.) ("washing the beads"), a magic ritual performed by a black minister in an Afro-Brazilian cult in order to identify the spirit that troubles a sick person.

**LAWYER LOOK 'PON BLACK NEGER WI' ONE EYE, BUT HIM LOOK 'PON HIM POCKET WID TWO** (Eng. Cr.) ("The lawyer looks upon the black nigger with one eye, i.e., with little attention, but he looks upon his pocket with two''), an Afro-Jamaican aphorism. (Beckwith, *Jamaica Proverbs*, p. 78.)

**LÉ** (Afr.), the smallest Afro-Brazilian drum, measuring from one and one-half to two and one-half feet.

**LE BAB'B ZAMI OU PREND DIFÉ METTÉ BAB' OU LATRAMP** (Fr. Cr.) (''When your friend's beard catches fire, put your beard to soaking''), an Afro-Haitian aphorism. (Courlander, *The Drum*, p. 336.)

**LECESNE, LOUIS CELESTE,** a Jamaican-born mulatto, the son of Louis Nicholas Lecesne, a French refugee from Saint Domingue (Haiti) and of a free black woman. He practiced a trade in Kingston and was also sergeant of militia. In 1823, he was accused of plotting a slave rebellion and of being an alien, and the government ordered his deportation to Haiti. In 1825, Lecesne appealed to the British Parliament, and, three years later, after being found to be a native-born British subject, he returned to Jamaica. He was awarded compensation for losses sustained by his illegal removal from the island.

**LEGAWU, NIGAWU** (Afr.), werewolf. In Trinidadian black folklore, a mythical werewolf whose activities are considered antisocial. There are many *legawu* tales.

**LEGBA** (Afr.), in Haiti, an African god, guardian of the crossroads, highways, and the entrance to every house, yard, and garden. He is one of the most important deities in the voodoo (q.v.) religion. Legba must be summoned before every ceremony may begin. Tuesday is his sacred day and the plum is reserved for him. Sometimes Legba is identified with St. Anthony. In Afro-Spanish and Afro-Brazilian cults, Legba appears as having different status and different attributes.

**LEGBA AVARDRA** (Afr.), an Afro-Haitian deity spoken of as a vagabond who continually wanders on the principal highways.

**LEGBA PIÉ CASSÉ** (Afr.), an Afro-Haitian god described as having paralyzed legs, with arms held stiff and crooked.

**LEGBA SÉ, ATTIBON LEGBA** (Afr.), in Haiti an important and powerful deity who guards the entrance of every house, yard, or garden. Of Dahomean origin, the god is generally conceived of as a limping old man, clad in tatters, but in his several manifestations he has more specific characteristics. He favors his servitors by giving them hidden treasures. He likes to eat cocks and male goats and to drink alcoholic beverages. Today, as in earlier times in Dahomey, the image of Legba Sé, made of clay, stands or sits before the entrance to many villages.

**LEI AUREA** ("Golden Law"), in Brazil, a law providing for the immediate abolition of slavery throughout the country. Parliament passed it in May 1888 but did not stipulate compensation for the slaveowners. The slaves of Brazil indulged in a delirium of enthusiasm such as the country had never seen.

**LEIDESDORF, WILLIAM ALEXANDER** (1810-1848), a black financier born in poverty in Saint Croix, Virgin Islands, in 1810. After emigrating to the United States, he became a successful cotton merchant in Louisiana. In 1841 he settled in San Francisco. There he began investing his money in real estate, finding it necessary to become a Mexican citizen. He was a prosperous businessman, acquiring wealth and fame. At his death, in 1848, he owned the largest estate in California.

**LEI DO RIO BRANCO** ("Rio Branco Law"), a law written by the baron of Rio Branco and passed by the Brazilian congress in March 1871. It provided for the gradual abolition of slavery, without disturbing the foundations of the plantation society and the economy. It emancipated all slave children born after passage of the law and set up a fund for the purchase and liberation of blacks by the government.

**LEI DO VENTRE LIVRE** (Pg.) ("Free Womb Law"), a law passed by the Brazilian Congress in 1869, at the request of the emperor, Pedro II, establishing an emancipation plan which provided for the freedom of all infants born to slave mothers. The purpose of the law was to effect the total abolition of slavery.

**LEMANO, LIAMANO** (Pg.), in Brazil, the spiritual and temporal head of Moslem slaves brought over during the colonial period. He was the supreme chief and master of worship among the Hausa (q.v.) and Fulani (q.v.) blacks. In religious ceremonies, the *lemano* directed the prayers and the reading of the Koran, while a chorus of women chanted in Arabic.

**LENGUA DE SÃO-TOMÉ**, a sixteenth-century Portuguese jargon spoken in Guinea (q.v.).

**LENKIE** (Afr.), an Afro-Jamaican word for tall and thin.

**LÉONARD, NICHOLAS-GERMAIN** (1744-1793), a poet and abolitionist born in BasseTerre, Guadeloupe, the son of a colonial administrator. As a young man Léonard was sent to France for his education. Recognized for his brilliance, he soon became popular in aristocratic circles and met Henriette de Berville, a wealthy aristocrat, who fell in love with him. Since he was only a poor man without even a degree, however, her parents opposed the marriage and put her in a convent after she refused to marry an aristocrat of their liking. She died a recluse, a tragedy Léonard carried with him all his life. To ease the pain of his loss, he wrote numerous poems about friendship and religion. At one time, he was French ambassador to Liège, and, in 1783, upon his return to Guadeloupe, he was appointed judge of Pointe-à-Pitre. He settled on the family estate of Sainte Rose where he spoke and wrote against slavery, consequently angering the white planters. Unhappy, he left for France in 1792. In revolutionary France, poets like Léonard were not particularly prized; hence, he decided to return to his native Guadeloupe, but got sick and died in a hospital in Nantes. Among his numerous works are *Idylles morales* (1766); *L'Heureux vieillard* (1767); *Epitre à un jeune homme* (s.d.); *Essai de littérature* (1769); *La Religion établie sur les ruines de l'idolâtrie* (1770); *Le Temple de Gnide* (1772); *L'Amour vengé* (1773); *La Nouvelle Clémentine* (1774); *Lettre des deux habitants de Lyon* (1783); and *Lettre sur un voyage aux Antilles* (1783). (Corzani, *Littérature antillaise, Poésie*, p. 55.)

**LERÓ** (Afr.), in the Afro-Caribbean region, a black dance.

**LÉRO, ETIÈNNE** (1909-1939), a black poet born in Martinique. Léro attended local schools and was later sent to Paris to further his education. While studying at the Sorbonne, in cooperation with other Martiniquans, he founded the journal *Légitime Défense*, which soon became the mouthpiece for the négritude (q.v.) movement. As a writer Léro violently rejected the bourgeois conventions and humanitarian hypocrisy imposed by white society on his native island. He tried to replace the traditional literary models offered him at school and proclaimed his allegiance to the proletariat and to black traditions. His poems appeared in his journal and in various literary magazines of the day.

**LESPÈS, ANTHONY** (b. 1907), a black Haitian writer. Lespès is deeply concerned with the social and economic conditions of Haiti's peasants. He often describes the poverty of blacks exploited by white aliens. Lespès defends the black's religious strength and his own sense of loyalty to the community and the country. His works include *Les Semences* (a novel, 1949); *Les Chefs de la lumière* (Port-au-Prince, 1955); *Compère général* (1955); *Les Arbres musiciens* (1957); *L'Espace d'un cillement* (1959); and *Romanceros aux étoiles* (1960).

**LESSER ATTORNEY**, in the colonial West Indies, an administrator of one or two small sugar estates (q.v.) appointed by an attorney (q.v.) as his deputy. He was sometimes commissioned by the absentee planter himself.

**LETTER OF PATENT,** in the colonial West Indies, a formal British Crown document granting land to colonists subject to the payment of royal taxes.

**LETTRE DE DEMANDE,** in Haiti, among literate blacks, a written proposal of marriage; in earlier days, it was written on flowered stationery.

**LEVA-PANCADA** (Pg.), in colonial Brazil, a young black slave assigned as a playmate of the white children of the planters. He was supposed to allow his master's sons to beat him.

**LEVENBAAR** (D.) ("deliverable"), in the Dutch slave code, a physically and mentally fit slave who could be put on the market. In 1662, all the label implied was that the slave was not blind or mutilated and that he had been able to walk onto the ship without any help. Later health stipulations became very strict.

**LEVILLOU, J.** (b. 1788), a Creole writer born in Martinique. Little is known about Levillou's life. In his book *Les Créoles ou la vie aux Antilles* (1815), he vividly describes the customs of blacks in the Antilles. He accepts the social role of the mulattoes, whom he feels combine the intelligence of the whites and the strength of the blacks, but he violently rejects racial equality as proclaimed by the French Revolution in 1791 and denounces the runaway slaves as a poisonous class. Levillou also portrays the tragic life of the mulattoes rejected by both whites and blacks. (Corzani, *Littérature antillaise, Prose*, p. 209.)

**LEWIS, GEORGE,** a black slave born in West Africa who was brought to Virginia. In 1775, Lewis was sold to a Jamaican planter. There he was able to buy his freedom. After his conversion to Christianity he became an itinerant Baptist preacher and traveled all over the island. Soon many slaves came to attend his services, assembling around him at night wherever he went. Lewis was one of several organizers of the so-called Native Baptist Movement (q.v.) at the end of the eighteenth century in Jamaica.

**LEWIS, MATTHEW,** an absentee West Indian planter and celebrated author known as "Monk" Lewis from the title of his famous Gothic novel, *Ambrosio, or The Monk*. A progressive planter, Lewis attempted to ameliorate the conditions of the black slaves on his Jamaican estate. In 1815, he prohibited whipping, accepted black evidence, sought to lessen toil by making extensive use of machines, and granted additional holidays. He also resolved to visit his possessions regularly and required in his will that his heir spend at least a few months there every third year. Among other works, Lewis wrote *Journal of a West Indian Proprietor Kept During a Residence in the Island of Jamaica* (London, 1834) in which he gives a detailed account of plantation operations and of slavery. (Brathwaite, *The Development*, pp. 123, 129, 190.)

**LEY MORET** (Sp.) ("Moret Law"), an antislavery bill introduced by colonial minister Segismundo Moret y Prendergast (q.v.), and approved by the Spanish Cortes on July 4, 1870. It granted the right of free birth to every child born of slave parents and proclaimed that all slaves born between September 17, 1868 and the date of publication of the law became the property of the state; masters were to be paid 125 Spanish pesetas for each such acquisition.

**LEY MORÚA** (Sp.) ("Morua Law"), a constitutional amendment passed by the Cuban Congress on May 2, 1910, forbidding the existence of political parties based on race or color. This bill, introduced by Senator Martín Morúa Delgado (q.v.), was bitterly attacked by the mulattoes since it directly affected the Colored People's Independent party (see PARTIDO INDEPENDIENTE DE LA GENTE DE COLOR).

**LEY PENAL CONTRA LOS TRAFICANTES EN ESCLAVOS** (Sp.) ("Penal Law Against Slave Traders"), a major Spanish law providing for the detention, confiscation, and destruction of any Spanish ship engaged in the slave trade. It was passed by the Cortes on February 28, 1845.

**LHÉRISON, JUSTIN,** (1873-1907), a black Haitian writer. Lhérison was a follower of French naturalism and a disciple of Honoré de Balzac. He sought to develop a national literature and often wrote in French Creole (q.v.), the language of the peasants. Lhérison felt that an author should draw inspiration from old customs and present a photographic image of people's passions, prejudices, and virtues. Among his works are *Myrtha, poème érotique* (Port-au-Prince, 1892); *Les chants de l'aurore; primes rimes* (Port-au-Prince, 1893); *Les fortunes de chez-nous* (Port-au-Prince, 1902); *La famille de Petite-Caille* (Port-au-Prince, 1905); *Zoune chez sa nainnaine* (Port-au-Prince, 1906); and *La Dessa-liniènne; chant nationale* (Port-au-Prince, s.d.).

**LIAMANO.** See LEMANO.

**LIBAMBO** (Afr.), in colonial Brazil, an instrument of torture used to punish serious offenses committed by black slaves. It gripped the unfortunate victim at the neck and also served to chain two slaves together.

**LIBERTO** (Sp.), in Cuba, a black child born to slave parents and freed by the Ley Moret (q.v.).

**LIBERTOS ORIENTALES, LOS** (Sp.) ("the Freedman of the Banda Oriental"), a special battalion of former slaves, which saw almost continuous service from 1816-1820, in Uruguay. They fought under Jose de Artigas, a Uruguayan liberator.

**LIBRO DE PALMEO** (Sp.), an account book which described the physical features of a slave, such as his height, age, sex, name, health, and port of entry. It was required by law in the Spanish colonies. See also PALMEO.

**LICENCIA DE ESCLAVOS** (Sp.). See ASIENTO DE NEGROS.

**LIELE, GEORGE** (circa 1733-1822), a Virginia-born black slave owned by a Baptist planter and apparently freed when the planter died. Around 1780 Liele was pastor of a black church in Savannah, Georgia. A former Loyalist, he decided to emigrate to the West Indies at the close of the American Revolution. In 1783, he arrived in Kingston, Jamaica. According to his own account, he was then about fifty years old and had a wife and four children. He built a church, founded the Native Baptist Movement (q.v.), and preached to the slaves around Kingston for several years. Charged with sedition, Liele, together with other black preachers, was jailed in 1794. His church began to fragment while he was in prison. Upon his release, Liele, like other black preachers (q.v.) became an itinerant minister in order to circumvent the ban against preachers. He visited England in 1822 at the invitation of the Baptist Mission and died that same year. He is also known as G. Lisle and G. Sharp. (Curtin, *Two Jamaicas*, p. 32.) See also BILL TO PREVENT PREACHING BY PERSONS NOT DULY QUALIFIED BY LAW.

**LIGHT-WORK PEOPLE.** See THIRD GANG.

**LIGNUM VITAE**, a tropical tree *(Guaiacum officinale)* used as medicine by blacks in Jamaica. To cure any bruise they grate the gum of the trees, mix it with rum, and apply it to the injured place.

**LILLY BILLY-GOAT HAB BEARD BUT BIG BULL HAB NONE** (Eng. Cr.) ("A little billy-goat has a beard, but a big bull has none"), an Afro-Jamaican aphorism. (Beckwith, *Jamaica Proverbs*, p. 79.)

**LIMA, JORGE MATEUS DE** (1895-1953), a Brazilian mulatto poet. Lima's philosophical, religious, and black themes are deeply rooted in the Brazilian northeast and in the plantation tradition. His modernist poetry reflects his interest in the cultural contribution of Afro-Brazilians to the nation as a whole and sets the pattern for the revival of the "Faithful Slave" image in postslavery literature. Among his works are *Essa Nega Fulô* (1928) and *Pae João Calunga* (a novel, 1935).

**LIMA, VICENTE,** a Brazilian mulatto scientist who has done serious research on black culture. He was the co-founder of the Centro de Cultura Afro-Brasileira (q.v.) in Recife in 1937 and is the author of *Xangô*, a well-documented study of black culture.

**LIMA BARRETO, AFONSO HENRIQUES DE** (1881-1922), a black Brazilian novelist who was a disciple of Honoré de Balzac. Lima Barreto studied at the Polytechnic School of Rio de Janeiro and afterwards became a public employee. He devoted his leisure hours to writing novels of urban life as seen in Rio de Janeiro, his native city; slavery also attracted his interest. He was a prolific writer among whose many works are *Vida e Morte de Gonzaga Sá* (Rio de Janeiro, s.d.); *Historias e Sonhos* (Rio de Janeiro, 1920); *Coisas do Jambon, Sátira e Folclore* (São Paulo, 1956); *Triste Fim de Polycarpo Quaresma* (São Paulo, 1956); and *Recordações do Escrivão Isaias Caminha* (São Paulo, 1961).

**LIMBA** (Afr.), in the Afro-Haitian pantheon, a gluttonous god with an insatiable appetite who lives in the rocks. He is said to kill and eat his followers.

**LIMPIEZA DE SANGRE** (Sp.) ("purity of blood"), a phrase originally used in Spain to describe a Catholic Spaniard without a trace of Jewish or Moorish blood. Later in the New World, it was used to block the mulattoes' efforts to be considered whites.

**LIMPIEZA DO CORPO** (Pg.), in the Afro-Brazilian *candomblé* (q.v.), a ritual performed by a cult priest consisting of rubbing the body of the faithful with corn oil and honey. It is usually done on Fridays.

**LINGLÉSOU** (Fr. Cr.), in Afro-Haitian folklore, a deity who lives in abysses and large boulders.

**LINGUA DA COSTA** (Pg.), in Brazil, a language spoken by Nagó (q.v.) slaves. In Bahia, it was used in the trade between the northeast and Lagos, Nigeria.

**LINGUA DA VACA** (Pg.) ("cow's tongue"), a derogatory name given to a dialect spoken by Yoruba (q.v.) slaves in colonial Brazil.

**LINHA** (Pg.), the religious service in some Afro-Brazilian cults.

**LISBÕA, ANTONIO FRANCISCO.** See ALEIJAÕDINHO.

**LISLE, GEORGE.** See LIELE, GEORGE.

**LITTLE CHRISTMAS,** in Jamaica, an old nickname among slaves for Easter holiday.

**LIVRO DE ASSENTO** (Pg.), in colonial Brazil, a ledger kept by plantation owners. Besides accounts, it contained family information and items of general interest, such as slave riots, epidemics and floods.

**LIXARI.** See VITRI.

**LIZARD NEBER PLANT CORN, BUT HIM HAB PLENTY** (Eng. Cr.) ("Lizard never plants corn but he has plenty"), an Afro-Jamaican aphorism. (Beckwith, *Jamaica Proverbs*, p. 80.)

**LO** (Afr.), among the Bush Negroes (q.v.) of Guiana, a matrilineal clan. (Bastide, *African Civilizations*, p. 53.)

**LOA** (Afr.), in Afro-Latin America, a generic term for a spirit, usually inherited in the family from generation to generation. Its origin is African. A *loa* protects and gives advice to a person and helps him to work better. Among Haitian blacks, *loas* are considered to be like children; they must be told what to do. If the *loas* are promised a sacrifice, the ceremony must be held on the set date; otherwise, the *loas* will cause their worshippers much trouble. It is believed that the government of *loas* is similar to human government; there are categories of *loas* as first, second, and third class, simple domestics, and those who have been condemned for their misdemeanors. There is no agreement regarding their nature, activities, and hierarchy. (Horowitz, *People and Cultures*, p. 502.)

**LOA BOSSAL** (Fr. Cr.), among Haitian blacks, the untamed spirit or god who animates any living creature. Its untrained and unpredictable behavior is dangerous; thus, it must be brought under proper control.

**LOA CREOLE,** in the Afro-Haitian pantheon, a spirit believed to have been born locally, in the country, as opposed to the *loas* who are of African origin.

**LOANDA.** 1. See LUANDA. 2. Probably scurvy, a common disease among slaves arriving at ports of entry in the New World; it swelled the body, rotted the gums, and caused sudden death.

**LOBISHOMEM** (Pg.), in Afro-Brazilian folklore, a mythical creature who roams around the countryside on moonlight nights, preferably on Fridays. Coming up behind a traveler or sneaking into the house after a child, he grasps his victims and sucks their blood.

**LOB-LOB** (Eng. Cr.), in Jamaica, a porridge or gruel of various kinds made from corn, manioc, and other ingredients. From the sailors' word *lobloly*, among slaves it became known as *lob-lob*. Although a staple food, it is said that the slaves disliked this thick, heavy stew, and when it was served to them they cried: "Oh, no. No more lob-lob."

**LOBLOLLY TREE,** a decorative West Indian tree, apparently of African origin.

**LOCKSMAN** (Eng. Cr.), in Jamaica, a member of a black cult.

**LOEKOE-MAN** (D.), in Surinam, a black sorcerer.

**LOKO ATTISOQUÉ** (Fr. Cr.), in the Afro-Haitian pantheon, a goddess, the wife of Loko Attisso (q.v.).

**LOKO ATTISSO** (Fr. Cr.), an Afro-Haitian god, healer and protector of the temple. In Dahomey (q.v.), he is one deity among the sky gods. (Courlander, *The Drum*, p. 324.)

**LOKO BASSIYÉ** (Fr. Cr.), an Afro-Haitian god of the sky invoked by Dahomean slaves in colonial times; a member of the Loko family of gods.

**LOKO DAHOMÉ** (Fr. Cr.), an Afro-Haitian sky god of Dahomean origin, protector of the family; a member of the Arada (q.v.) pantheon.

**LOKO DAINZO** (Fr. Cr.), an Afro-Haitian sky god, protector of his devotees.

**LOKO DAÏ PRÉ** (Fr. Cr.), an Afro-Haitian god, one of the many sky deities.

**LOKO TOKAMIWEZO** (Fr. Cr.), an Afro-Haitian deity, a member of the Loko family.

**LOLO** (Fr. Cr.), in the French Antilles, a small country store usually owned and operated by blacks.

**LOMBARD, JUAN,** a black Cuban leader in the uprising of the mulattoes that occurred on May 20, 1912. He was the chief organizer in Sagua la Grande. Unable to rally the black population to protest against the suppression of the Colored People's Independent party, he fled to the mountains. See PARTIDO INDEPENDIENTE DE LA GENTE DE COLOR.

**LONDON MISSIONARY SOCIETY (LMS),** an organization founded in London by David Bogue in 1795 to spread the Gospel among the heathen. The following year its affiliated societies, the Edinburgh Missionary Society (EMS) and the Glasgow Missionary Society (GMS), were also organized. Although it was supposed to remain an interdenominational group, it soon became Congregationalist like its founder. In 1798, the society began planning a mission to work among the slaves in Jamaica. After the abolition of the slave trade in 1808, it established missions in Tobago and in Demerara (British Guiana) where John Smith (q.v.) was one of its most active missionaries.

**LONG 'STORY MEK DEM KETCH RUN' AWAY NIGGER** (Eng. Cr.) ("A long story made them catch the runaway nigger"), an Afro-Jamaican aphorism from slavery times. (Beckwith, *Jamaica Proverbs*, p. 80.)

**LOOSE-PACKER,** a Guinea captain who, by providing good accommodations and better food for the slaves on the voyage to the West Indies, greatly reduced their mortality rate.

**LOPES, JOSÉ,** a black leader in the defense of a famous *quilombo* (q.v.), Buraco de Tatu, located in the state of Bahia, Brazil. After a dramatic attack by the government militia, Lopes and his followers were defeated, and the settlement was destroyed on September 2, 1763. (Price, *Maroon Societies*, pp. 222, 223.)

**LOPES BIXORDA, JORGE,** a Brazilian slave trader who, in 1536, unloaded a cargo of Guinea (q.v.) blacks in the city of Bahia. Apparently, this is the first record of Africans being imported into the newly established plantations. (Mendonça, *A Influencia*, p. 20.)

**LORD OF GUINEA,** a self-imposed title of John II, king of Portugal, who, in 1481, built the first castle at Elmina (q.v.) to promote trades in goods and slaves. (Mannix, *Black Cargoes*, p. 4.)

**LORO** (Sp.), the offspring of a white man and a black woman; the oldest Spanish racial term, recorded around 1475. (Alvarez Nazario, *El elemento negroide*, p. 354.)

**LOROKS.** See LURUKS.

**LOS RANCHOS,** in colonial Venezuela, a settlement of free blacks near the Coro region (circa 1750). This community had its own chiefs, police, and fields to grow food and keep animals, and included a patron saint and a cemetery.

**LOUD PEALS OF WHIPPING,** in the colonial West Indies, slave flogging (q.v.) in which every stroke could be heard from a distance away. (Brathwaite, *The Development*, p. 192.)

**LOUGAN** (Fr. Cr.), in the Antilles, a tropical system of agriculture consisting of clearing the forest and using the ashes of the burnt vegetation to fertilize the soil. It usually follows a cycle of four or five years.

**LOUP-GARO, LOUP-GAROU** (Fr. Cr.), in Afro-Haitian folklore, a mythical vampire. She is human in form, but she sheds her skin and assumes an animal shape at night when she roams the countryside seeking a victim.

**LOUS** (Fr. Cr.), in the French Antilles, a method used by blacks to preserve fruit.

**L'OUVERTURE, ISAAC** (1782-1854), a son of the liberator, Toussaint L'Ouverture (q.v.), born in Haiti. In 1797, Isaac was sent to Paris for his education. There he befriended Josephine (q.v.), Napoleon's wife. Later, the emperor sent Isaac and his brother Placide (q.v.) back to Haiti to convince their father to sign a peace agreement. He remained on the island, accompanied by his tutor, Abbé Coisnon, until his parents' exile to France in 1802. A poet and eloquent prose writer, he is credited with the authorship of *L'Haitiade*, an epic poem published in Paris in 1828. His autobiography was left unpublished at the time of this death.

**L'OUVERTURE, PAUL** (b. ca. 1744), a black leader who, like his brother Toussaint (q.v.), was born a slave on the Breda plantation in Haiti. He participated in the great slave rebellion of 1791. When his brother was exiled in 1802, he remained on the island in the service of France. Later he was assassinated by French colonists.

**L'OUVERTURE, PLACIDE,** a stepson of Toussaint L'Ouverture (q.v.), the black liberator. Placide was born in Haiti and attended local schools. In 1797, he was sent to France to continue his education. He attended school in Paris for three years. In 1801, the emperor Napoleon Bonaparte sent him and his brother Isaac (q.v.) back to the island with a conciliatory letter for their father. Placide was soon made a general in the army in Haiti and fought against French forces. In 1802, he followed his parents into exile and settled in Bayonne, France. The government later sent him to Ile Bell off the coast of France.

**L'OUVERTURE, TOUSSAINT** (circa 1744-1803), the great black patriot. L'Ouverture, born a slave on the Breda plantation near Le Cap François, Haiti, was the son of a black slave named Gao-Ginu. Because of his intelligence and loyalty, his master favored him with especially good treatment. A self-educated slave, he led the black rebellion of 1791. In 1793, he forced the British forces to withdraw from Haiti's coastal cities which they had occupied in alliance with the Spanish. In 1801, he conquered Santo Domingo and governed the whole island until Napoleon sent General Leclerc in 1802. The black leader fought stubbornly against the invaders, but soon a peace treaty was signed. L'Ouverture was then treacherously seized and taken to France where he died in prison in 1803.

**LOUVORES A OGUM** (Pg.) ("praises to Ogum"), a prayer honoring the African god Ogum, (q.v.), printed on red and white shields and hung on the walls of *candomblé* (q.v.) temples. These inscriptions are still seen in Bahía, Brazil. (Pierson, *Negroes*, p. 300.)

**LOUVORES A XANGÓ** (Pg.) ("praises to Xangó"), a prayer honoring the African god Xangó (q.v.) written on the walls of *candomblé* (q.v.) chapels in Bahia, Brazil.

**LOVE, JOSEPH ROBERT** (1839-1913), a black religious leader born in Nassau, Bahamas, in October 1839, the son of a shipwright. Educated in the United States for the priesthood in the Episcopal church, Love took orders in Florida and held several pastorates of black churches. In 1880, he entered the school of medicine at the University of Buffalo, New York. After graduation he settled in Port-au-Prince, Haiti. He was appointed a medical officer at the health department by the government and simultaneously acted as rector of the Church of the Redeemer in the same city. He moved to Kingston, Jamaica, in 1889 where he published *The Jamaica Advocate*, a weekly periodical in which he dealt with the black population's social problems. He soon became an influential leader. He was elected a member of the city council and later, in 1906, was a member of the House Assembly. He died in Kingston.

**LOVE BUSH, LOVE WEED,** in Jamaica, parasitic plants (genus *Cusenta*) which blacks believe bring success in love.

**LOVE DANCE,** in colonial Jamaica, a lascivious slave dance.

**LOVE WEED.** See LOVE BUSH.

**LUANDA,** an Angolan port built by the Portuguese in 1575 under the name of São Paulo de Loandas; capital of the Angola Colony (q.v.). It was the center of slave traffic to Brazil during the colonial period.

**LUBOLA, JUAN** (1635-1664), a black Jamaican slave leader of the Maroons (q.v.) who, in 1656, fought against British invaders of the island. He and his followers surrendered to the English in exchange for pardons and freedom. Lubola was made a colonel of a black regiment and was ordered to try to reduce the number of remaining Maroons. (Price, *Maroon Societies*, p. 231.)

**LUBOLO** (Afr.), a black dance performed during the noisy carnival processions in Montevideo, Uruguay (circa 1800).

**LUCIANO,** a black slave who was a leader in the Conspiracy of the Ladder (q.v.) in Cuba in 1844. A black of the Mandingo (q.v.) tribe, he was a counselor of the black king elected by the plotters. In his trial, he was described as "a sagacious and influential man with a privileged mind among his class." (Hall, *Social Control*, p. 58.)

**LUCUMI** (Afr.), Yoruba (q.v.) black slaves brought from West Africa into Cuba during the colonial period. They belonged to the Alkomy (or Ulkamy) Kingdom located at 10° latitude N between Benin (q.v.) and Ardra (q.v.).

**LUKU,** a black society of diviners in Surinam.

**LUKUMAN,** in Jamaica, a black diviner, often the head of certain African cults. Both the number and prestige of the *lukuman* have increased greatly since the abolition of slavery.

**LUNDÚ** (Afr.), an Afro-Brazilian song-dance, varying in style from a melancholy, slow type to a vigorous rhythmic movement with occasional syncopation. It began in the nineteenth century as a Neo-African dance, which some Brazilian musicologists claimed originated in the Congo (q.v.) or Angola (q.v.). It became entirely urbanized relatively early, being turned into a bourgeois social dance, and, in this form, was taken to Portugal and Spain. One expert held that either the *fandango* (q.v.) or the *bolero* (q.v.) might be a descendant of the *lundú*. The *lundú* was the first African-derived music accepted by the Brazilian bourgeoisie, and it brought into middle-class music both the flatted seventh and syncopation. (Roberts, *Black Music*, p. 78.)

**LUNDY** (Afr.), among West Indians, an African word for a sore or wound.

**LUNG-PLUNG** (Eng. Cr.), an Afro-Jamaican word for flour sauce.

**LUONI** (Afr.), in the West Indies, an African word for a baby standing or just learning to stand.

**LURUKS, LOROKS** (Eng. Cr.), in the West Indies, anything old, rubbish; a word used mainly by blacks.

**LUSOTROPICALISMO,** a theory developed by Gilberto de Mello Freyre (q.v.), stating that native Africans under Portuguese cultural influence have developed a unique western oriented cultural tradition quite different from the Anglo-Saxon or French influence on the Africans. The theory includes the concept of racial, social, and political equality.

**LUTIN** (Fr. Cr.), in Afro-Haitian folklore, the ghost of a child who dies before receiving baptism.

# m

**MA** ("grandmother"), a term of endearment used exclusively by black slaves in colonial Jamaica. It conveyed respect and love for the elderly woman who usually raised the children of slave parents working in the fields.

**MAAS, MARSA** (Eng. Cr.), an Afro-Jamaican term of intimate address for a man one's own age; formerly master. See also MASSA.

**MAAS-NIEGA, MASSA NIEGA** (Eng. Cr.), an Afro-Jamaican phrase for a fellow black, a friend.

**MABI** (Fr. Cr.), a fermented beverage prepared by blacks in the French Antilles.

**MABINGA** (Afr.), in Cuba, a lower class black.

**MABOUYA** (Fr. Cr.), among Haitian blacks, a small ground lizard.

**MACACO** (Afr.), in colonial Brazil, a black royal enclave, capital of Palmares (q.v.), residence of King Ganga Zumbá (q.v.). It was fortified with parapets full of caltrops, a big danger even when detected. Around 1676, the enclave itself consisted of some 1,000 huts. It was destroyed by government forces in 1697.

**MACAÍBA, MACAÚBA, MACAJUBA** (Pg.), in Brazil, a species of palm *(Acrocomia scelerocarpa Mart.)* that produces an oil used by black barbers to shave white customers in the colonial period. Its nuts yield an edible oil that is used in soap-making.

**MACAMBA** (Afr.), an Afro-Brazilian term for a fellow, a comrade.

**MACANDAL.** See MACKANDAL.

**MACAQUEIRO** (Pg.), in rural Brazil, a black seasonal laborer, usually illiterate and living on the fringes of society.

**MACARONI** (Eng. Cr.), a coin worth 1 shilling and 8 pence used during slavery times on Jamaican plantations.

**MACARY-BITTER** (Eng. Cr.), a shrub *(Picramnia antidesma)* which was one of the first medicinal herbs used by black herb dealers. The leaves are bitter, with a sweetish taste resembling that of licorice. It was used to cure afflictions connected with syphilis, yaws (q.v.), and intermittent fever. See also MAJOE BITTER.

**MACAULAY, ZACHARY** (1788-1838), an English abolitionist born on May 2, 1768, the son of John Macaulay by his second wife, Margaret Campbell. At the age of sixteen, Zachary was sent to be bookkeeper on an estate in Jamaica, of which he eventually became manager. He was deeply impressed with the miseries of the slave population. In 1792, he gave up his position in disgust and returned to England. He was soon appointed to the Council of the Sierra Leone Company (q.v.). In 1793, Macaulay sailed to the colony and, after reaching it, became governor. There he was also a clerk, preacher, and school teacher. After his health began to fail, he left Sierra Leone (q.v.), sailing to the West Indies in a slave ship so that he could become personally acquainted with the horrors of the voyage. After returning to Sierra Leone for a short time, he went back to England in 1799. He became an ardent abolitionist and was a driving force behind the movement to end the slave trade. Under his leadership the Society for the Mitigation and Gradual Abolition of Slavery throughout the British Dominions (q.v.) was founded in 1823. He visited Paris where he was made honorary president of the French Society for the Abolition of Slavery. Macaulay is greatly esteemed for his services in the emancipation of slaves.

**MACEO Y GRAJALES, ANTONIO** (1848-1896), a Cuban mulatto born in Santiago, Cuba on July 14, 1848. He fought in the Ten Years' War (1868-1878) and, after refusing to sign the Zanjón peace treaty, left the island to seek support for Cuban independence. He returned in 1895 in another attempt to win Cuba's freedom. In 1896, he was killed in action during the war of independence.

**MCFARLANE, BASIL** (b. 1922), a black poet, born in Kingston, Jamaica, the son of J.E.C. McFarlane (q.v.). McFarlane briefly attended Jamaica College and Calabar College, and in 1944, joined the Royal Air Force, serving for two years. He is mainly self-educated. He returned to Jamaica after World War II and since then he has been a government employee. He has written *Jacob and the Angel and Other Poems* (Georgetown, Guiana, 1952); his verses have appeared in the *London Mercury* and in *Life and Letters*.

**MCFARLANE, JOHN EBENEZER CLAIRE** (b. 1896), a black writer and scholar, born in Spanish Town, Jamaica. McFarlane was educated in private schools and at Cornwall College. Throughout the years he has held high positions in the Jamaican government, such as secretary, treasurer, and president of the Civil Service Association. As a scholar, he has contributed to the cultural life of his island and of the West Indies in general. He founded the Poetry League of Jamaica and was the editor of *Voices from Summerland*, the first anthology of Jamaican poetry. Among the many honors bestowed on him are his appointments as a fellow of the Royal Society of Arts and an officer of the Order of the British Empire. Among his works are *Beatrice, Narrative Poems* (Kingston, 1918); *Poems* (Kingston, 1924); *Daphne* (London, 1931); *The Challenge of Our Time: A Series of Essays and Addresses* (Kingston, 1954); and *The Magdalen* (Kingston, 1957).

**MCFARLANE, R.L.C.**, a young poet born in Jamaica and one of the leading writers in Jamaica of his generation. Among his works are *Selected Poems 1943-1945* (Kingston, 1952) and *Hunting the Bright Stream*; *Poems: 1954-1960* (Kingston, 1960).

**MACHADO DE ASSIS, JOAQUIN MARIA** (1839-1908), a Brazilian mulatto writer born in Rio de Janeiro on June 21, 1839. In his youth, Machado de Assis worked as a printer; later, he began writing poetry and fiction. Considered a master of the Portuguese language, he also translated many foreign works into Portuguese. He founded the Brazilian Academy of Literature and for many years served as its president. While he generally portrayed Afro-Brazilian characters in his novels with sympathy, he remained uncommitted in the long struggle to free the slaves which was then exciting all of Brazilian society. He married an aristocratic Portuguese woman and, right after the wedding, broke all relations with his stepmother, Maria Ines, a mulatto woman. Considered by many to be Brazil's greatest writer, Machado de Assis wrote poetry, plays, and novels. His most popular works of fiction are *Yayá (Iaiá)*; *Garcia* (1878); *Memórias Póstumas de Bráz Cubas* (1881); *Quincas Borba* (1891); *Dom Casmurro* (1900); and *Reliquias de Casa Velha* (1906).

**MACHO** (Pg.), in colonial Brazil, an instrument of torture made of iron or hard wood which hampered the movement of the victim's limbs until they became numb. It was used for serious crimes committed by black slaves.

**MACKANDAL** (circa 1715-1758), a black slave born on the Guinea Coast (q.v.) who was a leader of slave uprisings in Saint Domingue (Haiti). He claimed to be able to predict the future and to have had revelations. Mackandal finally persuaded plantation blacks that he was immortal and, for sixteen years, built up his bands. An expert in the use of poison, he and his followers poisoned whites as well as disobedient blacks within his own group. In 1758 he was betrayed, captured, and burned alive.

**MACKANDAL CONSPIRACY,** an unsuccessful slave rebellion organized by Mackandal (q.v.) in Saint Domingue in 1751. It was one of the first loosely planned uprisings on the island, preceding the great and bloody black revolution of 1791. (Hall, *Social Control*, p. 40.)

**MACKANDAL FETISH,** a sacred bundle containing incense, holy water, herbs, small crucifixes, and poison carried by the followers of the black leader Mackandal (q.v.) and believed to have magic power. On January 20, 1758, the government of Saint Domingue approved a law forbidding the manufacture and sale of this fetish. (Hall, *Social Control*, p. 41.)

**MCKAY, CLAUDE** (1890-1948), a poet born in Jamaica. McKay was also the first best-selling black writer in the United States. He was a member of the native constabulary and came to the United States on a student scholarship. Greatly influenced by the black fashion in Europe and by the Negro Renaissance (q.v.) after World War II, and attracted by the aethestic, musical, and cultural black primitivism, he sought to rehabilitate the black arts of both Africa and the New World. McKay rejected neither Christianity nor Europe. Although today his poetic idiom seems outmoded, his passion and powerful image make him an outstanding representative of British West Indian literature. Among his many works are *Constab Ballads* (London, 1912); *Spring in New Hampshire* (London, 1920); *Harlem Shadows* (New York, 1922); *Home to Harlem* (New York, 1928); *Banjo: A Story Without a Plot* (New York, 1929); *Gingertown* (New York, 1932); *Banana Bottom* (New York, 1933); *A Long Way from Home* (New York, 1937); *A Song of the Moon* (New York, 1937); and *Selected Poems* (New York , 1953).

**MACKRON** (Afr.), in colonial West Africa, a black slave declared by the ship surgeon to be unfit for sale in the West Indies. Slaves were examined in minute detail, with all the men, women, and children stark naked. Around 1676, British regulations required that a fit slave should not be above thirty-five years of age, or defective in his lips, eyes, or teeth, or gray-haired. A slave with venereal disease was also rejected. (Davidson, *Black Mother*, p. 92.)

**MACKY MASSA! MUCKY MASSA!** (Afr.) ("Good day, master!"), an African greeting used by West Indian slaves to hail their masters; today a term of address.

**MAÇOCA** (Pg.), an Afro-Brazilian dish made of manioc (see MANDIOCA) dough dried in the sun.

**MACOCO,** the capital of the black Republic of Palmares (q.v.).

**MACONGO TURTLE** (Eng. Cr.), in Jamaica, a black with some physical deformity.

**MACOO** (Afr.), among Jamaican blacks, a strange god who climbs poles and trees backwards.

**MACOTA** (Pg.), in colonial Brazil, a wise old black, generally one who was born in Africa; today any older person.

**MACOUTE** (Fr. Cr.), in Haiti, a black peasant carrying a basket; also the basket itself.

**MACULO, MAL-DE-BICHO,** in colonial Brazil, diarrhea accompanied by the prolapse of the anal sphincter; a disease very common among African blacks.

**MACUMBA** (Afr.), in Brazil, a fetishistic ceremony in which the black congregation invokes the gods and the spirits of the ancestors. All the members frequently go into spontaneous trances. It is accompanied by dances, songs, and prayers to the sound of the drum. It is an apparent survivor of ancestor cults among Angola (q.v.) blacks. See also QUIM-BANDA.

**MACUMBEIRO,** in Brazil, a black in charge of a *macumba* (q.v.) cult. In addition to his liturgical duties, a *maçumbeiro* often engages in the preparation of aphrodisiacs and in sexual incantations. He cooks aphrodisiac Afro-Brazilian dishes with exquisite condiments. He also practices sorcery.

**MACUTA** (Pg.), a Portuguese copper coin used in Angola (q.v.) by slave traders. It was worth as much as 30 reis.

**MACUTO** (Pg.), an Afro-Brazilian word for lie.

**MADA** (Eng. Cr.), in Jamaica, mother; also a title of respect for middle-aged and older women, particularly those with a special position in the black community, such as herb-healers and holders of religious offices. (Cassidy, *Jamaica Talk*, p. 223.)

**MADA CONTINNY** (Eng. Cr.), a character in an Anancy story (q.v.) whose name was known only to the animals she fostered. Anancy, disguised as a girl, learned her name from Bra Crab, one of her children; Mada Continny sang a song to each animal in turn, asking if it was responsible for divulging her name.

**MADAGASS** (Afr.), a generic term applied to black slaves brought to the West Indies from Madagascar. They were lighter in color and had less curly hair than the average Gold Coast (q.v.) slave. The colonists considered them very gentle and well suited to domestic labors.

**MADAME SARA,** in Haiti, a black woman peddler in the markets.

**MADDEN, ROBERT RICHARD** (1798-1886), an Irish writer, traveler, and abolitionist born on August 22, 1798. Madden studied medicine in Paris. In 1833, he went to Jamaica as a special magistrate appointed to administer the statute suppressing the slave traffic. In 1841, he served as a commissioner of inquiry into the administration of the British settlements in West Africa. He later became a special correspondent for the *Morning Chronicle* in Lisbon (1843-1846). Among his numerous works are *Address on Slavery in Cuba Presented to the General Antislavery Convention* (London, 1840) and *Poems by a Slave in the Island of Cuba, Recently Liberated, Translated from the Spanish by R.R. Madden, M.D., with the Story of the Early Life of the Black Poet, Written by Himself, to which Are Prefixed Two Pieces Descriptive of Cuban Slavery and the Slave Traffic* (London, 1840). The black poet in the latter work was Juan Francisco Manzano (q.v.).

**MADERA DE EBANO** (Sp.) ("ebony"), a phrase meaning a black slave used in the slave jargon in colonial Cuba and elsewhere. See also BOIS D'ÉBÈNE.

**MADRAS** (Fr. Cr.), in the French Antilles, a colorful headdress made of madras fabric worn by black women in the Caribbean, Senegal (q.v.), and elsewhere in Africa. The shape, the number of knots, and the color combination of madras indicate a woman's marital status and country of birth. See also CALENDRÉE.

**MÂE BENTA** (Pg.), in Brazil, a small cake made of wheat flour and eggs; sold by black women in the streets.

**MÂE D'AGUA** (Pg.), among Brazilian blacks, a supernatural being who lives in the water. The worship of this goddess is an integral part of many black cults, especially in Bahia. The belief in such a water spirit is very widespread in Brazil.

**MÂE DE SANTO** (Pg.), in Brazil, a black priestess who operates a black fetish cult. Her most important functions are to identify the deities, supervise the public ceremonies, and perform the sacred ritual designed to "fix" a spirit in the fetish. See also PAI DE SANTO.

**MÂE NEGRA** (Pg.) ("Black Mother"), a name given to Angola (q.v.) by Brazilian colonists around 1648 when the Brazilian governor, Salvador Correia de Sá, defeated the Dutch and took Luanda (q.v.). The colony then became what it had been in 1641, the principal source of slaves for Brazil. (Rodrigues, *Brazil and Africa*, p. 22.)

**MÂE-PRETA** (Pg.), in colonial Brazil, a mulatto nursemaid slave who raised white children. She was much respected, honored, and obeyed—even more than the child's natural parents. She gave the white infant her own milk, rocked the child in a cradle or hammock, and taught him his first words of halting Portuguese and his first prayers. (Freyre, *The Masters*, p. 369.)

**MAFEENA, MAFFIINA** (Eng. Cr.), an Afro-Jamaican word for a poor, ineffectual person.

**MAFOFO** (Afr.), in the Spanish Antilles, a word for a variety of *plátano* (q.v.), a staple food used to feed slaves in the colonial period. Also known as *chamaluco*, *fotico*, and *malango*.

**MAFUTO** (Afr.), in Jamaica, a vine used by the Maroons (q.v.) to disguise themselves when in ambush. Today blacks use it for tying bundles in building and basketry, and for fodder.

**MAGARA** (Afr.), a supposedly African concept meaning a life-force expressed in the living person by prosperity and happiness which come to him through the influence of his dead ancestors. This influence can be diminished or increased, but a person has a basic right to it regardless of the extent to which it operates. *Magara* has no moral connotations, as does the Western idea of dignity. While it too depends on the influence of others, it does not depend on another's judgment. This force is primarily a matter between an individual person and his gods. (Jahn, *Neo-African Literature*, pp. 107, 117, 123.)

**MAGBA** (Afr.), in Brazil, a black priest in charge of maintaining on earth the cult of Xangó (q.v.).

**MAGIC CHARMS,** symbols of magic power made by black sorcerers to protect or to hurt others. In Jamaica and elsewhere in the Caribbean, blacks believe these fetishes followed them across the sea from Africa. The small, rough figures of wood or stone, called *garde* or *garde-corps* (q.v.) and representing men and animals, are believed to have supernatural powers. It is said that through such magic charms sorcerers usually acquire absolute power over others. (Herskovits, *Life in a Haitian*, pp. 228-30.) See also ARRÊTÉ; DROGUE; WANGA.

**MAGIE** (Fr. Cr.), in Afro-Haitian tradition, the vast body of magico-medical practices prescribed and administered by black healers and sorcerers. It is believed that the knowledge of curative powers and roots is inherited from generation to generation.

**MAGLOIRE SAINT-AUDE, CLÉMENT** (b. 1912), a Haitian mulatto poet born and educated in Port-au-Prince. In 1931, he won the prize for literature given in France by the duke of Bauffremont. He is also a journalist who writes for Haitian and French newspapers and magazines. Among his works of poetry are *Dialogue de mes lampes* (Port-au-Prince, 1941); *Tabou* (Port-au-Prince, 1941); *Parias* (Port-au-Prince, 1949); *Ombres et reflets* (Port-au-Prince, 1952); *Déchu* (Port-au-Prince, 1956); and *Veillée* (Port-au-Prince, 1956).

**MAHOMET'S PARADISE,** a name given to Nicaragua, Central America, in colonial times by the Spanish settlers because of its mild climate, abundance of land, and beautiful Indian girls.

**MAIS, ROGER** (b. 1905), a black writer and politician born in Kingston, Jamaica. Mais attended schools on his native island. To earn a living he worked as a laborer, clerk, photographer, reporter, and editor. He entered politics with a newspaper editorial entitled "Now We Know," which provoked bitter public reaction and resulted in his internment for eighteen months. Among his works are *Face and Other Stones* (1942); *And Most of All Men* (a collection of poems and short stories, 1943); *The Hills Were Joyful Together* (London, 1953); *Brother Man* (London, 1954); and *Black Lightning* (London, 1955).

**MAISON DE SERVITUDE** (Fr. Cr.), among Haitian blacks, a hut located near the family house used as a place of worship for the gods. Its elaborateness varies according to the status of the members in the hierarchy of the cult. The doors are usually closed, with thorny acacia branches placed in front.

**MAÎT** (Fr. Cr.), in Afro-Haitian folklore, a word meaning master used to identify the names of gods, usually referring to their supernatural powers.

**MAÎT' BITATION** (Fr. Cr.), an Afro-Haitian god, protector of the family house.

**MAÎT' CARREFOUR** (Fr. Cr.), in the Afro-Haitian pantheon, a god who is the protector of roads and travelers. Each year on All Saints' Day, the faithful pay homage to this guardian of the highways by presenting him with money or food.

**MAÎT' CIMITIÈRE-BOUMBA** (Fr. Cr.), an Afro-Haitian god, protector of the cemeteries and the graves. Candles are lighted in his honor on Mondays and Fridays when the faithful visit their dead.

**MAÎT' CONTE** (Fr. Cr.), in Afro-Haitian folklore, a professional story-teller found everywhere in Haiti. He is a dramatic actor who interprets his characters as he goes along, thus providing different voices, singing, giving humorous or tragic emphasis, and changing his facial expressions to convey the temper and mood of the protagonists. He varies his themes according to circumstances and the responsiveness of his captive audience. The black storyteller is one of the most picturesque characters in Haitian culture.

**MAÎT' DAVID,** an Afro-Haitian deity who can speak pure French; persons possessed by him can read cards and tell fortunes.

**MAÎT' GRAN CHIMIN** (Fr. Cr.), in the Haitian pantheon, a deity who is master of the country roads. He is a spirit of supplication and must be placated with prayers and songs. An unpredictable master, he occasionally treats his followers with an iron hand.

**MAÎT' OGOUN** (Fr. Cr.), in the Afro-Haitian pantheon, one of the most powerful deities, identified with Saint Jacques. He is the master of fire and the helper of the sick. Maît' Ogoun is also a dispenser of rum, and rum is included in virtually all the rituals honoring him. The rum is often poured into a hot iron pot where it bursts into flames.

**MAÎT' SOURCE** (Fr. Cr.), in Afro-Haitian folklore, the god who is the master of fields and streams. Black peasants sacrifice a cock in his honor and offer him the first fruits because his good will has permitted a bountiful yield.

**MAÎT' TÊTE** (Fr. Cr.), among black Haitians, a spirit present in every child who acts as his protector for life. Since it is an inherited spirit, through a special ritual it can be replaced by a new one. This replacement must be done by a cult priest. The Maît' Tête must also be removed from the head of a dead person. If this is not done, the spirit of the deceased will reside under the waters and may cause trouble for the family. (Courlander, *The Drum*, pp. 21-22.)

**MAITRESS ESPAGNOL** (Fr. Cr.), an Afro-Haitian female deity; persons possessed or "mounted" by her speak Spanish exclusively.

**MAITRESS MAMBO** (Fr. Cr.), in the Afro-Haitian pantheon, a gentle female goddess who performs gay dances for her followers. Her favorite foods are eggs, flour, and fruit, and her abode is in the springs; she stammers.

**MAITURÚS** (Pg.), in Afro-Brazilian folklore, a supernatural being whose feet are backwards. Rural blacks fear her greatly. This Indian ghost entered into the magic world of black slaves early in the colonial period.

**MAJEUR** (Fr. Cr.), in Haiti, a term of derision employed by blacks for those peasants who evade their tasks, yet share in the feasting at the end of communal field work.

**MAJOE** (Afr.), in Jamaica, an old black woman who uses majoe bitter (q.v.) to cure inveterate ulcers, yaws (q.v.), venereal diseases, and the like. Among the Sande people in West Africa, Majoe was the leader of a secret society into which nearly all girls were initiated. Majoe is still used as a personal name among the Gullah blacks who live off the coast of Georgia in the United States.

**MAJOE BITTER** (Eng. Cr.), in colonial Jamaica, an African name applied to a plant *(Picramnia antidesma)* used by black healers to cure stubborn diseases. Formerly called macary-bitter (q.v.).

**MAJOR JONC** (Fr. Cr.), among Haitian blacks, the baton of a juggler who heads a noisy black group in carnival parades.

**MAKANDA** (Afr.), in Haiti, a sacred charm worn by blacks to protect themselves against various forms of black magic.

**MALAGÜETA, MALAGUETTA** (Afr.), a wild tree *(Amomis caryophyllata)* which produces a small, brown, spicy berry; used to prepare food and beverages. It was introduced to tropical America in slavery times from a region between Liberia and modern Ghana. It was thought to prevent dysentery and stomach disorders, and it was used to season the food of slaves in the West Indies. It has been known as African pepper, British pepper, Jamaican pepper, Paradise grain (q.v.), Guinea pepper (q.v.), and by several other names.

**MALAMBA** (Afr.), among Brazilian blacks, a term for misfortune, adversity, disgrace.

**MALAMBO** (Afr.), a rubber tree apparently brought to the Antilles from Africa during slavery times.

**MALAME** (Afr.), in Trinidad, a beverage made of pounded wild "coffee" beans. Black midwives give the drink to newly delivered women because it is thought to cleanse out the blood remaining after removal of the placenta.

**MALANGA, MALANGO** (Afr.), the edible root of the yautia plant *(Arum esculentum, Caladium esculentum, Colocasia esculentum),* a native-American plant widely used as a staple food for slaves. It is known throughout the Caribbean where its presence was documented in 1670. (Alvarez Nazario, *El elemento negroide*, p. 227.)

**MALANGAN** (Afr.), in Haiti, a kind of yam (q.v.) cultivated and eaten by blacks.

**MALANGO** (Afr.). See MALANGA.

**MALA RAZA** (Sp.), in the Spanish colonies, black slaves, considered to be members of an inferior race.

**MALAVA, MALAWA** (Afr.), among Afro-Jamaican blacks, a term for rum.

**MAL-DE-BICHO** (Pg.). See MACULO.

**MAL DE SIETE DÍAS** (Sp.), an infant sickness, a convulsive complaint called *espasmo*, that especially afflicted black slave children in Cuba. Around 1870, this malady was responsible for over 50 percent of the infant slave deaths on Cuban plantations. (Knight, *Slave Society*, p. 82.)
82.)

**MAL D'ESTOMAC, MAL DE STOMACH** (Fr. Cr.), in colonial Haiti and the Antilles, a kind of pleurisy peculiar to black slaves addicted to dirt-eating (q.v.).

**MAL DE UMBIGO** (Pg.), in Brazil, an infectious disease of the umbilical cord; a kind of tetanus that afflicted many slave infants on the plantations. See also MAL DE SIETE DÍAS.

**MALEMBA! MALEMBE!, MALENGA PAUNGAM** (Afr.) ("Good morning!"), in colonial Jamaica, an African greeting used by slaves on the plantations to hail each other.

**MALÊS** (Afr.). 1. In Brazil, a Moslem black slave; a term employed by the Berbers and Arabs for the Mandingo (q.v.) blacks. These slaves worshipped Allah and were very fond of wearing a talisman engraved with fragments of verse from the Koran in Arabic script. Many *malês* were literate and were trained in different crafts; the planters considered them their most valuable slaves, even though they were rebellious and were ever ready to flee to the wilderness. In 1905, it was estimated that one-third of the blacks in Bahia were *malês*. 2. A vigorous and flourishing Moslem sect with temples, leaders, and well-organized congregations; still active at the turn of the nineteenth century all over northeastern Brazil (Ramos, *The Negro*, p. 98.)

**MALGALHÃES, DOMINGOS JOSÉ GONÇALVES DE** (1811-1882), a Brazilian romantic poet. In 1836, Malgalhães published *Suspiros Poéticos* (Paris), a work which describes the misery of the black slaves who exist in a world that offers freedom for all but them. Malgalhães' slave, with his tears, songs, unending labors, and sufferings, would become a stock figure in literature. Malgalhães refers to the loss of slave ships at sea as God's way of punishing the slave traders.

**MALI** (Afr.), in Belize, a Black Carib (q.v.) dance in which the dancer pleads with a spirit to help someone who is ailing. A *mali* usually lasts for three days, with all the relatives of the sick person present.

**MALINGERING,** the feigning of illness to avoid work, a widespread practice among black slaves on many West Indian plantations. Some mothers deliberately infected their babies with yaws (q.v.) so that they might be released for a time from field labors.

**MALUNGA** (Afr.), in colonial Brazil, a bracelet worn by slaves as a sign of nobility.

**MALUNGO** (Afr.), in colonial Brazil, a young black slave who was a playmate of white boys on the plantations.

**MAMA LAOTÉ** (Afr.) ("Mother of All Nations"), in some Afro-Brazilian *candomblés* (q.v.), a goddess of Nigerian origin.

**MAMALOI** (Fr. Cr.), in Afro-Haitian cults, a black priestess who assists a minister in the services. She is usually a simple peasant woman, often a housewife, who feels able to participate actively in serving the deities.

**MAMA LOLA** (Pg.), in some Afro-Brazilian cults, a goddess who is the protector of lovers and of birth. She often wanders in the night, promoting trouble between husbands and wives.

**MAMAN-BILA** (Afr.), small, calcareous pebbles thought to have magical powers; worn by black slaves in Haiti around 1786. (Fouchard, *Les Marrons*, p. 522.)

**MAMA ZENFANT** (Fr. Cr.), in Trinidad, a kind of bean cultivated and eaten by blacks as a staple food.

**MAMBÍ** (Afr.). 1. In the Afro-Antilles, a term originally applied to runaway slaves and to half-wild animals. 2. In the nineteenth century, a Cuban revolutionary.

**MAMBO, MAMBU, MAMBU CAILLE** (Afr.), in Afro-Haitian cults, a priestess, an assistant of the *houngan* (q.v.).

**MAMETO** (Pg.), in Brazil, a circumcized black, usually a Moslem.

**MAMETO, PRINCE,** a popular black character in Afro-Brazilian *cuembé* (q.v.) plays. In some versions, the queen mother sends young Mameto to the court of a Congo king where he is killed in battle and is resucitated by a black sorcerer.

**MAMMA-YAW** (Eng. Cr.), the large central pustule of yaws (q.v.) around which the smaller ones cluster. It sometimes remains after all the others have healed. In the West Indies, this disease primarily affected black slaves.

**MAMMY** (Eng. Cr.), a black priestess in Jamaican revivalist cults.

**MAMPALA** (Eng. Cr.), in the West Indies, a man who deviates in his masculinity by being impotent, homosexual, or effeminate; applied to blacks.

**MAMPORA** (Afr.), a species of banana *(Musa sapientum)* grown especially for hog fodder and trap bait by black residents of the Colombia Pacific lowlands.

**MAMPULORIO** (Sp.), in Venezuela and the Antilles, an elaborate ceremony involving song and dance rituals; performed by blacks upon the death of a child.

**MANAFUNDO** (Pg.), in colonial Brazil, a black prince who leads a procession as part of the ritual for crowning a black king in carnival celebrations.

**MANCARRÓN** (Sp.), in the Dutch slave trade jargon, any black over forty years of age who was sick, blind, lame, or paralyzed, whose fair market value was low. This slave was classified by law (1662) as nondeliverable. (Goslinga, *The Dutch*, p. 357.)

**MANCEBÍA** (Pg.), ("concubinage"), in Brazil, a casual conjugal union outside marriage with no degree of permanency. In many cases, the woman involved is a mulatto, but rarely a black.

**MANCENILLIER** (Fr. Cr.), in the French Antilles, a tropical tree five to six feet high that produces a milky and poisonous juice which blacks believed to be blessed with magical powers.

**MANCHAS** (Pg.), in Brazil, deeply colored "stains" on either side of the buttocks characteristic of mixed-blood children. They are considered a sign of black ancestry and an index of subsequent dark pigmentation over the entire body. See also GENIPAPO.

**MANDINGA** (Afr.). 1. Among Afro-Brazilians, witchcraft, especially spells used by black women as sexual bait. 2. In the La Plata region, the devil. 3. Elsewhere a fetish or talisman worn by blacks against evil forces.

**MANDINGA, ANTON,** a black slave, an assistant of Luis de Mozambique (q.v.) the leader of a slave rebellion in the San Blas mountains on the isthmus of Panama in 1553. He and his chief were caught and pardoned by the Spaniards. (Rout. L. B., *The African Experience in Spanish America*, p. 118.)

**MANDINGEIRO** (Afr.), in colonial Brazil, a black sorcerer whose magic spells inspired dread and were often fatal. One of his various arts was to prepare aphrodisiac beverages for his plantation master to enable him to take care of his harem of black and mulatto women. (Freyre, *The Masters*, p. 336.)

**MANDINGO KINGDOM,** an ancient African state centered around the Upper Niger Valley. It embraced Islam between 1230 and 1255 and flourished during the fifteenth and sixteenth centuries when it extended to the Slave

Coast (q.v.) on the Gulf of Guinea (q.v.). Allied with the Portuguese in 1530, it became a source of black slaves for the Brazilian plantations. It began to decline in the seventeenth century and disintegrated as an empire in 1670. Later it was reduced to a small province whose ruler was a French vassal until modern times.

**MANDINGO SLAVES,** in the colonial West Indies and Brazil, Sudanese, nonblack slaves who converted to Islam and were brought mainly from the Mandingo Kingdom (q.v.). Of Arabic and Tuarge ancestry, they were tall, well built, hardy, and clever; they were favored for domestic work. They were known for their tendency toward group suicide, which they considered a means of freeing themselves from a cruel servitude and of escaping to a better world. In Bahia, Brazil, former Mandingo slaves conducted trade between their city and African towns such as Lagos and Ardra (q.v.).

**MANDIOCA** (Pg.) ("manihot"), the common name for a starch-producing plant *(Manihot utilissima)* native to tropical America. A member of the spurge family (Euphorbiaceae), it is also known as cassava, manioc, yuca, and tapioca plant. As an important source of starch, it became a staple food for black plantation slaves. The many varieties of manihots under cultivation throughout the tropics are usually grouped into bitter cassavas and sweet cassavas, depending upon the amount of poisonous hydrocyanic (prussic) acid present in the milky root sap.

**MANEIRAS** (Pg.), in colonial Brazil, a garment worn by black slave women with an opening in the back of the skirt, from the waist down, to permit it being slipped over the shoulders and hips.

**MANFUANFA** (Afr.), an Afro-Cuban word for leftovers.

**MANGE** (Fr. Cr.), among Haitian blacks, a feast, either social or religious.

**MANGÉ ASSOTOR** (Fr. Cr.), in Afro-Haitian folklore, a sacred feast to honor the *assotor* (q.v.) drum.

**MANGÉ DIRI** (Fr. Cr.), in rural Haiti, a rice harvest feast celebrated by blacks. In an elaborate ceremony, rice is shared with the family ancestors who have first rights and with close friends who have aided with the planting. While the food, consisting of several rice dishes, is being prepared, the farmer's relatives and friends play games and sing songs, and often a storyteller comes to entertain them. Before eating, the head of the family says prayers and drops a little food on the ground in honor of the dead and the ancestors, including the ones left behind in Africa. (Courlander, *The Drum*, pp. 60, 63.)

**MANGE LA BOTE** (Pg.), in Brazil, a band of musicians made up of black slaves kept by the plantation masters for the pleasure of family and friends.

**MANGÉ LOA** (Fr. Cr.), in Haiti, a sacred feast for the spirits celebrated by blacks.

**MANGÉ MARASSA** (Fr. Cr.), in rural Haiti, a socioreligious feast celebrated by black farmers to honor twins.

**MANGÉ MORT** (Fr. Cr.), a feast for the dead, a family ritual in several Afro-Haitian cults.

**MANGÉ MOUN** (Fr. Cr.), in Afro-Haitian folklore, the action of a spirit who "eats" his victim by sending a fatal illness or death-causing accident.

**MANGÉ SEC** (Fr. Cr.), in Afro-Haitian religion, a small offering given to the gods.

**MANGÉ YAM** (Fr. Cr.), in rural Haiti, an annual festival celebrating the harvest of yams (q.v.), considered the most vital of all staples. Blacks observe this event on November 25 each year. The festival is held to placate the ancestors so that they will insure the fertility of the fields. The rituals vary from region to region.

**MANGKISHIN** (Eng. Cr.), an Afro-Jamaican term for a particular person's death.

**MANGO** (Pg.), a tropical plant *(Mangifera indica)* that bears an oblong, yellowish-red fruit, with a thick ring, a fibrous, juicy pulp, and a hard stone. The Portuguese introduced the fruit into tropical America from India early in the colonial period. It soon became a staple food for black slaves working on the plantations.

**MANGONÉS, VICTOR MICHEL RAPHAEL** (1880-1949), a black poet born in Jérémie, Haiti. Mangónes was educated in his native city and in Port-au-Prince, where he obtained a degree in business and worked as a civil servant. His main theme is love. His published works are *Menuailles d'or et d'argent* (Port-au-Prince, 1933) and *Contes vrais; chroniques parlées* (Port-au-Prince, 1934).

**MANGUÁ** (Afr.), an Afro-Cuban word for money.

**MANI** (Afr.), a black chief or king in Angola (q.v.) (circa 1450).

**MANIBA.** See MANUBA.

**MANICONGO, MANI KONGO,** a sovereign of the Kongo Empire who, in 1483, established relations with Diogo Cão, the first Portuguese envoy to reach the Angola (q.v.) region, which later became the main source of slaves for Brazil.

**MANIEL, LE,** in colonial Saint Domingue (Haiti), a Maroon (q.v.) community organized around 1680. By 1784, it was well established with over 200 black slaves, most of them runaway slaves from the plantations. Two years later, the French authorities granted Le Maniel a vague sort of sovereignty. When the great slave rebellion of 1791, the Humanitarian Revolt (q.v.), unleashed its horrors, the blacks from this settlement, jealous of their independence, remained aloof from the conflict. At the beginning of the nineteenth century, in an independent Haiti, the descendants of Le Maniel were still grouped, if not in a little state of their own, at least in a society with strong links to its past. (Price, *Maroon Societies*, p. 143.)

**MANIGUA** (Sp.), in Cuba and elsewhere in the Antilles, a subtropical jungle. It is less dense than a tropical forest, but thick enough to make good cover and to provide food for those who know it. It usually consists of mountainous terrain covered by hardwood forests, evergreen bushes, shrubs, and vines. In the colonial period, the *manigua* was a favorite refuge for runaway black slaves; in modern times, it has become a haven for revolutionaries.

**MANIHOT.** See MANDIOCA.

**MANIPANSO** (Afr.), in Brazil, an idol worshipped by blacks.

**MANMAN.** See ASSOTOR.

**MANMAN' LEAU** (Fr. Cr.), an Afro-French word for mermaid.

**MAN NO DEAD, NO CALL HIM DUPPY** (Eng. Cr.) (If a man is not dead, don't call him duppy [q.v.]), an Afro-Jamaican aphorism implying that a sorcerer summons only the spirits of the dead, not those of the living. (Beckwith, *Jamaica Proverbs*, p. 82.)

**MANPLÉ, MANPLEY** (Bant.), an Afro-Caribbean word for a cheap rum made illegally.

**MANSA** (Afr.), an Afro-Brazilian word for king or emperor.

**MANSONG, JACK** (d. 1781), a Jamaican black slave, better known as Three-Fingered Jack. After leading an unsuccessful revolt of slaves on the plantation to which he belonged, he managed to escape to the mountains where, from his hideout in the region of Saint Thomas-in-the-East, he terrorized the island by his daring robberies and murders. He was recaptured and killed by the government militia in 1781. The story of Three-Fingered Jack is now part of Jamaican folklore. (Black, *History of Jamaica*, p. 114.)

**MANUBA, MANIBA** (Afr.), in Haiti, a black dance associated with Dahomean cults. It is accompanied by percussion music played on small drums hung around the neck. It is reportedly performed only by homosexual men.

**MANUÉ** (Pg.), in Brazil, a variety of cake made of corn flour, honey, and *dendé* palm oil (q.v.); a black delicacy sold by black women on the streets.

**MANUMIDO** (Sp.), in Gran Colombia, a slave child born free after 1821.

**MANUMISSION,** the formal freeing of a slave by his master or the government. In the Iberian legal system, manumission was a customary practice. For example, the fathers of illegitimate offspring often freed their mixed-blood children at the baptismal font. In Cuba and elsewhere, manumission was legalized through the *coartación* (q.v.). In Brazil in 1849, freed African black women outnumbered free African black men in all categories of manumission. This legal system of liberating slaves was very infrequent in the West Indies, although it sometimes occurred in favor of mulatto mistresses and mulatto children whose education was often provided for by their white fathers. In some cases, manumission was discouraged by laws such as those of Barbados and Grenada (circa 1784) which heavily fined a master who freed a slave. In 1816, the Jamaican Assembly decreed that manumission of slaves by will was legal. (Pescatello, *The African*, p. 169.)

**MANYO.** See MAYO.

**MANZANO, JUAN FRANCISCO** (1804-1854), a black Cuban poet. Manzano was born a slave, the illegitimate son of a slave woman, María del Pilar Manzano, and a mulatto father, Toribio Castro. His early childhood under the care of his master, the Marquis D. Juan Manzano, and his master's wife, Beatriz Juztis, was a happy one; at the age of six he was sent to school. When he was about eleven, his protectress, the marchioness, died, and his hardships under different masters began.

Around 1818, Manzano fled a plantation in Matanzas province and went to Havana where he was soon recaptured by his owner, D. Tomas Gener. Manzano began writing poetry. In 1821, his *Poesias líricas*, known as

*Cantos a Lesbia*, was published in Havana; this was done with his master's permission because, by law, a slave could not otherwise publish anything. His poems were read by the writer Domingo del Monte and by other intellectuals who collected 500 pesos, the price of his manumission (q.v.).

Manzano was freed in 1835 and in the following year published the now famous sonnet "Mis 30 años." At the request of his good friend del Monte, Manzano wrote *Apuntes biográficos* in 1834. His poems are scattered in various periodicals. In 1838, he published "Illusiones" in *El Album*, with an editor's note saying that the author was destitute. In *El Aguinaldo Habanero*, Manzano published "Una hora de tristeza," "El reloj adelantado," "La Cucuyera," "A Matanzas," and "Un sueño." His last published work was *Zafira* (1842), a play in five acts. His *Autobiografía* was translated by R. R. Madden (q.v.) and published in London in 1840.

**MÃO-DE-CABELO** (Pg.) ("scratching-hair"), among Brazilian blacks, a goblin with hairs for hands; a head-cutting monster much feared by children.

**MÃO-DE-COÇAR** (Pg.) ("scratching-hand"), in colonial Brazil, a black slave woman in charge of removing lice and cleansing her mistress's hair.

**MÃO-DE-PELO** (Pg.), an Afro-Brazilian hairy-handed goblin used to frighten children. It was visualized as an old black, ready to eat his penis or cut it off.

**MÃOZINHAS-DE-COÇAR** (Pg.) ("little scratching-hands"), in colonial Brazil, a comb made of ivory and used by black slaves to cleanse their mistresses' hair. The comb was once common among aristocratic families in Portugal.

**MAPOU** (Fr. Cr.), in Afro-Haitian folklore, a gigantic mythical tree, the secret meeting place of countless kinds of demons. It is said that on certain nights a chink of light can be seen through the trunk of the great *mapou*, in indicating that the demons are in macabre session.

**MAPOU TOMBÉ, CABRIT MANGÉ FÉ LI** (Fr. Cr.) ("The *mapou* tree falls, the goat eats its leaves"), an Afro-Haitian aphorism implying that when the mighty fall, they are helpless, even before the weak. (Courlander, *The Drum*, p. 336.)

**MAPUSSE!**, in Haiti, an exclamation having strong sexual connotations, used by blacks when dancing.

**MAR** (Pg.), an Afro-Brazilian cult centered around the worship of Christian saints, the ancestors, and the family spirits; supposedly of Bantu (q.v.) tradition.

**MARABOUT** (Fr. Cr.). In Haiti: 1. A black priest in several Afro-Haitian cults. 2. A peasant mulatto girl. 3. An ugly man. 4. Today in Africa, a Moslem holyman.

**MARABÚ** (Afr.), in Cuba, a leguminous plant *(Diagrostachys nutans, Benth)* introduced from Africa in slavery times. Since then, it has spread so rapidly, both by seed and underground rootstock, that today it covers hundreds of square miles with an impenetrable tangle and encroaches upon crops and pastureland. Because of its thorns, cattle can neither push through it nor eat it. It is a serious threat to the Cuban farmer.

**MARAÇA** (Afr.), an Afro-Brazilian word for twins. See also MARASSA.

**MARACATÚ** (Afr.), in Brazil, a carnival dance of African origin popular in Pernambuco. It is played by an ensemble of trumpets and percussion instruments.

**MARAFO** (Afr.), in rural Brazil, an African term for rum made of sugar cane (q.v.).

**MARAN, RENÉ** (1887-1960), a black poet and writer born in Fort-de-France, Martinique. In his novels Maran sought to reveal the social conditions of black peasants and used the Creole language. In his poetry he was a follower of the French Parnassian tradition and wrote inspired poems portraying the island landscape with marvelous and touching images. His works include *La maison de bonheur* (Paris, 1909); *La Vie intérieure* (Paris 1921), *Le Visage calme* (Paris, 1922); *Le Petit roi de chimérie* (Paris, 1924); *Djouma, chien de brousse* (Paris, 1927); *Bêtes de la brousse* (Paris, 1941); *Mbala l'éléphant* (Paris, 1943); *Bacouya, le cynocéphale* (Paris, 1953); and *Le Livre de souvenir* (Paris, 1959).

**MARANTA** (Afr.), an Afro-Jamaican word for mulatto.

**MARASSA** (Afr.), in Haiti, the spirit of twins who, following the traditional African belief, share a single soul. Should one die, the living twin must set aside for the other one a bit of all the food he eats or a small part of any gift given him.

**MARASSA BLANC** (Fr. Cr.), an Afro-Haitian deity, patron of white twins.

**MARASSA BOS** (Fr. Cr.), in Afro-Haitian religion, an untamed god, considered very savage and dangerous.

**MARASSA CAILLE** (Fr. Cr.), an Afro-Haitian god, protector of the crude chapel where black peasants gather to worship African deities and Christian saints.

**MARASSA DOÇA** (Fr. Cr.), in Afro-Haitian religion, a god who is the protector of the first child born after twins if it is a girl. See also MARASSA DOÇU.

**MARASSA DOÇU** (Fr. Cr.), in Afro-Haitian cults, a god who is the protector of the first child born after twins if it is a boy.

**MARASSA DOGUÉ** (Fr. Cr.), in Afro-Haitian religion, a deity who is the protector of consecutive twins and triplets.

**MARASSA GUINÉ** (Fr. Cr.), in Afro-Haitian folk religion, a deity who is the patron of twins when one is a boy and the other a girl.

**MARASSA-JUMEAY** (Fr. Cr.), in Martinique, the spirit of dead twins, highly revered by blacks.

**MARASSA TROIS** (Fr. Cr.), in Afro-Haitian religion, a god who is the patron of triplets.

**MARCELIN, FRÉDÉRIC** (1848-1917), a black Haitian poet. Marcelin, a follower of the naturalist movement, called for a national literature inspired by local themes and black peasant customs and traditions. He portrays the social reality of former slaves, their virtues and backwardness, with photographic exactness. His works include *Themistocle Epaminondas Labasterre: Petit récit haïtien* (Paris, 1901); *La Vengeance de mama: Roman haïtien* (Paris, 1903); *Autour de deux romans* (Paris, 1903); *Marillisse: Roman haïtien* (Paris, 1904); and *Au gré de souvenir* (Paris, 1913).

**MARCELIN, PHILIPPE THOBY.** See THOBY-MARCELIN, PHILIPPE.

**MARCELIN, PIERRE** (b. 1908), a Haitian poet born in Port-au-Prince. Marcelin was one of the leaders of the national movement called *indigénisme,* later known as négritude (q.v.). After attending local schools, he was sent to Paris to further his education. In 1927, while studying at the Sorbonne, he, together with his brother Philippe Thoby-Marcelin (q.v.), and other young intellectuals, founded *La Revue Indigène* (July 1927-February 1928) which became the mouthpiece for the black literary revival and gave it its name. He was interested in depicting black Haitian life, belief, and traditions, deeply rooted in the African past of the slaves. He tried to keep a balance between the Christian and Afro-Haitian elements. His works include *Canapé-vert* (New York, 1944); *La bête de Musseau* (New York, 1946); and *Le Crayon de Dieu* (Paris, 1952), which was written in collaboration with his brother, Philippe.

**MARCHANDE** (Fr. Cr.), in Haiti, a black woman who operated the retail produce trade in town markets. She often employed a number of hucksters to traverse the countryside to buy vegetables and fruits for resale. She would check her peddlers' findings and sales every evening or every week or month.

**MARDI KAMA.** See IBO KAMA.

**MARÉCHAUSSÉE** (Fr. Cr.), a permanent police force organized in 1717 in Saint Domingue (Haiti) to capture fugitive slaves, to protect travelers, and to fight against runaway blacks. The soldiers were slaves, free blacks, mulattoes, and professional bounty-hunters wearing clear identification; they inspected the plantations and immediately reported any slave unrest. Later the *maréchaussées* tried to protect the slaves from their masters' abuses and cruelty. (Hall, *Social Control*, pp. 76, 100.)

**MARGETSON, GEORGE REGINALD,** a deeply religious mulatto poet. Margetson, born in Saint Kitts, was inspired by Afro-Caribbean themes, especially by racial problems. His works include *England in the West Indies: A Neglected and Degenerating Empire* (Cambridge, Mass., 1906); *Ethiopia's Flight: The Negro Question or The White Man's Fear* (Cambridge, Mass., 1907); *Songs of Life* (Boston, 1910); and *The Fledgling Bard and the Poetry Society* (Boston, 1916).

**MARIAGE MYSTIQUE** (Fr. Cr.), a mystic marriage between an initiate and a god in several Afro-Haitian cults. It entails an elaborate ritual supervised by the priest of the sect. The person directly involved usually seeks wealth, social or political position, and the god's protection.

**MARIANDÁ** (Bant), **MARIANGOLA** (Afr.), in Cuba and elsewhere, a black dance popular during slavery times.

**MARIANO, JOSÉ,** an ardent Brazilian abolitionist very popular with the masses in Recife, Pernambuco, around 1880. He used illegal methods to liberate black slaves. An outspoken leader in the Chamber of Deputies and a man of great personal magnetism, he harangued large crowds on the streets, pleading the emancipation cause. In 1884, Mariano cooperated in the organization of the highly secret Thermite Club to conceal fugitive slaves and to expose planters' abuses. (Toplin, *The Abolition*, pp. 77, 190.)

**MARICONGO** (Afr.), in the Caribbean, a tropical perennial herb *(Musa paradisiaca)* or its fruit; a staple food for black slaves on colonial plantations. See also PLANTAIN.

**MARIFINGA** (Afr.), in Puerto Rico, an Afro-Spanish dish prepared with corn flour and spices.

**MARIMBA** (Afr.), a kind of xylophone, a keyboard instrument played with mallets, which is very popular in the Afro-Antilles. Brought by black slaves to the New World, it was a favorite instrument among slaves in Cuba around 1690. At that time it was simply called *congo* and *angola* referring to its origin. (Alvarez Nazario, *El elemento negroide*, p. 289.)

**MARIMBO** (Afr.), in rural Puerto Rico, a calabash produced by a vine *(Cucurbita lagenaria)* and used as a water or grain container.

**MARMAILLE** (Fr. Cr.), in Martinique, a term for people; often used by blacks.

**MAROON** (Eng. Cr.), in the West Indies and elsewhere, a fugitive black slave or one of the classes of blacks descended from runaway slaves. The Maroons' flight from the plantations was a classic problem from the beginning of the New World colonization; gradually during the seventeenth century, the number of Maroons increased greatly. Throughout the Caribbean, Maroon men organized small isolated communities in the forests and the mountains where they became skilled in guerrilla warfare and sometimes fought successfully against the planters and their enemies. Living in isolation, the Maroons learned how to survive in a primitive and hostile environment, maintaining a culture that possessed direct connections with both African and Indian New World plantation elements. Punishment for recaptured slaves ranged from castration to execution. (Price, *Maroon Societies*, p. 42.)

**MAROON BLISTER** (Eng. Cr.), in Jamaica, a strongly aromatic vine plant used by blacks to cure headaches.

**MAROON DEPORTATION,** the forced removal of 600 black Maroons (q.v.) from Jamaica to Nova Scotia ordered by the colonial Assembly in 1796. The deportation took place at the end of a bloody Maroon war (q.v.) between Maroons and Jamaican militiamen.

**MAROON FLUTE,** a primitive flute popular among the Maroons (q.v.) in colonial Jamaica.

**MAROON LANCE,** in Jamaica, a small tree *(Exostemia brachycarpum)* said to have been used by the Maroons (q.v.) to make lances.

**MAROON SETTLEMENTS,** in colonial Jamaica, communities organized by runaway slaves under a chief. Most of the inhabitants were African-born blacks. A Maroon (q.v.) hamlet usually had patches of plantains (q.v.) and yams (q.v.) in remote areas of the island for use during periods of retreat and emergency. Some of these communities had a sexually segregated pattern of settlement which helped protect the women and children from the savagery of white raiding parties. These rebel villages were numerous from 1625 to 1686 when they were overrun by the colonial militia. See also CUMBÉS; PALENQUE; and QUILOMBO.

**MAROON TALK,** an Afro-Jamaican dialect spoken by the Maroons (q.v.) in the colonial period.

**MAROON TOWNS,** in Jamaica, outlying villages settled by runaway slaves and supervised by a government superintendent. Around 1809, these Maroon (q.v.) communities included Trelawny, Accompong (q.v.), Moore Town, Charles Town, and Scotts Hall.

**MAROON WARS,** in Jamaica, bloody clashes between runaway slave communities and government forces. The first war, lasting from 1725 to 1739, ended with an agreement giving the rebels limited control of the various black towns. The second Maroon war lasted two years, from 1795 to 1797. The Maroons employed a highly effective guerrilla technique; the authorities retaliated with a scorched-earth policy and finally sent in 100 Cuban bloodhounds. The peace came after the removal of several hundred Maroons. See MAROON DEPORTATION.

**MAROON WEED,** in Jamaica, a tropical herb *(Echites echites)* used by blacks to cure sore legs, ground-itch fever, and other illnesses.

**MAROON WISS,** a vine used by Jamaican Maroons (q.v.) to camouflage themselves when fighting.

**MARRÉ** (Fr. Cr.), in the Afro-Haitian religion, the proper control of a spirit by its devotee.

**MARRIAGE SURINAM STYLE,** an expression used in colonial Surinam to refer to a marriage between a European and a mulatto woman. This marked tendency on the part of mixed-blood girls to marry or cohabit with white colonists continued in the nineteenth century.

**MARRONAGE** (Fr. Cr.), in the colonial West Indies and elsewhere, a common illegal flight of slave gangs (q.v.) from the plantations for the purpose of living as Maroons (q.v.). It was usually a massive escape with individual fugitives banding together under a chief. Systematic marronage struck at the foundation of the sugar estates (q.v.), presenting potential military and economic threats that brought terror to the colonists. The collective flight, especially of African-born blacks, resulted in strict laws and quick and brutal punishment for recaptured runaway slaves. Marronage did not have the same meaning in all colonies at all times. It has been calculated that in Saint Domingue (circa 1751) there were about 3,500 runaway blacks living in scattered, isolated communities which were legally settled and supervised by the government. (Price, *Maroon Societies*, p. 2.)

**MARSA.** See MAAS.

**MARSON, UNA M.** (b. 1905), a black poetess and playwright born in Santa Cruz, Saint Elizabeth, Jamaica. Marson has distinguished herself as a journalist, lecturer, and writer. From 1933 to 1935, she lived in London, where she was active in the League of Colored Peoples. Later, during World War II, she served as an editor and broadcaster of the West Indies programs of the BBC in London and also lectured widely throughout England. Her plays were produced in London and in Kingston, Jamaica. After the war, she returned to her native country. Among her works are *Tropic Reveries* (Kingston, 1931); *Heights and Depths* (Kingston, 1931); *The Moth and the Star* (Kingston, 1937); and *Towards the Stars* (London, 1945).

**MARTIN, FREDERICK,** a Moravian missionary whom N. L. Zinzendorf (q.v.), the founder of the Moravian church (q.v.), called "the apostle of the Negroes in the West Indies." In 1784, Martin organized one of the first missions for the conversion of slaves in Saint Thomas, Virgin Islands. From the beginning, he refused to accept the colonists' conviction that it was impossible to effect a real conversion of black slaves to Christianity. He imposed a strict discipline on the new Christians and attempted to ensure constant formal and informal supervision so that no convert would lapse from his new faith. He also created a formal church organization, incorporating a sacramental liturgy, class meetings, and a hierarchy of assistants. (Goveia, *Slave Society*, pp. 271, 275.)

**MARTIN, JUAN LUIS** (b. 1903), a prolific Cuban writer. Martin is concerned with Negro traditions and folklore, and has contributed greatly to the revival of African themes and values. Among his chief works are *Ecué Chango y Yamayá (ensayos sobre la sub-religíon de los afro-cubanos* (Havana, 1930); *De donde vinieron los negros de Cuba, los mandingos, gangás, carabeliés y ararás: Su historia, antes de la esclavitud* (Havana, 1939); and *Vocabulario de Ñáñigo y Lucumí; breve estudio de lingüística afro-cubana* (Havana, 1946).

**MARTINEZ, DOMINGO** (d. 1864), a Brazilian slave trader whose activities extended for thirty years, beginning in 1834 and continuing through the period of the rise of the palm oil trade and into the final twilight of the slave trade in the 1860s. He came to the Bight of Benin (q.v.), the center of his operations, in 1833 as a sailor on a slave ship. He established contacts between the king of Dahomey (q.v.) and the Brazilian planters and began exporting slaves to Bahia and other coastal cities in the northeast of Brazil. He soon became a rich merchant. In 1844 Martinez returned to Brazil where he set himself up as a man of property, but being without education, he was considered a socially unacceptable parvenu. He went back to the Bight of Benin in 1846. The king of Dahomey then made him his official representative in the slave trade, and Martinez again organized a prosperous business dealing with Brazilian planters in need of slave labor. As a result of increasing European penetration into the Bight of Benin, however, he lost his enterprise when the Dahomean king gave the French permission to trade in goods and slaves.

**MARTINIQUE** (Fr. Cr.), in Haiti, a black social dance performed at festivals, family gatherings, wakes, and in religious services. The name is sometimes also applied to the entire cycle of dances which follow burial rites. Also known as *juba* (q.v.).

**MÁSAMBA** (Afr.), in the Afro-Cuban dialect, a black lesbian.

**MASCARA** (Pg.), in colonial Brazil, an instrument of torture used to cover the face of persons who persisted in the habit of dirt-eating (q.v.); often used on children. (Ramos, *The Negro*, p. 34.)

**MASCORT** (Fr. Cr.), in rural Haiti, a dance performed by blacks after they completed their communal work in the fields.

**MAS ELE TEM CABELO RUIM** (Pg.) ("But his hair is bad"), in Brazil, an expression pointing to the kinky and woolly hair of a white person with light skin and fine facial features.

**MASH, MASH-MASH** (Eng. Cr.), in Jamaica, the small change left after spending a larger amount of money; a term used mainly by blacks.

**MASHER** (Eng. Cr.), in the West Indies, sandals made of canvas with corded soles; usually worn by blacks.

**MASH-MASH.** See MASH.

**MASINGA** (Bant.), in colonial Cuba, an Angolan-born slave.

**MASSA** (Eng. Cr.), in the colonial West Indies, a slave master, a planter.

**MASSA CAN DO NO WRONG** (Eng. Cr.), on Caribbean plantations, a principle accepted by exploited and powerless black slaves.

**MASSAMBARA** (Afr.), in Brazil, a kind of wild weed brought from Africa in slavery times.

**MASSAMBIE** (Afr.), in the West Indies, a kind of medicinal plant (species *Cleone*) imported from Mozambique in the colonial period.

**MASSANEAGA, MASSA-NIGGER, MAASA-NIEGA** (Afr.), in the West Indies, a fellow black, a friend.

**MASSA-TENKY, TENKY MASSA** (Eng. Cr.), an Afro-Jamaican word for a gift.

**MASSHU, MASU** (Twi), in the West Indies, an African word meaning to lift or pick up.

**MASUCAMBA** (Afr.), in Cuba, a black dance similar to the tango (q.v.).

**MASU GADU** (Afr.), the supreme diety among the Bush Negroes (q.v.) in Guiana; of Dahomean origin.

**MATA-BICHO** (Pg.), in Brazil and Angola (q.v.), the traditional habit among blacks of drinking a dose of brandy early in the morning as the best safeguard against the dreaded sickness called *mal-de-bicho* (q.v.) or *maculo* (q.v.).

**MATACUMBÉ** (Afr.), an Afro-Cuban term for key or reef, numerous along the Cuban coast.

**MATANGA** (Afr.), in Brazil, a black wake.

**MATI** (Afr.), in Surinam, a lower class black lesbian. A woman whose husband works in the forests may take a girl friend with whom she has a permanent sexual relationship. She often cohabits with the man as well. (Lier, *Frontier Society*, p. 286.)

**MATOMBO** (Afr.), an Afro-Brazilian word for a flower bed used for planting manihot. See MANDIOCA.

**MATOS, GREGORIO DO** (1633-1696), an early black satirical poet who used the theme of the black in his writings. He was a baroque writer and a member of the so-called Bahian School. His works form Brazil's first true native literature. He wrote a great number of unpublished poems of all kinds, in which he commented upon contemporary Bahian society and on the part blacks played in it. (Sayers, *The Negro*, p. 42.)

**MATTOS, JOAQUIN DE,** a black slave leader and hero in the unsuccessful rebellion of Hausa slaves (q.v.) in Bahia in 1835. His loyalty to his comrades was so great that during his trial he refused even to admit an acquaintance with his closest associates. Like all the rebels, Mattos was a devout Moslem. (Ramos, *The Negro*, p. 51.)

**MATUNGO** (Pg.), in Brazil, a set of iron bars used for bells in black music.

**MATUTENHO** (Pg.), in Brazil, a Portuguese Creole (q.v.) dialect spoken in rural areas by peasants of African ancestry.

**MATUWARI** (Afr.), a Portuguese-derived dialect spoken in Surinam originally developed from a Portuguese pidgin (q.v.) of the sixteenth century. It now contains a highly English-derived lexicon but appears to have retained an even higher proportion of African-related words.

**MAU OLHADO** (Pg.) ("evil eye"), a magical power that Afro-Brazilians believe brings death to plants, birds, and even small children. This folk belief is widespread in Afro-Latin America.

**MAX, JEAN.** See CASSIUS DE LINVAL, CLEMENCE.

**MAXAMBOMBA** (Afr.), in colonial Brazil, a two-team oxcart which was used on plantations to carry food for the two meals provided in the fields to slaves working far away from the big house.

**MAXIXE** (Afr.), an Afro-Brazilian dance which mixes black elements, rural folklore, and the rhythms of children's rounds. This hybrid dance, apparently brought from Africa, was one of the best known urban dances in the colonial period. Its syncopation is said to be African, and its rhythmic movements a late addition taken from the European polka.

**MAXWELL-HALL, AGNES** (b. 1894), a mulatto poetess born in Montego Bay. Maxwell-Hall was a member of a prominent Jamaican family. She was educated on her native island and was later sent to schools in New York, Boston, and London. Her father, the late Maxwell-Hall, had an observatory in the mountains at Kemshot where the writer owned and operated a dairy farm for several years. Her poems, such as "Jamaica Market" and "Lizard," as well as her short stories have been published in magazines in the United States and in England.

**MAYAMBA** (Afr.), in Haiti, a game of African origin using four chips made of shell, baked clay, or broken chinaware. One side of the chip is white, and the other is generally blue. Any number of players may participate, and, as in dice, all compete against the throwers. The *mayamba* is almost always a gambling game.

**MAYO, MANYO** (Afr.), in Haiti, a scapular worn by blacks to counteract the evil eye or some other magic.

**MAYOMBÉ** (Afr.). 1. In Cuba, a Yoruba (q.v.) cult centered around the worship of several African deities and the spirits of the dead. Today it has turned into black magic that includes a pact with the dead. The faithful believe that the dead are located in two separate places: their bodies, which are in the cemetery and their souls, in the bush (q.v.). 2. In the West Indies, a slave brought from the Congo (q.v.) region.

**MAYOMBERO** (Afr.), a black sorcerer initiated in the *mayombé* (q.v.), widespread in Cuba.

**MAYOMBO** (Afr.), a magic stick thought by black slaves in Haiti to protect the body in battle. Black soldiers carried this charm during the great uprisings of 1791-1798, the Humanitarian Revolt (q.v.). (Fouchard, *Les Marrons*, p. 522.)

**MAYORAL** (Sp.), in colonial Cuba, a black or mulatto slave who supervised other slaves working on the sugar plantations.

**MAYOYO** (Afr.), in Afro-Haitian folklore, a battery of rattles carried on a tall pole in some Congo (q.v.) religious services.

**MAYPOLE DANCERS,** a band of male black dancers who wear masks, twirl sticks, and wave colorful ribbons to the accompaniment of guitars, drums, and other African instruments. Some dancers are dressed as women. Maypole dancers are one of the several groups that compete for the attention and admiration of spectators during the celebration of Mardi Gras in Haiti.

**MAYUMBA** (Afr.), a kind of witchcraft in some Afro-Cuban cults.

**MAZAMORRA** (Sp.), in the Colombian Pacific lowlands, a name given by blacks to sand and gravel sluice tailings.

**MAZAMORRERO** (Sp.), in the Colombian Pacific lowlands, a black who reworks sluice ways abandoned by former slaveholders. (Whitten, *Black Frontiersmen*, p. 47.)

**MAZANZA** (Afr.), an Afro-Brazilian word for a negligent, lazy person.

**MAZOMBISMO** (Afr.), a Brazilian term for maladjustment, lack of initiative, want of interest in any kind of useful activity. It includes a deep scorn for everything other than quickly won fortune. In colonial times, it was characterized by a persistent and pervading longing that belittled native things and values, and looked to Portugal, Europe, and, later, France as models.

**MAZOMBO** (Afr.), a derogatory term for a Brazilian of foreign (especially Portuguese) parents who is sombre, melancholic, and sullen. In the colonial period, the term referred to a Brazilian-born person who was spiritually Portuguese and was constantly irritated because Brazil was not a replica of Portugal. See also MAZOMBISMO.

**MAZON** (Fr. Cr.), an Afro-Haitian religious dance performed in honor of certain deities.

**M'B** (Bant.), a prefix attached to Bantu (q.v.) words.

**MBALÁ** (Bant.), an Afro-Brazilian method of hunting in which the hunter disguises himself as a bush and thus tries to fool the animals.

**MBE** (Bant.), in the Dutch West Indies, a black matriarchal family group which settles around clusters of huts.

**MC** (Bant.), a prefix attached to Bantu (q.v.) or Angolan words.

**MEAGRE BROWN** (Eng. Cr.), in Jamaica, a racial term for a light brown person; not necessarily derogatory.

**MEBULA** (Bant.), in Brazil, a big tree *(Hexalobus Mbula Exell)* that produces a hardwood called *bula*; brought from Angola (q.v.) in slavery times.

**MEDIA CRIANDERA** (Sp.), in colonial Cuba, a black woman who suckled both her own infant and that of her mistress.

**MEDINA, MANUEL,** a mulatto slave born in Havana, Cuba, and owned by Don Carlos Rodriguez, a planter. Medina fought valiantly on the government side against the revolutionaries engaged in obtaining the island's independence. On August 9, 1862, the colonial authorities freed him as a reward for his heroism. (Calcagno, *Diccionario*, p. 411.)

**MEDINA Y CÉSPEDES, ANTONIO** (1824-1886), a mulatto poet born in Havana, Cuba, on June 13, 1824. At the age of nine Medina y Céspedes lost his father and, at age fifteen, he became a tailor to support his two sisters. Unable to attend school, he taught himself to read and write. Through his strong will and intellectual ambition, he attained fame as a writer and was later called "the light of his race." In 1861 he graduated as a teacher, and the following year a benefactor opened a school under his direction. Among his pupils were his own nine children and twelve poor blacks.

Medina y Céspedes was a friend and student of the black slave poet J. F. Manzano (q.v.). He collaborated on several periodicals, including *El Faro* and *El Avisador Comercial*. Some of his short stories such as "El calesero de alquiler" and "La vejez del sastre" and poems such as "Una visita al cementerio," "A mi lira," "Recuerdos de la infancia," and "La cena," have been published in magazines and newspapers. His works include *Lodoiska o la maldición* (Havana, 1849); *Don Canuto Ceibamocha, o el Guajiro generoso*, (a play, Havana, 1854); and *Jacobi Girondi*, a play staged in Madrid in 1880. He was writing a play, *La maldición y la hija del pueblo*, when he died. His sonnet "Amor a Dios" was published by the provincial press, and his poem "El suspiro de amor" was put to music. (Calcagno, *Diccionario*, p. 412.)

**MEKI-MAN** (Eng. Cr.), in Jamaica, a black *obeah* man (q.v.).

**MÉLANGE DE SANGS** (Fr.), the mixing of races between white colonists and black women in colonial Saint Domingue. This fusion of races, either physically or legally, was typical in the colony. A report dating from 1731 indicates that racial intermarriages were quite common in some parts of the island. (Hall, *Social Control*, p. 141.)

**MÊLÉ** (Fr.). See SANG MÊLÉ.

**MELHORANDO A RAÇA** (Pg.) ("improving the breed"), an idiom used in certain parts of Brazil expressing the prestige ordinarily attached to the so-called whiter child. Thus, a black mother would proudly say, when showing off her light-skinned child, "I am improving the breed." (Pierson, *Negroes*, p. 124.)

**MENDES, ODORICO** (1799-1864), a Brazilian poet. In 1812, Mendes wrote the first poem in Brazilian literature specifically dedicated to a suffering slave.

**MENELIQUE** (Pg.), in São Paulo, Brazil among people of Italian descent, a black or mulatto.

**MENEZES, TOBIAS BARRETO DE** (1838-1908), a Brazilian mulatto scientist and philosopher. As a man of letters and founder of the so-called Recife School of Arts and Letters, Menezes's fame rests in part on his book of verse, *Dias e Noites*. He was chiefly a philologist, however, devoted to the German language and German philosophy.

Menezes was apparently the first Afro-Brazilian to ask the kind of questions about his own identity which were later to play a big part in Brazilian literature: "Neither a pure Aryan nor a pure African nor a pure American —what am I then? An individual of a race or a subrace which is still evolving?" He was not concerned with slavery and the conditions of slaves in his time; rather, intellectually he was completely oriented toward Europe. He married a white woman, and attempted to dissociate himself from his African background. (Ramos, *The Negro*, p. 149.)

**MENOW WEED** (Afr.), in Jamaica, an African plant name applied to a weed *(Ruellia tuberosa)* frequently used by blacks to cure fevers; now usually called duppy gun.

**MENTO** (Eng. Cr.), in Jamaica, a popular black dance.

**MEN WITHOUT A COUNTRY,** an expression used in Panama to refer to West Indian blacks on the Isthmus whose citizenship status is sometimes uncertain. The second and third generations of Zone-born blacks find themselves on the margin of Panamanian society and have no feeling of belonging.

**MERCHANT FACTORS,** British merchants who, especially during the eighteenth century, supplied the West Indian planters with the long-term credit needed to support the trade in sugar estate (q.v.) staples, goods, and slaves. The factor usually charged an interest rate of 5 percent on advances of capital on credit; as planter debts accumulated, the interest payments increased correspondingly.

**MERECURE** (Fr. Cr.), in Venezuela and elsewhere in the Antilles, a big drum played by blacks.

**MERENGE, MÉRINGE** (Fr.), in Haiti and the Antilles, an old French song-dance popular at court in France. Today it is danced with a syncopated African beat. (Slonimzki, *Music*, p. 312.)

**MERRY-WANG** (Eng. Cr.), in colonial Jamaica, a kind of four-string African banjo made from a gourd with skin stretched over its largest section. An ornate handle was attached to the end of the gourd, giving the instrument the appearance of a primitive banjo. It was played with the fingers like a guitar. (Beckwith, *Black Roadways*, p. 211.)

**MESA DE CONSCIENCIA** (Pg.) ("Moral Tribunal"), established in Lisbon (1532) by the king of Portugal, João III, to aid in the resolution of juridical and administrative disputes, especially those having to do with moral and legal questions. In 1610, Luis Brandão, a Portuguese Jesuit residing in Luanda, Angola, answering a question regarding slavery put to him by another Jesuit Alonso de Sandoval (q.v.) from Cartagena, Colombia, argued that the Mesa de Consciencia in Lisbon never prohibited the slave traffic and that most slaves who said they had been kidnapped were probably lying. See *De Instauranda Aetiopum Salute* (Bogotá, 1956) p. 90. (Rout, L. B. *The African Experience in Spanish America*, p. 100.)

**MÉSALLIANCE** (Fr. Cr.), in Martinique and elsewhere in the Antilles, a marriage that contravenes the closed group's principal selection criteria. It applies when a white Creole marries a mulatto, or when an individual marries someone of a much lower social status. *Mésalliance* usually involves an element of racial stain for the whites.

**MESALLIÉ** (Fr. Cr.), in colonial Saint Domingue, a white colonist married to a black woman. He was considered an outcast.

**MESTIÇAGEM** (Pg.), in modern Brazil, a progressive form of racial mixing which, according to the Brazilian elite, will eventually absorb the African strain through the influence of European migration.

**MESTIÇO** (Pg.), in modern Brazil, a mulatto.

**MÉTAYE** (Fr.), in the French Antilles, a sharecropping system that keeps the black peasants tied to the traditional sugar estate (q.v.) economy.

**MÉTAYER** (Fr.), in Haiti, a small black farmer.

**MÉTIS** (Fr. Cr.), in the French Antilles, the offspring of a black man and an Indian woman.

**METRO** (Fr.), in Martinique and the French Antilles, a civil servant from metropolitan France.

**METTÉ N' ÂME** (Fr. Cr.), in the Afro-Haitian religion, a ritual used to restore a soul that has been taken from its body.

**MEU NEGO! MEU NEGRO!** (Pg.) ("my Negro!"), a term of endearment of intimate and special tenderness, spoken in soft tones by Brazilian whites in speaking to other whites, especially to lovers.

**MFUKA** (Bant.), the chief slave broker of the king of Angola (q.v.). Every slave in the kingdom was under the protection of a *mfuka*.

**MIÇANGA** (Afr.), an Afro-Brazilian word for cheap jewels such as beads.

**MICHEL, PIÈRRE,** (d. 1799), an African-born slave brought to Haiti as a young man. After being freed during the slave rebellion of 1791, he became a general and an aide of Toussaint L'Ouverture (q.v.). He was later accused of treason, and the Liberator ordered his execution on August 4, 1799. (Ott, *The Haitian Revolution*, p. 112.)

**MIDDLE PASSAGE,** the long voyage of slave cargoes from West Africa to the West Indies. The trip lasted from six to ten weeks, with all the slaves packed in small boats. The lack of food, the absence of refrigeration and bathing facilities, and rampant disease decimated the cargo. After 1650 the Middle Passage became notorious because of the overcrowded conditions on the ships and the extremely high death rate by suicide and sickness. See also CARABELAS; SHIPMATES.

**MIGUEL, KING,** a black slave, possibly an African native, who in 1552 led a rebellion of 800 blacks, mulattoes, and *sambo* (q.v.) against the Spaniards in Buria, a mining district (near the present city of Barquisimeto, Venezuela). He declared himself a king and created a court. For over two years he conducted a clever campaign against nearby Spanish settlements, stealing cattle, freeing other slaves, holding white hostages for random, and generally attempting to extend his control over the territory. He led attacks until 1555 when he was killed in a disastrous assault on the city of Barquisimeto. (Rout, L. B., *The African Experience in Spanish America*, p. 111.)

**MILATT PÔVRE QUE PAS CONNIN LI, ÉCRIT, CELA NÈG** (Fr. Cr.) ("The poor mulatto who can't read and write is a Negro"), an Afro-Haitian aphorism pointing to the low social status of blacks.

**MILE MONEY,** in the colonial West Indies, money paid for the return of a runaway slave proportionate to the number of miles his captor had to travel to bring him. The 1788 Act to Repeal set the rate of mile money at 1 shilling per mile for the first five miles and 6 pence per mile thereafter. (Cassidy, *Dictionary*, p. 300.)

**MILL-GANG,** in the West Indies, the slave labor force which tended the sugar mill (q.v.) while it was in operation.

**MILONGA MULANGA** (Pg.), an Afro-Brazilian dance.

**MIMBA** (Afr.), in the West Indies, an African day-name (q.v.) for a girl born on Saturday.

**MI MOUIN! KE FAI PÉ LABAT VINI POUEND OU!** (Fr. Cr.) ("My darling! I'll call Father Labat to come to take you away"), an Afro-Haitian aphorism used to frighten children. (Corzani, *Littérature antillaise, prose*, p. 46.) See also LABAT, JEAN BAPTISTE.

**MINA** (Pg.). 1. In colonial Brazil, a black woman who was a concubine and housewife of a white planter; usually a light-skinned female with near white features, she was considered to be an excellent sexual companion. 2. In modern Brazil, a black religious sect centered around the worship of Christian saints, the ancestors, and the family spirits.

**MINANA** (Afr.), a goddess of African origin worshipped by blacks in Trinidad. Her favorite foods are goat and fowl; her color is white with an orange band. (Herskovits, *Trinidad Village*, p. 331.)

**MINA SLAVES,** blacks exported to Brazil from the Gold Coast (q.v.) through the famous slave-trading post of Elmina (q.v.). They were considered to be both stronger and more vigorous than the Bantus (q.v.) and to have almost magical powers of discovering gold. These Sudanese blacks were famous for their physique, their proud, dignified bearing, and their culinary skill. Most of them were Moslem and literate. They were able to organize small ethnic communities on the plantations and in the mining district. When a delegation of the Society of Friends (Quakers) (q.v.) arrived in Rio de Janeiro in 1852, it was received by a commission of Mina freedmen, seventy of whom were to be repatriated to Benin (q.v.). They presented the English visitors with documents written in Arabic. (Freyre, *The Masters*, pp. 313, 318.)

**MINGONGO** (Afr.), in Brazil, an African name applied to an insect *(Bruchus nucleorum, Fabr.)* that attacks the *coco babaçu* tree. The blacks consider roasted *mingongo* a delicacy.

**MINGU** (Pg.), an Afro-Brazilian dish prepared with manihot (see *mandioca*), eggs, and sugar.

**MINHA NEGA!** (Pg.) ("My little Negress"), in Brazil, a phrase which a white man often employs in speaking to his white wife or mistress. The phrase has connotations of warm affection and sympathy. (Degler, *Neither Black nor White*, p. 3.)

**MINHOCA** (Pg.), an Afro-Brazilian generic term for earthworm, marine worm, leech, or other annelid.

**MINUTES OF THE EVIDENCE,** an official report of the British Parliament's investigations regarding the slave trade, published in four volumes in London, 1789-1791. Although these findings did not lead to the immediate abolition of the English slave trade, they did result in strict laws regarding the number of slaves a vessel could carry and in measures to protect the slaves while being transported to the West Indies. (Mannix, *Black Cargoes*, p. 291.)

**MIRA** (Fr. Cr.), in Haiti, a small gang of black peasants who come to help a neighbor with his work. A *mira* usually consists of ten or twelve men. (Herskovits, *Life in a Haitian*, p. 70.)

**MIRONGA** (Afr.), an Afro-Brazilian word meaning a secret.

**MISS** (Eng. Cr.), in the West Indies, a term of address such as Miss Polly or Miss Jane used by fellow slaves when talking to domestic female slaves. (Brathwaite, *The Development*, p. 175.)

**MISSANGA** (Afr.), in Brazil, a small, perforated glass bead used today to decorate women's attire such as turbans or headdresses. It is worn by black women in Bahia. These charms are among the most characteristic folk costumes of the country.

**MITTELHÖLZER, EDGAR AUSTIN** (1909-1965), native of Guiana, also known as H. Austin Woodsley, who was the best known novelist of his generation. His family was originally Swiss, an ancestor having emigrated in the eighteenth century. He himself emigrated to England where he lived in London and became popular as a watercolorist. He has an impressive list of novels, including *Corentyne Thunder* (London, 1941); *A Morning at the Office* (London, 1950); *A Morning in Trinidad* (Garden City, N.Y., 1950); *Shadows Move among Them* (London, 1951); *The Life and Death of Sylvia* (London, 1953); *My Bones and My Flute: A Ghost Story in the Old-Fashioned Manner* (London, 1955); *With a Carib Eye* (London, 1958); and *Uncle Paul* (London, 1963).

**MIXED COMMISSION, COURTS OF,** a joint tribunal established by England and Spain in 1817 to deal with the judiciary problems connected with the illegal trade of slaves between the West African coast and the New World. It was situated in Sierra Leone (q.v.) and, for a time, in Havana.

**MKONGO** (Bant.), a chief priest in the Afro-Cuban *santería* (q.v.).

**M'LEMBA** (Bant.), an Afro-Brazilian word for the deflowering of a virgin; symbolized in a sexual wedding dance called *quizomba* (q.v.).

**MOBICA** (Afr.), in colonial Brazil, a freed former black slave.

**MOÇA BRANCA** (Pg.) ("white girl"), a colloquial phrase used by black slaves to refer to brandy made of sugar cane (q.v.).

**MOÇAMBIQUE** (Afr.), a generic term applied to a black slave introduced into Brazil from the territory of Mozambique. Most of these slaves were brought in ships from India.

**MOCAMBO, MUCAMBO** (Afr.). 1. In early Brazilian history, a small, isolated settlement of runaway slaves. It grew out of the collective flights of African-born blacks who resisted both slavery and the assimilation of white culture. Also, a hut in such a community. 2. Today an urban hovel with thatched roof, unplastered walls, dirt floor, and usually no windows; used as a residence by many Afro-Brazilians.

**MOCO** (Afr.). 1. In colonial Jamaica, a slave shipped to the West Indies from Bonny. 2. Today, in colloquial usage, the term means ugliness or backwardness.

**MOCOTÓ** (Afr.), an Afro-Brazilian dish whose main ingredients are calves' feet and spices; made by black women and sold at home and on the streets.

**MODIFORD, SIR THOMAS,** a wealthy Barbadian planter who, around 1658, was an agent of the Royal African Company (q.v.) for the supply of slaves to the island. He was appointed governor to persuade his company to provide Jamaica with black slaves. (Craton and Walvin, *A Jamaican Plantation*, pp. 22-31.)

**MOEDA, MOIDORE** (Pg.), a Luso-Brazilian gold coin worth 4,000 reis and valued at 27s. 6d. in 1720. Around 1713, it became the most general and popular currency in the Slave Coast (q.v.), England and the Americans, including the British North American colonies before 1778. (Boxer, *The Portuguese Seaborne*, p. 164.)

**MOFONGO** (Bant.), an Afro-Caribbean dish made of fried or roasted plantain (q.v.) mixed with pork and spices; eaten mainly by blacks.

**MOIDORE.** See MOEDA.

**MOI SEUL JE SUIS NOBLE** (Fr. Cr.) ("I am the only noble"), a phrase attributed to Jean-Jacques Dessalines (q.v.), president of Haiti, in response to his black followers who were asking for the creation of a nobility. (Leyburn, *The Haitian People*, p. 214.)

**MOIN.** See MEVÉ.

**MOIN GRAND GOÛT** (Fr. Cr.) ("I am hungry"), an expression often heard in the urban slums of Haiti testifying to the extreme poverty of the black population.

**MOÏSE, RODOLPHE** (b. 1914), a black Haitian poet who was educated on his native island. Moïse took part in the 1946 revolution against President Elie Lescot and afterwards left for France where he studied sculpture. His main work is *Gueules de feu*, in which are included two of his best known poems, "Hymne ancestral" and "Crepuscule."

**MOLECÃO** (Pg.), in colonial Brazil, a black youth between eight and fifteen years of age whose fair market price in 1703 was 250 drams. (Boxer, *The Golden Age*, p. 33.)

**MOLEQUE.** See MULEQUE.

**MOLHO DE FERRUGEM** (Pg.), a thick Afro-Brazilian gravy made with meat juices.

**MONDAY,** among Afro-Jamaican blacks, an unlucky day for marriages and for paying debts.

**MONDÍ** (Pg.), an Afro-Brazilian word for disgrace, fight, or disagreement. ment.

**MONDONGO** (Afr.), in Brazil, an African black slave.

**MONDONGUE** (Afr.), an Afro-Haitian god who is fond of dogs. His favorite foods are dogs' ears and tails.

**MONEY CUFFEE** (Eng. Cr.), in Jamaica, a black who is financially well off and spends freely.

**MONEY WHITENS EVERYONE,** an idiom used in Panama to indicate that money breaks color barriers. A wealthy black can occupy any position open to whites.

**MONGA** (Afr.), an Afro-Hispanic word for a bad cold.

**MONGO** (Afr.), a merchant who, after the abolition of the slave trade (1808), continued buying slaves along the African coast and exporting them to the New World. He organized the illegal traffic with great ingenuity and obtained fabulous profits. Some of the *mongos* enjoyed almost royal power over coastal tribes by winning recognition as overlords from some of the black chiefs in the area. (Mannix, *Black Cargoes*, p. 229.)

**MONGO JOHN.** See ORMOND, JOHN.

**MONGOLA,** in the West Indies, an African ethnic group.

**MONGOLO,** in Brazil, a tropical tree introduced from Africa during slavery times.

**MONKEY BREADFRUIT** (Eng. Cr.), in the West Indies, a kind of bread-fruit (q.v.) *(Artocarpus communis)*, formerly a staple food for slaves.

**MONKEY-JESUS,** an Afro-Jamaican word for an ugly person, often applied to blacks.

**MONKEY PLAY DE FIDDLE MEK BABOON DANCE** (Eng. Cr.) ("The monkey plays the fiddle for the baboon to dance") an Afro-Jamaican aphorism suggesting that the "small" man must work while the powerful man enjoys life. (Beckwith, *Jamaica Proverbs*, p. 85.)

**MONTEAGUDO, BERNARDO DE** (1785-1825), a revolutionary, intellectual, political leader, lawyer, and collaborator with both San Martin and Bolivar in the wars of independence. Born of African ancestry in Tucuman, Argentina, Monteagudo was educated at the University of Chuquisaca (Bolivia). He was a diplomat who rose to the rank of Peruvian minister of war and the navy in 1822. He was assassinated in Lima three years later.

**MONTEIRO, MACIEL** (1804-1868), a Brazilian politician and poet. He proposed the abolition of slavery in a celebrated speech delivered in 1851.

**MOODY HYMN,** in Jamaica, a secular hymn sung by blacks at wakes.

**MOOMOO, MUMU** (Afr.), in the West Indies, an African word for a dumb person.

**MOON-GLOW** (Eng. Cr.), in Jamaica, a racial term for a person with light brown skin; generally used with favorable connotations.

**MOONGOOSE** (Eng. Cr.), in the West Indies, a black albino.

**MOONSHINE BABY** (Eng. Cr.), in the West Indies, a game played by black children at the full moon in which they choose a girl as "moonshine." The girl lies still on a wooden frame while the others outline her with bits of broken crockery which reflect the moonlight. The amusement comes, in part, from the players' remarks while outlining the "baby" and later filling in the outline with more mosaic bits.

**MOONSHINE DARLING** (Eng. Cr.), in Jamaica, a black dance held outdoors when the moon is full. Anyone can join in the fun, whether invited or not; the participants bring refreshments.

**MOONSHINE YAM** (Eng. Cr.), in the West Indies, a yellow or orange yam (q.v.) *(Dioscorea)* cultivated and eaten mainly by blacks.

**MOOS-MOOS, MUS-MUS** (Afr.), in the Caribbean region, an African dish made basically of turned meal or flour, with or without other ingredients. Cassava flour appears to be the most widely used.

**MORAND, FLORETTE,** a mulatto poetess born in Guadeloupe. Her poetry is inspired by the tropical islands of the region and the human sufferings of poor blacks, descendants of former slaves. She praises both the black race and French culture. She traveled throughout Europe and married in Italy, where she was greeted as the *fille des savanes.* In 1947, Morand was honored with a prize in poetry by the Association des Etudiants Guadeloupans in Paris; two years later, she received an award in Guadeloupe as a writer of French prose. Among her works are *Mon coeur est un oiseau des îsles* (Paris, 1955); *Biguines* (Paris, 1956); *Chanson pour ma savane* (Paris, 1958); *Tam-tam* (in Italian, Paris); and *Feux de brousse* (Paris, 1967). (Corzani, *Littérature antillaise, poésie*, p. 297).

**MORANT BAY REBELLION,** an uprising of about 400 black settlers which took place in Jamaica on October 11-12, 1865. The protesters, led by a Baptist named Paul Bogle (q.v.), assaulted the Moran Bay courthouse in Saint Thomas-in-the-East and set the building on fire. About fifteen government magistrates and other civilians were killed, and several estates were looted. The government suppressed the sedition immediately. Bogle and other Maroon (q.v.) leaders were caught, tried, and hanged.

**MORAVIA, CHARLES** (1875-1938), a Haitian poet born in Jérémie, Haiti, on June 17, 1875. Moravia was educated in his native town and in Port-au-Prince. He worked as a journalist, founding two newspapers, *La Plume* and *Le Temps*; he also served as a diplomat. His poetry is melancholic and tender. His works include *Ode à la mémoire de Toussaint L'Ouverture* (Port-au-Prince, 1903); *Roses et camélias* (Port-au-Prince, 1903); *Le Crête-à-Pierrot: Poème dramatique en trois tableaux et en vers* (Port-au-Prince, 1908); *Les Fils du tapissier* (Port-au-Prince, 1923); and *L'Amiral Killick* (Port-au-Prince, 1943).

**MORAVIAN CHURCH,** the Church of the United Brethren, an evangelical group reorganized by N. L. von Zinzendorf (q.v.) in Saxony in 1722. This was the first Protestant society to undertake the work of converting black slaves in the West Indies. The first missionaries sent by the founder arrived on December 13, 1732, on the Danish island of Saint Thomas. In the years that followed, the mission was extended from this island to Kingston, Jamaica (1754), Barbados (1765), and Tobago (1796). By 1835, the congregation in Saint Thomas included 9,508 slaves, but only 960 free blacks. (Farr, *Historical Dictionary*, p. 113.)

**MOREIRA, JULIANO** (1854-1911), a black Brazilian scientist, physician, and psychiatrist, a pioneer in the treatment of insanity in his country. His bibliography is lengthy and covers various aspects of psychiatry. In some of his scholarly studies, whose prestige extended to Europe, he took issue with the thesis that the black and mulatto are racially inferior. Among his works are *Ein neue pathologischer klinischer Bertrag zur Kentnis des Ainhums* (Leipzig, F. A. Brockhaus, s.d.) and *Impressoes de una Viagem ao Japão em 1928* (Rio de Janeiro, 1935).

**MORENA** (Pg.), in Brazil, especially in Bahia, an ideal type of femininity characterized as a mixed-blood woman of remarkable beauty with dark brown eyes and dark hair, quite wavy, perhaps even curly, and Caucasian features. She has the reputation of being more desirable than lighter Brazilian women and is commonly described as "more passionate." Poets and novelists, both professional and amateur, pour out ardent poems and romances in her honor, and songs are sung to her.

**MORENO** (Sp.), in Spanish America, a black; in Brazil, a mulatto.

**MORE RAIN, MORE REST; MORE GRASS GROW FE MASSA HORSE** (Eng. Cr.) ("More rain, more rest; more grass for master's horse"), an Afro-Jamaican aphorism from slavery times. (Beckwith, *Jamaica Proverbs*, p. 85.)

**MORET LAW.** See LEY MORET.

**MORET Y PRENDERGAST, SEGISMUNDO** (1838-1913), a Spanish politician and ardent abolitionist who, as colonial minister, was the proponent of the so-called Ley Moret (q.v.) in 1870 which outlawed slavery in the Spanish colonies.

**MORINGA** (Afr.), in Afro-Cuban folklore, a bogeyman, a fear-inspiring creature.

**MORISCO** (Sp.), in early sixteenth-century Mexico and elsewhere, the offspring of a Spanish man and mulatto woman. The child was considered one-quarter black.

**MORNING AT THE OFFICE, A,** a novel by the Guianian writer Edgar A. Mittelhölzer (q.v.) published in London in 1950. The author describes a cross-section of modern society in Trinidad where racial mixture, with its tensions, frustrations, and discrimination, has been traditional.

**MORNING MATCH** (Eng. Cr.), in Jamaica, the practice common to black smallholders of getting together with relatives and friends for the purpose of harvesting, cutting down bush (q.v.) planting yams (q.v.), and the like. See also COUMBITÉ.

**MORON, ALONSO GRASEANO** (1909-1971), a black educator and public servant who held several important government posts in the Virgin Islands. He served as the first black president of America's Hampton Institute in Virginia.

**MORPEAU, LOUIS** (1895-1926), a black writer, born in Aux Cayes, Haiti. Morpeau attended local schools and received his secondary education at the College of Saint Martial and at the Lycée National, both in Port-au-Prince. He became an educator, a writer, and a diplomat. He was a regular contributor to French periodicals. His books include *Pages de jeunesse et de foi* (1919); *Anthologie haïtienne des poètes contemporains, 1904-1920* (Port-au-Prince, 1920); *L'enterrement de la merlasse* (Paris, 1924); and *Anthologie d' un siècle de poésie haïtienne, 1817-1925* (Paris, 1925).

**MORRAYA MALA** (Sp.) ("bad hair"), a phrase applied in Puerto Rico to a person with kinky hair indicating black ancestry.

**MORRISSEAU-LEROY, FELIX** (b. 1912), a black Haitian poet and novelist. Morrisseau-Leroy is deeply interested in black tradition and social problems. As a member of the new *Ecole Indigéniste* (q.v.) in Haiti, he feels a deep solidarity with the people of Europe, Asia, Africa, and Latin America. In his writings, he emphasizes black peasant folklore and religion, together with the middle class and the alien white exploiters. Among his works are *Plénitudes* and *Ricolte*.

**MORTS EN BAS DE L'EAU** (Fr. Cr.) ("dead under the waters"), a phrase expressing the belief, common among blacks in Haiti, that the spirits of the dead continue living below the waters.

**MORTS-VIVANTS** (Fr. Cr.) ("dead-living persons), in Afro-Haitian religion, persons already dead and buried over whom the sorcerer has gained control and whom he employs as slaves to carry out his diabolical schemes.

**MORÚA DELGADO, MARTIN** (b. 1856), a black Cuban slave born in Matanzas province. Morúa Delgado was the son of a Spaniard who immigrated from Spain, Francisco Morúa, and of an African-born mother, Ines Delgado, who was brought to the island as a slave. Unable to attend school, he worked as a barrel maker on a plantation. A self-taught man, he became an expert in several foreign languages, a popular writer, and the founder and editor of several periodicals. Because of his revolutionary ideas, he was twice forced into exile in the United States. In 1900, he was elected senator, and in 1908 he was named president of the Senate, the first black man in Cuba to attain that position. In addition to writing essays on literature, he published two novels, *Sofia* (1890) and *La familia Unzúazu* (1901), both dealing with the inhumanity of chattel slavery. See also LEY MORUA.

**MORÚA YUANSÁ** (Afr.), a priest in the Afro-Cuban *santería* (q.v.).

**MOSCA NO LEITE** (Pg.), a derogatory term applied to a mixed-blood marriage in modern Brazil. It expresses a certain repugnance to such an alliance.

**MOSCOVADO.** See MUSCOVADO.

**MOSTRENCO** (Sp.), in the early colonial Antilles, a runaway slave. Once captured, he became a royal ward.

**MOTHER OF THE CUMINA,** a female assistant chief to the master of ceremonies in the Afro-Jamaican *cumina* (q.v.) cult. She is also referred to as the "black and white girl" and is either a relative or is appointed by the family holding the *cumina*.

**MOTHER THOMAS** (Eng. Cr.), among Afro-Jamaican laborers, a kind of open-guard machete worn so far down as to be useless.

**MOTOMPY** (Twi), in the West Indies, an African word for bleariness of the eyes.

**MOUCHOUE-FAULAS** (Afr.), in the Afro-Antilles, a colorful headdress worn by black women.

**MOUÉ PAS ESCLAVE!** (Fr. Cr.) ("I am not a slave"), an expression frequently used by Haitian blacks to express their deep dislike for any kind of work connected with the plantation, for it suggests the slavery of the old regime.

**MOUNE** (Fr. Cr.), an Afro-Haitian term for man or person.

**MOURNER'S HOUSE, MOURNIN' GROUN** (Eng. Cr.), in Trinidad, a hut or a room where initiates of the Shouter (q.v.) cult are kept in seclusion for a long period of time.

**MOUSSACHE** (Fr. Cr.), in the French-Antilles, dry manioc powder with the toxic and poisonous substances removed. The blacks use moussache to make cassava.

**MOUTH-WATER** (Eng. Cr.), in the Afro-Jamaican dialect, saliva—a translation from the African word *ono-mmiri* or "wash mouth"; a term commonly used by slaves in the colonial period.

**MOUVEMENT OUVRIER PAYSAN** (Peasant Labor Movement), a black political party organized by Daniel Figule in Haiti in 1946; its goal is social revolution.

**MOYEN** (Fr. Cr.), in Haiti, the middle-sized *arada* (q.v.) drum, played by blacks in rituals and social gatherings.

**MOYSE**, a famous black slave leader in the great Haitian slave rebellion of 1791. Affectionately called "nephew" by Toussaint L'Ouverture (q.v.), he later became second in command. After plotting an unsuccessful revolt against his chief, he was tried and executed on November 3, 1801. (Ott, *The Haitian Revolution*, pp. 58, 79.)

**MOZAMBIQUE.** See MOÇAMBIQUE.

**MOZAMBIQUE, LUIS DE,** a black slave, probably an African native, leader of a runaway slave settlement in the San Blas mountains in the isthmus of Panama, in 1553. He harassed the colonists for several years until the Madrid government pardoned his group. Later these slaves were settled in two towns, Santiago del Príncipe (1579) and Santa Cruz de la Real (1582). (Rout, L. B., *The African Experience in Spanish America*, p. 118.)

**MUAFA** (Afr.), an Afro-Brazilian word for drunkenness.

**MUAMBA** (Afr.). 1. An African basket used in Brazil for carrying goods; a knapsack. 2. An Afro-Brazilian word for a concealed article of merchandise for illicit or illegal sale.

**MUCAMA, MUCAMBA** (Pg.), in Brazil, a favorite black maid employed as a house servant and personal attendant.

**MUCAMA DE ESTIMAÇÃO** (Pg.), in colonial Brazil, a black wet nurse who often suckled her white master's children.

**MUCAMBA.** See MUCAMA.

**MUCAMBO** (Afr.). See MOCAMBO.

**MUCKASHANDY** (Eng. Cr.), among Jamaican blacks, a masquerade.

**MUCKEY** (Eng. Cr.), in Jamaica, the same as *massa* (q.v.) or mackey.

**MUDU, MUDUK** (Afr.), in the West Indies, a black albino.

**MUFTI** (Ar.), among Moslem Hausa slaves (q.v.) in Brazil, a judicial assessor in charge of settling community disputes regarding material possessions. (M. G. Smith, *The Plural Society*, p. 126.)

**MUFU, MUFUN** (Afr.), an Afro-Cuban term for white rice.

**MUGUA** (Afr.), an Afro-Brazilian word for a fellow, a comrade.

**MUGUNZÁ** (Afr.), an Afro-Brazilian delicacy made of boiled corn with sugar and *coco* (q.v.) milk.

**MUHAMMAD KABA,** an African-born slave who, around 1825, was settled on a plantation located in Manchaster Parish, Jamaica. As a leader of an Islamic group in the area, he received an official letter sent by the African king, Abu Bakr, a prominent *imam* (q.v.), exhorting the Moslem community to be true and faithful if they wished to go to Heaven. (Curtin, *Africa Remembered*, p. 163.)

**MUJANQUÉ** (Afr.), an Afro-Brazilian dish made from turtle eggs with sugar and fermented manihot flour (see MANDIOCA).

**MUJER DE ASIENTO** (Sp.), in colonial Spanish America, the principal wife of a black chief in a runaway slave community.

**MULAMBO** (Afr.), an Afro-Brazilian word for a rag or cloth.

**MULATA** (Sp.), a female mulatto.

**MULATARIA** (Pg.), in Brazil, a large group of lower class mulattoes.

**MULATA VELHA** (Pg.) ("Old Mulattress"), an honorific title conferred upon the city of Bahia because it was the first Brazilian town in which mulattoes were born.

**MULATEIRO** (Pg.), in Brazil, a tropical tree of the Amazon region; also known as *pau mulato* (mulatto tree).

**MULATERO** (Sp.), in Cuba, a white male fond of mulatto women.

**MULATINHA** (Pg.), in Brazil, a young mulatto woman.

**MULATINHO** (Pg.), in Brazil: 1. A young mulatto boy. 2. A variety of beans.

**MULATISMO**, in Brazil, a doctrine or opinion that mixed-blood offspring show a number of manners, attitudes, values, and behavior characteristic of the mulatto group.

**MULATO** (Sp.), in Afro-Latin America, any person of mixed European and black blood; a mulatto. In Brazilian society, a mulatto is clearly distinguished according to facial features, skin color, and type of hair. There are several categories of mulattoes as a result of the great degree of hybridism present since slavery times.

**MULATO AMARILLO** (Sp.), in the Afro-Antilles, a yellowish mulatto.

**MULATO BLANCO** (Sp.), in the Afro-Antilles, the offspring of a white man and a black woman.

**MULATO BRANCO** (Pg.), in Brazil, a white mulatto, the first-generation offspring of a white man and a black woman. He usually tends to look upon himself as a transition point in an inevitable whitening process. Brazilians generally consider him to be superior in vitality to both whites and blacks. He is thought of as "a native plant," better acclimated physically and spiritually than either the Europeans or the Africans. (Pierson, *Negroes*, p. 123.)

**MULATO CLARO** (Pg.), in Brazil, a yellowish mulatto.

**MULATO CUARTERÓN** (Sp.), a quadroon (q.v.).

**MULATO HOLANDÉS** (Sp.), a Dutch mulatto born in the Antilles; also called *criollo de Curazão* (q.v.).

**MULATO LOBO** (Sp.), in the Spanish Antilles, the offspring of a mulatto and an Indian.

**MULATO LORO** (Sp.), in the Spanish Antilles, a dark mulatto.

**MULATO MEMBRILLO** (Sp.), in the Spanish Antilles, a yellowish mulatto.

**MULATO MESTIÇO** (Pg.), a Brazilian-born mulatto.

**MULATO MORENO** (Pg.), in Brazil, a dark mulatto.

**MULATO MORISCO** (Sp.), in early Spanish America, the offspring of a white man and a mulatto woman.

**MULATO NO CALCULA Y EL NEGRO NO TIENE SESO, EL** (Sp.) ("The mulatto does not plan anything, and the Negro has no brain"), a derogatory racial aphorism.

**MULATO OSCURO** (Pg.), in Brazil, a very dark mulatto.

**MULATO PARDO** (Sp.), in the Spanish Antilles, the offspring of a black and an Indian.

**MULATO PRETO** (Pg.), in Brazil, a dark mulatto.

**MULATO PRIETO** (Sp.), in the Spanish Antilles, the offspring of a black man and a mulatto woman.

**MULATO TRIGUENHO** (Pg.), in Brazil, a light mulatto.

**MULATO VELHO** (Pg.), in Brazil, salted, dried fish.

**MULÂTRAILLE** (Fr. Cr.), in the French Antilles, a derogatory term for a mulatto whom black intellectuals identify with the white and therefore consider a traitor to his race. The *mulâtrailles* as a group are accused of being subservient to the whites and responsible for the injustices and misery of the black urban and peasant proletariat. (Coulthard, *Race and Colour*, p. 101.)

**MULÂTRE** (Fr. Cr.), in Haiti, a mulatto descendant of the French colonists who, by tradition, has helped make up the majority of the aristocracy. The *mulâtres* make up only about 2 percent of the total population, but by virtue of their prestige and position, until recently they have managed to control the conduct of the nation's affairs.

**MULÂTRESSE LIBRE** (Fr. Cr.). See FILLE DE COULEUR.

**MULATTO GIRL,** in the British West Indies, a young mixed-blood girl who was often sold as a prostitute to a white man. Around 1784 an observer stated that mulatto girls, during the flower of their age, were universally sacrificed to the lust of white men. (Pitman, "Slavery," p. 634.)

**MULATTO SAVINGS,** in colonial Brazil, free people of color employed as laborers on large estates along with those working as artisans, porters, messengers, street merchants, and the like, who accumulated considerable sums of money. They often invested their savings in buying slaves and in the slave trade, and in sending arms, money, and trade goods to individuals in Africa to mount raids on their homes or among neighboring tribes. (Pierson, *Negroes*, pp. 67-68.)

**MULATTO SLAVE,** in the West Indies, a mixed-blood slave ordinarily chosen by his master or mistress for the more delicate and exacting household tasks. As a privileged slave, he found opportunities to free himself and enter the free mulatto class. As a general policy, he filled positions requiring training and dexterity such as driver, overseer, and domestic.

**MULATTO SOCIAL MOBILITY,** in colonial Brazil, the ability of a mixed-blood male to strip himself of the social stigma of servile origin and advance rapidly and successfully in the social hierarchy. In 1774, a law gave free mulattoes access to all offices, honors, and dignities, without discrimination on the basis of color. (Pierson, *Negroes*, p. 162-63).

**MULATTO TREE,** in the West Indies, a term applied to birch trees *(Bursera gummifera)* characterized by smooth, papery, chestnut-colored bark and soft, white wood. Also known as birch of Jamaica.

**MULECA** (Pg.), in Brazil, a young black or mulatto girl.

**MULECÓN** (Sp.), in colonial Cuba and elsewhere, a young black slave, fourteen to eighteen years of age, who was newly imported from Africa.

**MULECOTE** (Pg.), in Brazil, a sturdily built black male youth.

**MULEQUE, MOLEQUE** (Pg.), in slavery times, a Brazilian-born young black, aged six to fourteen, who served as playmate, companion, and whipping boy for the white master's son. The big houses almost always had a schoolroom. Many of the *muleques* studied with the white children and together learned to read, write, do sums, and pray.

**MULEQUE COMPANHEIRO DE BRINQUEDO** (Pg.) ("young black playmate"), in colonial Brazil, a young black slave given to a child by its white parents. Of the same age and sex, the slave served as the child's playmate and almost constant companion.

**MULEQUE DE ESTIMAÇÃO** (Pg.) ("honored playmate"), in colonial Brazil, a young black slave who, as a playmate of the white children, gained a position as a member of the big house, becoming a favorite houseboy slave.

**MULEQUINHO** (Pg.), in Brazil, a small black boy.

**MULEQUITA** (Pg.), slave baby girl.

**MULEQUITO** (Pg.), slave baby boy.

**MULE SAY "BOCKRA WORK MUS' DONE"** (Eng. Cr.) (Mule say, "White men's work must be done"), an Afro-Jamaican aphorism from slavery times. (Beckwith, *Jamaica Proverbs*, p. 86.)

**MULHER DE CAMA** (Pg.) ("female of bed"), in Brazil, a black slave woman kept by the white colonists for extramarital relations; a concubine.

**MULHER DE COR** (Pg.) ("female of color"), in Brazil, a black woman.

**MULUNGÚ** (Afr.), a red-leafed Brazilian tree used by black slaves to make small, high-pitched drums.

**MUMMERS,** in Jamaica, John Canoe dancers (q.v.).

**MUMMINGS,** in colonial Jamaica, parades and dances organized by black slaves on the plantations and by town blacks to observe Christmas holidays. They were celebrated with competitive splendor to which masters and mistresses lent their aid with contributions for the three-day festival and with loans of their utensils and jewelry.

**MUMU** (Afr.), an Afro-Jamaican word for mule, clown, backward person.

**MUNDELLA WEZA** (Afr.), an Afro-Jamaican term for white man.

**MUNDEO** (Pg.), in Brazil, a trap placed on the path which animals take to go to the river to drink. It is made of planks, not fixed on the ground, but held together by *lianas* or vines which cross the path. The animal trips on the vines, pulling down the planks and crushing itself. The device is apparently of African origin.

**MUNGANGA** (Afr.), in Brazil, a pumpkin *(Cucurbita pepo)*, a favorite slave food.

**MUNGUNZÁ** (Afr.), an Afro-Brazilian dish consisting of grains of corn in a broth sometimes sweetened with coconut or cow's milk.

**MUNHAMBANA** (Afr.), a South African black ethnic group, many of whose members were brought to Brazil as slaves in colonial times.

**MUNZÚA** (Afr.), in Brazil, a fishing basket with a funnel-shaped opening, used by blacks.

**MUQUILA** (Afr.), an Afro-Brazilian term for tail.

**MURÉ** (Afr.), an Afro-Cuban word for a variety of mosquito.

**MURELL CAMPOS, JUAN** (1857-1896), a Puerto Rican mulatto composer and orchestra conductor. He organized an orchestra and gave concerts in several foreign countries.

**MURUNDU** (Afr.), an Afro-Brazilian term for ant hill. *Murundus* are taller in Africa than in Brazil; the underground tunnels extend for miles.

**MUSA, MUSSA** (Ar.), an Afro-Jamaican dish made of meal or flour, with or without other ingredients. Cassava *musa* appears to be the most common, along with banana and corn meal *musa*.

**MUSCOVADO, MOSCOVADO** (Eng. Cr.), in the colonial West Indies, unrefined sugar of lower quality which was sold to European refineries. This crude sugar was produced and packed by slaves. On some sugar estates (q.v.), particularly in the French territories, it was covered with a mass of wet clay to remove impurities. It was also called clayed sugar or plantation white. *Muscovado* was shipped in hogsheads, large casks holding 63 to 140 gallons.

**MUSENGA!** (Afr.), an African cheer used on Cuban plantations by black drivers (q.v.) to order the field slaves (q.v.) to start their daily tasks on the estate.

**MUSONGO** (Afr.), a chief black priest in the Afro-Cuban *santería* (q.v.).

**MUSSA** (Ar.). See MUSA.

**MUSSEQUE** (Afr.), in Luanda (q.v.), Angola (q.v.), a hillside black slum. See also FAVELA, SHANTY TOWN.

**MUSSURUMIN** (Ar.). In Brazil: 1. A black Islamic slave. 2. A black cult centered in the worshipping of Christian saints, the ancestors, and the family spirits; basically a Bantu (q.v.) tradition.

**MUSTEE** (Eng. Cr.), in the British West Indies, the offspring of a white man and a quadroon (q.v.) or octoroon (q.v.) woman.

**MUSTEFFINO** (Eng. Cr.), in the British West Indies, a child of a *mustee* (q.v.) mother and a white father, i.e., a child with one-sixteenth black and fifteen-sixteenths white parentage. By law he was "free of taint" and was ranked as a white person for all intents and purposes. (Cassidy, *Dictionary.*)

**MUSTIF** (Fr. Cr.), in colonial Saint Domingue, a native with only the slightest trace of black blood; he considered himself a white. See also MUSTEFFINO.

**MUTAMBA** (Bant.), in Brazil, an African name applied to a local plant by black slaves.

**MUTIRÃO** (Pg.), in Brazil, a mutual work party among slaves. See also COUMBITÉ.

**MUXIBA** (Bant.), an Afro-Brazilian word for spoiled meat, something rotten.

**MUXINGA** (Bant.), an Afro-Brazilian term for a whip or a whipping.

**MUXÔXÓ** (Bant.), an Afro-Brazilian word for a gesture of contempt or disdain made by pressing the lips and, with the aid of the tongue, uttering a sudden tsk-like sound while the chin is pushed sharply forward and upward. (Pierson, *Negroes*, p. 266.)

**MUXUANGO** (Bant.), in rural Brazil, a generic term applied to a rustic, often black individual, especially in the state of Rio de Janeiro.

**MUZAMBE** (Afr.), an Afro-Brazilian word for divination, foretelling.

**MWÉ, MOIN** (Fr. Cr.), "I," "me," in the French Creole (q.v.) dialect spoken in Haiti.

**MYAL** (Afr.), in the West Indies, a form of witchcraft of Fanti-Ashanti (q.v.) origin. It is not clearly distinguished from *obeah* (q.v.). At times it appears that *myal* destroys the evil effects of *obeah*, but this distinction is not consistent and may be no more than a defense made by slaves against the whites' opposition to *obeahism* (q.v.). (Cassidy, *Dictionary*.)

**MYAL CULT.** See MYALISM.

**MYAL DANCE,** in the West Indies, a ritual dance by which black slaves were initiated into a *myal* (q.v.) society. It was usually performed under the silk-cotton tree, a favorite haunt of the duppies (q.v.).

**MYALISM** (Afr.), in the West Indies, an old Fanti-Ashanti (q.v.) religion that flourished among black slaves in the colonial period. Today it has survived in the form of witchcraft.

**MYALIST,** in colonial West Indies, a black practitioner or adherent of myalism (q.v.).

**MYAL MAN,** in the West Indies, a sorcerer or priest of myalism (q.v.) who led its rituals. His duties were to prevent duppies (q.v.) from doing harm, to help people recover their lost shadows, and generally to propitiate the world of the spirits. Often by means of narcotics, he used to fall into a profound sleep or trance, after which he could reanimate dead bodies.

**MYAL SOCIETY,** in the colonial West Indies, a closed group of black slaves initiated into myalism (q.v.). The members believed they were invulnerable in fighting against the white men. It eventually became an antiwhite secret association.

**MYAL SONG,** in the West Indies, a song of the kind sung by blacks in the *myal* (q.v.) cult.

**MYAL WEED,** in Jamaica, a common weed *(Eryngium foetidum)* with a powerful aromatic odor. The *myal* (q.v.) man used it to revive people in a faint or fit during the cult rituals.

**MYAL WOMAN,** in the West Indies, a black woman practitioner of the *myal* (q.v.) cult.

**MYSTÈRES** (Fr. Cr.), in Haiti, African gods worshipped by blacks; a term synonymous with spirits and saints.

# n

**NABOT** (Fr.), in Saint Domingue, an instrument used to punish slaves consisting of an iron shackle weighing six, eight, or even ten pounds attached to the victim's foot. It was impossible to remove. On the eve of the slave rebellion in 1791, it was abolished and replaced by prison terms.

**ÑADUDU** (Afr.), in colonial Cuba, a newly arrived slave.

**NAGÓ** (Yor.), a term originally used to refer to a subgroup of the northern Yoruba Kingdom (q.v.), but gradually extended to include any Yoruba-speaking people and perhaps any slave sent to the New World from the Bight of Benin (q.v.). The latter group was comprised of several inland tribes, including the Arada, Fon, Ouidah, Popo, Oyo, and others. Nagó slaves were found in Cuba, the West Indies, and Brazil. See also ANAGÓ; LUCUMÍ; YORUBA SLAVES.

**NAGÓ-SHANGÓ** (Afr.), in northern Haiti, an African god who is restless and childish in his behavior. He lives in abysses, and his favorite foods are beef, guinea-fowl (q.v.), chickens, and birds.

**NAHIN, LUIZA,** an African-born princess who was violently uprooted and taken to Brazil where she was sold into slavery. A Moslem Hausa, she was one of the most outstanding leaders of the Hausa insurrection in 1835. Her house in Bahia became a center for the meetings of the chiefs during the great revolt. Luiza Nahin, mistress of a profligate and dissolute Portuguese planter, gave birth to the most famous Brazilian intellectual and abolitionist, Luiz da Gama (q.v.). Her end is obscure, but her name remains in history. and legend as a symbol of the black woman's courage and audacity.

**NAJAC, PAUL-E.** (b. 1928), a black poet born on April 26, 1928, and educated in Port-de-Paix, Haiti. Najac is the author of a single published volume of poems, *Amours, délices et orgues* (1949).

ÑALE (Afr.), an Afro-Cuban dance.

ÑALE LÉKE (Afr.), a necklace worn by blacks in Cuba.

NAMBU, NAMBO (Afr.). In Jamaica: 1. A field-bag used by blacks. 2. A temporary bag made by blacks in the field, usually of grass or debris.

ÑAME, GUAME, INHAME, NYAM, YAM (Afr.), a variety of tropical vine *(Dioscorea)* with edible, potato-like roots; a staple food for slaves in the colonial period. There are numerous varieties.

ÑAME AMARILLO, ÑAME DE GUINEA (Sp.), a variety of yam (q.v.) *(Dioscorea cayennensis Lam)* widely cultivated in colonial Cuba as a staple food for slaves.

ÑAME CIMARRÓN (Sp.), a kind of yam (q.v.) *(Dioscorea aerea bulbifera)* cultivated as a staple food for slaves in colonial Spanish America. Also known as *gunda* (q.v.).

ÑAME DE AGUA, ÑAME HABANERO (Sp.), a species of yam (q.v.) *(Dioscorea alata* or *Sativa L.)* which was a staple food for slaves in colonial Cuba and elsewhere in Spanish America.

ÑAME DE GUINEA (Sp.). See ÑAME AMARILLO.

ÑAME DE GUINEA BLANCO (Sp.), a species of yam (q.v.) *(Dioscorea rotundata Pon.)* grown as a staple food for slaves in colonial Spanish America.

ÑAME GULEMBO (Sp.), a kind of yam (q.v.) *(Rajania cordata L.)* extensively cultivated as food for slaves in colonial Cuba and elsewhere in the New World. It was introduced from India during the slave trade period.

ÑAME HABANERO (Sp.). See ÑAME DE AGUA.

ÑAMI-ÑAMI (Afr.) ("Eat!"), an expression used by black slaves in colonial Cuba.

NANÁ (Sp.), an Afro-Cuban goddess who lives in the rivers in the form of a snake. (Calorera, L., *Anaqó,* p. 217.)

ÑAÑA (Sp.), an Afro-Cuban word for mother; a term of endearment.

**NANAN** (Afr.), in Brazil, an African deity who controls the rain.

**NANCHON** (Fr. Cr.), a family or group of related Afro-Haitian deities having common features. Some are semi-independent, and they are thought to belong to one or two families or nations (q.v.).

**NANCHOU** (Fr. Cr.), an Afro-Haitian warrior deity.

**NANCY.** See ANANCY.

**NANCY BAG** (Eng. Cr.), in Afro-Jamaican folklore, a spider web. See also ANANCY.

**NANCY STORY.** See ANANCY STORY.

**NANGA** (Afr.), in Jamaica, a black tribal name.

**NANGALÉ** (Afr.), in the Afro-Cuban *santería* (q.v.), a ritual performed at dawn during the sacrifice of an animal to the god Olôrum (q.v.). The faithful dance, sing, pray, and lift sacred chocolate cups to heaven. (Cabrera, *Anagó*, p. 217.)

**ÑANGO** (Afr.), an Afro-Spanish word for broken limb.

**NANGOBAA** (Bant.), a tribal name for slaves brought to Puerto Rico and elsewhere in Spanish America during the colonial period. In the nineteenth century, there was a brotherhood of Nangobaas in San Juan with elected officers, such as a queen, who presided over the festivities. (Alvarez Nazario, *El elemento negroide*, p. 260.)

**NANHA** (Pg.), a black concubine of a white man; in Brazil, iaiá.

**NANHÁ.** See NHÁ.

**ÑÁÑIGO** (Afr.), in Cuba, a member of a secret black male society with priests, rites, and strict rules of conduct. Most of the faithful claim to have African ancestry. Each sect and every priest of the cult has a coat of arms. During the initiation rites, religious signs are drawn on the spot where the ceremony is to take place. These are used to trace out the mystical map of the land of the Efiks, the original founders of the cult. When a *ñáñigo* dies, his corpse is adorned with the same signs as on the day of his initiation. (Bastide, *African Civilizations*, p. 114.)

**ÑAÑIGUISMO** (Afr.), in Cuba, a legendary secret society of blacks which apparently originated among the Efiks of eastern Nigeria. It is said to have thousands of adherents in the countryside and in the cities of Havana and Matanzas. One important feature of the sect is the oath of secrecy required of the initiates. The beliefs of the cult emphasize the dangerous influences that threaten people, particularly those of African descent for whom Cuba is full of evil shadows. *Ñañiguismo*, however, confers protection in this world and the next. Among the many deities worshipped are the spirits of the dead. In the rituals, drums are given special significance as the voices of the gods. There is a syncretism of both African and Catholic ceremonies. See also ÑÁÑIGO.

**NANKA** (Afr.), an Afro-Jamaican word for a yellow snake.

**NANNY,** a legendary black woman, the chief sorcerer of the main gang of Windward Maroon (q.v.) rebels, who was killed by a slave named Cuffee in 1733. The whites of Jamaica dreaded her and rewarded the killer for his deed. Nanny played an important psychological role during the Maroon war (q.v.) by boosting the morale of the insurgents. (Price, *Maroon Societies*, p. 262.) See also NANNY TOWN.

**NANNY THATCH,** in Jamaica, a tree fern, the leaves or fronds of which are often used as thatch. To some extent, they resemble the leaves of long-thatch palm. Blacks used it to build their huts.

**NANNY TOWN,** a black town (q.v.) named after the famous Nanny (q.v.); the original Spanish Maroons (q.v.) settled it on the northern slopes of the Blue Mountains in Jamaica. Around 1690, it became a well-organized runaway slave settlement protected by the wilderness of the mountains. For three years the colonial militia attacked the village, which was finally destroyed in 1734. (Hamshire, *The British*, p. 140.)

**NAPPIER GRASS,** an African cultivated fodder grass *(Pennisetum purpureum)* common in the West Indies.

**ÑARA ÑARA** (Afr.), an Afro-Cuban word for lightning.

**NASAKO** (Afr.), in the Afro-Cuban *santería* (q.v.), a sorcerer, leader of the cult, who, dressed in rags and wearing a wig covered with crowns of feathers, presides over the rituals. When he invokes the gods of the cult known as *ñañiguismo* (q.v.), his hands and feet are garishly painted.

**NATAL TREE, NAVEL-STRING TREE,** in Jamaica, a term used by blacks to denote the coconut tree *(Coos nucifera)* under which the umbilical cord is buried. The fruit of this tree belongs to the child.

**NATION,** a generic term applied to a black ethnic group or race.

**NATIONALE PATIJ SURINAME** (D.) (National Surinam party), a political group organized in the Dutch colony in 1940 by representatives of the mulatto upper and middle class to promote the interests of the mulattoes.

**NATIVE BAPTIST MOVEMENT,** a strong religious revival movement among black slaves in Jamaica that began with the arrival of two black American preachers: George Liele (q.v.) and George Lewis (q.v.). The first congregation was established in Kingston around 1783. It rejected the whites' version of Christianity in favor of one more African in character, placing a great emphasis on "spirit" and a corresponding neglect of the Bible. In some congregations, it was required that the slave members be possessed by the spirit before baptism was administered. This meant that the spirit had to descend on the applicant in a dream, and, if the dream was judged satisfactory by the leader, the petitioner could then enter the church. It was an adaptation of the English Wesleyan practice. The leader became a spiritual guide and wielded great power over the group. A nationalist development in a slave society, the Native Baptist Movement was well established by 1830 and contributed greatly to the abolitionist campaign throughout the West Indies and England.

**NATIVE WEST INDIAN NEGRO,** in the colonial period, a black Creole born and raised in the Caribbean region. He was strongly influenced by European ideas, spoke an English patois rather than an African tongue, and was considered to be in a better mental state to receive instruction of any sort than were those slaves transported across the Atlantic.

**NAU, IGNACE** (1812-1845), a black writer born in Port-au-Prince, Haiti. Nau was educated in his native city where he attended L'Institution Jonathan Granville; he later studied in Paris and New York. He was a popular orator and an authority on colonial history. He lived and traveled in France, then returned to Haiti where he retired to his country estate to study and write at leisure. He participated in the publication of *Revue de colonies* (Paris, 1837).

**NAVEL-STRING TREE.** See NATAL TREE.

**NAYGA** (Eng. Cr.), in Jamaica, a black. The term is generally avoided by whites and when whites do use it, it is resented by blacks. Among blacks it is more or less derogatory, commonly implying extra blackness, backwardness, laziness, and the like.

**NAYGA HAIR** (Eng. Cr.), in Jamaica, a black's kinky hair.

**NAYGA-MAN** (Eng. Cr.), in Jamaica, a black.

**NAYGA-TRICK, NEGER-TRICK** (Eng. Cr.), in Jamaica, a story told by a black Creole to illustrate the tricks played or acts performed out of stupidity by African-born or more backward blacks.

**NAYGUR** (Eng. Cr.), in the West Indies, a derogatory term denigrating anything black. It is used by the upper, middle, and even lower class whites to voice disapproval of anything African.

**NDONGO** (Afr.). See ANGOLA AFRICAN STATE.

**NEACKA-NEACKA** (Afr.), in the West Indies, an African word meaning trash or rubbish.

**NEDERLANDSCHE MAATSCHAPPIJ TER BEVORDERING VAN DE AFSCHAFFING DER SLAVERNIIJ** (D.) (Netherlands Society for the Promotion of the Abolition of Slavery), a group organized in the Hague in 1842. Its members included prominent Protestant statesmen, such as J. W. Gefken, who later became attorney general of Surinam. They regarded emanicipation not as an end in itself, but as a means towards an end. In 1853, the society launched a monthly periodical which appeared until November 1862.

**NEEGRISH, NIGRISH** (Eng. Cr.), in the West Indies, a backward person.

**NEGA, NEGAR, NEGER** (Eng. Cr.), in the West Indies, a black.

**NEGERHOLLAND** (D.), a Dutch Creole dialect heavily mixed with West African elements; used in the Caribbean during the colonial period. The dialect was so highly developed that it had its own translation of the Bible (1818). It is now nearly extinct, but it is still spoken by a few blacks in the U.S. Virgin Islands, a former Dutch possession.

**NEGER POLITIEKE PARTIJ** (D.) (Negro Political party), a political group founded in Paramaribo, Surinam, in 1946 to promote the social and economic advancement of the black population.

**NEGER-TRICK** (Eng. Cr.). See NAYGA-TRICK.

**NÈGÈSSE IBO** (Fr. Cr.), an Afro-Haitian female deity, protector of the family.

**NEGRA** (Pg.). In Brazil: 1. A black female. 2. In the colonial period, a female slave.

**NEGRADA** (Pg.), in Brazil, a collective term for female blacks.

**NEGRA DE PAÑUELO** (Sp.), in Puerto Rico, a black woman wearing a colorful headdress. See also MADRAS.

**NÈGRE** (Fr. Cr.), in Haiti, an illiterate black peasant; a term used by mulattoes in the elite group.

**NEGREGADO** (Pg.), in Brazil, a word meaning unlucky, disgraceful, unhappy.

**NEGREIRO** (Pg.), a slave trader in colonial Brazil.

**NÉGRERIE** (Fr.), a *barracoon* (q.v.), a slave compound on the West African coast.

**NEGRERO** (Sp.), in the Spanish American colonies, a slave trader or a company engaged in the slave traffic. A *negrero* was considered to be cruel and brutal in dealing with slaves.

**NEGRIDÃO** (Pg.). In Brazil: 1. Blackness, darkness, gloom. 2. Perversity, crudeness; crime, black deed.

**NÈGRE SUCRIER** (Fr. Cr.), black boiler; in colonial Saint Domingue, a valuable skilled slave who was well trained in the delicate operations of boiling and refining sugar.

**NÉGRIER** (Fr.), a slave ship or a slave dealer.

**NÉGRILLON** (Fr.), "Little Negro," a black boy or girl.

**NEGRISMO** (Sp.). See AFROCUBANISMO.

**NÉGRITUDE** (Fr.), a philosophy developed by Aimé Césaire (q.v.), Léopold Senghor, and Léon Damas (q.v.), students in Paris in the 1930s, urging blacks to appreciate their cultural uniqueness and contributions to history. It is not a "return to Africa" movement or even the vindication of an African or Afro-American culture—something that Brazilian intellectuals regard as primitive or riddled with superstition. The doctrine is based on the physical survival of the black as one who mixed with other cultures to which he, as opposed to the white, has given fresh life and vitality. After World War II, négritude began to dissolve into a mass of ambiguous, contradictory images and ideologies for the intellectuals, messianism for the masses, and violent nationalism for the politicians. The term *négritude* first appeared in print in a poem by Aimé Césaire (q.v.) in *Cahier d'un retour au pays natal* (Paris, 1947) and has subsequently come into common use when neo-African art and literature are discussed. (Coulthard, *Race and Colour*, pp. 60-61, 67.)

**NEGRO** (Sp.). In Afro-Latin America: 1. A slave in the colonial period. 2. One who works hard (at manual labor). 3. A term of endearment meaning beautiful. (Pierson, *Negroes*, p. 378.)

**NEGRO, ANTONIO,** a black Brazilian slave who was a hero in the war against the Dutch in 1625. The king, Philip III, informed by the governor of the colony of Negro's bravery and courage, gave him his freedom at public expense. His Majesty ordered the building of a fortress on the site where Negro resisted the Dutch forces; Negro was further honored by an appointment as commander of the fortress. (Ramos, *The Negro*, p. 160.)

**NEGRO ATEZADO** (Sp.), a very dark-skinned black slave as opposed to a mulatto.

**NEGRO BICHADO** (Pg.) ("sick black"), in colonial Brazil, a sick black slave, especially one suffering from dysentery, chills, nematode worms, and other endemic illnesses.

**NEGRO BREAKDOWN** (Eng. Cr.), a noisy, lively, and rollicking dance popular among blacks in Jamaica.

**NEGRO BREAKFAST** (Eng. Cr.), in colonial Jamaica, a breakfast served about 11:00 A.M., when there was a pause for the slaves on the plantations.

**NEGRO BREEDING.** See SLAVE BREEDING.

**NEGRO BURIAL,** in the colonial West Indies, a pagan black slave interment made in the family garden. It was preceded by lively wakes during which wild dancing and other intemperate behavior were common.

**NEGRO CAFRE DE PASA** (Sp.) ("black with kinky hair"), in early colonial Mexico, a slave brought from East Africa; *pasa* referred to his kinky hair.

**NEGRO CALICO** (Pg.) ("calico black"), in the first quarter of the twentieth century, a poor Brazilian urban black, illiterate and oppressed, who did exclusively menial work; *calico* referred to the poor cloth he was dressed in as well as the dirtiness and shabbiness of his appearance. (Fernandes, *The Negro*, p. 76.)

**NEGRO CAROLO** (Sp.), in Afro-Spanish America, an insolent and contemptuous black.

**NEGRO CHURCHES,** in the colonial West Indies, Protestant missionary churches whose members were exclusively black slaves under the leadership of white ministers. At the end of the eighteenth century, these small Christian congregations enforced a zealous and strict religious discipline in contrast to the laxity and formalism in the established Church of England. Their missionaries were able to claim a degree of moral superiority for their converts who were trained to observe rigid adherence to the precepts of Christian virtue and ethics from which the whites continued to deviate sharply. (Goveia, *Slave Society*, p. 302.)

**NEGRO COCO,** in the West Indies, a tropical tree *(Cocos nucifera)* whose kernels, known as *copra*, and distilled sugar were staple foods for slaves in the colonial period.

**NEGRO-COUNTRY YAM** (Eng. Cr.), in the West Indies, a kind of Guinea yam (q.v.) *(Discorea alata)* with a foot-wide root. Slaves, blacks, and Europeans used it cut into pieces, boiled or roasted, and eaten as bread.

**NEGRO DAY** (Eng. Cr.), in Jamaica and elsewhere in the West Indies, the day set for slaves to work their own provision grounds on the sugar estates (q.v.).

**NEGRO DE ALUGEL** (Pg.), in colonial Brazil, a slave hired out by his or her owner for the owner's profit.

**NEGRO DE GANHO** (Pg.), in colonial Brazil, a semi-free slave living apart from his master, arranging his own employment. He was usually required to pay an established sum weekly to his owner, after which he might keep for his own use any balance remaining. He was employed as a porter, ironworker, mason, carpenter, printer, street merchant, or small shopkeeper. In Bahia they are reported to have been principally Yoruba slaves (q.v.), Hausa slaves (q.v.), and Gêgés (q.v.). (Pierson, *Negroes in Brazil*, pp. 38-39.)

**NEGRO DE RECADO** (Pg.) ("slave messenger"), in colonial Brazil, a black slave in charge of receiving and sending out his master's letters and messages.

**NEGRO DE SURRÃO** (Pg.), in Brazil, a mythical, old, ugly black man who carries a sack into which he stuffs little children. The children are scared of meeting him. This story underwent considerable modification as it was retold by the old nannies.

**NEGRO DRIVER** (Eng. Cr.), in the colonial West Indies, a trusted black or mulatto slave in charge of slave gangs (q.v.) working in the fields or in the sugar mill (q.v.) on a plantation.

**NEGRO FETICHERO** (Sp.) ("Negro sorcerer"), a well-mannered religious leader in the Afro-Cuban *santería* (q.v.).

**NEGRO FRANCISCO**, an antislavery novel by Antonio Zambrana Vázques (q.v.), a Cuban exile, published in Santiago, Chile, in 1875. Its subject, plot, and general atmosphere show the hardships and despotic conditions under which black slaves were exploited and abused by white planters.

**NEGRO FRUIT** (Eng. Cr.), in the West Indies, the kola nut (q.v.) tree *(Cola acuminata)* native to Africa, which produces seeds containing caffeine, oil, and a glucoside; a slave delicacy in the colonial period.

**NEGROFY** (Eng. Cr.), in the West Indies, a derogatory term meaning to infest with black ideas. Whites who defended slavery used this charge with great contempt against the opponents of the institution.

**NEGRO GROUND** (Eng. Cr.), in the West Indies, a portion of land on a plantation assigned to a slave to grow his own food.

**NEGRO HEROICO** (Pg.), the heroic black, a Brazilian literary character, embodying the black's virtues of patriotism and loyalty in war and peace.

**NEGRO HOUSE**, in the West Indies, a cottage built on a sugar estate (q.v.) for a free black laborer after emancipation (1838). It was well built, usually near a road, with a small parcel of land for a garden to be let by the former slave for a definite period of time. A Negro house was much more comfortable than the traditional thatched hut of the slave.

**NEGRO ITCH** (Eng. Cr.), in the West Indies, a malignant species of scabbies or eczema prevalent among black women; apparently of African origin.

**NEGRO LADINO** (Sp.) ("Spanish-speaking black"). 1. In the sixteenth century, a black slave born and living in Spain, Portugal, or the New World who was partially or totally assimilated into Iberian life and civilization. 2. An African-born black slave greatly acculturated after living for some years in the Hispanic world. (Alvarez Nazario, *El elemento negroide*, p. 19.)

**NEGRO MATUNGO** (Sp.) ("old useless slave"), in colonial Cuba, an aged black slave too old to work in the plantation fields.

**NEGRO NOVO** (Pg.) ("new Negro"), an African-born slave brought to Brazil in the colonial period.

**NEGRO PLAY**, in the West Indies, an entertainment among plantation blacks, including singing, dancing, and feasting. It often continues for several days.

**NEGRO-POT**, in Jamaica, a heavy iron cooking-pot such as that generally used by blacks over open fires. It usually has a flared top, round bottom, and small legs.

**NEGRO RELIGIOUS BROTHERHOOD.** See IRMANDADE.

**NEGRO RENAISSANCE**, a literary movement which began around 1920 in Harlem, a black ghetto of New York City. It was led by a group of descendants of the privileged class of freed blacks—those who had been free before the Civil War and who had migrated to the cities of the North at the turn of the century. Their ideology was primarily antibourgeois, exotic, and primitivist, and centered on a romanticization of Africa. They also stressed separatism, militant protest, irony, and a demand for racial equality. One of the leaders was a Jamaican black poet, Claude McKay (q.v.). Adherents of the movement affirmed self-confidence, love, and laughter, and used jazz music as their symbol. The Negro or Harlem Renaissance began to fade around 1941. (Jahn, *Neo-African Literature*, p. 193.)

**NEGRO SAINTS**, in Brazil, a number of Catholic saints worshipped exclusively by blacks. Among the most popular were Saint Benedict, Saint Iphigenia, and Our Lady of the Rosary. In Bahia, the Church of the Senhor do Bonfim was the place of worship for African blacks, Creole slaves, and mulattoes of the Nagó (q.v.) and Obatalá (q.v.) sects.

**NEGRO SLAVERY,** the title given to a series of at least sixteen pamphlets published in London (1823-1824) by British abolitionists. The series included *Slavery in British Guiana* (No. 1) and *Insurrections of Slaves in the West Indies . . .* (No. 7). (Ragatz, *The Fall*, p. 409.)

**NEGRO SOCIAL HIERARCHY,** in the colonial British West Indies, a hierarchical social ladder which descended as follows: free coloreds—those born free; freed coloreds—those manumitted; free blacks—those born free; and freed blacks—those manumitted. Unlike the whites, the social gradings within each of these groups were determined not only by occupation or income, but also by actual skin color and features. (Henriques, *Family and Colour*, p. 45.)

**NEGRO SQUATTER,** in the West Indies, after slave emancipation (1838), a former slave who preferred being idle on an estate to working for wages. He stayed in his hut and only occasionally performed labor, growing provision crops for sale in the local market.

**NEGRO-TOWN,** in early colonial Jamaica, a settlement built in the hills by Maroons (q.v.). It served as a base for raids upon the plantations.

**NEGRO TROOPS,** several companies of black slaves organized in the West Indies around 1795. The soldiers were recruited through purchase from among the best conditioned blacks on the island. The white planters viewed this experiment with horror. A deliberate arming of bondsmen to defend their masters marked the opening of a new epoch in interracial relations in the British islands.

**NEGRO VILLAGE,** in Jamaica and elsewhere in the Caribbean, a cluster of thatched huts built along irregular patterns at some distance from the great house on the plantation. Each dwelling had a small garden surrounded by tropical trees, including coconut, ackee, and breadfruit (q.v.).

**NEGRO-WORM** (Eng. Cr.), in Jamaica, the Guinea worm (q.v.) *(Filaria medinensis)*, a subcutaneous nematode worm that afflicted many African-born blacks on the island.

**NEGRO YAM,** in the West Indies, a species of yam (q.v.) *(Dioscorea sativa)* of coarser texture than white yam and eaten roasted or boiled by slaves. Formerly there were two kinds of Negro yam, the cassava-yam and the man-yam; the latter was considered better tasting.

**NEGRUME** (Pg.) 1. Darkness, obscurity. 2. Fog, mist, haze.

**NEMBANDA,** in Brazil, a black queen crowned during the Mardi Gras festivities. Around 1742, each church held its crowning as part of the carnival activities organized by several slave brotherhoods in Bahia and elsewhere in the northeast.

**ÑEÑEÑÉ** (Afr.), an Afro-Spanish word for foolishness.

**NEN-NEN** (Afr.), an Afro-Jamaican word for grandmother; also a term of address used in speaking to an old black woman.

**NENYAM, NENYAME** (Afr.). See NINYAM.

**NEO-AFRICAN LITERATURE,** a recent literary development reflecting the contact of two cultures; the traditional, nonwritten culture of Africa and the modern black culture whose written expression is greatly influenced by Western ideologies even when written by an African.

**NEPHRITIC TREE,** in the West Indies, a tree *(Pithecellobium)* once used by blacks as a medicine for kidney diseases; also known as black-bead shrub and bread-and-cheese.

**NEPTUNE, LOUIS** (b. 1927), a black writer born in Jacmel, Haiti, and educated in Port-au-Prince. Neptune was active on the journal *La Nouvelle Ruche* and in political circles. After the revolution of 1946, he left the island for Venezuela where he has spent the last years teaching French. Neptune has written one volume of poetry, *Gouttes de fiel* (Port-au-Prince, 1947).

**ÑEQUE** (Afr.), an Afro-Spanish word for a bewitched person, an unlucky individual.

**NEUVANGUE** (Afr.), in colonial Brazil, a black king crowned by black slaves as part of the Mardi Gras celebrations. In Bahía and other cities, the crowning was done in churches by members of slave religious brotherhoods. (Mendonça, *A Influencia*, p. 158.)

**NEW CALABAR,** a slave-trading port situated in the swampy Bight of Biafra (q.v.) through which many Ibo (q.v.) slaves were exported to the West Indies. See also OLD CALABAR.

**NEW-NAYA,** a Jamaican black who had rapidly advanced in the world.

**NEWTON, JOHN** (1725-1807), an English clergyman, a former slaver's captain, and a hymn writer. When Newton was sixteen, his father sent him to Jamaica. Later, he made many trips carrying slaves between West Africa and the West Indies. On March 9, 1748, the slaver (q.v.) on which Newton was traveling encountered a series of unprecedented storms. The superstitious crew regarded Newton as the cause of the danger because of his drinking habits and foul language, and he was nearly thrown overboard as a Jonah. Newton saw this incident as God's last invitation for him to be a good Christian, and he became a convert. After returning to England in 1764, he entered the clergy and, later in life, became a vehement antislavery advocate. His work *Thoughts Upon the Slave Trade* (London, 1788) presents a detailed account of the slave trade between the African Coast and West Indies.

**NGA** (Bant.), in Jamaica, an African word for mouth.

**NGANGA** (Bant.). 1. In Cuba, an African word for a large sacred pot believed to contain the saints of the *mayombé* (q.v.) cult. 2. Grandfather.

**NGOLA** (Bant.). 1. A pre-European name for the Angola Colony (q.v.) 2. The name of the ruler or king of Angola before the Portuguese conquest.

**NGOMA** (Bant.), in Brazil, an African word meaning the plantation's master.

**NGOMBE** (Bant.), in Brazil, an African term for cattle.

**NGUNGA** (Bant.), a small bell, an archaic African word formerly used in Brazil.

**NHÁ, NANHÁ** (Pg.), "Miss" or "Missy," a term of endearment used in slavery times in Brazil.

**NHÓ** (Pg.), an affectionate term for mister, master, or, more properly, *massa* (q.v.); used by slaves in colonial Brazil. See also IOIÓ.

**NHÔNHÔ** (Pg.), a white boy, the son of a planter in colonial Brazil; often a little rascal who abused his slave playmates.

**NICHÉ** (Sp.), a magic charm (q.v.) worn by the faithful in the Afro-Cuban folk religion.

**NICKOLLS, ROBERT,** a Barbadian clergyman, later dean of a church in

Middleham, England, who was an active opponent of slavery. In 1788, he published in London "A Letter to the Treasurer of the Society Instituted for the Purpose of Effecting the Abolition of the Slave Trade." Soon afterwards, 14,000 copies of this letter were distributed throughout England. (Ragatz, *The Fall*, p. 251.)

**NICOTINE-DAY,** the day, usually Monday, when some slave traders used to provide pipes and tobacco to the blacks aboard the ships sailing to the West Indies.

**NIFÉ** (Afr.), an Afro-Cuban term for the land of Africa.

**NIGAWU.** See LEGAWU.

**NIGER, PAUL** (1917-1962), a black writer, born Paul Béville in Guadeloupe. He later adopted the name of the African river. He was a fanatic follower of négritude (q.v.) and was violently anti-Christian. His writings are vituperative and disrespectful of established traditional values. In his poem *Je n'aime pas l'Afrique*, he uses heavy sarcasm and vulgar language whenever the Christian God speaks. He died in a plane crash in 1962 just as black African countries were gaining independence. Among his works are *Initiation* (Paris, 1954); *Les Puissants* (Paris, 1958); and *Les Grenouilles du Mont Kimbo* (Lausanne, 1964).

**NIGHT, JOAQUIN,** a black Cuban slave sorcerer accused of being implicated in the Conspiracy of the Ladder (q.v.) in 1844. He was tried and convicted of selling magic charms (q.v.) to the rebel black slaves. (Hall, *Social Control*, p. 58.)

**NIGHT-PLAY** (Eng. Cr.), among blacks in the West Indies, a celebration held on the second to eighth nights of a funeral.

**NIGHT-WALKING** (Eng. Cr.), in the West Indies, a field slave's (q.v.) practice of visiting friends or mates on other plantations after dark because the daily work occupied the time from dawn to sunset.

**NIGRISH.** See NEEGRISH.

**NIMBÚ** (Afr.), in Brazil, a religious song intoned by the priest in the black *umbanda* (q.v.) cult.

**NINE-DAY** (Eng. Cr.), in Jamaica, a period of mourning held by blacks after a funeral. The nine days (and nights) of activities include a wake, burial, singing of hymns, and dancing. On the ninth night, it is believed that the ghost of the dead has been put to rest. The observance of the nine-day varies considerably throughout the island.

**NINE-NIGHT,** in Jamaica, the celebration that concludes the nine-day (q.v.) period of funeral rituals in which ring-play games and storytelling are added to the other ceremonies.

**NINTH DAY AFTER BIRTH,** a momentous time in the life of a black infant in Jamaica. On this day a bath with a little rum poured into it is prepared for the child, and each member of the family must contribute a bit of silver "for the eyesight." To ward off evil spirits, indigo blue is added to the bath, the forehead is marked with a blue cross, and the midwife offers a prayer before bringing the baby out into the air. (Brathwaite, *The Development*, p. 214.)

**NINYAM, NENYAM, NYAMNYAM, NYMAN** (Afr.). In the West Indies: 1. Any foodstuff prepared for eating by blacks. 2. Specifically, yams (q.v.).

**NINYAM-SURREY** (Eng. Cr.), in Jamaica, a black who eats a great deal; a hearty eater.

**NISI OMÓ IYALA** (Afr.) ("Take care of your little grandson"), an Afro-Cuban expression.

**NIWORO** (Afr.), an Afro-Cuban term for town.

**NIYABINGI** (Afr.), in Jamaica, a society of "warriors" among the Rastafarian (q.v.) cult, patterned on a supposed secret African order.

**NIYAMAN** (Afr.), in Jamaica, a black member of the *niyabingi* (q.v.) cult.

**NIYARO** (Afr.), an Afro-Cuban term for ghost.

**NIYÉ** (Afr.), in the Afro-Cuban dialect, a toad (*Bufo* and allied genera).

**NOBLE NEGRO, THE,** a literary type figure who first appears in England in the novel *Oroonoko, or the History of the Royal Slave* (circa 1678) by Aphra Behn (q.v.). Here the black is depicted as a gallant warrior, a high-minded prince, an excellent conversationalist, and a modest lover. The Noble Negro symbolizing a national hero was a popular theme in Brazil during the romantic period (circa 1850); later (1880) the abolition movement (q.v.) made the figure a symbol of nationalism, beauty, and patriotism. See also OROONOKO.

**ÑOCO** (Afr.), an Afro-Cuban term for a man with one arm missing; an amputee.

**NOMMO** (Bant.), a Bantu (q.v.) concept meaning life force, a unity of spiritual-physical fluidity giving life to everything. *Nommo* influences things by means of the words used to name things. This principle apparently pervaded the minds of slaves in the West Indies and underlined the blacks' conviction that Christianity did not produce a deep change in them, except by the alteration of their names. This *nommo* was their alternative to Christianity; for this reason, many slaves did not wish to be baptized. (Brathwaite, *The Development*, p. 237; Jahn, *Muntu*, p. 124.)

**ÑONGO, ÑOÑO** (Afr.), an Afro-Spanish word for dumb, foolish.

**NOOKOO** (Afr.), mother death; a ghost among Jamaican blacks.

**NOONOO BUSH** (Afr.), in Jamaica, an aromatic medicinal plant *(Ocimum viride)* often used by black sorcerers in magic. Its origin seems to be Ashanti (q.v.).

**NORINGO, ÑORINGO** (Afr.), an Afro-Cuban word for a hairpin used by black women to fasten their hair.

**NOTE,** a legal contract issued by the European powers during the slavery period to build and control any slave-trading fort or castle on the West African Coast. This note acknowledged the African chief's title to the land where the fortress was located and fixed a yearly rent. Local chiefs fought for possession of the "notes" exactly as European powers battled for the highly profitable slave trade franchises. (Davidson, *Black Cargoes*, p. 30.)

**NOVENA** (Pg.), in colonial Brazil, a cruel slave whipping carried out at intervals of from nine to thirteen consecutive nights. Some slaves died before the end of the *novena.*

**NOVENARIO** (Sp.), in Cuba and elsewhere in Spanish America, a brutal slave punishment consisting of nine strokes daily over a period of nine days. See also NOVENA.

**NYAAMS** (Afr.), an Afro-Jamaican word for foolishness, nonsense, or something of no value; also weakling.

**NYAAMS-HEAD** (Eng. Cr.), among Jamaican blacks, a stupid, foolish person.

**NYAKA-NYAKA** (Afr.), an Afro-Jamaican term for a filthy-looking person.

**NYAM** (Afr.), an Afro-Jamaican word for a meal; also the act of eating voraciously. A West African term, possibly referring to a pagan ritual. See also NINYAM.

**NYAMA** (Afr.), an African religious belief centered in a hidden, mysterious, and pervading energy inherent in any black individual. This supersensitive power, enhanced through experience, education, and training, can be used for both constructive and destructive purposes. The belief in *nyama* was apparently institutionalized in the Afro-Latin American culture and tended to make the slaves rebellious. Black leaders gifted with *nyama* led various forms of uprisings and often inspired more respect and fear from their fellow slaves than did their masters or the colonial authorities. (Hall, *Social Control*, p. 34.) See also NOMMO.

**NYAMI-NYAMI** (Afr.), an Afro-Jamaican term for a greedy person.

**NYAMMING** (Eng. Cr.), an Afro-Jamaican word for a dish of curried goat.

**NYAMNYAM.** See NINYAM.

**NYANGA** (Afr.). In the Caribbean region, a Bantu (q.v.) word meaning: 1. Pride. 2. A person proud of himself. 3. To show oneself off, to strut proudly.

**NYATA NUOZ** (Afr.), an Afro-Jamaican term for a very flat, broad nose; a person having such a nose.

**NYMAN.** See NINYAM.

**NYONG** (Afr.), an Afro-Jamaican term for a young black.

**NZIMBU** (Bant.), on the African Atlantic Seaboard, sea shells, the most valued form of currency in slavery times (circa 1500-1700). These shells were obtained exclusively from the island of Luanda (q.v.) which was directly administered by a Portuguese royal representative. (Boxer, *The Portuguese Seaborne*, p. 98.)

**NZINGA** (d. 1663), a black queen of Matamba, Angola (q.v.), who for a long time was able to resist the attacks of Luso-Brazilian invaders searching for slaves. An expedition from Rio de Janeiro finally took Luanda (q.v.) in 1650 and intensified the activities in Angola, especially against Nzinga's kingdom. (Boxer, *The Portuguese Seaborne*, pp. 112, 160.)

**NZINGA A NKUWU** (d. 1506), a king of the Congo Empire who, on May 3, 1491, accepted baptism offered by the Portuguese and took the name of João I. He was the first African ruler to establish relations with the Europeans. Later he became disillusioned with the Portuguese when they began demanding slave labor for agricultural work in Portugal. (Birmingham, *Trade and Conflict*, p. 23.)

**NZINGA MVEMBA.** See AFFONSO I OF CONGO.

# O

**OALE** (Afr.), an Afro-Cuban word for dawn. (Cabrera, *Anagó*, p. 222.)

**OALÓYA** (Afr.), an Afro-Cuban term for square, market. (Cabrera, *Anagó*, p. 222.)

**OBÁ** (Afr.), among African-born slaves in colonial Brazil, a nobleman.

**OBÁBI** (Afr.), in Afro-Cuban religion, the son of Shangó (q.v.).

**OBADINA** (Afr.), in Afro-Cuban religion, a god worshipped as the king of the roads.

**OBATALÁ** (Afr.), an African god worshipped by blacks throughout Afro-Latin America. Among the Yoruba (q.v.) of Nigeria, he was a sky deity and protector of the town gates. In the New World, he was thought to form children in the womb and was therefore believed responsible for albinism and congenital deformities. Obatalá is variously identified with several Catholic saints and is worshipped under different names such as Babalá, Batalá, and Babará. (Courlander, *The Drum*, p. 322.)

**OBBONEY** (Afr.), an African god worshipped by Coromantee (q.v.) slaves in colonial Jamaica.

**OBEAH, OBIA, OBIAH** (Afr.). In the West Indies: 1. A bloody god of African origin worshipped by black slaves. His cult involved secret meetings at night, licentious dancing, blood sacrifices of chickens and goats, and, occasionally among French Creole (q.v.)-speaking slaves, the sacrifice of a human being, usually a child. 2. The Jamaican form of sorcery, a cult of fear, suspicion, and revenge. It is a form of black magic which was once counterbalanced by white magic or *myal* (q.v.). 3. The magic amulet used by an *obeah* man (q.v.). 4. The *obeah* materials which were supposed to have magic powers.

**OBEAHISM, OBEISM** (Afr.), the profession and practice of witchcraft.

**OBEAH MAN, OBEAH PROFESSOR** (Eng. Cr.), in the West Indies, a practitioner of black magic, a sorcerer. He can be a family adviser or a medicine man who sometimes burns poisonous herbs or uses blood, feathers, dog's teeth, rum, and other objects as charms to hurt or destroy people. The fear of his powers acts as a deterrent. In the colonial period, the *obeah* man had enormous influence among the plantation slaves. Also known as bush-man (q.v.). See also OBEAH.

**OBEAH STICK** (Eng. Cr.), in Jamaica, a sacred stick supposedly given magic properties through *obeah* rituals. See also OBEAH.

**OBEAH WOMAN** (Eng. Cr.), a black woman who practices sorcery or black magic; she employs her power against all kinds of people. Also known as bush-woman. See also OBEAH.

**OBEISANCE,** in several Brazilian black cults, a ritual bow to the fetishes or the religious leaders of the sect.

**OBEISM.** See OBEAHISM.

**OBGONI, OHOGOBO** (Afr.), in colonial Brazil, a powerful, secret Hausa society organized by black Moslem slaves in Bahia around 1812. The society generally follows the same pattern as similar societies in West Africa. On February 28, 1813, 600 Obgoni blacks rose in revolt in the city of Bahia, burning part of the city and killing many whites in the battle. The rebellion was crushed by government forces. Many slaves were executed, others were imprisoned, and some were deported to penal settlements in Angola (q.v.), Benguela (q.v.), and Mozambique. (Ramos, *The Negro*, p. 46.)

**OBI** (Afr.), in the West Indies, an African god who, according to black slaves, was incarnate in special concoctions of objects such as blood, feathers, teeth, broken bones, and grave dirt. A sorcerer could set Obi on an enemy.

**OBIA, OBIAH.** See OBEAH.

**OBI HORN** (Eng. Cr.), an Afro-Jamaican term for a goat's horn used as a container for *obeah* (q.v.) materials.

**OBI-RING** (Eng. Cr.), in Jamaica, a signet ring in which a hole has been drilled for an *obeah* (q.v.) charm.

**OBISHA** (Afr.). See BUSHA.

**OBI WEED,** in Jamaica, an unidentified herb used in black *obeah* (q.v.) rituals.

**OBO LOWÓ OLORUM** (Afr.) ("I left everything in God's hands"), an Afro-Cuban religious expression. (Cabrera, *Anagó*, p. 229.)

**OBONOEMAN** (Afr.), in Surinam, an *obeah* man (q.v.).

**OBROUNI** (Afr.), an Afro-Jamaican term for white man.

**OCHANE** (Afr.), in Afro-Haitian folklore, a sacred salutation sung by worshippers at the beginning of an evening service or of any festivity. Ochane is also used for dancing or for storytelling by a black family.

**OCHINCHIN** (Afr.), an Afro-Cuban delicacy made from watercress, greens, almonds, and stewed prawns. It is the favorite food of the god Ochún (q.v.).

**OCHÚN** (Afr.), in the Afro-Cuban religion, a Yoruba (q.v.) god of gold and sex.

**OCIO, JOSÉ DE JESÚS DEL,** a Cuban mulatto born in Matanzas province who was acclaimed as a poet. His only published book of poems is *El francés* (1835). (Calcagno, *Diccionario*, p. 457.)

**O CLARIM D'ALVORADA,** one of the first black journals in Brazil, founded in São Paulo in 1924 by Jaime d'Aguiar, a black. A group of distinguished black intellectuals gathered around this periodical, which also inspired the organization of a number of societies for literary and recreational purposes.

**OCTOROON, OCTAVON,** the offspring of a quadroon (q.v.) woman and a white man. In the colonial period it was thought that such a child was one-eighth one race and seven-eighths the other.

**OCU** (Afr.), an Afro-Brazilian term meaning to die.

**ODUM** (Afr.), in the West Indies, a tropical tree, the bark of which is used by black sorcerers to perform magic rituals.

**OFFICER BOY,** a slave ship's officer in charge of collecting duties to pay to African black kings for every slave sold by the traders to the slaver's (q.v.) captain. (Dow, *Slave Ships*, p. 135.)

**OGAN** (Afr.), in Afro-Haitian cults, an iron instrument used to sound the basic sacred rhythms, usually the blade of a hoe struck by a spike.

**ÔGAN** (Afr.), in Afro-Brazilian Yoruba (q.v.) cults, a male assistant to the head of a congregation. He takes care of the temple and acts as a public relations man.

**OGA-OGÓ** (Afr.) ("the glorious and high being"), a prayer honoring a Yoruba (q.v.) god worshipped in Afro-Cuban cults. (Ortiz Fernández, *Los negros*, p. 29.)

**O'GAVAN Y GUERRA, JUAN BERNARDO** (1808-1865), a priest, lawyer, and writer born in Santiago, Cuba. He was elected a Cuban representative to the Spanish Cortes in 1812. A proslavery politician, he wrote a pamphlet entitled *Observaciones sobre la suerte de los negros de Africa* (Madrid, 1821) in which he tried to justify the slave trade.

**OGÉ, VINCENT** (d. 1791), a wealthy mulatto born in Saint Domingue, Haiti. Ogé was educated on the island and in Paris where he joined Les Amis des Noirs, an influential abolitionist group. In 1789, he demanded that the French National Assembly in Paris free all the slaves in Saint Domingue; the rejection of his request convinced Ogé that the only recourse left was force. Before leaving France, he went to London to meet secretly with Thomas Clarkson (q.v.) and other abolitionist leaders. On his way to the island he bought arms in Charleston, South Carolina. With a small group of mulattoes, he attacked Le Cap Français in 1790, but he was defeated and fled to Spanish Santo Domingo. Ogé was extradited, tried, and executed on March 9, 1791.

**OGO** (Afr.), an African word for gold pebbles found in river beds in Minas Gerais, Brazil. (Mendonça, *A Influencia*, p. 159.)

**OGOUN, OGUM, OGUN** (Afr.), in Haiti and in Nigeria, a god of war identified with Saint James the Elder; his sacred day is Wednesday. His favorite foods are red cocks and red beans mixed with rice, and his color, red, is worn by his devotees. In West Africa, Ogoun is also considered a patron of hunters. In Haiti, he is the head of a large family of gods.

**OGOUN BADAGRI** (Afr.), in the Afro-Haitian pantheon, a god thought of as an ironworker and a warrior. Black peasants pray for his help in times of harvest and sickness. Badagri is the name of a town near the mouth of the Ogoun River in western Nigeria. (Courlander, *The Drum*, p. 321.) See also OGOUN.

**OGOUN CHANGÓ** (Afr.), an Afro-Haitian god, a member of the Ogoun (q.v.) family, and, like most of his brothers, a warrior and an iron worker. His altar is usually a pile of iron. In Nigeria, Ogoun and Changó were considered brothers closely associated with each other.

**OGOUN FERAILLE** (Afr.), an Afro-Haitian god considered the ancestor of a large family of deities. He is the patron of warriors and the forge, and his symbols are a machete, a hoe blade, and a piece of iron chain. In West Africa, he was believed to be a brother of Changó. Both of these deities have survived in the Haitian pantheon. See also OGOUN.

**OGOUN JÉROUGE** (Fr. Cr.), among Haitian blacks, a malevolent god with red eyes, a sign of bad behavior.

**OGOUN LAFLAMBEAU** (Fr. Cr.), an Afro-Haitian god of fire. When he appears at services, he plays with hot coals, hot iron, and flames.

**OGOUN PANAMA** (Fr. Cr.), in the Afro-Haitian pantheon, a god who acts as a guardian against sunstroke. He is usually seen wearing a Panama hat.

**OGUM.** See OGOUN.

**OGUN.** See OGOUN.

**OHOGOBO** (Afr.). See OBGONI.

**O HOMEM DE CÔR** (Pg.) ("The Colored Man"), the name of the first newspaper published in Brazil by Francisco de Paula Brito (q.v.), a mulatto writer. It appeared on September 14, 1833; after the fourth issue, its name was changed to *O Mulatto*. The paper was devoted to the interests of the mulattoes, stressing that every citizen must be admitted to public office on the basis of talent and virtue, not race or wealth. (Sayer, *The Negro*, p. 70.)

**OICOU** (Fr. Cr.), in the Afro-French Antilles, a Creole drink with a high percentage of alcohol.

**OI-LÁ.** See AI-LÁ.

**OIL-PLANT.** See WANGLA.

**OJÁ** (Afr.), in Brazil, a belt embroidered with beads worn by blacks.

**OKA** (Afr.), an Afro-Jamaican dish prepared with yam flour, cassava, and several other ingredients.

**OKAIA** (Afr.), in Brazil, a female black lover.

**OKÉ, OKÔ** (Afr.), an African god of the forest worshipped by blacks in Bahia, Brazil.

**OKORÓ** (Afr.), a sorcerer in the Afro-Cuban religion; an evildoer.

**OKOUME** (Afr.), in the Caribbean, an African tree used in light wood-work.

**OKRA** (Afr.), in the West Indies, a tall annual plant *(Hibiscus esculentus)*, widely cultivated among blacks chiefly for its edible pods, but also for medicinal and other uses.

**OKRA-FUNGI** (Fr. Cr.), in the West Indies, a favorite black dish prepared with corn flour, *quingombo* (q.v.), milk, or water, and pieces of fish.

**OKRA POLL, OKRO PARROT** (Eng. Cr.), in the West Indies, a name given by black fishermen to the wrasse (family *Labridae*), an edible, spiny-finned fish.

**OLANO, NUFLO DE,** a black slave, perhaps an African native, who was in the company of Vasco Nuñez de Balboa when in 1513 the latter claimed the South Sea for Spain (Rout, L. B., *The African Experience in Spanish America*, p. 75.)

**OLD-BADS** (Eng. Cr.), an Afro-Jamaican word for ragged, old clothes.

**OLD-BOY TREE,** in Jamaica, a banana tree grown in poor soil with a bunch that shoots straight up; formerly cultivated and eaten mainly by slaves.

**OLD BUBA** (Eng. Cr.), in Jamaica, an old black who acts overly young.

**OLD CALABAR,** a slave-trading post located in the Bight of Biafra (q.v.) through which many Ibibio and Efik (q.v.) slaves were brought to Afro-

Latin America. The Royal African Company (q.v.) exported black slaves from this port from 1673 to 1689.

**OLD-HIGE** (Eng. Cr.). In the West Indies: 1. A black witch who supposedly takes off her skin and flies at night to suck people's (especially babies') blood. 2. A nagging black woman.

**OLD MAN** (Eng. Cr.), in Jamaica, a spirit that comes down during black revivalist meetings and takes possession of the initiates.

**OLD MASSA** (Eng. Cr.), in colonial Jamaica, a slave's master; today a term of affectionate address to an old black man.

**OLD NIGGER,** in the West Indies, a derogatory term applied by blacks to other blacks.

**OLD-WITCH** (Eng. Cr.), in the West Indies, a practitioner of magic, male or female, old or young.

**OLHADOR** (Pg.), a black diviner in several Afro-Brazilian cults who often prescribes magic cures for many kinds of illnesses.

**OLOBÓ** (Afr.), an Afro-Brazilian term for a bitter paste, an African product.

**OLOCUM** (Afr.), a Yoruba (q.v.) god of the sea in Afro-Cuban religious cults.

**OLOFI** (Afr.), an Afro-Cuban god identified with the Holy Spirit; he is the eternal father of all the gods.

**OLÔRUM** (Afr.), in Afro-Latin America, a Yoruba (q.v.) god sometimes considered aloof and remote from the lives of men.

**OLÔRUM DIDÉ!** (Afr.) ("May God go with you!"), a religious expression common among black Moslems in Brazil.

**OLÔRUM MODUPÍ** (Afr.) ("May God protect you!), a religious expression common among black Moslems in Brazil.

**OLÔRUM ULUA** (Afr.), an Afro-Brazilian deity worshipped by black descendants of Yoruba (q.v.) Moslem slaves in Bahia and other cities. It is apparently a combination of two deities: the Yoruba Olôrum (q.v.) and Allah, the Moslem God. (Bastide, *African Civilizations*, p. 104.)

**OLUDUMARE** (Afr.) ("The One always just"), a Yoruba (q.v.) god worshipped in the Afro-Cuban folk religion.

**OMALÁ** (Afr.), in Brazil, a sacred meal prepared by the black followers of Xangó (q.v.) and taken to his altar as an offering.

**OMAN PRIM** (Eng. Cr.), in Jamaica, a black woman of rank who appears as a character in the Anancy story (q.v.) of African origin.

**OMELÉ** (Afr.), in Trinidad, a medium-size African drum.

**OMOLÚ** (Afr.), in Afro-Brazilian cults, a male deity who, in personified form, appears as a pestilence, especially smallpox. He usually dresses in black and red, and his favorite foods are goat and cock.

**O MULATTO** (Pg.), the title of a powerful antislavery novel by the Brazilian writer Aluizio Azevedo (q.v.), published in 1881 at the height of the abolition movement (q.v.). It tells the story of a mulatto youth educated in Portugal who, after returning to his native land, is murdered when he tries to take his place in white society.

**ONCLE ALUFA** (Afr.), in Brazil, a god who heads a family of malevolent spirits worshipped by Moslem slaves in the colonial period.

**O PAIZ** (Pg.), one of the most powerful abolitionist newspapers, founded in Rio de Janeiro on October 1, 1880. It immediately became the chief publication of the antislavery movement.

**OPA-SUMA** (Pg.), a sacred dance performed by Moslem slaves in their services during the colonial period.

**OPELÉ** (Afr.), in some Afro-Brazilian cults, a sacred vessel used by black sorcerers in magic rituals, especially in divination.

**OPELÉ IFÁ** (Afr.), a sacred metal chain worn by sorcerer followers of Ifá (q.v.), the god of divination, worshipped in Bahia and in other Brazilian cities. It is considered a precious gift of the god.

**OPILAÇÃO** (Pg.), an archaic term for a West African disease (ancylostomiasis) that afflicted a great number of black African slaves.

**OPÓ AFONGA CANDOMBLÉ** (Afr.) ("the Twelve Ministers of Candomblé"), a priestly hierarchy of the Xangó (q.v.) sect established in Bahia, Brazil. The whole organization of this cult is a direct borrowing from the royal court of the ancient kingdom of Oyo (q.v.) in West Africa. The black leader M. E. Bonfim (q.v.) traveled to Nigeria (circa 1930) expressly for initiation into the cult. (Bastide, *African Civilizations*, p. 130.)

**ORANGE WALK,** in the West Indies, a road lined with orange trees on a sugar estate (q.v.); also a grove of orange trees on a plantation.

**ORDENANZAS DE CÁCERES,** a legal code comprising eighty-eight ordinances, fifteen of which dealt with the slave system. It was proposed in 1574 by a judge from the Audiencia of Santo Domingo, Alonso de Cáceres, who, that year, had made an inspection of Cuban plantations in order to bring uniformity to their chaotic laws and practices. A large part of these ordinances was concerned with self-employed and hired-out slaves who, Cáceres felt, were leading too independent an existence. The code provided that no black slave, even if self-employed, could have his own house and required him to live with his master. The slaves working on the plantations had to be given sufficient clothing, and masters were forbidden to give them excessive and cruel punishment. (Klein, *Slavery*, pp. 73, 74.)

**ORISHA, ORIXA** (Afr.), a secondary deity in many African cults throughout the New World. Apparently, the *orisha* personifies some natural phenomenon and is presumed, on occasion, to manifest himself in human form and to speak his will. His presence is attested to by an abnormal psychic state, ordinarily called possession. There are many *orishas*, and they manifest themselves in prayer meetings held by black sects.

**ORISHABI, ORIXABI** (Afr.), a Yoruba (q.v.) goddess worshipped by blacks in Brazil; a diviner. She is highly respected and invoked at the beginning of all ceremonies of the cult.

**ORIXALÁ** (Afr.), an Afro-Brazilian bisexual deity symbolizing the reproductive energies of nature.

**ORIXA OKO** (Afr.), a Yoruba (q.v.) god, the protector of agriculture, greatly worshipped in Afro-Cuban religion.

**ORMOND, JOHN** (1790-1828), a mulatto slave trader nicknamed Mongo John born on the Guinea Coast (q.v.), the son of an English captain and a black woman who was the daughter of a local chief. Taken to England by his father, he left school on his father's death and returned to Guinea. He became a successful slave trader on the banks of the Pongo River where he established a system of *barracoons* (q.v.) with a private army. It is said that he enjoyed an annual income of $200,000. In 1828 he committed suicide.

**ORMSBY, BARBARA STEPHANIE** (b. 1899), a black poet born in Savanna-la-Mar, Jamaica. She was educated in Kingston and at the Whiteland College, Putney, England. She has written poetry since childhood. (Hughes, *The Poetry*, p. 402.)

**ORÔ** (Afr.), a ghost that according to devotees appears in macumba rituals in the Bahia region. Its origin is unknown.

**OROBÓ** (Afr.), the name of a well-known *quilombo* (q.v.) located approximately 150 miles west of the port of Bahia, Brazil. Destroyed in 1797, it exists today as a small country town. (Pierson, *Negroes*, p. 49.)

**ÔRÔBÔ** (Afr.), in Brazil, a sacred fruit imported from Africa and used in several Afro-Brazilian cults.

**OROONOKO, OR THE HISTORY OF THE ROYAL SLAVE,** a novel written by Aphra Behn (q.v.), published in London, circa 1678, based on a legend popular in literary circles in England and France. Oroonoko, the grandson and heir of an African king, fell in love with Imoinda, daughter of the king's general. The king, infuriated upon learning of this affair, ordered Imoinda to be sold out of the country as a slave. Oroonoko himself was kidnapped, taken to Surinam, and sold to a local planter. There he discovered Imoinda, and both tried unsuccessfully to escape. Oroonoko, in fear of losing his love, killed her and attempted to take his own life, but was prevented from doing so and was cruelly executed.

**ORTIZ, ADALBERTO** (b. 1914), an Ecuadorian writer concerned with blacks. His main interest is the survival of the African descendants in the tropical jungle. His main characters are blacks and mulattoes whom he portrays as victims of racial prejudice and extreme misery. His works include *Juyungo: Historia de un negro, una isla y otros negros* (Buenos Aires, 1944); *Tierra son y tambor: Cantares negros y mulatos* (Mexico, 1944); *Camino y puerto de la angustia* (Mexico, 1945); *Los contrabandistas* (Mexico, 1947); *La mala espalda: Once relatos de aqui y de allá* (Guayaquil, Ecuador, 1952); and *El vigilante insepulto* (Guayaquil, Ecuador, 1954).

**ORTIZ FERNÁNDEZ, FERNANDO** (1880-1969), a Cuban scholar and writer born in Havana. Ortiz Fernández was educated in his native city and abroad. The first scientist to recognize the black's part in Cuban life, he claims that the experience of both the blacks and whites is integral to the island's social history. His works include *Hampa afrocubana: Los negros brujos* (1916); *Glosario de afro-cubanismos* (1923); and *Los cabildos afro-cubanos* (1923).

**ORU** (Afr.), in the Afro-Cuban religion, the rhythms by which the gods are called to take possession of the initiates.

**ORUNGAN** (Afr.), an Afro-Brazilian male god closely related to the cult of Ifá (q.v.). He is the husband of the goddess Orixabi (q.v.).

**ORUNGAN, A JUBA O!** (Afr.) ("Orungan, we respect you!"), an African prayer said in Brazil by a priest of Ifá (q.v.) in the service honoring Orungan (q.v.).

**ORUNKO** (Afr.), a prayer meeting which in some Afro-Brazilian black cults takes place at the end of the initiation service, when the candidates reveal their new magic names to the congregation.

**OSENGA** (Afr.), the name of a black *quilombo* (q.v.) organized in the interior of northeast Brazil around 1670.

**OSHALÁ.** See OXALÁ.

**OSHÓ-OSHÚ** (Afr.), in the Cuban folk religion, an African god who is the protector of hunters and travelers. He is represented by a man holding a bow and arrow. In Cuba, Oshó-Oshú is identified with Saint Albert, and in Bahia, Brazil, with Saint George. (Ortiz Fernandez, *Los negros brujos*, p. 34.)

**OSHUN.** See OXUN.

**OSHUN-MANRÊ** (Afr.). See OXUN-MANRÊ.

**OSNABURGH LINEN,** in the West Indies, a rough linen that was issued to slaves for their clothing. On every well-regulated sugar estate (q.v.) the annual allowance was ten to twenty yards to every man, seven to fifteen yards to every woman, and proportionately smaller amounts to every child. Osnaburgh linen was one of the principal textile exports from Liverpool in 1700. (Davidson, *Black Cargoes*, p. 69.)

**OUANGA, OWANGA** (Afr.), in Haiti, a charm obtained from black sorcerers to cast a spell upon an enemy; used in aggressive magic.

**OUBATALÁ** (Afr.). See OBATALÁ.

**OUGAN** (Afr.). See ÔGAN.

**OUIDAH.** See AJUDÁ.

**OUNCE "TRADE,"** a unit of currency used in slave trading in Dahomey (q.v.) around 1793; 1 ounce "trade" was worth 40s. 0d., or 16,000 cowries, weighing 42 pounds. (Davidson, *Black Cargoes*, p. 91.)

**OUVRI BAYÉ POU' MOIN!** (Fr. Cr.) ("Open the gate for me!"), in Afro-Haitian religious cults, a prayer addressed to the god Legba (q.v.) requesting his help in communicating with other gods.

**OVERLOOK BEAN** (Eng. Cr.), a large bean plant *(Canavalia ensiformis)* believed by Jamaican blacks to have a magic "overlooking" influence on provision grounds.

**OVERSEER,** in the colonial West Indies, a manager of a sugar estate (q.v.).

**OWANGA** (Afr.). See OUANGA.

**OXALÁ, OSHALÁ** (Afr.), an Afro-Brazilian bisexual deity symbolizing the reproductive energies of nature. He is represented by lemon-green shells and is honored on Fridays.

**OXÉ** (Afr.), in Brazil, a black priest of a *candomblé* (q.v.) possessed by the god Xangó (q.v.).

**OXOSSI** (Afr.), an African god worshipped in several black cults in Bahia, Brazil.

**OXUN, OSHUN** (Afr.), in Brazil, a Yoruba (q.v.) goddess, the protectress of the waters. Her fetish is a stone worn smooth by a river stream, and her insignia are small bells. She eats mainly fish, she-goat, hen, and beans.

**OXUN-ABAIÔ** (Afr.), magic blue beads worn by Afro-Brazilian followers of the Oxun (q.v.) cult.

**OXUN-APARÁ** (Afr.), sacred yellow beads worn by devotees of the African goddess Oxun (q.v.).

**OXUN-MANRÊ** (Afr.), an Afro-Brazilian god represented by the rainbow.

**OYA** (Afr.), in Trinidad, an African goddess living in the air who is characterized as the wind. She likes to eat she-goat and chicken of any color except black. Her day of worship is Wednesday, and she is identified with Saint Catherine.

**OYO** (Afr.), an old, and at one time powerful, West African kingdom. Centuries before the Europeans arrived on the shores of Guinea (q.v.), its rulers were engaged in the slave trade with caravans crossing the Sahara. Beginning in the sixteenth century, it became entangled in the export of slaves overseas. Oyo was the capital of the Yoruba (q.v.) region.

**OZEWO, ZEWO** (Afr.), in Trinidad, an African male god of the Shangó (q.v.) cult worshipped by blacks and thought to be the supreme god. He likes to eat only pigeons, and his favorite color, worn by his devotees, is orange. (Herskovits, *Trinidad Village*, p. 333.)

# P

**PACHORÔ** (Pg.), a bull's tail, thought to have magic powers and used by black priests in the Afro-Brazilian *gêgé-nagó* (q.v.) cult.

**PAÇOCA, PACOKA** (Pg.), an Afro-Brazilian dish made from cashew-nut kernels roasted and pounded in a pestle with flour, water, and sugar.

**PACQUET-CONGO** (Fr. Cr.), in Haiti, feathered dolls carried by blacks and thought to be powerful protective charms.

**PADA.** See PATA.

**PADIAL Y VIZCARRONDO, LUIS** (1832-1879), a politician and army officer born in Puerto Rico. An ardent abolitionist, he expounded his ideas in the Spanish Cortes around 1865.

**PADOLY, IVES** (b. 1937), a mulatto poet born in Fort-de-France, Martinique. Padoly was educated at the Lycée Schoelcher and has worked as a teacher in his native city. A traditional poet, he feels deeply the tropical beauty of his island, and his quiet, soft inspiration is often touched by the human aspirations and preoccupations of the black people. He sometimes writes his poems in the Creole language. Among his works are *Le Missel Noir*, (Fort-de-France, 1961) and *Poèmes pour adultes* (forthcoming). (Corzani, *Littérature antillaise, poésie*, p. 293.)

**PADREJEAN**, a black slave born in Tortuga who, in 1679, settled on the coast of Saint Domingue. There he organized a rebellion against the white colonists and burned several plantations. The governor of the island destroyed his Maroon (q.v.) settlement and killed Padrejean and his black followers. (Fouchard, *Les Marrons*, p. 474.)

**PADRINO** (Sp.), in colonial Spanish America, a white planter or government official who acted as a third party between a runaway slave looking for pardon and his master.

**PAEN** (Pg.), in the West Indies, a sort of petticoat worn by slave children.

**PAGÉ.** See PAJÉ.

**PAGELANÇA** (Pg.), an Afro-Brazilian folk pageant with mixed Christian and African themes and choreography.

**PAGEM** (Pg.), in colonial Brazil, a young black slave companion who played with the master's growing children, taking them on trips, to and from school, and on hunting excursions.

**PAHOUIN, FANG** (Afr.), a black ethnic group in Gabon, West Africa, from which many slaves were brought to the French Antilles in the colonial period. The slaves from this tribe were known for their work in the plastic arts.

**PAI DE ESHU** (Pg.), a black priest of the Afro-Brazilian Exu (q.v.) cult.

**PAI DE SANTO** (Pg.), a black priest of the Afro-Brazilian candomblé cult. His main responsibility is to preside at public ceremonies and to identify a "manifesting" spirit in a seance. In addition, he is an adviser on business and politics and aids in the curing and prevention of disease. See also MÃE DE SANTO.

**PAI JOÃO,** in Brazil, a popular term referring to the image of the black as humble, docile, mild. This image is very remote from the historical black slave, who gave ample evidence of his capacity for resistance and even revolt.

**PAI JOAQUIN** (Pg.), in some Afro-Brazilian cults, the patron saint or principal spirit, thought to be an ancestor from the West African coast incarnate in the officiating black priest. Pai Joaquin advises the congregation through the priest and always inquires about the health of each of the faithful, the way an elder does in Angola (q.v.). He also often intervenes in petty family affairs and quarrels. (Ramos, *The Negro*, p. 102.)

**PAJÉ, PAGÉ** (Pg.), in Afro-Brazilian folklore, a medicine man.

**PALANQUIN** (Pg.), in colonial Brazil, a sedan chair used by the wealthiest, most aristocratic persons and planters. It was carried by black slaves in colored livery frock coats and blue and red kilts.

**PALAVER** (Eng.), a common term used by Europeans and Africans for any sort of talks, negotiations, or disputes held among slave traders. Purchasing blacks was a lengthy process, generally involving considerable bargaining skill. (Davidson, *Black Cargoes*, pp. 27, 45.)

**PALENQUE** (Sp.), in Spanish America, a small, isolated settlement organized by runaway black slaves. In Cuba, around 1750, it consisted of fifteen to twenty huts made of twigs and mud, and protected by a stockade built of sharpened bamboo poles fixed firmly in the ground and covered with dried leaves and branches with magic paraphernalia. There were fields with beans, yam (q.v.), manihot, corn, and greens to supplement foraging and stealing from the plantations. Some of the *palenques* grew strong and lasted for many years. (Price, *Maroon Societies*, pp. 52-55.) See also CUMBÉ; QUILOMBO.

**PALENQUERO CREOLE,** a Spanish-based dialect spoken by blacks in Colombia.

**PALÉS MATOS, LUIS,** a poet born in Puerto Rico. After being educated in local schools, Palés Matos became a country schoolteacher, a newspaperman, and a lecturer at the University of Puerto Rico. One of the first poets inspired by the African theme, he advanced beyond the usual descriptive African exoticism and created an onomatopoeic style exemplified in some of his famous poems such as "Pueblo negro" (1925), "Danza negra" (1926), and "Bombó" (1930). His major works are *Azaleas* (1915), and *Tuntun de Pasa y Grifería* (1937).

**PALMAR** (Pg.), in colonial northeast Brazil, an inland area along rivers covered by palm trees, where runaway slaves settled in scattered communities. Around 1643, near Alagõas, there were two *palmares* harboring some 5,000 blacks. (Price, *Maroon Societies*, p. 174.)

**PALMARES, REPUBLIC OF,** a large, fortified black settlement organized by runaway slaves around 1640 in the state of Pernambuco, Brazil. Its founders were mainly African-born and Bantu (q.v.)-speaking black slaves who had escaped from the northeast plantations. By 1670, Macoco, the capital of a federation of *quilombos* (q.v.), had 1,500 huts and a native black king, Ganga Zumbá (q.v.), who had a palatial residence for members of his family, government officials, and a well-trained army. There were fields planted with all kinds of vegetables and irrigated by means of ponds and canals. Between 1679 and 1694, Palmares withstood several military expeditions. Finally, on February 5-6, 1694, it was taken by government forces after twenty days of siege. Many defenders were killed or taken captive, and all its leaders were tried and executed. Palmares is thought to have been an incipient African state, established by black slaves in a reaction to a slaveholding society which was foreign to the form of bondage with which they were familiar. (Hanke, *History of Latin American*, V. 1, p. 239.)

**PALMARISTA** (Pg.), in colonial Brazil, a runaway black slave who settled in a *palmar* (q.v.).

**PALMEO** (Sp.), a system of establishing the legal physical features of any slave before he could be sold in the Spanish colonies. It included a medical check by a surgeon, a measuring of the slave's height, and an age estimate. The *palmeo* was done at the port of entry. See also LIBRO DE PALMEO.

**PALMERSTON, HENRY J. T., LORD** (1784-1865), a British statesman and secretary of the Foreign Office, who, in 1835, signed an agreement with Spain and Portugal allowing the seizure of any slave vessel.

**PALMERSTONIAN CRUSADE,** an antislavery traffic campaign organized by Lord H.J.T. Palmerston (q.v.) in 1830 when he took over the British Foreign Office.

**PALMETTO GROVE,** a runaway slave refuge organized around 1632 and located to the southeast of Providence Island off the coast of Costa Rica. (Hamshire, *The British in the Caribbean*, p. 44.)

**PALMO** (Sp.), a Spanish unit of length equivalent to 8½ inches, or a quarter of a "vara"; a standard used for measuring slave height.

**PAMONHA** (Pg.), an Afro-Brazilian dish made of green corn, coconut milk, butter, cinnamon, anise, and sugar; cooked in tubes made of corn leaves.

**PAN.** See PÃO.

**PANAN** (Pg.), in Afro-Brazilian *candomblés* (q.v.), an initiation ceremony during which the novice relearns the behavior appropriate to a secular life which he had supposedly forgotten during the several weeks he was required to spend in seclusion.

**PANDEGOS DA AFRICA** (Pg.), the name of a black carnival club in Bahia, Brazil. In the tumultuous, noisy carnival parades, its members depicted African themes. In 1899, the Pandegos da Africa prepared a float representing the Zambesi River with King Labossi on one of its banks surrounded by his ministers Aná, Oman, and Abato. (Pierson, *Negroes*, p. 100.)

**PANDO** (Sp.), a fish basket used for small river fish by Afro-Hispanic blacks in the Colombian Pacific lowlands.

**PANGA** (Sp.). See IMBABURA.

**PANGGE** (Afr.), in the language of the Saint Thomas African cult, to greet.

**PANGO** (Pg.), in colonial Brazil, a tropical tree *(Cannabi indica)* whose hardwood was used by black slaves to make smoking pipes.

**PANNIER** (Fr. Cr.), a saddlebag used by blacks in Haiti to transport produce.

**PANNO** (Pg.), a palm-leaf cloth used as a medium of exchange for slaves in Angola (q.v.) during the colonial period. (Bowser, *The African Slave*, p. 348.)

**PANO DA COSTA** (Pg.) ("cloth of the coast"), in Brazil, a garment of African origin worn by certain black women. It consists of a long, heavy, striped cotton cloth worn either slung over the shoulder and pinned under the opposite arm or wrapped once or twice in a wide fold about the waist and tied rather tightly.

**PANYARING,** slave kidnapping in colonial West Africa.

**PÃO, PAN, PANO** (Pg.) ("stick, bread, and cloth"), a saying stressing the three basic requirements of plantation slaves in Brazil. (Bastide, *Les Religions africaines*, p. 88.)

**PÃO-DE-LÓ DE ARROZ** (Pg.), an Afro-Brazilian rice cake, a food staple for slaves on the plantations.

**PÃO-DE-LÓ DE MINHO** (Pg.), a corn cake eaten by slaves on Brazilian plantations.

**PAPA-BOIS** (Fr. Cr.), in Trinidadian black folklore, a short, hairy, human-like creature with a funny head a little like an animal's. As the guardian of animals, he takes vengeance on wasteful hunters who kill animals but use little of what they kill.

**PAPA-FIGO** (Pg.), in Afro-Brazilian folklore, a goblin who eats the livers of children.

**PAPALOI** (Fr. Cr.). In Haiti: 1. In colonial times, a Catholic priest. 2. Today, a black medicine man, a shaman, who is thought to have magic power given by the spirits to cure any illness.

**PAPÃO** (Pg.), in Afro-Brazilian folklore, an imaginary monster or goblin used to frighten children.

**PAPA PIE** (Fr. Cr.), in Haitian black folklore, a god of military appearance who never laughs. Dressed in a red and gray robe, he lives at the bottoms of rivers and ponds. He speaks with a piercing voice and likes to eat goat meat and cocks.

**PAPA ZACA** (Fr. Cr.), among Haitian black peasants, the god of agriculture, protector of the farmers. He is a crude peasant with a big appetite and the voice and behavior of a goat. Papa Zaca wears a blue denim jacket and carries a *macoute* (q.v.).

**PAPA ZAO** (Fr. Cr.), an Afro-Haitian deity, protector of the family.

**PAPIAMENTO,** a Spanish-based Creole spoken in the Dutch West Indies since colonial times. It probably derives from an earlier Portuguese pidgin much influenced lexically by Dutch and African elements. Its origin was possibly a Portuguese trade jargon used in West Africa during the slave period. Also called Curacaleño and Curassesse.

**PARACUMBÉ** (Sp.), an Afro-Spanish dance popular in Colombia.

**PARADISE GRAIN.** See MALAGÜETA.

**PARA GRASS.** See ANGOLA GRASS.

**PARANUT** (Afr.), a large tropical tree *(Bertholletea exelsa)* that produces a dozen or more three-sided nuts inside pear-shaped shells. The nut kernels are rich in oil and delicious to eat. It was a standard slave food throughout plantation America. Also called Brazilian nut.

**PARCEL** (Eng.), in slave trade jargon, a group of black slaves selected at random who, because of pestilence, short provisions, or rebellion, were thrown into the sea by Guinea captains during the Middle Passage (q.v.) to the West Indies. (Mannix, *Black Cargoes*, p. 125.)

**PARDAVASCO** (Pg.), in Brazil, a dark-skinned individual approaching the mulatto; the offspring of a black and mulatto.

**PARDO** (Pg.), a vague Brazilian term for mulatto; a racial mixture of white and black.

**PARDO LIBRE** (Sp.), in colonial Spanish America, a generic legal term for any freedman—black, mulatto, or Indian.

**PARET, TIMOTHÉE** (1887-1942), a black poet born in Jérémie, Haiti. After attending local schools, Paret obtained a law degree at Port-au-Prince University, following which he practiced law and served as minister of justice. He wrote for many periodicals and his poetry shows his ardent patriotism. Among his works are *Lueurs sereines: Journal rétrospectif d'un célibataire: Jeannine, essai de nouvelle en vers* (Port-au-Prince, 1908); *L'Ame vibrante, amour tragique, lueurs sereines* (Paris, 1913); *Fleurs détachées* (Port-au-Prince, 1917); *Nouvelle floraison* (Angers, 1917); and *L'Ame vibrante* (Paris, 1922).

**PARROT EYE,** in Jamaica, a black albino.

**PARTIDO INDEPENDIENTE DE LA GENTE DE COLOR** (Sp.) (Colored People's Independent party), a Cuban political group organized legally in 1906. Its leaders were two black generals, heroes of the War of Independence (1898): Evaristo Estenoz and Pedro Ivonet (q.v.). The party was abolished by law in 1912 because of its racial policy. See also LEY MORÚA.

**PARTI PROGRESSISTE MARTINIQUAIS** (Fr.) (Progressive Martiniquan party), on the island of Martinique, a political group with strong support among young blacks and led by the poet Aimé Césaire (q.v.).

**PARTY NEGRO** (Eng. Cr.), in Jamaica, a slave member of any of the expeditionary parties sent by the government from 1730 to 1739 against the Maroons (q.v.) and the runaways who had joined them. The white planters considered the party Negro to be both loyal and brave. (Cassidy, *Dictionary*, p. 341.)

**PASA** (Sp.), in Spanish America, kinky hair characteristic of blacks.

**PASIERO** (Eng. Cr.), in Jamaica, a traveler, a passenger; in slavery times, the term probably meant shipmate (q.v.).

**PASSAGE D'ALLIANCE** (Fr. Cr.), in Afro-Haitian folklore, a special ceremony held by a black sorcerer to identify a thief or other guilty person. A ring is suspended on a string over a person's head. If it moves in a regular, pendulous way, the person is deemed innocent; if it swings in a circle, he is judged guilty.

**PASSÉ BALÉ** (Fr. Cr.), an Afro-Haitian ritual performed by a black sorcerer to identify a criminal. A person sits in a low chair and small branches and leaves of the *balai* (broom) are placed under the chair and fastened to its legs. A guilty person will supposedly cause the branches to vibrate.

**PASSÉ-MAGUNZA** (Fr. Cr.), in Trinidad, a black song-dance.

**PASURÍN, PASUSO** (Sp.), in Puerto Rico, kinky hair.

**PATA, PADA** (Afr.). An Afro-Jamaican word for: 1. A wooden frame used for shelter during cultivation of the fields. 2. An outside rustic kitchen or a wash-place; apparently of African origin.

**PATO, PATU**, an Afro-Jamaican word for an ugly person.

**PATOIS** (Fr.), another name for French Creole (q.v.), the language spoken by blacks in Haiti and elsewhere.

**PATROCINADO** (Sp.), in Cuba, a young black who was born free according to the Ley Moret (q.v.) of 1870, but was subjected to a state patronage until the age of eighteen. The master, now called patron, was obliged to care for the young black, but he also had the privilege of utilizing his labor without pay until the child reached legal age. From then on the black youth was entitled to half the wages of a free man.

**PATROCINIO, JOSÉ DO** (1854-1905), a Brazilian mulatto leader of the abolition movement (q.v.). He was the son of a priest and a black vegetable vendor. Through his own efforts and protectors, he was able to attend the university. He became a politician, writer, spokesman for abolition, and a great journalist. No phase of the struggle for the freedom of the slaves escaped his energetic and tireless efforts. After the abolition of slavery in 1888, he went into semi-oblivion and died indigent and forgotten. Among his writings are several novels: *Motta Coqueño ou a pena de morte* (Rio de Janeiro, 1877), an historical work concerned with the evils of slavery; *Os Retirantes* (Rio de Janeiro, 1879); *Pedro hespanho* (Rio de Janeiro, 1884).

**PATRONATO** (Sp.), in Cuba, a system of trusteeship established by the Ley Moret (q.v.) of 1870 by which former slaves remained attached to their owners until the age of eighteen. See also PATROCINADO.

**PATU**. See PATO.

**PATÚA** (Pg.), in Brazil, written prayers, sometimes verses from the Koran, which were written or printed in Arabic characters and worn close to the body by black Moslem slaves in the colonial period. It was thought that they protected the faithful against disease, accidents, and even death. (Pierson, *Negroes*, p. 258.)

**PATU EYE** (Eng. Cr.), in the West Indies, a black albino.

**PAULINAIRE,** a black slave leader of a slave rebellion on the island of Dominica in January 1791. The uprising was the result of a dispute over the number of days off that the slaves were to have. The blacks wanted three days for themselves, but the planters refused. The insurrection was crushed, and Paulinaire was tried and executed.

**PAVILLON** (Fr. Cr.), in Haiti, the court of a black chapel.

**PAW-PAW, POPO** (Afr.), a tribal name applied by Europeans to any slave coming from the vicinity of Whydah (see AJUDÁ) Dahomey (q.v.), and shipped to the New World from ports located on the Slave Coast (q.v.).

**PAWNS,** in West Africa, a slave trade term for black hostages left on shipboard by black native dealers who borrowed trade goods to use in obtaining slaves from the interior of the continent. This practice became common around 1750. (Mannix, *Black Cargoes*, p. 87.)

**PAXICÁ** (Pg.), an Afro-Brazilian ragout made of turtle's liver and seasoned with salt, lemon, and Indian pepper.

**PAYÉ SORTI** (Fr. Cr.) ("pay-to-go"), among Haitian blacks, the tip given to a troupe of musicians when it stops to play before a person's house.

**PAYETTE** (Fr. Cr.), a lascivious Afro-Haitian dance.

**PAYÓN** (Sp.), a clay-domed baking oven in which blacks of the Pacific lowlands of Gran Colombia bake corn bread or wheat bread for family consumption and sometimes for sale.

**PÉ** (Fr. Cr.), in the Afro-Haitian religion, the *hounfort's* (q.v.) simple altar where the food brought to the spirits is placed. Also on the *pé* are jugs with the souls of the faithful, plates holding votive offerings, and the decorated gourd rattles of the black priest.

**PEACE OF UTRECHT.** See UTRECHT, PEACE OF.

**PEÇA DA AFRICA** (Pg.) ("African slave"), an early Portuguese term for a slave imported from Africa to Portugal and then to Brazil. Two royal decrees, one signed on October 17, 1516, and the other on October 15, 1586, ordered that African slaves should be taken to Lisbon first, where a 10 percent tax was collected, and then to Brazil where another import duty was deducted at the port of entry. (Mendonça, *A Influencia*, p. 21.)

**PEÇA DE INDIAS,** in colonial Brazil, a 1678 law defining a slave as "a Negro from fifteen to twenty-five years old; from eight to fifteen, and from twenty-five to thirty-five, three pass for two; beneath eight, and from thirty five to forty-five, two pass for one; sucking infants follow their mothers without account; all above forty-five, with some disease, are valued by arbiters." The slaves were registered and marketed like any other merchandise. The prices they brought normally varied in accordance with their age, sex, physical condition, and the use for which they were intended. (Boxer, *The Golden Age*, pp. 5, 7.)

**PEÇANHA, NILO** (1864-1924), a Brazilian politician of black ancestry who was president of the country from June 1909 to November 1910. As a young lawyer, he fought for the emancipation of slaves, and, in 1890, he was elected deputy to the Constituent Assembly. In 1912 Peçanha won reelection to the Senate, and, in 1917, he was appointed minister of foreign affairs.

**PÉ-DE-MOLEQUE** (Pg.) ("black boy's foot"), a kind of cake made out of fermented manihot (see MANDIOCA) dough mixed with peanuts; a favorite black delicacy.

**PEDRA BONITA** (Pg.), a legendary monument, resembling a dolmen, marking the exact location of an enchanted country where many black slaves and whites believe a new Jerusalem would be established by King Sebastião. Around 1855 thousands of slaves fled from the *fazendas* (q.v.) and took refuge in the region of Pedra Bonita in the state of Pernambuco.

**PEDRE,** an Angolan-born black slave who, around 1656, organized a bloody uprising in Guadeloupe. The aims of the plot included the establishment of two Cap-Terre Angolan kingdoms, one at Basse-Terre and the other at Cap-Terre. With the help of loyal slaves the French militia defeated the rebels. Pedre was caught, put to trial, and executed. (Hall, *Social Control*, p. 62.)

**PEDROSO, REGINO** (b. 1896), a Cuban-born poet of black and Chinese ancestry. In his youth, Pedroso worked in the sugar cane fields and on the railroad and later was employed in the Ministry of Education. He reacted violently against the exploitation of the black workers who were kept in dire poverty by the rich and the wealthy classes. In his writings, he championed the aesthetic values of black primitivism as a source of inspiration in poetry and music. His works include *Nosotros* (Havana, 1933); *Antología Poetica: 1918-1938* (Havana, 1935); *Mas allá canta el mar* (Havana, 1939); Bolivar, *sinfonía de libertad, poemas* (Havana, 1945); and *El ciruelo de Yan Pei Fu, poemas chinos* (Havana, 1955).

**PEGGANNING** (Eng. Cr.), in Jamaica, the black's Easter holidays.

**PEIA QUEIMADA** (Pg.), among Afro-Brazilians, a children's game described as sadistic. It apparently originated in slavery times.

**PEIXOTO, JOSÉ INACIO DE ALVARENGA** (1744-1793), a Brazilian poet of the Escola Mineira who wrote a poem, "Canto Genethiaco," in which he pays tribute to the children of Africa who work hard on the plantations and are valiant soldiers.

**PEJI** (Afr.), in Afro-Brazilian cults, a shrine or special room of a chapel containing the sacred fetishes, the vessels for food, and drink for the spirits, and the symbols of each spirit such as a spade, sword, or hat. In addition, the room usually contains a trunk filled with the ceremonial paraphernalia used during the festivities.

**PEKEIN MAMA** (Fr. Cr.), in Haiti,.a black midwife.

**PELO BUENO** (Sp.), in Puerto Rico, a white person's "nice" hair as opposed to a black's "bad," kinky hair.

**PELO DE PASA** (Sp.), in Puerto Rico, the black's kinky hair.

**PELO MALO** (Sp.), in Puerto Rico, the black's "bad" or kinky hair; a derogatory term used to indicate African racial features.

**PEMI** (Eng. Cr.), in Trinidad, a dish make of boiled cornmeal, a black delicacy.

**PEPPER-POT** (Eng. Cr.), a favorite West Indian dish, a kind of vegetable soup made with a leaf or two of cabbage, calalu (q.v.), beans, tomato, pumpkin, and okra (q.v.), boiled with salt or pork and flavored with red peppers. See also SPANISH CALALU.

**PEQUENA LAVOURA** (Pg.), in colonial Brazil, small-scale or subsistence agriculture.

**PEQUENINO** (Pg.) ("very little"), a Portuguese term used by slave traders in Africa during the slavery period. See also PICKANINNY.

**PEREIRA, NUÑNO MARQUES** (d. 1728), a Brazilian traveler and writer. Pereira is best known for *Compendio Narrativo do Peregrino da America* (circa 1725), a very popular novel, the first part of which underwent five printings between 1728 and 1765. The book recounts the trip a visitor made to Brazil, including his stops at the *fazendas* (q.v.) and his observations on the planters' lives and their homes. The descriptions of the slaves are very detailed. (Sayers, *The Negro*, p. 47.)

**PERE-PERE** (Afr.), an Afro-Jamaican word for small things, scraps; hence something of little value.

**PÈRE-SAVANT**, in the Afro-Haitian folk religion, a black preacher and healer. A fusion of African diviner and magician, he baptizes, performs weddings, and also practices magic. Pères-Savants flourished after the 1791 slave revolution when all French priests and teachers were expelled from Haiti.

**PÉREZ Y SANTA CRUZ, LAUREANO,** a black Cuban poet. In 1828 he published in *Poesías Líricas* (Paris) which contained a prologue by the famous Spanish writer Francisco Martínez de la Rosa.

**PERISTYLE** (Fr. Cr.), the roofed court of an Afro-Haitian country chapel.

**PERROS CAZADORES, PERROS DE BUSCA** (Sp.) ("bloodhounds"), in colonial Cuba, a special breed of bloodhound used to hunt runaway slaves. These dogs were big, fierce, broad-toothed, and well trained for their work. On December 14, 1795, 100 of these dogs, along with forty handlers, were introduced into Jamaica. (Black, *History of Jamaica*, p. 140.)

**PESSOA DE COR** (Pg.), in Brazil, a mulatto.

**PESSOAL DE CASA** (Pg.) ("domestic slave"), in colonial Brazil, a domestic black slave with higher social status than a field slave (q.v.).

**PETERS, CHARLES,** a Dominican friar, rector of a church in Dominica, West Indies. Peters preached two sermons on Good Friday and Easter, 1800, urging slave masters to adopt equitable and judicious measures for the welfare of black slaves and denouncing the practice of overworking them. A heated controversy ensued. The priest was summoned before the local council and found it advisable to resign his duties and hastily leave the island. A local paper described him as a "diminutive wolf in sheep's clothing" and recommended that he "exchange his gown for the party-coloured trappings of the French Republicans." (Ragatz, *The Fall*, pp. 284, 285.)

**PÉTION, ALEXANDER SABÉS** (1770-1818), a Haitian soldier and statesman born in Port-Au-Prince, Haiti, April 2, 1770. He was the son of a mulatto woman and a white man, Pascal Sabés. He later adopted the name Pétion in honor of the French revolutionary Pétion Dilleneuve. He received part of his education in a military school in France and at about the age of twenty joined the militia in Haiti. One of the leaders of the Haitian Revolution against the French, he was president of the Haitian Republic of the South from 1807 to 1818. Pétion was known to his fellow Haitians as "Bon Coeur."

**PETITE BANDE** (Fr. Cr.) ("small gang"), in the colonial French Antilles, a gang of slave children working under a black overseer on a plantation. See also PICKANINNY GANG; THIRD GANG.

**PETIT BLANC** (Fr. Cr.) ("small white), in colonial Jamaica, staff members of a sugar estate (q.v.) such as attorneys, doctors, preachers, tavern keepers, and artisans. Today in Martinique the term is used to refer to a poor white, usually with a large family, who often lives in less than moderate circumstances but does not give the impression of misery or physical degradation. (Comitas and Lowenthal, *Slaves, Free Men*, p. 250.)

**PETIT BON ANGE** (Fr. Cr.) ("good little angel"), in Afro-Haitian folklore, a ghost which, on its owner's death, takes refuge in the water for a whole year. At the end of this period, it is brought back by a sorcerer and is put in a sacred pot and placed on an altar to be worshipped by the cult's followers.

**PETIT NOM** (Fr. Cr.) ("small name"), among Afro-Haitians, a child's nickname known only to the father and mother until the infant is old enough to guard its secret character.

**PETIT PROPIÉTAIRE** (Fr. Cr.) ("small landholder"), in Haiti, a former slave who owned a small plot of land on which he grew tropical commodities such as cotton, rice, coffee, and tobacco for sale in the local market.

**PETRAS DE SANTA BÁRBARA.** See ITÁS DA XANGÓ.

**PÉTRO,** one of the two classes of spirits worshipped in the Afro-Haitian cults. All these deities are of local black origin and are regarded as separated from the so-called African group or Rada (q.v.). This sect originated around 1768 under the leadership of a powerful sorcerer, Don Pétro (q.v.). (Leyburn, *The Haitian People*, p. 145.)

**PETUN** (Fr. Cr.), an archaic term for tobacco in the Afro-French Antilles.

**PHACOCHÈRE** (Fr. Cr.), in the Afro-French Antilles, a kind of African boar with big feet and a brownish, bristly coat.

**PHEBA, PHIBBA** (Afr.), in the West Indies, an African day-name (q.v.) given to a female born on Friday; now seldom used. It corresponds to the male day-name of Cuffee (q.v.).

**PHELPS, ANTHONY** (b. 1928), a black poet born in Port-au-Prince, Haiti. After his early education on the island, Phelps attended Seton Hall University in the United States. After his return to Haiti he became active in politics and was imprisoned by Haitian president François Duvalier. In 1964 he left the country and settled in Montreal where he resumed his writing career. While in Haiti, he wrote a number of radio sketches. Phelps is considered one of the foremost Haitian writers. He has written *Les Enchainés*, an unpublished novel dealing with the 1946 revolution. His volumes of poetry are *Eté* (1960); *Présence* (1962); *Eclats de silence* (1962); *Points cardinaux* (1966); *Mon pays que voici* (1968); and *Les Dits du fou-aux-cailloux* (1968).

**PHENOTYPICAL COLOR,** in West Indian society, the color of an individual, indicative of his racial background and an important factor in defining the individual's status in society. In terms of prestige, there is an overt order of rank which places white phenotypes at the highest point and black phenotypes at the lowest. (M. G. Smith, *The Plural Society*, p. 60.)

**PHIBBA.** See PHEBA.

**PHILOTECTE, RENÉ** (b. 1932), a black poet born in Jéremie, Haiti. After finishing his education in Port-au-Prince Philotecte taught at the Fernand

Prosper High School. He is the leading poet of his generation. His published works include *Saison des hommes* (1960); *Margha* (1961); and *Les Tambours du soleil* (1962).

**PHYSICIAN.** See SLAVER SURGEON.

**PIABA** (Afr.), an Afro-Caribbean name for a wild herb *(Hyptis pectinata)* often used in black folk medicine.

**PIACAM, PIACAM** (Fr. Cr.) ("go slow"), an expression used by blacks in the French Antilles.

**PIAN** (Afr.), a skin disease that affected black slaves brought from Africa to the New World. It caused swollen ulcers of a yellowish color; synonymous with syphillis and bubas.

**PIANGI, PYANGII** (Afr.), in the Caribbean, an African word for slight, small, weak.

**PIANO DE CUIA** (Pg.). See AGÊ.

**PIAYE** (Fr. Cr.). See QUIMBOIS.

**PICAROON,** in the West Indies and elsewhere, a rogue; also applied to someone who tries to climb the social ladder through chicanery and other dubious activites.

**PICCONG** (Eng. Cr.), in the West Indies, a verbal contest of insults, an institutionalized form of abuse used in early versions of the modern *calipso* (q.v.).

**PICHINCHAT, PHILIPPE,** a mulatto leader in the 1791 Haitian revolution. He was educated in Haiti and in France where he joined the mulattoes' party. Later he fought with black forces against the white colonists.

**PICKANINNY,** a black child.

**PICKANINNY GANG, PICKNEY GANG,** in colonial Jamaica, a group of slave children from nine to twelve years of age employed on a sugar estate (q.v.) for the lightest work. See also THIRD GANG.

**PICKLING** (Eng. Cr.), in the West Indies, the rubbing of salt into the wounds black slaves received from being whipped; although painful, it prevented infection.

**PICKNEY** (Eng. Cr.), in Jamaica, a black child, especially a very young child. See also PICKANINNY.

**PICKNEY CHRISTMAS, PIGANINNY CHRISTMAS** (Eng. Cr.), in the West Indies, Easter holidays celebrated by black slaves. Though a shorter holiday than the Christmas one, it featured a noisy and merry carnival with gay, colorful parades through the streets.

**PICKNEY GANG** (Eng. Cr.). See PICKANINNY GANG.

**PICKNEY MUMMA** (Eng. Cr.), in the West Indies, a nursing mother or the mother of a small child. Among slaves, these women were given extra provisions and certain privileges.

**PIÉ CASSÉ** (Fr. Cr.), an Afro-Haitian god who crawls because of his broken feet.

**PIÈRRE-LOA** (Fr. Cr.), in Afro-Haitian cults, the stone in which a *loa* (q.v.) or spirit is believed to reside.

**PIERRE-MAMMAN,** a large sacred stone placed in the center of a room which Haitian blacks believe to be the residence of the family god, the protector of the hut.

**PIEZA DE INDIAS** (Sp.), in colonial Spanish America, a prime black slave, sound in mind and limb, usually between the ages of eighteen and thirty, and seven Spanish *palmos* (1.70m.) tall. A *pieza de Indias* was actually a measure of potential labor, not of individuals. This was because the Spanish imperial economy required a given amount of labor power and not a given number of people. Accordingly, the number of slaves delivered was always greater than the number of *piezas de Indias* specified in an *asiento* (q.v.). (Pescatello, *The African*, p. 37.)

**PIEZA DE ROZA** (Sp.), in Spanish America, a black slave employed to grow food for the master's house. See also FIELD SLAVE.

**PIGANINNY CHRISTMAS.** See PICKNEY CHRISTMAS.

**PIGEON PEA,** in the Caribbean, a variety of pea *(Cajanus cajan)*, formerly a staple food for slaves. Also called Angola pea (q.v.) and Congo pea.

**PIGMENTOCRACY.** See COLOROCRACIA.

**PILDÉ** (Sp.), among blacks of the Pacific Colombian lowlands, a drug comparable to lysergic acid diethylamide (LSD) taken by sorcerers to gain knowledge of the supernatural world. (Whitten, *Black Frontiersmen*, p. 102.)

**PIMENTA DA COSTA** (Pg.), in colonial Brazil, a generic term for an African pepper that was one of the main foods eaten by slaves on the plantations.

**PIMENTÃO** (Pg.), in Brazil, guinea red pepper *(Capsicum cordiforme)*, possibly of African origin.

**PIMENTEL, ESTEVÃO,** in colonial Brazil, a free mulatto, a blacksmith by trade who in 1847 as chief of a secret society, led a slave revolt in a black town located in the forest of Santa Catarina, near Petropolis. (Price, *Maroon Society*, p. 198.)

**PIMIENTA DE MALAGÜETA** (Pg.). See MALAGÜETA.

**PIMPÃO** (Pg.), in Brazil, a black ruffian or dandy.

**PINGA** (Pg.), an Afro-Brazilian word for a low-priced rum.

**PINGÉ** (Fr. Cr.), in Haiti, a form of wrestling performed by blacks in carnival festivals.

**PIQUET** (Fr. Cr.), in southern Haiti, a black experienced in fighting who hires himself out as a mercenary.

**PIQUETTE** (Fr. Cr.), in Haiti, a piece of sharpened bamboo or hard wood, planted in the earth to protect gardens. Its point is dipped into poison and placed in the ground with the sharpened end up. An unwary intruder who steps on a *piquette* may die of his wound.

**PIRÃO** (Pg.), an Afro-Brazilian dish made from manihot flour and spices.

**PISTON** (Fr. Cr.), among Haitian blacks, any wind instrument resembling a trumpet.

**PLAÇAGE** (Fr. Cr.), among Haitian blacks, a traditional type of polygamy that allows a man to have several mating partners or wives in separate dwellings. This companionship is for pleasure and provides a degree of home life without incurring any legal obligation on either person. *Plaçage* has no overtones of licentiousness and does not connote disreputable behavior.

**PLACÉE** (Fr. Cr.), in Haiti, a black woman who takes a mate without a formal marriage. See also PLAÇAGE.

**PLÁCIDO** (1809-1844), pseudonym for the mulatto poet Diego Gabriel de la Concepción Valdez born in Havana in March 1809 to a mulatto father and a Spanish dancer. Educated in local schools, in 1834 he published his first poem, "La siempreviva," dedicated to the Spanish poet Francisco Martínez de la Rosa. He wrote lyrics for ballads like "Licterical" and erotic sonnets like "La flor de caña," and touched deeply on his inner feelings in "La Fatalidad" and "A la Condesa Merlin." Accused of taking part in the Conspiracy of the Ladder (q.v.), Plácido was tried and executed in 1844. Before his execution, he wrote his most inspired poems: "Plegaria a Dios," translated into several languages, "Despedida a mi madre," and "Adios a mi lira." Among his numerous works are *Poesías de Plácido* (Mantanzas, 1836); *El veguero: Poesías cubanas dedicadas por Plácido a sus amigos de Villa-Clara* (Matanzas, 1841); *El hijo de maldicion: Poema del tiempo de las cruzadas* (Matanzas, 1843); and *Poemas de Plácido* (New Orleans, 1847).

**PLANTAIN,** a tropical perennial plant *(Musa paradisia)* or its fruit, a staple food for black slaves in the New World. The plant consists of long vertical sheathing leafstalks overlapping one another and crowned by broad expanding leaves and a bunch of fruit weighing 40 to 60 or more pounds. When roasted and eaten before maturity it resembles the potato; the powdered dried fruit has been compared with rice.

**PLANTAIN-WALK,** in the West Indies, a grove or plantation of plantain (q.v.) trees on a sugar estate (q.v.).

**PLANTER CLASS,** in tropical America, a group of powerful and wealthy pioneers, owners of large sugar estates (q.v.) that produced sugar for overseas markets using massive slave labor. The planter class was basically the same all over the New World, but during the colonial period it developed distinctive features because of the European backgrounds of the plantation systems introduced into the various colonies.

**PLANTER HIGGLER,** in Jamaica, a black trader or middleman who may grow part of his stock himself, but who more often travels long distances to buy a large quantity of one commodity which he then transports even greater distances, often over fifty miles, to market.

**PLANTERS' CLUB OF LONDON,** an organization of West Indian absentee planters living in Great Britain, established before 1740 and continuing in existence for several decades thereafter. Its membership consisted of proprietors only and was distinct from the merchant groups of the time. Later (circa 1780), the two groups coalesced, forming the Society of West Indian Planters and Merchants (q.v.). (Ragatz, *The Fall*, p. 57.)

**PLANTING ATTORNEY,** in colonial Jamaica, the chief manager of a plantation; he was appointed and paid by the owner in England. His business was to see that everything was properly conducted on the plantation. If there were any complaints by the black slaves, remedies were in his hands.

**PLANTING SUGAR ESTATE,** in the colonial West Indies, a slave sugar estate (q.v.) located inland on higher ground. Here the black, moist soil, accumulated perhaps from rotten vegetable substances, produced abundant crops.

**PLANTOCRACY,** a generic term often used by scholars to refer to the socioeconomic plantation system introduced into the New World.

**PLÁTANO** (Sp.), a plant commonly subdivided into two species, the plantain (q.v.) proper *(Musa Paradisiaca)* and the banana *(Musa sapientum).* Both belong to one family, *Musaceae*, which originated in southeastern Asia. The plantain was nearly always cooked and served as a staple in the diet of the plantation slaves. Some, perhaps all, of the bananas were brought from the Old World by the Spaniards and the Portuguese.

**POCOMANIA** (Sp.), in Jamaica and elsewhere in the West Indies, an African cult influenced by Christian worship, apparently introduced by African slaves around 1850. In its revival meetings, the faithful are driven to frenzy by rhythmic drumming, and some fall almost unconscious, possessed by spirits.

**POETAS DE COLOR** (Sp.) *(Colored Poets)*, a curious book published in Havana in 1868 by Francisco Calcagno (q.v.), a Cuban scholar. Calcagno includes biographical notes on six black poets who were born slaves; the best known are Plácido (q.v.), the pseudonym of Diego Gabriel de la Concepción Valdez, and Juan F. Manzano (q.v.)

**POIS D' ANGOLA, POIS DE BOIS** (Fr. Cr.), in the Caribbean, an Angola pea (q.v.) *(Pistum sativum)*, the fruit of a shrubby tree that produces in seven to eight years. Its seed, resembling a kind of bean, was a staple food for plantation slaves. It may have been imported from Africa in the colonial period.

**POLINKS,** in the West Indies, areas of black, moist soil in the hills up to ten miles from the slaves' huts which the slaves cleared and tended themselves. These *polinks* were required by a law passed in Jamaica in 1678 which stipulated that proprietors should, under penalty, provide an acre for every five blacks. (Brathwaite, *The Development*, p. 133.)

**POLYDOR,** a black leader of a Maroon settlement (q.v.) in the mountains of Saint Domingue near the Spanish border. Around 1725, he organized a band of runaway slaves to attack the plantations and, for several years, killed white colonists. In 1734, Polydor was killed by government forces. (Fouchard, *Les Marrons*, p. 485.)

**POMBEIRO, PUMBO** (Pg.), in colonial Brazil, a half-caste slave trader who usually traveled throughout the interior looking for slaves to sell to the plantations of the northeast. In Africa, especially in Angola (q.v.), *pombeiros* were sometimes itinerant blacks or mulattoes who purchased slaves from the inland chiefs and took them to Luanda (q.v.) for sale.

**POMBINHA** (Pg.), in Afro-Brazilian folklore, an aphrodisiac herb used by black sorcerers to help cure impotence. Its origin is Portuguese.

**POMBO** (Pg.). See POMBEIRO.

**POMPÉE,** a black slave chief of a Maroon settlement (q.v.) in the Blue Mountains in Haiti. He resisted the colonist forces for some years but, in 1747, was taken prisoner and executed. (Fouchard, *Les Marrons*, p. 488.)

**PONG-FINGER** (Eng. Cr.), in the West Indies, a black game in which large stones or coconut husks are passed rhythmically around a ring of seated people.

**PONTOS RISCADOS** (Pg.), magic drawings chalked on the dancing grounds where the initiates of the Bantu *candomblé* (q.v.) of Rio de Janeiro, Brazil perform their ritual dances. They are crude and simple patterns, designed to ensure success in magic. See also VÈVÉ.

**POOR WHITES,** in the West Indies, English descendants of indentured or bond servants, usually convicts, assigned to planters to work in conditions very similar to slavery for a given period of years. At the end of their sentence, many of the former servants established small farms on the islands. Their descendants have remained a dispossessed class to this day. The unity within their group was, and is, provided by color. (Henriques, *Family and Colour*, p. 45.)

**PORRES, MARTÍN DE** (1579-1639), a Lima-born mulatto, the son of a Spaniard and a black woman. In 1601, he was accepted as a lay brother in the Dominican Order. He was beatified in the Catholic church by papal bull on August 8, 1837.

**PORTEUS, BEILBY** (1731-1808), a bishop of Chester and later of London, born in York on May 8, 1731, the youngest of the nineteen children of Robert Porteus. Both his parents were natives of Virginia and lived there on their own estate until 1720 when they left for England to provide a better education for the children. Beilby entered Christ College, Cambridge, in 1748. A few years later he was ordained deacon and, in 1776, was promoted to the bishopric of Chester. He took a deep interest in the welfare of black slaves in the West Indies, first by preaching and later in writings. The Society for the Conversion and Religious Instruction of the Negroes in the West Indies was organized under his auspices around 1791.

**PORTO CABESSE** (Fr. Cr.), in Afro-Haitian cults, the central part of the chapel through which the gods are believed to make their entrance into the dancing space and where they remain until they are invoked.

**PORTO SEGURO,** a city port that was founded around 1850 on the West African coast by repatriated *gêgê* black slaves from Brazil. Porto Seguro was also the name of a port near Bahia. (Pierson, *Negroes*, p. 33.)

**PORTUGUESE CREOLE,** a Portuguese-based dialect widely used on three islands off the West African coast—Cape Verde (q.v.), Amobón, and São Tomé (q.v.)—and in Asia. It is relatively uniform, although in sharp contrast to standard Portuguese.

**PORTUGUESE PIDGIN,** an extinct Portuguese-based speech used during the slave trade in West Africa. In the sixteenth century, it replaced Arabic and Malay as the trade language of the Far East and was employed by all nationalities, from India to Indonesia and as far north as Japan. Portuguese pidgin has played a role in the development of modern Afrikaans in South Africa and of Negerholland in the Caribbean.

**PORTUGUESE WEST AFRICA.** See ANGOLA COLONY.

**PO' TEAU MITAN, PO' TEAU PLANTÉ,** (Fr. Cr.), in Afro-Haitian cults, the center part of a chapel where the rituals take place.

**POTÉ COLÉ** (Fr. Cr.) ("pull together"), an Afro-Haitian expression applied in northern Haiti to a combined program organized in 1959 by the Haitian and U.S. governments to increase the production of rice and other vegetables among black peasants. The program concentrated on graphic demonstrations of how to grow and market green vegetables.

**POTESTAD DOMINICA** (Sp.), in the Spanish American colonies, the master's authority over bondsmen, vested in slaveholders by the civil laws.

**POTO** (Fr. Cr.), in Haiti, red and black beans *(Phaseolus)* that blacks consider to be endowed with magical powers.

**POTS** (Eng. Cr.), in colonial Jamaica, a fresh broth highly seasoned with peppers and okra (q.v.), a staple food for slaves.

**POT TÊTE** (Fr. Cr.), in Afro-Haitian religion, a sacred pot in which the spirits of the ancestors are thought to live. It is kept in a place of honor in chapels all over the countryside.

**POTTOCHS** (Eng. Cr.), in the West Indies, iron rings put around a slave's neck as punishment for having run away.

**POUIN** (Fr. Cr.), in Afro-Haitian folklore, a magic charm (q.v.).

**POVEDA, JOSÉ MANUEL** (1888-1926), a post-modernist Cuban poet and essayist who was a pioneer in the *afrocubanismo* movement (q.v.). He was interested first in black folklore and later in the social conditions of the black population in general. He wrote *Versos Precursores* (Manzanillo, Cuba, 1917).

**POWER KEY** (Eng. Cr.), in the Jamaican Pocomania (q.v.) cult, a sacred stone placed on the altar and covered with a black cloth with a white cross on it. It is used by black sorcerers as a charm to control supernatural powers.

**PRAEDIAL LARCENY,** a criminal provision of the so-called class legislation enacted by the Assembly in Jamaica after the emancipation of the slaves in 1838. This offense came to embrace not only the theft of cultivated crops, but also the gathering of wild products from any land at all.

**PRAEDIAL SLAVE.** See FIELD SLAVE.

**PRAYER KEY** (Eng. Cr.), in Jamaica, a charm associated with black cults.

**PRAZERO** (Pg.), in East Africa, a chieftain, owner of a slave-run estate given to him by the Portuguese. He was an absolute master: he owned the land and he established tributes to be collected from petty chiefs residing on his property. In default of payment in goods (usually ivory), slaves were accepted. Some of these grantees lived in great luxury and comfort. See also PRAZO.

**PRAZO** (Pg.), a land grant given by the Portuguese Crown to black chiefs in the interior of Africa. The *prazo* system, which originated in the late sixteenth century, was abolished by the government in 1832. It shaped the colonization of Mozambique and other areas in Africa. See also PRAZERO.

**PRAZO DA CORÕA** (Pg.), a Crown land grant bestowed by the king to Portuguese colonists in Africa.

**PREACHY-PREACHY,** in the West Indies, an expression referring to the continual and repetitive style of preaching used by black healers.

**PRECEITO** (Pg.), a ritualistic obligation imposed on the initiates by a priest in some of the *candomblé* (q.v.) rituals in Brazil.

**PREDIKANT** (D.), in Brazil, a Calvinist preacher, very active during the Dutch domination in the northeast (1624-1648).

**PREGO** (Pg.), in Bahia, Brazil, a very dark black boy.

**PREGUNTAR POR SU ABUELA** (Sp.) ("to ask for somebody's grand-mother"), an expression used in Puerto Rico and elsewhere with reference to a person who hides his black ancestry.

**PRESIDENT CLERMEIL.** See GÉNÉRAL CLERMEIL.

**PRESSOIR, CHARLES FERNAND** (b. 1910), a black writer born in Haiti. Pressoir was educated in local schools and in England and France. In 1928, he received his baccalaureate in Paris. After returning to Port-au-Prince, he received a law degree and later was elected president of the Creole Academy. He studied and wrote about black folklore, using the Creole language in some of his works. His publications include *En rythme des coumbites* (Port-au-Prince, 1933); *Débats sur le créole et le folklore* (Port-au-Prince, 1947); and *Sè-t poè-m ki so-t nan mo-n*; *Sept poèmes qui viennent de la montagne* (Port-au-Prince, 1954).

**PRETALHÃO** (Pg.), in Brazil, a tall, stout black.

**PRETO** (Pg.), in Brazil, a very dark-skinned black.

**PRETO-AÇA** (Pg.), in Brazil, a black albino.

**PRETO COMO CARVÃO** (Pg.), in Brazil, a black "dark as coal."

**PRETO DE ALUGEL, PRETO DE GANHO** (Pg.), in colonial Brazil, a black slave hired out by his master for the master's profit.

**PRETO RETINTO** (Pg.), in Bahia, Brazil, a very dark black.

**PRETO RICO** (Pg.), in Brazil, a wealthy black, usually the owner of a small estate in the countryside.

**PRET' SAVANNE** (Fr. Cr.), a black minister in some Afro-Haitian sects. His status and function are partially those of a Catholic priest whom he replaced after the slave revolt of 1791 when the French clergy left the country. Today, although illiterate, the *pret' savanne* has a respected place in the black community, operating within an African framework.

**PRICE-MARS, JEAN** (b. 1876), a black Haitian scholar, one of the first intellectuals of the Antillanité (q.v.) movement. He was deeply concerned with the customs, beliefs, folk tales, and religion of the impoverished Haitian black masses, seeing in them a magnificent source of inspiration for poets and writers. He set the tone for the black renaissance in Haiti and elsewhere. His works include *Ainsi parle l'oncle* (1928); *Une Etape de l'évolution haïtiènne* (1929); and *Le Sentiment de la valeur personnelle chez Henry Christophe* (1933).

**PRIMEIRO DOS BRANCOS** (Pg.) ("the First among the Whites"), an honorific title given by Dahomean kings (circa 1730) to Portuguese and Brazilian slave traders operating in Ajudá (q.v.).

**PRINCE DE BUNDO,** a black impostor who claimed to be the grandson of an African king. In his trial, held in Jamaica in 1816, he declared that he was born in Staines, England, and that, in 1776, he attended Oxford University and afterwards married a Polish princess. But the court found that he was actually a black slave who had been born in Barbados and had been sent to England by his master as servant of one of his sons. He was condemned as a charlatan and exiled to England. (Brathwaite, *The Development*, p. 195.)

**PRINCE OF ANNAMABOE,** the son of the king of Annamaboe on the Gold Coast (q.v.) who, together with his younger brother, was sent to school in England on a slaving ship around 1740. The captain seized the two brothers and took them to the West Indies where he sold them into slavery. When the story reached England, the youths were released by order of the British government which duly paid their ransom. The prince and his brother were taken to England and were placed under the care of the earl of Halifax for their education. Horace Walpole mentioned them in his London diary entry for March 23, 1749. Before returning to Africa, both youngsters were received by the king. (Davidson, *Black Mother*, p. 274.)

**PINGAR UM ESCRAVO** (Pg.) ("to drip a slave"), in colonial Brazil, a particularly cruel form of punishment for runaway slaves, consisting of letting drops of boiling water fall on the victim.

**PRIVILEGED FREE COLORED PERSON,** in colonial Jamaica, any free mulatto to whom, after petitioning, the Assembly gave the rights of persons born of white parents. There were certain restrictions which varied with the individual. Between 1772 and 1796, at least sixty-seven petitions, involving 512 free mulattoes and only one free black, had passed before the Assembly. (Brathwaite, *The Development*, p. 171.)

**PROCURADOR SÍNDICO DE ESCLAVOS** (Sp.) ("legal defender of slaves"), a Cuban magistrate whose duties included the legal protection of slaves. He was charged with assuring them the right to purchase their freedom, even against the will of their masters, and to seek court protection in all formal proceedings. During the eighteenth century, each locality was supposed to have a *procurador síndico*. (Klein, *Slavery in the Americas*, p. 78.)

**PROGGING DAY** (Eng. Cr.), among Afro-Jamaicans, market day, the day for obtaining the goods one wants.

**PROTOME MÉDICATO** (Sp.), a royal tribunal in charge of examining and licensing physicians.

**PROTOMÉDICO** (Sp.), a royal licensed physician whose duty included health inspection of slave cargoes at ports of entry.

**PROTECTOR DE ESCLAVOS,** in Cuba and elsewhere, an ordinary court official in charge of protecting slaves living in towns. His intervention was required in disputes with their masters regarding family affairs, thefts, injuries and the like. See also PROCURADOR SÍNDICO DE ESCLAVOS.

**PROVINCIA NEGRA** (Sp.). See BLACK PROVINCE.

**PUITA** (Afr.), a small cylindrical drum played by blacks in Brazil.

**PULLER** (Eng. Cr.), in Jamaica, an *obeah* man (q.v.).

**PUMBO** (Pg.). See POMBEIRO.

**PUMPKIN GUTS** (Eng. Cr.), an Afro-Jamaican term for the nonedible inside of a pumpkin *(Cucurbita pepo)*. The blacks used magic to try to prevent the plant from growing this internal waste.

**PUNGO** (Afr.), in Brazil an aphrodisiac herb employed by black sorcerers in the Rio de Janeiro region.

**PUNTEE** (Afr.), an Afro-Jamaican term for an amulet blessed by a sorcerer, usually hung on the trees or laid down on the ground to keep thieves away from the gardens and the orchards.

**PUSS** (Eng. Cr.), in Jamaica, a black albino.

**PUSSERY** (Eng. Cr.), an Afro-Jamaican word for trickery, stealing.

**PUSS-EYE,** in the West Indies, a black albino.

**PYANGII** (Afr.). See PIANGI.

# q

**QUACO** (Afr.). In the West Indies: 1. An African day-name (q.v.) for a boy born on Wednesday. 2. A rough and ignorant black.

**QUADRILLE,** an Afro-Antilles dance thought to be an adaptation of an old French quadrille. In Martinique, it is performed by two pairs of black dancers who follow the contortions, movements, and swings indicated by a leader.

**QUADROON,** the offspring of a mulatto woman and a white man with one-quarter black blood.

**QUAKER,** a member of a religious sect founded by George Fox (q.v.). In 1671, following their founder's advice, Quakers condemned slavery in the West Indies. In 1727, the London Yearly Meeting of Quakers denounced the slave traffic and censured members who participated in it. A few years later (1758), all persons engaged in slavery were excluded from the society. The Quakers were among the most active abolitionists in England and the West Indies. (Ragatz, *The Fall*, p. 240.)

**QUAMIN, KWAAMIN** (Afr.), in the West Indies, an African day-name (q.v.) given to a boy born on Saturday.

**QUAMINA,** a black slave leader of an uprising in Demerara, a British colony, that took place on August 17, 1823. The rebels burned plantations and imprisoned planters, attorneys (q.v.), managers, and other white people. None of them was hurt or killed. While Quamina and others prepared to march to Georgetown, the capital, a fight broke out and Quamina was killed. (Jakobsson, *Am I Not*, p. 319.)

**QUAO, CAPTAIN,** a Coromantee (q.v.) black slave leader of the Maroon wars (q.v.) in Jamaica. He signed a treaty with the Jamaican authorities which ensured the liberty of all his followers and their rights to own land in the vicinity of his town (ca. 1740?). (Price, *Maroon Societies*, p. 257.)

**QUAQUA** (Afr.), in Jamaica, an African dish made of cassava or starch, mixed with pork and flavored with other ingredients. It was served to slaves in the colonial period.

**QUASÁ** (Afr.), among Colombian blacks, a tube-shaped flute made from bamboo.

**QUASHEBA.** See QUASHIBA.

**QUASHEE, QUASHI, QUASHIE** (Afr.). In the West Indies: 1. An African day-name (q.v.) for a boy born on Sunday. 2. A stupid black, a fool; a backward individual who refuses improvement. 3. A black who is crafty, artful, rarely grateful for small services, often deceitful and over-reaching. The *quashee* personality pattern includes falsehood and contempt for truth. (Cassidy, *Dictionary*).

**QUASHEE CREOLE.** See JAMAICAN ENGLISH CREOLE.

**QUASHI, QUASHIE.** See QUASHEE.

**QUASHIBA, QUASHEBA** (Afr.). In the West Indies: 1. An African day-name (q.v.) for a girl born on Sunday. 2. The mulatto concubine of a white man. 3. An uneducated black or mulatto woman.

**QUATTIE, QUATTY,** an Afro-Jamaican term for a coin worth 1½d.; also called tup, especially in western Jamaica.

**QUAW** (Afr.). In the West Indies: 1. An African day-name (q.v.) for a boy born on Thursday. 2. A stupid, ugly person; one from the remote countryside. 3. A black albino.

**QUAWY, QUAWE, QUAY** (Afr.), in Jamaica, a black albino.

**QUEEN,** in Jamaica, the reigning leader of an *obeah* (q.v.) cult. This matron, dressed with splendor, possesses some degree of authority over the other members of the sect.

**QUEEN DOVE,** a black woman leader in revivalist cults in Jamaica.

**QUEEN OF THE ANTILLES,** a name given to Saint Domingue around 1790 when it was the wealthiest French colony. It had 792 sugar estates (q.v.), a black population of 455,000, and a level of production nearly equal to that of all British tropical American possessions combined. (Ragatz, *The Fall*, p. 204).

**QUEEN OF THE CUMINA.** See MOTHER OF THE CUMINA.

**QUENG** (Afr.), an Afro-Jamaican word for a weird creature.

**QUENGA** (Afr.), in Brazil, an African dish made of okra (q.v.) and chicken.

**QUENTÃO** (Pg.), in Brazil, homemade sugar cane (q.v.) brandy with ginger sold by black women in courtyards and streets.

**QUERINO, MANOEL** (1851-1923), a black scholar and abolitionist born in San Amaro, Bahía, in July 1851. Querino voiced his convictions against slavery in a series of newspaper articles in Bahía. A gifted artist, Querino taught art and painted churches. He wrote *Artistas Bahianos* (1909); *As Artes na Bahía* (1913); and *O Colono Preto como Factor do Civilização* (1918).

**QUIABEIRO** (Pg.), in Brazil, a fruit tree *(Hibiscus)* brought from Africa during slavery times.

**QUIABO** (Pg.), the fruit of the *quiabeiro* (q.v.) tree used by blacks in magic rituals.

**QUIBANDO** (Afr.), in Brazil, a Bantu (q.v.) idiom for the first of June. (Mendonça, *A Influencia*, p. 164.)

**QUIBEBE** (Afr.), an Afro-Brazilian dish made of mashed pumpkin or potato.

**QUIBUNGO** (Afr.), in Afro-Brazilian folklore, a monster, half-man and half-animal, who swallows children through a hole in his back.

**QUIER, JOHN,** an English physician who, after studying in London and Leyden, came to Jamaica and settled at Lluida where he treated thousands of slaves in a career that spanned fifty-six years. Around 1770, Quier perfected an inoculation against smallpox and measles that greatly reduced the mortality which these two scourges caused among slaves. (Craton, *A Jamaican Plantation*, p. 133.)

**QUILOMBO** (Afr.), in colonial Brazil, an isolated and secluded settlement of runaway slaves, usually in the interior of the country. Surrounded by ditches and palisades, it was governed by an elected black chief. Food was obtained by cultivating corn, manioc, sweet potatoes, beans, and the like; the settlement also had hunting, fishing, and trading of animal skins and forest edibles for arms, clothing, and food. The size varied from fifty huts to several thousand. The first *quilombo* in Bahia dates back almost to the beginning of the slave trade in 1575. After 1750, the number of *quilombos* increased greatly. Some were well organized, and there were a few settled exclusively by black Africans. They disappeared with the abolition of slavery in 1888. The term *quilombo* came into usage in the eighteenth century. (Price, *Maroon Societies*, pp. 194-200.)

**QUILOMBOLA** (Afr.), in Brazil, a runaway slave settled in a *quilombo* (q.v.).

**QUIMAMA** (Afr.), an Afro-Brazilian dish made of wheat flour, salt, and spicy ingredients.

**QUIMBANDA** (Afr.), in Afro-Brazilian cults, the high priest of the sect, a combination of priest, sorcerer, and fortune-teller.

**QUIMBANDA CABOCLO,** among blacks of the Amazon region, the soul of a medicine man.

**QUIMBANDEIRO** (Afr.), in colonial Brazil, a black sorcerer.

**QUIMBEMBE** (Afr.), an African word for a poor hut in Brazil.

**QUIMBEMBEQUE** (Afr.), in Brazil, magic charms (q.v.) which black children wear around their necks.

**QUIMBÊTE** (Afr.), in Brazil, a black dance accompanied by percussion instruments.

**QUIMBOIS, PIAYE** (Fr. Cr.), divination by means of a magic beverage prepared by a sorcerer; sorcery. *Quimbois* is very popular among blacks in Martinique.

**QUIMBOISEUR** (Fr. Cr.), in Martinique, a black soothsayer, a practitioner of magic. See also QUIMBOIS.

**QUIMBOMBO** (Afr.), an Afro-Brazilian term for a sorcerer who sometimes acts as a priest in black cults.

**QUIMBÔTO** (Afr.), the name of a black sorcerer, one of the main characters in the Afro-Brazilian plays known as *cucumby* (q.v.). In one of the several versions, Quimbôto accompanies the prince Mameto when the queen mother sends him to the court of the powerful king of the Congo. In a confrontation between the ambassador's warriors and the king's troops, Mameto is killed, but the great Quimbôto restores him to life.

**QUIMBUMBIA** (Afr.), in Afro-Cuban folklore, a magic game usually played at night as part of religious rituals; apparently of African origin.

**QUIMBUNDA** (Afr.), a Bantu (q.v.) tongue spoken by black slaves brought from Angola (q.v.) to northeast Brazil.

**QUIMZUMBA** (Afr.), in colonial Brazil, a song-dance performed by slaves brought from Angola (q.v.).

**QUINDEMBO** (Afr.), in Cuba, a black dance.

**QUINDIM** (Afr.). In Brazil: 1. An amorous sexual longing of a mulatto girl. 2. Darling, a term of endearment. 3. An Afro-Brazilian delicacy, a kind of sweetmeat mixed with egg, coconut, and sugar.

**QUINGOMBO** (Afr.), in Brazil and elsewhere, a seed plant used by blacks for medicinal purposes and for its sweet scent or flavor. It was introduced from Africa and was documented in 1694. (Alvarez Nazario, *El elemento negroide*, p. 223.)

**QUINGUINGU** (Afr.), in colonial Brazil, the overnight cleaning by black slaves of the millstones of a sugar mill (q.v.).

**QUINTROON,** in the colonial West Indies, the offspring of a white man and a "white" black woman; practically a white person.

**QUITA-CHÉ-CHÉ** (Fr. Cr.), in Haiti, a black ritual dance to stop the rain.

**QUITANDA** (Afr.), in Brazil, a vegetable and fruit stand in a market attended by a black woman.

**QUITANDA DA YAŬO** (Afr.), in Brazil, a black *candomblé* (q.v.) ritual in which all the objects used by a female novice during her months' or year-long probation period are sold at public auction. (Ramos, *As Culturas Negras*, p. 87.)

**QUITANDEIRA** (Pg.), in Brazil, a woman who makes and sells homemade sweets and pastries in the streets; a street peddler, usually a black woman.

**QUITUBIA** (Afr.), a legendary Brazilian slave, a symbol of the Noble

Negro (q.v.), described in a famous poem written by José Basilio da Gama (q.v.) in the eighteenth century.

**QUITUTE** (Afr.), an Afro-Brazilian dish.

**QUIZILA** (Afr.), in Brazil, the repugnance that blacks feel for certain foods.

**QUIZOMBA** (Afr.), a Bantu (q.v.) wedding dance very popular in Angola, (q.v.), brought to Brazil in slavery times. It has greatly influenced typical Brazilian black dances such as *samba* (q.v.) and *batuques* (q.v.).

**QUIZUMBA** (Afr.), in colonial Brazil, melodies sung by slaves in African tongues.

# r

**RAAD** (D.), a colonial council organized in Curaçao by the Dutch government around 1673 to administer the West Indian colonies. At the beginning, the council's members were appointed by the governor, and a few were elected. But soon the planters and the slave traders gained control of the body.

**RABELLO, LAURINDO** (1826-1864), a mulatto poet born in Rio de Janeiro, the son of poverty-stricken parents. The hardships of his youth are evident in his strong sentiment of rebellion towards society; his deep-rooted feelings of frustration exploded later in his powerful and moving satires. After receiving a medical degree, he became an army physician. He died at the age of thirty-eight. His main work, *Obras Poeticas*, was published posthumously by his friends.

**RACIAL DEMOCRACY**, a concept advanced by the Brazilian scholar Gilberto Freyre (q.v.). It states that, in Brazil, the black social problem has been solved without conflict and hatred through constant racial assimilation and intermarriages among whites and blacks. (Degler, *Neither Black nor White*, p. 6.)

**RADA** (Afr.), in Haiti, a group of deities of Dahomean and Nigerian derivation. Their role during the slavery period was one of appeasers and conformists, giving solace to the exploited African masses. Although their names and number vary a great deal, all these gods are characterized by their piety, reconciliation, and thanksgiving.

**RADE** (Fr. Cr.), in Afro-Haitian cults, a religious habit worn by the faithful to fulfill a vow; usually made in the color sacred to the respective god.

**RAIMOND, JULIEN,** a mulatto born in Saint Domingue who was a wealthy planter and slaveowner. He was little concerned with the abolition of slavery and the rise of the blacks as such, but rather concentrated on demanding that the freedmen of color be accorded the same rights and privileges as the whites on the island. In 1784, he went to France as an agent for the mulatto party. He resided in southern France until 1789 or 1790 when he settled in Paris. His writings were popular, especially his published brochures against the white colonists. He wrote a well-documented book on racial discrimination entitled *Observations sur l'origine et le progrès de prejugé des colons blancs contre les hommes de couleur* (Paris, 1791).

**RAINHA DOS CONGOS** (Pg.), in colonial Brazil, in several slave religious brotherhoods, a black woman elected and crowned queen who presided at church and carnival festivities. See also REI DOS CONGOS.

**RAISING THE COLOR,** in the West Indies, a phrase justifying and sanctioning concubinage between whites and blacks as a means of elevating the blacks to the status and prestige of the whites. (M. G. Smith, *The Plural Society*, p. 138.)

**RAIZ DE GAMBÁ** (Pg.), the root of an herb *(Petiveria aliacea)*, a narcotic plant used by black sorcerers in Brazil.

**RAMADAN** (Ar.), the holy month of fasting and prayers prescribed by Islam; observed by black Moslem slaves in colonial Brazil.

**RAMBLING SHEPHERD,** in the *cumina* (q.v.) cult, a black diviner with a special knowledge of the spirit world.

**RAMSAY, JAMES** (1733-1789), a minister and philanthropist, born on July 25, 1733 in England. While Ramsay was a navy surgeon, he assisted a slaver (q.v.) infested with the plague and became absorbed with the problems of abolition. He received holy orders from the bishop of London and settled in the West Indies where he labored among the slaves for twenty years. As naval chaplain in Saint Kitts, he became embroiled with the planters when he gave the slaves religious instructions and launched an attack on the slave trade. He published a booklet entitled *Objections to the Abolition of the Slave Trade, with Answers* (1788).

**RANCHADOR, RANCHEADOR** (Sp.), in colonial Cuba, a white slave hunter who, accompanied by bloodhounds, led expeditions into the mountains in search of runaway slaves. Soon after colonization (circa 1540), the *ranchadores* became a professional group. They were very hardy, abstemious men, dressed in checked shirts, wide checked trousers, straw hats, and rawhide shoes. Each hunter kept three dogs, hunting with two of them at a time. (Klein, *Slavery*, p. 70.)

**RANCHO** (Pg.), an Afro-Brazilian Christmas play distinguished by its gaudy and showy black characters and the number of musical instruments.

**RAPARIQUEIRO** (Pg.), in colonial Brazil, a plantation owner's son.

**RAPPEL** (Fr. Cr.), in Afro-Haitian cults, a sacred drum beaten in prayer meetings. The faithful believe it is the voice of the spirits.

**RARA** (Afr.). In Haiti: 1. A black band consisting of several African and native instruments such as the *marimba* (q.v.), *lambi* (q.v.), *papaya-stem* (piston), and drums of several sizes; featured at religious and social gatherings. 2. A noisy black carnival.

**RAS** (Afr.), in Jamaica, a common abbreviation of Rastafari (q.v.).

**RASH-MAN** (Eng. Cr.), in the West Indies, a black *obeah* man (q.v.).

**RASTA MAN**, an adherent of the black Rastafari (q.v.) cult.

**RASTAFARI, RASTAFARIAN** (Afr.), in Jamaica and elsewhere, an extremist black sect whose members think of themselves as the chosen people and regard their repatriation to Africa as a matter of right. Until recently the emperor of Ethiopia was the group's god. They usually refuse to work for anyone but their own kind and claim to be different from and superior to all other blacks. The men frequently let their beards and hair grow as a mark of distinction.

**RATTLE-DRUM, RATTLER, RATTLING DRUM**, an Afro-Jamaican treble drum (the smaller of a pair of drums often played together) with which the more complex rhythms are produced, while the bass drum keeps a steady beat.

**REAL COMPAÑÍA MERCANTIL DE LA HABANA** (Sp.), a private concern formed in 1740 to take over the transportation to, and the sale of, African slaves in Cuba. It was the first attempt to boost the trade in slaves and to stir the waning interest in agriculture. It disposed of its slaves for cash, credit, or pledged crop returns. In this way, the company dominated, though never monopolized, Cuba's major exports of sugar, tobacco, and hides before 1763. (Knight, *Slave Society*, p. 9.)

**REBAMBARAMBA, LA** (Sp.), a black ballet by Cuban composer Amadeo Roldán inspired by the black musical tradition. After its first performance in Havana in 1928, at the height of the *afrocubanismo* movement (q.v.), its popularity decreased rapidly. Its rumba (q.v.) rhythm and jazz type of music made it one of the first successful attempts to create an African art in which the technical realization was subordinated to the beat and blood of the new African aesthetic.

**REBOUÇAS, ANDRÉ** (1838-1898), a black engineer and abolitionist born in Bahia on January 13, 1838. In close cooperation with other Brazilians, both white and black, Rebouças struggled to end slavery. He served in government and private enterprise, amassing a considerable fortune, part of which he spent on supporting journals, magazines, and societies that were working for the freedom of the slaves. After the fall of the monarchy in 1889, Rebouças resigned his professorship at the Escola Politécnica of Rio de Janeiro to accompany Emperor Dom Pedro II into exile. After the death of the emperor, he retired to the Azores where he died in 1898.

**RECLAME DO PIXE** (Pg.), in Bahía, a descriptive term for a very black Afro-Brazilian.

**RED,** in Jamaica, a term referring to the combination of light or yellowish skin with kinky hair or other Negroid features; often used by blacks in a derogatory sense.

**REDCAM, THOMAS HENRY MCDERMOT** (1870-1933), a black writer born in Clarendon, Jamaica, and educated at the Church of England Grammar School in Kingston. After he had already started a career as a schoolmaster, Redcam took up journalism. He migrated to the United States where he worked on newspapers and magazines in New York and San Francisco. He was a correspondent during World War I, and in 1922, he became an associate editor of Hearst International Magazine. His books include biographies, novels, and historical works such as *The Caribbean and the French in the West Indies.* Among his books of verse are *Pierrot Wounded and Other Poems* (1919) and *Pan and Peacock* (1928).

**RED DISEASE OF GUIANA,** in the West Indies, a kind of leprosy that afflicted black slaves; also called *cocobay* (q.v.).

**RED-HEAD,** in Jamaica, a tropical plant *(Asclepias curassavica)* highly valued by blacks as a medicinal herb.

**RED IBO,** in Jamaica, a light-colored person with Negroid characteristics, so-called because the Ibo (q.v.) slaves were originally of lighter color than the rest of the blacks. The term is now used in an insulting manner.

**REDI MOESOE** (D.), in colonial Surinam, a corps of black soldiers consisting of slaves who were released from bondage upon being selected for the corps. Organized in 1772, it was in charge of fighting and capturing runaway slaves. (Lier, *Frontier Society*, p. 59.)

**RED LEG,** in Barbados, a fair or white person of very low economic status.

**RED NAYGA** (Eng. Cr.), a mulatto with very light skin but kinky hair who may pass for white or Jamaica white.

**RED PEA SOUP,** a famous Afro-Jamaican dish made of red kidney beans, cabbage, tomato and pumpkin, with salt beef or pork.

**REDS AND BLUES.** See BLUES AND REDS.

**RED SKIN,** in Jamaica, a person with a light-colored (but not white) complexion; mulatto or lighter. The term is not necessarily an insult.

**RED SORREL,** in the West Indies, a tropical tree *(Hibiscus sabdariffa)* whose pods are used by blacks to make cool drinks, marmalade, and jellies.

**RED WOOD,** in the West Indies, a kind of tree with reddish wood *(Erythroxylon)*, formerly exported from Jamaica as dye-wood; also called guinea-wood (q.v.).

**REGISTRATION BILL,** an antislavery bill that the British Parliament enforced in 1819, ordering the formal enrollment of black slaves and forbidding British subjects in the United Kingdom from purchasing unlisted slaves or using them as security for loans.

**REGLAMENTO DE ESCLAVOS** ("Slaves' Law"), a law promulgated in Cuba on November 14, 1842, regulating slavery, with stringent provisions for the law's enforcement. Among its aims were to better the condition of the blacks and to render the domestic development of the race more certain. It provided for gradual manumission (q.v.) and for decreasing the African slave trade. (Aimes, *A History of Slavery*, p. 149.)

**REGLAMENTO SOBRE EDUCACIÓN, TRATO Y OCUPACIONES QUE DEBEN DAR A SUS ESCLAVOS LOS DUEÑOS O MAYORDO-MOS DE ESTA ISLA** (Sp.), a detailed slave code adopted in Puerto Rico in 1826 consisting of forty-eight articles and reflecting some of the principles of the unimplemented code of 1789. Its provisions covered five major areas: religion and hispanization, slave welfare and recreation, slaves' rights and benefits, public protection measures, and the administrative procedure for implementing the code. (Knight, *Slave Society*, p. 128.)

**REID, VICTOR STAFFORD** (b. 1913), a black journalist and novelist born and educated in Jamaica. He is one of the best known writers of works on African themes. His novel *The Leopard* (London, 1958) is an extraordinary piece of fantasy writing. Another of his works is *New Day* (New York, 1949).

**REI DOS CONGOS,** in some religious brotherhoods in colonial Brazil, a black slave elected and crowned as the presiding officer during church and secular festivities. See also RAINHA DOS CONGOS.

**RENDEIRO** (Pg.), in colonial Brazil, a free mulatto artisan.

**RENVOYÉ** (Fr. Cr.), in the Afro-Haitian religion, the ritual of banishing a spirit or a god who has been troubling a family.

**REPEATER DRUM,** in Jamaica, a small, tightly strung, double-membraned drum used by blacks to play the melody in drumming for *obeah* (q.v.) dancing.

**REPOSOIR** (Fr. Cr.), in the Afro-Haitian religion, the preferred seat of a god; this can be a tree, plant, spring, or mountain.

**REPUBLIC OF NIRGUA.** See SAN BASILIO.

**REPUBLIC OF PALMARES.** See PALMARES, REPUBLIC OF.

**REPUTED WHITE,** in colonial Jamaica, an individual categorized as belonging to the white group; a near-white usually enjoying the political and inheritance rights of the white population.

**RÉRÉ** (Afr.), in Afro-Brazilian cults, a black messenger or servant of a spirit, often a mischievous, child-like sprite. *Réré* is a transitory status of an initiate before he or she becomes a full-fledged member of the sect. (Bastide, *African Civilizations*, p. 122.)

**RESQUARDO** (Sp.), in Afro-Cuban religion, protective charms such as strings, beads, or any other object properly blessed by a sorcerer.

**REST DANCE,** in Jamaica, an inactive black dance, that features hugging but little movement.

**RETINTO** (Sp.), a derogatory term employed in Peru to identify a very dark-skinned person.

**RETIRÉ D'ÂME** (Fr. Cr.), in the Afro-Haitian religion, the ritual by which a soul is removed from the body.

**REVENANT** (Fr. Cr.), among Haitian blacks, the spirit of a neglected dead person which returns to persecute his relatives.

**REVOLUÇÃO PRAIERA** (Pg.), in Brazil, one of the last rebellions of Moslem slaves in Bahía organized by the mulatto Figereido in 1848. Its purpose was to massacre the planters, expel the Portuguese, and divide the plantations into small lots to be distributed to black slaves. (Bastide, *Les Religions africaines*, p. 142.)

**REZADOR** (Pg.), in rural Brazil, a layman, sometimes an old black, who gathers countrymen around a private chapel and leads prayers, litanies, and novenas.

**RIBEIRO, JULIO** (1845-1890), a Brazilian novelist who dealt with slavery. As a naturalist writer, his descriptions of black characters are sometimes negative. The slaves appear as irrational, dirty victims of sordid pleasures. Among his works are *A Carne* (1888) and *Os Homens de Sangue* (1889).

**RIBEIRO DA ROCHA, MANOEL,** a black Brazilian freedman and priest who studied canon law at Coimbra University, Portugal. He published *Ethiope Resgatado, Empenhado, Sustentado, Corregido, Instruido e Liberado* (q.v.) (Lisboa, 1758) in which he enthusiastically advocated the abolition of the slave trade. This was the beginning of numerous statutes and restrictive measures against the trade, which coincided with the development of the abolition movement (q.v.) in England. (Ramos, *The Negro*, p. 18.)

**RICEY COCO** (Eng. Cr.), an Afro-Jamaican dish made of rice flavored with coconut milk, sugar, and spices.

**RICH AS A CREOLE,** a popular phrase in Europe around 1785 stressing the extraordinary wealth of the Caribbean planters at the time.

**RIGAUD, ANDRÉ,** a Haitian mulatto leader, the son of a white man and a black woman. Educated in Bordeaux, France, and trained as a soldier, he enlisted as a volunteer in the French army which fought in the American War of Independence. After returning to Saint Domingue, he practiced his goldsmith trade until the outbreak of the slave revolt. He fought with Toussaint L'Ouverture (q.v.), but, in a power struggle, he lost his position. In 1801, he fled to France. Napoleon deported him to Madagascar.

**RIGAUD, MILO** (b. 1904), a Haitian poet inspired by Afro-American folklore. As a follower of Price-Mars (q.v.), Rigaud was very interested in writing about the daily life of the black peasants and voodoo (q.v.). Among his works are *Rites et rythmes* (Vienne, 1932); *Jésus ou Legba, ou Les dieux se battent* (Poitiers, 1933); and *Tassos* (1933).

**RIGHTS OF ENGLISHMEN,** a political movement organized by Jamaican planters in 1831 who claimed for themselves basic political rights, such as making laws for their own government by their own representatives as did the people of England.

**RIMLAND,** a cultural term applied by geographers to the Euro-African-Caribbean region as opposed to the Euro-Indian Mainland. This delimitation is based in part upon the racial makeup of the population of the two segments. In general, the dominant strain of the Rimland is Negroid, or part Negroid, even where blacks do not form a majority as in Cuba, Puerto Rico, and some segments of the Caribbean coast of Central America. The racial differentiation is only a symptom, however, of the far more important contrasts which stem from cultural orientation, human habitat, and the economic and political organization of land and population.

**RING,** in Jamaica, a black game played by a ring of players.

**RING PLAY,** in Jamaica, a playing of games by a ring of players as at wakes, nine-night (q.v.), and similar occasions.

**RING SONG,** in the West Indies, a folk tune sung by slaves. A soloist and a chorus often expressed laments or complaints about an overseer's harsh treatment. The song was usually improvised.

**RINGWORM,** in the West Indies, any of several fungi causing a contagious disease of the skin. The disease afflicted a great number of black slaves. It was characterized by ring-shaped, discolored body patches covered with blisters and scales, and by disorders of the scalp.

**RINGWORM BUSH,** in the West Indies, a tropical shrub *(Cassia alata)*, the juice of whose leaves was used by slaves to cure infections caused by ringworm (q.v.).

**RINGWORM YAWS,** in the West Indies, one of the effects of yaws (q.v.) that scourged slaves; it resembled ringworm (q.v.) infections.

**RIPE BANANA** (Eng. Cr.), in the West Indies, a black albino.

**RITI** (Afr.), in the French Antilles, an African monochord viola played by blacks to accompany satirical songs.

**RIO BRANCO LAW.** See LEI DO RIO BRANCO.

**RIVER MAID,** in West Indian folklore, a black female deity associated with rivers and streams who is worshipped in revivalist sects and for whom propitiatory offerings are left at springs and deep holes; also known as *maman de l'eau* in Saint Lucia and Granada. Another synonym is river mumma.

**RIVIEL, EL,** among blacks of the Colombian Pacific lowlands, a ghostly cannibal, a dangerous "living-dead," who is able to move freely in the world, on the sea, in Hell, in the sky, and in other worlds.

**RIVIÈRE, ROMAINE,** a black female slave who, around 1792, gathered a large number of slaves and attacked Léogâne, a village in Martinique. She proclaimed herself a prophetess and daughter of the Virgin Mary. (Fouchard, *Les Marrons*, p. 538.)

**ROÇA** (Pg.), in colonial Brazil, a small cultivated plot near the plantation center where slaves raised coffee, corn, and beans for their own consumption.

**ROCHA, JOSÉ JOAQUÍN DA,** a black Brazilian painter in Bahia who was at the height of his career around 1777. Da Rocha was a master in the development of polychrome imagery. One of his best paintings is "The Visitation" which he painted for the main altar of the Church of Santa Clara da Misericordia in Bahia, Brazil.

**ROCHELA** (Pg.), in colonial Brazil, a settlement organized in the wilderness by fugitive slaves. A *rochela* sometimes became so large and its leaders so aggressive that it threatened nearby towns. See also ARINGA; PALENQUE; QUILOMBO.

**RODA,** in colonial Brazil, a foundling asylum where many mulatto children of masters and their black mistresses were raised.

**RODRÍGUEZ, AGUSTIN BALDOMERO** (1826-1862), a black Cuban poet born in Villaclara. Rodríguez was the son of a cobbler. Unable to attend school, he taught himself to write and read. His book of verses,

*Pucha Silvestre*, is a sad autobiography of his unhappy childhood. (Calcagno, *Diccionario*, p. 550.)

**RODRÍGUEZ, LUIS FELIPE,** a Cuban writer who published a short story, "Danza Lucumí," in the *Revista Avance* of February 1930. The tale describes an old black, a cane cutter all his life, who between his bouts of drunkenness remembers how he and his father "were brought from Africa and were dumped on the Cuban shores, like sacks of dried meat."

**RODRIGUEZ, MANUEL DEL SOCORRO** (1758-1818), a mulatto scientist, newspaperman, and poet born in Bayamo, Cuba, on April 1, 1758. While working as a carpenter, Rodriguez learned to read and write. In 1783, a special tribunal awarded him a degree in sciences and mathematics. He was taken to Bogotá, Nueva Granada, by the viceroy, José de Ezpeleta y Veyre, and appointed librarian in that city. There Rodriguez participated in the publication of several papers, including *El Semanario* (1781), *Papel Periódico* (1791), *Correo Curioso* (1795), and *Redactor Americano de Bogotá*. He was a co-founder with José Caldas of the Observatorio Astronómico where he taught cosmography until his death. Baron von Humboldt visited the observatory and praised Rodriguez for his work. Among his published writings are *Elogios en honor de Carlos III* (New York, 1827); *Las delicías de España* (poems); and *La Constitución feliz* (circa 1812). (Calcagno, *Diccionario*, p. 546.)

**ROGUING JOE** (Eng. Cr.), in Jamaica, a bag carried on the shoulders to stow pilfered things; also the black man who carries one.

**ROLLING-CALF,** in Afro-Antilles folklore, an imaginary monster in the form of a calf with fiery eyes who haunts the roads at night. Wicked people are said to "turn rolling-calf" when they die.

**ROLL ROCK-STONE,** an Afro-Jamaican song-game in which twelve players sit in a circle. The leader sings the song, and the others join the chorus while passing around the circle, from player to player, stones about the size of bricks. (Cassidy, *Jamaica Talk*, p. 275.)

**ROMANS AFRICAINS** (Fr.), African tales popular in Western Europe around 1750-1780.

**RONDE** (Fr. Cr.), in rural Haiti, the amount of collective work that can be done, usually on a reciprocal basis, by a small group of black peasants in half a day. It is a system of mutual aid in agriculture by which a group of men band together to work on each member's land in turn.

**RONIER, RONDIER,** in the French Antilles, a tall tropical palm whose leaves produce a kind of syrup or palm wine, a favorite black beverage.

**ROPER, THOMAS,** a Jamaican mulatto sergeant who, in 1805, was tried and condemned for mutiny in Spanish Town, Jamaica. At the age of sixty, he was fined 4,000 pounds and sentenced to two years in solitary confinement for abusing his colonel in the militia and "white people in general." (Brathwaite, *The Development*, p. 195.)

**ROOKAW** (Afr.), in Jamaica, a crude musical instrument similar to the jawbone. It is played in black revivalist and Pocomania (q.v.) cults.

**ROSIERS, COMTE DE** (1766-1828), a black political leader and poet born in Jacmel, Haiti. He is also known as Juste Chanlatte. Rosiers was an ardent follower of King Christophe (q.v.), but at Christophe's death he joined his enemies and enrolled in the Republican party. Later he became the editor of *Telegraphe*, the official periodical of the country. Among his works are *Recueil de chants et de couplets* (Sans Souci, Haiti) and *Poèmes patriotiques*.

**ROUMAIN, JACQUES** (1907-1944), a black Haitian writer, journalist, and political leader. Born of an aristocratic family, he was educated in Port-au-Prince and Europe. With other intellectuals of his generation, he studied at the University of Paris. In 1927, he returned to Haiti. Roumain became a co-founder of *La Revue Indigène* (1927-1928), a literary journal that gave its name to the neo-Haitian movement called *Indigénisme*. He was attracted by the aesthetic and cultural aspects of black primitivism and wanted to rehabilitate black tradition, both in Africa and in the New World, as a basis for a constructive projection towards the future. Among his works are *Bois d'ébène* (Port-au-Prince, 1939); *La Montagne ensorcelée* (Port-au-Prince, 1931); *Les Fantoches* (Port-au-Prince, 1931); and *Gouverneurs de la rosée 1896-1907* (Port-au-Prince, 1944). See also *ECOLE INDIGÉNISTE.*

**ROUMER, EMILE** (b. 1903), a poet born in Jérémie, Haiti, associated with *La Revue Indigène* (1927-1928). He was inspired by black peasant life, its customs and traditions. As in his poem "Marabout de mon coeur," he praises the mulatto girls for their beauty and simplicity and, in the fashion of the movement, is touched by the serenity of the black woman. Among his works are *Poèmes d'Haïti et de France* (1909) and *La Chanson des lambis* (1928).

**ROUND-THATCH PALM,** in the West Indies, a thatch palm (family *Arecaceae*) with round (rather than long) leaves used by blacks to build their huts.

**ROUPA DE-VER-A-DEUS** (Pg.), in colonial Brazil, the Sunday-best clothes worn by blacks slaves to attend church services.

**ROWING SHANTIES,** in the West Indies, traditional black tunes sung while sailing into the open sea to fish or when the men return home with their catch. The captain usually leads the song, and the crew answers in chorus.

**ROYAL AFRICAN COMPANY,** an English commercial company organized in 1663 for purposes of trade between England, the west coast of Africa, and the West Indies. Several members of the royal family were shareholders in this enterprise, which, for a quarter of a century, enjoyed a national monopoly handling slaves. Between 1690 and 1713, this company provided Jamaica with 34,480 slaves. It was suppressed in 1750 when the slave trade was taken over by a committee of merchants with the help of government subsidies. (Mannix, *Black Cargoes*, p. 69.)

**ROYAL MAROON,** a black born and settled in central Jamaica, a descendant of former slaves. See also MAROON.

**ROYAL TIMBIN.** See TIMBIN.

**RUBANIERS** (Fr. Cr.), in Haiti, bands of male black dancers, some of them attired as women, who wave their colored ribbons around portable poles. Also called Maypole dancers.

**RUCUMBO** (Pg.), an Afro-Brazilian musical instrument consisting of a flexible arch with a wire; played with a bow.

**RUDENESS** (Eng. Cr.), in Jamaica, a term for sexual intercourse, a term used mainly by blacks.

**RUM** (Pg.), in Brazil, a big drum played by blacks in fetish rituals.

**RUMBA** (Afr.), an Afro-Cuban song-dance of varied rhythms, often with a different pattern in every bar. In the slums of Havana, the *rumba* is often accompanied by a musical ensemble of domestic utensils such as bottles, pans, and spoons. It is a carnival dance and is frequently used as a political campaign song.

**RUMBA BOX,** an Afro-Antilles musical instrument that stimulates the tones of the base viol. It consists of four pieces of metal of different gauges attached to a box (the resonance chamber); the pieces vibrate when they are plucked with the fingers and are tuned to correspond to the strings.

**RUMMARIAN** (Eng. Cr.), in Jamaica, a black who habitually drinks too much rum.

**RUMPI** (Pg.), a medium-sized Afro-Brazilian drum played by blacks in religious and secular festivities.

**RUNDOWN,** in Jamaica, a sauce made by boiling coconut down until it resembles custard. Salt or pickled fish, banana, or other ingredients may be added. It is served in a bowl in the middle of the table into which bread is dipped. It is favorite black delicacy.

**RUN DUPPY,** among Afro-Jamaicans, the ritual used to drive away an evil spirit in revivalist meetings.

**RUNNING YAWS,** among former West Indian slaves, a variety of crab-yaws (q.v.) characterized by peeling and fissuring of the sole of the foot and its periphery.

**RYDIM** (Eng. Cr.), among West Indian blacks, the hips or buttocks, so-called because of their swaying motion.

**RYGIN** (Eng. Cr.), in Jamaica, a word for angry, heated; used mainly by blacks.

# S

**SÁ, JOSÉ BERNARDINO DE,** a Portuguese slave trader who, around 1834-1835, established a trade post with agents south of the equator to buy slaves for the Brazilian market. He used English fabrics for his bartering and the Portuguese flag for his ships, and had no difficulties with the British cruisers patrolling the African coast to confiscate slavers. Sá was knighted by the Portuguese government with the title of Baron de Vila Nova do Minho. (Rodrigues, *Brazil and Africa*, p. 179.)

**SAB,** a romantic antislavery novel by the Cuban writer Gertrudis Goméz de Avellaneda (1841) in which the hero, Sab, a mulatto slave, is depicted at the same time as a Noble Negro (q.v.) and a rebellious one, a victim of white society. The novel condemns slavery as an institution which destroys the life of generous men like Sab. The book appeared ten years before Harriet Beecher Stowe's *Uncle Tom's Cabin* (1851).

**SABÃO DA COSTA** (Pg.) ("soap from the Coast"), in colonial Brazil, special soap imported from Africa in slavery times.

**SABBAT-FOOT,** in Jamaica, a lame or deformed foot, presumably that of a slave unable to work on Saturdays.

**SABINADA,** a slave rebellion organized in Bahia, Brazil, in 1837 by Sabino Alvares da Rocha Vieira, a mulatto physician who was a leader of the abolition movement (q.v.) in Brazil.

**SABLE VENUS,** a romantic, sensuous young black girl who is the subject of a painting by Thomas Stothard of the Royal Academy (circa 1792) bearing the title "The Voyage of the Sable Venus from Angola to the West Indies." In the painting, the ship that carries the Sable Venus is an immense scallop shell in which she sits upright on a velvet throne. Later the canvas was reproduced with an anonymous poem boasting that the black beauty yields nothing to Botticelli's white Venus and that slave women are preferable to English girls at night, being both passionate and accessible. (Mannix, *Black Cargoes*, pp. 112-13.)

**SABO** (Afr.), in the West Indies, a bean *(Fevillea cordifobia)* used by blacks as an antidote against infection.

**SACI-PERERÊ** (Pg.), in Brazil, a mythical being, a little black with one leg who, according to popular belief, pursues travelers or lies in ambush for them.

**SACKA** (Eng. Cr.), an Afro-Jamaican word for a loose gown worn by black women.

**SACO, JOSÉ ANTONIO** (1797-1878), a writer born on May 7, 1797, in Bayamo, Cuba. As a member of a wealthy family, Saco was educated in Havana and the United States. Later he traveled widely in Europe and lived in Madrid. Saco was a nationalist and fought hard for the independence of the island and the abolition of slavery. Among his works are *Supresión del tráfico de esclavos en la isla de Cuba* (1845) and *Historia de la esclavitud desde los tiempos más remotos hasta nuestros días* (1893).

**SACUÉ** (Afr.), in Brazil, a species of Angola (q.v.) fowl.

**SADACA DO ALAMBI** (Ar.) ("I offer this [a ring] in the name of God"), a ritual statement made by a bridegroom while taking a bride in a Moslem ceremony held by Hausa slaves (q.v.) in colonial Brazil. (Ramos, *As Culturas Negras*, p. 146.)

**SAGABAMO** (Afr.), an assistant judge among Moslem Hausa slaves (q.v.) in Brazil.

**SAGO** (Afr.), an African grass brought to Brazil during the slavery period; also known as *santo* grass.

**SAGWA** (Afr.), in the West Indies, a black stage show performed by a medicine man who paints his face, charms snakes, and sells ointment.

**SAIA GRANDE** (Pg.), in Brazil, a large, full skirt of varying combinations of colors, ordinarily some twelve to fifteen feet in circumference at the hem; it is worn bouffant, spread out by a heavily starched underskirt. This was a popular costume among mulatto women in Bahía until the end of the nineteenth century. (Pierson, *Negroes*, p. 246.)

**SAINT,** in the West Indies, an abolitionist whose activities incited the greatest indignation among planters.

**SAINT JOHN,** in Afro-Haitian religion, a nervous god, a wanderer without a fixed abode who is usually dressed in a black and white silk robe. His favorite foods are black cattle and white sheep, and he drinks champagne and other alcoholic beverages.

**SAINVILLE, LEONARD** (b. 1910), a historian born of poor parents in Lorrain, Martinique. After attending schools and teaching on the island, Sainville left for France in 1931. Following his graduation from the Sorbonne in Paris, he was drafted into the army. In 1939, he wrote a dissertation about the social conditions of the French-speaking blacks in the Antilles. After being a professor in Paris for twenty-one years, he left for Senegal (q.v.) to pursue his investigations in African history. Among his published works are *Victor Schoelcher* (1950); *Dominique, nègre esclave* (1951); and *Au fond du bourg: Romanciers et conteurs africains* (anthology, v. I, 1963; v. II, 1968.)

**SAKA** (Afr.), in Brazil, gifts exchanged among Moslem Hausa slaves (q.v.).

**SAKARA** (Afr.), in Trinidad, a sacrifice to the spirits of the ancestors; of African origin.

**SAKU** (Eng. Cr.), in the West Indies, a crocus bag (q.v.) carried by blacks; the term is also found in the Gullah dialect in the United States.

**SALABANDA** (Afr.), in Afro-Cuban religion, a major god identified with Saint Peter.

**SALACIÓN** (Sp.), in Afro-Cuban religion, a black magic incantation or spell cast by a black sorcerer to cause illnesses and suffering.

**SALAH** (Ar.), in Brazil, a prayer which, according to Moslem usage, was to be recited five times a day while kneeling and facing Mecca.

**SALAH PUBLICA** (Ar.), the public prayer meeting of Moslem slaves in Brazil led by the *imam* (q.v.).

**SALALAI-ALEI-ISALAMA** (Ar.) ("Unique and True God, you are our Guiding Prophet!"), a Moslem prayer recited by Hausa slaves (q.v.) in Brazil.

**SALANDAIN, SALIDAIN,** in Jamaica, a wild plant *(Bocconia frutescens)* used by blacks for cleaning floors. Also called John-Crow (q.v.) bush.

**SALDANHA, JOSÉ DE NATIVIDADE** (1796-1830), a mulatto poet born in Pernambuco, Brazil, the son of a priest and a mulatto girl. While studying at the University of Coimbra, Portugal, Saldanha wrote poetry, later published under the title, *Poesias*, in which he praised black heroes such as Henrique Dias (q.v.). He was an ardent nationalist and participated in an unsuccessful attempt to organize the Republic of the Equator (1824) in the Northeast. After defeat he was forced into exile and lived in various European countries and in the United States.

**SALIDAIN.** See SALANDAIN.

**SALLO, SALO** (Afr.), in Jamaica, a black feast and dance gathering.

**SALLY WATER,** in Jamaica, a phrase from the refrain of the song "Little Sally Water" and from several black games. It has its origin in English children's games.

**SALO.** See SALLO.

**SALT,** in the colonial West Indies, the allowance of salt meat or fish given out to each slave at stated times. Each black was legally entitled to a weekly provision of salt.

**SALT-FISH,** in the West Indies, a codfish preserved with salt which was imported from the North American colonies; a staple food for slaves.

**SALTO ATRÁS** (Sp.), in the Spanish colonies, an offspring with Negroid features born in a white family. He was considered to be a step backward in the racial lineage.

**SALTWATER CREOLE** (Eng. Cr.), a black offspring born to slaves on the voyage from Africa to the West Indies.

**SALTWATER NEGRO,** in the West Indies, a black slave born in Africa and brought across the ocean; he was considered to be proud and recalcitrant. Unlike many Creole slaves (q.v.), the saltwater Negroes had a tendency to run away and take to the hills.

**SAMAMBAIA** (Afr.), a type of weed brought from Africa to Brazil in slavery times.

**SAMBA** (Pg.), in modern Brazil, a generic term used to refer to any airs and dances characterized by a vivid rolling rhythm and loosely danced in fast tempo. It has several regional variations called by different names such as *samba-carioca* and *samba-canção*.

**SAMBA-MPUNGI** (Afr.), in Afro-Cuban religion, a major god of the *mayombé* cult (q.v.).

**SAMBANGA** (Afr.), an Afro-Brazilian word for a foolish or stupid person who often comes by as an uninvited guest.

**SAMBÉ** (Afr.), in Cuba, a children's game of African origin.

**SAMBÍ** (Afr.), in Afro-Cuban music, a string instrument with a drum case; played with a bow.

**SAMBO** (Afr.), in the colonial West Indies, the offspring of a mulatto and a black, thought to be about three-quarters black.

**SAMBO BACKRA** (Afr.), in colonial times in the West Indies, a term of respect for a *sambo* (q.v.). See also BACKRA.

**SAMBUMBIA** (Afr.). 1. An Afro-Cuban beverage made of sugar syrup, popular in the eighteenth century. 2. In the modern Afro-Antilles, a cheap, fermented palm wine.

**SAMFAI** (Afr.), in Jamaica, an *obeah* man (q.v.) or other person professing to have magic power.

**SAMMY BLACKIE,** in the West Indies, a dark-skinned person.

**SAN BASILIO,** a famous runaway slave settlement in the highlands near the city of Cartagena, organized by a black slave, probably an African native, named Dionisio (or Domingo) Bioho. Between 1599-1606 he led attacks on nearby *haciendas* (q.v.) and terrorized travelers attempting to journey inland from Cartagena. A number of expeditions against the rebels failed miserably. Therefore in 1612 and 1613 Governor Diego Fernández de Velasco offered amnesty and freedom to all who would abandon the settlement. Among those who did was Bioho, who later was accused of sedition and was arbitrarily imprisoned and executed in 1619. (Rout, L.B., *The African Experience in Spanish America*, p. 110.)

**SÁNCHEZ, JOSÉ,** a Cuban mulatto who, around 1660, distinguished himself as a volunteer soldier in the militia. He saw duty at the Havana fortress in the defense of Matanzas against European forces and in campaigns against runaway slaves in the mountains. Sanchez, like other mulatto soldiers, took part in expeditions to Florida in defense of Saint Augustine. He retired from service with the rank of captain. (Klein, *Slavery*, p. 215.)

**SANCHO, IGNATIUS** (1729-1780), a black born on board a slaver (q.v.) while traveling from the African coast to the West Indies. He was brought to England as a child and raised in the Western tradition. He was a protegé of the duke of Montagu. After having served the family as a butler for over twenty years, he then wrote a book based on letters he exchanged with several prominent people, including Laurence Sterne and the duchess of Kent. They were published under the title *Letters of the Late Ignatius Sancho, an African; To which are Prefixed Memoirs of his Life* (2 v., London, 1782).

**SANCHY,** in the West Indies, the name given to a slave converted to Methodism around 1815 when it was a force in the abolition of slavery.

**SANCTIONES CONCILLI DOMINICANI, 1622** (The Ordinances of the Council of the Dominican Friars), one of the first religious councils in the New World concerned specifically with the basic task of determining if the black slaves had been properly admitted into the church. It ordered that the baptism must be repeated if the slave had been sprinkled with holy water by the traders in Africa or on the sea. It established that, at a slave's wedding, two blessings should be given. It also demanded that no master put slaves to work on festive days under penalty of a fine of 10 silver pounds for the first transgression. (Klein, *Slavery*, p. 92.)

**SANDOVAL, ALONSO DE** (1576-1652), a Spanish-born Jesuit brought to Lima, Peru, at the age of six by his widower father. In 1593, he joined the Society of Jesus. Around the same time he went to Cartagena de Indias to work with the slaves. He was a mentor of his assistant Pedro Claver (see EL APÓSTOL DE LOS NEGROS). His labors among the slaves who arrived and lived in the city during the first half of the seventeenth century formed the experimental background for his theoretical and practical work, *De Instauranda Aetiopum Saluti: Naturaleza, Policia Sagrada i Profana, Costumbrei, Ritos, Disciplina i catechismo evangelico de todos etiopes* (Seville, 1627). The work is divided into four books. Book I deals with the history and geography of Africa; Book II outlines the evils under which the black suffers; and Books III and IV discuss the practical side of the black slave ministry in the New World.

**SANDUNGA** (Afr.), an Afro-Cuban term for a mulatto girl, considered to be an ideal sexual partner.

**SANGA** (Afr.), among Bush Negroes (q.v.) in Guiana, a gang of men armed with guns, machetes, and spears who rush headlong into an attack, the method of warfare used in Africa in the past.

**SANGAREE,** an oath taken among slaves to stick by each other, made by sucking a few drops of each other's blood. The *sangaree* was a widespread custom among black slaves brought from West Africa to the New World. (Dow, *Slave Ships*, p. 176.)

**SANG-MÊLÉ,** in colonial Saint Domingue, a mulatto, the offspring of a white man and a mulatto woman. The Code Noir (q.v.), promulgated in 1685, placed no restrictions upon inheritance of property by a *sang-mêlé*, whether legitimate or not.

**SANIM, LUIZ,** a Brazilian Moslem Hausa slave (q.v.), a leading chief in the massive uprising of slaves that took place in Bahia in 1835. He was tried and sentenced to 600 lashes. (Ramos, *The Negro*, p. 50.)

**SANKEY HYMN,** among Jamaican blacks, a hymn accompanied by the beat of a drum; it is sung at wakes on the night of a death.

**SANROMA, JOAQUÍN,** a Puerto Rican Abolitionist, one of the founders of the Sociedad Abolicionista Española (q.v.) in Madrid in 1864. For a brief period in 1879, he was president of the society.

**SANSA** (Afr.), in Brazil, an African musical instrument played by slaves.

**SANSAN** (Afr.), in Trinidad, a dish made of pounded corn mixed with salt or sugar and eaten dry, mainly by blacks.

**SANS MAMAN** (Fr. Cr.), in rural Haiti, the poorest, landless black peasant.

**SANTA** (Eng. Cr.), in Jamaica, a drink prepared with fruit juice, sugar, rum, and other ingredients; formerly a favorite of slaves.

**SANTA CRUZ Y ESPEJO, FRANCISCO JAVIER EUGENIO** (1740 or 1747-1796), a mulatto scholar and man of letters born in Quito, Ecuador. His father was an Indian and his mother a mulatto daughter of a slave. At twenty years of age he graduated as a doctor of medicine. He died in prison where he had been sent because of his revolutionary writings.

**SANTERÍA** (Sp.), in Cuba, a black cult centered in the worship of Christian saints and African deities, predominantly Yoruba (q.v.) from Nigeria or

Lucumi. It is a growing sect and has spread throughout the entire island. Its membership is mainly black and mulatto.

**SANTERO** (Sp.), in the Afro-Cuban *santería* (q.v.), a black leader of the cult. His house is used by the faithful to pray, dance, and eat the sacred food put out for the saints.

**SÃO TOMÉ,** a small, offshore island in the Gulf of Guinea (q.v.) occupied by the Portuguese around 1471. From here, early in the seventeenth century, the sugar cane (q.v.) plantation system was introduced into Brazil. Soon after, it was converted into a slave-trading base. In 1532, the Portuguese Crown granted each Brazilian planter the right to import a maximum of 120 slaves from São Tomé. Slaves were bartered nearly exclusively for sugar. The French sacked the port in 1709. (Ramos, *The Negro*, p. 17.)

**SARÁ** (Ar.), in Brazil, a religious service performed by black Moslems.

**SARAMAKAN,** a dialect spoken by Bush Negroes (q.v.) in the upper reaches of the Surinam or Saramakka River. It appears to be a tonal language, containing Portuguese, English, and African elements (especially Kikongo). The total number of speakers of Saramakan does not exceed 20,000.

**SARARÁ** (Afr.), in northeast Brazil, a light-skinned black with reddish or blondish, but kinky hair; facial features may vary.

**SASABONSUM** (Afr.), in Jamaica, an African god whose favorite residence is the giant silk-cotton tree (q.v.). He is feared as the witches' god, who can give magic powers to his faithful.

**SAUDADE** (Pg.), among Luso-Brazilians especially in the colonial period, homesickness and nostalgia, a deep sadness and longing for the homeland that deeply pervades the Brazilian character. See also BANZO.

**SAVAGE AFRICA,** a stereotype that originated late during the slave trade when the original (fifteenth and sixteenth centuries) attitudes of equality and mutual respect between Africans and Europeans vanished. The white slave traders took advantage of the strife among African chieftains to increase the profitable slave traffic. Finally, in the nineteenth century, outright invasion and occupation brought a belief in European superiority over wild Africa. Enslavement was then thought to be a means of civilizing savage black Africans. (Davidson, *Black Mother*, p. 160.)

**SCHOLTEN, PETER CARL FREDERICK VON** (1784-1854), a Danish nobleman, governor of Saint Thomas in 1823 and of all the Virgin islands in 1827. Von Scholten was known for his compassion for the slaves whose emancipation he proclaimed in 1848. This action was so unpopular with the planters that he resigned and submitted himself to trial in Denmark. He was acquitted of all charges on April 29, 1852. The mulatto Anne Helgaard (q.v.) was his mistress. (Farr, *Historical Dictionary*, p. 120.)

**SCIENCE,** in Jamaica, *obeah* (q.v.).

**SCIENCE MAN,** in Afro-Jamaican cults, an *obeah* man (q.v.).

**SCOTTISH MISSIONARY SOCIETY,** a society that undertook work among the slaves in the West Indies before emancipation. Three workers arrived in Jamaica in 1800, but two died shortly after landing, and the third, losing heart, became a teacher. A quarter of a century later, the organization had not yet resumed its activities on the island. (Ragatz, *The Fall*, p. 282.)

**SCRAMBLE,** a slave trader's practice of selling healthy blacks by setting standard prices for each man, woman, boy and girl in the cargo. Once the prices were agreed upon with purchasers, the purchasers scrambled for their pick of the slaves. (Mannix, *Black Cargoes*, p. 129.)

**SCRAPER,** in Jamaica, a crude musical instrument similar in principle to the jawbone. It consists of a corrugated stick across which a smooth stick is rubbed. It is played by blacks in revivalist cults.

**SCRATCH COCO** (Eng. Cr.), in the West Indies, wild varieties of *coco (Colocasia)* used by blacks to scratch the mouth or throat.

**SCRATCH-SCRATCH, KRACH-KRACH** (Eng. Cr.), in the West Indies, a skin disease that causes one to scratch continually; it afflicted slaves.

**SCRATCH WITHE,** in Jamaica, a kind of withe pudding used by blacks as a plaster for itchy skin conditions.

**SCREECH-OWL,** in the West Indies, a black albino.

**SEAL,** in Jamaica, in black balm-yard (q.v.) rituals, a sort of altar on the ground. It is consecrated, and the priestess of the cult often works on the seal and draws visions.

**SEA-LETTER,** an official U.S. document authorizing a foreign ship to fly the American flag and giving her immunity from inspection by warships in the crossing between Africa and the New World. Many slavers (q.v.) took advantage of this protection. From 1834 to 1836, the American consul in Havana, Cuba, openly issued sea-letters to any slave ship requesting them. It is believed that two-thirds of the slavers on the African Coast claiming American nationality were provided with this document. (Mannix, *Black Cargoes*, p. 208.)

**SEA-MAHMY,** in Afro-Jamaican folklore, a mermaid, a mythical creature believed to inhabit the sea and the streams.

**SEASONING OF SLAVES,** the process of full acclimatization of the slaves in the New World. In the West Indies, this period lasted three years. It has been estimated that one-fourth of the blacks who reached Jamaica around 1788 died during the first eleven months of seasoning, mostly by suicide. (Ragatz, *The Fall*, p. 87.)

**SEA YAM,** in the West Indies, a species of big, white yam (q.v.) *(Dioscorea)* possibly brought from Africa in slavery times.

**SEBASTIANISMO** (Pg.) ("Sebastianism"), a conviction held by Sebastianistas (q.v.) that King Sebastian of Portugal, killed in the battle of Alcácer-Quibir (1578), Morocco, shall return to his throne which was taken after his death by King Philip II of Spain. Later it came to mean a firm hope that in times of social struggle and political unrest, a saviour will appear to save oppressed people. *Sebastianismo* has been a recurrent phenomenon in Brazilian politics. See also SEBASTIANISTA.

**SEBASTIANISTA** (Pg.) ("Sebastianist"), a firm believer that King Sebastian of Portugal, killed in the battle of Alcácer-Quibir, (1578), Morocco will return as a saviour to rescue his oppressed people. *Sebastianistas* have appeared from time to time during social unrests as a powerful force.

**SEBLEJACK** (Eng. Cr.), in the West Indies, a tropical climbing shrub *(Paulinian barbadensis* and *P. jamaicensis)* used to make whips in slavery times.

**SECKEY.** See SEKI.

**SECONDARY WHITE,** any white settler in Jamaica and the West Indies around 1820, either a lesser landed proprietor or an employee on a plantation or in a commercial house. He frequently had black slave concubines and educated his offspring by sending the sons to schools in England and the daughters to local institutions. (M. G. Smith, *The Plural Society*, p. 94.)

**SECOND GANG,** on West Indian plantations, the slave gang (q.v.) of medium strength, composed of young boys and girls who were employed chiefly in weeding the canes, carrying fodder, caring for animals, and doing other work adapted to their stamina. A mulatto foreman supervised them.

**SECONDIER** (Fr. Cr.), in the Afro-Haitian religion, the player of a small drum.

**SECOND TABLE,** in the black Pocomania (q.v.) cult, the second phase of the service when the Bible is removed and fallen angels are invoked; it is followed by tramping and possession.

**SEDE** (Pg.), on a Brazilian plantation, the nucleus of buildings, including the mill and its installations, the planter's residence, slave quarters, storehouses, and vegetable gardens.

**SEIGNING** (Eng. Cr.), in the West Indies, a cooperative fishing group engaged in catching schools of small fish that come close to the shore. The nets are thrown by crews of six black fishermen; each man on the beach commonly belongs to one (or more) crews. (Abrahams, *Deep the Water*, p. 26.)

**SEIGNORIAL SLAVOCRACIA** (Pg.), a term applied by some historians to the paternalistic plantation social order based on a landed aristocracy and slavery and established in Brazil from its colonization to the abolition of slave labor in 1888.

**SEITA** (Pg.), an Afro-Brazilian cult center with a large, lower class congregation and a highly complex organization of ritual and belief. The older and more respected *seitas* are commonly considered to be of Nagó (q.v.) (Yoruba) or Gêgé (q.v.) (Ewe) origin, or represent a fusion in Brazil of these two apparently closely related ethnic groups. In some of these sects, the ceremonies are carried out in Bantu (q.v.)-based dialects.

**SEITA MALÊ** (Pg.), a Moslem sect organized by Hausa slaves (q.v.) in different urban centers in colonial Brazil.

**SEKI, SECKEY** (Afr.), in Jamaica, a black female concubine.

**SEMANA YORUBA** (Pg.), in Brazil, a week of four days, following the Yoruba (q.v.) calendar observed by black slaves.

**SENEGAL,** the name of both the river and free republic in Africa. The mouth of the Senegal River was explored by the Portuguese around 1451. In the first quarter of the sixteenth century, traders frequently ventured to the upper part of the river, populated by black ethnic groups, to barter for gold, ivory, and slaves. After 1700, Portuguese and other Europeans began establishing trading posts on the banks of the river and its effluents to buy slaves for the New World market.

**SENEGALESE SLAVES,** a generic term applied to black slaves brought from the Senegal River region to the West Indies and elsewhere. In the eighteenth century, some planters considered them to be the brightest of all African slaves, well fitted for the trades and domestic service. They became good drivers (q.v.), were dependable, and could be easily disciplined, but were not thought capable of performing arduous labor. (Ragatz, *The Fall*, p. 85.)

**SENEGAMBIA,** the westernmost projection of Africa, essentially the land between two navigable rivers, the Senegal (q.v.) (controlled by the French) and the Gambia (controlled by the English). According to European geographers of the eighteenth century, it was populated in the north by the Moslem Fula herdsmen, the Wolof (see GELOFE), and the tall and slender Serer, and south of the Gambia by the Felup, with the Mandingo farmers and merchants living in wide sections of the interior.

**SENHOR DE BONFIM,** in Bahia, Brazil, a famous shrine where Our Lord of the Happy Death was worshipped, mainly by slaves. Today it is the center of devotion of the black and mulatto population.

**SENHOR DE ENGENHO** (Pg.), in colonial Brazil, the proprietor of a sugar plantation.

**SEÑOR DE CUADRILLA,** in colonial Colombia, the owner of a slave gang (q.v.) working in the mines. The *señor de cuadrilla* fed and clothed his men adequately and took care of the sick. Each slave usually received six plantains (q.v.) a day, a small weekly portion of maize and salt, and, in some camps, two pounds of salt pork or beef per week. (Pescatello, *The African*, p. 101.)

**SENSAMAYÁ,** in Afro-Cuban religion, a goddess sometimes represented by a snake.

**SENSAY, SENSA, SENSEH** (Eng. Cr.), a West Indian name for a frizzled or ruffled breed of fowl with feathers standing out in opposite directions. The black population regard it as an object of myth and magic, and its eggs, crow, and cackling are regarded as ominous.

**SENZALA** (Pg.), in colonial Brazil, the plantation slave quarters. It consisted of a huge compound with a big strong gate and was subdivided into dozens of small adjoining cubicles of about twelve square feet for each family. In some cases, the quarters were separate shanties consisting of small cabins covered with mud and grass or palm trunks; they were often windowless. The *senzala* played a basic role in acculturating the African slaves to the language, religion, morality, and customs of the white Portuguese colonists.

**SEPRE** (Afr.), in the West Indies, a variety of maiden plantain (q.v.) *(Plantago)*; of African origin.

**SERÃO** (Pg.), in Brazil, night work performed by slaves that often lasted until 10:00 or 11:00 P.M. On the sugar estates (q.v.), the production of sugar and rum was an all-night task for at least fifteen consecutive weeks every season. The *serão* was among the most burdensome work performed by slaves.

**SERVICE MAN,** in Jamaica, a black *obeah* man (q.v.).

**SERVI DE MAIN** (Fr. Cr.), in the Afro-Haitian religion, a priest who officiates in the two most important blacks cults, the Pétro (q.v.) and the Arada (q.v.).

**SERVITEUR** (Fr. Cr.), in the Afro-Haitian religious cults, any initiate possessed by a god.

**SÉSÉ** (Afr.), in the West Indies, a quarrel or argument among blacks.

**SESMARIA** (Pg.), in colonial Brazil, a royal land grant usually encompassing nine square miles; many grantees possessed anywhere from one to a dozen such estates. It gave rise to the plantation system worked by African slaves. In 1822, the land grants were abolished.

**SESMERIO** (Pg.), in Brazil, a recipient of a *sesmaria* (q.v.) who was supposed to be a Christian and pay a tithe to the Order of Christ, a medieval military religious brotherhood.

**SET** (Eng. Cr.), in the West Indies, to apply the magic powers of *obeah* (q.v.); usually done by a black sorcerer.

**SET DUPPY** (Eng. Cr.), to have a spell or curse put by an *obeah* man (q.v.) upon one's enemy.

**SET GIRLS,** in colonial Jamaica at the end of the eighteenth century, a group of girls or others dressed alike for the Christmas celebrations. The practice was apparently introduced from Saint Domingue and later became mingled with the John Canoe (q.v.) Christmas celebrations. The set girls, however, sought elegance in costume and dancing, while John Canoe was grotesque, wild, and noisy. (Cassidy, *Dictionary*, p. 402.)

**SET OBEAH,** in Jamaica, to initiate a magic charm (q.v.) to do a person harm.

**SET-UP,** in Jamaica, a black wake or similar ritual for the dead; the custom varies locally on the island.

**SEU NEGRINHO HUMILDE** (Pg.) ("your humble little Negro"), a phrase of endearment and tender feeling used by whites in addressing other whites. It was part of a standard style of writing in colonial Brazil.

**SEYA,** in the West Indies, a black *obeah* man (q.v.).

**SEYMOUR, ARTHUR, J.** (b. 1914), a black writer born in British Guiana and educated at Queen's College, Georgetown. After graduation, he worked as an assistant information officer for the government. He was editor of *Kykoveral*, a twice-a-year literary magazine, and president of the British Guiana Writers' Association. Among his books of verse are *Verse* (Georgetown, 1937); *More Poems* (Georgetown, 1940); *Over Guiana, Clouds* (Georgetown, 1944); *Suns in My Blood* (Georgetown, 1944); and *Six Songs* (Georgetown, 1946).

**SHADOW,** in the West Indies, that part of one's soul, in African belief, thought to be manifested during life by one's shadow. The concept is now confused or combined with that of ghost.

**SHADOW-CATCHER** (Eng. Cr.), among West Indian blacks, a myal man (q.v.) who harms by depriving persons of their shadows (souls) or setting death upon them. See also SHADOW.

**SHADOW-CATCHING,** among West Indian blacks, the release of a shadow (q.v.) that has been bound by a black sorcerer and its restoration to its owner.

**SHAKA** (Afr.), in the West Indies, a rattle usually made of a calabash on a stick with seeds inside; used by blacks as a musical instrument. Also called *shaker* and *shaky*.

**SHAKEFOOT,** in Jamaica, a wild black dance.

**SHAKER, SHAKY.** See SHAKA.

**SHAKY-SHEKIES** (Eng. Cr.), in the Caribbean and elsewhere a rattle instrument of African origin made of gourds or cylindrical tin boxes "pierced with small holes, and filled with beads, shots or gravel;" used in black music as a kind of metronome. (Brathwaite, *The Development*, p. 226.)

**SHAM-SHAM** (Afr.), a dish made of ground, parched corn which, if mixed with sugar, is called *asham*. It is a West Indian black delicacy.

**SHANGÓ** (Afr.), a male god of Nigerian origin who acts as servant of the Ogun (q.v.) deities, particularly Ogun Badagu and Ogun Batala. In Cuba, Shangó is sometimes identified with thunder and lightning and throws stones from the sky. In Haiti and elsewhere, he is the spirit of a lucky warrior now living peacefully in a palace. See also XANGÓ.

**SHANGÓ-OBEAH** (Afr.), in Trinidad and elsewhere, a black cult in which magic plays an important role.

**SHANTEY, SHANTIES,** in the West Indies and elsewhere, improvised work songs sung in chorus by blacks while sailing, fishing, loading ships, or moving a house. (Abrahams, *Deep the Water*, p. 10.)

**SHANTYING, CHANTYING,** throughout the Caribbean, the habit of singing by groups of workers, especially blacks. The songs may be improvised for the occasion, or, more commonly, they may come from the international store of shanties, including those associated with the sea traders in the days of the large sailing vessels. (Abrahams, *Deep the Water*, p. 3.)

**SHANTY-MAN,** a West Indian black singer of improvised work songs.

**SHANTY TOWN,** in the West Indies, an urban slum inhabited by poor lower class blacks.

**SHAPAMAN** (Afr.), the god of smallpox and medicine in some Afro-Brazilian cults; his origin is Yoruba (q.v.).

**SHARP, GEORGE.** See LIELE, GEORGE.

**SHARP, GRANVILLE** (1735-1813), an English abolitionist born on November 10, 1735, the ninth and youngest son of Thomas Sharp. In 1765, he befriended a black, Jonathan Strong (q.v.), whom he found in destitute condition in the streets of London where he had been abandoned by his master, David Lisle. Two years later, Lisle threw Strong into prison as a runaway slave, but Sharp procured his release and prosecuted Lisle for assault and battery. Sharp became chairman of the Society for Effecting the Abolition of the Slave Trade (q.v.). Soon after, he entered into correspondence with the Antislavery Society in Philadelphia which had just been reorganized with Benjamin Franklin as president.

**SHARP, SAMUEL,** a freed black slave, who was one of the leaders in the Baptist War (q.v.) in Montego Bay, Jamaica, in 1831. The uprising was strongly influenced by the Native Baptist Movement (q.v.). (Curtin, *Two Jamaicas*, p. 85.)

**SHAY-SHAY, SHEY-SHEY** (Eng. Cr.), in Jamaica, an old Maroon (q.v.) dance consisting of slow movements characterized by strange postures of the body, shaking of the hips, and foot stamping. It is highly erotic.

**SHELL-BLOW** (Eng. Cr.), in colonial Jamaica, a blowing of a shell as a signal to the slaves on the plantations to begin or cease work.

**SHELL-SHELL,** small bits of shell-like things; specifically, the chitinous wing-covers of fireflies that black *obeah* men (q.v.) sell to rural blacks in Jamaica.

**SHELL-TURN-IN,** the blowing of a shell to indicate the cessation of work by plantation slaves at the noon hour in the West Indies.

**SHELL-TURN-OUT,** on West Indian sugar estates (q.v.) the blowing of a shell to signify the end of the day's slave labors. It is not clear when this practice was introduced.

**SHEPHERD, SHEPHERDESS,** in Afro-West Indian revivalist cults, titles of the leaders, male and female.

**SHERLOCK, PHILIP M.** (b. 1902), a writer born in Portland, Jamaica.

Sherlock was educated in Kingston and later received a college degree in England. He had a long career as a schoolmaster, librarian, and officer of public education in Jamaica. He also did research on black folklore and published a number of books for use in the schools. One of his best known works is *Three Finger Jack's Treasure* (London, 1961).

**SHEY-SHEY.** See SHAY-SHAY.

**SHIM-SHAM** (Eng. Cr.), an old-fashioned African dance popular throughout the Caribbean.

**SHIPMATES,** African slaves who had made the Middle Passage (q.v.) to the New World in the same ship. In the West Indies, this experience developed close friendships. Considered almost as strong as a blood relationship, it passed from one generation to another so that a young man felt that the shipmate of his father was his own relative as well. The love and affection of shipmates for each other was proverbial, and the bonds uniting them were so strong that sexual intercourse between them was considered incestuous. (Curtin, *Two Jamaicas*, p. 26.)

**SHOLA** (Afr.). See ASHOLA AGUENGUE.

**SHORT-BAG,** a small bag used by West Indian blacks to carry food, small tools, and other necessities to work in the fields.

**SHOUTER** (Eng.), in the West Indies, a member of a religious sect found among blacks and marked by the use of ceremonies resembling African rituals.

**SHOUTER HOME,** in Trinidad, a room in a private house which is used for holding black revivalist prayer meetings.

**SHOW-BELLY,** in Jamaica, a black pregnant woman.

**SHUM-SHUM,** an Afro-Jamaican dish made of corn and sugar.

**SICÁ** (Afr.), an African dance popular among slaves in the Caribbean.

**SIDE-PORK** (Eng. Cr.), in the West Indies, a black albino.

**SIDOGAN** (Afr.), a black priestess in some Afro-Brazilian cults.

**SIERRA LEONE,** in slavery times, a large, ill-defined coastal zone that extended roughly from the Casamance in the north to Cape Mount in the south, including the coastline of Guinea-Conakry, Guinea-Bissau, and a very small part of Senegal (q.v.) and Liberia as well. Today, it is an independent West African republic.

**SIERRA LEONE COMPANY,** an English corporation founded in 1791 by William Wilberforce (q.v.), Granville Sharp (q.v.), and Henry Thornton for the purpose of forming a colony of liberated slaves in the Sierra Leone coastal zone. See also SIERRA LEONE.

**SIERRA LEONE SLAVES,** a generic term applied loosely to slaves exported to the New World from scattered settlements located along the seashore of Sierra Leone (q.v.).

**SIGNO DE SALOMÃO** (Pg.), among blacks in Brazil, a charm painted or carved on the door of the house or tattooed on an individual's arm, leg, or chest. It is used against evil or the machinations of enemies. (Pierson, *Negroes*, p. 258.)

**SIKAN** (Afr.), in Afro-Cuban folklore, a mythic woman of the society of *ñáñigos* (q.v.) who receives the souls of dead initiates.

**SILENT WAKE** (Eng. Cr.), in the West Indies, the first night of a black wake characterized by singing the whole night.

**SILICEO, SEBASTIÁN DE,** a Castilian slave trader who, together with Antonio García (q.v.), obtained a slave *asiento* (q.v.) on December 15, 1674, to import blacks into the Spanish colonies.

**SILK-COTTON TREE,** a tropical tree *(Bombax)* considered by West Indian blacks to be a favorite haunt of spirits and ghosts.

**SILVA, ESTEVÃO** (d. 1801), a black painter born in Rio de Janeiro. His favorite subjects were slaves and nature. (Ramos, *The Negro*, p. 138.)

**SILVA ALVARENGA, MANOEL IGNÁCIO DA** (1749-1814), a mulatto born in Vila Rica, Minas Gerais, Brazil, the son of a poor musician. He studied at Coimbra University in Portugal from 1773 to 1776 where he was a protegé of the marques de Pombal. He returned to Brazil and distinguished himself as a poet and public servant. He wrote on Brazilian themes, but seldom mentioned Africa or black subjects. Among his works are *O desertor: Poema Heroi-Comico* (Coimbra, 1774); *O Templo de Neptuno*

(Lisbon, 1777); *Glaura, Poemas Eróticos* (Lisbon, 1798); *Obras Poéticas* (Rio de Janeiro, 1864); and *Poemas Eróticos* (Lisbon, 1889).

**SILVA CUNHA, GASPAR DE,** a Brazilian black slave leader in the unsuccessful Hausa slave (q.v.) revolt in Bahía in 1835.

**SILVEIRA, VICENTE,** a Cuban mulatto poet born in Camaguey. His only known published work is *Flores y espinas* (Habana, 1873). (Calcagno, *Los poetas de color*, p. 48.)

**SILVER ROLL EMPLOYEE,** a West Indian black working for the U.S. government in the Panama Canal. This classification was used until 1947. See also GOLD AND SILVER ROLL.

**SILVER THATCH,** in the West Indies, a tropical palm *(Thrinax argentea)*, the leaves of which are used by blacks for thatch (q.v.).

**SIMALO** (Fr. Cr.), an Afro-Haitian male god believed responsible for man's physical proportions and bodily strength.

**SIMBA** (Afr.), in Haiti, an African god who is the patron of rain and drinking water.

**SIMBI** (Afr.), an Afro-Haitian male god who lives in calabash trees.

**SIMBI DLEAU,** in the Haitian pantheon, a friendly deity, patron of streams and springs, who is often symbolized as a snake. Ponds are sometimes constructed for him near a chapel.

**SIMBI GRAND BASS,** an Afro-Haitian god, patron of the forests.

**SIMIDOR** (Fr. Cr.), in Haiti, a black singer of folk songs; especially a man who leads the singing at *coumbités* (q.v.).

**SIMPSON, LOUIS** (b. 1923), a black poet born in Kingston, Jamaica. He attended primary and secondary schools in his native city and later studied at Columbia University in New York. During World War II, he interrupted his studies to serve in England. At the end of the conflict, he resumed his education in Paris. His major published work is *The Arrivistes: Poems 1940-1948* (New York, 1949).

**SINGBE, JOSEPH.** See CINQUE, JOSEPH.

**SINGING MEETING,** in the West Indies, a hymn-singing meeting held by blacks on the night after a funeral.

**SINHÁ** (Pg.), in Brazil, a term employed by slaves in addressing white ladies.

**SINHÁ-DONA** (Pg.), in Brazil, a term used by slaves to address young white girls. Also called *sinhá-moça*.

**SINHAMA** (Pg.), in Brazil, an affectionate term for a black nurse or nanny.

**SINHAZINHA** (Pg.), in Brazil, a term of endearment employed by slaves in addressing their mistress's daughter.

**SINHÓ** (Pg.), in Brazil, a term of address used by slaves in talking to their master.

**SINHÓ-MOÇO** (Pg.), in Brazil, a term used by slaves to address young white men.

**SÍNDICO DE ESCLAVOS** (Sp.). See PROTECTOR DE ESCLAVOS.

**SIRO** (Fr. Cr.), in Haiti, a favorite sweet drink of blacks.

**SLABBER-SAUCE,** a sauce made of palm-oil mixed with flour, water, and pepper that was served to blacks on board ship during the trip from West Africa to the Caribbean. (Dow, *Slave Ships*, p. 144.)

**SLAVE-AND-SUGAR VOYAGE,** a loosely organized and profitable journey by a merchant who usually represented a big commercial company or an entrepreneur. The trip started in an English port, touched the west coast of Africa, and, after crossing the Atlantic, returned to the port of call. Such a trip lasted several months.

**SLAVE BAPTISM,** all African slaves were required by Portuguese law to be baptized into the Christian religion before they left their native shores. This was ordered on penalty of forfeiture to the state. The mark of the Royal Crown upon slaves' breasts signified that they had undergone this ceremony and that the king's duties had been paid. The Spanish law also ordered the baptism of slaves and the payment of the Crown's taxes at the port of entry in the New World. (Pierson, *Negroes*, p. 92.)

**SLAVE BREEDING,** common practice in slaveowning regions. In colonial Brazil, the black slave woman was considered the most productive feature of slavery. In the West Indies around 1788, however, the birth and rearing of slaves were regarded as more expensive than buying new blacks from Africa.

**SLAVE CATCHER,** in the West Indies, a trusted black slave in charge of capturing runaway slaves.

**SLAVE CLOTHING,** in the West Indies, little clothing was worn. Up to the age of puberty, black children went naked. Adult black males wore loincloths or drawers, and they sometimes added shirts on Sundays and canvas jackets in the cooler months. Adult black females wore loincloths, smocks, or shirts. Field blacks rarely wore hats or sandals. Around 1678, a master needed to spend only 25 pounds per annum on clothing. This would buy three pairs of coarse canvas drawers per man and two cheap skirts per woman. Black garments were usually made of blue cloth, the same as apprentices' costumes in England. (Dunn, *Sugar and Slaves*, pp. 283-84.)

**SLAVE COAST,** the shoreline of the Gulf of Guinea (q.v.) between the Volta River and the Niger River Delta, a chief slave-trading center in the seventeenth and eighteenth centuries. It included the famous Ajudá Fort (q.v.), also known as Whydah.

**SLAVE CONCUBINE CHILD,** in Jamaica, an illegitimate child. He or she took the mother's status and would become free only if manumitted, a condition hardly likely unless the father owned the mother or otherwise secured her manumission (q.v.). The manumission of the child of a slave concubine often left the mother herself in slavery. The child was the lawful property of the mother's owner. (M. G. Smith, *The Plural Society*, p. 135.)

**SLAVE CONTROL,** in the West Indies, the control of a large number of African-born and Creole slaves. It was a constant worry, especially in the rural areas. On the plantations, a strict and often inhuman discipline was imposed on field slaves (q.v.), and they were systematically oppressed.

**SLAVE COTTAGES,** on Caribbean plantations, wooden huts built by the slaves themselves on the estate grounds. They were often barely high enough for the occupant to stand up straight. Thatched roofs were common, while the floors were made of earth. They were seldom placed with much regard to order, but because they were intermingled with fruit trees, particularly the banana, the avocado-pear, and the orange, they sometimes gave a pleasing and picturesque appearance.

**SLAVE-COURT,** in Jamaica, a court established by an Act of the Assembly in 1817 for the purpose of inquiring into, hearing, and determining all manners of offenses for which slaves were liable to punishment by death or confinement to hard labor. (Cassidy, *Dictionary*, p. 412.)

**SLAVE DEHUMANIZATION,** in the British West Indies, a system based on the systematic denial of all basic human rights to slaves. It involved forcibly moving them around between the estates, transporting and listing them like animals, destroying their family structure, and dragooning them to work for long periods of time on an inadequate diet with no material or spiritual reward in sight. (Craton and Walfin, *A Jamaican Plantation*, p. 142.)

**SLAVE ELITE.** See HEAD PEOPLE.

**SLAVE FACTOR,** a commercial agent, usually employed by a slave trade company, engaged in buying slaves from local black chieftains along the West African coast. In the West Indies, the factor was an independent middleman who sold blacks to local planters. Around 1796, a West Indian merchant in charge of retail sales received a commission of 15 percent on the gross amount and 5 percent more on the net proceeds. (Mannix, *Black Cargoes*, p. 128.)

**SLAVE FACTORY,** on the west coast of Africa, a commercial establishment engaged in the purchase and sale of slaves for New World planters. The heart of the factory was the *barracoon* (q.v.). Between 1746 and 1759, scores of these trading posts were scattered along the shore line from Senegal (q.v.) south to the mouth of the Niger. Some were very elaborate communities but most were ramshackle affairs holding ten to twenty slaves controlled by a white merchant who was condemned to spend his life on the fever-ridden coast.

**SLAVE FAMILY STRUCTURE,** in the West Indies, there was no formal family life among slaves. Breeding was usually carried on by casual mating. Slaves, like the land, the cattle, and the factory plant, were generally regarded simply as units of economic value, without moral or spiritual personality.

**SLAVE FOOD ALLOWANCE,** the amount of food given to ordinary slaves by their master. In the West Indies and elsewhere, it was scarcely enough to assure survival. In 1788, the legislature of Saint Kitts reported that the slaves there were generally allowed 4 to 9 pounds of flour, corn, peas, or beans, and 4 to 8 herrings or other salted fish per slave per week. (Goveia, *Slave Society*, p. 138.)

**SLAVE FORK,** in the West Indies, a forked piece of wood placed around a slave's neck by slave catchers (q.v.) to prevent escape.

**SLAVE FUNERAL,** in the West Indies, marked by no formal church religious service. The funeral of a slave was usually celebrated by feasts and dances, as in Africa, although a formal group ritual was held with an abundance of magic-religious ceremonies.

**SLAVE GANG,** a group of slaves working in the fields, organized by age. In the colonial West Indies, there were at least three kinds of slave gangs. See FIRST GANG; SECOND GANG; THIRD GANG.

**SLAVEHOLDER,** in the West Indies, an owner of African or Creole slaves (q.v.).

**SLAVE HOSPITAL.** See HOT HOUSE PIECE.

**SLAVE HUCKSTER,** in the West Indies, a black slave who sold vegetables and fruits in the streets or in the markets, especially at the slave Sunday market (q.v.).

**SLAVE HUNTING DOGS,** dogs trained to catch runaway slaves. They were large-sized, stronger, and heavier than ordinary hounds, usually with cropped ears and a rather pointed nose which widened towards the back of the jaw. They were trained not to kill, but to hold the fugitive at bay and seize him only in case of resistance. See also RANCHADOR.

**SLAVE JETTISONING,** on slaving ships, the practice of throwing slaves overboard in case of massive contagious epidemic or of short provisions, especially during the Middle Passage (q.v.) to the New World. If the slaves died of thirst or illness, the loss fell on the owner of the vessel, but if they were thrown into the sea, it was considered legal jettisoning and was covered by insurance. (Mannix, *Black Cargoes*, pp. 125-26.)

**SLAVE LAND ALLOTMENT,** a small patch of land on sugar estates (q.v.) given to field slaves (q.v.) to grow food for their own support. This practice was widespread throughout the West Indies.

**SLAVE LAWS,** in the West Indies, a juridical system based upon the legal concept of property in persons. It was accepted in the statute law of England and was governed by the principles of common law. Slaves were considered merchandise when first imported into the islands, but after their sale they could be transferred only by conveyance as real property.

**SLAVE MARRIAGE,** in the colonial West Indies, not a legal institution. As property, slaves were prohibited from forming juridical relationships of marriage which would interfere with or restrict their owner's property rights. Originally, the situation was further complicated by the fact that far more male than female slaves were imported into the islands. Permanent mating relationships were eventually established for spouses by their kinship or lineage groups which varied in type and constitution from one ethnic group to another. There were also differences in ceremonial procedures and in the exchange of property by virtue of which a marriage was completed. (M. G. Smith, *The Plural Society*, p. 107.)

**SLAVE MOTHERHOOD,** in the Caribbean plantation economy, rarely rewarded. Occasionally (circa 1794), a slave mother was given an English pound by her master. Few pregnant mothers were released from work to care for their children since too few of their young survived. The miscarriage rate was very high as a result of insufficient diet and lack of medical care. (Craton and Malvin, *A Jamaican Plantation*, p. 140.)

**SLAVE NAME,** throughout the Caribbean, the African name, and for others new names as given by their masters. In plantation records, the list of names suggests a fairly even distribution between African and English names. Slaves might be distinguished from each other as Ebo Jack, Coromantee Jack, Congo Jack, and the like. In the seventeenth century, the favorite name was Sambo. Other African names included Mingo, Cuffee, Quaco, Cubbenah, and Yambo for males, and Adjaba, Affrad, Phibba, and Quatha for females. English names were especially popular such as Jack, Robin, Tom, Will, Harry, and Dick for males, and Doll, Mame, Bess and Betty for females. The planters often used similar names for their slaves and their cows. (Dunn, *Sugar and Slaves*, p. 252.)

**SLAVE POLYGAMOUS MATING,** in the British West Indies, a widespread practice. Concubines were separated spatially, the majority living in their own huts; some of them with their children, might belong to adjoining estates. The slave father provided the mother with an allowance and assistance, and held her responsible for the care of the child. (M. G. Smith, *The Plural Society*, p. 108.)

**SLAVE PREACHER,** in the West Indies, an inspired black slave who preached and held religious meetings on a plantation. He was often an itinerant unorthodox minister, not always recognized as an acceptable man of God by the white missionaries. He taught the slaves their religious duties, insisting on the necessity of prayer, fasting at least one day a week, and not working on Saturdays and Sundays. He requested fowls and hogs as expiatory sacrifices. His powerful influence among slaves was considered a social threat, as a result of which, in 1806, the Jamaican Assembly imposed severe restrictions on the activities of black preachers. (Brathwaite, *The Development*, p. 162.) See also BILL TO PREVENT PREACHING BY PERSONS NOT DULY QUALIFIED BY LAW.

**SLAVE PRICE,** in the New World, a widely varying price because, beyond the original cost, the slaver had to pay extra charges, such as port duties, brokerage fees, and wages of native labor. Around 1708, the price of a slave on the African coast was 5 pounds; this increased to 10 pounds once the slave reached the West Indies. In 1786, the cost of a slave delivered on board ship on the African coast was over 27 pounds; the same black slave price, after deducting factorage, was over 40 pounds in the Caribbean. (Mannix, *Black Cargoes*, p. 99.)

**SLAVE PROPERTY RIGHTS,** in the West Indies, two classes of slave property rights: 1. rights *in rem* with respect to material possessions, held commonly by all slaves in the plantation community; and 2. rights *in personam* which were held against the master or his agent for future allowances, usufruct, holidays, and so forth. The majority of rights *in rem* were customary and lacked legal sanction; their infringement gave rise to, or followed, disputes within the slave community. The majority of rights *in personam*, however, were sanctioned by law and were regarded by slaves as reciprocal return for their labor. (M. G. Smith, *The Plural Society*, p. 104.)

**SLAVER.** 1. A slave trader, usually a European, who often had to cruise along the west coast of Africa to pick up a dozen captives here and a dozen there, enduring long weeks and months in pestilential misery and paying the price with an appallingly high death rate in his own ranks. His job was made more difficult when the demand for slaves increased in the West Indies and elsewhere. 2. A vessel specifically equipped to carry slaves from the west coast of Africa to the New World; it was always extremely crowded. A cargo of approximately 100 tons was calculated to accommodate 220 to 250 slaves. In general, a slave had only as much room as a man in a coffin, both in length and breadth.

**SLAVER HOUSE,** a slave-trade term for a temporary shelter on the deck of a slaver (q.v.) where extra passengers were piled up during the two months' trip across the Atlantic. These "houses" ran from mast to mast with a roof supported by the ship's booms.

**SLAVER SURGEON,** a physician hired by the slaver's (q.v.) captain to examine the slaves before their sale. As part of the examination, he made them jump and stretch out their arms quickly, and he looked in their mouths to judge their age. The sick ones were rejected. Following the surgeon's examination, the selected slaves were branded. After 1788, the law required that a trained surgeon be on board, and a premium was placed upon proper care for the Africans. The English government offered 100 to 500 pounds to all captains and medical men who made the transatlantic passage with a mortality rate of 2 percent or less, and half this amount was paid if losses in the human cargo did not exceed 3 percent. (Ragatz, *The Fall*, pp. 25-52.)

**SLAVERY TANK,** in the West Indies, a water tank of the kind that was used during slavery days.

**SLAVE SEASONING.** See SEASONING OF SLAVES.

**SLAVE SUNDAY MARKET,** in the British Caribbean and elsewhere, an assemblage of hundreds of slaves and mulattoes in market towns where field slaves (q.v.) were allowed to sell the surplus produce grown on the patches of plantation land assigned to them.

**SLAVE WARDSHIP,** in 1820, the master's guardianship of slaves extended to their wives, children, and junior kinsmen through a law passed by the Jamaican assembly. Later old slaves were also included. In this way, the slaves and their kinsmen were placed under the absolute power of their owners. (M. G. Smith, *The Plural Society*, p. 124.)

**SLAVE WOMAN MATING,** in Jamaica and elsewhere, a temporary and unstable situation. There was no formal procedure for establishing slave unions except for the house-building and the feast for a girl's first mating. The unions were dissolved without any formality. Since the owner was interested only in the children, his female slaves were free to mate as they pleased.

**SLAVE WORKDAY,** on Cuban sugar estates (q.v.) circa 1850, during the yearly producing season of five to seven months, twenty hours long, allowing only three to four hours' sleep a night. The burden was lightened for women in their seventh or eighth month of pregnancy. The slaves often fell asleep standing up and were struck if they were found doing so. In the West Indies and Brazil, the same extremely intense labor regime was maintained. Slave labor on coffee estates in Cuba and Brazil was usually sixteen hours a day; without adequate food, slaves sometimes worked from 3 A.M. until 9 or 10 P.M. (Hall, *Social Control*, pp. 17-18.)

**SLAVOCRACIA** (Pg.) ("slavocracy"), a system of economic exploitation rooted in the Brazilian land. It served to entrench old and traditional families, consolidate an externally well-bred upper caste, and extend the influence of a plantation order which was tied to the Portuguese home market by mercantilism, navigation acts, and the control of sugar prices by European merchants.

**SMALL GANG.** See THIRD GANG.

**SMITH, JOHN** (1790-1824), an agent of the London Missionary Society (q.v.) among the slaves of Demerara, British Guiana, who was accused in 1823 of having incited them to revolt. He was tried, convicted, and condemned to death. He died in prison the following year, before his execution.

**SMITH, MARY ANN ABLE,** an American-born Methodist missionary who came to Jamaica (circa 1803) as a result of her opposition to the American Revolution. She and eight others are believed to have been the first Methodists on the island. By January 1822, the congregation was reported to have over 600 members in Kingston and 8,000 on the island. (Brathwaite, *The Development*, p. 209.)

**SMOKE TRADING,** a slave-trade method employed on the Grain Coast (q.v.) and elsewhere. Standing offshore, a European slaver (q.v.) vessel would fire a gun to attract attention. The Africans, if they had rice or pepper or slaves to sell, would send up smoke signals and launch a canoe through the surf. This traditional smoke signal meant trade.

**SNAKE-ROOT,** a plant *(Eryngium foetidum)* used by blacks to "revive" supposedly dead people in *myal* (q.v.) rituals.

**SOBA** (Afr.), an Angolan chief, a provider of slaves for the Brazilian market from the early sixteenth century.

**SOBADO** (Afr.), a tax paid to Angolan petty kings for slaves sold to Portuguese merchants.

**SOBO** (Afr.), an Afro-Haitian god who appears as a handsome military officer. He is found everywhere, but prefers living under trees.

**SOBRADOS E MUCAMBOS** (Pg.) *(The Mansions and the Shanties),* a well-known essay by Gilberto Freyre (q.v.) published in 1936. It describes the emergence and growth of Brazilian civilization from the patriarchal family, black slavery, and a single-crop economy. It is the continuation of the *Casa Grande e Senzala* (q.v.). Both books have acquired a permanent place in Brazil as national classics.

**SOCIEDAD ABOLICIONISTA ESPAÑOLA** (Sp.) (Spanish Abolitionist Society), an abolitionist group organized in Madrid, Spain on December 7, 1864. That same year, to voice its concern and to inform the public regarding the evils of slavery, the society founded a periodical entitled *El Abolicionista Español* (q.v.).

**SOCIEDADE ABOLICIONISTA 20 DE MAYO** (Pg.) (The 20th of May Abolitionist Society), an important antislavery organization established in Rio de Janeiro, Brazil in 1880. It played a decisive role in denouncing slavery and in convincing the government and Congress to speed the emancipation of the slaves.

**SOCIEDADE EMANCIPADORA DOS ESCRAVOS** (Pg.) (Society for the Emancipation of Slaves), an abolitionist group founded in Rio de Janeiro, Brazil, on March 20, 1870. It soon became the leading institution engaged in the suppression of slavery.

**SOCIÉTÉ CONGO,** in rural Haiti, an informal neighborhood group organized by blacks for mutual aid. Its name indicates an African origin, and it seems to be related to a kind of cooperative work traditional among the people of Dahomey (q.v.).

**SOCIÉTÉ DES AMIS DES NOIRS** (Fr.) (Society of Friends of the Negroes), a group established in Paris, France in 1788, largely by mulattoes from Saint Domingue. It proposed to abolish not only the slave trade but also slavery itself in all French possessions, including Saint Domingue. Its membership included prominent Frenchmen of the time, such as A. N. de Condorcet and the marquis de Lafayette.

**SOCIÉTÉ POUR L'ABOLITION DE L'ESCLAVAGE** (Fr.) (The Society for the Abolition of Slavery), a group organized in Paris, France in 1834 for the purpose of emancipating the slaves in the French colonies. In 1838, it proposed a draft of an emancipation law in the French Assembly.

**SOCIETY FOR EFFECTING THE ABOLITION OF THE SLAVE TRADE,** an association founded in London, England in May 1787 by a distinguished group of abolitionists under the chairmanship of Granville Sharp (q.v.). An office was opened to enlist new members and to collect funds; within a year, 2,760 pounds were received in subscription for a pamphlet by Thomas Clarkson (q.v.) entitled *A Summary View of the Slave-Trade and of the Probable Consequences of its Abolition.* The society entered into correspondence with the Antislavery Society in Philadelphia and with the Société des Amis des Noirs (q.v.) in Paris.

**SOCIETY FOR THE MITIGATION AND GRADUAL ABOLITION OF SLAVERY THROUGHOUT THE BRITISH DOMINIONS,** a group organized in London, England in January 1823 by prominent British Quakers (q.v.) and a number of society leaders under the leadership of Zachary Macaulay (q.v.). Sir Thomas Fowell Buxton (q.v.), its spokesman, opened the parliamentary battle in May 1823 by moving "that the state of slavery is repugnant to the principles of the British Constitution and the Christian religion."

**SOCIETY FOR THE PROPAGATION OF THE GOSPEL IN FOREIGN PARTS (SPG),** a British missionary society which began its activities by teaching religion to the slaves of the Codrington Estates (q.v.), bequeathed to the Society in 1710 by Christopher Codrington (q.v.), a former governor of Barbados. The SPG took a special interest in the religious situation of the slaves in Jamaica after the parliamentary decision in 1823 concerning the amelioration of the conditions of slaves in the British colonies.

**SOCIETY OF WEST INDIA PLANTERS AND MERCHANTS,** a coalition of sugar producers and sugar traders organized in London, England in 1780 to influence Parliament and to secure favorable trade regulations for the West Indies. It formed a powerful lobby seeking to secure the passage of bills which would be beneficial to the slaveowners and to block those bills held to be inimical. Its strength was further increased by the membership of both estate owners and West Indian traders in Parliament.

**SODRE-PEREIRA, JERONYMO,** a Brazilian professor of medicine from Bahia. On March 5, 1879, Sodre-Pereira proposed plans for the emancipation of slaves in Brazil. He predicted that the slaves' provocative actions in rural areas would cease on the day of abolition, bringing peace and prosperity to the plantation owners. He was elected to the Chamber of Deputies in 1879.

**SOINAGE** (Fr. Cr.), in the Afro-Haitian religion, the magic bath administered by a god to children.

**SON AFROCUBANO** (Sp.), a hybrid Spanish-African dance and song in syncopated rhythm. It is a Cuban extension of a popular tune with black melodies and ritualistic African words.

**SON ENTERO, EL** (Sp.), a book of poetry published in Buenos Aires in 1947 by the Cuban poet Nicolás Guillén. It is a milestone in the *afrocuban-*

*ismo* (q.v.) literary movement. Guillén's inspiration revolves around the axis of rhythm, and his final pages, the starkest and most universal, are filled with pure and exquisite sounds.

**SOONGA, WOLONGO** (Afr.), small oily white seeds of a plant (Zesamuum or *sesamum Africanum)* common throughout the Caribbean today. It is sold in shops and is used by blacks in cakes, folk medicine, and *obeah* (q.v.) rituals.

**SORONG** (Afr.), in the French Antilles, an African harp with sixteen to thirty-two chords; it is a variety of a *kora* (q.v.).

**SORREL,** in the West Indies, a tropical plant *(Hibiscus sabdoriffa)* used by blacks to make cool drinks, jelly, and marmalade. In colonial times, the flowercups and capsulae were boiled and fermented to make sorrel wine, a favorite drink among plantation slaves.

**SORTEO DE ESCLAVOS** (Sp.) ("drawing of slaves"), in Puerto Rico, an annual drawing of lots among slaves (1833-1886). Those whose names appeared in the drawing were given freedom at once. (Díaz Soler, *Historia,* p. 229.)

**SOSUMA** (Afr.). See SUSUMBA.

**SOSUMA BERRY** (Afr.), in Jamaica, a wild and cultivated tropical herb *(Solanum mammosum)* used by blacks in preparing salt-fish (q.v.) and in other dishes.

**SOUL FOOD,** in Jamaica, salt-fish (q.v.), preferably cooked with ackee; a dish often eaten by slaves in colonial times.

**SOULLESS,** in Afro-Haitian folklore, a word referring to a mythical being deprived of his soul by a black sorcerer. The faithful believe that a soulless creature can be used at will by a practitioner of magic for evil purposes.

**SOUSA, JOÃO DA CRUZ E** (1862-1898), a Brazilian-born black poet of pure African descent. Throughout his life, Sousa was subjected to innumerable sufferings and humiliation because of his race; many of his poems express his sadness and grief. In his poetry, he adopted a basic symbolism of color: white for the white man, the European, Christianity, and virtue, but also sterility, the cold and death-bringing snow; black for lust and fetishism, but also for life, fertility, creative power, and pain. Although he saw African cultures through European eyes, he tragically felt the presence of both, and the racial conflict drew him to the pessimism of Schopenhauer. He is the creator of a "nocturnal" poetry in which blackness is beautiful, an idea which was a forerunner of *négritude* (q.v.). Among his works are *Missal* (1893); *Broqueis* (1893); *Evocações* (1898); *Pharaões* (1900); and *Ultimos Sonetos* (1900).

**SOUZA, FRANCISCO FELIX DE** (d. 1849), an important Brazilian slave trader who, between 1815 and 1840, made Whydah or Ajudá (q.v.) the most famous slave-trading post in West Africa. He was appointed a state minister by King Ghezo of Dahomey (q.v.) in 1818 and was given special trading privileges. He was very prosperous and lived in a state of princely splendor. Long before his death, however, his fortune melted away, and he died in poverty.

**SOUZA E SILVA, J. J. NORBERTO** (1820-1891), a Brazilian poet inspired by African themes and the history of slaves. He was an ardent defender of the black tradition as a creative force in literature. His main work is an unfinished volume of poetry entitled *Palmares: fragmentos de um Poema Zumbi* (1850).

**SOWING-MATCH,** among Jamaican black peasants, a contest of seed-sowing.

**SPAANSE BOK** (D.) ("the Spanish whip"), in colonial Surinam, a legal penalty imposed on slaves for minor offenses. It consisted of placing weights on the feet or head of the accused, with the hands tied together, the knees drawn up between them, and a stick inserted through the opening between the knees and the hands and planted firmly in the ground. (Lier, *Frontier Society*, p. 130.)

**SPANISH CALALU,** in Jamaica, a tropical plant *(Phytolacca octandra)* cultivated by blacks in their gardens and used in soup or broth, and as a green.

**SPANISH DOG,** in Jamaica, a bloodhound imported from Cuba to track down Maroons (q.v.) and runaway slaves.

**SPANISH DUPPY,** in the West Indies, a ghost of a person who died in slavery times.

**SPECKLE** (Eng. Cr.), in the West Indies, a black albino.

**SPECULUM ORIS,** an iron mouth-opener used by guards during the Middle Passage (q.v.) to open the mouths of slaves who refused to eat.

**SPELL** (Eng. Cr.), on West Indian plantations, the shift of a slave gang (q.v.) working in the fields. A Negro driver (q.v.) was in charge of supervising this operation.

**SPIDER-RAIL,** in Afro-Caribbean folklore, an imaginary monster, half-spider and half unspecified; possibly an allusion to Anancy (q.v.) the spider, who was a sort of spider-man.

**SPIRIT SICKNESS,** in the West Indies, a mental illness caused by a malignant spirit. It is supposedly cured by a black *obeah* man (q.v.).

**SPIRIT WEED,** in the West Indies, a tropical bush *(Eryngium foetidum)* used by black sorcerers to rub away evil spirits.

**SPOTTING,** in Jamaica, a kind of religious dance step; possibly an African survival.

**SPREE,** in the West Indies, a black girl friend.

**SPREE-CHILD,** in Jamaica, a smartly dressed black woman.

**SPUR YAWS,** in the West Indies, a variety of contagious skin disease (framboesia) in which a spur-like growth emerges from the sole of the foot. This illness was common among slaves.

**SPYING-MAN,** in Afro-Jamaican revivalist cults, the minister believed to have powers of divination and special knowledge of the spirit world.

**SQUAW-MAN,** in the Panama Canal Zone, a white American who marries a lower class black Panamanian girl at the bottom of the Zonian social ladder. For marrying across racial lines, the squaw-man is accused of having "gone native."

**STAND THERE** (Eng. Cr.), a magic formula to prevent someone or something from moving. Some Afro-Jamaican blacks believe that by using the formula, a thief who enters a man's field can be made to stay on the spot until the owner comes and gives him a flogging (q.v.).

**STATION GUARD,** in Afro-Jamaican revivalist cults, an officer whose duty is to guard a "station" in the ceremony.

**STEPHEN-BASKET,** in Jamaica, a small basket with a slightly raised center and somewhat flaring sides; used by Maroons (q.v.).

**STIPENDARY MAGISTRATE,** in Jamaica during the period 1833-1838, a special judge sent from England for the purpose of adjudicating disputes over work, wages, and manumission (q.v.) of former slaves.

**STOCKMAN SLAVE,** on West Indian plantations, a skilled slave involved in the process of refining sugar. He worked in small groups under an appointed driver (q.v.).

**STOMACH EVIL,** in the British Caribbean, a disease resulting from dirt-eating (q.v.); very common among black slaves in the colonial period.

**STRIPED-HOLLAND,** in the West Indies, a striped variety of Holland cloth which at one time was widely used for clothing among slaves.

**STRONG, JONATHAN,** a black slave brought to London by his master, David Lisle, a planter from Barbados. Lisle abused Strong and eventually abandoned him on the streets. Granville Sharp (q.v.), the abolitionist, found him one day, ill, and placed him in a hospital where he was cured. Some time later, Lisle saw Strong again, claimed him as his property and sold him to John Kerr for 30 pounds. As soon as this news reached Sharp, he approached the lord mayor of London for help. The lord mayor intervened and secured a hearing on the incident which resulted in the slave's release in 1765. (Ragatz, *The Fall*, p. 245.)

**STRUM-STRUM,** in the West Indies, a crude stringed instrument played by blacks; a precursor of the banjo.

**SUÁREZ Y ROMERO, ANSELMO** (1818-1871), a Cuban intellectual and writer who fought for the abolition of slavery and the political independence of the island. He is the author of the antislavery novel *Francisco, El ingenio o las delicias del campo* (New York, 1880) (q.v.).

**SUBUPIRA** (Afr.), the name of a famous *quilombo* (q.v.) established by runaway slaves (circa 1660) in the interior of Brazil.

**SUCIA,** among Black Caribs (q.v.), a female nature-spirit who haunts cemeteries. She lures men into the forest by assuming the form of the woman they are in love with and then drives them mad.

**SUCUSUMUCO** (Afr.), an Afro-Cuban word for overcoat.

**SUDANESE SLAVES,** a generic term applied to black slaves brought from the Slave Coast (q.v.) to Brazil during the colonial period. Included among these blacks were various ethnic groups such as the Yoruba (q.v.) Fanti, and Ashanti (q.v.). Broadly speaking, the planters consider these Sudanese slaves to be more intelligent, more robust. and more hard-working than the Bantu (q.v.).

**SUGAR AND WATER,** in the West Indies, a soft drink made of local brown (or new or wet) sugar and water, sometimes with added lime leaves. Black peasants drink it hot as morning tea.

**SUGAR BARONS,** wealthy West Indian planters who developed the islands into prosperous colonies during the colonial period. They organized a capitalistic sugar industry based on slavery.

**SUGAR CANE,** an exceptionally tall perennial grass *(Saccharum officinarum)* cultivated in tropical and subtropical regions of the New World. In the early fifteenth century, Portuguese and Spanish navigators introduced sugar cane into the islands of Madeira, the Azores, and Cape Verde (q.v.). Columbus apparently carried stalks of sugar cane to Hispaniola (Santo Domingo) in 1492, but not until 1506 did the Spaniards successfully transplant it there. In the short span of thirty years following its introduction into the Caribbean, cane cultivation had spread widely and became recognized as one of the most valuable crops in the New World. As sugar cultivation continued to expand, the industry demanded additional labor. When the Indians showed little aptitude for this type of work, the plantation owners imported slaves from Africa. Ultimately, the slave system became inextricably interwined with the production of sugar for the international market.

**SUGAR ESTATE,** in the West Indies, a sugar plantation which, around 1750, varied from about 300 to 3,000 acres in size. In the eighteenth century, a 900-acre estate was considered average in Jamaica. On a typical tropical plantation, there were three building complexes: the owner's residence with his family and domestic slaves; the mill with the boiling and curing houses, the distillery, the blacksmith's and carpenter's sheds and trash houses; and, at a certain distance, the slave quarters. There were also a cattle yard, a poultry pen and sometimes, separate from all this, a slave hospital. Surrounding these structures were the estate lands.

**SUGAR ISLANDS,** a name given to the West Indies when English interest in the slave trade had been intensified by the acquisition of the colonies, beginning with Barbados in 1603.

**SUGAR LATIFUNDIUM,** in the sugar plantation sphere of the New World, a large agrarian property, usually owned by a family or corporation, where sugar and its byproducts are produced for large national or international markets. The latifundium is only the territorial expression of a complicated socioeconomic capitalistic system of industrial machinery, transportation, technicians, workers, and people engaged in producing sugar, rum, and other manufactured goods. This huge feudal territory is practically outside the jurisdiction of public law, being regulated by the norms of private property.

**SUGAR MILL,** on New World tropical plantations, a factory compound consisting mainly of a huge wheel and boiling house, with its chimney belching smoke during crop-time. Adjacent to the boiling house are the trash house and the distillery. The size, the degree of sophistication of the machinery, and the production capacity vary considerably.

**SUHMAN** (Afr.), among Surinamese blacks, a powerful charm, a gift of the gods, by which a sorcerer can supposedly bewitch a person causing death or bodily injury.

**SUKUBAKARIONGO** (Afr.), in Afro-Cuban religion, a goatskin which is stretched like a flag and carried by a sorcerer in a woman's dress during the services.

**SUKUYAN** (Afr.), in Trinidad, a mythical vampire which blacks believe can cause evil to human beings.

**SUMAN** (Afr.), in Jamaica, a fetish that blacks believe can mediate between man and the gods. It is regarded as an attribute or token of divine power.

**SUNDAY JINAL,** in the West Indies, a black Sunday preacher.

**SUN-MAN,** in Jamaica, an *obeah* man (q.v.).

**SUPERCARGO,** the merchant in charge of buying slaves along the west coast of Africa. He was required to know not only the state of the trade (the supply of slaves and ships), but also the varying values of different standards of payment. Coins were seldom, if ever, used. Supercargoes dealt mostly in rolls of tobacco, pipes of rum, and firearms, or, more generally, in lengths of iron and copper or in pots and basins of brass.

**SURGEON.** See SLAVER SURGEON.

**SURUMBA** (Afr.), among Afro-Hispanics in Colombia, panela or brown sugar.

**SURUSIÉ** (Fr. Cr.), among Black Caribs (q.v.) , a healer who cures with herbs.

**SURVEYRA** (Eng. Cr.), in Trinidad, a black female official of the Shouter (q.v.) sect in charge of surveying the place where a service is to be held and of designating the water for baptism. She must keep out all evil.

**SUSU** (Afr.). See ESUSU.

**SUSUM** (Afr.), in the Afro-Caribbean religion, the soul or spirit of man; the inner force of emotions.

**SUSUMBA, SUSUMBER, SOSUMA** (Afr.), in Jamaica, a common bush with berries about the size of small cherries used by blacks to season saltfish (q.v.) and other meals; it grows wild. Also known as gulley beans.

**SYLVAIN, GEORGE** (1865-1898), a black writer and poet born in Puerto Plata, Dominican Republic. Sylvain was one of the beloved and gifted patrons of the arts in Haiti where he settled and wrote. Educated in Haiti and Paris, he served as ambassador to France and to the Vatican. He thought that Haitian literature should be written in French Creole (q.v.). His works include *Confidences et mélancolies, poésies* (1885-1898), *Précedées d'une notice sur la poésie haïtienne par l'auteur* (Paris, 1901); and *Cri? Crac?* (Paris, 1901).

**SYLVAIN, NORMIL** (1901-1929), a black writer born in Port-au-Prince, Haiti. Sylvain attended schools in his native city and received a medical degree from the University of Port-au-Prince in 1926. He practiced medicine, but he was also deeply interested in literature. In association with other young writers, he took part in the foundation of *La Revue Indigène*, initiating the Negro Renaissance (q.v.) in the Caribbean. At the same time he promoted better medical care in the country, was one of the founders of the Association de Médecine Haïtienne, and served as editor of the *Annales de la Médecine Haïtienne.*

**SYMBOL,** in the West Indies, a frenzied black revivalist service in which an initiate, possessed by a spirit, speaks unknown tongues.

# t

**TA** (Afr.), in the West Indies, grandfather, a term of endearment used by black slaves; it conveyed esteem, affection, and respect for the old man who took care of children born to slaves. Today in Jamaica the term is applied to a sister.

**TAA** (Afr.), in the Caribbean, a variety of yam (q.v.) *(Dioscorea)* often eaten by blacks.

**TAATA,** in the West Indies, grandfather, a term used by slaves in colonial times. This term was common among a number of West African languages. See also TA.

**TABAQUE** (Afr.). See ATABAQUE.

**TABARENHO,** a Brazilian Portuguese-based Creole dialect spoken in rural areas by peasants of African ancestry.

**TABOCAS,** the name of a black *quilombo* (q.v.) organized by runaway slaves in the wilderness of northeast Brazil around 1660.

**TACHA** (Sp.), a legal term for a slave's physical or moral defect, such as disobedience, rebelliousness, and laziness.

**TACKY,** a Coromantee (q.v.) black slave leader of a rebellion in Jamaica in 1760, who had previously been a petty king in Africa. Making his plans with great care and in secrecy, Tacky gathered a small party of trusted followers, mostly Coromantees like himself, and attacked, robbed, and burned several plantations. The revolt was crushed by government forces. Tacky was killed while fleeing, and many of his followers committed suicide rather than surrender. (Black, *History of Jamaica*, p. 93.)

**TACOOMA** (Afr.), in Anancy stories (q.v.), the most often-named son of

Anancy. His personality is dull, but he is small and cute and sometimes is seen in opposition to Anancy.

**TAFIA** (Afr.), a distilled raw rum, a favorite black beverage in Haiti.

**TAHAN** (Afr.), in the French Antilles, a small African drum.

**TAHKI-TAHKI,** in Surinam, an English-based dialect with African, Portuguese, and other elements; spoken by blacks in towns.

**TAILLE BAS** (Fr. Cr.), a sensuous hip dance favored by blacks in Haiti.

**TAKE BUSH, TAKE HOUSETOP,** (Eng. Cr.), in Afro-Jamaican English, to flee to a place of shelter.

**TAKE UP WORK,** in Jamaica with reference to a *busha* (q.v.) or black head-man, to look over and judge the amount of work a black man has done in order to pay him.

**TAKWA** (Afr.), an Ibo (q.v.) deity worshipped in several Afro-Haitian rituals. According to black belief, he speaks unknown languages.

**TALAWA** (Afr.), an Afro-Jamaican word for dangerous. It is said of a black girl who sets no limits in sexual matters.

**TALBOOM, LÉON,** a white Creole writer and critic born in Bouillante, Guadeloupe. After attending local schools, Talboom left the island for Paris where he became an art critic. An admirer of blacks, he sometimes considered them demigods, a source of innocence and primeval goodness kept in isolation by the savage tropics as a spiritual reserve for mankind. In his praise of blackness, Talboom, anticipated the négritude (q.v.) movement. His major work is *Karukera* (1921).

**TALKEE, TALKEE-TALKEE,** a leave pass given to a slave on special occasions to prove his identity or the legitimacy of his business. All black slaves in colonial Jamaica were to have *talkees.* The term did not become official in the laws until as late as 1788. (Cassidy, *Jamaica Talk*, p. 215.)

**TALKING COWS,** the quiet ruminating of cows that some blacks believe is a deep silence that keeps the secrets of the spirits. This so-called animal talk had often been reported from African fields. It is part of Afro-Caribbean folklore.

**TALLET, JOSÉ ZACARÍAS** (b. 1893), a Cuban author and a leader of the *afrocubanismo* (q.v.) literary movement. With Ramón Guirao (q.v.) and Alejo Carpentier (q.v.), he belonged to the new school of exotic sensitivity inspired by black dance and music. His only poem, "La rumba," first appeared in the Cuban journal *Atenei* (August 1928). The poem describes black figures, male and female, who are caught in a frantic contortion of Afro-Cuban dancing and singing, African instruments, rum-drinking, and voodoo (q.v.) possession. In this poetry, words are only rhythms, and dance becomes hypnotic physical and sexual movements. His major work is *La semilla estéril* (Havana, 1951.)

**TAMBAQUE.** See ATABAQUE.

**TAMBO** (Bant.), in the West Indies, a Bantu (q.v.) word meaning a bow-shaped bird trap.

**TAMBORES DO JONGO** (Pg.), drums made of iron or wood which are part of black orchestras in Brazil; their origin is Angolan.

**TAMBORITO** (Sp.), in Panama, the highest expression of folk art, combining dance, music, lyrics, and instruments. It is said to have originated with the dances of black slaves when they gathered in the yards of their plantation quarters.

**TAMBOURINE** (Fr. Cr.), an Afro-Haitian miniature tow-headed drum played by blacks in their festivals.

**TAMBOUR MERINGOUIN** (Fr. Cr.), in Haiti, a musical bow, not a drum, consisting of a string attached on one end to a tree branch and on the other to a cowhide drumhead which covers a hole in the ground that serves as a resonator.

**TAMBRAN SEASON (TIME),** among Jamaican blacks, the time of year (January to March) when tamarinds *(Tamarindus indica)* are in season but other products are scarce; hence hard times.

**TAMBÚ** (Pap.), in the Netherlands Antilles, a bittersweet black dance-song played with a four-string guitar accompaniment to improvised lyrics in Papiamento (q.v.).

**TAMINA** (Pg.), in Brazil, a food ration served in a bowl to black slaves on the plantations.

**TANA** (Eng. Cr.), in the West Indies, a rough bundle made with trash, bark, and soft materials, and used by blacks to carry possessions back from the fields.

**TANCO Y BOSMENIEL, FÉLIX** (1797-1871), a Cuban writer and ardent abolitionist. Tanco y Bosmeniel may be the author of the first antislavery novel ever written in Spanish America. The book, entitled *Pedro y Rosalía*, was written in 1838 but not published until 1925. It concerns the love of a planter's son for Rosalía, a black slave.

**TAN-DE, TANDEH** (Eng. Cr.) ("stand there"), a phrase used by blacks in Jamaica.

**TANGA** (Afr.), in colonial Brazil, an African garment worn by slaves of both sexes; it covers the body from the waistline down to the feet.

**TANGAMÃO, TANGANHÃO** (Pg.), a Portuguese or Brazilian fugitive who settled on the West African coast as a slave trader. He usually lived in black villages where, with his mulatto descendants, he functioned as intermediary in the barter-trade for gold, ivory, and slaves. In dealing with European merchants, he spread the Portuguese language along the shoreline from Senegal (q.v.) to Angola (q.v.).

**TANGO** (Afr.), a lascivious black dance popular among slaves in the region of Rio de la Plata at the beginning of the nineteenth century. Originally part of Mardi Gras celebrations, it has survived in the modern Argentine tango.

**TAN-PAM-MI** (Eng. Cr.). In the West Indies: 1. A satchel or field-bag used by blacks to carry food or other supplies. 2. Old ragged work clothes, especially if dirty; formerly worn by slaves.

**TAPAS** (Afr.), in Brazil, slaves, possibly converts to Islam, imported from the Slave Coast (q.v.) through the port of Lagos, Nigeria. In the Bahia slave uprising of 1835, six black *tapas* were brought to trial. The *tapa* language was spoken in Bahia during the entire nineteenth century. (Pierson, *Negroes*, pp. 35, 45.)

**TAPUYA,** in colonial Brazil, a name given by the Indians to the black slaves.

**TARDON, RAPHAËL** (1911-1961), a writer born in Fort-de-France, Martinique, of a rich mulatto family. After attending local schools, Tardon studied at the University of Paris where he took a degree in history. He worked for the French government in Africa and the Antilles, and later fought in the underground during World War II. As a writer, he opposed all kinds of racism, including the négritude (q.v.) movement led by his country-man Aimé Césaire (q.v.). He refused to collaborate on the periodical *Présence Africaine*, published in Paris, arguing that the Antilles were not African islands, and that all efforts to connect this area with Africa were regressive. He was a brilliant raconteur. Among his works are *Bleu des îles* (1946); *Le Combat de Schoelcher* (1948); *La Caldeira* (1948); *Christ au poing* (1950); *Toussaint L'Ouverture, le Napoléon noir*, (1951); and *Noirs et blancs* (1961).

**TARIMBA** (Pg.), in colonial Brazil, a slave's bed made of boards sup-ported on two sawhorses and covered with a mat of woven grass.

**TASA DE NEGRO,** in Spanish America, a sales tax on each slave paid by the slave trader at the port of entry. It was established by Philip II in 1560.

**TASK SERVICE,** in the West Indies, a work system for slaves established around 1784. Each slave was required to do a definite task each day; once this was completed, he was at liberty to work for himself and accumulate savings to buy his freedom.

**TAYERA** (Afr.), in Afro-Brazilian folklore, a black play in which a black queen is the central figure.

**TCHA-TCHA** (Afr.), in Haiti, a common gourd rattle played by blacks.

**TEA,** in Jamaica, usually included in the black peasant's first meal of the day.

**TEAMEETING,** in Trinidad, a general practice common to black small-holders of getting together to help each other with tasks such as reaping, harvesting, cutting bushes and trees, planting crops, and moving or building a house. See also COUMBITÉ.

**TECEBA** (Afr.), an Islamic rosary with three series of thirty-three beads each; it ends with a wooden ball instead of a crucifix. Each series begins with a special prayer in Arabic. This sacred string was brought to Brazil by slaves, possibly Hausa, most of whom settled in Bahia.

**TEJUPABA** (Pg.), in Brazil, a field-sack in which slave mothers were obliged to leave their infants. They would place the child in the sack and bury half the body in a hole in the ground; in this way, their children could not creep off into the pasture, barnyard, stable, or jungle. (Freyre, *The Masters*, p. 378.)

**TEKREHKI** (Afr.), in the West Indies, an African bag or sack plaited like a mat and used by blacks in the fields.

**TELEMAGUE, HAROLD MILTON** (b. 1911), a black poet born in Plymouth, Tobago. Telemague, the son of a sailing schooner captain, began his education in a Moravian school at Bethesda and later attended high school at Scarborough. After graduation from the Government Training College for teachers, he worked as a school teacher on the island and then became headmaster of the large Fyzabad Intermediate E.C. School. Among his works are *Burn Bush* (Trinidad, 1947) and *Scarlet* (Georgetown, Guiana, 1953).

**TEMME** (Afr.). 1. An African ethnic name and language from Sierra Leone (q.v.). 2. A slave of Temme origin; in Jamaica this implies short stature.

**TEMPER-BUSH,** in Jamaica, a magic herb *(Anyris)* used by black sorcerers.

**TEM PINTA** (Pg.) (''He has a touch of tarbush''), in Brazil, an expression applied to a black who tries to appear white.

**TEMPTING-POWDER,** in the West Indies, a magic love potion given by an *obeah* man (q.v.).

**TEMSANGUE** (Pg.) (''He has blood''), an expression used in Brazil to point out a white person with black blood.

**TEM SANTO** (Pg.) (''having a saint''), a phrase applied to a black who, after being possessed by a specific god, has an obligation to care for him. The initiate has usually gone through rituals and learned the secrets, language, and dances of the god, and knows how to care for him properly. This possession is common in Brazilian *candomblés* (q.v.).

**TEMTEM.** See TENTEN.

**TENER PARIENTES EN LA COSTA** (Sp.) (''To have relatives on the coast of Africa''), an insulting expression suggesting that a person has black blood; one of the most offensive affronts for a native Puerto Rican.

**TENGOSO** (Afr.), an Afro-Hispanic word for loathing; also boredom, or drudgery.

**TENGUE** (Afr.), an Afro-Cuban term for a spoiled child.

**TENKY-MASSA** (Afr.), an Afro-Jamaican expression for a gift such as a piece of land given rent-free to a black peasant to be cultivated.

**TENTE EN EL AIRE** (Sp.), an old Afro-Hispanic expression applied to a mulatto indicating neither progress nor regression in the whitening process.

**TENTEN, TEMTEM** (Pg.), in Brazil, the motions a child makes in learning to walk; a term of endearment used by the old black wet nurse.

**TERESA A RAINHA** (Pg.), a former black queen from Cabinda who was condemned to slavery after she was caught committing adultery (circa 1580). Soon after, she was sold to a Portuguese merchant and taken to Brazil. When she arrived at her owner's plantation, she still wore bands of gold-plated copper on her arms and legs, and her companions showed her much respect. At the beginning she refused to work, but soon, under duress, she accepted her fate. (Rodrigues, *Brazil and Africa*, p. 43.)

**TERREIRO** (Pg.). In Brazil: 1. The ground of an Afro-Brazilian cult center. 2. The cult itself. 3. Space, ordinarily swept bare, immediately around a rural house.

**TETE-FATHER,** among Afro-Jamaicans, a life name given to a black father whose child dies on the ninth day after birth.

**TEXEIRA E SOUZA, ANTONIO GONÇALVES** (1812-1861), an outstanding mulatto writer born in Cabo Frio, Rio de Janeiro. Of humble origin, through hard efforts he was able to obtain only a rudimentary education. He was a carpenter by trade. His writings cover every field of literature: poetry, fiction, and theater. His novels are full of mystery, intrigue, and romantic adventure. Among his works are *O tres días de um Noivado*; *Contos Lyricos*; *O Cavalleiro Teutonico*; *ou A Freira de Marien-burg, Tragedia em 5 Actos* (Rio de Janeiro, 1855).

**THATCH,** in the West Indies, any of the tropical palms *(Calyptronum Swartzii)* whose leaves were used by slaves to build their huts. Today, the poor still use thatch as a building material.

**THATCH HOUSE,** in the West Indies, a slave hut on the plantations.

**THATCH WALK,** on Afro-Caribbean plantations, a grove of thatch trees used by slaves as building material.

**THEIR CHILDREN STAND IN THE PARENTS' SITUATION,** an official policy approved by the Jamaican Assembly (circa 1796) stating that a slave could make no social advancement or own property, being himself property (by custom); he did not possess the right of self-defense, except against another slave. In law and custom, a black was presumed to be a slave until he could prove otherwise, and there was no way in which he could legally disprove the whites' assumption of his inferiority. (Brathwaite, *The Development*, p. 191.)

**THINGS,** in the West Indies, magical materials such as dirt, egg-shells, bones, and herbs used by black sorcerers in their rituals.

**THIRD GANG,** on Caribbean plantations, a group of slave children from nine to twelve years of age and old people who were given the lightest work in the fields. An old slave woman was in charge of the group.

**THOBY-MARCELIN, PHILIPPE** (b. 1904), a black writer born in Port-au-Prince, Haiti, where he attended school. He later studied at Saint Marcial College where he was awarded a law degree. He wrote several novels and, for many years, was a translator at the Organization of American States in Washington, D. C. Among his works are *La Négresse adolescente* (Port-au-Prince, 1932); *Dialogue avec la femme endormie* (Port-au-Prince, 1941); *Lago-Lago* (Port-au-Prince, 1944); and *A fond perdu* (Paris, 1953).

**THOMAREL, ANDRÉ** (b. 1893), a black poet born in Saint-Claude, Guadeloupe. Thomarel attended local schools and continued his education in Fort-de-France, Martinique when his parents moved there in 1904. He fought in World War I and, in 1919, returned to the island and became a school principal. He was very active in local politics and, just before World War II, served as a minister of the colonies in Paris. After the war, he traveled to Africa to study the sources of Afro-Antilles civilization. He was a poet in prose, enchanted with the tropical world of his native islands. His works include *Coeurs meurtris* (1922); *Amours et Equisses* (1927); *Parfums et saveurs des Antilles* (1935); *Regrets et esquisses* (1936); *Naïma, fleur de Maghreb* (1949); *Les Mille et un antillais* (1951); and *Nuits tropicales* (1960).

**THOUGHTS AND SENTIMENTS ON THE EVIL AND WICKED TRAFFIC OF SLAVERY, AND COMMERCE OF THE HUMAN SPECIES, HUMBLY SUBMITTED TO THE INHABITANTS OF GREAT-BRITAIN BY OTTOBAH CUGOANO, A NATIVE OF AFRICA,** a vivid autobiographical story of the kidnapping and enslaving of Ottobah Cugoano (q.v.) published in London in 1787.

**THOUGHTS UPON THE AFRICAN SLAVE TRADE,** a detailed account by the Reverend John Newton (q.v.) of the buying and transporting of slaves between the African coast and the West Indies, published in London in 1788.

**THREAD-BAG** (Eng. Cr.), in Jamaica, a small cloth bag tied or drawn closed with a thread or small strings and often hung around the neck. It is used chiefly by black higglers (q.v.) for carrying their money.

**THREE-CORNERED TRADE,** a name given to the Manchester-Guinea-West Indies trade which consisted mainly of exchanging European goods for slaves, palm oil, and ivory in Africa, then transporting these goods to the West Indies where they were exchanged for sugar, rum, and rawhide to be sold in England.

**THREE-FINGERED JACK.** See MANSONG, JACK.

**THREE-FOOT HORSE,** in Afro-Jamaican folklore, a ghost that gallops through the moonlight faster than any living steed, fatally wounding anyone it comes upon. On dark nights or under the shadow of a tree, one is safe from attack. The three-foot horse is ridden by a whooping-boy (q.v.)

**THREE-QUARTER DAY,** in Jamaica, 9:00 A.M., so called by blacks because three-quarters of the working day still remain.

**THROWING A BOX,** in British Guiana, the black peasant's general practice of bringing together relatives, neighbors, and friends to reap a harvest, plant crops, cut down bushes and trees, and do other communal work. See also TEAMEETING.

**THUNDER-STONE,** in the West Indies, a stone which has supposedly fallen after a clap of thunder; used by black sorcerers as a charm for divination or healing.

**TIATIA.** See ASSON.

**TI BAKA.** In Afro-Haitian folklore: 1. Little demon. 2. The name of a small Pétro (q.v.) drum.

**TI COUMBA** (Fr. Cr.), in Haiti, a black religious dance. See also MACUMBA.

**TIGNON MADRAS** (Fr. Cr.), in Haiti, a colored headpiece worn by black women.

**TIJEAN PETRO,** a malevolent Afro-Haitian deity who preys on children from inside the foliage of the coconut palm (q.v.).

**TIJEAN PIED FIN,** a malevolent Afro-Haitian spirit, brother of Tijean Petro (q.v.).

**TIJEAN QUINTO,** a quarrelsome Afro-Haitian spirit who is usually dressed like a policeman; he likes to eat goat and drink white beer.

**TI KANMBO** (Afr.), in Haiti, a bamboo stamper instrument used by blacks as a substitute for a drum.

**TIMBA** (Afr.), an Afro-Caribbean word for drum.

**TIMBEQUE** (Afr.), a black dance popular in Puerto Rico.

**TIMBIN, ROYAL TIMBIN** (Afr.), an Afro-Jamaican word meaning a sore or lame foot.

**TIOMOUN** (Fr. Cr.), a small child who temporarily lives with people other than his parents; part of a widespread institution in Haiti whereby poor parents entrust their children to friends and acquaintances living in a city, often for the purpose of attending school. Such a child repays the cost of keeping him in the family by running errands. When the *tiomoun* grows older, he returns home. (Herskovitz, *Life in a Haitian*, p. 103.)

**TIROLIEN, GUY** (b. 1917), a black poet and politician born in Pinte-à-Pitre, Haiti. Tirolien attended local schools and was later sent to Paris where he studied political science. While a student, he joined the négritude (q.v.) group led by Léopold S. Senghor, Aimé Césaire (q.v.), and Léon Damas (q.v.). He was taken prisoner during World War II. After the liberation of France, Tirolien became interested in the Negro Renaissance (q.v.) in the Antilles, Africa, and the United States. He was an overseas administrator of the French government in Cameroon and the Sudan. Since African independence, he has worked for the government of Nigeria and as a United Nations representative in Mali. His works include *Balles d'or* (Paris, 1960), as well as numerous essays, novels, and journal articles.

**TI-TAI** (Eng. Cr.), an Afro-Jamaican word for anything used for tying, especially string and withes.

**TITAN DE BRONCE** (Sp.), a nickname given to the Cuban mulatto hero Antonio Maceo y Grajales (q.v.).

**TI-TANE** (Fr. Cr.), in the French Antilles, a young black lady who is sexually promiscuous.

**TITINGÓ** (Afr.), an Afro-Hispanic word for fight, scandal.

**TITTLE DRUM** (Eng. Cr.), an Afro-Jamaican term for rattle drum.

**TOCKY,** a Portuguese unit of currency used in slave trading in Dahomey (q.v.) around 1793; 1 tocky was worth 1/5d. or 40 cowries.

**TOMO,** a black slave who, around 1727, was sent by the king of Dahomey (q.v.), Trudo Adato, with his favorite captain, Bullfinch Lambe, to learn all about England and report back to the king. Captain Bullfinch later took Tomo to Barbados where he sold him to a gentleman in Maryland. (Pope-Hennessy, *Sins of the Fathers*, p. 101.)

**TOM-TOM,** in Haiti, a purée made of banana and considered a black delicacy.

**TONNELLE** (Fr. Cr.), in Haiti, a temporary thatched shelter used for religious dancing.

**TONTON** (Fr. Cr.), in Haiti, a term of endearment used by blacks for an uncle or any old man.

**TONTON BANANE** (Fr. Cr.), in Martinique, a thick paste (dough) made of boiled green bananas flavored with spicy ingredients.

**TONTON MACOUTES** (Fr. Cr.), in Haiti, a secret police used by the government to control, persecute, and sometimes liquidate its political enemies; often called the "President's body-guard of armed thugs."

**TOOMBAH** (Afr.), in the West Indies, a small drum with shells inside; a favorite instrument among blacks.

**TOQUE DE BUZIO** (Pg.), a Brazilian currency equal to 20 reis; used in the slave trade.

**TORNA-ATRÁS** (Sp.), in colonial Spanish America, a mulatto.

**TORSO** (Pg.), in Brazil, a turban of cotton or silk bound around the head and worn by black women; probably an Islamic fashion brought from Africa during the colonial period.

**TOUMENT** (Afr.), an African deity of Ibo (q.v.) origin worshipped in some Afro-Haitian cults.

**TOUSSAINT L'OUVERTURE.** See L'OUVERTURE, TOUSSAINT.

**TOWN HIGGLER,** in Jamaica, a black woman trader who rents market stalls to sell produce. See also HIGGLER.

**TRABAJAR COMO NEGRO** (Sp.) ("to work like a Negro"), an expression used in the Afro-Caribbean area meaning to work hard and long.

**TRABALHO É PARA CACHORRO E NEGRO** (Pg.) ("work is for a dog and a black"), a Brazilian aphorism referring to the traditional identification of manual labor with black slave work. It is considered inappropriate for an aristocrat to labor as lower class people do.

**TRADESMAN SLAVE,** in Jamaica (circa 1820), a black slave craftsman working on plantations in a small group under a black or white overseer. These specialized slaves were highly valued.

**TRAITEMENT** (Fr. Cr.), in Haiti, magic healing done by black sorcerers with herbs and charms.

**TRAJE DOMINGUEIRO** (Pg.), clothes worn by slaves on Sundays in colonial Brazil.

**TRANCAZO** (Sp.), in Puerto Rico, *dengué* fever (q.v.).

**TRANGO-MANGO** (Pg.), in Afro-Brazilian folklore, a goblin with seven sets of teeth; used to frighten children.

**TRAPICHE** (Sp.), a primitive sugar cane (q.v.) mill constructed with gears and rollers and operated by animal power and a few slaves. It was introduced by the Spaniards in Hispaniola, Cuba, and other hispanic areas early in the sixteenth century. See also INGENIO DE AZÚCAR.

**TRATA DE NEGROS** (Sp.) ("slave trade"), the first official recognition of the institution of black slavery in the New World. In 1501, Nicolás de Ovando, governor of the Indies, was authorized by the Spanish Crown to take to Hispaniola Christianized slaves born on the peninsula. In 1518, the first license to transport and sell blacks in quantity directly from Africa to America was granted by Charles V to a Flemish favorite, Laurent de Gouvernat. This was the official beginning of the slave trade. (Haring, *The Spanish Empire*, pp. 203-204.)

**TRAY GIRLS,** in urban Jamaica, black women who carry their total stock of produce (garlic, peppers, cabbage, onions, and other items) on a tray or flat basket for sale on the streets or in the market.

**TRÉ, TROJE** (Fr. Cr.), in the Afro-Antilles, a flat-bottomed open receptacle with a low rim used by black women to carry produce for sale on the streets or in the market.

**TREFU** (Afr.), among the Bush Negroes (q.v.) of Guiana, a ritual taboo on eating certain foods; its origin is Ashanti (q.v.).

**TREMPÉ** (Afr.), in Haiti, an alcoholic beverage prepared with rum and aromatic leaves; a favorite black drink.

**TREN JAMAIQUINO** (Sp.), a steam engine for the sugar mills (q.v.), an English invention introduced into Jamaica around 1825. Soon after its use spread to Cuba and elsewhere. It revolutionized the production of sugar by reducing the slave force and greatly increasing production.

**TRIANGLE TRADE,** the intra-empire trade among Britain, West Africa, and the American colonies. It specialized in certain tropical crops, needed foodstuffs, and manufactured goods. Products were shipped across the Atlantic, usually in April, June, or August. See also THREE-CORNERED TRADE.

**TRICKSTER HERO,** in Afro-Caribbean folklore, the main character of the animal tales such as the spider Anancy (q.v.); its origin is African. See ANANCY STORY.

**TRINDADE, SOLANO,** a mulatto Brazilian poet deeply inspired by black themes. He was one of the founders of the Centro de Cultura Afro-Brasileira (q.v.) in 1937. Among his works are *Poemas d'uma Vida Simples* (Rio de Janeiro, 1945); *Seis Tempos de Poesia* (São Paulo, 1958); and *Cantares ao meu Povo* (São Paulo, 1961).

**TRIUNFO EUCHARISTICO** (Pg.) ("The Eucharistic Triumph"), the title of a play (Lisbon, 1734) written by members of Irmandade (q.v.) dos Irmãos Pretos da Nossa Senhora do Rosario, Minas Gerais, Brazil. The play illustrates the penchant of the Portuguese for outward splendor and the fondness of slaves for dancing. (Boxer, *The Golden Age*, p. 178.)

**TROCA DA CABEÇA** (Pg.), in Afro-Brazilian folklore, a magic ritual in which a sorcerer removes a disease from a sick person for the purpose of transferring it to another individual.

**TROCA DIA** (Pg.), in Brazil and elsewhere, an African-style cooperative work group widely spread throughout the New World.

**TROIS-SEPT** (Fr. Cr.), an Afro-Haitian card game.

**TROJE.** See TRÉ.

**TRONCO** (Pg.), in Brazil, an instrument of torture made of iron or hardwood which held a slave at the ankle, often for days.

**TROOPING,** in black revivalist cults in the Caribbean, the action of inducing, by hyperventilation, semiconsciousness and ultimately frenzy. Also called trumping and laboring.

**TRUNK FLEET** (Eng. Cr.), in colonial Jamaica, a string of nine or ten black slave girls carrying trunks filled with their mistress's clothes.

**TUDERATION** (Eng. Cr.), in Jamaica, a word used in black dialect humor.

**TUESDAY,** in Jamaica, a lucky day for blacks to go out to look for work; should a man fail to find work on one Tuesday, he will not try again until the following Tuesday.

**TUMBA, TUMBE** (Afr.), in Jamaica, a drum; a variety of banjo played by black Maroons (q.v.).

**TUMBA DE ARCO** (Pg.), in Brazil, a covered bier used exclusively by the white population during colonial times. In 1720, a Colored Brotherhood of Bahia asked King João V for the privilege of being buried in a *tumba de arco*. It represented an advance over the *esquife* (q.v.) permitted to the slaves by law.

**TUMBADERO,** in Cuba, a special room on a sugar estate (q.v.) for slave flogging (q.v.).

**TUMBE.** See TUMBA.

**TUMBEIRO** (Pg.), a slave ship transporting blacks from Africa to Brazil. The name *tumbeiro* (undertaker) referred to the high mortality rate during the Atlantic crossing, especially in the vessels from Guinea (q.v.); the trip lasted thirty-five to fifty days.

**TUMBLE DOWN** (Eng. Cr.), in Jamaica, the first pregnancy of an unwed black girl.

**TUMBOZOO** (Afr.), an Afro-Jamaican word for a big foot, the result of elephantiasis that often afflicted black slaves.

**TUMPA TOE** (Eng. Cr.), in the Caribbean, a stump-like remnant of toes or of the whole foot resulting from jiggers' (q.v.) infestation; a scourge among slaves.

**TUM-TUM,** an Afro-Jamaican drum with a goatskin head played by blacks.

**TUNDA** (Sp.), among blacks of the Pacific Colombian lowlands, a mythical, terrifying being who seeks bad children and frightens them to death.

**TUNDA-CUMBÉ** (Afr.), in colonial Brazil, a gang of runaway slaves and mulattoes, all with criminal records, who pillaged the houses of the planters, killed and ate livestock, and maltreated the women and children.

**TUNGTUNGO** (Afr.), an Afro-Cuban word meaning the rhythmic beating of a drum played by blacks.

**TUN-TUN, TUN-TUS,** in Jamaica, a term of endearment used by blacks for a child or sweetheart.

**TUN-TUN DE PASA Y GRIFERÍA** (Sp.), a book of Afro-Antillean poetry by Luis Palés Matos (San Juan, 1937) in which he evokes an African background with elephants, hippopotami, and baobab trees in an amusing and playful rhythm. It was considered a great contribution to the literature of the Negro Renaissance (q.v.).

**TUN-TUS.** See TUN-TUN.

**TUOTO** (Afr.), in the West Indies, an African word meaning a small cake made of flour and brown sugar, sometimes with shredded coconut.

**TURN-BILL** (Eng. Cr.), in Jamaica, a machete with a turned or hooked end used by blacks in the fields to pull forward the branches of stalks that are to be cut.

**TURNBULL, DAVID,** a British abolitionist who, in 1838, arrived at Santiago, Cuba from Demerara, the British Antilles. He visited the mines and sugar estates (q.v.) in the Guinea (q.v.) and Mantanzas districts, and reported his observations in a book, *Travels in the West, Cuba* (London, 1840). His accounts brought violent reactions among the Cuban planters. When his friend, Lord Palmerston (q.v.) appointed him British consul and superintendent of free Africans on the island, the government recognized his status as a diplomat but rejected his position as supervisor of free slaves. He left Cuba in 1842. (Calcagno, *Diccionario*, p. 628.)

**TURN-COLOUR MAN** (Eng. Cr.), in Jamaica, a derogatory term for a nearly white person.

**TUTÚ** (Pg.), in Afro-Brazilian folklore, a goblin used to frighten children.

**TUTÚ DE FEIJÃO** (Pg.), an Afro-Brazilian dish made of salt pork, bacon, beans, and manihot flour.

**TUYÉ-LEVÉ** (Fr. Cr.), in Haiti, witchcraft in which a black sorcerer kills someone through magic powers, then takes him out of the grave, restores him to life and makes him a servant slave.

**TWI**, an African language spoken by slaves in the New World.

**TWO-SIDE BASKET** (Eng. Cr.), in the West Indies, an African square-cornered basket with a lid and handle made of palm thatch. See also BANKRA.

**TYMBALE**, an Afro-Haitian musical instrument consisting of a large cylindrical drum with heads at both ends.

# u

**UANTUAFUNO** (Afr.), in Brazil, a black colorfully dressed as a vassal of an African king. He formed part of a happy and noisy gang in traditional Afro-Brazilian festivals, especially carnivals.

**UIANI,** among Black Caribs (q.v.), Satan.

**ULAMA** (Ar.), in Brazil, a highly respected Islamic teacher among Moslem slaves.

**ULUÉ** (Afr.), the head of a black slave religious brotherhood in the Afro-Cuban religion. He used to organize, direct, and preside over the group.

**UMAN-KRA** (Afr.), among the Bush Negroes (q.v.) of Guiana, a spirit taken from the mother by the Supreme Being and implanted in each child at birth; it vanishes at the moment of death. This spirit, of Fanti-Ashanti (q.v.) origin, symbolizes clan affiliation.

**UMBALU** (Afr.), among Afro-Caribbean blacks, a fraternity in charge of performing funerary rituals.

**UMBANDA** (Afr.), an Afro-Brazilian cult which is today flourishing throughout Brazil. Apparently developed from the *macumba* (q.v.), it includes Indian and Catholic elements, with a priesthood, a set of dogmas, and a liturgy; it emphasizes a strong belief in the worship of black ancestors. It represents a black syncretism that, at least in the major urban centers, has moved on from the old spontaneous slave and Indian practices into a Brazilian religious ideology, parallel to the development of political nationalism among the proletariat. (Bastide, *African Civilizations*, pp. 87, 221.)

**UMBANDISTA** (Afr.), in Brazil, a follower of the Umbanda (q.v.) sect.

**UM POUCO DA RAÇA** (Pg.) (''a little color''), an expression applied in

Brazil to a person of African decent whose desire to marry a white woman is not opposed, provided he also belongs to the upper class.

**UNCREOLIZED,** in the Caribbean, a term that usually pertained to black slaves who had not yet adapted Creole speech and manners of living.

**UNDER-OVERSEER** (Eng. Cr.), in Jamaica, a bookkeeper; in slavery times, a young man kept on each plantation whose duties included going to the fields with the blacks or staying at home with the keys to the stores which were constantly in demand.

**UNFORTUNATE CIRCUMSTANCES OF BIRTH,** a legal term used in colonial Jamaica and elsewhere to refer to mulattoes. The majority of this group, offspring of a white father and a black woman, usually attempted to cling to their white ancestry.

**UNGGURU** (Afr.), in Jamaica, a black albino.

**UNIÃO DAS SEITAS AFRO-BRASILEIRAS DA BAHIA** (Pg.) (Union of the Afro-Brazilian Sects of Bahia), a religious organization founded on August 3, 1937, for the purpose of attaining official recognition of religious liberty for the Bahian blacks. A general council of the union, formed by each congregation, is responsible for the control of all the sects.

**UNIDADE** (Pg.) ("a unit"), a Portuguese word for slave used in West Africa during the slave trade.

**UNIVERSAL NEGRO IMPROVEMENT ASSOCIATION (UNIA),** an international organization founded by Marcus Garvey (q.v.) in Kingston, Jamaica, in 1918 to foster a great black community that would eventually unify the black race. The group was based on ideas of racial purity; it rejected mulattoes, considering them traitors and boot-licking agents of subserviency to the whites.

**UN NOIR AU POUVOIR** (Fr.) ("A Negro to power"), a party slogan advocating François Chevalier as candidate for the presidency of Haiti in 1946.

**UN PIED, UN MAIN, UN JÉ** (Fr. Cr.) (one foot, one hand, one eye), an Afro-Haitian god.

**UPLIFTING THE TABLE** (Eng. Cr.), in Jamaican black revivalist cults, a prayer meeting to seek understanding and prophecy.

**URHOBO,** an ethnic group located in the Niger River Delta south of Benin City from which slaves were imported into the West Indies around 1815. (Curtin, *The Atlantic Slave*, p. 293.)

**URUBÁ,** in colonial Brazil, a black slave with a tattooed face.

**URUCONGO** (Afr.), in colonial Brazil, a melancholic slave song.

**USINA** (Pg.), in Brazil, a modern sugar refinery.

**UTRECHT, PEACE OF,** a series of treaties signed in Utrecht (1713) by Spain, England, and other countries. One of its main provisions was to grant England the exclusive right to supply the Spanish colonies with slaves. Of all the British colonies in the New World, Jamaica was the greatest beneficiary of this agreement.

# V

**VACCINE** (Fr. Cr.), a bamboo trumpet played by blacks in sequence; the nearest musician taps a second rhythm on the side of the single-note instrument. The instrument and the playing technique are from Africa. In Haiti, there are *vaccine* orchestras of three and four instruments which walk through a village followed by dancers during Holy Week festivities. Also called BOIS BOURIGNE.

**VAGABOND GANG,** in colonial Jamaica, a special group of slave offenders who, instead of being sent to prison, were condemned to hard labor in this gang, sometimes serving life sentences. In May 1795, on the Worthy Park plantation, in Jamaica, the vagabond gang included thirteen offenders —nine men and four women. (Craton and Walvin, *A Jamaican Plantation*, p. 144.)

**VAI,** an ethnic group settled along the Atlantic seashore in Liberia from which a few slaves were brought to the West Indies around 1844. (Curtin, *The Atlantic Slave*, p. 291.)

**VALDEZ, DIEGO GABRIEL DE LA CONCEPCIÓN.** See PLÁCIDO.

**VALENTÍN,** a black Cuban slave leader on the *ingenio* (q.v.) Nueva Vizcaya and on the other estates in the Yumuri district during the Conspiracy of the Ladder (q.v.) in March 1844. The slaves eventually elected him king, and he had about 6,000 blacks under his command. (Hall, *Social Control*, p. 58.)

**VALIENTE, JUAN,** a black slave, apparently an African native, who with the permission of his owner, Alonso Valiente, joined Pedro de Alvarado's army as it was moving from Guatemala to Peru in 1534. This black man distinguished himself in Chile with Almagro in 1536 and once again with Pedro de Valdivia four years later. Valiente was undoubtedly a fierce fighter, for, as a result of his exploits in battles against the Araucanian Indians in 1546, Valdivia, then governor of Chile, rewarded him with an estate near the capital of Santiago. Juan subsequently married Juana de Valdivia, the governor's ex-slave, in 1548, and two years later he became the first known black to receive an encomienda (a fief of tribute-paying Indians). A few years later, he was killed along with his benefactor by the Araucanian Indians in the battle of Tucapel in 1553. The irony of his life was that land-lord or not, Juan Valiente was still a slave. In 1550 he had hired Esteban de Sosa, a Spanish official, to negotiate with his old master for the purchase of his freedom. Sosa took the money, but he did little else before returning to Europe. Even before Juan was killed, Alonso Valiente had learned of his whereabouts and initiated legal proceedings to reclaim both the slave and whatever property he might have accumulated. The story of Juan Valiente mirrors the general and legal position of the African in Spanish America: he might garner fame and fortune, but the stigma of his origin was always upon him. (Rout, L. B., *The African Experience in Spanish America*, p. 76.)

**VALONGO** (Pg.), a large slave market in Rio de Janeiro, Brazil, famous for its cruel spectacles, details of which have been described in the accounts of many foreign travelers.

**VANJOU** (Fr. Cr.), in Haiti, a cooperative group of fifteen to twenty black laborers who hire themselves out to work on behalf of one particular landowner in return for food, drink, and a social gathering. See also COUMBITÉ.

**VARELA, FAGUNDES** (1841-1875), a Brazilian poet. Varela wrote *Cantos Meridionais* in which he praises the suffering slaves; in one of the poems, "O Escravo," Varela describes the toil, tribulations, and dreams of distant Africa that torment the soul of the black. If the slave, says the poet, had defended himself by calling upon the African wind, it would have sum-moned to his aid the beasts of the jungle. Varela had only occasional interest in the black slaves, however, and he apparently did not feel any deep kin-ship with the darker Brazilians.

**VASCULHADOR** (Pg.), in Brazil, a black cleaner of chimneys, roofs, and walls.

**VASSA, GUSTAVUS.** See EQUIANO, OLAUDAH.

**VASSOURA-DE-BRUXA** (Pg.), in Afro-Brazilian cults, magic branches used in sorcery by blacks. Also known as VASSOURA-DE-FEITICEIRIA.

**VASSOURA DO DESPACHO** (Pg.), in Afro-Brazilian cults, the sacred broom used by a black sorcerer to chase away evil spirits.

**VATAPÁ** (Pg.), an Afro-Brazilian dish made of fish and dried shrimp with *dendé* oil, peanuts, and various spices.

**VAUDOUX HYMN** (Fr. Cr.). See VOODOO HYMN.

**VAUDOUX SECT** (Fr. Cr.). See VOODOO SECT.

**VAUGHAN, H. A.** (b. 1901), a black poet born in Barbados. Vaughn attended local schools and completed his education in England. On his return to the island, he entered politics and was elected a member of the Barbados House of Assembly, later becoming a district magistrate. In 1945, he published *Sandy Land and Other Poems*.

**VAVAL, DURACINÉ (b.** 1879), a black poet born in Aux Cayes, Haiti. After finishing his primary and secondary education in his country, he was sent to Paris where he received a law degree. On his return to Port-au-Prince, he worked as a school teacher, then practiced law, and was appointed a civil judge. At one time, he was chief of the Haitian legation in London. Among his numerous publications are *L'Art dans la vie* (1900); *Conférences historiques* (1907); *Coup d'oeil sur l'état financier de la république* (1907); *Littérature haïtienne* (Paris, 1911); *Les Stances haïtiennes* (Paris, 1912); and *L'Ame noir* (Paris, 1933).

**VAZ COELHO, ANTONIO,** a free black born in Brazil'who, around 1790, made several voyages to Ardra (q.v.) on the Slave Coast (q.v.). He later organized a profitable business in the slave trade and became a very respectable businessman. It is said that he introduced the idea of mounting swivel guns on war canoes. (Davidson, *Black Mother*, p. 275.)

**VELHO LOURENÇO,** in Afro-Brazilian folklore, an elderly, mythical black slave believed to be a friendly spirit who gives spiritual and material assistance to his devotees.

**VENDA** (Pg.), in colonial Brazil, a plantation-owned country store that served the sugar estate (q.v.) slave population. Today it is a rural grocery store that sells coarse textiles, dry goods, liquors, knick-knacks and tin dishes to renters, sharecroppers, and poor blacks.

**VENDER UN NEGRO ALMA EN BOCA Y HUESOS EN COSTAL** (Sp.), the selling of a slave without responsibility on the part of the seller for any sickness or vices which the slave might have; a slave trade idiom used in the Spanish Antilles. (Alvarez Nazario, *El elemento negroide*, p. 359.)

**VENTAILLAGE** (Fr. Cr.), in Afro-Haitian cults, a special ritual in which the priest takes a sacrificial cock in each hand, then walks along the line of the faithful, dancing and swinging the bird up and down before him.

**VENTE GRAN' GOUT PAS GAIN ZOREILLE** (Fr. Cr.) ("A starving belly doesn't have ears"), an aphorism from slavery times still used by blacks in Haiti. (Courlander, *The Drum*, p. 336.)

**VERANDA** (Eng. Cr.), in the West Indies, an open gallery or portico, usually roofed, attached to the exterior of the great house (q.v.) on the plantations.

**VERDE ISLANDS.** See CAPE VERDE ISLANDS.

**VERMEHALI, LOS VERMEJALES,** a Maroon settlement (q.v.) and its inhabitants organized around 1656 on a plateau in the mid-interior of Jamaica. These runaway slaves, the remnants of early Spanish settlers on the island, put up strong resistance to the invading British forces. When the blacks moved some miles to the west of the original site, they carried the name with them. (Price, *Maroon Societies*, p. 257.)

**VERNEGEREN** (D.), in Surinam, a derogatory term for a wretched black; a Dutch-derived word stressing the low moral and social status of the blacks. (Lier, *Frontier Society*, p. 270.)

**VERVINE** (Eng. Cr.), the vervaine of Jamaica *(Stachy-tarpheta jamaicensis)*, much valued by blacks as a tea and in folk remedies. The leaves of the vervaine plant were used by slaves as a refreshing morning tea, sweetened to taste.

**VESTIMENTO BAHIANO** (Pg.), in Bahia, Brazil, a colorful costume worn by black women. It includes a long, loose-flowing white cotton blouse, a turban of cotton or silk, strapless leather sandals, and numerous necklaces of coral, cowries, or glass beads, with a metal chain often of silver, earrings of turquoise, coral, silver, or gold, and bracelets of iron, copper, or other metal. This costume is commonly worn on feast days. (Pierson, *Negroes*, p. 246.)

**VÈVÉ** (Fr. Cr.), in Afro-Haitian cults, magic drawings for the gods traced on the ground of a temple by a priest using white flour and ashes. When the spirits answer the summons, the *vèvés* have served their purpose and are scraped out. These drawings are composed of a multiplicity of cabalistic symbols—heart shapes, stars, interlocked V's, flags, machetes, circles, mortar shapes, and so on—each with its own specific meaning. The *vèvé* sometimes becomes openly pictorial. (Courlander, *The Drum*, p. 124). See also PONTOS.

**VIDAL DE NEGREIROS, ANDRÉ,** a white Brazilian captain who, in 1645 leading an army of blacks, mulattoes, and Indians, fought and defeated the Dutch invaders in northeast Brazil. Later, in the 1660s, he became a governor of Angola (q.v.). His administration was irregular, and he committed acts of violence, among others, that of deporting Angola slaves to Pernambuco to labor on the sugar plantations. (Rodrigues, *Brazil and Africa*, p. 24.)

**VIDE** (Fr. Cr.), in the French Antilles, a wild and noisy parade of black singers and dancers; usually part of the Mardi Gras celebration.

**VIENS-VIENS** (Fr. Cr.), in Afro-Haitian folklore, ordinary ghosts of dead persons to whom God has given the right to live and wander on earth.

**VIENTRE LIBRE** (Sp.) (''Free Womb''), a decree issued by the Cuban governor, Francisco Serrano, on September 29, 1868, freeing all slaves born after that date. It officially committed the Spanish government to the principle of abolition of slavery in Cuba and Puerto Rico.

**VILLATTE,** a Haitian mulatto politician who, in 1791, led a slave rebellion. He opposed Toussaint L'Ouverture (q.v.). On March 20, 1796, Villatte defeated the colonist forces and imprisoned the French governor. L'Ouverture demanded the release of the French official and defeated Villatte, who then fled the country.

**VILLAVERDE, CIRILO** (1812-1894), a Cuban nationalist who was well known as the author of the antislavery novel *Cecilia Valdez* (q.v.). Because of his political activities, Villaverde lived most of his life in New York working as a teacher and writing for periodicals.

**VILLEVALIEX, CHARLES SÉGUY** (1835-1923), a Haitian black poet influenced by the romantic movement. He published *Les primavères* (Paris, 1866).

**VIMBINDINQUE** (Afr.), in colonial Haiti, a black secret society based on ethnic group affiliation, but including members recruited from the population at large. According to tradition, it was a predatory group, often holding cannibalistic rites. Bizarre tales and legends disseminated by the white colonists have resulted in a large body of folklore about the group's activities.

**VINE-GANG,** on West Indian plantations, a group of young slaves up to the age of sixteen who engaged in light field work or acted as assistants to wagoners, pen-keepers, domestic staff, and so forth.

**VINTEM BRANCO** (Pg.), in some Afro-Brazilian cults a silver coin which is included as a charm in the offering to the ancestors.

**VIRER** (Fr. Cr.), in Afro-Haitian cults, a graceful ceremony of greeting during which each faithful, advancing towards the priest, honors him as their god's representative.

**VIRTUE, VIVIAN L.** (b. 1911), a black poet born in Kingston, Jamaica. After finishing elementary school, Virtue entered Kingston College. He contributed to such magazines as *Life and Letters* and the *London Mercury*. He is an officer of the Poetry League of Jamaica and a member of the Royal Society of Literature of England. His first collection of poems, *Wings of the Morning*, appeared in 1938.

**VISARIA** (Pg.), in Brazil, a slave's song, sung in Portuguese.

**VISSUNGO** (Afr.), a work song sung by slave diamond-miners in Minas Gerais, Brazil. There were special *vissungos* for the morning, mid-day, and afternoon. The lyrics included a mixture of Portuguese and African words.

**VITRI, LIXARI** (Afr.), among Afro-Brazilian Moslems, the fifth and last prayer of the day; recited in the evening.

**VIVA THE BROWN PEOPLE!** a popular battle cry in racially troubled Panama praising the West Indian or Spanish-speaking blacks.

**VIZCARRONDO Y CORONADO, JULIO L. DE** (1830-1899), a Puerto Rican writer and journalist. After attending local schools, Vizcarrondo was sent to continue his education in Philadelphia. There he married Harriet Brewster, possibly a Quaker (q.v.) from the same city. In 1854, he returned to the island and immediately began emancipating his own slaves and denouncing abuses practiced on slaves before the courts. As a result, he was exiled by the government and went back to Philadelphia. In 1863, he traveled to Spain, arriving in Madrid on July 4, 1863. The following year he organized the Sociedad Abolicionista Española (q.v.) in Madrid which included among its members leading politicians such as Emilio Castelar, Juan Valera, Fernán Caballero, Mateo Praxedes Sagasta, Segismundo D. Moret y Prendergast (q.v.) and Nicolás Salmerón (Corwin, *Spain and the Abolition*, p. 154.)

**VON-VON** (Fr. Cr.), a bull roarer—a thin flat piece of wood whirled on the end of a cord; played by Haitian blacks at the time of the Rada (q.v.) festival, usually on Good Friday.

**VOODOO** (Afr.), in Haiti, a complex of African belief and ritual governing in large measure the religious life of the black peasantry. It is an integrated system of concepts concerning human activities, the relationship between the natural world and the supernatural, and the ties between the living and the dead. It has its own cause-and-effect systems to explain otherwise inexplicable or unpredictable events and thus establishes order where there might otherwise be chaos. It provides guidelines for personal and social behavior, including the duties of the faithful to the gods. The word *voodoo* means spirit in Ewe (q.v.), a West African language.

**VOODOO DANCE** (Fr. Cr.), in Haiti, the most public aspect of the black peasant religion. It is an important social occasion, and its success is measured by the numbers in attendance and the enthusiasm of the participants. It is an important ritual and an opportunity for recreation.

**VOODOO HYMN** (Fr. Cr.), an African battle hymn sung by the slaves at the time of the great black revolt in Haiti in 1791, especially at the secret meetings held prior to the uprising. It was a sacred hymn, expressed in African words incomprehensible to the white colonists. (Fouchard, *Les Marrons*, pp. 536-37.)

**VOODOO SECT** (Fr. Cr.), originally an African secret society introduced into Saint Domingue by black slaves early in the colonial period.

**VOZ DA RAÇA, A** (Pg.) ("The Voice of the Race"), a bimonthly publication under the direction of Raōl Amaral which first appeared in São Paulo, Brazil on March 18, 1933. It undertook several campaigns on behalf of the Brazilian blacks, seeking to better their economic and social conditions. It also proposed the foundation of libraries, recreational and musical groups, theaters and sporting associations to integrate the black population with the rest of the nation.

**VROMAN, MARY ELIZABETH** (b. 1925), a black writer born in Kingston, Jamaica. After attending local schools, Vroman went to the United States where she enrolled at a state college in Alabama. She was the first black woman to gain membership in the Screen Writers Guild. Two of her short stories, "See How They Run" and "And Have No Charity," have been published in the *Ladies Home Journal*. "See How They Run" was made into the motion picture *Bright Road* (1953). She has also written *Esther*, a novel (1963), and *Shaped to Its Purpose*, a history of Delta Sigma Theta Sorority (1964). (Hughes, *The Best Short Stories*, p. 506.)

# W

**WAGATY** (Afr.), an Afro-Jamaican word for clumsy.

**WAGA-WAGA** (Afr.), in the West Indies, an African term for plentiful, opulent.

**WAGONER SLAVE,** on West Indian plantations, a skilled slave who operated in small productive units under a white overseer or under a white tradesman practicing the same specialty. These slaves were highly valued on the sugar estates (q.v.).

**WAITING-BOY,** in Jamaica, a young black male about fifteen years of age who used to wait on a gentleman; a personal attendant.

**WAJA** (Eng. Cr.), in Jamaica, a tropical plant of the cocoa family highly valued as food by blacks; also called *toya*.

**WAKEE** (Afr.), in the West Indies, an African ethnic name and language; a slave of this origin.

**WALCOTT, DEREK** (b. 1930), a black poet born in Saint Lucia and one of the leading West Indian poets of today. Walcott attended schools on his native island. He has written and taught in Trinidad and Jamaica and has traveled widely. Among his works are *The Sea at Dauphin: A Play in 1 Act* (Mona, Jamaica, 1958); *Ione: A Play with Music* (Mona, Jamaica, 1957); *Drums' Colours* (Port-of-Spain, Trinidad, 1961); *In a Green Night; Poems, 1948-1960* (London, 1962); *Malcauchon, or, Six in the Rain: A Play in 1 Act* (Kingston, s.d.); and *Ti Jean: A Play in 1 Act* (Mona, Jamaica, s.d.).

**WALCOTT, RODERICK,** a poet and playwright born in Saint Lucia. His works include *The Harrowing of Benjy: A Character Study in Two Scenes* (Mona, Jamaica, 1958); *A Flight of Sparrows* (Kingston, s.d.); *Malfinis, or, the Heart of a Child* (Kingston, s.d.); and *Shrove Tuesday March: A Play of the Stellband* (Kingston, s.d.).

**WALK,** in the West Indies, a grove usually planted with trees, often fruit trees. The term usually appears in toponyms such as Banana———, Chocolate———, Cocoa———, Coffee———, Gungo———, Pear———, Peas———, Pimento———, Plantain———, Prickle———, and Thatch ———. (Cassidy, *Dictionary*, p. 460.)

**WALK-AND-NYAM** (Eng. Cr.), an Afro-Jamaican expression for one who lives off others; a "sponge."

**WALK-DANDY-DUDE** (Eng. Cr.), in Jamaica, a finely dressed black.

**WALK GOOD!** ("Safe journey!"), an exclamation common among Jamaican blacks; used when a person is setting out on a journey, although not necessarily a long one.

**WALKING BUCKRA,** an Afro-Jamaican phrase for a beggar or vagabond, usually a black. See also BACKRA.

**WALKING SAAL** (Eng. Cr.), among Jamaican blacks, provisions, specifically meat.

**WALK THE PLANK,** the practice on slaving ships of throwing slaves into the sea in case of rebellion, massive sickness, or short provisions. This was a common practice among Guinea (q.v.) captains carrying black cargoes to the West Indies during the seventeenth and eighteenth centuries. (Mannix, *Black Cargoes*, p. 125.) See also SLAVE JETTISONING.

**WALROND, ERIC** (1895-1966), a black writer born in British Guiana. Walrond was educated in the Panama Canal Zone and then attended City College of New York and Columbia University. In his youth, he traveled extensively throughout Europe, settling for a while in France and later living in London. His exotic short stories of the West Indies were published in *Tropic Death* (1926) which appeared during Harlem's Negro Renaissance (q.v.) when Walrond lived in New York. He later worked on a book about his years in the Panama Canal Zone. (Hughes, *The Best Short Stories*, p. 506.)

**WAMBO** (Afr.), a black leader of some African cults in Trinidad.

**WAMPARA** (Eng. Cr.), in the West Indies, a machete of various sizes and shapes used by blacks in the sugar fields.

**WANÁRAGUA** (Afr.), among black Caribs (q.v.), a male dance performed on Christmas Day and on January 6 by a group of men dressed in short, full skirts, blouses with yokes and long, full sleeves, colored stockings, masks, and elaborate headdresses with feathers and ribbons. This dance has two names—one is *wanárangua*, which means mask, and the other is John Canoe (q.v.).

**WANGA, WENGA** (Afr.). 1. In Jamaica, a black dance characterized by raising one's shoulders and moving one's arms. 2. In Afro-Haitian folklore, a charm that works evil magic.

**WANGLA, WONGALA** (Afr.), among Afro-Jamaicans, a magic tree *(Rosamum orientale)* believed to have *obeah* (q.v.) power. It should be planted in the provision ground and the seeds carefully gathered. The burning of *wangla* branches with pepper and salt on a road on which a thief passes will give him Jamaica leprosy; the burning of the seeds will make the thief's skin strip off. Also called oil-plant. (Beckwith, *Black Roadways*, pp. 128-29.)

**WANIKA** (Afr.), in Jamaica, an African woman's name.

**WAR,** in colonial West Africa, a slave trade term for a raiding expedition organized by black chiefs into the interior of the continent to obtain captives for sale to the West Indian planters. These wars were carried out by the king's soldiers, from 300 to 3,000 at a time, who attacked and set fire to a village and seized the inhabitants. (Mannix, *Black Cargoes*, p. 95.)

**WARI, WARRI** (Afr.), an Afro-Jamaican game played with small balls moved in holes in a board. It is also played with nickels and formerly was played with marbles.

**WARM FIRE** (Eng. Cr.), among Afro-Jamaicans, to warm oneself at the fire.

**WARM-MOUTH,** in Jamaica, a term of slave origin for the first meal of the day.

**WARRI.** See WARI.

**WARRIOR SHEPHERD,** in the West Indies, an officer of black revivalist cults who protects the temple from human and evil intrusions; sometimes called captain.

**WART-BUSH** (Eng. Cr.), in the West Indies, any wild milky plant or milkweed (genus *Asclepias*) with milky juice used by blacks to remove warts.

**WART-HERB** (Eng. Cr.), in Jamaica, any tropical, wild milkweed used by blacks in folk medicine, especially to eradicate skin tumors and the like.

**WASH-BELLY** (Eng. Cr.), an Afro-Jamaican word for the last child that a black woman bears.

**WASH-HEAD** (Eng. Cr.), among Afro-West Indians, washed cassava which has been cleaned and wrung.

**WASH-MOUTH,** in the West Indies, early morning tea; the first meal of the day. The term originated in slavery times.

**WASH-PAY** (Eng. Cr.), in the British Caribbean, a kind of porridge made from green corn and spices; a black delicacy.

**WATCH-DEAD** (Eng. Cr.), in Jamaica, a black funeral wake on the first night after the death of the deceased.

**WATCHMAN,** in Afro-West Indian revivalist cults, a magical bundle put into a provision ground to frighten thieves away. Watchmen are commonly composed of pieces of wood-ant's nests, the roots of a particular grass, grave dirt, bunches of feathers, and the like.

**WATCHMAN, THE,** a small weekly paper edited in Kingston, Jamaica, in 1830 by two free colored men, Robert Osborn and Edward Jordon (q.v.). It was the organ of the mulattoes. In his editorials, Jordon expressed great indignation at the white minority's failure to aid the free mulattoes.

**WATER BUSH,** among Afro-Jamaicans, small branches put on top of a container to keep it from splashing when being carried.

**WATER COCONUT,** in the West Indies, a tropical palm *(Cocos nucifera)* whose fruit is picked green for the sake of its water rather than for the ripe nut meat; formerly a standard slave drink.

**WATER FETCHER,** in Jamaica, the smallest of a litter of pigs. In slavery times, the term referred to black children who had the task of fetching water to the home.

**WATER GRASS,** in the Caribbean, a tropical creeping plant with juicy stems highly valued by blacks in folk medicine.

**WATER LEMON,** in the West Indies, a wild and cultivated plant *(Passifora* *laurifolia* and *L. maliformis)* that formerly supplied wild hogs and plantation slaves with food in season.

**WATER-MAN,** on Caribbean plantations, a slave in charge of irrigating the fields.

**WATER-MAW,** an Afro-Jamaican word for the bladder of a cow.

**WATER-OATS,** in the West Indies, a tropical wild rice *(Zizania aquatica)* eaten by slaves instead of grain.

**WATER SHEPHERD,** a black officer in the revivalist cults.

**WATER-WEED,** in Jamaica, a wild marigold *(Wedelia tribolata)* used by blacks as "bush tea" (q.v.); in magic, it is burnt to keep away the duppies (q.v.).

**WATERY-YAWS** (Eng. Cr.). See GUINEA CORN.

**WAT-LEF** (Eng. Cr.), an Afro-Jamaican word for leftover food.

**WATHIQA** (Ar.), a pastoral letter supposedly sent to Jamaica (circa 1827-1828) by Abu Bakr, a West African Moslem ruler. It circulated in the Moslem slave community, eventually reaching Muhammad Kaba (q.v.), a slave in Manchester Parish. The paper exhorted all of Mahomet's followers to be true and faithful if they wished to go to Heaven. The *wathiqa* was destroyed by Kaba's wife at the time of the slave rebellion of 1832. (Curtin, *Africa Remembered*, p. 163.)

**WATRA-MANIA** (Afr.), in colonial Surinam, an African religious dance popular among slaves. It was believed that during *watra-mania* dances the initiates were possessed by the gods. This is one of the most tenacious African rites in modern Surinam. Since 1874, it has been punishable by imprisonment. (Lier, *Frontier Society*, p. 290.)

**WATSON, SAMUEL,** an English Quaker (q.v.) sent to Antiqua in 1776 where he opened a mission for the conversion of plantation slaves. This congregation was very prosperous. During the years 1769 to 1792, the number of black converts increased from 14 to 7,400, the majority of whom were baptized.

**WATTLE-PANE,** in the West Indies, a panel of wattling separating the kitchen from the bedroom in blacks' houses; formerly used by slaves in building their huts.

**WATTLE-WOOD,** in the West Indies, a tropical tree *(Loetia thammia)* used by blacks in wattling.

**WAWEE,** tribal and language names of African slaves brought to Jamaica.

**WEDDING-BESSIE,** in Jamaica, a black woman who is a frequent attendant at weddings.

**WEDGEWOOD, JOSIAH** (1730-1795), the eminent English potter who, in 1787, engraved a medallion portraying a slave with the famous sentence, "Am I Not a Man and a Brother?" (q.v.). In 1795, the abolitionists adopted it as an official seal.

**WEEDING GANG,** in the colonial West Indies, a group of slaves including young slaves about twelve years old, the weaker slaves, and those who suffered from chronic ailments, all of whom were employed in the lighter jobs on the sugar estates (q.v.). See also PICKNEY GANG; THIRD GANG.

**WEED-MAN, WEDDY,** in Jamaican revivalist cults, a black *obeah* man (q.v.) believed to know the poisonous and medicinal uses of weeds.

**WEEKEND COUNTRY HIGGLER,** in rural Jamaica, a black woman who buys produce from areas within about 25 miles of Kingston and sells it in surrounding villages on weekends.

**WE-FI-DU, WA-FIDU, WEH-FE-DO** (Afr.), in Jamaica, a locally made hat of palm thatch worn by blacks; often one with a very wide brim.

**WEIGHT,** among Afro-Jamaicans, a quantity of goods constituting a unit in marketing; specifically, 13 or 7½ pounds of fish, 28 pounds of potatoes, and the like. When selling by the pound, it is common to give 13 pounds for 12, although there is no name for this practice. (Cassidy, *Dictionary*, p. 466.)

**WELL-HANDED** (Eng. Cr.), in Jamaica, a sugar estate (q.v.) owner well provided with black laborers.

**WENGA** (Afr.). See WANGA.

**WENYA-WENYA** (Afr.), an Afro-Jamaican word for thin, fine, meager; not fat.

**WERE-WERE** (Afr.), in the Caribbean region, an African word for small, worthless things.

**WERLEIGH, CHRISTIAN** (1895-1945), a black poet born in Cap Haitien, Haiti. Educated in local schools, he became a professor of rhetoric. His works include *Le Psalmiste dans l'Ouragan* (1930) and *Le Psalmiste dans la lumière* (1934).

**WESLEY, JOHN** (1703-1791), an English evangelist preacher, the founder of Methodism. He was ordained a priest in the Church of England at Oxford in 1728, but he led a group gathered around his brother Charles, derisively called Methodists for their methodical habits of study and religious duties. He went to Georgia, in the United States in 1735 with the intention of working among black slaves, but he returned to England soon after. On May 24, 1738, at a religious meeting in London, Wesley experienced an assurance of salvation through faith in Christ alone. This conviction formed the basis of his message to the world. In 1758, he baptized two slaves brought to England from the West Indies by Nathanial Gilbert (q.v.), thus reawakening his interest in slaves. In 1772, he called the slave trade the "execrable sum of all villainies"; two years later, he published his book, *Thoughts upon Slavery.*

**WESLEY(AN),** in Jamaica, a Methodist-sponsored group labor activity featuring singing to which slaves were called by the sound of a horn.

**WESLEY HORN,** in colonial Jamaica, a horn with which black slaves were called to religious meetings. It was also commonly used in slave days as a signal to begin or cease work on the sugar estates (q.v.).

**WESLEY-WESLEY!,** in Jamaica, a Methodist religious singing-meeting attended by slaves. It was later transferred to a "sing" accompanying a communal work-party.

**WEST AFRICA SLAVING SQUADRON,** a British naval force consisting of a dozen or more vessels stationed along the African coast to capture slaving ships after the abolition of the slave trade in 1808.

**WEST INDIA COMPANY,** a corporation organized in London and established in 1825 by act of Parliament to make loans to West Indian planters against Caribbean property. Abolitionists opposed it on the basis that such an enterprise would result in the mortgaging of human beings and would adversely affect the entire slave population.

**WEST INDIA CONSUMER,** a user of Caribbean products whom the abolitionists (circa 1787) accused of being the principal cause both of the continuance of the slave trade and of slaving itself. In England, every person who habitually consumed one West Indian item produced by slaves was considered guilty of the crime of murder. (Ragatz, *The Fall*, p. 260.)

**WEST INDIA FACTOR,** in the West Indies, a commercial agent who earned a double profit in dealing with the estate owners; facing little competition he became extremely wealthy. Part of the factor's earnings came from the illegal importation of slaves.

**WEST INDIA MANGO,** in the Caribbean region, an old name for the tree *(Grias cauliflora)* whose fruit was formerly pickled like the mango (q.v.) by plantation slaves.

**WEST INDIES COMPANY,** a commercial corporation organized by the Dutch government in 1621 to engage in slave trade between the African coasts and the Dutch West Indies. It enjoyed a monopoly over the slave trade until 1666. In 1674, a second West Indies Company with a more limited charter was established, but it was never successful. In 1791, when all Dutch West Indies colonies came under the jurisdiction of the States General, it was dissolved. (Hiss, *Netherlands America*, pp. 56, 58.)

**WEST INDIES LTD.,** a book of poems (1934) by the Cuban poet Nicolás Guillen. Evoking an atmosphere of dancing and sexuality, with dynamic rhythms and vivid descriptions of blacks, the author elicits a growing social concern for the economic and cultural poverty of the former slaves in Cuba.

**WET SUGAR,** on Caribbean plantations, sugar usually made of unrefined cane sugar with some of the molasses still in it. This "new sugar" is consumed mainly by poor blacks.

**WHANGRA** (Afr.). See WANGLA.

**WHATEVER NEGER SAY IF A NO SO A NEARLY SO** ("Whatever the *obeah* man [the sorcerer] says, if it does not come to pass exactly as predicted, it comes to pass nearly so"), an Afro-Jamaican aphorism. (Beckwith, *Jamaica Proverbs*, p. 115.)

**WHEELING SHEPHERD,** in West Indian black revivalist cults, an officer whose specialty is to whirl like a dervish around the ceremonial circle, sometimes with a glass of holy water on his head which he does not spill.

**WHEN FUMFUM COME, 'STORY COME** ("A beating brings out the truth"), an Afro-Jamaican aphorism from slavery times. (Beckwith, *Jamaica Proverbs*, p. 118.)

**WHISTLING COWBOY,** in Afro-Jamaican folklore, a magic being, ghost or duppy (q.v.) associated with the rolling-calf (q.v.).

**WHITE-A-MIDDLE,** in Jamaica, a person who is half Maroon (q.v.) or half black.

**WHITE COCKROACH,** in the West Indies, a black albino.

**WHITE CREOLE,** a male born in the West Indies. In Jamaica, white Creoles were classified by occupation (circa 1820) into three groups: planters, professionals, and merchants. (M. G. Smith, *The Plural Society*, p. 73.)

**WHITE EBOE,** in the West Indies, a black albino; a term of abuse.

**WHITE FLUX** (Eng. Cr.), among West Indian blacks, a discharge of mucus in dysentery.

**WHITE FOWL,** in the West Indies, a mushroom or other edible fungus eaten by blacks. Blacks have looked upon fungi as a substitute for meat since slavery times.

**WHITE JEG,** in the West Indies, a poor white.

**WHITE LABOUR,** in Jamaica, a black albino.

**WHITE-MAN,** in the West Indies, a black albino.

**WHITE SAGE,** in the West Indies, a tropical wild bush *(Lantana camara)* which blacks used in folk medicine.

**WHITE SHOT** (Eng. Cr.), in colonial Jamaica, a white man, or a band of whites, bearing arms to suppress rebellious slaves.

**WHITE SORREL,** in the Caribbean, a tropical plant *(Hibiscus sabdariffa)* whose pods are used by blacks to make sorrel (q.v.) wine and jellies.

**WHITE SQUALL,** an Afro-Jamaican word meaning hunger. The term has been in usage since slavery times.

**WHITEWASHING** (Eng. Cr.), in Jamaica, an archaic term for the religious conversion of a slave when the conversion is made for reasons of convenience or to save one's life.

**WHITE YAM,** in the West Indies, a fine white-fleshed yam *(Dioscorea alata)*, a staple food for slaves in the colonial period.

**WHITEY-WHITEY** (Eng. Cr.), in Jamaica, a black albino.

**WHOOPING-BOY** (Eng. Cr.), a ghost or duppy (q.v.) which blacks believe appears only at certain seasons of the year and in certain places. He manifests himself at night with loud whoopings and whip cracking.

**WHYDAH.** See AJUDÁ.

**WIESING.** See WISI.

**WIFE,** in colonial Jamaica, a euphemism applied to an overseer's black mistress.

**WIG** (Eng. Cr.), in Jamaica, a haircutting style for black men.

**WILBERFORCE, WILLIAM** (1759-1833), a British statesman, humanitarian, and antislavery champion born in Hull, Yorkshire, the son of a rich merchant. A brilliant man, Wilberforce was a member of the better London clubs and a friend of William Pitt, Benjamin Franklin, and other distinguished personalities of his time. The Society for Effecting the Abolition of the Slave Trade (q.v.) asked him to become its spokesman. Together with Thomas Clarkson (q.v.), he decided to work for the total abolition of slavery. As a member of Parliament, he secured passage of the bill abolishing the slave trade in 1807. He died just a month before Parliament passed a bill abolishing slavery in all British possessions.

**WILD BASIL** (Eng. Cr.), in the West Indies, a tropical herb *(Ocimum micranthum)* valued by blacks in folk medicine. Its leaves were made into a tea to help relieve fever, and they were also rubbed over the body.

**WILD CLARY** (Eng. Cr.), in the West Indies, a tropical wild plant *(Heliotropium indicum)* which blacks use in folk medicine.

**WILD COCO,** in the West Indies, a variety of wild cocoa *(Colocasia esculenta)* which grows like potatoes, with a broad leaf in the shape of a heart. Blacks use it as a sauce to salt meat. Also called ground-coco.

**WILD HOOD,** in the West Indies, a tropical wild vine whose leaves are used by blacks to prepare soups and stews.

**WILD NEGRO,** in the Caribbean region, a Maroon (q.v.) or a runaway slave.

**WILLIAMS, CHARLES D.** (1849-1815), a black Haitian poet of the romantic school who took Victor Hugo as a model. He published *La voix du coeur; pages de la 20ème année, suivi de Paris-souvenirs* (Paris, 1886).

**WILLIAMS, FRANCIS** (b. 1700), a mulatto born in Jamaica to free parents of African descent. Protégé of the duke of Montague, Williams was picked to be the subject of an experiment aimed at discovering whether, by proper education and proper instruction at school and at a university, a black might not be found as capable in literature as a white person. He attended English schools and then was sent to Cambridge University. When George Holdane became governor of Jamaica, Williams wrote a panegyric in his honor in Latin entitled *Integerrimus et fortissiums vire, Giorgius Holdane* (George Holdane, a Man of the Greatest Heroism and Courage).

**WILLIAMS, JAMES,** a black writer born in Jamaica who was an apprenticed laborer. He published *A Narrative of Events since the First of August, 1834.*

**WINDWARD COAST,** in eighteenth-century Africa, the region along the east-west coast, mainly the present-day Ivory Coast (q.v.) and Liberia. In the nineteenth century, slave traders sometimes used the term for the area on either side of Sierra Leone (q.v.). The Windward Coast was a source of slaves brought to the New World.

**WINDWARD MAROONS,** a large group of Maroons (q.v.) who settled in the uninhabited northeastern region of Jamaica around 1656. These runaway slaves peopled Nanny Town (q.v.), Guys' Town (q.v.), Charles, or Crawford Town in Saint George Parish, and Moore Town in Portland. Their best known leaders were Captains Cuffee (q.v.), Kishee (q.v.), and Quao (q.v.).

**WINTI CULT,** an Afro-Christian sect among the Bush Negroes (q.v.) of

Guiana. One of its special rites is an ecstatic dance during which the initiates are possessed by spirits. (Lier, *Frontier Society*, p. 290.)

**WISDOM-WEED** (Eng. Cr.), in Jamaica, one or more herbs thought by black Rastafarians (q.v.) to have the property of giving wisdom.

**WISHING COW,** in the West Indies, a cow whom blacks believe wishes someone's death.

**WISI, WIESING,** in Surinam, poisoning or casting spells. The fear of *wisi* has lived on undiminished in the lives of African descendants of the slaves.

**WISI MAN,** in Surinam, a black sorcerer.

**WITCHCRAFT.** See OBEAH.

**WIZARD (MAN),** in the Caribbean region, a black sorcerer.

**WOLOF.** See GELOFE.

**WOLONGO** (Afr.). See SOONGA.

**WOMAN-BE-DAMNED,** in Jamaica, a cooking arrangement whereby black workmen may dispense with the help of a female cook.

**WOMAN OF COLOUR,** in Jamaica, a woman of mixed white and black ancestry. This term was current in the latter part of the eighteenth century, although "brown" is the preferred Jamaican term.

**WONGALA.** See WANGLA.

**WOOD LIZARD** (Eng. Cr.). See WOOD-SLAVE.

**WOOD-SKIN,** in Afro-Jamaican folk tales, the bark of a tree.

**WOOD-SLAVE, WOOD LIZARD,** among Jamaican blacks, a term applied to a small lizard that dwells in rotten wood.

**WOODSLEY, H. AUSTIN.** See MITTELHÖLZER, EDGAR AUSTIN.

**WOOD SORREL,** in the West Indies, tropical herbs *(Oxalis cornuculata* and *O. corymbosa)* used by blacks in folk medicine.

**WORKING** (Eng. Cr.), in Afro-Caribbean revivalist cults, any ceremony in which "workings of the spirit" are sought. It includes protection from evil spirits and divination.

**WORK-MAN,** in Jamaica, a sorcerer.

**WORK SPORT** (Eng. Cr.), the traditional Jamaican practice among black smallholders of getting together with relatives, neighbors, and friends for the purpose of reaping a harvest, cutting bushes and trees, or building or moving a house. See also COUMBITÉ.

**WORM-GRASS** (Eng. Cr.), in the West Indies, a tropical herb *(Spigelia anthelma)* used by black peasants to destroy worms.

**WORM WEED,** in the West Indies, a tropical herb *(Chenopodium ambrosioides)* used by blacks in folk medicine, especially as a vermifuge. Also called *simikantrak*.

**WURRO-WURRO, WURRU-WURRU** (Yor.), in the West Indies, a Yoruba (q.v.) word meaning untidy, rough, in a confused mess.

# X

**XACÔCO** (Afr.), an Afro-Brazilian term for a prattler, gossip; a backbiter.

**XANGÓ** (Afr.), in Brazil, one of most powerful African deities and his cult. As a god of lightning and thunder, his fetish is a meteoric stone. In the temple, his statue is surrounded by collars of white and red, a lance, and a small staff—his divine emblems. His feast is Wednesday, and roosters and sheep are sacrificed to him. See also XANGÓ CULT.

**XANGÓ CULT,** an elaborate system of worship in honor of the African god Xangó (q.v.). It is noisy and exuberant, with practically no repression of individual impulses. Its work songs, feast-day melodies, and cradle lullabies are filled with an African joyfulness. See also SHANGÓ.

**XANGOLINÉ** (Afr.), a Moslem saint honored by Hausa slaves (q.v.) in Brazil.

**XAPANAN** (Afr.), an Afro-Brazilian god who protects against smallpox.

**XAQUE-XAQUE** (Afr.), an Afro-Brazilian hollow metal musical instrument, shaped like a dumbell, each of whose enlarged extremities contains small pebbles. When shaken, it produces a sound similar to its name. See also CHOCALHO.

**XAXÁ** (Afr.), in colonial West Africa, a black official who represented the king of his ethnic group at a slave-trading post. He was in charge of delivering slaves and collecting taxes. (Mendonça, *A Influencia*, p. 174.)

**XAXÁ, QUEEN,** the daughter of the king of Dahomey (q.v.) who, around 1820, was sent by her father to Brazil to attend school. She later married Manoel José de Souza Lopes, a wealthy Brazilian slave trader operating in the kingdom.

**XAXARÁ** (Afr.), in Brazil, a sacred straw bundle decorated with beads, a symbol of the African god Omolú (q.v.).

**XAYÁ** (Afr.), along the African coast, a black official representing a tribal chief at a slave-trading post.

**XENDENQUE** (Afr.), in Pernambuco, Brazil, a small, slim black.

**XEQUERÊ** (Afr.), in Brazil, an African musical instrument played by blacks.

**XÉRÊ, XERÉRÉ** (Afr.), in Afro-Brazilian cults, a small copper vessel full of pebbles and used in fetish rituals.

**XERÉM** (Afr.), in Afro-Brazilian fetish cults, a sacred copper bell, a symbol of Xangô (q.v.).

**XERÉRÉ.** See XÉRÊ.

**XIBÁ** (Afr.), in Brazil, a noisy black dance.

**XIBAMBA** (Afr.), in Afro-Brazilian folklore, a mythical she-mule without a head.

**XICUA** (Afr.), in Brazil, an African basket used by blacks.

**XIMANGATA** (Afr.), a black slave used as a guide by African chiefs traveling inland.

**XIN-XIN** (Afr.), an Afro-Brazilian delicacy made from chicken with dried shrimp, onions, jerimum kernels, and *dendé* palm oil (q.v.).

**XUANDA** (Afr.), in Mozambique, a slave of a Portuguese planter during the colonial period.

**XYLOPHON.** See MARIMBA.

# Y

**YABA, YABBA** (Afr.), in Jamaica crudely glazed earthenware vessels in all sizes; sometimes the clay itself. These African utensils are called *ayawa* in Twi (q.v.). (Cassidy, *Dictionary*, p. 483.)

**YACÓ** (Afr.), in Afro-Caribbean cults, a protective charm worn by blacks.

**YAGA-YAGA, YEGE-YEGE, YAGGA-YAGGA,** (Afr.), an Afro-Jamaican word for rags, tatters; old unwanted things.

**YAM, NYAM** (Afr.), in the West Indies, a tropical plant *(Dioscorea alata)* with thick, edible, starchy roots. Transplanted from Africa to Haiti in the colonial period, it became the most vital of all staples in the slave diet. It spread throughout the tropical New World and has now become the standard food of black peasants. When the yams are plentiful, especially in Haiti, there is food for the winter months and a sense of well-being; when the yam crop is poor, there is insecurity and even hunger. In black cults, the yam is the symbol of fertility, tied to the worship of the ancestors.

**YAM-BANK,** in the West Indies, a prevalent term for what is usually called a yam-hill (q.v.).

**YAM-BEAN,** in Jamaica, an edible bean *(Pachyrhizus tuberosus)* with a tuber-like yam (q.v.) cultivated mainly by blacks.

**YAM FESTIVAL.** See MANGÉ YAM.

**YAM-HILL,** in the West Indies, the heap of earth into which the yam-head is planted by black peasants. See YAM-BANK.

**YAMIGAN** (Afr.), in Haiti, a magic bundle used by blacks in folk medicine.

**YAM MANGO** (Afr.), in the West Indies, a variety of mango (q.v.) *(Mangifera indica)* with firm, pale yellow flesh considered to resemble that of yellow yams (q.v.); cultivated and eaten mainly by black peasants.

**YAMPEE** (Afr.), in the West Indies, a small variety of yam (q.v.) *(Dioscorea)* with fine, white flesh; formerly a staple food for slaves.

**YAM WALK** (Eng. Cr.), in the Caribbean area, a yam (q.v.) field usually cultivated by blacks.

**YANGA** (Afr.), in Jamaica, a black dance characterized by shaking or swaying and provocative movements; hands on hips, the dancer pushes pelvis and knees back and forth to a fast rhythm.

**YANGA, NYANGA** (Bant.), the best known slave leader in Mexican history. Probably an Angolan native, Yanga claimed to be a Congolese prince and in 1608 established a runaway slave town in the highlands of what today is east central Veracruz state. From there he and his band regularly attacked traffic on the Mexico City-Veracruz highway and raided the *haciendas* (q.v.) in the area. The Spaniards began a campaign against them in 1609. In 1611 Yanga and his band were finally defeated. Viceroy Don Luis de Velazco conceded him and his followers their freedom as long as they remained in peace, took no fugitives, and obeyed the laws. Eventually in 1612 a settlement was founded for them, the town of San Lorenzo de los Negros de Córdoba. (Rout, L.B., *The African Experience in Spanish America*, p. 106.)

**YANGKUKU APIKIBO** (Afr.), in Jamaica, a preserved Africanism for Maroon (q.v.) children.

**YANSAN** (Afr.), in Afro-Brazilian cults, a female deity manifested in wind and storm and in her fetish, a meteorite. Dressed in red, she carries a sword as her insignia. Her favorite foods are goat and hen. (Pierson, *Negroes*, p. 283.)

**YANVALOU** (Fr. Cr.), a dance and rhythm characteristic of Afro-Haitian cults. It is a personal invocation to the *loas* (q.v.) or spirits, especially Legba (q.v.), to come down and "mount" or possess the dancer and "ride" him. (Jahn, *Muntu*, pp. 42, 43.)

**YARA** (Afr.), a Yoruba (q.v.) black mermaid worshipped in Afro-Brazilian cults.

**YARD** (Eng. Cr.), in Jamaica, the land around and including a dwelling; a piece of private property usually owned by blacks.

**YARD-CHILD** (Eng. Cr.), a term used by blacks in the West Indies for a black child who lives in the household of his father rather than away from him in the household of his unmarried mother.

**YATWA** (Afr.), in the Caribbean region, a dish made of breadfruit (q.v.) and coconut, a black delicacy.

**YAUÕ** (Afr.), in some Afro-Brazilian cults, a young black girl who is being prepared to serve as a sacred dancer or an attendant of the gods and priests. During the initiation period, she must remain in the ceremonial house, subject to a series of taboos. Among these are prohibitions against going outside, sexual intercourse, and the use of certain foods. (T. L. Smith, *Brazil*, p. 538.)

**YAW, YAWS,** in the West Indies, a disease (framboesia) which greatly afflicted black slaves on plantations. It was characterized by blisters, a very destructive distemper, eruptive appearances on the body, and swollen eyes.

**YAWS BUSH,** in Jamaica, a vine *(Cissus sicyoides)* whose leaves were used by slaves to cure the sores produced by yaws (q.v.).

**YAWS-CHILDREN** (Eng. Cr.), black children suffering from yaws (q.v.) who, in slavery times, were kept in a separate house.

**YAWS-FILTH** (Eng. Cr.), in the West Indies, the pustules of papillary yaws (q.v.), a disease that afflicted slaves in the colonial period.

**YAWS-HOSPITAL, YAWS-HOUSE** (Eng. Cr.), on Jamaican plantations, a house on sugar estates (q.v.) where slaves with yaws (q.v.) were isolated until the disease had run its course.

**YAW SORE** (Eng. Cr.), in the West Indies, the pustule of the skin caused by yaws (q.v.).

**YAWS-TRASH** (Eng. Cr.), in the West Indies, the remains of yaws (q.v.) after the initial phase of the disease has subsided.

**YAWSY, YAWY** (Eng. Cr.), in the West Indies, a person affected with yaws (q.v.).

**YAWSY-KENGE** (Eng. Cr.), in the West Indies, one who has yaws (q.v.).

**YAWSY-SKIN** (Eng. Cr.), one whose skin shows the scars and other effects of yaws (q.v.).

**YAW TAINT** (Eng. Cr.), in the West Indies, an effect of yaws (q.v.) thought to carry over from one generation of black slaves to the next, predisposing the second toward contracting the disease.

**YAW WEED,** a tropical shrub *(Morinda royoc)* once used as a medicine in treating yaws (q.v.).

**YAWY.** See YAWSY.

**YAYA** (Afr.). 1. In the Afro-Caribbean region, a term of endearment used by blacks in addressing their grandmothers or mothers. 2. In Brazil, a term of address used by slaves in talking to girls and young ladies of the Casa Grande (q.v.), or "Big House," on the plantations.

**YEARLY-NIGHT** (Eng. Cr.), in Jamaica, a funeral wake held among blacks on the first anniversary of a death.

**YEGE-YEGE.** See YAGA-YAGA.

**YELLOW** (Eng. Cr.), in Jamaica, a term for a skin color which is mulatto. or lighter. It sometimes has unfavorable connotations.

**YELLOW BALSAM,** in the Caribbean region, an aromatic tropical shrub *(Croton flavens)* which blacks sometimes use in baths.

**YELLOW BLAST** (Eng. Cr.), on the Caribbean sugar estates (q.v.), a disease contracted from sugar cane (q.v.); it formerly afflicted black slaves.

**YELLOW CANDLEWOOD,** in the West Indies, a tropical tree *(Cassia emarginata)* whose yellow wood burns easily, whence its name; widely used by slaves as firewood.

**YELLOW MANGO,** in the Caribbean region, a common variety of mango (q.v.) *(Mangifera indica)* often used as food for slaves in the colonial period.

**YELLOW NICKER (NIKAL)** (Eng. Cr.), in the West Indies, a tropical plant *(Coesalpina bonduc)* and its yellow fruit whose hard seed is used by black children to play games. Some blacks use the plant for medicinal purposes.

**YELLOW SORREL,** in the Caribbean, a variety of a tropical plant *(Hibiscus sabdariffa)* whose leaves are used by blacks to make a cool fermented drink, jellies, and tarts.

**YELLOW TAIL,** in Jamaica, a common food fish *(Ocyrus chrysurus)*; among blacks, the word has come to symbolize prettiness.

**YELLOW THISTLE,** in Jamaica, a tropical herb *(Argemone mexicana)* which blacks use in folk medicine, especially for children's colds.

**YELLOW YAM** (Eng. Cr.), in the West Indies, a variety of yam (q.v.) *(Dioscorea cayennensis)* very popular with planters as a standard food for slaves in the colonial period.

**YEMANJÁ, YEMANYÁ** (Afr.), in Afro-Latin American cults, a female deity born from Obatalá (q.v.) and worshipped as the goddess of rivers and streams where she lives. Her fetish is a marine shell; her day of worship is Saturday; and she dresses in red, dark blue, and rose, carrying as insignia a fan and a sword. Yemanjá's favorite foods are pigeon, maize, cock, and castrated he-goat.

**YERBA CANGÁ** (Sp.), in Puerto Rico, an African grass *(Jussiacea augustifobra)* used as fodder. Also called *yerba de clan*.

**YERBA DE GUINEA** (Sp.), in Puerto Rico, an African grass *(Panicum maximum Jacq.)* used to feed cattle.

**YERBA KIKUYO** (Sp.), in Puerto Rico, an African grass *(Pennisetum clandistinum Coiv.)* used in folk medicine since slavery times.

**YGAÇABA** (Afr.), an African deity, son of Yara (q.v.), worshipped in some Afro-Brazilian cults.

**YONGA** (Afr.), in the West Indies, a wild black dance in which the body is shaken in all directions.

**YONYÓN** (Afr.), in the Spanish Antilles, a wild edible mushroom *(Agaricus campestris)* which blacks have used to prepare several dishes since slavery times.

**YORKA** (Afr.), among Guianan Bush Negroes (q.v.), a wandering soul which leaves the body at the moment of death and roams far from its owner's countryside. (Bastide, *African Civilizations*, p. 100.)

**YORUBA KINGDOM,** an ancient black kingdom located in central-western Nigeria, apparently originating in the northern fringes of the forest. Before the Europeans arrived, it was already a highly urbanized and industrialized state, experienced in the art of working iron, copper, and glassware. It traded with the Mediterranean cities across the Sahara. The slave trade in the area reached a high development when the Portuguese reached the Guinea (q.v.) or Gold Coast (q.v.), around 1510. See also YORUBA SLAVES.

**YORUBA SLAVES,** brought in great numbers to the New World, especially to Cuba and Brazil, where they were known as Lucumi in Cuba and Nagós in Brazil. They were usually exported through the port of Lagos on the Slave Coast (q.v.). In Brazil, they were thought to be robust, courageous, hard-working, and better tempered than other races, and they were noted for their intelligence. In 1826, the Yoruba slaves of Bahía set up a *quilombo* (q.v.) in the hinterland at Urubú, not far from the city. They fought valiantly against the government troops but were ultimately subdued. (Ramos, *The Negro*, pp. 26, 47.)

**YOU NEVER SEE A KICKIN' COW WIDOUT A KICKIN' CALF** ("You never see a kicking cow without a kicking calf"), an Afro-Jamaican aphorism.

**YOYÓ, IOIÓ** (Pg.), in northeast Brazil, an old term formerly used by slaves in addressing their masters and today occasionally applied to members of a mulatto family by their intimate friends.

**YUBA.** See JUBA.

**YUBÁ** (Afr.), in Puerto Rico, an African dance.

**YUCCA,** any of a genus *(Yucca)* of plants of the lily family, sometimes arborescent, producing a starchy tuber used as a filler in soups and stews or fried like potatoes; a staple food for slaves on the plantations.

**YUKA** (Afr.), in Afro-Cuban folklore, a profane dance played to the beat of a drum.

**YUMMA** (Afr.), a religious doll worshipped by Maroons (q.v.) in Jamaica representing Old Nanny (q.v.), "Queen" of the Maroons at the time of their first treaty with the whites (circa 1725). The figure was brought out, washed, and dressed annually at Christmas time. (Beckwith, *Black Roadways*, p. 191.)

**YUN SEUL DWET PAS CAPAB' MANGÉ GOMBO** (Fr. Cr.) ("A single finger can't eat okra"), an old Afro-Haitian maxim meaning that when food is eaten by picking it with the fingers, cooperation is necessary. (Courlander, *The Drum*, p. 337.)

**YUYUNGO,** a novel about black life by Ecuadorian writer Adalberto Ortiz (1943). Set in the Pacific jungle dividing Ecuador and Colombia, it is a picturesque account of the adventures of a poor black who runs away from his home to live and travel in the forests and along the rivers of this isolated region. *Yuyungo* documents this hitherto unknown country and arouses awareness of the hardships and poverty of its black settlers.

# Z

**ZABUMBA** (Afr.), an Afro-Brazilian drum played by blacks, especially at Mardi Gras and similar black festivals.

**ZAFACÓN** (Sp.), in the Spanish Caribbean, an old barrack divided into many apartments of two small rooms each where plantation workers live; it originated in slavery times.

**ZAFFAI' MOUTON PAS ZAFFAI' CABRIT** (Fr. Cr.) ("The sheep's affair is none of the goat's business"), an Afro-Haitian aphorism. (Courlander, *The Drum*, p. 336.)

**ZAFRA** (Sp.), in the Caribbean region, the sugar cane (q.v.) harvest, roughly a period of 100 days and the highest pitch of activity on the sugar estates (q.v.). In the colonial period, it was the season when slaves had to work long hours performing the hardest and most demanding tasks.

**ZAKA** (Afr.), in Haiti, an African deity who is the protector of agriculture. He is a real peasant and is thought to be avaricious, suspicious, a lover of litigation, and greedy for profit. He hates city people but loves the countryside. Baskets are his symbol; lightning and thunder his signs. Also called Azaka Tonner and Thunder Azaka.

**ZAKA GROLI** (Afr.), in Haiti, an African god worshipped by black peasants; a member of the Congo-Guinée (q.v.) family of gods.

**ZAKA L'OREILLE,** an African deity, a member of the Congo-Guinée (q.v.) family of gods worshipped by black peasants in rural Haiti as a protector against storms.

**ZAMBA** (Afr.), in Senegal (q.v.), the common name for a second-born son. (Curtin, *Africa Remembered*, p. 6.)

**ZAMBAIGO** (Afr.), in early Spanish America, a term for a person of mixed black and Indian blood; eventually shortened to *zambo* (q.v.). In Spanish, called ZAMBO DE INDIO.

**ZAMBANGO** (Afr.), in Puerto Rico, a term referring to a person with kinky hair, considered a Negroid physical feature.

**ZAMBÉ** (Afr.), an African drum played by blacks in northeastern Brazil.

**ZAMBI, NZAMBI** (Afr.), in Brazil, a great Angolan deity worshipped in several black cults.

**ZAMBI, KING,** in Brazil, a black leader, the nephew of Ganga Zumbá (q.v.) and organizer of the Palmares Republic (q.v.). In 1685, Zambi rebelled against his uncle, killed him, gathered a small force of runaway slaves, and proclaimed himself king of Palmares. This was the beginning of the most turbulent and decisive period in the existence of the kingdom. He fortified the settlement and defended it by a series of fences and stockades which made it nearly invincible. It resisted many attacks by regular troops until 1695 when it was partially conquered, and Zambi was defeated and killed. (Ramos, *The Negro*, p. 61.)

**ZAMBIAPONGO, ZAMBIAPUNGO** (Afr.), an Angolan deity worshipped in several black cults in Bahia, Brazil; called Zambi-ampungu in Angola, (q.v.). (Ramos, *O Negro*, p. 94.)

**ZAMBO, SAMBO** (Afr.), in Spanish America, the offspring of a black and Indian couple. In early colonial times, *zambos*, whether slaves or freedmen, were on the lowest rung of the social ladder. If free, they paid tribute and had to reside, by law, with recognized employers under penalty of being consigned to the mines or to public works.

**ZAMBO DE INDIO** (Sp.). See ZAMBAIGO.

**ZAMBO'S REPUBLIC,** a loosely organized settlement of runaway slaves in the modern province of Esmeraldas, Ecuador, which, from 1587 to 1620, gained dominance over various local Indian tribes. Its black population is reported to have comprised around 5,000 people. These Africans were apparently from the Guinea Coast (q.v.). (Whitten, *Black Frontier*, p. 40.)

**ZAMBRANA VÁZQUES, ANTONIO** (1846-1922), a Cuban revolutionary writer and abolitionist. As a result of his political activities, he was exiled to Santiago, Chile where he published his famous antislavery novel *El negro Francisco: Novela de costumbres cubanas* (1875). He also published *La República de Cuba* (New York, 1873) and *La poesía de la historia* (San José, Costa Rica).

**ZANGBETO,** a sacred society in Dahomey (q.v.), West Africa that influenced similar groups of slaves in prerevolutionary Haiti.

**ZANGE** (Afr.), in Afro-Haitian religion, a secondary deity.

**ZANGO** (Afr.), a black cult practiced in Pernambuco, Brazil.

**ZAO LANGÉ** (Afr.), in Haiti, an African deity of Ibo (q.v.) origin.

**ZAO PIMBA** (Afr.), an Afro-Haitian god, a member of the Pétro (q.v.) family.

**ZAPE** (Afr.), an African ethnic group of the Bakongo tribes located in central and southern Africa from which slaves were taken to Spanish America.

**ZARABANDA** (Afr.), in Cuba, a Congo-Yoruba cult apparently associated with Zarabang (q.v.), a Yoruba (q.v.) god.

**ZARABANG** (Afr.), an Afro-Cuban god of Yoruba (q.v.) origin; a war god who performs black magic to hurt his devotees' enemies. As a sorcerer he has a pact with the dead.

**ZARABE** (Afr.), an African ethnic group located in Senegambia (q.v.) from which black slaves were brought to Colombia early in the colonial period.

**ZEAUBEAUPS** (Fr. Cr.), in Afro-Haitian folklore, mythical human cannibals, fearsome beings, who meet in the darkness of the night in their assembly hall inside the *mapou* (q.v.) tree.

**ZEE ROOVERS** (D.), Dutch slave traders in the Antilles.

**ZEFERINA,** a Yoruba (q.v.) slave woman, the leader of a runaway settlement formed by black Yoruba slaves outside the city of Bahia, Brazil. In

1826, she organized a revolt against the plantation masters. The uprising was put down by government troops, and Zeferina and her people were imprisoned. (Ramos, *The Negro*, p. 47.)

**ZEFRE** (Afr.), an African ethnic group of Senegambia (q.v.) from which slaves were imported into Colombia and elsewhere early in the colonial period.

**ZELADOR** (Pg.), in the Afro-Brazilian *candomblé* (q.v.) cult, the caretaker of a saint and the shrine. A black *zelador* usually has more than one saint and tries to honor each on the proper day of the week, as well as at the end of the year. He often learns a large number of prayers, dances, and herbal cures. His healing powers induce blacks to worship his saints.

**ZELADOR DE SANTO** (Pg.), an assistant of the *zelador* (q.v.) in the Afro-Brazilian *candomblé* (q.v.). His duties are to clean and decorate the shrine, to watch the fetishes at regular intervals, and to renew the food and drink offerings.

**ZELLA** (Afr.), in Jamaica, a funeral drum played by blacks at a dead person's home for the celebration of the nine-night (q.v.) in Pocomania (q.v.) rituals.

**ZEPAULE** (Fr. Cr.), in Afro-Haitian folklore, a supplication dance in which the movements are made primarily by the shoulders; in French, *les épaules*.

**ZESSE** (Afr.), in Haiti, an African dance popular among black peasants.

**ZEWO.** See OZEWO.

**ZEZEGARY, ZIZIGARY** (Afr.), in the West Indies, a name under which *wangla* (q.v.) was imported at the end of the eighteenth century, although it had already long been known and used. For a time it was a standard treatment for dysentery among slaves. (Cassidy, *Dictionary*, p. 489.)

**ZIMBO** (Afr.), a cowrie (q.v.) shell used as medium of exchange for slaves in Angola (q.v.).

**ZIN** (Fr. Cr.), a sacred iron pot used in Afro-Haitian rituals; occasionally it is made of clay.

**ZINGZANG** (Eng. Cr.), a swing, a word used mainly by blacks in Jamaica.

**ZINZENDORF, NIKOLAUS LUDWIG, GRAF VON** (1700-1760), a prominent German nobleman who reorganized the Moravian Brothers, Church of the United Brethren, (Unitas Fratrum) in Saxony in 1722. As early as 1728, the devout count proposed preaching the gospel to the slaves in the West Indies. By the end of 1732, he sent the first missionaries to the Caribbean: Leonard Dober, a potter, and David Nitschmann, a carpenter. They arrived in 1732 at the Danish Island of Saint Thomas where they began to preach to the slaves. Von Zinzendorf himself visited Saint Thomas in 1739 to gain personal knowledge of the work done in favor of the "heathens." (Goveia, *Slave Society*, p. 271.) See also ZINZENDORF MISSIONS.

**ZINZENDORF MISSIONS,** a series of Moravian mission stations established to convert the slaves in the Caribbean. The first mission was opened in Saint Thomas, West Indies, in 1732. Another station was organized in Jamaica in 1754. See also ZINZENDORF, NIKOLAUS LUDWIG, GRAF VON.

**ZION REVIVAL,** in Jamaica, a traditional black pagan cult often exploited by politicians to arouse popular black protest against cultural and religious domination by whites. Its rituals are performed in the open air around a pole on which a box is mounted containing the Bible (Christianity), two wooden swords, a small ladder, and two wheels—the ladder for Jacob and Moses, the swords and the wheels as symbols of weapons against alien domination. It practices baptism by immersion, within a pagan setting, and has a clerical organization which includes several "equerries" called upon to restrain the faithful when conversion and frenzy become excessive. (Frucht, *Black Society*, p. 311.)

**ZIZIGARY** See ZEZEGARY.

**ZO** (Afr.), an Afro-Haitian god of fire; he is of Dahomean origin.

**ZOBEL, JOSEPH** (b. 1915), a black writer born in Rivière Salie, Martinique. Through his mother's hard work, he was able to attend schools on his native island. Later, after World War II, he studied ethnology and literature in Paris and, for several years, taught in France. In 1951, he moved to Senegal (q.v.) where he became artistic director for Dakar radio. Although he has written some poetry, Zobel is known primarily as a novelist. He describes with deep sympathy the unknown world of rural laborers, fishermen, and masses and, in a poetic and touching peasant language, brings to life Afro-Antillean society, giving reality to the "jours immobiles." Much of his fiction is autobiographical. His main works are

*Diabl'a, roman antillais* (Paris, 1947); *Laghia de la mort* (Paris, 1946); *Les Jours immobiles* (Paris, 1946); *La Rue Cases-Nègres* (Paris, 1950); *La Fête à Paris* (Paris, 1953); *Le Soleil partagé* (Paris, 1964); and *Incantation pour un retour au pays natal, poème* (Paris, 1965).

**ZOMBIE, ZUMBI** (Afr.), in Haiti and elsewhere in the Caribbean, a soulless robot who is a person killed and resurrected by a black sorcerer. Such a supernatural being has no will, and the sorcerer exploits him without respite until the time "set by God" for his natural death. Often zombies are completely dominated by their masters who utilize them for evil designs. (Herskovits, *Life in a Haitian*, p. 346.)

**ZOMBIE ERRANT** (Fr. Cr.), in Afro-Haitian folklore, the spirit of a human being who died in an accident. This mythical creature inhabits the woods by day and walks on the roads by night, as he lives out the period of earthly existence assigned to him by God.

**ZONA-ZUMBA** (Afr.), a black leader, the brother of the famous Ganga Zumbá (q.v.), king of Palmares (q.v.). Zona-Zumba was a ruler of one of the several small and less protected communities of the black kingdom in Brazil.

**ZONE OF EXASPERATION,** in Brazil and elsewhere in Afro-Latin America, the crowded critical area of contact between the actual level at which the masses are presently living and that on which they now feel entitled to live. These ghetto areas, populated mainly by black descendants of plantation slaves urbanized after the emancipation (1888), are the famous *favelas* (q.v.) that surround the great modern metropoles of Brazil. This ever-widening zone of poverty has attained dangerous and critical proportions in recent times. (T. L. Smith, *Brazil*, p. 692.)

**ZORÔ** (Afr.), an Afro-Brazilian dish made of shrimp, okra (q.v.), and spices.

**ZOZO** (Afr.), an ethnic group located in Senegambia (q.v.) from which slaves were brought to Colombia and elsewhere in Spanish America early in the colonial period.

**ZOZO BEF** (Fr. Cr.), a leather whip used on horses and burros by Haitian blacks; formerly a dreadful instrument of torture used to punish slaves. Literally "bull penis."

**ZOZO RAIDE PAS GAINYAIN ZOREILLE** (Fr. Cr.) ("A hard penis has no ears"), an old black aphorism in Haiti. (Courlander, *The Drum*, p. 336.)

**ZUMBI,** in colonial Brazil, a black chief of a *quilombo* (q.v.).

**ZUNDU,** a great black leader of several runaway settlements in the interior of northeast Brazil. For years he fought heroically against overwhelming odds. In 1757, he chose death to defeat. (Ramos, *The Negro*, p. 43.)

**ZUNGÚ** (Afr.), in Brazil, an African word for fight.

**ZUNGUS** (Afr.), during the Brazilian empire (circa 1845), shanties with foul-smelling rooms where black prostitutes used to practice their art. The *zungus* were owned and operated by free black street vendors in Rio de Janeiro and other cities.

**ZUZARDS** (Fr. Cr.), in Saint Domingue, a battalion of about 200 black slaves who, in 1792, promised help and loyalty to the mulatto revolutionary party. They fought with great bravery, but after the defeat of the slave rebellion the victorious mulattoes and white colonists betrayed them and deported them to Mexico. (Ott, *The Haitian Revolution*, p. 98.)

**ZUZU, ZUZU-MAN** (Afr.), in Jamaica, an African word for sorcerer or *obeah* man (q.v.).

**ZUZU WAPP** (Eng. Cr.), in Jamaica, a children's ring game in which one player, named *zuzu wapp*, chases another and beats him; a favorite game of black children.

# Bibliography

## DICTIONARIES AND GLOSSARIES

Alvarez, Nazario, Manuel. *El elemento negroide en el español de Puerto Rico*. San Juan, Puerto Rico: Instituto de Cultura Puertorriqueña, 1974.

Cabrera, Lydia. *Anagó; Vocabulario Lucumí; (El yoruba que se habla en Cuba)*. Miami, Fla.: Cabrera y Rojos, 1970.

Calcagno, Francisco. *Diccionario biográfico cubano: Corresponde hasta 1878*. New York: N. Ponce de Leon, 1878-1886.

Cassidy, Frederick Gomes and R. B. Le Page. *Dictionary of Jamaican English*. Cambridge: Cambridge University Press, 1967.

Collymore, Frank. *Notes for a Glossary of Words and Phrases of Barbadian Dialect*. Bridgetown, Barbados: Advocate Co., 1957.

Farr, Kenneth B. *Historical Dictionary of Puerto Rico and U.S. Virgin Islands*. Metuchen, N. J.: Scarecrow Press, 1973.

Houaiss, Antonio and C. B. Avery. *The New Appleton Dictionary of the English and Portuguese Languages*. New York: Appleton-Century-Crofts Inc., 1964.

Jourdain, Anne Marie Louise. *Le Vocabulaire du parleur créole de la Martinique*. Paris: Librarie C. Klincksieck, 1956.

Macedo Soares, Antonio Joaquim de. *Diccionario brasileiro de lingua portuguesa; Elucidario Etimológico Crítico*. Rio de Janeiro: Ministerio de Educação e Cultura, 1875-1888. 2 vols.

Martin, Michael R. and G. H. Lovett. *Encyclopedia of Latin American History*. New York: Bobbs-Merrill Co., Inc., 1968.

Mendonça, R. M. *A Influencia Africana no Portugués do Brasil*. São Paulo: Companhia Editora Nacional, 1973.

Merriam-Webster. *Webster's Third New International Dictionary of the English Language Unabridged*. Springfield, Mass.: G. & C. Merriam Co., 1971.

Ortiz Fernández, Fernando. *Glosario de afronegrismos*. Habana: Imprensa El Siglo XX, 1924.

Ribes Tovar, Federico. *Enciclopedia puertorriqueña ilustrada; The Puerto Rican Heritage Encyclopedia*. San Juan, Puerto Rico: Plus Ultra Educational Publishers, Inc., 1970.

## BOOKS AND MONOGRAPHS


Abrahams, Roger D. *Deep the Water, Shallow the Shore: Three Essays on Shanty-ing in the West Indies.* Austin, Tex./London, American Folklore Society, University of Texas Press, 1974.

Aimes, Herbert H.S. *A History of Slavery in Cuba 1511 to 1868.* New York: Octagon Books, Inc., 1967.

Alagoa, Ebiegberi Joe. *The Small Brave City-State: A History of Nembe-Brass in the Nigeria Delta.* Madison: University of Wisconsin Press, 1964.

Alden, Daniel, ed. *Colonial Roots of Modern Brazil.* Berkeley: University of California Press, 1973.

Bailey, Helen M. *Latin America: The Development of Its Civilization.* Englewood Cliffs, N.J.: Prentice-Hall Inc., 1968.

Bastide, Roger. *African Civilizations in the New World.* New York: Harper & Row, 1971.

———. *Les Religions africaines au Brésil.* Paris: Presses Universitaires de France, 1961.

Beckwith, M. Warren. *Black Roadways: A Study of Jamaican Folk Life.* Chapel Hill: University of North Carolina Press, 1929.

———. *Jamaica Proverbs.* New York: Negro University Press, 1970.

Berrow, F. Raphael and Pradel Pompilus. *Histoire de la littérature haïtienne; Illustrée par les textes.* Port-au-Prince: Editions Caribes, 1975.

Biesanz, John B. and M. Biesanz. *The People of Panama.* New York: Columbia University Press, 1955.

Birmingham, David. *Trade and Conflict in Angola: The Mbundu and Their Neighbors under the Influence of the Portuguese, 1483-1790.* London/New York: Oxford University Press, 1966.

Black, C. V. *History of Jamaica.* London/Glasgow: Collin-Clear-Type Press, 1958.

Bowser, Frederick P. *The African Slave in Colonial Peru, 1524-1650.* Stanford, Calif., Stanford University Press, 1974.

Boxer, C. R. *The Dutch in Brazil, 1624-1654.* Oxford: Clarendon Press, 1957.

———. *Four Centuries of Portuguese Expansion, 1415-1825: A Succinct Survey.* Johannesburg: Witwatersrand University Press, 1965.

———. *The Golden Age of Brazil, 1695-1750.* Berkeley: University of California Press, 1964.

———. *The Portuguese Seaborne Empire, 1415-1825.* London: Hutchinson Co., 1969.

Brathwaite, *The Development of Creole Society in Jamaica, 1770-1820.* London: Oxford University Press, 1971.

Cabrera, Lydia. *Refranes de negros viejos.* Habana: Ediciones C.R., 1955.

———. *La sociedad secreta Abakua.* Habana: Ediciones C.R., 1958.

Calcagno, Francisco. *Los poetas de color; Plácido, Manzano, Rodríguez, Echemendia, Silveira, Medina.* Habana; Imprenta Militar de la V. de Soler y Compañia, 1878.

Carneiro, Edison. *Ladinos e Crioulos; Estudos sobre o Negro no Brasil.* Rio de Janeiro: Editora Civilização, Brasileira, 1964.

————. *Negros Bantús; Notas de Ethnographia Religiosa e de Folclore.* Rio de Janeiro: Editora Civilização Brasileira, 1937.

Carvalho-Neto, Paulo de. *History of Ibero-American Folklore and Mestizo Cultures.* Oosterhout, Netherlands: Anthropological Publications, 1969.

Cassidy, Frederick Gomes. *Jamaica Talk: Three-Hundred Years of English Language in Jamaica.* London: Macmillian and Co., 1961.

Castedo, Leopoldo. *A History of Latin American Art and Architecture from Pre-Colombian Times to the Present.* New York: Praeger Inc., 1969.

Chase, Gilbert. *Art in Latin America.* New York: The Free Press, 1970.

Comitas, David and D. Lowenthal, ed. *Slaves, Free Men, Citizens: West Indian Perspectives.* Garden City, N.Y.: Anchor Press/Doubleday, 1973.

Corwin, Arthur F. *Spain and the Abolition of Slavery in Cuba, 1817-1968.* Austin: University of Texas Press, 1967.

Corzani, Jack. *Littérature antillaise, poésie.* Fort-de-France: Emile Gros Desormeaux, 1971.

————. *Littérature antillaise, prose.* Fort-de-France: Emile Gros Desormeaux, 1972.

Coulthard, G. R. *Race and Colour in Caribbean Literature.* New York: Oxford University Press, 1962.

Courlander, Harold. *The Drum and the Hoe: Life and Lore of the Haitian People.* Berkeley: University of California Press, 1960.

———— and R. Bastien. *Religion and Politics in Haiti.* Washington, D.C.: Institute for Cross-Cultural Research, 1964.

Craton, Michael and James Walvin. *A Jamaican Plantation: The History of Worthy Park, 1670-1970.* Toronto: University of Toronto Press, 1970.

Curtin, Philip D. *Africa Remembered: Narratives by West Africans from the Era of the Slave Trade.* Madison/Milwaukee: University of Wisconsin Press, 1967.

————. *The Atlantic Slave Trade: A Census.* Madison/Milwaukee: University of Wisconsin Press, 1969.

————. *Two Jamaicas.* New York: Greenwood Press, 1968.

Damas, Léon Gontran. *Poètes d'expression française d'Afrique Noire, Madagascar, Réunion, Guadaloupe, Martinique, Indochine, Guyane, 1900-1945.* Paris: Editions du Seuil, 1947.

Davidson, Basil. *Black Mother: The Years of African Slave Trade.* Boston: Little, Brown & Co., 1961.

————. *A History of West Africa.* Garden City, N.Y.: Prentice-Hall Inc., 1966.

Degler, Carl N. *Neither Black nor White: Slavery and Race Relations in Brazil and the United States.* New York: Macmillan Co., 1971.

Diaz Soler, Luis M. *Historia de la esclavitud negra en Puerto Rico.* San Juan: Universidad de Puerto Rico, Editorial Universitaria, 1970.

Diffie, Bailey Wallis. *Latin American Civilization, Colonial Period.* New York: Octagon Books, 1967.

Dow, George Francis. *Slave Ships and Slaving.* Salem, Mass.: Marine Research Society, 1927.

Dunn, Richard S. *Sugar and Slaves: The Rise of the Planter Class in the West Indies, 1624-1713.* Chapel Hill: University of North Carolina Press, 1972.

Eisenberg, Peter L. *The Sugar Industry in Pernambuco.* Berkeley: University of California Press, 1974.

Engerman, Stanley L. and E. D. Genovese. *Race and Slavery in the Western Hemisphere: Quantitative Studies.* Princeton, N.J.: Princeton University Press, 1975.

Fernandes, Florestan. *The Negro in Brazilian Society.* New York: Columbia University Press, 1969.

Foner, Laura. *Slavery in the New World: A Reader in Comparative History.* Englewood Cliffs, N.J.: Prentice-Hall Inc., 1969.

Foner, Philip Sheldon. *The Spanish-Cuban-American War and the Birth of American Imperialism, 1895-1902.* New York: Monthly Review Press, 1972. 2 vols.

Fouchard, Jean. *Les Marrons de la liberté.* Paris: Editions de l'Ecole, 1972.

Freyre, Gilberto. *The Mansions and the Shanties: The Making of Modern Brazil.* New York: Alfred A. Knopf, 1963. (Translated from the Portuguese by Harriet de Onis.)

———. *The Masters and the Slaves (Casa Grande e Senzala): A Study in the Development of Brazilian Civilization.* New York: Alfred A. Knopf, 1970. (Translated from the Portuguese by S. Putnam.)

Frucht, Richard. *Black Society in the New World.* New York: Random House, 1971.

Goslinga, Cornelius C. *The Dutch in the Caribbean and on the Wild Coast, 1580-1680.* Gainesville: University of Florida Press, 1971.

Goveia, Elsa V. *Slave Society in the British Leeward Islands at the End of the Eighteenth Century.* New Haven, Conn.: Yale University Press, 1965.

Hall, Gwendolyn Midlo. *Social Control in Slave Plantation Societies.* Baltimore, Md.: Johns Hopkins Press, 1971.

Hamshire, Cyrill. *The British in the Caribbean.* Cambridge, Mass.: Harvard University Press, 1972.

Hanke, Lewis. *History of Latin American Civilization: Sources and Interpretations.* Boston: Little, Brown & Co., 1973. 2 vols.

Haring, C. H. *The Spanish Empire in America.* New York: Harcourt, Brace & World, 1963.

Henriques, Fernando. *Family and Colour in Jamaica.* London: MacGibon and Kee Ltd., 1968.

Herskovits, Melville J. *Life in a Haitian Valley.* New York: Octagon Books Inc., 1964.

———. *Rebel Destiny.* Freeport, N.Y.: Books for Libraries Press, 1971.

———. *Trinidad Village.* New York: Alfred A. Knopf, 1964.

Hiss, Philip Hanson. *Netherlands America: The Dutch Territories in the West.* New York: Duell, Sloan and Pearce Inc., 1943.

Horowitz, Michael M. *People and Cultures.* Garden City, N.Y.: Natural History Press, 1971.

Hughes, Langston, ed. *The Best Short Stories by Negro Writers: An Anthology from 1899 to the Present.* Boston: Little, Brown & Co., 1967.

———. *The Poetry of the Negro, 1740-1949.* Garden City, N.J.: Doubleday, 1949.

Hurwitz, Samuel J. and E. F. Hurwitz, *Jamaica: A Historical Portrait.* New York: Praeger, 1971.

Hutchinson, Harry W. *Village and Plantation Life in Northeastern Brazil.* Seattle: University of Washington Press, 1957.

Hymes, Dell, ed. *Pidginization and Creolization of Languages.* Cambridge: Cambridge University Press, 1971.

Jahn, Janheinz. *Muntu: An Outline of the New African Culture.* New York: Grove Press Inc., 1961.
————. *Neo-African Literature: A History of Black Writing.* New York: Grove Press Inc., 1968.
———— and C. P. Dressler. *Bibliography of Creative African Writing.* Nendeln, Liechtenstein: Kraus-Thomson Organization Limited, 1971.
Jakobsson, Stiv. *Am I Not a Man and a Brother?* Uppsala, Sweden: Almqvist and Wiksell, 1972.
James, C.L.R. *The Black Jacobins: Toussaint L'Ouverture and the San Domingo Revolution.* New York: Vintage Press, 1963.
Johnston, Harry H. *The Negro in the New World.* London: Methuen & Co., 1910.
Klein, Herbert S. *Slavery in the Americas: A Comparative Study of Virginia and Cuba.* Chicago, Ill.: University of Chicago Press, 1967.
Knight, Franklin W. *Slave Society in Cuba during the Nineteenth Century.* Madison: University of Wisconsin Press, 1970.
Lewis, Gordon. *The Growth of the Modern West Indies.* New York: Monthly Review Press, 1968.
Leyburn, James G. *The Haitian People.* New Haven, Conn.: Yale University Press, 1941.
Lier, Rudolf A.-J. van. *Frontier Society: A Special Analysis of the History of Surinam.* The Hague: Martinus Nijhoof, 1971.
Liss, S. B. and P. K. Liss. *Man, State and Society in Latin American History.* New York, Praeger, 1972.
McCloy, Shelby Thomas. *The Negro in the French West Indies.* Lexington: University of Kentucky Press, 1966.
Mannix, Daniel P. *Black Cargoes: A History of the Atlantic Slave Trade, 1518-1865.* New York: Viking Press, 1962.
Mellafe, Rolando. *La esclavitud en Hispano-America.* Buenos Aires: EUDEBA, 1964.
Montejo, Esteban. *The Autobiography of a Runaway Slave.* New York: Pantheon Books, 1968. (Edited by M. Barnett; translated from the Spanish by J. Innes.)
Moses, Bernard. *The Spanish Dependencies in South America: An Introduction to the History of Their Civilization.* New York: Cooper Square Publishers, 1965. 2 vols.
Nina Rodrigues, Raymundo. *Os Africanos no Brasil.* São Paulo: Companhia Editora Nacional, 1965.
Olien, Michael D. *Latin Americans: Contemporary Peoples and Their Cultural Traditions.* New York: Holt, Rinehart & Winston, 1973.
Oliver, Roland and J. D. Fage. *A Short History of Africa.* New York: New York University Press, 1968.
Ortiz Fernández, Fernando. *Los negros brujos (apuntes para un estudio de la etnología criminal).* Miami: Ediciones Universal, 1973.
Ott, Thomas O. *The Haitian Revolution.* Knoxville: University of Tennessee Press, 1973.
Pescatello, Ann M. *The African in Latin America.* New York: Alfred A. Knopf, 1975.
Pierson, Donald. *Negroes in Brazil, a Study of Race Contact at Bahia.* Chicago: University of Chicago Press, 1942.

Pilling, William. *The Emancipation of South America, Being a Condensed Translation of the History of San Martin by Bartolomé Mitre.* With an introduction by A. Curtis Wilgus. New York: Cooper Square Publishers, Inc., 1969.

Polanyi, Karl. *Dahomey and the Slave Trade: An Analysis of an Archaic Economy.* Seattle: University of Washington Press, 1966.

Pompilus, Pradel. *Manuel illustré d'histoire de la littérature haïtienne.* Port-au-Prince: H. Dechamps, 1961.

Pope-Hennessy, James. *Sins of the Fathers: A Study of the Atlantic Slave Traders, 1441-1807.* New York: Capricorn, 1969.

Price, Richard, ed. *Maroon Societies.* New York: Anchor Press/Doubleday, 1973.

Ragatz, Lowell Joseph. *The Fall of the Planter Class in the British Caribbean, 1763-1833.* New York: Octagon Books Inc., 1963.

Ramos, Arthur. *As Culturas Negras.* Rio de Janeiro: Livraria Editora da Casa do Estudiante do Brasil, 1972.

———. *The Negro in Brazil.* Washington, D.C.: Associated Publishers Inc., 1951.

———. *O Negro brasileiro.* São Paulo: Companhia Editora Nacional, 1951.

Roberts, John Storm. *Black Music of Two Worlds.* New York: Praeger, 1972.

Rodman, Selden. *Haiti: The Black Republic.* New York: Devin-Adair Co., 1961.

Rodrigues, Jose H. *Brazil and Africa.* Berkeley: University of California Press, 1965.

Roett, Riordan. *Brazil in the Sixties.* Nashville, Tenn.: Vanderbilt University Press, 1972.

Rout, Leslie B., Jr. *The African Experience in Spanish America.* London: Cambridge University Press, 1976.

Sayers, Raymond S. *The Negro in Brazilian Literature.* New York: Hispanic Institute in the United States, 1956.

Senna, Nelson de. *Africanos no Brasil.* Belo Horizonte, Brasil: Oficinas Gráficas Queiroz Breyner Limitada, 1940.

Shapiro, Norman R., ed. *Negritude, Black Poetry from Africa and the Caribbean.* New York: October House, 1970.

Simey, T. S. *Welfare and Planning in the West Indies.* Oxford: Clarendon Press, 1946.

Slonimzki, Nicolas. *Music of Latin America.* New York: Capo Press, 1972.

Smith, M. G. *The Plural Society in the British West Indies.* Berkeley: University of California Press, 1965.

Smith, T. Lynn. *Brazil: People and Institutions.* Baton Rouge: Louisiana State University Press, 1972.

Stein, Stanley J. *Vassouras: A Brazilian Coffee County, 1850-1900.* Cambridge, Mass.: Harvard University Press, 1957.

Toplin, Robert Brent. *The Abolition of Slavery in Brazil.* New York: Atheneum, 1972.

Voorhoeve, Jan and Ursy H. Lichtveld. *Creole Drum: An Anthology of Creole Literature in Surinam.* New Haven, Conn.: Yale University Press, 1975.

Wagenheim, Karl. *The Puerto Ricans: A Documentary History.* New York: Praeger, 1973.

Wagley, Charles. *An Introduction to Brazil.* New York: Columbia University Press, 1963.

Whitten, Norman E. *Black Frontiersmen: A South American Case.* Cambridge, Mass.: Shenkman Publishing Co., 1974.

Woodson, Carter G. *The African Background: Outline or Handbook for the Study of the Negro.* New York: Negro University Press, 1968.


ARTICLES AND PERIODICALS

Carranca y Trujillo, Raúl. "El Estatuto jurídico de los esclavos en las postrimerías de la colonización española." In: *Revista de Historia de América*, vol. I, no. 3, 1938, pp. 20-60.

Clemence, Stella R. "Deed of Emancipation of a Negro Woman Slave, Dated Mexico, September 14, 1585." In: *The Hispanic American Historical Review*, vol. X, 1930, pp. 51-57.

Debien, Gabriel. "Le Marronage aux Antilles Françaises an XVIII$^e$ siècle." In: *Caribbean Studies*, vol. VI, no. 3, 1966, pp. 3-44.

Hernández y Sánchez-Barbaó, Mario. "David Turnbull y el problema de la esclavitud en Cuba." In: *Anuario de Estudios Americanos*, vol. XIV, 1957, pp. 241-99.

Ivy, James W. "The Wisdom of the Haitian Peasant, Or Some Haitian Proverbs Considered." In: *Journal of Negro History,* Washington, D.C., vol. XXVI, 1941, pp. 485-98.

Jaramillo Uribe, Jaime. "Esclavos y señores en la sociedad colombiana del Siglo XVIII." In: *Anuario Colombiano de Historia Social y de las Culturas*, Bogota, vol. I, 1963.

Kent, Marian D. de B. "Palmares: An African State in Brazil." In: *Journal of African History*, vol. VI, 1965, pp. 161-75.

King, James E. "The Colored Castes and the American Representation in the Cortes of Cádiz." In: *Hispanic American Historical Review*, vol. XXXIII, 1953, pp. 33-64.

Malagón, Javier. "Un documento del siglo XVIII para la historia de la esclavitúd en las Antillas." In: *Imago Mundi*, vol. I, no. 2, 1955, pp. 38-56.

Marquez de la Plata, Fernando. "Documentos relativos a la introducción de esclavos negros en America." In: *Revista de Historia y Geografía*, Santiago, Chile, nos. 61 and 62, 1928.

Ohe, Enrique y Conchita Ruiz-Burruecos. "Los portugueses en la trata de esclavos negros de las postrimerías del siglo XVI." In: *Moneda y Credito*, Madrid, vol. LXXXV, 1963, pp. 3-40.

Pavy, David. "The Provenience of Colombian Negroes." In: *The Journal of Negro History*, Washington, D.C., vol. LII, 1967, pp. 35-58.

Pitman, F. W. "Slavery on the British West India Plantations in the Eighteenth Century." In: *The Journal of Negro History*, Washington, D.C., vol. XI, 1926, pp. 584-668.

Price, R. and S. Price. "Saramaka Onomastics: An Afro-American Naming System." In: *Ethnology*, vol. XI, 1972, pp. 341-67.

Rigaud, Odette Mennisson. "Le Rôle du vaudou dans l' indépendence d'Haiti." In: *Présence Africaine*, nos. 17-18, 1958, pp. 43-67.

Romero, Fernando. "The Slave Trade and Negro in South America." In: *Hispanic American Historical Review*, vol. XXIV, 1944, pp. 368-86.

Sheridan, Richard B. "Africa and the Caribbean in the Atlantic Slave Trade." In: *American Historical Review*, vol. LXXVII, 1922, pp. 15-35.

Wesley, Charles H. "The Emancipation of the Free Colored Population in the British Empire." In: *The Journal of Negro History*, Washington, D.C., vol. XIX, no. 2, 1934, pp. 137-70.

Williams, Mary W. "The Treatment of Negro Slaves in the Brazilian Empire: A Comparison with the United States of America." In: *The Journal of Negro History*, Washington, D.C., vol. XV, 1930, pp. 315-36.

Zavala, Silvio. "Los Trabajadores antillanos en el siglo XVI." In: *Revista de Historia de América*, vol. I, no. 3, 1938, pp. 60-89.

# General Subject Index

Abolition, 5, 8, 12, 31(2), 36, 40(5), 69, 90, 97, 103, 116–117, 127(2), 128–129, 129(2), 132, 134, 158, 176, 190, 212, 233, 258, 259, 263, 264, 283, 304, 321, 341, 347, 350, 358, 371, 375, 403, 413, 419, 428, 440(6), 441, 452, 463–464, 473, 484; acts promulgating, 5, 8, 9, 70–71, 109, 176(2), 269(3), 272, 472

Africans, names for in the New World, 29(2), 71–72, 77, 85, 93, 102, 121, 134, 172, 182, 202, 255, 264, 308, 310, 318, 319, 320, 333, 337, 338, 344, 346, 376, 377, 466(2)

Afrocubanismo, 14, 53, 113, 223, 389, 402, 441–442, 451

Anancy Stories. *See* Folklore, Afro-Jamaican

Antillanité. *See* Movements, nationalist, in the Arts

Blacks
—customs among, 57, 109, 165, 170, 171, 192–193, 226, 231(2), 252, 260, 266, 271, 294–295, 308, 376, 414
—housing for, 73, 100, 103(2), 151, 187, 190, 198, 264, 339, 345, 347, 397, 410, 427, 455, 502
—names for: Americas, 138, 203, 232, 236, 292, 323, 343, 344, 383(2), 395; Antilles, 67, 198, 221; Barbados, 404; Brazil, 12, 88, 100, 124, 150, 174, 240, 283, 286, 293, 294, 313, 318, 331(3), 334, 342(2), 343, 344, 369, 371, 390, 391(6), 403, 452, 467, 489; Colombia, 299, 311; Cuba, 14, 67, 102, 123, 154, 220, 273, 282, 287, 331, 346; Ecuador, 121; Haiti, 214, 216, 219, 224, 342; Jamaica, 70, 76, 77, 80, 89, 92, 94, 96, 135, 150, 152, 164, 168(2), 169, 196, 217(4), 218, 221, 224, 225, 228, 262(2), 266, 286, 320, 321, 340, 341(2),

348, 351, 353, 360, 374, 393, 395, 403(2), 404(2), 409, 412, 433, 466, 476(2), 484; Panama, 125(3), 313, 431; Peru, 406; Puerto Rico, 122, 130, 324; Spain, 277, 346; Surinam, 96, 167(2), 471; West Indies, 12, 77, 119, 148, 168, 193, 196, 221, 222, 229, 287, 294, 308, 327, 340, 341, 361, 376, 393, 395(3), 408, 416(2), 429, 443
—social and political organization among: Brazil, 24, 36, 40, 119, 144, 176, 192, 199, 241, 295, 333, 371, 374, 462, 466; Cuba, 98–99, 112, 203, 225–226, 243; Haiti, 143(2), 145, 146, 164, 167, 214, 225, 317, 326, 385, 409, 440, 458, 469, 472; Jamaica, 12, 159, 164, 185, 197, 324, 466, 487; Martinique, 374; Surinam, 216, 341; Trinidad, 205, 453; Uruguay, 139–140; West Indies, 166, 251, 256, 423

Candomblé, 23, 82, 107, 108, 114, 158, 174, 188, 236(2), 243, 248, 257, 274, 279(2), 293, 363, 366, 371, 387, 390, 398, 454, 500(2)

Clothing used by blacks: Brazil, 3, 63, 296, 372, 410, 414, 452, 459, 460, 471; Caribbean, 86, 96, 133; French Antilles, 49, 142, 167, 287; Guiana, 255; Haiti, 457; Jamaica, 414, 480; West Indies, 150, 165, 308, 365, 369, 433, 445

Conspiracy of the Ladder, 141. *See also* Slave rebellions

Creole. *See* Dialects

Cult leaders: Afro-Brazilian, 8, 20, 23, 39, 46, 47, 102, 107, 117, 176, 239, 243, 248, 264, 286, 288, 289, 358, 366, 369(2), 397; Afro-Caribbean, 187; Afro-Cuban, 3, 4, 104, 176, 177, 179, 237, 242, 310, 318, 325, 333, 339, 345, 420, 465; Afro-Haitian,

# Name Index ———————————

Persons are listed under their countries of origin or countries of major involvement with other countries of involvement given in parentheses. *Italicized* page numbers indicate a main entry in the dictionary.

Marcelin, Pierre, 302–303
Michel, Pièrre, 315
Möise, Randolphe, 319
Moravia, Charles, 322
Morpeau, Louis, 324
Morrisseau-Leroy, Félix, 107, *324*
Moyse, 326
Najac, Paul-E., 336
Nau, Ignace, 340
Neptune, Louis, 348
Ogé, Vincent, 123, 134, *358*
Padrejean, 368
Paret, Timothée, 374
Pétion, Alexander Sabes, 125, 162, 193, *380*
Phelps, Anthony, 381
Philotecte, René, 381–382
Pichinchat, Philippe, 382
Polydor, 387
Pompée, 387
Pressoir, Charles Fernand, 390
Price-Mars, Jean, 18, *391*, 407
Raimond, Julien, 134, *401*
Rigaud, André, 406–407
Rigaud, Milo, 407
Rosiers, Comte de, 410
Roumain, Jacques, 410
Roumer, Emile, 410
Sylvain, Normil, 448
Thoby-Marcelin, Philippe, 456
Tirolien, Guy, 458
Toussaint L'Ouverture (*see* Haiti: L'Ouverture, Toussaint)
Vaval, Duraciné, 470
Villatte, 472
Villevaliex, Charles Séguy, 472
Werleigh, Christian, 481
Williams, Charles D., 485

**Holland**

Coymans, Baltazar, 147

**Italy**

Grillo, Domingo, 218

**Jamaica**

Accompang, Captain, 7
Bedward, Alexander, 65
Bethune, Leber, 71
Bogle, Paul, *79*, 322
Campbell, George, 107
Carbery, H. D., 112

Clark, Dugald, 127
Cudjoe, Captain, 7, *152*
Cuffee, 152
Cuffee, Captain, *152*, 257
Gordon, George William, 213
Hollar, Constance, 232
Jonson, Ben, *68*, 69
Jordon, Edward, *251*, 478
Kishee, Captain, 258
Knibb, William, 59, *259*
Lecesne, Louis Celeste, 268
Lewis, George, *271*, 340
Lewis, Matthew, 271–272
Liele, George, 273
Lisle, George (*see* Jamaica: Liele, George)
Love, Joseph Robert (Haiti, Bahamas), 279
Lubola, Juan, 280
McFarlane, Basil, 283–284
McFarlane, John Ebenezer Claire, 284
McFarlane, R. L. C., 284
McKay, Claude, 56–57, *285*, 346
Mais, Roger, 289
Mansong, Jack, 299
Marson, Una M., 306
Maxwell-Hall, Agnes, 310
Muhammad Kaba, *327*, 479
Nanny, *339*, 496
Ormsby, Barbara Stephanie, 364
Prince de Bundo, 391–392
Quao, Captain, 394
Quier, John, 396
Redcam, Thomas Henry McDermot, 403
Reid, Victor Stafford, 405
Roper, Thomas, 410
Sharp, Samuel, 428
Sherlock, Philip M., 429–430
Simpson, Louis, 431
Smith, Mary Ann Able, 439
Tacky, 449
Virtue, Vivian L., 473
Vroman, Mary Elizabeth, 474
Williams, Francis, 485
Williams, James, 485

**Martinique**

Bonaparte, Josephine, *82*, 278
Bonnevile, René, 83
Boukman, Daniel, 84
Césaire, Aimé, 103, *120*, 157, 183, 342, 343, 453, 458
Chalonec, Frantz, 121

**Virgin Islands**

Blyden, Edward Wilmot, 78
Helgaard, Anne, *229*, 421
Kingo, Johannes Christian, 258
Leidesdorf, William Alexander, 269
Martin, Frederick, 306–307
Morón, Alonso Graseano, 324

Scholten, Peter Carl Frederick Von, 421

**West Indies**

Baxter, John, *64*, 209
Ben Johnson, 68–69
Gilbert, Nathaniel, *209*, 481
Saint, 415

## ABOUT THE AUTHOR

BENJAMIN NUNEZ (retired) was Professor of Latin American Civilization and Linquistics at West Chester State College in West Chester, Pennsylvania (1967-1978), and at Georgetown University in Washington, D.C. (1957-1967). His writings on linguistics and Latin American affairs have appeared in books and scholarly journals.